IBM International Technical Support Organization

Introduction to the New Mainframe: z/OS Basics

March 2011

SG24-6366-02

Third Edition (March 2011)

Contents

Notices

This information was developed for products and services offered in the U.S.A.

IBM may not offer the products, services, or features discussed in this document in other countries. Consult your local IBM representative for information on the products and services currently available in your area. Any reference to an IBM product, program, or service is not intended to state or imply that only that IBM product, program, or service may be used. Any functionally equivalent product, program, or service that does not infringe any IBM intellectual property right may be used instead. However, it is the user's responsibility to evaluate and verify the operation of any non-IBM product, program, or service.

IBM may have patents or pending patent applications covering subject matter described in this document. The furnishing of this document does not give you any license to these patents. You can send license inquiries, in writing, to:
IBM Director of Licensing, IBM Corporation, North Castle Drive, Armonk, NY 10504-1785 U.S.A.

The following paragraph does not apply to the United Kingdom or any other country where such provisions are inconsistent with local law: INTERNATIONAL BUSINESS MACHINES CORPORATION PROVIDES THIS PUBLICATION "AS IS" WITHOUT WARRANTY OF ANY KIND, EITHER EXPRESS OR IMPLIED, INCLUDING, BUT NOT LIMITED TO, THE IMPLIED WARRANTIES OF NON-INFRINGEMENT, MERCHANTABILITY OR FITNESS FOR A PARTICULAR PURPOSE. Some states do not allow disclaimer of express or implied warranties in certain transactions, therefore, this statement may not apply to you.

This information could include technical inaccuracies or typographical errors. Changes are periodically made to the information herein; these changes will be incorporated in new editions of the publication. IBM may make improvements and/or changes in the product(s) and/or the program(s) described in this publication at any time without notice.

Any references in this information to non-IBM Web sites are provided for convenience only and do not in any manner serve as an endorsement of those Web sites. The materials at those Web sites are not part of the materials for this IBM product and use of those Web sites is at your own risk.

IBM may use or distribute any of the information you supply in any way it believes appropriate without incurring any obligation to you.

Information concerning non-IBM products was obtained from the suppliers of those products, their published announcements or other publicly available sources. IBM has not tested those products and cannot confirm the accuracy of performance, compatibility or any other claims related to non-IBM products. Questions on the capabilities of non-IBM products should be addressed to the suppliers of those products.

This information contains examples of data and reports used in daily business operations. To illustrate them as completely as possible, the examples include the names of individuals, companies, brands, and products. All of these names are fictitious and any similarity to the names and addresses used by an actual business enterprise is entirely coincidental.

COPYRIGHT LICENSE:

This information contains sample application programs in source language, which illustrate programming techniques on various operating platforms. You may copy, modify, and distribute these sample programs in any form without payment to IBM, for the purposes of developing, using, marketing or distributing application programs conforming to the application programming interface for the operating platform for which the sample programs are written. These examples have not been thoroughly tested under all conditions. IBM, therefore, cannot guarantee or imply reliability, serviceability, or function of these programs.

Trademarks

IBM, the IBM logo, and ibm.com are trademarks or registered trademarks of International Business Machines Corporation in the United States, other countries, or both. These and other IBM trademarked terms are marked on their first occurrence in this information with the appropriate symbol (® or ™), indicating US registered or common law trademarks owned by IBM at the time this information was published. Such trademarks may also be registered or common law trademarks in other countries. A current list of IBM trademarks is available on the Web at `http://www.ibm.com/legal/copytrade.shtml`

The following terms are trademarks of the International Business Machines Corporation in the United States, other countries, or both:

AD/Cycle®	Language Environment®	S/390®
AIX®	Lotus®	Sysplex Timer®
BladeCenter®	MVS™	System Storage DS®
C/370™	NetView®	System Storage®
CICSPlex®	Open Class®	System z10®
CICS®	OS/390®	System z9®
DB2®	Parallel Sysplex®	System z®
Domino®	PowerVM™	System/390®
DRDA®	POWER®	Tivoli®
DS8000®	PR/SM™	VisualAge®
ECKD™	Processor Resource/Systems	VTAM®
ESCON®	Manager™	WebSphere®
eServer™	QMF™	z/Architecture®
FICON®	Query Management Facility™	z/OS®
FlashCopy®	RACF®	z/VM®
GDPS®	Rational®	z/VSE™
Geographically Dispersed	Redbooks®	z10™
Parallel Sysplex™	Redbooks (logo) ®	z9®
HiperSockets™	Resource Measurement	zSeries®
IBM®	Facility™	
IMS™	RMF™	

The following terms are trademarks of other companies:

Java, and all Java-based trademarks are trademarks of Sun Microsystems, Inc. in the United States, other countries, or both.

Microsoft, Windows, and the Windows logo are trademarks of Microsoft Corporation in the United States, other countries, or both.

Intel, Intel logo, Intel Inside logo, and Intel Centrino logo are trademarks or registered trademarks of Intel Corporation or its subsidiaries in the United States and other countries.

UNIX is a registered trademark of The Open Group in the United States and other countries.

Linux is a trademark of Linus Torvalds in the United States, other countries, or both.

Other company, product, or service names may be trademarks or service marks of others.

Preface

This IBM® Redbooks® publication provides students of information systems technology with the background knowledge and skills necessary to begin using the basic facilities of a mainframe computer. It is the first in a planned series of book designed to introduce students to mainframe concepts and help prepare them for a career in large systems computing.

For optimal learning, students are assumed to have successfully completed an introductory course in computer system concepts, such as computer organization and architecture, operating systems, data management, or data communications. They should also have successfully completed courses in one or more programming languages, and be PC literate.

This book can also be used as a prerequisite for courses in advanced topics or for internships and special studies. It is not intended to be a complete text covering all aspects of mainframe operation or a reference book that discusses every feature and option of the mainframe facilities.

Others who will benefit from this book include experienced data processing professionals who have worked with non-mainframe platforms, or who are familiar with some aspects of the mainframe but want to become knowledgeable with other facilities and benefits of the mainframe environment.

As we go through this course, we suggest that the instructor alternate between text, lecture, discussions, and hands-on exercises. Many of the exercises are cumulative, and are designed to show the student how to design and implement the topic presented. The instructor-led discussions and hands-on exercises are an integral part of the course material, and can include topics not covered in this textbook.

In this course, we use simplified examples and focus mainly on basic system functions. Hands-on exercises are provided throughout the course to help students explore the mainframe style of computing.

At the end of this course, you will know:

► Basic concepts of the mainframe, including its usage, and architecture
► Fundamentals of z/OS®, a widely used mainframe operating system
► Mainframe workloads and the major middleware applications in use on mainframes today
► The basis for subsequent course work in more advanced, specialized areas of z/OS, such as system administration or application programming

How this text is organized

This text is organized in four parts, as follows:

- ► Part 1, "Introduction to z/OS and the mainframe environment" on page 1 provides an overview of the types of workloads commonly processed on the mainframe, such as batch jobs and online transactions. This part of the text helps students explore the user interfaces of z/OS, a widely used mainframe operating system. Discussion topics include TSO/E and ISPF, UNIX® interfaces, job control language, file structures, and job entry subsystems. Special attention is paid to the users of mainframes and to the evolving role of mainframes in today's business world.

- ► Part 2, "Application programming on z/OS" on page 297 introduces the tools and utilities for developing a simple program to run on z/OS. This part of the text guides the student through the process of application design, choosing a programming language, and using a runtime environment.

- ► Part 3, "Online workloads for z/OS" on page 399 examines the major categories of interactive workloads processed by z/OS, such as transaction processing, database management, and web serving. This part includes discussions about several popular middleware products, including IBM DB2®, CICS®, and IBM WebSphere® Application Server.

- ► Part 4, "System programming on z/OS" on page 527 provides topics to help the student become familiar with the role of the z/OS system programmer. This part of the text includes discussions of system libraries, starting and stopping the system, security, network communications, and the clustering of multiple systems. We also provide an overview of mainframe hardware systems, including processors and I/O devices.

In this text, we use simplified examples and focus mainly on basic system functions. Hands-on exercises are provided throughout the text to help students explore the mainframe style of computing. Exercises include entering work into the system, checking its status, and examining the output of submitted jobs.

How each chapter is organized

Each chapter follows a common format:

- ► Objectives for the student
- ► Topics that teach a central theme related to mainframe computing
- ► Summary of the main ideas of the chapter
- ► A list of key terms introduced in the chapter

- ► Questions for review to help students verify their understanding of the material
- ► Topics for further discussion to encourage students to explore issues that extend beyond the chapter objectives
- ► Hands-on exercises to help students reinforce their understanding of the material

The team who wrote this book

John Kettner revised the second edition of this text. He is a Consulting IT Architect in the Systems z and zEnterprise sales group. He has 37 years of mainframe experience and holds a Bachelor of Science degree in Computer Science from L.I.U. His specialties are working with customers with IBM System z® internals, technical newsletters, and customer lecturing. John has written several IBM Redbooks and contributes to various education programs throughout IBM.

Special thanks to the following advisors:
Rick Butler, Bank of Montreal
Timothy Hahn, IBM Raleigh
Pete Siddall, IBM Hursley

The first edition of this text was produced by technical specialists working at the International Technical Support Organization, Poughkeepsie Center, who also reviewed and revised the third edition:

Mike Ebbers has worked with mainframe systems at IBM for 32 years. For part of that time, he taught hands-on mainframe classes to new hires just out of college. Mike currently creates IBM Redbooks, a popular set of product documentation that can be found at:

http://www.ibm.com/redbooks

Wayne O'Brien is an Advisory Software Engineer at IBM Poughkeepsie. Since joining IBM in 1988, he has developed user assistance manuals and online help for a wide variety of software products. Wayne holds a Master of Science degree in Technical Communications from Rensselaer Polytechnic Institute (RPI) of Troy, New York.

In addition, the following technical specialist helped produce the first edition of this text while working at the International Technical Support Organization, Poughkeepsie Center:

Bill Ogden is a retired IBM Senior Technical Staff Member. He holds a Bachelor of Science degree in Electrical Engineering and a Master of Science degree in Computer Science. He has worked with mainframes since 1962 and with z/OS since it was known as OS/360 Release 1/2. Since joining the ITSO in 1978, Bill has specialized in encouraging users new to the operating system and associated hardware.

Acknowledgements

The following people are gratefully acknowledged for their contributions to this project:

Dan Andrascik is a senior at the Pennsylvania State University, majoring in Information Science and Technology. Dan is proficient in computer languages (C++, Visual Basic, HTML, XML, and SQL), organizational theory, database theory and design, and project planning and management. During his internship with the ITSO organization at IBM Poughkeepsie, Dan worked extensively with elements of the IBM eServer™ zSeries® platform.

Rama Ayyar is a Senior IT Specialist with the IBM Support Center in Sydney, Australia. He has 20 years of experience with the MVS™ operating system and has been in the IT field for over 30 years. His areas of expertise include TCP/IP, security, storage management, configuration management, and problem determination. Rama holds a Master's degree in Computer Science from the Indian Institute of Technology, Kanpur.

Emil T. Cipolla is an information systems consultant in the United States with 40 years of experience in information systems. He holds Master's degrees in Mechanical Engineering and Business Administration from Cornell University. Emil is currently an adjunct instructor at the college level.

Mark Daubman is a senior at St. Bonaventure University, majoring in Business Information Systems with a minor concentration in Computer Science. As part of his internship with IBM, Mark worked extensively with many of the z/OS interfaces described in this textbook. After graduation, Mark plans to pursue a career in mainframes.

Myriam Duhamel is an IT Specialist in Belgium. She has 20 years of experience in application development and has worked at IBM for 12 years. Her areas of expertise include development in different areas of z/OS (such as COBOL, PL/I, CICS, DB2, and WebSphere MQ). Myriam currently teaches courses in DB2 and WebSphere MQ.

Per Fremstad is an IBM-certified I/T Specialist from the IBM Systems and Technology group in IBM Norway. He has worked for IBM since 1982 and has extensive experience with mainframes and z/OS. His areas of expertise include the web, WebSphere for z/OS, and web enabling of the z/OS environment. He teaches frequently on z/OS, zSeries, and WebSphere for z/OS topics. Per holds a Bachelor of Science degree from the University of Oslo, Norway.

Luis Martinez Fuentes is a Certified Consulting IT Specialist (Data Integration discipline) with the Systems and Technology Group, IBM Spain. He has 20 years of experience with IBM mainframes, mainly in the CICS and DB2 areas. He is currently working in technical sales support for new workloads on the mainframe. Luis is a member of the Iberia Technical Expert Council, which is affiliated with the IBM Academy of Technology. Luis teaches about mainframes at two universities in Madrid.

Miriam Gelinski is a staff member of Maffei Consulting Group in Brazil, where she is responsible for supporting customer planning and installing mainframe software. She has five years of experience in mainframes. She holds a Bachelor's degree in Information Systems from Universidade São Marcos in Sao Paulo. Her areas of expertise include the z/OS operating system, its subsystems, and TSO and ISPF.

Michael Grossmann is an IT Education specialist in Germany with nine years of experience as a z/OS system programmer and instructor. His areas of expertise include z/OS education for beginners, z/OS operations, automation, mainframe hardware, and Parallel Sysplex®.

Olegario Hernandez is a former IBM Advisory Systems Engineer in Chile. He has more than 35 years of experience in application design and development projects for mainframe systems. He has written extensively on the CICS application interface, systems management, and grid computing. Olegario holds a degree in Chemical Engineering from Universidad de Chile.

Roberto Yuiti Hiratzuka is an MVS system programmer in Brazil. He has 15 years of experience as a mainframe system programmer. Roberto holds a degree in Information Systems from Faculdade de Tecnologia Sao Paulo (FATEC-SP).

John Kettner, whose contributions were noted earlier.

Georg Müller is a student at the University of Leipzig in Germany. He has three years of experience with z/OS and mainframe hardware. He plans to complete his study with a Master's degree in Computer Science next year. For this textbook, Georg wrote topics about WebSphere MQ and HTTP Server, coded sample programs, and helped to verify the final sequence of learning modules.

Rod Neufeld is a Senior Technical Services Professional in Canada. He has 25 years of experience in MVS and z/OS system programming. His areas of expertise include z/OS systems software and support, Parallel Sysplex, and business continuance and recovery. Rod holds an Honors Bachelor of Science degree from the University of Manitoba.

Paul Newton is a Senior Software Engineer in the Dallas, Texas, IBM Developer Relations Technical Support Center. He has 25 years of experience with IBM mainframe operating systems, subsystems, and data networks. Paul holds a degree in Business Administration from the University of Arizona.

Bill Seubert is a zSeries Software Architect in the United States. He has over 20 years experience in mainframes and distributed computing. He holds a Bachelor's degree in Computer Science from the University of Missouri, Columbia. His areas of expertise include z/OS, WebSphere integration software, and software architecture. Bill speaks frequently to IBM clients about integration architecture and enterprise modernization.

Henrik Thorsen is a Senior Consulting IT Specialist at IBM Denmark. He has 25 years of mainframe experience and holds an Master of Science degree in Engineering from the Technical University in Copenhagen and a Bachelor of Science degree in Economics from Copenhagen Business School. His specialties are z/OS, Parallel Sysplex, high availability, performance, and capacity planning. Henrik has written several IBM Redbooks and other documents and contributes to various education programs throughout IBM and the zSeries technical community.

Andy R. Wilkinson is an IT Specialist in the United Kingdom. He has 25 years of experience in reservation systems and z/OS system programming, and has worked at IBM for six years. His areas of expertise include hardware configuration and SMP/E. Andy holds a degree in Materials Science and Technology from the University of Sheffield and a degree in Computing from the Open University.

Lastly, special thanks to the editors at the ITSO center in Poughkeepsie, New York:

► Terry Barthel
► Ella Buslovich and Linda Robinson (graphics)
► Alfred Schwab

Now you can become a published author, too!

Here's an opportunity to spotlight your skills, grow your career, and become a published author - all at the same time! Join an ITSO residency project and help write a book in your area of expertise, while honing your experience using leading-edge technologies. Your efforts will help to increase product acceptance and customer satisfaction, as you expand your network of technical contacts and relationships. Residencies run from two to six weeks in length, and you can participate either in person or as a remote resident working from your home base.

Find out more about the residency program, browse the residency index, and apply online at:

ibm.com/redbooks/residencies.html

Comments welcome

Your comments are important to us!

We want our books to be as helpful as possible. Send us your comments about this book or other IBM Redbooks publications in one of the following ways:

► Use the online **Contact us** review Redbooks form found at:

ibm.com/redbooks

► Send your comments in an email to:

redbooks@us.ibm.com

► Mail your comments to:

IBM Corporation, International Technical Support Organization
Dept. HYTD Mail Station P099
2455 South Road
Poughkeepsie, NY 12601-5400

Stay connected to IBM Redbooks

► Find us on Facebook:

http://www.facebook.com/IBMRedbooks

► Follow us on Twitter:

http://twitter.com/ibmredbooks

- ► Look for us on LinkedIn:

  http://www.linkedin.com/groups?home=&gid=2130806

- ► Explore new Redbooks publications, residencies, and workshops with the IBM Redbooks weekly newsletter:

  https://www.redbooks.ibm.com/Redbooks.nsf/subscribe?OpenForm

- ► Stay current on recent Redbooks publications with RSS Feeds:

  http://www.redbooks.ibm.com/rss.html

Summary of changes

This section describes the technical changes made in this edition of the book and in previous editions. This edition might also include minor corrections and editorial changes that are not identified.

Summary of Changes
for SG24-6366-02
for Introduction to the New Mainframe: z/OS Basics
as created or updated on April 6, 2011.

March 2011, Third Edition

This revision reflects the addition, deletion, or modification of new and changed information described below.

New and changed information
This edition adds information about the IBM System z Enterprise hardware.

August 2009, Second Edition

This revision reflects the addition, deletion, or modification of new and changed information described below.

New and changed information
- ► Chapters 1 through 3 were updated with the latest System z hardware and software information.
- ► Chapter 8 received additional information about application development on the mainframe.
- ► Added Appendix F, which includes the Console Operator commands.

Part 1

Introduction to z/OS and the mainframe environment

Welcome to mainframe computing! We begin this text with an overview of the mainframe computer and its place in today's information technology (IT) organization. We explore the reasons why public and private enterprises throughout the world rely on the mainframe as the foundation of large-scale computing. We discuss the types of workloads that are commonly associated with the mainframe, such as batch jobs and online or interactive transactions, and the unique manner in which this work is processed by a widely used mainframe operating system, that is, z/OS.

Throughout this text, we pay special attention to the people who use mainframes and to the role of the new mainframe in today's business world.

1

1

Introduction to the new mainframe

Objective: As a technical professional in the world of mainframe computing, you need to understand how mainframe computers support your company's IT infrastructure and business goals. You also need to know the job titles of the various members of your company's mainframe support team.

After completing this chapter, you will be able to:

- ► List ways in which the mainframes of today challenge the traditional thinking about centralized computing versus distributed computing.

- ► Explain how businesses make use of mainframe processing power, the typical uses of mainframes, and how mainframe computing differs from other types of computing.

- ► Outline the major types of workloads for which mainframes are best suited.

- ► Name five jobs or responsibilities that are related to mainframe computing.

- ► Identify four mainframe operating systems.

- ► Describe how IBM zEnterprise System is used to address IT problems.

Refer to Table 1-1 on page 42 for a list of key terms used in this chapter.

1.1 The new mainframe

Today, mainframe computers play a central role in the daily operations of most of the world's largest corporations, including many Fortune 1000 companies. While other forms of computing are used extensively in various business capacities, the mainframe occupies a coveted place in today's e-business environment. In banking, finance, health care, insurance, public utilities, government, and a multitude of other public and private enterprises, the mainframe computer continues to form the foundation of modern business.

e-business:
The transaction of business over an electronic medium, such as the Internet.

The long-term success of mainframe computers is without precedent in the information technology (IT) field. Periodic upheavals shake world economies and continuous, often wrenching, change in the Information Age has claimed many once-compelling innovations as victims in the relentless march of progress. As emerging technologies leap into the public eye, many are just as suddenly rendered obsolete by some even newer advancement. Yet today, as in every decade since the 1960s, mainframe computers and the mainframe *style* of computing dominate the landscape of large-scale business computing.

Why has this one form of computing taken hold so strongly among so many of the world's corporations? In this chapter, we look at the reasons why mainframe computers continue to be the popular choice for large-scale business computing.

1.2 The System/360: A turning point in mainframe history

Mainframe development occurred in a series of *generations* starting in the 1950s. First generation systems, such as the IBM 705 in 1954 and its successor generation, the IBM 1401 in 1959, were a far cry from the enormously powerful and economical machines that were to follow, but they clearly had characteristics of mainframe computers. The IBM 1401 was called the Model T of the computer business, because it was the first mass-produced digital, all-transistorized, business computer that could be afforded by many businesses worldwide. These computers were sold as business machines and served then, as now, as the central data repository in a corporation's data processing center.

System/360:
The first general purpose computer, introduced in 1964.

In the 1960s, the course of computing history changed dramatically when mainframe manufacturers began to standardize the hardware and software they offered to customers. The introduction of the IBM System/360 (or S/360) in 1964 signaled the start of the third generation: the first general purpose computers. Earlier systems were dedicated to either commercial or scientific computing. The revolutionary S/360 could perform both types of computing, as long as the customer, a software company, or a consultant provided the programs to do so.

In fact, the name S/360 refers to the architecture's wide scope: 360 degrees to cover the entire circle of possible uses.

The S/360 was also the first of these computers to use *microcode* to implement many of its machine instructions, as opposed to having all of its machine instructions hardwired into its circuitry. Microcode (or *firmware*) consists of stored microinstructions, not available to users, that provide a functional layer between hardware and software. The advantage of microcoding is flexibility, where any correction or new function can be implemented by just changing the existing microcode, rather than replacing the computer.

Over the passing decades, mainframe computers have steadily grown to achieve enormous processing capabilities. Today's mainframes have an unrivaled ability to serve users by the tens of thousands, manage petabytes[1] of data, and reconfigure hardware and software resources to accommodate changes in workload, all from a single point of control.

1.3 An evolving architecture

An *architecture* is a set of defined terms and rules that are used as instructions to build products. In computer science, an architecture describes the organizational structure of a system. An architecture can be recursively decomposed into parts that interact through interfaces, relationships that connect parts, and constraints for assembling parts. Parts that interact through interfaces include classes, components, and subsystems.

Starting with the first large machines, which arrived on the scene in the 1960s and became known as "Big Iron" (in contrast to smaller departmental systems), each new generation of mainframe computers has included improvements in one or more of the following areas of the architecture:[2]

► More and faster processors

► More physical memory and greater memory addressing capability

► Dynamic capabilities for upgrading both hardware and software

► Increased automation along with hardware error checking and recovery

► Enhanced devices for input/output (I/O) and more and faster paths (*channels*) between I/O devices and processors

---

[1] Quadrillions of bytes.

[2] Since the introduction of the S/360 in 1964, IBM has significantly extended the platform roughly every ten years: System/370 in 1970, System/370 Extended Architecture (370-XA) in 1983, Enterprise Systems Architecture/390 (ESA/390) in 1990, and z/Architecture® in 2000. For more information about earlier mainframe hardware systems, see Appendix A, "A brief look at IBM mainframe history" on page 633.

- More sophisticated I/O attachments, such as LAN adapters with extensive inboard processing

- A greater ability to divide the resources of one machine into multiple, logically independent and isolated systems, each running its own operating system

- Advanced clustering technologies, such as Parallel Sysplex, and the ability to share data among multiple systems

- Emphasis on utility savings with power and cooling reduction

- An expanded set of application runtime environments, including support for POSIX applications, C, C++, Java™, PHP, web applications, SOA[3], and web services

Despite the continual changes, mainframe computers remain the most stable, secure, and compatible of all computing platforms. The latest models can handle the most advanced and demanding customer workloads, yet continue to run applications that were written in the 1970s or earlier.

How can a technology change so much yet remain so stable? It evolved to meet new challenges. In the early 1990s, the client-server model of computing, with its distributed nodes of less powerful computers, emerged to challenge the dominance of mainframe computers. In response, mainframe designers did what they have always done when confronted with changing times and a growing list of user requirements: They designed new mainframe computers to meet the demand. With the expanded functions and added tiers of data processing capabilities, such as web serving, autonomics, disaster recovery, and grid computing, the mainframe computer is poised to ride the next wave of growth in the IT industry.

Today's mainframe generation provides a significant increase in system scalability over the previous mainframe servers. With increased performance and total system capacity, customers continue to consolidate diverse applications on a single platform. New innovations help to ensure it is a security-rich platform that can help maximize the resources and their utilization, and can help provide the ability to integrate applications and data across a single infrastructure. The current mainframe is built using a modular design that supports a packaging concept based on *books*. One to four books can be configured, each containing a processor housing that hosts the central processor units, memory, and high speed connectors for I/O. This approach enables many of the high-availability, nondisruptive capabilities that differentiate it from other platforms.

---

[3] Service-oriented architecture

Figure 1-1 shows the mainframe's continued growth improvements in all directions. Although some of the previous generation of machines have grown more along one graphical axis for a given family, later families focus on the other axes. The balanced design of today's mainframe achieves improvement equally along all four axes.

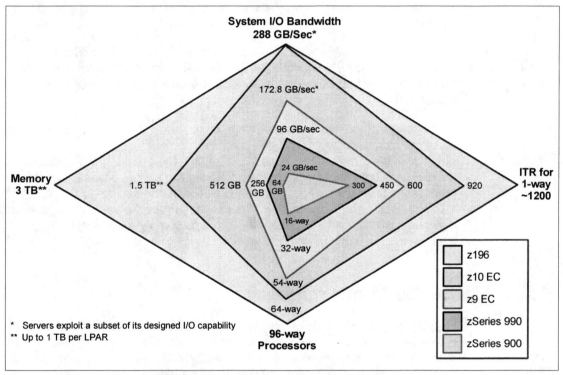

Figure 1-1   Growth of the mainframe and its components

The evolution continues. Although the mainframe computer has retained its traditional, central role in the IT organization, that role is now defined to include being the primary hub in the largest distributed networks. In fact, the Internet itself is based largely on numerous, interconnected mainframe computers serving as major hubs and routers.

Today's mainframe has taken on an additional critical role as an energy efficient system. As energy costs are increasing at a rate of 2.8% per year, energy costs to power equipment often exceed the purchase cost of the hardware itself.

Market researchers, such as International Data Corporation (IDC), have conducted studies that compare the total worldwide server spending to total server power and cooling expenditure on a global basis and found that customers are spending more than twice as much on power and cooling as they are spending on total server purchases. The power and cooling issues that data center managers face are not stand-alone challenges. These issues can have a cascading impact on other facilities issues, such as wiring, floor space, and lighting.

The mainframe also contains an "energy meter." The mainframe's power consumption today is 0.91 watts per MIPS and is expected to decrease with future models. As such, the mainframe has become an environmentally friendly platform to run a business with on a global basis.

As the image of the mainframe computer continues to evolve, you might wonder: Is the mainframe computer is a self-contained computing environment, or is it one part of the puzzle in distributed computing? The answer is that the new mainframe is both. It is a self-contained processing center, powerful enough to process the largest and most diverse workloads in one secure "footprint." It is also just as effective when implemented as the primary server in a corporation's distributed server farm. In effect, the mainframe computer is the definitive platform in the client-server model of computing.

1.4 Mainframes in our midst

Despite the predominance of mainframes in the business world, these machines are largely invisible to the general public, the academic community, and indeed many experienced IT professionals. Instead, other forms of computing attract more attention, at least in terms of visibility and public awareness. That this is so is perhaps not surprising. After all, who among us needs direct access to a mainframe? And, if we did, where would we find one to access? The truth, however, is that we are *all* mainframe users, whether we realize it or not (more on this later).

Most of us with some personal computer (PC) literacy and sufficient funds can purchase a notebook computer and quickly put it to good use by running software, browsing websites, and perhaps even writing papers for college professors to grade. With somewhat greater effort and technical prowess, we can delve more deeply into the various facilities of a typical Intel®-based workstation and learn its capabilities through direct, hands-on experience, with or without help from any of a multitude of readily available information sources in print or on the web.

Mainframes, however, tend to be hidden from the public eye. They do their jobs dependably (indeed, with almost total reliability) and are highly resistant to most forms of insidious abuse that afflict PCs, such as email-borne viruses and trojan horses. By performing stably, quietly, and with negligible downtime, mainframes are the example by which all other computers are judged. But at the same time, this lack of attention tends to allow them to fade into the background.

Furthermore, in a typical customer installation, the mainframe shares space with many other hardware devices: external storage devices, hardware network routers, channel controllers, and automated tape library "robots," to name a few. The mainframe is physically no larger than many of these devices and generally does not stand out from the crowd of peripheral devices. There are different classes of mainframe to meet diverse needs of customers. The mainframe can grow in capacity as businesses grow.

So, how can we explore the mainframe's capabilities in the real world? How can we learn to interact with the mainframe, learn its capabilities, and understand its importance to the business world? Major corporations are eager to hire new mainframe professionals, but there is a catch: some previous experience would help.

1.5 What is a mainframe

First, let us review terminology. Today, computer manufacturers do not always use the term *mainframe* to refer to mainframe computers. Instead, most have taken to calling any commercial-use computer, large or small, a *server*, with the mainframe simply being the largest type of server in use today. We use the term mainframe in this text to mean computers that can support thousands of applications and input/output devices to simultaneously serve thousands of users.

Servers are proliferating. A business might have a large server collection that includes transaction servers, database servers, email servers, and web servers. Large collections of servers are sometimes called *server farms* (in fact, some data centers cover areas measured in *acres*). The hardware required to perform a server function can range from little more than a cluster of rack-mounted personal computers to the most powerful mainframes manufactured today.

Server farm:
A large collection of servers.

A mainframe is the central data repository, or *hub,* in a corporation's data processing center, linked to users through less powerful devices such as workstations or terminals. The presence of a mainframe often implies a centralized form of computing, as opposed to a distributed form of computing.

Centralizing the data in a single mainframe repository saves customers from having to manage updates to more than one copy of their business data, which increases the likelihood that the data is current.

The distinction between centralized and distributed computing, however, is rapidly blurring, as smaller machines continue to gain in processing power and mainframes become ever more flexible and multi-purpose. Market pressures require that today's businesses continually reevaluate their IT strategies to find better ways of supporting a changing marketplace. As a result, mainframes are now frequently used in combination with networks of smaller servers in a multitude of configurations. The ability to dynamically reconfigure a mainframe's hardware and software resources (such as processors, memory, and device connections), while applications continue running, further underscores the flexible, evolving nature of the modern mainframe.

Although mainframe hardware has become harder to pigeon-hole, so, too, have the operating systems that run on mainframes. Years ago, in fact, the terms defined each other: a mainframe was any hardware system that ran a major IBM operating system.[4] This meaning has been blurred in recent years because these operating systems can be run on small systems.

Platform:
A computer architecture (hardware and software).

Computer manufacturers and IT professionals often use the term *platform* to refer to the hardware and software that are associated with a particular computer architecture. For example, a mainframe computer and its operating system (and their predecessors[5]) are considered a platform. UNIX on a Reduced Instruction Set Computer (RISC) system is considered a platform somewhat independently of exactly which RISC machine is involved. Personal computers can be seen as several different platforms, depending on which operating system is being used.

So, let us return to our question: What is a mainframe? Today, the term mainframe can best be used to describe a *style* of operation, applications, and operating system facilities. Here is a working definition, "A mainframe is what businesses use to host the commercial databases, transaction servers, and applications that require a greater degree of security and availability than is commonly found on smaller-scale machines."

---

[4] The name was also traditionally applied to large computer systems that were produced by other vendors.

[5] IBM System/390® (S/390®) refers to a specific series of machines, which have been superseded by the IBM System z machines. Nevertheless, many S/390 systems are still in use. Therefore, keep in mind that although we discuss the System z in this course, almost everything discussed also applies to S/390 machines. One major exception is 64-bit addressing, which is used only with System z.

Mainframe:
A highly secured computer system designed to continuously run large, mixed workloads at high levels of utilization while meeting user-defined service level objectives.

Early mainframe systems were housed in enormous, room-sized metal boxes or frames, which is probably how the term mainframe originated. The early mainframe required large amounts of electrical power and air-conditioning, and the room was filled mainly with I/O devices. Also, a typical customer site had several mainframes installed, with most of the I/O devices connected to all of the mainframes. During their largest period, in terms of physical size, a typical mainframe occupied 2,000 to 10,000 square feet (200 to 1000 square meters). Some installations were even larger.

Starting around 1990, mainframe processors and most of their I/O devices became physically smaller, while their functionality and capacity continued to grow. Mainframe systems today are much smaller than earlier systems, and are about the size of a large refrigerator.

In some cases, it is now possible to run a mainframe operating system on a PC that emulates a mainframe. Such emulators are useful for developing and testing business applications before moving them to a mainframe production system.

Figure 1-2 shows the old and new mainframes.

Figure 1-2   The old and the new mainframes

Clearly, the term mainframe has expanded beyond merely describing the physical characteristics of a system. Instead, the word typically applies to some combination of the following attributes:

▶ Compatibility with System z operating systems, applications, and data.

▶ Centralized control of resources.

▶ Hardware and operating systems that can share access to disk drives with other systems, with automatic locking and protection against destructive simultaneous use of disk data.

- A *style* of operation, often involving dedicated operations staff who use detailed *operations procedure books* and highly organized procedures for backups, recovery, training, and disaster recovery at an alternative location.

- Hardware and operating systems that routinely work with hundreds or thousands of simultaneous I/O operations.

- Clustering technologies that allow the customer to operate multiple copies of the operating system as a single system. This configuration, known as Parallel Sysplex, is analogous in concept to a UNIX cluster, but allows systems to be added or removed as needed, while applications continue to run. This flexibility allows mainframe customers to introduce new applications, or discontinue the use of existing applications, in response to changes in business activity.

- Additional data and resource sharing capabilities. In a Parallel Sysplex, for example, it is possible for users across multiple systems to access the same databases concurrently, with database access controlled at the *record level*.

- Optimized for I/O for business-related data processing applications supporting high speed networking and terabytes of disk storage.

As the performance and cost of such hardware resources as the central processing unit (CPU) and external storage media improve, and the number and types of devices that can be attached to the CPU increase, the operating system software can more fully take advantage of the improved hardware.

1.6 Who uses mainframe computers

So, who uses mainframes? Just about *everyone* has used a mainframe computer at one point or another. If you ever used an automated teller machine (ATM) to interact with your bank account, you used a mainframe.

Today, mainframe computers play a central role in the daily operations of most of the world's largest corporations. While other forms of computing are used extensively in business in various capacities, the mainframe occupies a coveted place in today's e-business environment. In banking, finance, health care, insurance, utilities, government, and a multitude of other public and private enterprises, the mainframe computer continues to be the foundation of modern business.

Until the mid-1990s, mainframes provided the *only* acceptable means of handling the data processing requirements of a large business. These requirements were then (and are often now) based on large and complex batch jobs, such as payroll and general ledger processing.

The mainframe owes much of its popularity and longevity to its inherent reliability and stability, which is a result of careful and steady technological advances that have been made since the introduction of the System/360 in 1964. No other computer architecture can claim as much continuous, evolutionary improvement, while maintaining compatibility with previous releases.

Because of these design strengths, the mainframe is often used by IT organizations to host the most important, *mission-critical* applications. These applications typically include customer order processing, financial transactions, production and inventory control, payroll, and many other types of work.

One common impression of a mainframe's user interface is the 80x24-character "green screen" terminal, named for the old cathode ray tube (CRT) monitors from years ago that glowed green. In reality, mainframe interfaces today look much the same as those for personal computers or UNIX systems. When a business application is accessed through a web browser, there is often a mainframe computer performing crucial functions "behind the scene."

Many of today's busiest websites store their production databases on a mainframe host. New mainframe hardware and software products are ideal for web transactions because they are designed to allow huge numbers of users and applications to rapidly and simultaneously access the same data without interfering with each other. This security, scalability, and reliability is critical to the efficient and secure operation of contemporary information processing.

Corporations use mainframes for applications that depend on scalability and reliability. For example, a banking institution could use a mainframe to host the database of its customer accounts, for which transactions can be submitted from any of thousands of ATM locations worldwide.

Businesses today rely on the mainframe to:

► Perform large-scale transaction processing (thousands of transactions per second)[6]

► Support thousands of users and application programs concurrently accessing numerous resources

► Manage terabytes of information in databases

► Handle large-bandwidth communication

The roads of the information superhighway often lead to a mainframe.

---

[6] The IBM series of mainframe computers, for example, the IBM System z10® Enterprise Class (EC), can process over a staggering *one billion* transactions per day.

1.6.1 Two mainframe models

Mainframes are available with a variety of processing capabilities to suit the requirements of most business organizations. In the case of IBM, for example, each mainframe model provides for subcapacity processors from granular processing requirements up to the full range of high-end computing.

Let's look at two entries from IBM (Figure 1-3):

► System z Business Class (BC)
► System z Enterprise Class (EC)

Figure 1-3   System z Business Class and Enterprise Class

The System z Business Class (BC) could be said to be intended for small to midrange enterprise computing, and delivers an entry point with granular scalability and a wide range of capacity settings to grow with the workload. The BC provides for a maximum of up to 10 configurable PUs.

The BC shares many of the characteristics and processing traits of its larger sibling, the Enterprise Class (EC). This model provides granular scalability and capacity settings on a much larger scale and is intended to satisfy high-end processing requirements. As a result, the EC has a larger frame to house the extensive capacity that supports greater processing requirements. The EC offers up to 64 configurable CPs.

1.7 Factors contributing to mainframe use

The reasons for mainframe use are many, but most generally fall into one or more of the following categories:

- ▶ Reliability, availability, and serviceability
- ▶ Security
- ▶ Scalability
- ▶ Continuing compatibility
- ▶ Evolving architecture
- ▶ Extensibility
- ▶ Lower total cost of ownership (TCO)
- ▶ Environmental friendliness

Let us look at each of these categories in more detail.

1.7.1 Reliability, availability, and serviceability

The *reliability, availability,* and *serviceability* (RAS) of a computer system have always been important factors in data processing. When we say that a particular computer system "exhibits RAS characteristics", we mean that its design places a high priority on the system remaining in service at all times. Ideally, RAS is a central design feature of all aspects of this computer system, including the applications. RAS is ubiquitous in the mainframe.

RAS has become accepted as a collective term for many characteristics of hardware and software that are prized by mainframe users. The terms are defined as follows:

Reliability   The system's hardware components have extensive self-checking and self-recovery capabilities. The system's software reliability is a result of extensive testing and the ability to make quick updates for detected problems.

One of the operating system's feature is a Health Checker that identifies potential problems before they impact availability or, in worst cases, cause system or application outages.

Availability   The system can recover from a failed component without impacting the rest of the running system. This applies to hardware recovery (the automatic replacing of failed elements with spares) and software recovery (the layers of error recovery that are provided by the operating system). The highest levels of availability are obtained with DB2 and the Parallel Sysplex on the System z architecture.

Serviceability The system can determine why a failure occurred. This allows for the replacement of hardware and software elements while impacting as little of the operational system as possible. This term also implies well-defined units of replacement, either hardware or software.

A computer system is available when its applications are available. An available system is one that is reliable, that is, it rarely requires downtime for upgrades or repairs. And, if the system is brought down by an error condition, it must be serviceable, that is, easy to fix within a relatively short period of time.

Mean time between failure (MTBF) refers to the availability of a computer system. The new mainframe and its associated software have evolved to the point that customers often experience months or even *years* of system availability between system downtimes. Moreover, when the system is unavailable because of an unplanned failure or a scheduled upgrade, this period is typically short. The remarkable availability of the system in processing the organization's mission-critical applications is vital in today's 24x7 global economy. Along with the hardware, mainframe operating systems exhibit RAS through such features as storage protection and a controlled maintenance process.

System z servers are among the most secure servers on the market, with mean time between failures (MTBF) measured in decades. In fact, the System z is designed for up to 99.999% availability with Parallel Sysplex clustering. The System z is designed to provide superior qualities of service to help support high volume, transaction-driven applications, and other critical processes. It supplies tremendous power and throughput for information-intensive computing requirements.

Beyond RAS, a state-of-the-art mainframe system might be said to provide *high availability* and *fault tolerance*. Redundant hardware components in critical paths, enhanced storage protection, a controlled maintenance process, and system software designed for unlimited availability all help to ensure a consistent, highly available environment for business applications in the event that a system component fails. Such an approach allows the system designer to minimize the risk of having a *single point of failure* (SPOF) undermine the overall RAS of a computer system.

Enterprises many times require an on demand operating environment that provides responsiveness, resilience, and a variable cost structure to provide maximum business benefits. The mainframe's Capacity on Demand (CoD) solutions offer permanent or temporary increases in processor capacity and additional memory. This robust serviceability allows for on going upgrades during concurrent workload execution.

1.7.2 Security

One of a firm's most valuable resources is its data: customer lists, accounting data, employee information, and so on. This critical data needs to be securely managed and controlled, and, simultaneously, made available to those users authorized to see it. The mainframe computer has extensive capabilities to simultaneously share, but still protect, the firm's data among multiple users.

In an IT environment, data security is defined as protection against unauthorized access, transfer, modification, or destruction, whether accidental or intentional. To protect data and to maintain the resources necessary to meet the security objectives, customers typically add a sophisticated security manager product to their mainframe operating system. The customer's security administrator often bears the overall responsibility for using the available technology to transform the company's security policy into a usable plan.

A secure computer system prevents users from accessing or changing any objects on the system, including user data, except through system-provided interfaces that enforce authority rules. The mainframe provides a secure system for processing large numbers of heterogeneous applications that access critical data.

The mainframe's built-in security throughout the software stack means that z/OS, due to its architecture design and use of registries, will not suffer from buffer overflow related problems caused by virii that are characteristic of many distributed environments.

Hardware enabled security offers unmatched protection for workload isolation, storage protection, and secured communications. Built-in security embedded throughout the operating system, network infrastructure, middleware, application and database architectures deliver secured infrastructures and secured business processing, which fosters compliance. The mainframe's cryptography executes at multiple layers of the infrastructure, which ensures protection of data throughout its life cycle.

In this course, we discuss one example of a mainframe security system in Chapter 18, "Security on z/OS" on page 595.

The IBM System z joins previous IBM mainframes as the world's only servers with the highest level of hardware security certification, that is, Common Criteria Evaluation Assurance Level 5 (EAL5). The EAL5 ranking gives companies confidence that they can run many different applications running on different operating systems, such as z/OS, z/VM®, z/VSE™, z/TPF and Linux®-based applications containing confidential data, such as payroll, human resources, e-commerce, ERP and CRM systems, on one System z divided into partitions that keep each application's data secure and distinct from the others.

That is, the System z architecture is designed to prevent the flow of information among logical partitions on a single system.

Data is the key to running your business. DB2 and zSeries hardware and software give you the controls to safely and effectively administer it. DB2 uses security functions in the operating system. With multilevel security, users can implement sophisticated security in their DB2 applications without writing their own code and be better positioned to obtain auditor certification.

DB2 uses cryptographic functions in the hardware. Both security and cryptographic functions enable delivery of leading-edge security at low levels of granularity, for example, individual rows and columns instead of tables.

EAL5 certification for zSeries and z/Os demonstrates that the zSeries can be an essential building block for server consolidation and the integration of on demand applications and traditional corporate workloads on a single server. This is desirable for reasons of economy, flexibility, security, or management.

1.7.3 Scalability

It has been said that the only constant is *change*. Nowhere is that statement truer than in the IT industry. In business, positive results can often trigger a growth in IT infrastructure to cope with increased demand. The degree to which the IT organization can add capacity without disruption to normal business processes or without incurring excessive overhead (nonproductive processing) is largely determined by the *scalability* of the particular computing platform.

Scalability:
Scalability is a desirable property of a system, which indicates its ability to either handle growing amounts of work in a graceful manner or to be readily enlarged.

By scalability, we mean the ability of the hardware, software, or a distributed system to continue to function well as it changes in size or volume, for example, the ability to retain performance levels when adding processors, memory, and storage. A scalable system can efficiently adapt to more work, with larger or smaller networks performing tasks of varying complexity. The mainframe provides functionality for both vertical and horizontal scaling, where software and hardware collaborate to accommodate various application requirements.

As a company grows in employees, customers, and business partners, it usually needs to add computing resources to support business growth. One approach is to add more processors of the same size, with the resulting overhead, to manage this more complex setup. A company can consolidate its many smaller processors into fewer, larger systems because the mainframe is a *shared everything* (SE) architecture. This is different from a *shared nothing* architecture. Through the shared everything design, you have near-continuous availability for your business applications, which gives you a competitive advantage, allowing you to grow your business on demand.

Mainframes exhibit scalability characteristics in both hardware and software, with the ability to run multiple copies of the operating system software as a single entity called a system complex, or *sysplex*. We further explore mainframe clustering technology and its uses in 2.9, "What is a sysplex" on page 69.

The ease of this platform's scalability is due to the mainframe's inherent virtualization capability, which has evolved over several decades through its balanced synergy design.

1.7.4 Continuing compatibility

Mainframe customers tend to have a large financial investment in their applications and data. Some applications have been developed and refined over decades. Some applications were written many years ago, while others may have been written "yesterday." The ability of an application to work in the system or its ability to work with other devices or programs is called *compatibility*.

Compatibility: The ability of a system both to run software requiring new hardware instructions and to run older software requiring the original hardware instructions.

The need to support applications of varying ages imposes a strict compatibility demand on mainframe hardware and software, which have been upgraded many times since the first System/360 mainframe computer was shipped in 1964. Applications *must* continue to work properly. Thus, much of the design work for new hardware and system software revolves around this compatibility requirement.

The overriding need for compatibility is also the primary reason why many aspects of the system work as they do, for example, the syntax restrictions of the job control language (JCL) that is used to control job scheduling and execution. Any new design enhancements made to the JCL must preserve compatibility with older jobs so that they can continue to run without modification. The desire and need for continuing compatibility is one of the defining characteristics of mainframe computing.

Absolute compatibility across decades of changes and enhancements is not possible, of course, but the designers of mainframe hardware and software make it a top priority. When an incompatibility is unavoidable, the designers typically warn users *at least a year* in advance that software changes might be needed.

1.7.5 Evolving architecture

Technology has always accelerated the pace of change. New technologies enable new ways of doing business, shifting markets, changing customer expectations, and redefining business models. Each major enhancement to technology presents opportunities. Companies that understand and prepare for changes can gain advantage over competitors and lead their industries. To support an on demand business, the IT infrastructure must evolve to support it.

At its heart, the data center must transition to reflect these needs, the data center must be responsive to changing demands, it must be variable to support the diverse environment, it must be flexible so that applications can run on the optimal resources at any point in time, and it must be resilient to support an always open for business environment.

For over four decades, the mainframe has been the leading technology in data and transaction serving. Each new generation of this platform provides a strong combination of past mainframe characteristics plus new functions designed around scalability, availability, and security.

1.7.6 Extensibility

In software engineering, extensibility is a system design principle where the implementation takes future growth into consideration. It is a systemic measure of the ability to extend a system and the level of effort required to implement the extension. Extensions can be added through the addition of new functionality or through modification of existing functionality. The mainframe's central theme is to provide for change while minimizing impact to existing system functions.

The mainframe, as it becomes more autonomic, takes on tasks not anticipated in its original design. Its ultimate aim is to create the definitive self-managing computer environment to overcome its rapidly growing maturity and to facilitate expansion. Many built-in features perform software management, runtime health checking, and transparent hardware hot-swapping.

Also, extensibility comes in the form of cost containment and has been with the mainframe for a long time in different forms. One aspect is that it is a share-everything architecture. Its component and infrastructure reuse is characteristic of its design.

1.7.7 Total cost of ownership

Many organizations are under the false impression that the mainframe is a server that will be accompanied by higher overall software, hardware, and people costs. Most organizations do not accurately calculate the total costs of their server proliferation, largely because chargeback mechanisms do not exist, because only incremental mainframe investment costs are compared to incremental distributed costs, or because total shadow costs are not weighed in. Many organizations also fail to recognize the path length delays and context switching of running workloads across many servers, which typically adds up to a performance penalty that is non-existent on the mainframe. Also, the autonomic capabilities of the mainframe (reliability, scalability, and self-managing design) may not be taken into consideration.

Distributed servers encounter an efficiency barrier where adding incremental servers after a certain point fails to add efficiency. The total diluted cost of the mainframe is not used correctly in calculations; rather, the delta costs attributed to an added workload often make the comparisons erroneous.

In distributed servers, the cost per unit of work never approximates the incremental cost of a mainframe. However, over time, it is unlikely that a server farm could achieve the economies of scale associated with a fully loaded mainframe regardless of how many devices are added. In effect, there is a limit to the efficiencies realizable in a distributed computing environment. These inefficiencies are due to shadow costs, execution of only one style of workload versus a balanced workload, underutilization of CPUs, people expenses, and real estate cost of a distributed operations management.

1.7.8 Environmentally friendly

Refurbishing existing data centers can also prove cost-prohibitive, such as installing new cooling units that require reconfigured floors. The cost of power over time must also be considered in data center planning.

With the rising trends in energy costs is an accompanying trend towards high density distributed servers that stress the power capacity of today's environment. However, this trend has been met with rising energy bills, and facilities that do not accommodate new energy requirements. Distributed servers result in power and cooling requirements per square foot that stress current data center power thresholds.

Because these servers have an attractive initial price point, their popularity has increased. At the same time, their heat has created a problem for data centers whose total utility usage is consumed entirely by the energy proliferating servers. The mainframe's virtualization uses the power of many servers using a small hardware footprint. Today's mainframe reduces the impact of energy cost to a near-negligible value when calculated on a per logical server basis because more applications, several hundred of them, can be deployed on a single machine.

With mainframes, fewer physical servers running at a near constant energy level can host multiple virtual software servers. This setup allows a company to optimize the utilization of hardware, and consolidate physical server infrastructure by hosting servers on a small number of powerful servers. With server consolidation onto a mainframe, often using Linux, companies can achieve better hardware utilization, and reduce floor space and power consumption, thus driving down costs.

The mainframe is designed to scale up and out, for example, by adding more processors to an existing hardware frame, and using existing MIPS, which retain their value during upgrades. (With distributed systems, the hardware and processing power is typically replaced after just three to four years of use.) By adding MIPS to the existing mainframe, more workloads can be run more cost-effectively without changing the footprint. There is no need for another server that would in turn require additional environmental work, network, and cooling. For example, the IBM System z Integrated Facility for Linux (IFL) CPUs can easily run hundreds of instances of Linux at an incremental cost of 75 watts of power.

1.8 Typical mainframe workloads

Most mainframe workloads fall into one of two categories: batch processing or online transaction processing, which includes web-based applications (Figure 1-4).

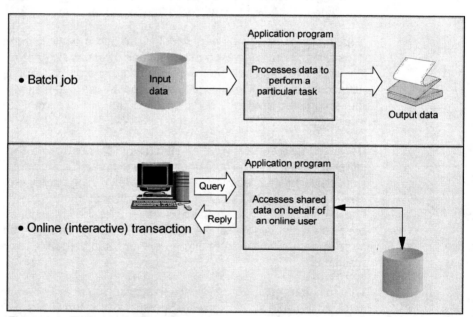

Figure 1-4   Typical mainframe workloads

These workloads are discussed in several chapters in this text; the following sections provide an overview.

1.8.1 Batch processing

One key advantage of mainframe systems is their ability to process terabytes of data from high-speed storage devices and produce valuable output. For example, mainframe systems make it possible for banks and other financial institutions to perform end-of-quarter processing and produce reports that must be sent to customers (for example, quarterly stock statements or pension statements) or to the government (for example, financial results). With mainframe systems, retail stores can generate and consolidate nightly sales reports for review by regional sales managers.

Batch processing: The running of jobs on the mainframe without user interaction.

The applications that produce these statements are *batch* applications, that is, they are processed on the mainframe without user interaction. A *batch job* is submitted on the computer, reads and processes data in bulk (perhaps terabytes of data), and produces output, such as customer billing statements. An equivalent concept can be found in a UNIX script file or a Windows® command file, but a z/OS batch job might process millions of records.

While batch processing is possible on distributed systems, it is not as commonplace as it is on mainframes, because distributed systems often lack:

- ► Sufficient data storage
- ► Available processor capacity, or *cycles*
- ► Sysplex-wide management of system resources and job scheduling

Mainframe operating systems are typically equipped with sophisticated job scheduling software that allows data center staff to submit, manage, and track the execution and output of batch jobs.[7]

Batch processes typically have the following characteristics:

- ► Large amounts of input data are processed and stored (perhaps terabytes or more), large numbers of records are accessed, and a large volume of output is produced.

- ► Immediate response time is usually not a requirement. However, batch jobs often must complete within a "batch window," a period of less-intensive online activity, as prescribed by a *service level agreement* (SLA). This window is shrinking, and batch jobs are now often designed to run concurrently with online transactions with minimal resource contention.

---

[7] In the early days of the mainframe, punched cards were often used to enter jobs into the system for execution. "Keypunch operators" used card punches to enter data, and decks of cards (or batches) were produced. These were fed into card readers, which read the jobs and data into the system. As you can imagine, this process was cumbersome and error-prone. Nowadays, it is possible to transfer the equivalent of punched card data to the mainframe in a PC text file. We discuss various ways of introducing work into the mainframe in Chapter 7, "Batch processing and the job entry subsystem" on page 273.

- Information is generated about large numbers of users or data entities (for example, customer orders or a retailer's stock on hand).

- A scheduled batch process can consist of the execution of hundreds or thousands of jobs in a pre-established sequence.

During batch processing, multiple types of work can be generated. Consolidated information, such as profitability of investment funds, scheduled database backups, processing of daily orders, and updating of inventories, are common examples.

Figure 1-5 on page 25 shows a number of batch jobs running in a typical mainframe environment. Consider the following elements at work in the scheduled batch process:

1. At night, numerous batch jobs running programs and utilities are processed. These jobs consolidate the results of the online transactions that take place during the day.

2. The batch jobs generate reports of business statistics.

3. Backups of critical files and databases are made before and after the batch window.

4. Reports with business statistics are sent to a specific area for analysis the next day.

5. Reports with exceptions are sent to the branch offices.

6. Monthly account balance reports are generated and sent to all bank customers.

7. Reports with processing summaries are sent to the partner credit card company.

8. A credit card transaction report is received from the partner company.

9. In the production control department, the operations area is monitoring the messages on the system console and the execution of the jobs.

10. Jobs and transactions are reading or updating the database (the same one that is used by online transactions) and many files are written to tape.

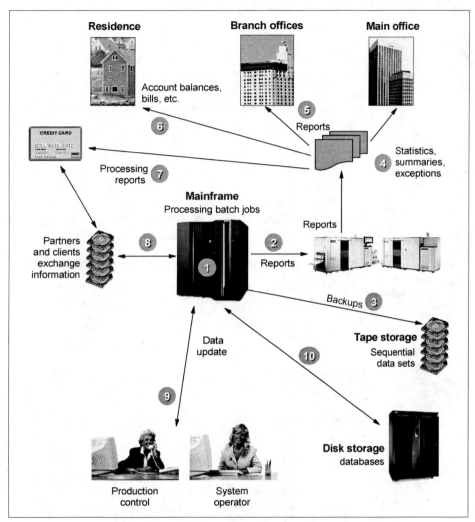

Figure 1-5   Typical batch use

Attention: Today's mainframes can run standard batch processing, such as COBOL, and UNIX and Java programs. These run times can execute either as stand-alone jobs or participate collaboratively within a single job stream. This makes batch processing extremely flexible when integrating different execution environments centrally on a single server.

1.8.2 Online transaction processing

Transaction processing that occurs interactively with the user is referred to as *online transaction processing* (OLTP). Typically, mainframes serve a vast number of *transaction systems*. These systems are often mission-critical applications that businesses depend on for their core functions. Transaction systems must be able to support an unpredictable number of concurrent users and transaction types. Most transactions are executed in short time periods (fractions of a second in some cases).

One of the main characteristics of a transaction system is that the interactions between the user and the system are short. The user performs a complete business transaction through short interactions, with an immediate response time required for each interaction. These systems are currently supporting mission-critical applications; therefore, continuous availability, high performance, and data protection and integrity are required.

Online transaction processing (OLTP): Transaction processing that occurs interactively with the user.

Online transactions are familiar to most people. Examples include:

► ATM machine transactions, such as deposits, withdrawals, inquiries, and transfers

► Supermarket payments with debit or credit cards

► Purchase of merchandise over the Internet

For example, inside a bank branch office or on the Internet, customers are using online services when checking an account balance or directing fund balances.

In fact, an online system performs many of the same functions as an operating system:

► Managing and dispatching tasks
► Controlling user access authority to system resources
► Managing the use of memory
► Managing and controlling simultaneous access to data files
► Providing device independence

Some industry uses of mainframe-based online systems include:

► Banks: ATMs, teller systems for customer service, and online financial systems

► Insurance: Agent systems for policy management and claims processing

► Travel and transport: Airline reservation systems

► Manufacturing: Inventory control and production scheduling

► Government: Tax processing, and license issuance and management

How might the users in these industries interact with their mainframe systems? Multiple factors can influence the design of a company's transaction processing system, including:

- ▶ Number of users interacting with the system at any one time.

- ▶ Number of transactions per second (TPS).

- ▶ Availability requirements of the application. For example, must the application be available 24 hours a day, seven days a week, or can it be brought down briefly one night each week?

Before personal computers and intelligent workstations became popular, the most common way to communicate with online mainframe applications was with 3270 terminals. These devices were sometimes known as "dumb" terminals, but they had enough intelligence to collect and display a full screen of data rather than interacting with the computer for each key stroke, saving processor cycles. The characters were green on a black screen, so the mainframe applications were nicknamed "green screen" applications.

Based on these factors, user interactions vary from installation to installation. For many of the applications now being designed, many installations are reworking their existing mainframe applications to include web browser-based interfaces for users. This work sometimes requires new application development, but can often be done with vendor software purchased to "re-face" the application. Here, the user often does not realize that there is a mainframe behind the scenes.

In this book, there is no need to describe the process of interacting with the mainframe through a web browser, as it is exactly the same as any interaction a user would have through the web. The only difference is the machine at the other end.

Online transactions usually have the following characteristics:

- ▶ A small amount of input data, a few stored records accessed and processed, and a small amount of data as output

- ▶ Immediate response time, usually less than one second

- ▶ A large numbers of users involved in large numbers of transactions

- ▶ Round-the-clock availability of the transactional interface to the user

- ▶ Assurance of security for transactions and user data

In a bank branch office, for example, customers use online services when checking an account balance or making an investment.

Figure 1-6 shows a series of common online transactions using a mainframe.

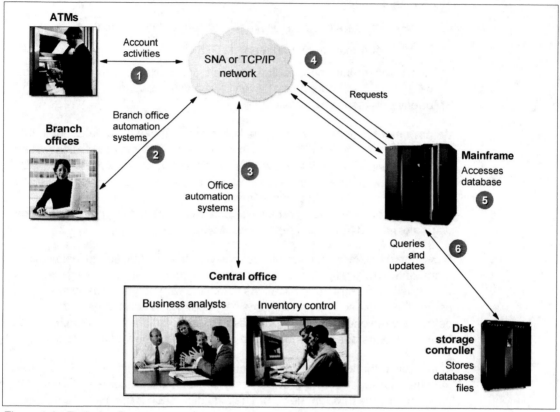

Figure 1-6   Typical online use

Where:

1. A customer uses an ATM, which presents a user-friendly interface for various functions: withdrawal, query account balance, deposit, transfer, or cash advance from a credit card account.

2. Elsewhere in the same private network, a bank employee in a branch office performs operations, such as consulting, working with fund applications, and money ordering.

3. At the bank's central office, business analysts tune transactions for improved performance. Other staff use specialized online systems for office automation to perform customer relationship management, budget planning, and stock control.

4. All requests are directed to the mainframe computer for processing.

5. Programs running on the mainframe computer perform updates and inquiries to the database management system (for example, DB2).

6. Specialized disk storage systems store the database files.

1.8.3 Speciality engines to characterize workload

The mainframe provides customers with the capability to characterize their server configuration to the type of workload they elect to run on it. The mainframe can configure CPUs as speciality engines to off load specific work to separate processors, which alleviates the general CPUs to continue processing standard workloads, increasing the overall ability of the mainframe to complete more batch jobs or transactions. In these scenarios, the customer can benefit from greater throughput, which eases the overall total cost of ownership. These speciality processors are described in Chapter 2, "Mainframe hardware systems and high availability" on page 45.

1.9 Roles in the mainframe world

Mainframe systems are designed to be used by large numbers of people. Most of those who interact with mainframes are users, that is, people who use the applications that are hosted on the system. However, because of the large number of users, applications running on the system, and the sophistication and complexity of the system software that supports the users and applications, a variety of roles are needed to operate and support the mainframe system.

Figure 1-7 shows the many roles in the mainframe environment.

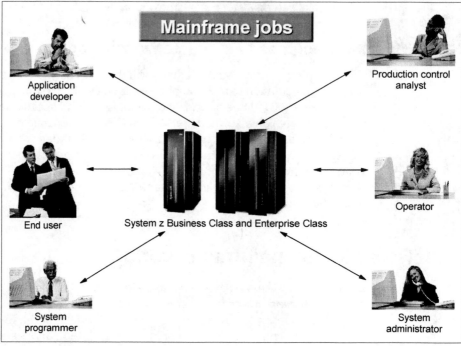

Figure 1-7   Who's who in the mainframe world

In the IT field, these roles are referred to by a number of different titles. This text uses the following:

▶ System programmers

▶ System administrators (for example, DBA, storage, network, security, and performance)

▶ Application designers and programmers

▶ System operators

▶ Production control analysts

In a distributed systems environment, many of the same roles are needed as in the mainframe environment. However, the job responsibilities are often not as well defined. Since the 1960s, mainframe roles have evolved and expanded to provide an environment on which the system software and applications can function smoothly and effectively and serve many thousands of users efficiently.

Although it may seem that the size of the mainframe support staff is large and unwieldy, the numbers become comparatively small when one considers the number of users supported, the number of transactions run, and the high business value of the work that is performed on the mainframe. This situation relates to the cost containment mentioned earlier.

This book is concerned mainly with the system programmer and application programmer roles in the mainframe environment. There are, however, several other important jobs involved in the upkeep of the mainframe, and we touch on some of these roles to give you a better idea of what is going on behind the scene.

Mainframe activities, such as the following, often require cooperation among the various roles:

► Installing and configuring system software

► Designing and coding new applications to run on the mainframe

► Introduction and management of new workloads on the system, such as batch jobs and online transaction processing

► Operation and maintenance of the mainframe software and hardware

In the following sections, we describe each role in more detail.

> **Important:** A feature of the mainframe is it requires fewer personnel to configure and run it than another server environment. Many of the administration roles are automated and offer the means to incorporate rules, allowing the system to run autonomously with no manual intervention. These rules are based on installation policies that become integrated with the configuration.

1.9.1 Who is the system programmer

In a mainframe IT organization, the *system programmer* plays a central role. The system programmer installs, customizes, and maintains the operating system, and also installs or upgrades products that run on the system. The system programmer might be presented with the latest version of the operating system to upgrade the existing systems, or the installation might be as simple as upgrading a single program, such as a sort application.

System programmer: The person who installs, customizes, and maintains the operating system.

The system programmer performs the following tasks:

► Planning hardware and software system upgrades and changes in configuration

► Training system operators and application programmers

- Automating operations
- Performing capacity planning
- Running installation jobs and scripts
- Performing installation-specific customization tasks
- Integration-testing the new products with existing applications and user procedures
- System-wide performance tuning to meet required levels of service

The system programmer must be skilled at debugging problems with system software. These problems are often captured in a copy of the computer's memory contents called a *dump*, which the system produces in response to a failing software product, user job, or transaction. Armed with a dump and specialized debugging tools, the system programmer can determine where the components have failed. When the error has occurred in a software product, the system programmer works directly with the software vendor's support representatives to discover whether the problem's cause is known and whether a patch is available.

System programmers are needed to install and maintain the *middleware* on the mainframe, such as database management systems, online transaction processing systems, and web servers. Middleware is a software "layer" between the operating system and the user or user application. It supplies major functions that are not provided by the operating system. Major middleware products such as DB2, CICS, and IMS™ can be as complex as the operating system itself, if not more so.

Attention: For large mainframe shops, it is not unusual for system programmers to specialize in specific products, such as CICS, IMS or DB2.

1.9.2 Who is the system administrator

The distinction between system programmer and system administrator varies widely among mainframe sites. In smaller IT organizations, where one person might be called upon to perform several roles, the terms may be used interchangeably.

System administrator: The person who maintains the critical business data that resides on the mainframe.

In larger IT organizations with multiple departments, the job responsibilities tend to be more clearly separated. System administrators perform more of the day-to-day tasks related to maintaining the critical business data that resides on the mainframe, while the system programmer focuses on maintaining the system itself.

One reason for the separation of duties is to comply with auditing procedures, which often require that no one person in the IT organization be allowed to have unlimited access to sensitive data or resources. Examples of system administrators include the database administrator (DBA) and the security administrator.

Although system programmer expertise lies mainly in the mainframe hardware and software areas, system administrators are more likely to have experience with the applications. They often interface directly with the application programmers and users to make sure that the administrative aspects of the applications are met. These roles are not necessarily unique to the mainframe environment, but they are key to its smooth operation nonetheless.

In larger IT organizations, the system administrator maintains the system software environment for business purposes, including the day-to-day maintenance of systems to keep them running smoothly. For example, the database administrator must ensure the integrity of, and efficient access to, the data that is stored in the database management systems.

Other examples of common system administrator tasks can include:

► Installing software
► Adding and deleting users and maintaining user profiles
► Maintaining security resource access lists
► Managing storage devices and printers
► Managing networks and connectivity
► Monitoring system performance

In matters of problem determination, the system administrator generally relies on the software vendor support center personnel to diagnose problems, read dumps, and identify corrections for cases in which these tasks are not performed by the system programmer.

1.9.3 Who are the application designers and programmers

The application designer and application programmer (or application developer) design, build, test, and deliver mainframe applications for the company's users and customers. Based on requirements gathered from business analysts and users, the designer creates a design specification from which the programmer constructs an application. The process includes several iterations of code changes and compilation, application builds, and unit testing.

During the application development process, the designer and programmer must interact with other roles in the enterprise. For example, the programmer often works on a team with other programmers who are building code for related application program modules. When completed, each module is passed through a testing process that can include function, integration, and system-wide tests. Following the tests, the application programs must be acceptance tested by the user community to determine whether the code actually satisfies the original user requirement.

In addition to creating new application code, the programmer is responsible for maintaining and enhancing the company's existing mainframe applications. In fact, this is often the primary job for many of today's mainframe application programmers. Although mainframe installations still create new programs with Common Business Oriented Language (COBOL) or PL/I, languages such as Java and C/C++ have become popular for building new applications on the mainframe, just as they have on distributed platforms.

Widespread development of mainframe programs written in high-level languages such as COBOL and PL/I continues at a brisk pace, despite rumors to the contrary. Many thousands of programs are in production on mainframe systems around the world, and these programs are critical to the day-to-day business of the corporations that use them. COBOL and other high-level language programmers are needed to maintain existing code and make updates and modifications to existing programs. Also, many corporations continue to build new application logic in COBOL and other traditional languages, and IBM continues to enhance their high-level language compilers to include new functions and features that allow those languages to continue to take advantage of newer technologies and data formats.

These programmers can benefit from state-of-the-art integrated development environments (IDEs) to enhance their productivity. These IDEs include support for sophisticated source code search and navigation, source code re-factoring, and syntax highlighting. IDEs also assist with defining repeatable build processing steps and identifying dependent modules that must be re-built after changes to source code have been developed.

We look at the roles of application designer and application programmer in more detail in Part 2, "Application programming on z/OS" on page 297.

1.9.4 Who is the system operator

The system operator monitors and controls the operation of the mainframe hardware and software. The operator starts and stops system tasks, monitors the system consoles for unusual conditions, and works with the system programming and production control staff to ensure the health and normal operation of the systems.

System operator:
The person who monitors and controls the operation of the mainframe hardware and software.

As applications are added to the mainframe, the system operator is responsible for ensuring that they run smoothly. New applications from the Applications Programming Department are typically delivered to the Operations Staff with a *run book* of instructions. A run book identifies the specific operational requirements of the application, which operators need to be aware of during job execution. Run book instructions might include, for example, application-specific console messages that require operator intervention, recommended operator responses to specific system events, and directions for modifying job flows to accommodate changes in business requirements[8].

The operator is also responsible for starting and stopping the major subsystems, such as transaction processing systems, database systems, and the operating system itself. These *restart operations* are not nearly as commonplace as they once were, as the availability of the mainframe has improved dramatically over the years. However, the operator must still perform an orderly shutdown and startup of the system and its workloads, when it is required.

In case of a failure or an unusual situation, the operator communicates with system programmers, who assist the operator in determining the proper course of action, and with the production control analyst, who works with the operator to make sure that production workloads are completing properly.

1.9.5 Who is the production control analyst

Production control analyst:
The person who ensures that batch workloads run to completion without error or delay.

The production control analyst is responsible for making sure that batch workloads run to completion without error or delay. Some mainframe installations run interactive workloads for online users, followed by batch updates that run after the prime shift when the online systems are not running. While this execution model is still common, worldwide operations at many companies with live, Internet-based access to production data are finding the "daytime online/night time batch" model to be obsolete. However batch workloads continue to be a part of information processing, and skilled production control analysts play a key role.

---

[8] Console messages were once so voluminous that operators often had a difficult time determining whether a situation was really a problem. In recent years, tools to reduce the volume of messages and automate message responses to routine situations have made it easier for operators to concentrate on unusual events that might require human intervention.

A common complaint about mainframe systems is that they are inflexible and hard to work with, specifically in terms of implementing changes. The production control analyst often hears this type of complaint, but understands that the use of well-structured rules and procedures to control changes, a strength of the mainframe environment, helps prevent outages. In fact, one reason that mainframes have attained a strong reputation for high levels of availability and performance is that there are controls on change and it is difficult to introduce change without proper procedures.

1.9.6 What role do vendors play

A number of vendor roles are commonplace in the mainframe shop. Because most mainframe computers are sold by IBM, and the operating systems and primary online systems are also provided by IBM, most vendor contacts are IBM employees. However, independent software vendor (ISV) products are also used in the IBM mainframe environment, and customers use original equipment manufacturer (OEM) hardware, such as disk and tape storage devices, as well.

Typical vendor roles are:

► *Hardware support* or *customer engineer*

Hardware vendors usually provide onsite support for hardware devices. The IBM hardware maintenance person is often referred to as the customer engineer (CE). The CE provides installation and repair service for the mainframe hardware and peripherals. The CE usually works directly with the operations teams if hardware fails or if new hardware is being installed.

► *Software support*

A number of vendor roles exist to support software products on the mainframe[9]. IBM has a centralized *Support Center* that provides entitled and extra-charge support for software defects or usage assistance. There are also information technology specialists and architects who can be engaged to provide additional pre- and post-sales support for software products, depending upon the size of the enterprise and the particular customer situation.

► *Field technical sales support, systems engineer*, or *client representative*

For larger mainframe accounts, IBM and other vendors provide face-to-face sales support. The vendor representatives specialize in various types of hardware or software product families and call on the part of the customer organization that influences the product purchases.

---

[9] This text does not examine the marketing and pricing of mainframe software. However, the availability and pricing of middleware and other licensed programs is a critical factor affecting the growth and use of mainframes.

At IBM, the technical sales specialist is referred to as the *field* technical sales support (FTSS) person, or by the older term, systems engineer (SE).

For larger mainframe accounts, IBM frequently assigns a client representative, who is attuned to the business issues of a particular industry sector, to work exclusively with a small number of customers. The client representative acts as the general *single point of contact* (SPOC) between the customer and the various organizations within IBM.

1.10 z/OS and other mainframe operating systems

Much of this text is concerned with teaching you the fundamentals of z/OS, which is the foremost IBM mainframe operating system. We begin discussing z/OS concepts in Chapter 3, "z/OS overview" on page 91. It is useful for mainframe students, however, to have a working knowledge of other mainframe operating systems. One reason is that a given mainframe computer might run multiple operating systems. For example, the use of z/OS, z/VM, and Linux on the same mainframe is common.

Mainframe operating systems are sophisticated products with substantially different characteristics and purposes, and each could justify a separate book for a detailed introduction. Besides z/OS, four other operating systems dominate mainframe usage: z/VM, z/VSE, Linux on IBM System z, and z/TPF.

1.10.1 z/VM

z/Virtual Machine (z/VM) has two basic components: a *control program* (CP) and a single-user operating system (CMS). As a control program, z/VM is a *hypervisor* because it runs other operating systems in the virtual machines it creates. Any of the IBM mainframe operating systems such as z/OS, Linux on System z, z/VSE, and z/TPF can be run as *guest systems* in their own virtual machines, and z/VM can run any combination of guest systems.

The control program artificially creates multiple virtual machines from the real hardware resources. To users, it appears as though they have dedicated use of the shared real resources. The shared real resources include printers, disk storage devices, and the CPU. The control program ensures data and application security among the guest systems. The real hardware can be shared among the guests, or dedicated to a single guest for performance reasons. The system programmer allocates the real devices among the guests. For most customers, the use of guest systems avoids the need for larger hardware configurations.

z/VM's other major component is the Conversational Monitor System (CMS). This component of z/VM runs in a virtual machine and provides both an interactive user interface and the general z/VM application programming interface.

1.10.2 z/VSE

z/Virtual Storage Extended (z/VSE) is popular with users of smaller mainframe computers. Some of these customers eventually migrate to z/OS when they grow beyond the capabilities of z/VSE.

Compared to z/OS, the z/VSE operating system provides a smaller, less complex base for batch processing and transaction processing. The design and management structure of z/VSE is excellent for running routine production workloads consisting of multiple batch jobs (running in parallel) and extensive, traditional transaction processing. In practice, most z/VSE users also have the z/VM operating system and use this as a general terminal interface for z/VSE application development and system management.

z/VSE was originally known as Disk Operating System (DOS), and was the first disk-based operating system introduced for the System/360 mainframe computers. DOS was seen as a temporary measure until OS/360 would be ready. However, some mainframe customers liked its simplicity (and small size) and decided to remain with it after OS/360 became available. DOS became known as DOS/VS (when it started using virtual storage), then VSE/SP, and later VSE/ESA, and most recently z/VSE. The name VSE is often used collectively to refer to any of the more recent versions.

1.10.3 Linux on IBM System z

Several (non-IBM) Linux distributions can be used on a mainframe. There are two generic names for these distributions:

- ► Linux on S/390 (uses 31-bit addressing and 32-bit registers)
- ► Linux on System z (uses 64-bit addressing and registers)

The phrase *Linux on System z* is used to refer to Linux running on an S/390 or System z system, when there is no specific need to refer explicitly to either the 31-bit version or the 64-bit version.

We assume students are generally familiar with Linux and therefore we mention only those characteristics that are relevant for mainframe usage. Those characteristics include the following:

► Linux uses traditional count key data (CKD)[10]disk devices and SAN-connected SCSI-type devices. Other mainframe operating systems can recognize these drives as Linux drives, but cannot use the data formats on the drives, that is, there is no sharing of data between Linux and other mainframe operating systems.

► Linux does not use 3270 display terminals, while all other mainframe operating systems use 3270s as their basic terminal architecture.[11] Linux uses X Window System based terminals or X Window System emulators on PCs; it also supports typical ASCII terminals, usually connected through the *telnet* protocol. The X Window System is the standard for graphical interfaces in Linux. It is the middle layer between the hardware and the window manager.

► With the proper setup, a Linux system under z/VM can be quickly cloned to make another, separate Linux image. The z/VM emulated LAN can be used to connect multiple Linux images and to provide an external LAN route for them. Read-only file systems, such as a typical /usr file system, can be shared by Linux images.

► Linux on a mainframe operates with the ASCII character set, not the (Extended Binary Coded Decimal Interchange Code) EBCDIC[12] form of stored data that is typically used on mainframes. Here, EBCDIC is used only when writing to such character-sensitive devices as displays and printers. The Linux drivers for these devices handle the character translation.

1.10.4 z/TPF

The z/Transaction Processing Facility (z/TPF) operating system is a special-purpose system that is used by companies with high transaction volume, such as credit card companies and airline reservation systems. z/TPF was once known as Airline Control Program (ACP). It is still used by airlines and has been extended for other large systems with high-speed, high-volume transaction processing requirements.

---

[10] CKD devices are formatted such that the individual data pieces can be accessed directly by the read head of the disk.

[11] There is a Linux driver for minimal 3270 operation, in restrictive modes, but this is not commonly used. 3270 terminals were full-screen buffered non-intelligent terminals, with control units and data streams to maximize efficiency of data transmission.

[12] EBCDIC is a coded character set of 256 8-bit characters that was developed for the representation of textual data. EBCDIC is not compatible with ASCII character coding. For a handy conversion table, see Appendix D, "EBCDIC - ASCII table" on page 661.

z/TPF can use multiple mainframes in a loosely-coupled environment to routinely handle tens of thousands of transactions per second, while experiencing uninterrupted availability that is measured in years. Large terminal networks, including special-protocol networks used by portions of the reservation industry, are common.

1.11 Introducing the IBM zEnterprise System

Multitier workloads and their deployment on heterogeneous infrastructures are commonplace today. Creating and maintaining these high-level qualities of service from a large collection of distributed components demands significant knowledge and effort. It implies acquiring and installing extra equipment and software to ensure availability and security, monitoring, and managing. Additional manpower and skills are required to configure, administer, troubleshoot, and tune such a complex set of separate and diverse environments. Due to platform functional differences, the resulting infrastructure will not be uniform regarding those qualities of service or serviceability.

IBM introduced zEnterprise System, which is the first of its kind. It was purposefully designed to help overcome fundamental problems of today's IT infrastructures and simultaneously provide a foundation for the future. The zEnterprise System brings about a revolution in the end-to-end management of diverse systems, while offering expanded and evolved traditional System z capabilities.

With zEnterprise, a system of systems can be created where the virtualized resources of both the zEnterprise 196 (z196) and selected IBM blade-based servers, housed in the zEnterprise BladeCenter® Extension (zBX), are pooled together and jointly managed.

End-to-end solutions based on multi-platform workloads can be deployed across the zEnterprise System structure and benefit from System z's traditional qualities of service, including high availability, and simplified and improved management of the virtualized infrastructure.

Because many mission-critical workloads today have one or more components on System z, using System z environments for z/OS databases and other capabilities, the ability to co-locate all of the workload components under the same management platform and thereby benefit from uniformly high qualities of service should be quite appealing and provide tangible benefits and a rapid return on investment (ROI).

For the first time it is possible to deploy an integrated hardware platform that brings mainframe and distributed technologies together, producing a system that can start to replace individual islands of computing and that can work to reduce complexity, improve security, and bring applications closer to the data they need.

1.12 Summary

Today, mainframe computers play a central role in the daily operations of most of the world's largest corporations, including many Fortune 1000 companies. Although other forms of computing are used extensively in business in various capacities, the mainframe occupies a coveted place in today's e-business environment. In banking, finance, health care, insurance, utilities, government, and a multitude of other public and private enterprises, the mainframe computer continues to form the foundation of modern business.

The new mainframe owes much of its popularity and longevity to its inherent richness in reliability and stability, a result of continuous technological advances since the introduction of the IBM System/360 in 1964. No other computer architecture in existence can claim as much continuous, evolutionary improvement, while maintaining compatibility with existing applications.

The term *mainframe* has gradually moved from a physical description of the IBM larger computers to the categorization of a style of computing. One defining characteristic of the mainframe has been a continuing compatibility that spans decades.

The roles and responsibilities in a mainframe IT organization are wide and varied. It takes skilled staff to keep a mainframe computer running smoothly and reliably. It might seem that there are far more resources needed in a mainframe environment than for small, distributed systems. But, if roles are fully identified on the distributed systems side, a number of the same roles exist there as well.

Several operating systems are currently available for mainframes. This text concentrates on one of these, z/OS. However, mainframe students should be aware of the existence of the other operating systems and understand their positions relative to z/OS.

Table 1-1 lists the key terms used in this chapter.

Table 1-1 Key terms used in this chapter

architecture	availability	batch processing	compatibility	e-business
mainframe	online transaction processing (OLTP)	platform	production control analyst	run book
scalability	System/360	system operator	system programmer	zEnterprise System

1.13 Questions for review

To help test your understanding of the material in this chapter, perform the following tasks:

1. List ways in which the mainframe of today challenges the traditional thinking about centralized computing versus distributed computing.

2. Explain how businesses make use of mainframe processing power, and how mainframe computing differs from other types of computing.

3. List some of the factors that contribute to mainframe use.

4. List three strengths of mainframe computing, and outline the major types of workloads for which mainframes are best suited.

5. Name five jobs or responsibilities that are related to mainframe computing.

6. This chapter mentioned at least five operating systems that are used on the mainframe. Choose three of them and describe the main characteristics of each one.

1.14 Topics for further discussion

Here are topics for further discussion:

1. What is a mainframe today? How did the term arise? Is it still appropriate?

2. Why is it important to maintain system compatibility for older applications? Why not simply change existing application programming interfaces whenever improved interfaces become available?

3. Describe how running a mainframe can be cost effective, given the large number of roles needed to run a mainframe system.

4. What characteristics, good or bad, exist in a mainframe processing environment because of the roles that are present in a mainframe shop? (Efficiency? Reliability? Scalability?)

5. Describe some similarities and differences between application development for mainframe systems compared to other systems.

6. Most mainframe shops have implemented rigorous systems management, security, and operational procedures. Have these same procedures been implemented in distributed system environments? Why or why not?

7. Can you find examples of mainframe use in your everyday experiences? Describe them and the extent to which mainframe processing is apparent to users. Examples might include the following:

   a. Popular websites that rely on mainframe technology as the back-end server to support online transactions and databases.

   b. Multitiered applications that interface with mainframe resources.

   c. Mainframes used in your locality. These might include banks and financial centers, major retailers, transportation hubs, and the health and medical industries.

8. Can you find examples of distributed systems in everyday use? Could any of these systems be improved through the addition of a mainframe? How?

9. How is today's mainframe environment-friendly? Discuss with examples.

2

Mainframe hardware systems and high availability

Objective: As a new z/OS system programmer, you need to develop a thorough understanding of the hardware that runs the z/OS operating system. z/OS is designed to make full use of mainframe hardware and its many sophisticated peripheral devices. You should also understand how the hardware and software achieves near-continuous availability through concepts such as Parallel Sysplex and "no single points of failure."

After completing this chapter, you will be able to:

- ▶ Discuss System/360 (S/360) and IBM System z hardware design.
- ▶ Explain processing units and disk hardware.
- ▶ Explain how mainframes differ from PC systems in data encoding.
- ▶ List some typical hardware configurations.
- ▶ Describe platform performance management features.
- ▶ Explain how Parallel Sysplex can achieve continuous availability.
- ▶ Explain dynamic workload balancing.
- ▶ Explain the single system image.

Refer to Table 2-1 on page 88 for a list of key terms used in this chapter.

2.1 Introduction to mainframe hardware systems

This chapter provides an overview of mainframe hardware systems, with most of the emphasis on the processor "box."

For detailed descriptions of the major facilities of z/Architecture, the book *z/3 Principles of Operation* is the standard reference. You can find this and other IBM publications at the z/OS Internet Library website at the following address:

`http://www-03.ibm.com/systems/z/os/zos/bkserv/`

Let us begin this chapter with a look at the terminology associated with mainframe hardware. Knowing the various meanings of the terms *systems*, *processors*, *CP*s, and so on, is important for your understanding of mainframe computers.

CPU:
Synonymous with *processor*.

In the early S/360 days, a system had a single processor, which was also known as the central processing unit (CPU). The terms *system*, *processor*, and *CPU* were used interchangeably. However, these terms became confusing when systems became available with more than one processor. Today the mainframe has a rich heritage of terms, as shown in Figure 2-1.

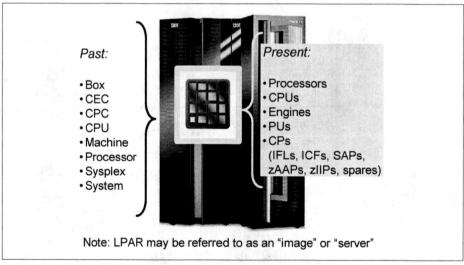

Past:

- Box
- CEC
- CPC
- CPU
- Machine
- Processor
- Sysplex
- System

Present:

- Processors
- CPUs
- Engines
- PUs
- CPs
  (IFLs, ICFs, SAPs, zAAPs, zIIPs, spares)

Note: LPAR may be referred to as an "image" or "server"

Figure 2-1   Terminology overlap

The term *box* may refer to the entire machine or model; the expression refers to its shape. The abbreviation *CPC* is used for the Central Processor Complex that houses the central processing units (CPUs).

CPC:
The physical collection of hardware that includes main storage, one or more central processors, timers, and channels.

Processor and CPU can refer to either the complete system box, or to one of the processors within the system box. Although the meaning may be clear from the context of a discussion, even mainframe professionals must clarify which processor or CPU meaning they are using in a discussion. System programmers use the term CPC to refer to the mainframe "box" or centralized processing hub. In this text, we use the term CPC to refer to the physical collection of hardware that includes main storage, one or more central processors, timers, and channels.

Partitioning and some of the terms in Figure 2-1 on page 46 are discussed later in this chapter, although the term *sysplex* is an idiom made up of two words: system and complex, which suggests multiple systems. Briefly, all the S/390 or z/Architecture processors within a CPC are *processing units* (PUs). When IBM delivers the CPC, the PUs are characterized as CPs (for normal work), Integrated Facility for Linux (IFL), Integrated Coupling Facility (ICF) for Parallel Sysplex configurations, and so on.

In this text, we hope the meanings of *system* and *processor* are clear from the context. We normally use system to indicate the hardware box, a complete hardware environment (with I/O devices), or an operating environment (with software), depending on the context. We normally use processor to mean a single processor (CP) within the CPC.

In some text, you may see a logical partition (LPAR) defined as an image or server. This represents an operating system instance, such as z/OS, z/VM, or Linux. You can run several different operating systems within a single mainframe by partitioning the resources into isolated servers. The term LPAR is covered in more detail later in this chapter.

2.2 Early system design

The central processor box contains the processors, memory,[1] control circuits, and interfaces for *channels*. A channel provides an independent data and control path between I/O devices and memory. Early systems had up to 16 channels; the largest mainframe machines at the time of this writing can have over 1000 channels. A channel can be considered as a high speed data bus.

Channels connect to *control units*. A control unit contains logic to work with a particular type of I/O device. A control unit for a printer would have much different internal circuitry and logic than a control unit for a tape drive, for example. Some control units can have multiple channel connections providing *multiple paths* to the control unit and its devices.

---
[1] Some S/360s had separate boxes for memory. However, this is a conceptual discussion and we ignore such details.

Today's channel paths are dynamically attached to control units as the workload demands. This provides a form of virtualizing access to devices. We will discuss this topic later in the chapter.

Control units connect to *devices*, such as disk drives, tape drives, communication interfaces, and so on. The division of circuitry and logic between a control unit and its devices is not defined, but it is usually more economical to place most of the circuitry in the control unit.

Figure 2-2 shows a conceptual diagram of a S/360 system. Current systems are not connected this way. However, this figure helps explain the background terminology that permeates mainframe discussions.

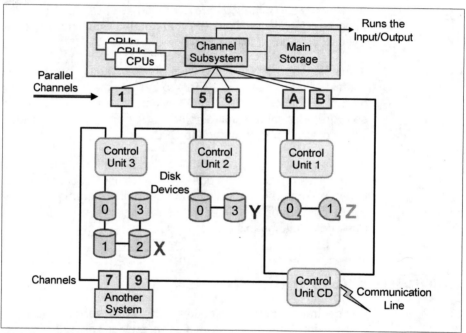

Figure 2-2   Simple conceptual S/360

The channels in Figure 2-2 are *parallel channels* (also known as *bus and tag channels*, named for the two heavy copper cables they use). A bus cable carries information (one byte each way), and a tag cable indicates the meaning of the data on the bus cable. The maximum data rate of the parallel channel is up to 4.5 MBps when in streaming mode, and the maximum distance achieved with a parallel channel interface is up to 122 meters (400 feet).

Attention: Parallel channels are no longer used by the latest mainframes and are mentioned here for completeness of this topic.

Each channel, control unit, and device has an address, expressed as a hexadecimal number. The disk drive marked with an X in Figure 2-2 on page 48 has address 132, as shown in Figure 2-3.

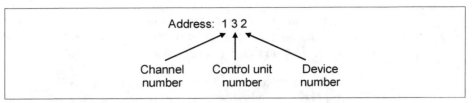

Address: 1 3 2

Channel   Control unit   Device
number   number   number

Figure 2-3   Device address

The disk drive marked with a Y in the figure can be addressed as 123, 523, or 623, because it is connected through three channels. By convention, the device is known by its lowest address (132), but all three addresses could be used by the operating system to access the disk drive. Multiple paths to a device are useful for performance and for availability. When an application wants to access disk 123, the operating system will first try channel 1. If it is busy (or not available), it will try channel 5, and so on.

Figure 2-2 on page 48 contains another S/360 system with two channels connected to control units used by the first system. This sharing of I/O devices is common in all mainframe installations because the mainframe is a share-everything architecture. Tape drive Z is address A11 for the first system, but is address 911 for the second system. Sharing devices, especially disk drives, is not a simple topic and there are hardware and software techniques used by the operating system to control exposures, such as updating the same disk data at the same time from two independent systems.

> **Attention:** A technique used to access a single disk drive by multiple systems is called *multiple allegiance*.

As mentioned, current mainframes are not used exactly as shown in Figure 2-2 on page 48. Differences include:

▶ Parallel channels are not available on the newest mainframes and are slowly being displaced on older systems. They are described here for the completeness of the topic.

ESCON:
Enterprise
Systems
Connection

▶ Parallel channels have been replaced with Enterprise Systems CONnection (ESCON®) and FIber CONnection (FICON®) channels. These channels connect to only one control unit or, more likely, are connected to a *director* (switch) and are optical fibers.

▶ Current mainframes can have over one thousand channels and use two hexadecimal digits as the channel portion of an address.

- ▶ Channels are generally known as channel path identifiers (CHPIDs) or physical channel identifiers (PCHIDs) on later systems, although the term *channel* is also correct. The channels are all integrated in the main processor box.

The device address seen by software is more correctly known as a device number (although the term *address* is still widely used) and is indirectly related to the control unit and device addresses.

For more information about the development of the IBM mainframe since 1964, see Appendix A, "A brief look at IBM mainframe history" on page 633.

2.3 Current design

Current CPC designs are considerably more complex than the early S/360 design. This complexity includes many areas:

- ▶ I/O connectivity and configuration
- ▶ I/O operation
- ▶ Partitioning of the system

I/O channels are part of the channel subsystem (CSS). They provide connectivity for data exchange between servers, or between servers and external control units (CU) and devices, or networks.

2.3.1 I/O connectivity

Figure 2-4 on page 51 shows a recent configuration. A real system would have more channels and I/O devices, but this figure illustrates key concepts. Partitions, ESCON channels, and FICON channels are described later.

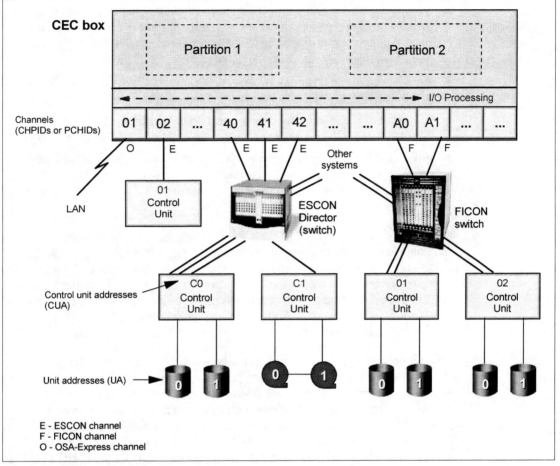

Figure 2-4   Recent system configuration

Briefly, partitions create separate logical machines (servers) in the CPC. ESCON and FICON channels are logically similar to parallel channels, but they use fibre connections and operate much faster. A modern system might have 300 - 500 channels or CHPIDs.[2] Key concepts partly illustrated here include the following:

► ESCON and FICON channels connect to only one device or one port on a switch.

► Most modern mainframes use switches between the channels and the control units. The switches are dynamically connected to several systems, sharing the control units and some or all of its I/O devices across all the systems.

---

[2] The more recent mainframe machines can have up to a maximum of 1024 channels, but an additional setup is needed. The channels are assigned in a way that only two hexadecimal digits are needed for CHPID addresses.

▶ CHPID addresses are two composed of two hexadecimal digits.

▶ Multiple partitions can sometimes share CHPIDs. This is known as *spanning*. Whether this is possible depends on the nature of the channel type and control units used through the CHPIDs. In general, CHPIDs used for disks can be shared.

▶ An I/O subsystem layer exists between the operating systems in partitions (or in the basic machine if partitions are not used) and the CHPIDs.

▶ The largest machine today can support up to four Logical Channel Subsystems (LCSSs), each having a maximum of 256 channels.

▶ InfiniBand (IFB) is used as the pervasive, low-latency, and high-bandwidth interconnect that has low processing impact and is ideal for carrying multiple traffic types. Beginning with the z10, it replaces the Self Timed Interface (STI) cable.

An ESCON director or FICON switch is a sophisticated device that can sustain high data rates through many connections. (A large director might have 200 connections, for example, and all of them can be passing data at the same time.) The director or switch must keep track of which CHPID (and partition) initiated which I/O operation so that data and status information is returned to the right place. Multiple I/O requests, from multiple CHPIDs attached to multiple partitions on multiple systems, can be in progress through a single control unit.

The I/O control layer uses a control file known as an I/O Control Data Set (IOCDS) that translates physical I/O addresses (composed of CHPID numbers, switch port numbers, control unit addresses, and unit addresses) into *device numbers* that are used by the operating system software to access devices. These numbers are loaded into a special storage area called the Hardware Save Area (HSA) at power-on. The HSA is not addressable by users and is a special component of the mainframe central storage area. A device number looks like the addresses we described for early S/360 machines except that it can contain three or four hexadecimal digits.

Many users still refer to these as "addresses" even though the device numbers are 16-bit (2 byte) arbitrary numbers between x'0000' and x'FFFF'. The newest mainframes, at the time of the writing of this book, have two layers of I/O address translations between the real I/O elements and the operating system software. The second layer was added to make migration to newer systems easier.

Modern control units, especially for disks, often have multiple channel (or switch) connections and multiple connections to their devices. They can handle multiple data transfers at the same time on the multiple channels. Each disk device unit is represented by a unit control block (UCB) in each z/OS image.

The UCB is a small piece of virtual storage describing the characteristics of a device to the operating system and contains the device address to denote status as well as tracking the progress of the I/O to the device. As an example, under certain conditions, if a disk device is busy servicing an I/O, another I/O to the same device is queued up with a "device busy" condition recorded within the UCB.

Attention: There is a feature to allow multiple I/Os to execute concurrently against the same disk device without queuing. This functionality allows a device to contain more than one access path using a base address along with aliases. It is implemented through the Enterprise Storage System (ESS) using a feature called Parallel Access Volumes (PAVs).

Figure 2-5 shows an overview of device addressing.

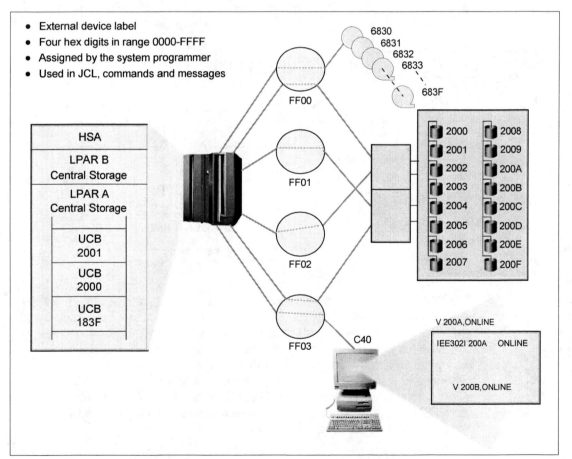

Figure 2-5   Device addressing

2.3.2 System control and partitioning

There are many ways to illustrate a mainframe's internal structure, depending on what we want to emphasize. Figure 2-6, while highly conceptual, shows several of the functions of the internal system controls on current mainframes. The internal controllers are microprocessors, but use a much simpler organization and instruction set than mainframe processors. They are usually known as *controllers* to avoid confusion with mainframe *processors*.

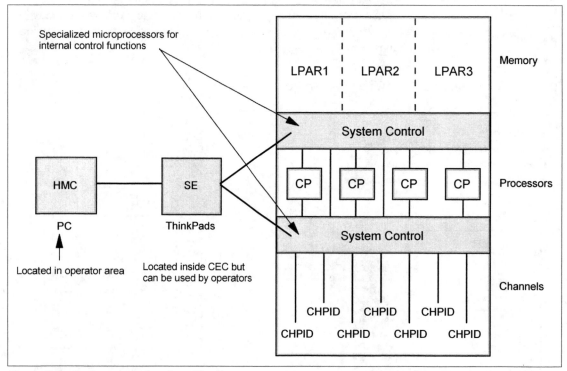

Figure 2-6   System control and partitioning

The IBM mainframe can be partitioned into separate logical computing systems. System resources (memory, processors, and I/O devices) can be divided or shared among many such independent logical partitions (LPARs) under the control of the LPAR hypervisor, which comes with the standard Processor Resource/ Systems Manager (PR/SM™) feature on all mainframes. The hypervisor is a software layer to manage multiple operating systems running in a single central processing complex. The mainframe uses a Type 1 hypervisor. Each LPAR supports an independent operating system (OS) loaded by a separate initial program load (IPL) operation.

For many years, there was a limit of 15 LPARs in a mainframe; today's machines can be configured with up to 60 logical partitions. Practical limitations of memory size, I/O availability, and available processing power usually limit the number of LPARs to less than these maximums. Each LPAR is considered an isolated and distinct server that supports an instance of an operating system (OS). The operating system can be any version or release supported by the hardware. In essence, a single mainframe can support the operation of several different OS environments, as shown in Figure 2-7.

Attention: A Type 1 (or native) hypervisor is software that runs directly on a given hardware platform (as an operating system control program). A Type 2 (or hosted) hypervisor is software that runs within an operating system environment such as VMWare.

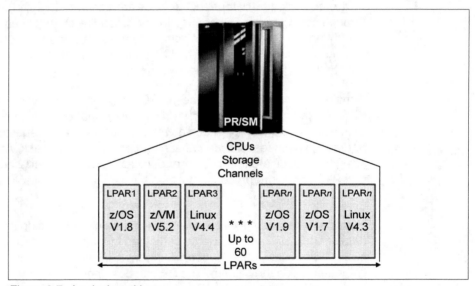

Figure 2-7   Logical partitions

System administrators assign portions of memory to each LPAR; memory also known as central storage (CSTOR) cannot be shared among LPARs. CSTOR, which is also referred to as *main storage*, provides the system with directly addressable, fast-access electronic storage of data. Both data and programs must be loaded into central storage (from input devices) before they can be processed by the CPU. The maximum central storage size is restricted by hardware and system architecture.

Attention: Prior to the current storage addressing scheme (64-bit), z/OS used another form of storage called Expanded Storage (ESTOR). This form of electronic storage is addressable in 4 KB blocks. Expanded storage was originally intended to bridge the gap in cost and density between main storage and auxiliary media by serving as a high-speed backing store for paging and for large data buffers. It is mentioned here for completeness because other operating systems on the mainframe still use this form of storage.

The system administrators can assign dedicated processors (noted as CPs in Figure 2-6 on page 54) to specific LPARs or they can allow the system to share and dispatch any or all the processors to the LPARs using an internal load-balancing algorithm.

Channels serve as a communication path from the mainframe to an external device such as disk or tape. I/O devices are attached to the channel subsystem through control units. The connection between the channel subsystem and a control unit is called a channel path. Channels Path Identifiers (CHPIDs) are assigned to specific LPARs or can be shared by multiple LPARs, depending on the nature of the devices on each channel.

A mainframe with a single processor (CP processor) can serve multiple LPARs. PR/SM has an internal dispatcher (Hipervisor) that can allocate a portion of the processor to each LPAR, much as an operating system dispatcher allocates a portion of its processor time to each process, thread, or task. An LPAR can be assigned a dedicated processor or dedicated several processors. Alternatively, an LPAR can share processors with other LPARS. The latter is the configuration norm.

Partitioning control specifications are, in part, contained in an input/output control data set (IOCDS) and are partly contained in a system *profile*. The IOCDS and profile both reside in the Support Element (SE), which is simply a mobile computer inside the system. The SE can be connected to one or more Hardware Management Consoles (HMCs), which are desktop personal computers used to monitor and control hardware, such as the mainframe microprocessors. An HMC is more convenient to use than an SE and can control several different mainframes.

HMC:
A console used to monitor and control hardware, such as the mainframe microprocessors.

Working from an HMC, an operator prepares a mainframe for use by selecting and loading a profile and an IOCDS. These create LPARs and configure the channels with device numbers, LPAR assignments, multiple path information, and so on. This is known as a Power-on Reset (POR). By loading a different profile and IOCDS, the operator can completely change the number and design of LPARs and the appearance of the I/O configuration. In some circumstances, this can be nondisruptive to running operating systems and applications.

2.3.3 Characteristics of LPARs

Logical partitions are, in practice, equivalent to separate mainframes. Each LPAR runs its own operating system (OS). This OS can be any mainframe operating system; there is no need to run z/OS, for example, in each LPAR. The installation planners may elect to share I/O devices across several LPARs, but this is a local decision.

The system administrator can assign one or more system processors for the exclusive use of an LPAR. Alternately, the administrator can allow all processors to be used on some or all LPARs. Here, the system control functions (often known as microcode or firmware) provide a dispatcher to share the processors among the selected LPARs. The administrator can specify a maximum number of concurrent processors executing in each LPAR. The administrator can also provide weightings for different LPARs, for example, specifying that LPAR1 should receive twice as much processor time as LPAR2.

The operating system in each LPAR is performs an IPL separately, has its own copy[3] of its operating system, has its own operator console (if needed), and so on. If the system in one LPAR fails or is taken down for maintenance, it has no effect on the other LPARs.

In Figure 2-7 on page 55, for example, we might be running a production z/OS in LPAR1, a test version of z/VM in LPAR2, and Linux on System z in LPAR3. If our total system has 8 GB of memory, we might assign 4 GB to LPAR1, 1 GB to LPAR2, 1 GB to LPAR3, and keep 2 GB in reserve for future use. The operating system consoles for the two z/OS LPARs might be in completely different locations.[4]

There is no practical difference between, for example, three separate mainframes running z/OS (and sharing most of their I/O configuration) and three LPARs on the same mainframe doing the same thing. In general, neither z/OS, the operators, or the applications, can detect the difference.

Minor differences include the ability of z/OS (if permitted when the LPARs were defined) to obtain performance and utilization information across the complete mainframe system and to dynamically shift resources (processors and channels) among LPARs to improve performance.

> **Note:** There is an implementation using a SYStem comPLEX (SYSPLEX) where LPARs can communicate and collaborate sharing resources.

---

[3] Most, but not all, of the z/OS system libraries can be shared.
[4] Linux does not have an operator console in the sense of the z/OS consoles.

2.3.4 Consolidation of mainframes

There are fewer mainframes in use today than there were 20 years ago because of corporate mergers and data center consolidations. In some cases, applications were moved to other types of systems, because there is no such thing as a "one size fits all" solution. However, in most cases the reduced number is due to consolidation, that is, several smaller mainframes have been replaced with a fewer but larger systems. Today's mainframe is considerably more powerful than past generations.

An additional reason for consolidation is that mainframe software (from many vendors) can be expensive, often costing more than the mainframe hardware. It is usually less expensive to replace multiple software licenses for smaller machines with one or two licenses for larger machines. Software license costs are often linked to the power of the system, yet the pricing curves favor a small number of large machines.

Software license costs for mainframes have become a dominant factor in the growth and direction of the mainframe industry. There are several factors that make software pricing difficult. We must remember that mainframe software is not a mass market item like PC software. The growth of mainframe processing power in recent years has been exponential rather than linear.

The relative power needed to run a traditional mainframe application (a batch job written in COBOL, for example) is far less than the power needed for a new application (with a GUI interface, written in C and Java). The consolidation effect has produced powerful mainframes, which might need only 1% of their power to run an older application, but the application vendor often sets a price based on the total power of the machine, even for older applications.

As an aid to consolidation, the mainframe offers software virtualization, through z/VM. z/VM's extreme virtualization capabilities, which have been perfected since its introduction in 1967, make it possible to virtualize thousands of distributed servers on a single server, resulting in the significant reduction in the use of space and energy.

Mainframes require fewer staff when supporting hundreds of applications. Because centralized computing is a major theme when using the mainframe, many of the configuration and support tasks are implemented by writing *rules* or creating a policy that manages the infrastructure automatically. This is a tremendous savings in time, resources, and cost.

2.4 Processing units

z/Architecture:
An IBM
architecture for
mainframe
computers and
peripherals. The
System z family
of servers uses
this
architecture.

Figure 2-1 on page 46 lists several different types of processors in a system. These are all z/Architecture processors that can be used for different workload characterization purposes.[5] Several of these purposes are related to software cost control, while others are more fundamental.

All these start as equivalent processor units[6] (PUs) or engines. A PU is a processor that has not been *characterized* for use. Each of the processors begins as a PU and is characterized by IBM during installation or at a later time. The potential characterizations are:

- ▸ Central processor (CP)

  This is a processor available to the general operating system and application software.

- ▸ system assist processor

  Every modern mainframe has at least one system assist processor; larger systems may have several. The system assist processors execute internal code[7] to drive the I/O subsystem. A system assist processor, for example, translates device numbers and real addresses of CHPIDs, control unit addresses, and device numbers. It manages and schedules an I/O by selecting an available path to control units. It also has a supplementary role during error recovery. Operating systems and applications cannot detect system assist processors, and system assist processors do not use any "normal" memory. system assist processors are considered co-processors or input /output processors (IOP) because you cannot perform an IPL from this engine type.

- ▸ Integrated Facility for Linux (IFL)

  This is a processor used exclusively by a Linux LPAR or Linux running under z/VM. An IPL of the LPAR performed only to run either operating environment. This processor type is accompanied with special user licensing incentives. Because these incentives reduce cost, they are not counted towards the overall capacity of the machine.[8] This can make a substantial difference in software costs.

---

[5] Do not confuse these processors with the controller microprocessors. The processors discussed in this section are full, standard mainframe processors.

[6] This discussion applies to the current System z machines at the time of the writing of this book. Earlier systems had fewer processor characterizations, and even earlier systems did not use these techniques.

[7] IBM refers to this as Licensed Internal Code (LIC). It is often known as microcode (which is not technically correct) or as firmware. It is not user code.

[8] Some systems do not have different models; in this case, a *capacity model number* is used.

> **Note:** A Linux LPAR can use general central processors, but licensing incentives do not apply.

- z/OS Application Assist Processor (zAAP)

  The z/OS Application Assist Processor (zAAP) provides for license incentives that allow you to run Java applications at a reduced cost. You can integrate and run e-business Java workloads on the same LPAR as your database, helping to simplify and reduce the infrastructure required for web applications. zAAP runs with general CPs in a z/OS LPAR. When Java code is detected, z/OS switches that instruction set to the zAAP processor, freeing up the general CP to perform other, non-Java work. This potentially offers a means to provide greater throughput. The zAAP engine is not counted towards the capacity of the model machine.

  With later versions of z/OS, all XML System Services validation and parsing that execute in TCB mode (which is problem state mode, as in most application workloads) might be eligible for zAAP processing, meaning that middleware and applications requesting z/OS XML System Services can have z/OS XML System Services processing execute on the zAAP.

- z/OS Integrated Information Processor (zIIP)

  The z/OS Integrated Information Processor (zIIP) provides for license incentives allowing you to optimize certain database workload functions at a reduced cost, such as business intelligence (BI), enterprise resource planning (ERP), and customer relationship management (CRM). When certain database code is detected, z/OS switches that instruction set to the zIIP processor, freeing up the general CP to perform other work. The zIIP runs with general CPs in a z/OS LPAR and is not counted towards the capacity of a machine model.

  z/OS Communications Server uses the zIIP for eligible IPSec network encryption workloads as well as XML System Services that are enabled to take additional advantage of the zIIP for preemptable SRB eligible XML workloads.

> **Attention:** Specialty engines may be used further as new releases of z/OS are announced.

► Integrated Coupling Facility (ICF)

This Integrated Coupling Facility processor exclusively uses the Coupling Facility Control Code (CFCC) and License Internal Code (LIC). A Coupling Facility is, in effect, a large memory scratch pad used by multiple systems to coordinate work by sharing resources between LPARs or used for workload balancing when configured for a Parallel Sysplex. ICFs must be assigned to separate LPARs that then become Coupling Facilities. The ICF are not visible to normal operating systems or applications.

► Spare

An uncharacterized PU functions as a "spare." If the system controllers detect a failing CP or system assist processor, it can be replaced with a spare PU. In most cases, this can be done without any system interruption, even for the application running on the failing processor.

► Various forms of *Capacity on Demand (CoD)* and similar arrangements exist whereby a customer can enable additional CPs at certain times (for example, unexpected peak loads or year end processing requirements).

2.4.1 Subcapacity processors

Some mainframes have models that can be configured to operate slower than the potential speed of their CPs. This is widely known as running *subcapacity*; IBM uses the term *capacity setting*. Subcapacity processors allow customers to choose a server size to best meet business requirements. Smaller incremental steps between capacity settings can allow customers to manage their growth, and their costs, in smaller increments. This task is accomplished by using microcode to insert null cycles into the processor instruction stream. The purpose, again, is to control software costs by having the minimum mainframe model that meets the application requirements.

Specialty engines such as IFLs, system assist processors, zAAPs, zIIPs, and ICFs are not eligible for this feature and always function at the full speed of the processor because these processors "do not count" in software pricing calculations.[9]

---

[9] This is true for IBM software but may not be true for all software vendors.

2.5 Multiprocessors

All the earlier discussions and examples assume that more than one processor (CP) is present in a system (and perhaps in an LPAR). It is possible to purchase a current mainframe with a single processor (CP), but this is not a typical system.[10] The term *multiprocessor* means several processors (CP processors) and implies that several processors are used by a copy of z/OS. The term also refers to the ability of a system to support more than one processor and the ability to allocate tasks between them.

Multiprocessor: A CPC that can be physically partitioned to form two operating processor complexes.

All operating systems today, from PCs to mainframes, can work in a multiprocessor environment. However, the degree of integration of the multiple processors varies considerably. For example, pending interrupts in a system (or in an LPAR) can be accepted by any processor in the system (or working in the LPAR). Any processor can initiate and manage I/O operations to any channel or device available to the system or LPAR. Channels, I/O devices, interrupts, and memory are owned by the system (or by the LPAR) and not by any specific processor.

This multiprocessor integration appears simple on the surface, but its implementation is complex. For maximum performance, the ability of any processor to accept any interrupt sent to the system (or to the LPAR) is especially important.

Each processor in a system (or in an LPAR) has a small private area of memory (8 KB starting at real address 0 and always mapped to virtual address 0) that is unique to that processor. This is the Prefix Storage Area (PSA) and it is used for instruction execution, interrupts, and error handling. A processor can access another processor's PSA through special programming, although this is normally done only for error recovery purposes. A processor can interrupt other processors by using a special instruction (SIGP, for Signal Processor). Again, this is typically used only for error recovery.

---

[10] All current IBM mainframes also require at least one system assist processor, so the minimum system has two processors: one CP and one system assist processor. However, the use of "processor" in the text usually means a CP processor usable for applications. Whenever discussing a processor other than a CP, we always make this clear.

2.6 Disk devices

IBM 3390 disk drives are commonly used on current mainframes. Conceptually, this is a simple arrangement, as shown in Figure 2-8.

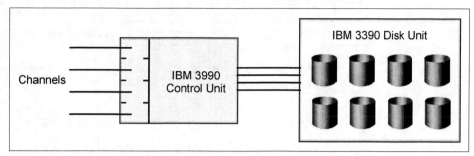

Figure 2-8   Initial IBM 3390 disk implementation

The associated control unit (3990) typically has up to four Fibre Channel connections connected to one or more processors (probably with a switch), and the 3390 unit typically has eight or more disk drives. Each disk drive has the characteristics explained earlier. This illustration shows 3990 and 3390 units, and it also represents the concept or architecture of current devices.

Figure 2-9 shows the architecture of current devices.

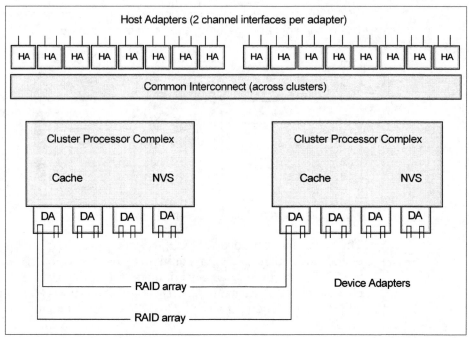

Figure 2-9   Current 3390 implementation

IBM has a wide range of product offerings that are based on open standards and that share a common set of tools, interfaces, and innovative features. The IBM System Storage® DS® family and its member, the DS8000®, gives customers the freedom to choose the right combination of solutions for their current needs and the flexibility for the infrastructure to evolve as their needs change. The System Storage DS family is designed to offer high availability and multi-platform support, which helps cost-effectively adjust to an evolving business world.

The 2105 unit is a sophisticated device. It emulates a large number of control units and 3390 disk drives. It contains up to 11 TB of disk space, has up to 32 channel interfaces, 16 GB cache, and 284 MB of non-volatile memory (used for write queuing). The Host Adapters appear as control unit interfaces and can connect up to 32 channels (ESCON or FICON).

The physical disk drives are commodity SCSI-type units (although a serial interface, known as SSA, is used to provide faster and redundant access to the disks). A number of internal arrangements are possible, but the most common involves many RAID 5 arrays with hot spares. Practically everything in the unit has a spare or fallback unit.

The internal processing (to emulate 3990 control units and 3390 disks) is provided by four high-end RISC processors in two processor complexes; each complex can operate the total system. Internal batteries preserve transient data during short power failures. A separate console is used to configure and manage the unit.

The 2105 offers many functions not available in real 3390 units, including FlashCopy®, Extended Remote Copy, Concurrent Copy, Parallel Access Volumes, Multiple Allegiance, a huge cache, and so on.

A simple 3390 disk drive (with control unit) has different technology from the 2105 just described. However, the basic architectural appearance to software is the same. This allows applications and system software written for 3390 disk drives to use the newer technology with no revisions.[11]

There have been several stages of new technology implementing 3390 disk drives; the 2105 is the most recent of these. The process of implementing an architectural standard (in this case, the 3390 disk drive and associated control unit) with newer and different technology while maintaining software compatibility is characteristic of mainframe development. As we mentioned, maintaining application compatibility over long periods of technology change is an important characteristic of mainframes.

2.7 Clustering

Clustering has been done on mainframes since the early S/360 days, although the term *cluster* is seldom used in terms of mainframes. A clustering technique can be as simple as a shared DASD configuration where manual control or planning is needed to prevent unwanted data overlap.

Additional clustering techniques have been added over the years. In the following sections, we discuss three levels of clustering:

► Basic Shared DASD
► CTC rings
► Parallel Sysplex

Most z/OS installations today use one or more of these levels; a single z/OS installation is relatively rare.

---

[11] Some software enhancements are needed to use some of the new functions, but these are compatible extensions at the operating system level and do not affect application programs.

In this discussion, we use the term "image". A z/OS server (with one or more processors) is a *z/OS image*. A z/OS image might exist on a mainframe (with other LPARs), or it might run under z/VM (a hypervisor operating system mentioned in 1.10, "z/OS and other mainframe operating systems" on page 37). A system with six LPARs, each a separate z/OS system, has six z/OS images.

2.8 Basic shared DASD

A basic shared DASD environment is shown in Figure 2-10. The figure shows z/OS images, but these could be any earlier version of the operating system. This could be two LPARs in the same system or two separate systems; there is absolutely no difference in the concept or operation.

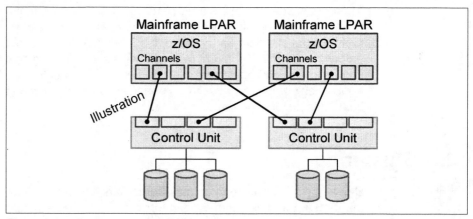

Figure 2-10   Basic shared DASD

The capabilities of a basic shared DASD system are limited. The operating systems automatically issue RESERVE and RELEASE commands to a DASD before updating the volume table of contents (VTOC) or catalog. (As we discuss in Chapter 5, "Working with data sets" on page 203, the VTOC and catalog are structures that contain metadata for the DASD, indicating where various data sets reside.) The RESERVE command limits access to the entire DASD to the system issuing the command, and this lasts until a RELEASE command is issued. These commands work well for limited periods (such as updating metadata). Applications can also issue RESERVE/RELEASE commands to protect their data sets for the duration of the application. This is not automatically done in this environment and is seldom done in practice because it would lock out other systems' access to the DASD for too long.

A basic shared DASD system is typically used where the operations staff controls which jobs go to which system and ensures that there is no conflict, such as both systems trying to update the same data at the same time. Despite this limitation, a basic shared DASD environment is useful for testing, recovery, and careful load balancing.

Other types of devices or control units can be attached to both systems. For example, a tape control unit, with multiple tape drives, can be attached to both systems. In this configuration, the operators can then allocate individual tape drives to the systems as needed.

2.8.1 CTC rings

The channel-to-channel (CTC) function simulates an input/output (I/O) device that can be used by one system control program (SCP) to communicate with another SCP. It provides the data path and synchronization for data transfer. When the CTC option is used to connect two channels that are associated with different systems, a loosely coupled multiprocessing system is established. The CTC connection, as viewed by either of the channels to which it connects, has the appearance of an unshared input/output (I/O) device.

Figure 2-11 shows the next level of clustering. This level has the same shared DASD as discussed previously, but also has two *channel-to-channel* (CTC) connections between the systems. This is known as a *CTC ring*. (The ring aspect is more obvious when more than two systems are involved.)

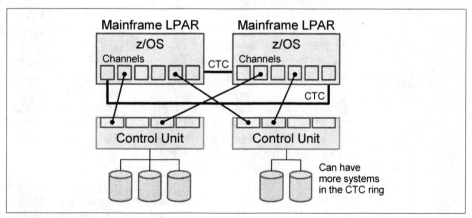

Figure 2-11   Basic sysplex

z/OS can use the CTC ring to pass control information among all systems in the ring. The information that can be passed this way includes:

▶ Usage and locking information for data sets on disks. This allows the system to automatically prevent unwanted duplicate access to data sets. This locking is based on JCL specifications provided for jobs sent to the system, as explained in Chapter 6, "Using Job Control Language and System Display and Search Facility" on page 241.

▶ Job queue information, such that all the systems in the ring can accept jobs from a single input queue. Likewise, all systems can send printed output to a single output queue.

▶ Security controls that allow uniform security decisions across all systems.

▶ Disk metadata controls, so that RESERVE and RELEASE disk commands are not necessary.

To a large extent, batch jobs and interactive users can run on any system in this configuration because all disk data sets can be accessed from any z/OS image. Jobs (and interactive users) can be assigned to whichever system is most lightly loaded at the time.

When the CTC configurations were first used, the basic control information shared was locking information. As we discuss in 3.7.5, "Serializing the use of resources" on page 140, the z/OS component performing this function is called the *global resource serialization (GRS) function*; this configuration is called a GRS ring. The primary limitation of a GRS ring is the latency involved in sending messages around the ring.

CTC connection:
A connection between two CHPIDs on the same or different processors, either directly or through a switch.

A different CTC configuration was used before the ring technique was developed. This required two CTC connections from every system to every other system in the configuration. When more than two or three systems were involved, this became complex and required a considerable number of channels.

The earlier CTC configurations (every-system-to-every-system or a ring configuration) were later developed into a basic *sysplex* configuration, which includes control data sets on the shared DASD. These data sets are used for consistent operational specifications for all systems and to retain information over system restarts.

Configurations with shared DASD, CTC connections, and shared job queues are known as *loosely coupled systems*. (Multiprocessors, where several processors are used by the operating system, are sometimes contrasted as *tightly coupled systems*, but this terminology is seldom used. These are also known as Symmetrical MultiProcessors (SMPs); the SMP terminology is common with RISC systems, but is not normally used for mainframes.)

2.9 What is a sysplex

A systems complex, commonly called a *sysplex*, is one or more (up to 32 LPARs) z/OS images joined into a cooperative single unit using specialized hardware and software. It uses unique messaging services and can share special file structures contained within couple facility (CF) data sets.

A sysplex is an instance of a computer system running on one or more physical partitions where each can run a different release of a z/OS operating system. Sysplexes are often isolated to a single system, but Parallel Sysplex technology allows multiple mainframes to act as one. It is a clustering technology that can provide near-continuous availability.

A conventional large computer system also uses hardware and software products that cooperate to process work. A major difference between a sysplex and a conventional large computer system is the improved growth potential and level of availability in a sysplex. A sysplex generally provides for resource sharing between communicating systems (tape, consoles, catalogues, and so on). The sysplex increases the number of processing units and z/OS operating systems that can cooperate, which in turn increases the amount of work that can be processed. To facilitate this cooperation, new products were developed and past products were enhanced.

2.9.1 Parallel Sysplex

Parallel Sysplex: A sysplex that uses one or more Coupling Facilities.

A *Parallel Sysplex* is a symmetric sysplex using multisystem data-sharing technology. This is the mainframe's clustering technology. It allows direct, concurrent read/write access to shared data from all processing servers in the configuration without impacting performance or data integrity. Each LPAR can concurrently cache shared data in the CF processor memory through hardware-assisted, cluster-wide serialization and coherency controls.

As a result, when applications are "enabled" for this implementation, the complete benefits of the Parallel Sysplex technology are made available. Work requests that are associated with a single workload, such as business transactions or database queries, can:

► Dynamically be balanced across systems with high performance

► Improve availability for both planned and unplanned outages

► Provide for system or application rolling maintenance

► Offer scalable workload growth both vertically and horizontally

► View multiple-system environments as a single logical resource

An important design aspect of a Parallel Sysplex is synchronizing the TOD clocks of multiple servers, which allows events occurring on different servers to be properly sequenced in time. As an example, when multiple servers update the same database and database reconstruction is necessary, all updates are required to be time stamped in proper sequence.

In the past, a separate device known as the Sysplex Timer® was required to keep the TOD clocks of all participating servers synchronized with each other to within a small number of microseconds. It was dictated by the fastest possible passing of data from one server to another through the Coupling Facility (CF) structure.

Today's implementation uses the Server Time Protocol (STP), which is a server-wide facility that is implemented in the Licensed Internal Code (LIC). STP presents a single view of time to Processor Resource/Systems Manager™ (PR/SM), and is designed to provide the capability for multiple mainframe servers to maintain time synchronization with each other. It is the follow-up to the Sysplex Timer.

The Sysplex Timer distributes time to multiple servers in a star pattern, that is, the Sysplex Timer is the star, and its time signals distribute out from it to all attached servers. The signals from the Sysplex Timer are used to increment or step the TOD clocks in the attached server. Unlike the Sysplex Timer, STP passes time messages in layers, or strata. The top layer (Stratum 1) distributes time messages to the layer immediately below it (Stratum 2). Stratum 2 in turn distributes time messages to Stratum 3 and so on.

In a timing network based on STP, a stratum is used as a means to define the hierarchy of a server in the timing network. A Stratum 1 server is the highest level in the hierarchy in the STP network.

Figure 2-12 shows the hardware components of a Parallel Sysplex that make up the key aspects in its architecture. It includes several system files or data sets placed on direct access storage devices (DASD).

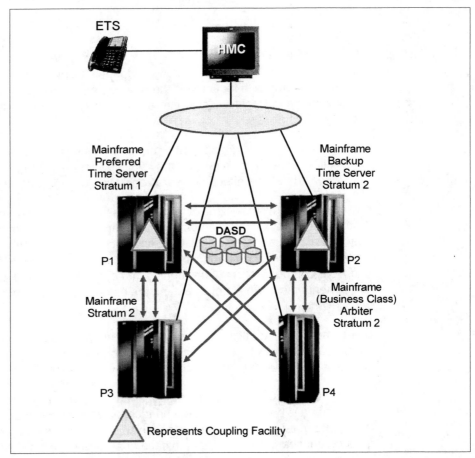

Figure 2-12   Sysplex hardware overview

2.9.2 What is a Coupling Facility

A Parallel Sysplex relies on one or more Coupling Facilities (CFs). A Coupling Facility enables high performance multisystem data sharing. The CF contains one or more mainframe processors and a special licensed built-in operating system.

A CF functions largely as a fast scratch pad. It is used for three purposes:

► Locking information that is shared among all attached systems

► Cache information (such as for a data base) that is shared among all attached systems

► Data list information that is shared among all attached systems

z/OS applications on different LPARs often need to access the same information, sometimes to read it and other times to update it. Sometimes several copies of the data exist and with that comes the requirement of keeping all the copies identical. If the system fails, customers need a way to preserve the data with the most recent changes.

Linking a number of images together brings with it special considerations, such as how the servers communicate and how they cooperate to share resources. These considerations affect the overall operation of z/OS systems.

Implementing a sysplex significantly changes the way z/OS systems share data. As the number of systems increase, it is essential to have an efficient means to share data across systems. The Coupling Facility enables centrally accessible, high performance data sharing for authorized applications, such as subsystems and z/OS components, that are running in a sysplex. These subsystems and components then transparently extend the benefits of data sharing to their applications.

Use of the Coupling Facility (CF) significantly improves the viability of connecting many z/OS systems together in a sysplex to process work in parallel. Data validity is controlled by a data management system such as IMS or DB2.

Within a single z/OS system, the data management system keeps track of which piece of data is being accessed or changed by which application in the system. It is the data management system's responsibility to capture and preserve the most recent changes to the data, in case of system failure. When two or more z/OS systems share data, each system contains its own copy of a data management system. Communication between the data management systems is essential. Therefore, multisystem data sharing centers on high performance communication to ensure data validity among multiple data management systems requiring high speed data accessing methods implemented through the Coupling Facility feature.

The information in the CF resides in memory and a CF typically has a large memory. A CF can be a separate system or an LPAR can be used as a CF.

Figure 2-13 shows a small Parallel Sysplex with two z/OS images. Again, this whole configuration could be in three LPARs on a single system, in three separate systems, or in a mixed combination.

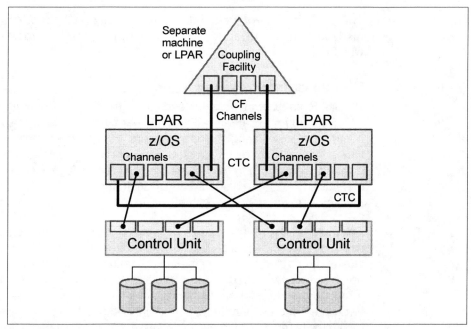

Figure 2-13   Parallel Sysplex

In many ways, a Parallel Sysplex system appears as a single large system. It has a single operator interface (that controls all systems). With proper planning and operation, complex workloads can be shared by any or all systems in the Parallel Sysplex, and recovery (by another system in the Parallel Sysplex) can be automatic for many workloads.

> **Note:** The Coupling Facility is usually illustrated as a triangle in the diagrams used in IBM publications.

2.9.3 Clustering technologies for the mainframe

Parallel Sysplex technology helps ensure continuous availability in today's large systems environments. A Parallel Sysplex allows the linking up to 32 servers with near linear scalability to create a powerful commercial processing clustered system. Every server in a Parallel Sysplex cluster can be configured to share access to data resources, and a "cloned" instance of an application might run on every server.

Parallel Sysplex design characteristics help businesses run continuously, even during periods of dramatic change. Sysplex sites can dynamically add and change systems in a sysplex, and configure the systems for no single points of failure.

Through this state-of-the-art cluster technology, multiple z/OS systems can be made to work in concert to more efficiently process the largest commercial workloads.

Shared data clustering

Parallel Sysplex technology extends the strengths of IBM mainframe computers by linking up to 32 servers with near linear scalability to create a powerful commercial processing clustered system. Every server in a Parallel Sysplex cluster has access to all data resources, and every "cloned" application can run on every server. Using mainframe coupling technology, Parallel Sysplex technology provides a "shared data" clustering technique that permits multi-system data sharing with high performance read/write integrity.

This "shared data" (as opposed to "shared nothing") approach enables workloads to be dynamically balanced across servers in the Parallel Sysplex cluster. It enables critical business applications to take advantage of the aggregate capacity of multiple servers to help ensure maximum system throughput and performance during peak processing periods. In the event of a hardware or software outage, either planned or unplanned, workloads can be dynamically redirected to available servers, thus providing near-continuous application availability.

Nondisruptive maintenance

Another unique advantage of using Parallel Sysplex technology is the ability to perform hardware and software maintenance and installation in a nondisruptive manner.

Through data sharing and dynamic workload management, servers can be dynamically removed from or added to the cluster, allowing installation and maintenance activities to be performed while the remaining systems continue to process work. Furthermore, by adhering to the IBM software and hardware coexistence policy, software and hardware upgrades can be introduced one system at a time. This capability allows customers to roll changes through systems at a pace that makes sense for their business.

The ability to perform rolling hardware and software maintenance in a nondisruptive manner allows businesses to implement critical business functions and react to rapid growth without affecting customer availability.

2.10 Intelligent Resource Director

Intelligent Resource Director can be viewed as Stage 2 of Parallel Sysplex. Stage 1 provides facilities to let you share your data and workload across multiple system images. As a result, applications that support data sharing could potentially run on any system in the sysplex, thus allowing you to move your workload to where the processing resources were available.

However, not all applications support data sharing, and there are many applications that have not been migrated to data sharing for various reasons. For these applications, IBM has provided Intelligent Resource Director, which gives you the ability to move the resource to where the workload is.

Intelligent Resource Director uses facilities in z/OS Workload Manager (WLM), Parallel Sysplex, and PR/SM to help you derive greater value from your mainframe investment. Compared to other platforms, z/OS with WLM already provides benefits, such as the ability to drive a processor at 100% while still providing acceptable response times for your critical applications. Intelligent Resource Director amplifies this advantage by helping you make sure that all those resources are being used by the right workloads, even if the workloads exist in different logical partitions (LPARs).

Intelligent Resource Director is not actually a product or a system component; rather, it is three separate but mutually supportive functions:

► WLM LPAR CPU Management

This function provides the means to modify an LPAR weight to a higher value to move logical CPUs to an LPAR that is missing its service level goal.

► Dynamic Channel-path Management (DCM)

Dynamic Channel-path Management is designed to dynamically adjust the channel configuration in response to shifting workload patterns.

DCM is implemented by exploiting functions in software components, such as WLM, I/O, and hardware configuration. This supports DASD controller to have the system automatically manage the number of I/O paths available to disk devices.

► Channel Subsystem I/O Priority Queueing (CSS IOPQ)

z/OS uses this function to dynamically manage the channel subsystem priority of I/O operations for given workloads based on the performance goals for these workloads as specified in the WLM policy.

The Channel Subsystem I/O Priority Queueing works at the channel subsystem level, and affects every I/O request (for every device, from every LPAR) on the CPC.

> **Note:** I/O prioritization occurs in a microcode queue within the system assist processor.

2.11 Platform Performance Management with zEnterprise

A key strength of the mainframe is its ability to run multiple workloads concurrently across multiple system images, and you learn how to manage those workloads according to performance goals that you set. With the IBM zEnterprise System (zEnterprise) mainframe, this concept is extended to include performance management capability for both traditional System z and the IBM zEnterprise BladeCenter Extension (zBX) hardware environments.

For multitier applications that span System z hardware and zBX hardware, this extended capability enables dynamic adjustments to CPU allocations to ensure that those applications are provided with sufficient resources.

To manage work on these attached platforms (known as an *ensemble*), you classify the workload running into *service classes* and set its level of importance by defining goals for it that express the expectation of how the work should perform using performance policies.

> **Attention:** An ensemble is a collection of one or more zEnterprise nodes (including any attached zBX) that are managed as a single logical virtualized system by the IBM zEnterprise Unified Resource Manager (zManager), through the use of a Hardware Management Console.

The IBM zEnterprise Unified Resource Manager (zManager) uses these policy definitions to manage the resources for each workload in an ensemble.

In contrast, for z/OS workload management (WLM), which you will read about in Chapter 3, "z/OS overview" on page 91, a workload is a customer-defined collection of work to be tracked, managed, and reported as a unit. So for z/OS workload management, a workload is not an amount of work, but rather a type of work that is meaningful to customers. Customers use business goals or functions to define z/OS WLM workloads, for example, a z/OS WLM workload might represent all the work started by a particular business application, or all the work created by one company group, such as sales or software development, or all the work processed by a subsystem, such as DB2 for z/OS.

The Unified Resource Manager performance policies do not replace the z/OS WLM policy. The performance monitoring and management done by the Unified Resource Manager performance management function is at a different scope than z/OS WLM and the policies are separate. The major performance management functions of Unified Resource Manager are:

► The ability to define Platform Workloads, which is a grouping of the virtual servers (AIX® partitions on POWER® blades, z/VM virtual machines, and PR/SM LPARs) that support business applications. Consider a three-tiered application with a web server running on a POWER blade, IBM WebSphere Application Server running in a Linux on System z z/VM guest, and DB2 in a z/OS partition. The workload would be the three virtual servers.

► The ability to define a performance policy for a Platform Workload that is used to monitor and manage the virtual servers in that Platform Workload. This performance policy allows goal-oriented performance objectives and workload importance to be set for the virtual servers in the Platform Workload.

► Provide performance monitoring in the context of the Platform Workload. This monitoring indicates whether the virtual servers in the Platform Workload are achieving their goals. If not, it helps determine which virtual servers are contributing to the performance problem.

2.12 Typical mainframe system growth

An integral characteristic of the mainframe is extensibility. This is a system design principle where the implementation takes into consideration future ease of growth to extend a system's infrastructure. Extensions can be made through the addition of new functionality or through modification of existing functionality. The central objective is to provide for change while minimizing the impact to existing system functions. You will see this design theme throughout this publication.

Today's mainframe supports size and capacity in various ways. It is difficult to provide a definitive set of guidelines to portray what are considered small, medium, and large mainframe shops, because infrastructure upgrades can be readily made.

IBM further enhances the capabilities of the mainframe by using optimized capacity settings with subcapacity central processors. There is great granularity by using subcapacity engines and high scalability (with up to 64 engines on a single server).

Here are a few other examples:

- ► Customer Initiated Upgrade (CIU): The CIU feature enables a customer to order permanent capacity upgrades rapidly and download them without disrupting applications already running on the machine. When extra processing power becomes necessary, an administrator simply uses a two step process:

  a. Navigates to special web-based link to order an upgrade.

  b. Uses the Remote Service Facility on the Hardware Management Console (HMC) to download and activate preinstalled inactive processors (uncharacterized engines) or memory.

- ► On/Off Capacity on Demand (On/Off CoD): This feature is available through CIU, and uses On/Off CoD for temporary increases in processor capacity. With temporary processor capacity, customers manage both predictable and unpredictable surges in capacity demands. They can activate and deactivate quickly and efficiently as the demands on their organization dictates to obtain additional capacity that they need, when they need it, and the machine will keep track of its usage. On/Off CoD provides a cost-effective strategy for handling seasonal or period-end fluctuations in activity and may enable customers to deploy pilot applications without investing in new hardware. Free tests are available for this feature.

- ► Capacity Backup (CBU): Customers can use CBU to add temporary processing capacity to a backup machine in the event of an unforeseen loss of server capability because of an emergency. With CBU, customers can divert entire workloads to backup servers for up to 90 days.

2.13 Continuous availability of mainframes

Parallel Sysplex technology is an enabling technology, allowing highly reliable, redundant, and robust mainframe technologies to achieve near-continuous availability. A properly configured Parallel Sysplex cluster is designed to remain available to its users and applications with minimal downtime.

Here are some examples:

- ► Hardware and software components provide concurrency to facilitate nondisruptive maintenance, such as Capacity Upgrade on Demand, which allows processing or coupling capacity to be added one engine at a time without disruption to running workloads. In addition, CP sparing is used if there is a processor failure (another one is brought online transparently).

- ► DASD subsystems employ disk mirroring or RAID technologies to help protect against data loss, and exploit technologies to enable point-in-time backup, without the need to shut down applications.

- Networking technologies deliver functions such as VTAM® Generic Resources, Multi-Node Persistent Sessions, Virtual IP Addressing, and Sysplex Distributor to provide fault-tolerant network connections.

- I/O subsystems support multiple I/O paths and dynamic switching to prevent loss of data access and improved throughput.

- z/OS software components allow new software releases to coexist with lower levels of those software components to facilitate rolling maintenance.

- Business applications are "data sharing-enabled" and cloned across servers to allow workload balancing to prevent loss of application availability in the event of an outage.

- Operational and recovery processes are fully automated and transparent to users, and reduce or eliminate the need for human intervention.

- z/OS has a Health Checker to assist in avoiding outages. This uses "best practices," identifying potential problems before they impact availability. It produces output in the form of detailed messages and offers suggested actions to take.

Parallel Sysplex is a way of managing this multi-system environment, providing such benefits as:

- No single points of failure
- Capacity and scaling
- Dynamic workload balancing
- Systems management technologies
- Single system image
- Compatible change and nondisruptive growth
- Application compatibility
- Disaster recovery

These benefits are described in the remaining sections of this chapter.

2.13.1 No single points of failure

In a Parallel Sysplex cluster, it is possible to construct a parallel processing environment with no single points of failure. Because all of the systems in the Parallel Sysplex can have concurrent access to all critical applications and data, the loss of a system due to either hardware or software failure does not necessitate loss of application availability.

Peer instances of a failing subsystem executing on remaining healthy system nodes can take over recovery responsibility for resources held by the failing instance. Alternatively, the failing subsystem can be automatically restarted on still-healthy systems using automatic restart capabilities to perform recovery for work in progress at the time of the failure. While the failing subsystem instance is unavailable, new work requests can be redirected to other data-sharing instances of the subsystem on other cluster nodes to provide continuous application availability across the failure and subsequent recovery. This provides the ability to mask planned as well as unplanned outages to the user.

Because of the redundancy in the configuration, there is a significant reduction in the number of single points of failure. Without a Parallel Sysplex, the loss of a server could severely impact the performance of an application, as well as introduce system management difficulties in redistributing the workload or reallocating resources until the failure is repaired. In a Parallel Sysplex environment, it is possible that the loss of a server may be transparent to the application, and the server workload can be redistributed automatically within the Parallel Sysplex with little performance degradation. Therefore, events that otherwise would seriously impact application availability, such as failures in central processor complex (CPC) hardware elements or critical operating system components, would, in a Parallel Sysplex environment, have reduced impact.

Even though they work together and present a single image, the nodes in a Parallel Sysplex cluster remain individual systems, making installation, operation, and maintenance nondisruptive. The system programmer can introduce changes, such as software upgrades, one system at a time, while the remaining systems continue to process work. This allows the mainframe IT staff to roll changes through its systems on a schedule that is convenient to the business.

2.13.2 Capacity and scaling

The Parallel Sysplex environment can scale nearly linearly from 2 to 32 systems. This can be a mix of any servers that support the Parallel Sysplex environment. The aggregate capacity of this configuration meets every processing requirement known today.

The mainframe offers subcapacity settings for general CPs. If you do not need the full strength of a full cycle CP, you have the option for a smaller setting. There are ranges of subcapacity settings, as defined by the model of the machine.

2.13.3 Dynamic workload balancing

The entire Parallel Sysplex cluster can be viewed as a single logical resource to users and business applications. Just as work can be dynamically distributed across the individual processors within a single SMP server, so too can work be directed to any node in a Parallel Sysplex cluster having available capacity. This capability avoids the need to partition data or applications among individual nodes in the cluster or to replicate databases across multiple servers.

Workload balancing also permits a business to run diverse applications across a Parallel Sysplex cluster while maintaining the response levels critical to a business. The mainframe IT director selects the service level agreements required for each workload, and the workload management (WLM) component of z/OS, along with subsystems such as CP/SM or IMS, automatically balance tasks across all the resources of the Parallel Sysplex cluster to meet these business goals. The work can come from a variety of sources, such as batch, SNA, TCP/IP, DRDA®, or WebSphere MQ.

There are several aspects to consider for recovery. First, when a failure occurs, it is important to bypass it by automatically redistributing the workload to use the remaining available resources. Secondly, it is necessary to recover the elements of work that were in progress at the time of the failure. Finally, when the failed element is repaired, it should be brought back into the configuration as quickly and transparently as possible to again start processing the workload. Parallel Sysplex technology enables all these tasks.

Workload distribution

After the failing element has been isolated, it is necessary to non-disruptively redirect the workload to the remaining available resources in the Parallel Sysplex. In the event of failure in the Parallel Sysplex environment, the online transaction workload is automatically redistributed without operator intervention.

Generic resource management

Generic resource management provides the ability to specify a common network interface to VTAM. This ability can be used for CICS terminal owning regions (TORs), IMS Transaction Manager, TSO, or DB2 DDF work. If one of the CICS TORs fails, for example, only a subset of the network is affected. The affected terminals are able to immediately log on again and continue processing after being connected to a different TOR.

2.13.4 Systems management technologies

The Parallel Sysplex solution satisfies a major customer requirement for 24x7 availability, while providing techniques for achieving enhanced Systems Management consistent with this requirement. Some of the features of the Parallel Sysplex solution that contribute to increased availability also help to eliminate some Systems Management tasks. Examples include:

- ► Workload management component
- ► Sysplex Failure Manager
- ► Automatic Restart Manager
- ► Cloning and symbolics
- ► z/OS resource sharing

Workload management component

The idea of z/OS Workload Manager (WLM) is to make a contract between the installation (user) and the operating system. The installation classifies the work running on the z/OS operating system in distinct service classes and defines goals for them that express the expectation of how the work should perform. WLM uses these goal definitions to manage the work across all systems.

The workload management component of z/OS provides sysplex-wide throughput management capabilities based on installation-specified performance policy goals written as rules. These rules define the business importance of the workloads. WLM attains the performance goals through dynamic resource distribution. This is one of the major strengths of z/OS.

WLM provides the Parallel Sysplex cluster with the intelligence to determine where work needs to be processed and in what priority. The priority is based on the customer's business goals and is managed by sysplex technology.

Sysplex Failure Manager

The Sysplex Failure Management (SFM) policy allows the installation to specify failure detection intervals and recovery actions to be initiated in the event of the failure of a system in the sysplex.

Without SFM, when one of the systems in the Parallel Sysplex fails, the operator is notified and prompted to take some recovery action. The operator may choose to partition the non-responding system from the Parallel Sysplex, or to take some action to try to recover the system. This period of operator intervention might tie up critical system resources required by the remaining active systems.

Sysplex Failure Manager allows the installation to code a policy to define the recovery actions to be initiated when specific types of problems are detected, such as fencing off the failed image that prevents access to shared resources, logical partition deactivation, or central storage acquisition, to be automatically initiated following detection of a Parallel Sysplex failure.

Automatic Restart Manager

Automatic Restart Manager (ARM) enables fast recovery of subsystems that might hold critical resources at the time of failure. If other instances of the subsystem in the Parallel Sysplex need any of these critical resources, fast recovery makes these resources available more quickly. Even though automation packages are used today to restart the subsystem to resolve such deadlocks, ARM can be activated closer to the time of failure.

ARM reduces operator intervention in the following areas:

► Detection of the failure of a critical job or started task

► Automatic restart after a started task or job failure

  After an abend of a job or started task, the job or started task can be restarted with specific conditions, such as overriding the original JCL or specifying job dependencies, without relying on the operator.

► Automatic redistribution of work to an appropriate system following a system failure

  This action removes the time-consuming step of human evaluation of the most appropriate target system for restarting work.

Cloning and symbolics

Cloning refers to replicating the hardware and software configurations across the different physical servers in the Parallel Sysplex, that is, an application that takes advantage of parallel processing might have identical instances running on all images in the Parallel Sysplex. The hardware and software supporting these applications could also be configured identically on all systems in the Parallel Sysplex to reduce the amount of work required to define and support the environment.

The concept of *symmetry* allows new systems to be introduced and enables automatic workload distribution in the event of failure or when an individual system is scheduled for maintenance. It also reduces the amount of work required by the system programmer in setting up the environment.

Note that symmetry does *not* preclude the need for systems to have unique configuration requirements, such as the asymmetric attachment of printers and communications controllers, or asymmetric workloads that do not lend themselves to the parallel environment.

System symbolics are used to help manage cloning. z/OS provides support for the substitution values in startup parameters, JCL, system commands, and started tasks. These values can be used in parameter and procedure specifications to allow unique substitution when dynamically forming a resource name.

z/OS resource sharing

A number of base z/OS components have discovered that the IBM Coupling Facility shared storage provides a medium for sharing component information for the purpose of multi-system resource management. This medium, called IBM z/OS Resource Sharing, enables sharing of physical resources, such as files, tape drives, consoles, and catalogs, with improvements in cost, performance, and simplified systems management. This is *not to be confused* with Parallel Sysplex data sharing by the database subsystems. Resource Sharing delivers immediate value even for customers who are not using data sharing, through native system usage delivered with the base z/OS software stack.

One of the goals of the Parallel Sysplex solution is to provide simplified systems management by reducing complexity in managing, operating, and servicing a Parallel Sysplex, without requiring an increase in the number of support staff and without reducing availability.

2.13.5 Single system image

Even though there could be multiple servers and z/OS images in the Parallel Sysplex and a mix of different technologies, the collection of systems in the Parallel Sysplex should appear as a single entity to the operator, the user, the database administrator, and so on. A single system image brings reduced complexity from both operational and definition perspectives.

Regardless of the number of system images and the complexity of the underlying hardware, the Parallel Sysplex solution provides for a single system image from several perspectives:

▶ Data access, allowing dynamic workload balancing and improved availability

▶ Dynamic Transaction Routing, providing dynamic workload balancing and improved availability

▶ A user interface, allowing logon to a logical network entity

▶ Operational interfaces, allowing easier Systems Management

Single point of control

It is a requirement that the collection of systems in the Parallel Sysplex can be managed from a logical single point of control. The term "single point of control" means the ability to access whatever interfaces are required for the task in question, without reliance on a physical piece of hardware. For example, in a Parallel Sysplex of many systems, it is necessary to be able to direct commands or operations to any system in the Parallel Sysplex, without the necessity for a console or control point to be physically attached to every system in the Parallel Sysplex.

Persistent single system image across failures

Even though individual hardware elements or entire systems in the Parallel Sysplex fail, a single system image must be maintained. This means that, as with the concept of single point of control, the presentation of the single system image is not dependent on a specific physical element in the configuration. From the user point of view, the parallel nature of applications in the Parallel Sysplex environment must be transparent. An application should be accessible regardless of which physical z/OS image supports it.

2.13.6 Compatible change and nondisruptive growth

A primary goal of Parallel Sysplex is continuous availability. Therefore, it is a requirement that changes, such as new applications, software, or hardware, be introduced non-disruptively, and that they be able to coexist with current levels. In support of compatible change, the hardware and software components of the Parallel Sysplex solution allow the coexistence of two levels, that is, level N and level N+1. This means, for example, that no IBM software product will make a change that cannot be tolerated by the previous release.

2.13.7 Application compatibility

A design goal of Parallel Sysplex clustering is that no application changes be required to take advantage of the technology. For the most part, this has held true, although some affinities need to be investigated to get the maximum advantage from the configuration.

From the application architects' point of view, three major points might lead to the decision to run an application in a Parallel Sysplex:

► Technology benefits

   Scalability (even with nondisruptive upgrades), availability, and dynamic workload management are tools that enable an architect to meet customer needs in cases where the application plays a key role in the customer's business process.

With the multisystem data sharing technology, all processing nodes in a Parallel Sysplex have full concurrent read/write access to shared data without affecting integrity and performance.

► Integration benefits

Because many applications are historically S/390- and z/OS-based, new applications on z/OS get performance and maintenance benefits, especially if they are connected to existing applications.

► Infrastructure benefits

If there is already an existing Parallel Sysplex, it needs little infrastructure work to integrate a new application. In many cases, the installation does not need to integrate new servers. Instead, it can use the existing infrastructure and make use of the strengths of the existing sysplex. With Geographically Dispersed Parallel Sysplex™ (GDPS®) connecting multiple sysplexes in different locations, the mainframe IT staff can create a configuration that is enabled for disaster recovery.

2.13.8 Disaster recovery

GDPS:
An application that improves application availability and disaster recovery in a Parallel Sysplex.

Geographically Dispersed Parallel Sysplex (GDPS) is the primary disaster recovery and continuous availability solution for a mainframe-based multisite enterprise. GDPS automatically mirrors critical data and efficiently balances workload between the sites.

GDPS also uses automation and Parallel Sysplex technology to help manage multisite databases, processors, network resources, and storage subsystem mirroring. This technology offers continuous availability, efficient movement of workload between sites, resource management, and prompt data recovery for business-critical mainframe applications and data. With GDPS, the current maximum distance between the two sites is 100 km (about 62 miles) of fibre, although there are some other restrictions. This provides a synchronous solution that helps ensure that there is no loss of data.

There is also GDPS/XRC, which can be used over extended distances and should provide a recovery point objective of less than two minutes (that is, a maximum of two minutes of data would need to be recovered or is lost). This disaster recovery (DR) solution across two sites can be separated by virtually unlimited distance.

Today's DR implementations provide several types of offerings, including two and three site solutions. The code has been developed and enhanced over a number of years, to use new hardware and software capabilities, to reflect best practices based on IBM experience with GDPS customers since its inception, and to address the constantly changing requirements of clients.

2.14 Summary

Being aware of various meanings of the terms systems, processors, CPs, and so on is important to understanding mainframe computers. The original S/360 architecture, based on CPUs, memory, channels, control units, and devices, and the way these are addressed, is fundamental to understanding mainframe hardware, even though almost every detail of the original design has been changed in various ways. The concepts and terminology of the original design still permeate mainframe descriptions and designs.

zAAP/zIIP: Specialized processing assist units configured for running selective programming on the mainframe.

The ability to partition a large system into multiple logical partitions (LPARs) is now a core requirement in practically all mainframe installations. The flexibility of the hardware design, allowing any processor (CP) to access and accept interrupts for any channel, control unit, and device connected to a given LPAR, contributes to the flexibility, reliability, and performance of the complete system. The availability of a pool of processors (PUs) that can be configured (by IBM) as customer processors (CPs), I/O processors (system assist processors), dedicated Linux processors (IFLs), dedicated Java-type processors (zAAPs), specialized services for DB2/XML (zIIPs) and spare processors is unique to mainframes and, again, provides great flexibility in meeting customer requirements. Some of these requirements are based on the cost structures of some mainframe software.

In addition to the primary processors just mentioned (the PUs, and all their characterizations), mainframes have a network of controllers (special microprocessors) that control the system as a whole. These controllers are not visible to the operating system or application programs.

Since the early 1970s, mainframes have been designed as multiprocessor systems, even when only a single processor is installed. All operating system software is designed for multiple processors; a system with a single processor is considered a special case of a general multiprocessor design. All but the smallest mainframe installations typically use clustering techniques, although they do not normally use the terms *cluster* or *clustering*.

As stated previously, a clustering technique can be as simple as a shared DASD configuration where manual control or planning is needed to prevent unwanted data overlap. More common today are configurations that allow sharing of locking and enqueueing controls among all systems. Among other benefits, this automatically manages access to data sets so that unwanted concurrent usage does not occur.

The most sophisticated of the clustering techniques is a Parallel Sysplex. This technology allows the linking up to 32 servers with near linear scalability to create a powerful commercial processing clustered system. Every server in a Parallel Sysplex cluster has access to all data resources, and every "cloned" application can run on every server. When used with coupling technology, Parallel Sysplex provides a "shared data" clustering technique that permits multisystem data sharing with high performance read/write integrity. Sysplex design characteristics help businesses run continuously, even during periods of dramatic change. Sysplex sites can dynamically add and change systems in a sysplex, and configure the systems for no single points of failure.

Through this state-of-the-art cluster technology, multiple z/OS systems can be made to work in concert to more efficiently process the largest commercial workloads.

Table 2-1 lists the key terms used in this chapter.

Table 2-1 Key terms used in this chapter

Automatic Restart Manager (ARM)	central processing complex (CPC)	central processing unit (CPU)
channel path identifier (CHPID)	channel-to-channel (CTC) connection	Coupling Facility
ESCON channel	Geographically Dispersed Parallel Sysplex (GDPS)	Hardware Management Console (HMC)
logical partition (LPAR)	multiprocessor	Parallel Sysplex
single point of control	z/Architecture	System z Specialty Processors.

2.15 Questions for review

To help test your understanding of the material in this chapter, answer the following questions:

1. Why does software pricing for mainframes seem so complex?

2. Why does IBM have so many models (or "capacity settings") for recent mainframe machines?

3. Why does the power needed for a traditional COBOL application not have a linear relationship with the power needed for a new Java application?

4. *Multiprocessing* means running several processors simultaneously (available to the operating system and applications). What does *multiprogramming* mean?

5. What are the differences between loosely coupled systems and tightly coupled systems?

6. What z/OS application changes are needed for it to work in an LPAR?

7. What z/OS application changes are needed to work in a Parallel Sysplex?

8. How do specialty processors help applications?

9. How do disaster recovery solutions benefit a global business?

2.16 Topics for further discussion

Visit a mainframe installation, if possible. The range of new, older, and much older systems and devices found in a typical installation is usually interesting and helps to illustrate the sense of continuity that is so important to mainframe customers. Then consider the following questions:

1. What are the advantages of a Parallel Sysplex presenting a single image externally? Are there any disadvantages?

2. Why is continuous availability required in today's marketplace?

3. How might someone justify the cost of the "redundant" hardware and the cost of the software licences required to build a Parallel Sysplex?

2.17 Exercises

Here are some exercises you can perform:

► To display the CPU configuration:

   a. Access SDSF from the ISPF primary option menu.
   b. In the command input field, enter /D M=CPU and press Enter.
   c. Use the ULOG option in SDSF to view the command display result.

► To display the page data set usage:

   a. In the command input field, enter /D ASM and press Enter.
   b. Press PF3 to return to the previous screens.

► To display information about the current Initial Program Load (IPL):

   a. Use ULOG option in SDSF to view the command display result.
   b. In the command input field, enter /D IPLINFO and press Enter.

Attention: The forward slash is the required prefix for entering operator commands in SDSF.

3

z/OS overview

Objective: As the newest member of your company's mainframe IT group, you need to know the basic functional characteristics of the mainframe operating system. The operating system taught in this course is z/OS, a widely used mainframe operating system. z/OS is known for its ability to serve thousands of users concurrently and for processing large workloads in a secure, reliable, and expedient manner.

After completing this chapter, you will be able to:

► List several defining characteristics of the z/OS operating system.
► Give examples of how z/OS differs from a single-user operating system.
► List the major types of storage used by z/OS.
► Explain the concept of virtual storage and its use in z/OS.
► State the relationship between pages, frames, and slots.
► List several software products used with z/OS to provide a complete system.
► Describe several differences and similarities between the z/OS and UNIX operating systems.
► Understand z/OS Workload Manager concepts.
► Describe features to optimize workloads.

Refer to Table 3-2 on page 161 for a list of key terms used in this chapter.

91

3.1 What is an operating system

In simplest terms, an *operating system* is a collection of programs that manage the internal workings of a computer system. Operating systems are designed to make the best use of the computer's various resources, and ensure that the maximum amount of work is processed as efficiently as possible. Although an operating system cannot increase the speed of a computer, it can maximize its use, thereby making the computer seem faster by allowing it to do more work in a given period of time.

A computer's *architecture* consists of the functions the computer system provides. The architecture is distinct from the physical design, and, in fact, different machine designs might conform to the same computer architecture. In a sense, the architecture is the computer as seen by the user, such as a system programmer. For example, part of the architecture is the set of machine instructions that the computer can recognize and execute. In the mainframe environment, the system software and hardware comprise a highly advanced computer architecture, the result of decades of technological innovation.

3.2 What is z/OS

The operating system we discuss in this course is z/OS[1], a widely used mainframe operating system. z/OS is designed to offer a stable, secure, continuously available, and scalable environment for applications running on the mainframe.

z/OS today is the result of decades of technological advancement. It evolved from an operating system that could process only a single program at a time to an operating system that can handle many thousands of programs and interactive users concurrently. To understand how and why z/OS functions as it does, it is important to understand some basic concepts about z/OS and the environment in which it functions. This chapter introduces some of the concepts that you need to understand the z/OS operating system.

In most early operating systems, requests for work entered the system one at a time. The operating system processed each request or *job* as a unit, and did not start the next job until the one being processed had completed. This arrangement worked well when a job could execute continuously from start to completion. But often a job had to wait for information to be read in from, or written out to, a device such as a tape drive or printer.

---

[1] z/OS is designed to take advantage of the IBM System z architecture, or z/Architecture, which was introduced in the year 2000. The z in the name was selected because these systems often have zero downtime.

Input and output (I/O) take a long time compared to the electronic speed of the processor. When a job waited for I/O, the processor was idle.

Finding a way to keep the processor working while a job is waiting would increase the total amount of work the processor could do without requiring additional hardware. z/OS gets work done by dividing it into pieces and giving portions of the job to various system components and subsystems that function interdependently. At any point in time, one component or another gets control of the processor, makes its contribution, and then passes control along to a user program or another component.

Today's z/OS operating system is a share-everything runtime environment that provides for resource sharing through its heritage of virtualization technology. It uses special hardware and software to access and control the use of those resources, ensuring that there is little underutilization of its components.

Further optimization for specific workloads

The latest z/OS provides for optional optimization features to accelerate processing of specific workloads. This functionality is provided by blade extension servers. A *blade server* is a stripped down server computer with a modular design optimized to minimize the use of physical space and energy.

The common theme with these specialized hardware components is their relatively seamless integration within the mainframe and operating system environments.

IBM has introduced the IBM zEnterprise BladeCenter Extension (zBX), which is a heterogeneous hardware infrastructure that consists of a BladeCenter chassis attached to a IBM zEnterprise 196 (z196). A BladeCenter chassis can contain IBM blades or optimizers.

The zBX components are configured, managed, and serviced the same way as the other components of the System z server. Despite the fact that the zBX processors are not System z PUs and run purpose- specific software, the zBX software does not require any additional administration effort or tuning by the user.

In short, zBX further extends the degree of integration in the mainframe. zBX provides, within the System z infrastructure, a cost optimized solution for running data warehouse and business intelligence queries against DB2 for z/OS, with fast and predictable response times, while retaining the data integrity, data management, security, availability, and other qualities of service of System z.

3.2.1 Hardware resources used by z/OS

The z/OS operating system executes in a processor and resides in processor storage during execution. z/OS is commonly referred to as the system software or base control program (BCP).

Mainframe hardware consists of processors and a multitude of peripheral devices such as disk drives (called direct access storage devices (DASD)), magnetic tape drives, and various types of user consoles; see Figure 3-1. Tape and DASD are used for system functions and by user programs executed by z/OS.

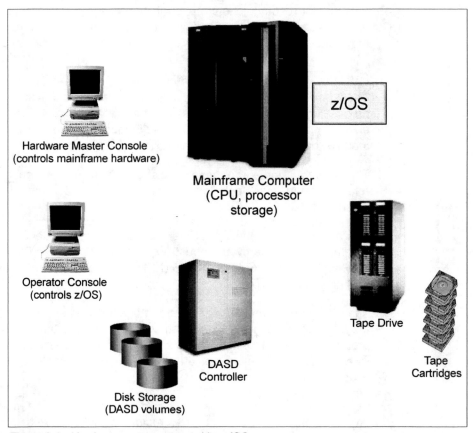

Figure 3-1   Hardware resources used by z/OS

Today's z/OS provides a new disk device geometry called Extended Address Volume (EAV) that enables support for over 223 gigabytes (262,668 cylinders) per disk volume in its initial offering. This helps many larger customers that have the 4-digit device number limitation begin consolidation of disk farms.

The mainframe offers several types of I/O adapter cards that include open standards, allowing flexibility for configuring high bandwidth for any device type.

All hardware components offer built-in redundancy, ensuring reliability and availability, from memory sparing to cooling units. Today's mainframe also has a *capacity provisoning* capability to monitor z/OS utilization of system workloads. This feature allows CPUs to be turned on and off dynamically.

To fulfill a new order for a z/OS system, IBM ships the system code to the customer through the Internet or (depending on the customer's preference) on physical tape cartridges. At the customer site, a person, such as the z/OS system programmer, receives the order and copies the new system to DASD volumes. After the system is customized and ready for operation, system consoles are required to start and operate the z/OS system.

The z/OS operating system is designed to make full use of the latest IBM mainframe hardware and its many sophisticated peripheral devices. Figure 3-1 on page 94 presents a simplified view of mainframe concepts that we build upon throughout this course:

▶ Software: The z/OS operating system consists of load modules or *executable code*. During the installation process, the system programmer copies these load modules to *load libraries* (files) residing on DASD volumes.

▶ Hardware: The system hardware consists of all the channels[2], control units[3], devices, and processors that constitute a mainframe environment.

▶ Peripheral devices: These devices include tape drives, DASD, and consoles. There are many other types of devices, some of which were discussed in Chapter 2, "Mainframe hardware systems and high availability" on page 45.

▶ Processor storage: Often called real or central storage (or memory), this is where the z/OS operating system executes. Also, all user programs share the use of processor storage with the operating system.

Figure 3-1 on page 94 is not a detailed picture. Not shown, for example, are the hardware control units that connect the mainframe to the other tape drives, and consoles.

The standard reference for descriptions of the major facilities of z/Architecture is *z/Architecture Principles of Operation*, SA22-7832. You can find this and related publications at the z/OS Internet Library website:

`http://www.ibm.com/servers/eserver/zseries/zos/bkserv/`

---

[2] A channel is the communication path from the channel subsystem to the connected control unit and I/O devices.

[3] A control unit provides the logical capabilities necessary to operate and control an I/O device.

3.2.2 Multiprogramming and multiprocessing

The earliest operating systems were used to control single-user computer systems. In those days, the operating system would read in one job, find the data and devices the job needed, let the job run to completion, and then read in another job. In contrast, the computer systems that z/OS manages are capable of *multiprogramming*, or executing many programs concurrently. With multiprogramming, when a job cannot use the processor, the system can suspend, or *interrupt*[4], the job, freeing the processor to work on another job.

z/OS makes multiprogramming possible by capturing and saving all the relevant information about the interrupted program before allowing another program to execute. When the interrupted program is ready to begin executing again, it can resume execution just where it left off. Multiprogramming allows z/OS to run thousands of programs simultaneously for users who might be working on different projects at different physical locations around the world.

z/OS can also perform *multiprocessing*, which is the simultaneous operation of two or more processors that share the various hardware resources, such as memory and external disk storage devices. The techniques of multiprogramming and multiprocessing make z/OS ideally suited for processing workloads that require many input/output (I/O) operations. Typical mainframe workloads include long-running applications that write updates to millions of records in a database, and online applications for thousands of interactive users at any given time. In contrast, consider the operating system that might be used for a single-user computer system. Such an operating system would need to execute programs on behalf of one user only. In the case of a personal computer (PC), for example, the entire resources of the machine are often at the disposal of one user.

Multiprocessing: The simultaneous operation of two or more processors that share the various hardware resources.

Many users running many separate programs means that, along with large amounts of complex hardware, z/OS needs large amounts of memory to ensure suitable system performance. Large companies run sophisticated business applications that access large databases and industry-strength middleware products. Such applications require the operating system to protect privacy among users, as well as enable the sharing of databases and software services.

Thus, multiprogramming, multiprocessing, and the need for a large amount of memory mean that z/OS must provide function beyond simple, single-user applications. The sections that follow explain, in a general way, the attributes that enable z/OS to manage complex computer configurations. Subsequent portions of this text explore these features in more detail.

---

[4] Interrupt capability permits the CP to switch rapidly to another program in response to exception conditions and external stimuli.

3.2.3 Modules and macros

z/OS is made up of programming instructions that control the operation of the computer system. These instructions ensure that the computer hardware is being used efficiently and is allowing application programs to run. z/OS includes sets of instructions that, for example, accept work, convert work to a form that the computer can recognize, keep track of work, allocate resources for work, execute work, monitor work, and handle output. A group of related instructions is called a *routine* or *module*. A set of related modules that make a particular system function possible is called a *system component*. The workload management (WLM) component of z/OS, for example, controls system resources, while the recovery termination manager (RTM) handles system recovery.

Grouping of sequences of instructions that perform frequently-used system or application functions can be invoked with executable macro[5] instructions, or *macros*. z/OS has macros for functions such as opening and closing data files, loading and deleting programs, and sending messages to the computer operator.

3.2.4 Control blocks

As programs execute work on a z/OS system, they keep track of this work in storage areas called *control blocks*. Controls blocks contain status data, tables, or queues. In general, there are four types of z/OS control blocks:

► System-related control blocks
► Resource-related control blocks
► Job-related control blocks
► Task-related control blocks

Each system-related control block represents one z/OS system and contains system-wide information, such as how many processors are in use. Each resource-related control block represents one resource, such as a processor or storage device. Each job-related control block represents one job executing on the system. Each task-related control block represents one unit of work.

Control block:
A data structure that serves as a vehicle for communication in z/OS.

Control blocks serve as vehicles for communication throughout z/OS. Such communication is possible because the structure of a control block is known to the programs that use it, and thus these programs can find needed information about the unit of work or resource. Control blocks representing many units of the same type may be chained together on queues, with each control block pointing to the next one in the chain.

The operating system can search the queue to find information about a particular unit of work or resource, which might be:

---

[5] Macros provide predefined code used as a callable service within z/OS or application programs.

- An address of a control block or a required routine

- Actual data, such as a value, a quantity, a parameter, or a name

- Status flags (usually single bits in a byte, where each bit has a specific meaning)

z/OS uses a huge variety of control blocks, many with specialized purposes. This chapter discusses three of the most commonly used control blocks:

- Task control block (TCB): Represents a unit of work or *task*.

  It serves as a repository for information and pointers associated with a task. Various components of the z/OS place information in the TCB and obtain information from the TCB.

- Service request block (SRB): Represents a request for a system service.

  It is used as input to the SCHEDULE macro when scheduling a routine for asynchronous execution.

- Address space control block (ASCB): Represents an address space.

  It contains information and pointers needed for Address Space Control.

3.2.5 Physical storage used by z/OS

Conceptually, mainframes and all other computers have two types of physical storage[6]:

Central storage:
Physical storage on the processor.

- Physical storage located on the mainframe processor itself. This is memory, often called processor storage, real storage, or *central storage* (CSTOR).

- Physical storage external to the mainframe, including storage on direct access devices, such as disk drives, and tape drives. For z/OS usage, this storage is called page storage or *auxiliary storage*.

---

[6] Many computers also have a fast memory, local to the processor, called the processor cache. The cache is not visible to the programmer or application programs or even the operating system directly.

One difference between the two kinds of storage relates to the way in which they are accessed, as follows:

▶ Central storage is accessed synchronously with the processor, that is, the processor must wait while data is retrieved from central storage[7].

Auxiliary storage:
Physical storage external to the mainframe, including storage on direct access devices, such as disk drives and tape drives.

▶ Auxiliary storage is accessed asynchronously. The processor accesses auxiliary storage through an input/output (I/O) request, which is scheduled to run amid other work requests in the system. During an I/O request, the processor is free to execute other, unrelated work.

As with memory for a personal computer, mainframe central storage is tightly coupled with the processor itself, whereas mainframe auxiliary storage is located on (comparatively) slower, external disk and tape drives. Because central storage is more closely integrated with the processor, it takes the processor much less time to access data from central storage than from auxiliary storage. Auxiliary storage, however, is less expensive than central storage. Most z/OS installations use large amounts of both.

Note: There is another form of storage called expanded storage (ESTOR). Expanded storage was offered as a relatively inexpensive way of using high speed processor storage to minimize I/O operations. Since the introduction of z/OS with 64-bit addressing, this form of storage was not required anymore, but other operating systems, such as z/VM, still use it.

3.3 Overview of z/OS facilities

An extensive set of system facilities and unique attributes makes z/OS well suited for processing large, complex workloads, such as those that require many I/O operations, access to large amounts of data, or comprehensive security. Typical mainframe workloads include long-running applications that update millions of records in a database and online applications that can serve many thousands of users concurrently.

---

[7] Some processor implementations use techniques such as instruction or data prefetching or "pipelining" to enhance performance. These techniques are not visible to the application program or even the operating system, but a sophisticated compiler can organize the code it produces to take advantage of these techniques.

Figure 3-2 provides a "snapshot" view of the z/OS operating environment.

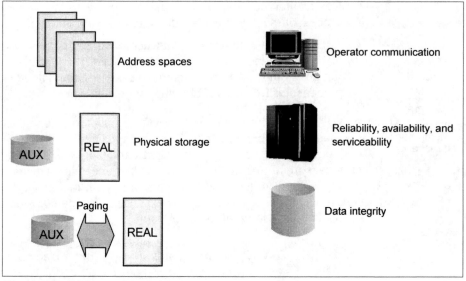

Figure 3-2   z/OS operating environment

These facilities are explored in greater depth in the remaining portions of this book, but are summarized here:

► An address space describes the virtual storage addressing range available to a user or program.

The address space is an area of contiguous virtual addresses available to a program (or set of programs) and its data requirements. The range of virtual addresses available to a program starts at 0 and can go to the highest address permitted by the operating system architecture. This virtual storage is available for user code and data.

Because it maps all of the available addresses, an address space includes system code and data and user code and data.

Thus, not all of the mapped addresses are available for user code and data.

- ► Two types of physical storage are available: central storage and auxiliary storage (AUX). Central storage is also referred to as *real storage* or *real memory*.

  - – The Real Storage Manager (RSM) controls the allocation of central storage during system initialization, and pages[8] in user or system functions during execution.

  - – The auxiliary storage manager controls the use of page and swap data sets. z/OS moves programs and data between central storage and auxiliary storage through processes called paging and swapping.

- ► z/OS dispatches work for execution (not shown in the figure), that is, it selects programs to be run based on priority and the ability to execute and then loads the program and data into central storage. All program instructions and data must be in central storage when executing.

- ► An extensive set of facilities manages files stored on direct access storage devices (DASDs) or tape cartridges.

- ► Operators use consoles to start and stop z/OS, enter commands, and manage the operating system.

z/OS is further defined by many other operational characteristics, such as security, recovery, data integrity, and workload management.

3.4 Virtual storage and other mainframe concepts

z/OS uses both types of physical storage (central and auxiliary) to enable another kind of storage called *virtual storage*. In z/OS, each user has access to virtual storage, rather than physical storage. This use of virtual storage is central to the unique ability of z/OS to interact with large numbers of users concurrently, while processing the largest workloads.

3.4.1 What is virtual storage

Virtual storage means that each running program can assume it has access to all of the storage defined by the architecture's addressing scheme. The only limit is the number of bits in a storage address. This ability to use a large number of storage locations is important because a program may be long and complex, and both the program's code and the data it requires must be in central storage for the processor to access them.

---

[8] See 3.4, "Virtual storage and other mainframe concepts" on page 101.

z/OS supports a 64-bit addressing scheme, which allows an address space (see 3.4.2, "What is an address space" on page 102) to address, theoretically, up to 16 exabytes[9] of storage locations. In reality, the mainframe will have *much less* central storage installed. How much less depends on the model of the computer and the system configuration.

To allow each user to act as though this much storage really exists in the computer system, z/OS keeps only the active portions of each program in central storage. It keeps the rest of the code and data in files called *page data sets* on auxiliary storage, which usually consists of a number of high-speed direct access storage devices (DASDs).

Virtual storage, then, is this combination of real and auxiliary storage. z/OS uses a series of tables and indexes to relate locations on auxiliary storage to locations in central storage. It uses special settings (bit settings) to keep track of the identity and authority of each user or program. z/OS uses a variety of storage manager components to manage virtual storage. This chapter briefly covers the key points in the process.

This process is shown in more detail in 3.4.4, "Virtual storage overview" on page 107.

> **Terms:** Mainframe workers use the terms central storage, real memory, real storage, and main storage interchangeably. Likewise, they use the terms virtual memory and virtual storage synonymously.

3.4.2 What is an address space

The range of virtual addresses that the operating system assigns to a user or separately running program is called an *address space*. This is the area of contiguous virtual addresses available for executing instructions and storing data. The range of virtual addresses in an address space starts at zero and can extend to the highest address permitted by the operating system architecture.

For a user, the address space can be considered as the runtime container where programs and their data are accessed.

Address space: The range of virtual addresses that the operating system assigns to a user or program.

z/OS provides each user with a unique address space and maintains the distinction between the programs and data belonging to each address space. Within each address space, the user can start multiple tasks by using *task control blocks* (TCBs) that allow multiprogramming.

---

[9] An exabyte is slightly more than one billion gigabytes.

In other ways, a z/OS address space is like a UNIX process, and the address space identifier (ASID)[10] is like a process ID (PID). Further, TCBs are like UNIX threads in that each operating system supports processing multiple instances of work concurrently.

However, the use of multiple virtual address spaces in z/OS holds some special advantages. Virtual addressing permits an addressing range that is greater than the central storage capabilities of the system. The use of multiple virtual address spaces provides this virtual addressing capability to each job in the system by assigning each job its own separate virtual address space. The potentially large number of address spaces provides the system with a large virtual addressing capacity.

With an address space, errors are confined to that address space, except for errors in commonly addressable storage, thus improving system reliability and making error recovery easier. Programs in separate address spaces are protected from each other. Isolating data in its own address space also protects the data.

z/OS uses address spaces for its own services that are working on behalf of executing applications. There is at least one address space for each job in progress and one address space for each user logged on through TSO, telnet, rlogin, or FTP (users logged on z/OS through a major subsystem, such as CICS or IMS, are using an address space belonging to the subsystem, not their own address spaces). There are many address spaces for operating system functions, such as operator communication, automation, networking, security, and so on.

Address space isolation

The use of address spaces allows z/OS to maintain the distinction between the programs and data belonging to each address space. The private areas[11] in one user's address space are isolated from the private areas in other address spaces, and this provides much of the operating system's security. There are two private areas: One below the 16 MB line (for 24-bit addressing) and one above the 16 MB line (for 31-bit addressing), as shown in Figure 3-12 on page 120.

Each address space also contains a common area that is accessible to every other address space. Because it maps all of the available addresses, an address space includes system code and data and user code and data. Thus, not all of the mapped addresses are available for user code and data.

---

[10] An ASID is a 2-byte numeric identifier assigned to the Address Space Control Block.

[11] The private area of an address space is where user application programs execute, as opposed to the common area, which is shared across all address spaces.

The ability of many users to share the same resources implies the need to protect users from one another and to protect the operating system itself. Along with such methods as storage keys[12] for protecting central storage, data files, and programs, separate address spaces ensure that users' programs and data do not overlap.

> **Important:** Storage protection is one of the mechanisms implemented by z/Architecture to protect central storage. With multiprocessing, hundreds of tasks can run programs accessing physically any piece of central storage. Storage protection imposes limits on what a task can access (for read or write) within central storage locations with its own data and programs, or, if specifically allowed, to read areas from other tasks. Any violation of this rule causes the CP to generate a program interrupt or storage exception. All real addresses manipulated by CPs must go through the storage protection verification before being used as an argument to access the contents of central storage. For each 4 KB block of central storage, there is a 7-bit control field called a *storage key*.

Address space communication

In a multiple virtual address space environment, applications need ways to communicate between address spaces. z/OS provides two methods of inter-address space communication:

▶ Scheduling a service request block (SRB), which is an asynchronous process

▶ Using cross-memory services and access registers, which is a synchronous process

A program uses an SRB to initiate a process in another address space or in the same address space. The SRB is asynchronous in nature and runs independently of the program that issues it, thereby improving the availability of resources in a multiprocessing environment. We discuss SRBs further in "What is a service request block" on page 136.

A program uses cross-memory services to access another user's address spaces directly (see 3.8, "Cross-memory services" on page 143 for more information). You might compare z/OS cross-memory services to the UNIX Shared Memory functions, which can be used on UNIX without special authority.

---

[12] Keys are bit settings within the program status word (the currently executing instruction) used by z/OS to compare storage being accessed by the program.

Unlike UNIX, however, z/OS cross-memory (XM) services require the issuing program to have special authority, controlled by the authorized program facility (APF). This method allows efficient and secure access to data owned by others, data owned by the user but stored in another address space for convenience, and for rapid and secure communication with services, such as transaction managers and database managers. Cross memory is also implemented by many z/OS subsystems[13] and products.

Cross memory can also be synchronous, enabling one program to provide services coordinated with other programs. In Figure 3-3, synchronous cross-memory communication takes place between Address Space 2, which gets control from Address Space 1 when the program call (PC) is issued. Address Space 1 had previously established the necessary environment before the PC instruction transferred control to an Address Space 2 called a *PC routine*. The PC routine provides the requested service and returns control to Address Space 1.

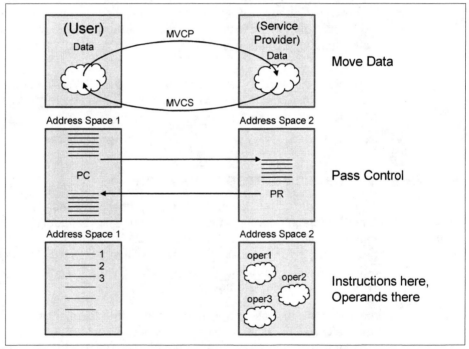

Figure 3-3   Synchronous cross memory

---

[13] A subsystem is middleware used by applications to perform certain system services. Subsystem examples are DB2, IMS, and CICS.

The user program in Address Space 1 and the PC routine can execute in the same address space, as shown in Figure 3-3 on page 105, or in different address spaces. In either case, the PC routine executes under the same TCB as the user program that issued the PC. Thus, the PC routine provides the service synchronously.

Cross memory is an evolution of virtual storage and has three objectives:

► Move data synchronously between virtual addresses located in distinct address spaces.

► Pass control synchronously between instructions located in distinct address spaces.

► Execute one instruction located in one address space while its operands are located in another address space.

> **Important:** Address spaces are distinct runtime containers that are isolated from one another through the z/OS architecture. Cross-memory services, used to access another address space, are performed under special authorized instructions and access privileges used only by certain system functions.

Using cross-memory services is described in *z/OS MVS Programming: Extended Addressability Guide*, SA22-7614. You can find this and related publications at the z/OS Internet Library website:

`http://www.ibm.com/servers/eserver/zseries/zos/bkserv/`

3.4.3 What is dynamic address translation

Dynamic address translation (DAT) is the process of translating a virtual address during a storage reference into the corresponding real address. If the virtual address is already in central storage, the DAT process may be accelerated through the use of translation lookaside buffers. If the virtual address is not in central storage, a page fault interrupt occurs, and z/OS is notified and brings the page in from auxiliary storage.

Looking at this process more closely reveals that the machine can present any one of a number of different types of storage faults.[14] A type, region, segment, or page fault is presented depending on at which point in the DAT structure invalid entries are found. The faults repeat down the DAT structure until a page fault is presented and the virtual page is brought into central storage either for the first time (there is no copy on auxiliary storage) or by bringing the page in from auxiliary storage.

---

[14] An address not in real storage.

DAT is implemented by both hardware and software through the use of page tables, segment tables, region tables, and translation lookaside buffers. DAT allows different address spaces to share the same program or other data that is for read only. This is because virtual addresses in different address spaces can be made to translate to the same frame of central storage.

Otherwise, there would have to be many copies of the program or data, one for each address space.

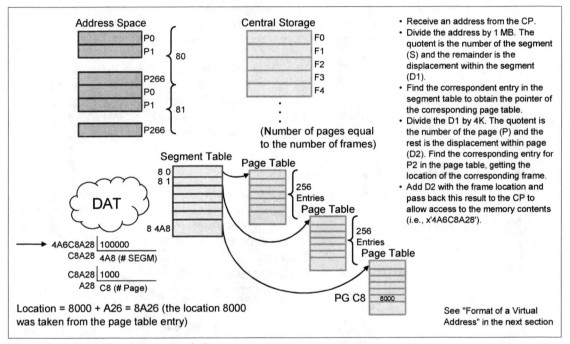

Figure 3-4   Dynamic address translation

3.4.4 Virtual storage overview

Recall that for the processor to execute a program instruction, both the instruction and the data it references must be in central storage. The convention of early operating systems was to have the entire program reside in central storage when its instructions were executing. However, the entire program does not really need to be in central storage when an instruction executes. Instead, by bringing pieces of the program into central storage only when the processor is ready to execute them, and moving them out to auxiliary storage when it does not need them, an operating system can execute more and larger programs concurrently.

How does the operating system keep track of each program piece? How does it know whether it is in central storage or auxiliary storage, and where? It is important for z/OS professionals to understand how the operating system makes this happen.

Physical storage is divided into areas, each the same size and accessible by a unique address. In central storage, these areas are called *frames*; in auxiliary storage, they are called *slots*. Similarly, the operating system can divide a program into pieces the size of frames or slots and assign each piece a unique address. This arrangement allows the operating system to keep track of these pieces. In z/OS, the program pieces are called *pages*. These topics are discussed further in "Frames, pages, and slots" on page 111.

Pages are referenced by their virtual addresses and not by their real addresses. From the time a program enters the system until it completes, the virtual address of the page remains the same, regardless of whether the page is in central storage or auxiliary storage. Each page consists of individual locations called bytes, each of which has a unique virtual address.

Format of a virtual address

As mentioned, virtual storage is an illusion created by the architecture, in that the system seems to have more memory than it really has. Each user or program gets an address space, and each address space contains the same range of storage addresses. Only those portions of the address space that are needed at any point in time are actually loaded into central storage. z/OS keeps the inactive pieces of address spaces in auxiliary storage. z/OS manages address spaces in units of various sizes. DAT may use from two to five levels of tables and is broken down as follows:

Page   Address spaces are divided into 4 KB units of virtual storage called pages.

Segment   Address spaces are divided into 1 MB units called segments. A segment is a block of sequential virtual addresses spanning megabytes, beginning at a 1 MB boundary. A 2 GB address space, for example, consists of 2048 segments.

Region   Address spaces are divided into 2 - 8 GB units called regions. A region is a block of sequential virtual addresses spanning 2 - 8 GB, beginning at a 2 GB boundary. A 2 TB address space, for example, consists of 2048 regions.

A virtual address, accordingly, is divided into four principal fields: bits 0 - 32 are called the region index (RX), bits 33 - 43 are called the segment index (SX), bits 44 - 51 are called the page index (PX), and bits 52 - 63 are called the byte index (BX).

A virtual address has the format shown in Figure 3-5.

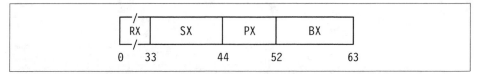

Figure 3-5   Virtual address format

As determined by its address-space-control element, a virtual address space can be a 2 GB space consisting of one region, or as large as a 16 EB space. The RX part of a virtual address for a 2 GB address space must be all zeros; otherwise, an exception is recognized.

The RX part of a virtual address is itself divided into three fields. Bits 0 - 10 are called the region first index (RFX), bits 11 - 21 are called the region second index (RSX), and bits 22 - 32 are called the region third index (RTX). Bits 0 - 32 of the virtual address have the format shown in Figure 3-6.

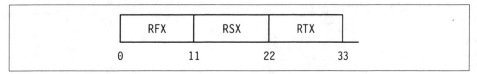

Figure 3-6   Virtual address format of bits 0 - 32

A virtual address in which the RTX is the left most significant part (a 42-bit address) is capable of addressing 4 TB (4096 regions), one in which the RSX is the left most significant part (a 53-bit address) is capable of addressing 8 PB (four million regions), and one in which the RFX is the left most significant part (a 64-bit address) is capable of addressing 16 EB (8 billion regions).

How virtual storage addressing works in z/OS

As stated previously, the use of virtual storage in z/OS means that only the pieces of a program that are currently active need to be in central storage at processing time. The inactive pieces are held in auxiliary storage.

Figure 3-7 shows the virtual storage concept at work in z/OS.

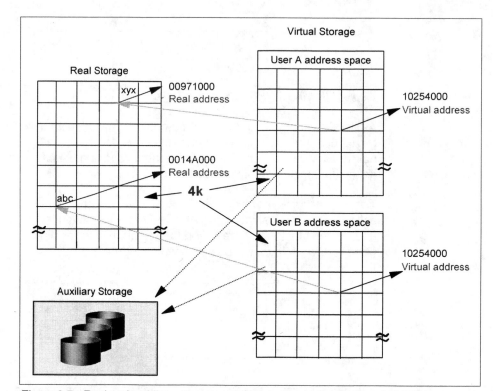

Figure 3-7   Real and auxiliary storage combine to create the illusion of virtual storage

In Figure 3-7, observe the following:

▶ An address is an identifier of a required piece of information, but not a description of where in central storage that piece of information is. This allows the size of an address space (that is, all addresses available to a program) to exceed the amount of central storage available.

▶ For most user programs, all central storage references are made in terms of virtual storage addresses.[15]

▶ Dynamic address translation (DAT) is used to translate a virtual address during a storage reference into a physical location in central storage. As shown in Figure 3-7, the virtual address 10254000 can exist more than once, because each virtual address maps to a different address in central storage.

▶ When a requested address is not in central storage, a hardware interruption is signaled to z/OS and the operating system pages in the required instructions and data to central storage.

---

[15] Some instructions, primarily those used by operating system programs, require real addresses.

Frames, pages, and slots

When a program is selected for execution, the system brings it into virtual storage, divides it into pages of 4 KB, and transfers the pages into central storage for execution. To the programmer, the entire program appears to occupy contiguous space in storage at all times. Actually, not all pages of a program are necessarily in central storage, and the pages that *are* in central storage do not necessarily occupy contiguous space.

The pieces of a program executing in virtual storage must be moved between real and auxiliary storage. To allow this action, z/OS manages storage in units, or *blocks*, of 4 KB. The following blocks are defined:

- ► A block of central storage is a *frame*.
- ► A block of virtual storage is a *page*.
- ► A block of auxiliary storage is a *slot*.

Frame:
In central storage, areas of equal size that are accessible by a unique address.

A page, a frame, and a slot are all the same size: 4 KB. An active virtual storage page resides in a central storage frame. A virtual storage page that becomes inactive resides in an auxiliary storage slot (in a paging data set). Figure 3-8 shows the relationship of pages, frames, and slots.

Slot:
In auxiliary storage, areas of equal size that are accessible by a unique address.

In Figure 3-8, z/OS is performing paging for a program running in virtual storage. The lettered boxes represent parts of the program. In this simplified view, program parts A, E, F, and H are active and running in central storage frames, while parts B, C, D, and G are inactive and have been moved to auxiliary storage slots. All of the program parts, however, reside in virtual storage and have virtual storage addresses.

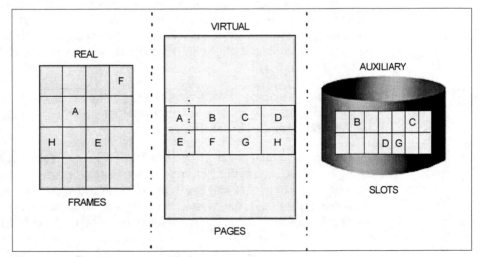

Figure 3-8   Frames, pages, and slots

3.4.5 What is paging

As stated previously, z/OS uses a series of tables to determine whether a page is in real or auxiliary storage, and where. To find a page of a program, z/OS checks the table for the virtual address of the page, rather than searching through all of physical storage for it. z/OS then transfers the page into central storage or out to auxiliary storage as needed. This movement of pages between auxiliary storage slots and central storage frames is called *paging*. Paging is key to understanding the use of virtual storage in z/OS.

z/OS paging is transparent to the user. During job execution, only those pieces of the application that are required are brought in, or *paged in*, to central storage. The pages remain in central storage until no longer needed, or until another page is required by the same application or a higher-priority application and no empty central storage is available. To select pages for paging out to auxiliary storage, z/OS follows a "Least Used" algorithm, that is, z/OS assumes that a page that has not been used for some time will probably not be used in the near future.

How paging works in z/OS

In addition to the DAT hardware, and the segment and page tables required for address translation, paging activity involves a number of system components to handle the movement of pages and several additional tables to keep track of the most current version of each page.

To understand how paging works, assume that DAT encounters an invalid page table entry during address translation, indicating that a page is required that is not in a central storage frame. To resolve this page fault, the system must bring the page in from auxiliary storage. First, however, it must locate an available central storage frame. If none is available, the request must be saved and an assigned frame freed. To free a frame, the system copies its contents to auxiliary storage and marks its corresponding page table entry as invalid. This operation is called a *page-out*.

After a frame is located for the required page, the contents of the page are copied from auxiliary storage to central storage and the page table invalid bit is set off. This operation is called a *page-in*.

Paging can also take place when z/OS loads an entire program into virtual storage. z/OS obtains virtual storage for the user program and allocates a central storage frame to each page. Each page is then active and subject to the normal paging activity, that is, the most active pages are retained in central storage while the pages not currently active might be paged out to auxiliary storage.

Page stealing

z/OS tries to keep an adequate supply of available central storage frames on hand. When a program refers to a page that is not in central storage, z/OS uses a central storage page frame from a supply of available frames.

When this supply becomes low, z/OS uses *page stealing* to replenish it, that is, it takes a frame assigned to an active user and makes it available for other work. The decision to steal a particular page is based on the activity history of each page currently residing in a central storage frame. Pages that have not been active for a relatively long time are good candidates for page stealing.

Unreferenced interval count

z/OS uses a sophisticated paging algorithm to efficiently manage virtual storage based on which pages were most recently used. An unreferenced interval count indicates how long it has been since a program referenced the page. At regular intervals, the system checks the reference bit for each page frame. If the reference bit is off, that is, the frame has not been referenced, the system adds to the frame's unreferenced interval count. It adds the number of seconds since this address space last had the reference count checked. If the reference bit is on, the frame has been referenced, and the system turns it off and sets the unreferenced interval count for the frame to zero. Frames with the highest unreferenced interval counts are the ones most likely to be stolen.

z/OS also uses various storage managers to keep track of all pages, frames, and slots in the system. These storage managers are described in 3.4.8, "Role of storage managers" on page 115.

3.4.6 Swapping and the working set

Swapping: The process of transferring an entire address space between central storage and auxiliary storage.

Swapping is the process of transferring all of the pages of an address space between central storage and auxiliary storage. A swapped-in address space is active, having pages in central storage frames and pages in auxiliary storage slots. A swapped-out address space is inactive; the address space resides on auxiliary storage and cannot execute until it is swapped in.

While only a subset of the address space's pages (known as its *working set*) would likely be in central storage at any time, swapping effectively moves the entire address space. It is one of several methods that z/OS uses to balance the system workload and ensure that an adequate supply of available central storage frames is maintained.

Swapping is performed by the System Resource Manager (SRM) component, in response to recommendations from the Workload Manager (WLM) component. WLM is described in 3.5, "What is workload management" on page 126.

3.4.7 What is storage protection

Up to now, we have discussed virtual storage mostly in the context of a single user or program. In reality, of course, many programs and users are competing for the use of the system. z/OS uses the following techniques to preserve the integrity of each user's work:

▶ A private address space for each user
▶ Page protection
▶ Low-address protection
▶ Multiple storage protect keys

How storage protect keys are used

Under z/OS, the information in central storage is protected from unauthorized use by means of multiple storage protect keys. A control field in storage called a key is associated with each 4 K frame of central storage.

When a request is made to modify the contents of a central storage location, the key associated with the request is compared to the storage protect key. If the keys match or the program is executing in key 0, the request is satisfied. If the key associated with the request does not match the storage key, the system rejects the request and issues a program exception interruption.

When a request is made to read (or fetch) the contents of a central storage location, the request is automatically satisfied unless the fetch protect bit is on, indicating that the frame is fetch-protected. When a request is made to access the contents of a fetch-protected central storage location, the key in storage is compared to the key associated with the request. If the keys match, or the requestor is in key 0, the request is satisfied. If the keys do not match, and the requestor is not in key 0, the system rejects the request and issues a program exception interruption.

How storage protect keys are assigned

z/OS uses 16 storage protect keys. A specific key is assigned according to the type of work being performed. As Figure 3-9 shows, the key is stored in bits 8 through 11 of the program status word (PSW). A PSW is assigned to each job in the system.

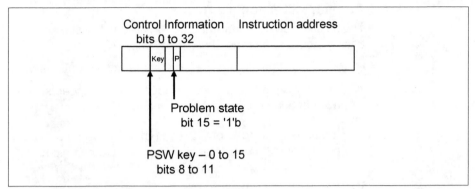

Figure 3-9   Location of the storage protect key

Storage protect keys 0 through 7 are used by the z/OS base control program (BCP) and various subsystems and middleware products. Storage protect key 0 is the master key. Its use is restricted to those parts of the BCP that require almost unlimited store and fetch capabilities. In almost any situation, a storage protect key of 0 associated with a request to access or modify the contents of a central storage location means that the request will be satisfied.

Storage protect keys 8 through 15 are assigned to users. Because all users are isolated in private address spaces, most users (those whose programs run in a virtual region) can use the same storage protect key. These users are called V=V (virtual = virtual) users and are assigned a key of 8. Some users, however, must run in a central storage region. These users are known as V=R (virtual = real) users and require individual storage protect keys because their addresses are not protected by the DAT process that keeps each address space distinct. Without separate keys, V=R users might reference each other's code and data. These keys are in the range of 9 through 15.

3.4.8 Role of storage managers

Central storage frames and auxiliary storage slots, and the virtual storage pages that they support, are managed by separate components of z/OS. These components are known as the real storage manager (not *central* storage manager), the auxiliary storage manager, and the virtual storage manager. Here, we describe the role of each briefly.

Real storage manager

The real storage manager (RSM) keeps track of the contents of central storage. It manages the paging activities described earlier, such as page-in, page-out, and page stealing, and helps with swapping an address space in or out. RSM also performs *page fixing* (marking pages as unavailable for stealing).

Auxiliary storage manager

The auxiliary storage manager (ASM) uses the system's page data sets, to keep track of auxiliary storage slots, specifically:

- ▶ Slots for virtual storage pages that are not in central storage frames.
- ▶ Slots for pages that do not occupy frames, but, because the frame's contents have not been changed, the slots are still valid.

When a page-in or page-out is required, ASM works with RSM to locate the proper central storage frames and auxiliary storage slots.

Virtual storage manager

The virtual storage manager (VSM) responds to requests to obtain and free virtual storage. VSM also manages storage allocation for any program that must run in real storage, rather than virtual storage. Real storage is allocated to code and data when they are loaded in virtual storage. As they run, programs can request more storage by means of a system service, such as the GETMAIN macro. Programs can release storage by using the FREEMAIN macro.

VSM keeps track of the map of virtual storage for each address space. It sees an address space as a collection of 256 *subpools,* which are logically related areas of virtual storage identified by the numbers 0 to 255. Being logically related means the storage areas within a subpool share characteristics, such as:

- ▶ Storage protect key
- ▶ Whether they are fetch protected, pageable, or swappable
- ▶ Where they must reside in virtual storage (above or below 16 MB)
- ▶ Whether they can be shared by more than one task

Some subpools (numbers 128 to 255) are predefined by use by system programs. Subpool 252, for example, is for programs from authorized libraries. Others (numbered 0 to 127) are defined by user programs.

Attention: Every address space has the same virtual storage mapping. z/OS creates a segment table for each address space.

3.4.9 A brief history of virtual storage and 64-bit addressability

Addressability:
A program's
ability to
reference all of
the storage
associated with
an address
space.

In 1970, IBM introduced System/370 (S/370), the first of its architectures to use virtual storage and address spaces. Since that time, the operating system has changed in many ways. One key area of growth and change is addressability.

A program running in an address space can reference all of the storage associated with that address space. In this text, a program's ability to reference all of the storage associated with an address space is called *addressability*.

S/370 defined storage addresses as 24 bits in length, which meant that the highest accessible address was 16,777,215 bytes (or 2^{24}-1 bytes).[16] The use of 24-bit addressability allowed MVS/370, the operating system at that time, to allot to each user an address space of 16 MB. Over the years, as MVS/370 gained more functions and was asked to handle more complex applications, even access to 16 MB of virtual storage fell short of user needs.

With the release of the System/370-XA architecture in 1983, IBM extended the addressability of the architecture to 31 bits. With 31-bit addressing, the operating system (now called MVS Extended Architecture (MVS/XA)) increased the addressability of virtual storage from 16 MB to 2 GB. In other words, MVS/XA provided an address space for users that was 128 times larger than the address space provided by MVS/370. The 16 MB address became the dividing point between the two architectures and is commonly called the *line* (see Figure 3-10).

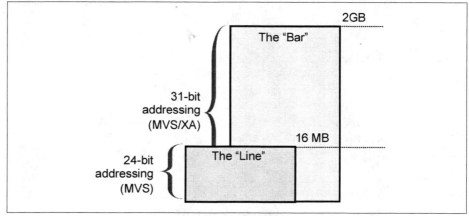

Figure 3-10   31-bit addressability allows for 2 GB address spaces in MVS/XA

---

[16] Addressing starts with 0, so the last address is always one less than the total number of addressable bytes.

The new architecture did not require customers to change existing application programs. To maintain compatibility for existing programs, MVS/XA remained compatible for programs originally designed to run with 24-bit addressing on MVS/370, while allowing application developers to write new programs to use the 31-bit technology.

To preserve compatibility between the different addressing schemes, MVS/XA did not use the *high-order bit* of the address (Bit 0) for addressing. Instead, MVS/XA reserved this bit to indicate how many bits would be used to resolve an address: 31-bit addressing (Bit 0 on) or 24-bit addressing (Bit 0 off).

With the release of IBM eServer zSeries mainframes in 2000, IBM further extended the addressability of the architecture to 64 bits. With 64-bit addressing, the potential size of a z/OS address space expands to a size so vast we need new terms to describe it. Each address space, called a 64-bit address space, is 16 EB in size (an exabyte is slightly more than one billion gigabytes).

The new address space has logically 2^{64} addresses. It is 8 billion times the size of the former 2 GB address space, or 18,446,744,073,709,600,000 bytes (Figure 3-11).

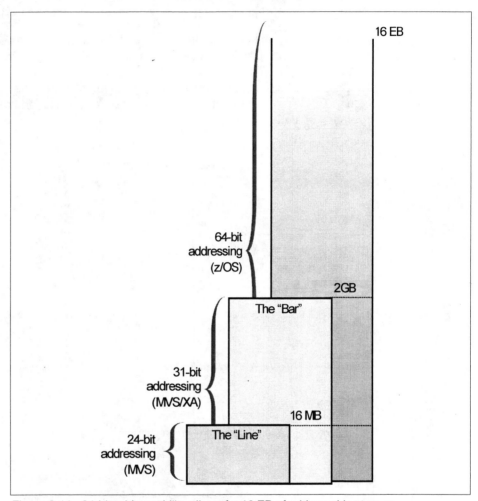

Figure 3-11   64-bit addressability allows for 16 EB of addressable storage

We say that the potential size is 16 EB because z/OS, by default, continues to create address spaces with a size of 2 GB. The address space exceeds this limit only if a program running in it allocates virtual storage above the 2 GB address. If so, z/OS increases the storage available to the user from 2 GB to 16 EB.

A program running on z/OS and the zSeries mainframe can run with 24-, 31-, or 64-bit addressing (and can switch among these if needed). To address the high virtual storage available with the 64-bit architecture, the program uses 64-bit-specific instructions. Although the architecture introduces the unique 64-bit instructions, the program can use both 31-bit and 64-bit instructions as needed.

For compatibility, the layout of the storage areas for an address space is the same below 2 GB, providing an environment that can support both 24-bit and 31-bit addressing. The area that separates the virtual storage area below the 2 GB address from the user private area is called the *bar*, as shown in Figure 3-12. The user private area is allocated for application code rather than operating system code.

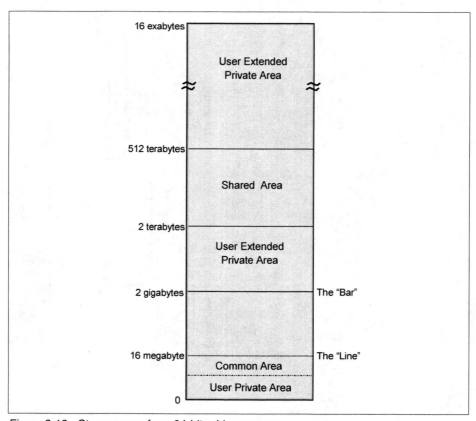

Figure 3-12   Storage map for a 64-bit address space

Here is a summary of each virtual storage layer shown in Figure 3-12:

$0 - 2^{31}$ For compatibility, storage addresses below the bar are addressed as before.

$2^{31} - 2^{32}$ A 2 GB address is considered the "bar."

$2^{32} - 2^{41}$ The low non-shared area (user private area) starts at 4 GB and extends to 2^{41}.

$2^{41} - 2^{50}$ Shared area (for storage sharing) starts at 2^{41} and extends to 2^{50} or higher, if requested.

$2^{50} - 2^{64}$ High non-shared area (user private area) starts at 2^{50} or wherever the shared area ends, and goes to 2^{64}.

In a 16 EB address space with 64-bit virtual storage addressing, there are three additional levels of translation tables, called region tables: region third table (R3T), region second table (R2T), and region first table (R1T). The region tables are 16 KB in length, and there are 2048 entries per table. Each region has 2 GB.

Segment tables and page table formats remain the same as for virtual addresses below the bar. When translating a 64-bit virtual address, after the system has identified the corresponding 2 GB region entry that points to the Segment table, the process is the same as that described previously.

3.4.10 What is meant by below-the-line storage

z/OS programs and data reside in virtual storage that, when necessary, is backed by central storage. Most programs and data do not depend on their real addresses. Some z/OS programs, however, do depend on real addresses and some require these real addresses to be less than 16 MB. z/OS programmers refer to this storage as being "below the 16 MB line."

In z/OS, a program's attributes include one called *residence mode* (RMODE), which specifies whether the program must reside (be loaded) in storage below 16 MB. A program with RMODE(24) must reside below 16 MB, while a program with RMODE(31) can reside anywhere in virtual storage.

Examples of programs that require below-the-line storage include any program that allocates a data control block (DCB). Those programs, however, often can be 31-bit residency mode (RMODE(31)), as they can run in 31-bit addressing mode (AMODE(31)). z/OS reserves as much central storage below 16 MB as it can for such programs and, for the most part, handles their central storage dependencies without requiring them to make any changes.

Thousands of programs in use today are AMODE(24) and therefore RMODE(24). Every program written before MVS/XA was available, and not subsequently changed, has that characteristic. There are relatively few reasons these days why a new program might need to be AMODE(24), so a new application likely has next to nothing that is RMODE(24).

3.4.11 What is in an address space

Another way of thinking of an address space is as a programmer's map of the virtual storage available for code and data. An address space provides each programmer with access to all of the addresses available through the computer architecture (earlier, we defined this characteristic as addressability).

z/OS provides each user with a unique address space and maintains the distinction between the programs and data belonging to each address space. Because it maps all of the available addresses, however, an address space includes system code and data and user code and data. Thus, not all of the mapped addresses are available for user code and data.

Understanding the division of storage areas in an address space is made easier with a diagram. The diagram shown in Figure 3-13 is more detailed than needed for this part of the course, but is included here to show that an address space maintains the distinction between programs and data belonging to the user, and those belonging to the operating system.

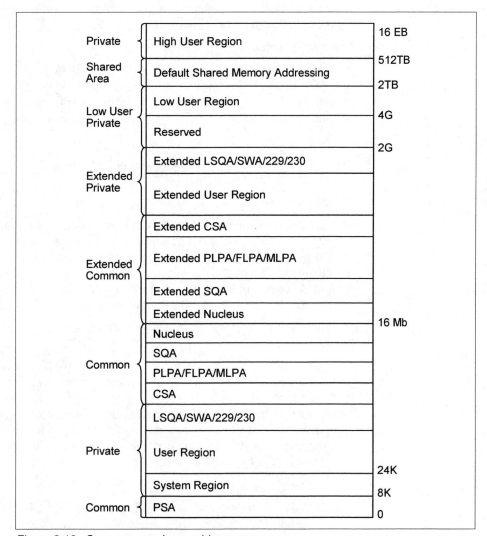

Figure 3-13   Storage areas in an address space

Figure 3-13 on page 123 shows the major storage areas in each address space. These are described briefly as follows:

► All storage above 2 GB

This area is called *high virtual storage* and is addressable only by programs running in 64-bit mode. It is divided by the high virtual shared area, which is an area of installation-defined size that can be used to establish cross-address space viewable connections to obtained areas within this area.

► Extended areas above 16 MB

This range of areas, which lies above the line (16 MB) but below the bar (2 GB), is a kind of "mirror image" of the common area below 16 MB. They have the same attributes as their equivalent areas below the line, but because of the additional storage above the line, their sizes are much larger.

► Nucleus

This is a key 0, read-only area of common storage that contains operating system control programs.

► System queue area (SQA)

This area contains system level (key 0) data accessed by multiple address spaces. The SQA area is not pageable (fixed), which means that it resides in central storage until it is freed by the requesting program. The size of the SQA area is predefined by the installation and cannot change while the operating system is active. Yet it has the unique ability to "overflow" into the CSA area as long as there is unused CSA storage that can be converted to SQA.

► Pageable link pack area (PLPA), fixed link pack area (FLPA), and modified link pack area (MLPA)

This area contains the link pack areas (the pageable link pack area, fixed link pack area, and modified link pack area), which contain system level programs that are often run by multiple address spaces. For this reason, the link pack areas reside in the common area that is addressable by every address space, therefore eliminating the need for each address space to have its own copy of the program. This storage area is below the line and is therefore addressable by programs running in 24-bit mode.

► CSA

This portion of common area storage (addressable by all address spaces) is available to all applications. The CSA is often used to contain data frequently accessed by multiple address spaces. The size of the CSA area is established at system initialization time (IPL) and cannot change while the operating system is active.

- ▶ LSQA/SWA/subpool 228/subpool 230

  This assortment of subpools, each with specific attributes, is used primarily by system functions when the functions require address space level storage isolation. Being below the line, these areas are addressable by programs running in 24-bit mode.

- ▶ User Region

  This area is obtainable by any program running in the user's address space, including user key programs. It resides below the line and is therefore addressable by programs running in 24-bit mode.

- ▶ System Region

  This small area (usually only four pages) is reserved for use by the region control task of each address space.

- ▶ Prefixed Save Area (PSA)

  This area is often referred to as "Low Core." The PSA is a common area of virtual storage from address zero through 8191 in every address space. There is one unique PSA for every processor installed in a system. The PSA maps architecturally fixed hardware and software storage locations for the processor. Because there is a unique PSA for each processor, from the view of a program running on z/OS, the contents of the PSA can change any time the program is dispatched on a different processor. This feature is unique to the PSA area and is accomplished through a unique DAT manipulation technique called *prefixing*.

Given the vast range of addressable storage in an address space, the drawing in Figure 3-13 on page 123 is not to scale.

Each address space in the system is represented by an address space control block (ASCB). To represent an address space, the system creates an ASCB in common storage (system queue area (SQA)), which makes it accessible to other address spaces.

3.4.12 System address spaces and the master scheduler

Many z/OS system functions run in their own address spaces. The master scheduler subsystem, for example, runs in the address space called *MASTER* and is used to establish communication between z/OS and its own address spaces.

When you start z/OS, master initialization routines initialize system services, such as the system log and communication task, and start the master scheduler address space. Then, the master scheduler may start the job entry subsystem (JES2 or JES3). JES is the primary job entry subsystem.

On many production systems JES is not started immediately; instead, the automation package starts all tasks in a controlled sequence. Then other subsystems are started. Subsystems are defined in a special file of system settings called a parameter library (PARMLIB). These subsystems are *secondary subsystems*.

Each address space created has a number associated with it, called the address space ID (ASID). Because the master scheduler is the first address space created in the system, it becomes address space number 1 (ASID=1). Other system address spaces are then started during the initialization process of z/OS.

At this point, you need only understand that z/OS and its related subsystems require address spaces of their own to provide a functioning operating system. A short description of each type of address space follows:

▶ System

z/OS system address spaces are started after initialization of the master scheduler. These address spaces perform functions for all the other types of address spaces that start in z/OS.

▶ Subsystem

z/OS requires the use of various subsystems, such as a primary job entry subsystem (JES) (described in Chapter 7, "Batch processing and the job entry subsystem" on page 273). Also, there are address spaces for middleware products, such as DB2, CICS, and IMS.

Besides system address spaces, there are, of course, typically many address spaces for users and separately running programs, for example:

▶ TSO/E address spaces are created for every user who logs on to z/OS (described in Chapter 4, "TSO/E, ISPF, and UNIX: Interactive facilities of z/OS" on page 165).

▶ An address space is created for every batch job that runs on z/OS. Batch job address spaces are started by JES.

3.5 What is workload management

For z/OS, the management of system resources is the responsibility of the workload management (WLM) component. WLM manages the processing of workloads in the system according to the company's business goals, such as response time. WLM also manages the use of system resources, such as processors and storage, to accomplish these goals.

3.5.1 What does WLM do

In simple terms, WLM has three objectives:

- ► To achieve the business goals that are defined by the installation, by automatically assigning sysplex resources to workloads based on their importance and goals. This objective is known as *goal achievement*.

- ► To achieve optimal use of the system resources from the system point of view. This objective is known as *throughput*.

- ► To achieve optimal use of system resources from the point of view of the individual address space. This objective is known as *response* and *turnaround time*.

Goal achievement is the first and most important task of WLM. Optimizing throughput and minimizing turnaround times of address spaces come after that task. Often, these latter two objectives are contradictory. Optimizing throughput means keeping resources busy. Optimizing response and turnaround time, however, requires resources to be available when they are needed. Achieving the goal of an important address space might result in worsening the turnaround time of a less important address space. Thus, WLM must make decisions that represent trade-offs between conflicting objectives.

Workload management: A z/OS component that manages system resources according to stated business goals.

To balance throughput with response and turnaround time, WLM performs the following actions:

- ► Monitors the use of resources by the various address spaces.

- ► Monitors the system-wide use of resources to determine whether they are fully utilized.

- ► Determines which address spaces to swap out (and when).

- ► Inhibits the creation of new address spaces or steals pages when certain shortages of central storage exist.

- ► Changes the dispatching priority of address spaces, which controls the rate at which the address spaces are allowed to consume system resources.

- ► Selects the devices to be allocated, if a choice of devices exists, to balance the use of I/O devices.

Other z/OS components, transaction managers, and database managers can communicate to WLM a change in status for a particular address space (or for the system as a whole), or to invoke WLM's decision-making power.

For example, WLM is notified when:

- ► Central storage is configured into or out of the system.
- ► An address space is created.
- ► An address space is deleted.
- ► A swap-out starts or completes.
- ► Allocation routines can choose the devices to be allocated to a request.

Up to this point, we have discussed WLM only in the context of a single z/OS system. In real life, customer installations often use clusters of multiple z/OS systems in concert to process complex workloads. Remember our earlier discussion of clustered z/OS systems (a sysplex).

WLM is particularly well-suited to a sysplex environment. It keeps track of system usage and workload goal achievement across all the systems in the Parallel Sysplex and data sharing environments. For example, WLM can decide the z/OS system on which a batch job should run, based on the availability of resources to process the job quickly.

WLM also plays a role in the zEnterprise System environment. In a zEnterprise System, the Unified Resource Manager (Unified Resource Manager) can provide goal-based hardware performance management, monitoring, and data collection. Through interaction with optional guest platform management providers that customers install and start on virtual servers, the Unified Resource Manager augments hardware performance reports by including operating system statistics and application performance data. On z/OS, administrators configure WLM to activate and manage the guest platform management providers that collect data for the Unified Resource Manager.

3.5.2 How is WLM used

A mainframe installation can influence almost all decisions made by WLM by establishing a set of *policies* that allow an installation to closely link system performance to its business needs. Workloads are assigned goals (for example, a target average response time) and an importance (that is, how important it is to the business that a workload meet its goals).

Before the introduction of WLM, the only way to inform z/OS about the company's business goals was for the system programmer to translate from high-level objectives into the detailed technical terms using various parameter settings that the system could understand. This action provided a pre-established runtime environment where if the workload changed during the the IPL, the parameter values remained unchanged, creating artificial constraints and thresholds that did not match the true capacity of the machine's resources.

Service level agreement (SLA):
A written agreement of the service to be provided to the users of a computing installation.

This static form of a configuration required highly skilled staff, and could be protracted, error-prone, and eventually in conflict with the original business goals.

Further, it was often difficult to predict the effects of changing a system setting, which might be required, for example, following a system capacity increase. This situation could result in unbalanced resource allocation, in which work is deprived of a critical system resource. This way of operating, called compatibility mode, was becoming unmanageable as new workloads were introduced, and as multiple systems were being managed together.

Using *goal mode* system operation, WLM provides fewer, simpler, and more consistent system externals that reflect goals for work expressed in terms commonly used in business objectives, and WLM and System Resource Manager (SRM) match resources to meet those goals by constantly monitoring and adapting the system. Workload Manager provides a solution for managing workload distribution, workload balancing, and distributing resources to competing workloads.

WLM policies are often based on a service level agreement (SLA), which is a written agreement of the information systems (IS) service to be provided to the users of a computing installation. WLM tries to achieve the needs of workloads (response time) as described in an SLA by attempting the appropriate distribution of resources without overcommitting them through firmware algorithms. In this situation, resources are matched to a workload transparently without administrator intervention. Equally important, WLM maximizes system use (throughput) to deliver maximum benefit from the installed hardware and software platform.

> **Summary:** Using today's zEnterprise workload management functionality provides a sophisticated means for managing hardware and software for goal oriented performance objectives.

3.6 I/O and data management

Nearly all work in the system involves data input or data output. In a mainframe, the channel subsystem (CSS) manages the use of I/O devices, such as disks, tapes, and printers. The operating system must associate the data for a given task with a device, and manage file allocation, placement, monitoring, migration, backup, recall, recovery, and deletion.

The channel subsystem directs the flow of information between the devices and main storage. A logical device is represented as a subchannel to a program and contains the information required for sustaining an I/O.

The CSS uses one or more channel path identifiers (known as CHPIDs) as communication links. The CHPID is assigned a value between 0 - 255 in each CSS. There can be one or more CSSs defined within a mainframe. Control units provide the logical capabilities to operate and control an I/O device.

The input/output architecture (Figure 3-14) is a major strength of the mainframe.

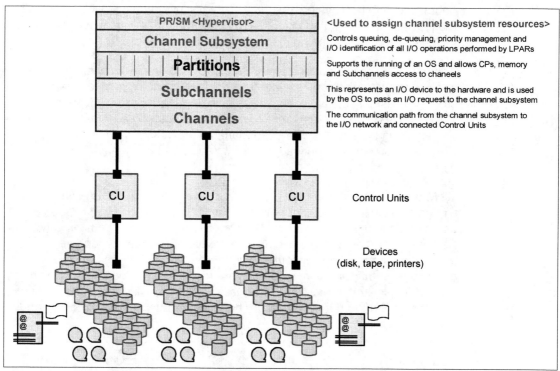

Figure 3-14   Input/output architecture

It uses a special processor called the system assist processor to schedule and prioritize I/O. This processor is dedicated to driving the mainframe's channel subsystem, up to 100,000 I/O operations per second and beyond. Each model mainframe comes with a default number of system assist processors, ranging from one to eleven, although more system assist processors can be added as required. The channel subsystem can provide over 1000 high-speed buses, one per single server. The system assist processor runs special Licensed Internal Code (LIC)[17] and takes responsibility during the execution of an I/O operation. The system assist processor relieves the OS (and consequently, general CP involvement) during the setup of an I/O operation.

---

[17] LIC is IBM microcode or software programs that the customer is not able to read or alter.

It does the scheduling of an I/O, that is, it finds an available channel path to the device and guarantees that the I/O operation starts. system assist processor, however, is not in charge of the movement between central storage (CS) and the channel. The system assist processor, which is inherent in this platform's design, is architected into the I/O subsystem, providing a rich quality of service.

3.6.1 Data management

Data management activities can be done either manually or through the use of automated processes. When data management is automated, the system uses a policy or set of rules known as Automatic Class Selection (ACS) to determine object placement, manage object backup, movement, space, and security. Storage management policies reduce the need for users to make many detailed decisions that are not related to their business objectives.

A typical z/OS production system includes both manual and automated processes for managing data. ACS applies to all data set types, including database and UNIX file structures.

Depending on how a z/OS system and its storage devices are configured, a user or program can directly control many aspects of data management, and in the early days of the operating system, users were required to do so. Increasingly, however, z/OS installations rely on installation-specific settings for data and resource management, and add-on storage management products to automate the use of storage.

The primary means of managing storage in z/OS is by using the DFSMS component, which is discussed in Chapter 5, "Working with data sets" on page 203.

3.7 Supervising the execution of work in the system

To enable multiprogramming, z/OS requires the use of a number of supervisor controls, as follows:

► Interrupt processing

Multiprogramming requires that there be some technique for switching control from one routine to another so that, for example, when routine A must wait for an I/O request to be satisfied, routine B can execute. In z/OS, this switch is achieved by *interrupts*, which are events that alter the sequence in which the processor executes instructions. When an interrupt occurs, the system saves the execution status of the interrupted routine and analyzes and processes the interrupt.

► Creating dispatchable units of work

To identify and keep track of its work, the z/OS operating system represents each unit of work with a control block. Two types of control blocks represent dispatchable units of work: *task control blocks* (TCBs), which represent tasks executing within an address space, and *service request blocks* (SRBs), which represent higher priority system services.

► Dispatching work

After interrupts are processed, the operating system determines which unit of work (of all the units of work in the system) is ready to run and has the highest priority, and passes control to that unit of work.

► Serializing the use of resources

In a multiprogramming system, almost any sequence of instructions can be interrupted and resumed later. If that set of instructions manipulates or modifies a resource (for example, a control block or a data file), the operating system must prevent other programs from using the resource until the interrupted program has completed its processing of the resource.

Several techniques exist for serializing the use of resources; *enqueuing* and *locking* are the most common (a third technique is called *latching*). All users can use enqueuing, but only authorized routines can use locking to serialize the use of resources.

3.7.1 What is interrupt processing

An interrupt is an event that alters the sequence in which the processor executes instructions. An interrupt might be planned (specifically requested by the currently running program) or unplanned (caused by an event that might or might not be related to the currently running program). z/OS uses six types of interrupts, as follows:

► Supervisor calls or SVC interrupts

These occur when the program issues an SVC to request a particular system service. An SVC interrupts the program being executed and passes control to the supervisor so that it can perform the service. Programs request these services through macros, such as OPEN (open a file), GETMAIN (obtain storage), or WTO (write a message to the system operator).

► I/O interrupts

These occur when the channel subsystem signals a change of status, such as an I/O operation completing, an error occurring, or when an I/O device, such as a printer, has become ready for work.

- External interrupts

  These can indicate any of several events, such as a time interval expiring, the operator pressing the interrupt key on the console, or the processor receiving a signal from another processor.

- Restart interrupts

  These occur when the operator selects the restart function at the console or when a restart SIGP (signal processor) instruction is received from another processor.

- Program interrupts

  These are caused by program errors (for example, the program attempts to perform an invalid operation), *page faults* (the program references a page that is not in central storage), or requests to monitor an event.

- Machine check interrupts

  These are caused by machine malfunctions.

When an interrupt occurs, the hardware saves pertinent information about the program that was interrupted and, if possible, disables the processor for further interrupts of the same type. The hardware then routes control to the appropriate interrupt handler routine. The program status word (PSW) is a key resource in this process.

How is the program status word used

The program status word (PSW) is a 128-bit data area in the processor that, along with a variety of other types of registers (control registers, timing registers, and prefix registers) provides details crucial to both the hardware and the software. The current PSW includes the address of the next program instruction and control information about the program that is running. Each processor has only one current PSW. Thus, only one task can execute on a processor at a time.

The PSW controls the order in which instructions are fed to the processor, and indicates the status of the system in relation to the currently running program. Although each processor has only one PSW, it is useful to think of three types of PSWs to understand interrupt processing:

- Current PSW
- New PSW
- Old PSW

The current PSW indicates the next instruction to be executed. It also indicates whether the processor is enabled or disabled for I/O interrupts, external interrupts, machine check interrupts, and certain program interrupts. When the processor is enabled, these interrupts can occur. When the processor is disabled, these interrupts are ignored or remain pending.

There is a new PSW and an old PSW associated with each of the six types of interrupts. The new PSW contains the address of the routine that can process its associated interrupt. If the processor is enabled for interrupts when an interrupt occurs, PSWs are switched using the following technique:

1. Storing the current PSW in the old PSW associated with the type of interrupt that occurred

2. Loading the contents of the new PSW for the type of interrupt that occurred into the current PSW

The current PSW, which indicates the next instruction to be executed, now contains the address of the appropriate routine to handle the interrupt. This switch has the effect of transferring control to the appropriate interrupt handling routine.

Registers and the PSW

Mainframe architecture provides registers to keep track of things. The PSW, for example, is a register used to contain information that is required for the execution of the currently active program.

Mainframes provide other registers, as follows:

▶ *Access registers* are used to specify the address space in which data is found.

▶ *General registers* are used to address data in storage, and also for holding user data.

▶ *Floating point registers* are used to hold numeric data in floating point form.

▶ *Control registers* are used by the operating system itself, for example, as references to translation tables.

z/Architecture Principles of Operation, SA22-7832 describes the hardware facilities for the switching of system status, including CPU states, control modes, the PSW, and control registers. You can find this and other related publications at the z/OS Internet Library website:

`http://www.ibm.com/servers/eserver/zseries/zos/bkserv/`

Figure 3-15 gives an overview of registers and the PSW.

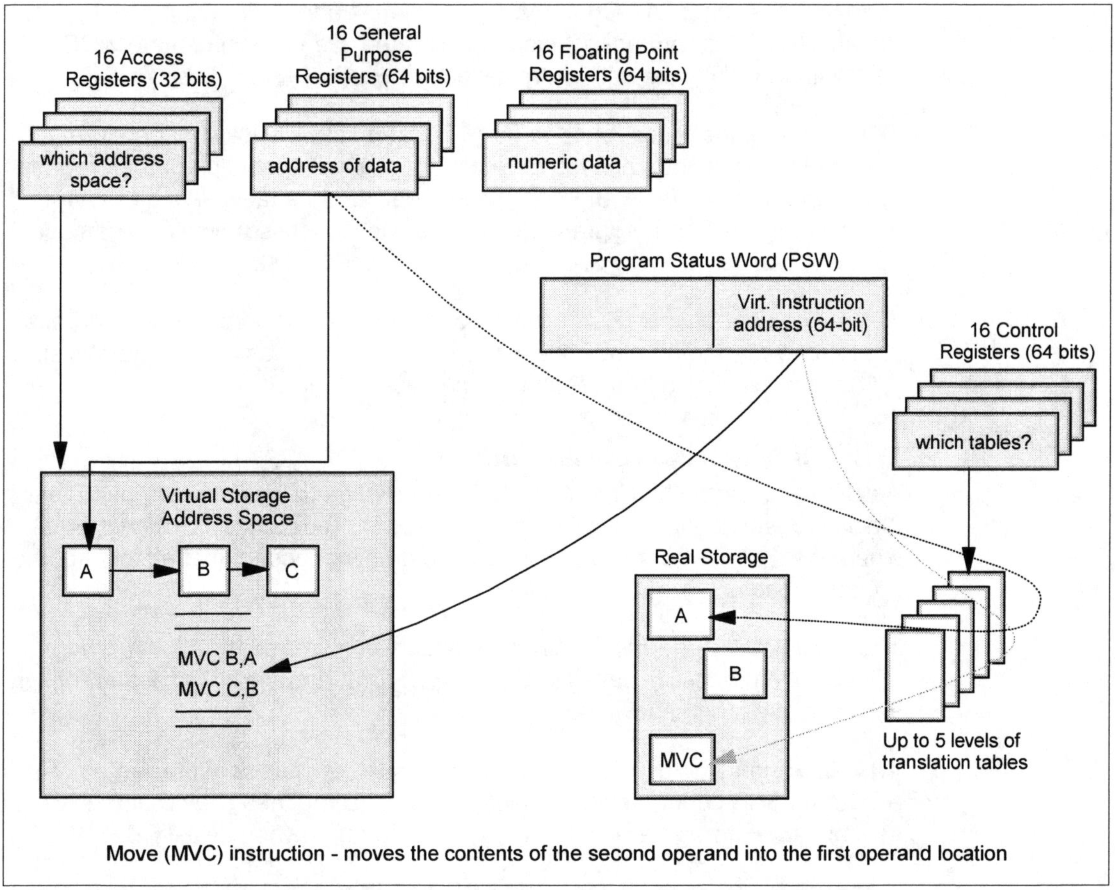

Figure 3-15   Registers and the PSW

3.7.2 Creating dispatchable units of work

In z/OS, dispatchable units of work are represented by two kinds of control blocks:

► Task control blocks (TCBs): These represent tasks executing within an address space, such as user programs and system programs that support the user programs.

► Service request blocks (SRBs): These represent requests to execute a system service routine. SRBs are typically created when one address space detects an event that affects a different address space; they provide one mechanism for communication between address spaces.

What is a task control block

A TCB is a control block that represents a task, such as your program, as it runs in an address space. A TCB contains information about the running task, such as the address of any storage areas it has created. Do not confuse the z/OS term *TCB* with the UNIX data structure called a *process control block* (PCB).

TCBs are created in response to an ATTACH macro. By issuing the ATTACH macro, a user program or system routine begins the execution of the program specified on the ATTACH macro, as a subtask of the attacher's task. As a subtask, the specified program can compete for processor time and can use certain resources already allocated to the attacher's task.

The region control task (RCT), which is responsible for preparing an address space for swap-in and swap-out, is the highest priority task in an address space. All tasks within an address space are subtasks of the RCT.

What is a service request block

An SRB is a control block that represents a routine that performs a particular function or service in a specified address space. Typically, an SRB is created when one address space is executing and an event occurs that affects another address space.

The routine that performs the function or service is called the *SRB routine*, initiating the process is called *scheduling an SRB*, and the SRB routine runs in the operating mode known as *SRB mode*.

An SRB is similar to a TCB in that it identifies a unit of work to the system. Unlike a TCB, an SRB cannot "own" storage areas. SRB routines can obtain, reference, use, and free storage areas, but the areas must be owned by a TCB.

In a multiprocessor environment, the SRB routine, after being scheduled, can be dispatched on another processor and can run concurrently with the scheduling program. The scheduling program can continue to do other processing in parallel with the SRB routine. As mentioned earlier, an SRB provides a means of asynchronous inter-address space communication for programs running on z/OS.

Only programs running in a mode of higher authority called a *supervisor state* can create an SRB. These authorized programs obtain storage and initialize the control block with, for example, the identity of the target address space and pointers to the code that process the request. The program creating the SRB then issues the SCHEDULE macro and indicates whether the SRB has global (system-wide) or local (address space-wide) priority. The system places the SRB on the appropriate dispatching queue, where it remains until it becomes the highest priority work on the queue.

SRBs with a global priority have a higher priority than that of any address space, regardless of the actual address space in which they will be executed. SRBs with a local priority have a priority equal to that of the address space in which they will be executed, but higher than any TCB within that address space. The assignment of global or local priority depends on the "importance" of the request, for example, SRBs for I/O interrupts are scheduled at a global priority, to minimize I/O delays.

Using an SRB is described in the *z/OS MVS Authorized Assembler Services Guide*, SA22-7605. You can find this and related publications at the z/OS Internet Library website:

```
http://www.ibm.com/servers/eserver/zseries/zos/bkserv/
```

3.7.3 Preemptable versus non-preemptable

Which routine receives control after an interrupt is processed depends on whether the interrupted unit of work was preemptable. If so, the operating system determines which unit of work should be performed next, that is, the system determines which unit or work, of all the work in the system, has the highest priority, and passes control to that unit of work.

A non-preemptable unit of work can be interrupted, but must receive control after the interrupt is processed. For example, SRBs are often non-preemptable.[18] Thus, if a routine represented by a non-preemptable SRB is interrupted, it receives control after the interrupt has been processed. In contrast, a routine represented by a TCB, such as a user program, is usually preemptable.[19]

If the routine is interrupted, control returns to the operating system when the interrupt handling completes. z/OS then determines which task, of all the ready tasks, will execute next.

3.7.4 What does the dispatcher do

New work is selected, for example, when a task is interrupted or becomes non-dispatchable, or after an SRB completes or is suspended (that is, an SRB is delayed because a required resource is not available).

---

[18] SRBs can be made preemptable by the issuing program, to allow work at an equal or higher priority to have access to the processor. Also, client SRBs and enclave SRBs are preemptable. These topics are beyond the scope of this book.
[19] A TCB is non-preemptable when it is executing an SVC.

In z/OS, the dispatcher component is responsible for routing control to the highest priority unit of work that is ready to execute. The dispatcher processes work in the following order:

1. Special exits

   These are exits to routines that have a high priority because of specific conditions in the system. For example, if one processor in a multi-processing system fails, alternate CPU recovery is invoked by means of a special exit to recover work that was being executed on the failing processor.

2. SRBs that have a global priority

3. Ready address spaces in order of priority

   An address space is ready to execute if it is swapped in and not waiting for some event to complete. An address spaces's priority is determined by the dispatching priority specified by the user or the installation.

   After selecting the highest priority address space, z/OS (through the dispatcher) first dispatches SRBs with a local priority that are scheduled for that address space and then dispatches TCBs in that address space.

If there is no ready work in the system, z/OS assumes a state called an *enabled wait* until fresh work enters the system.

Models of the System z hardware can have from one to 64 central processors (CPs).[20] Each and every CP can be executing instructions at the same time. Dispatching priorities determine when ready-to-execute address spaces get dispatched.

> **Attention:** At the time of the writing of this book, due to the current PR/SM architecture, the maximum number of customizable CPs is 64 on the EC model, although when fully loaded, the MCMs can physically contain up to 77, including system assist processors and spares.

z/OS and dispatching modes

The mainframe was originally designed as a Symmetric Multi Processor (SMP) involving a multiprocessor computer architecture where two or more identical general purpose processors can connect to a single shared main memory. SMP architecture is the most common multiprocessor system used today.

---

[20] The IBM z10 Enterprise Class machine can be ordered with up to 64 CPs (the model numbers correspond to the maximum number of processors that can be ordered in the server).

When System z acquired special purpose processors, its computing paradigm was supplemented by adding Asymmetric Multi Processing (ASMP), which uses separate specialty processors such as zAAP and zIIP engines for executing specific software stacks. ASMP allowed the z/OS dispatcher to offload eligible workloads to non-general purpose CPs. This increases overall throughput and helps scalability. (See 2.4, "Processing units" on page 59 for more information.)

One of the engineering challenges with SMP using large server designs was to maintain near-linear scalability as the number of CPUs increases. Performance and throughput do not double when doubling the number of processors. There are many factors, including contention for cache and main memory access. These factors become increasingly difficult to mitigate as the number of CPUs increases. The design goal for delivering maximum performance is to minimize those factors. Each new mainframe model supports a higher maximum number of CPUs, so this engineering challenge becomes ever more important.

HiperDispatch helps address the problem through a combination of hardware features, z/OS dispatching, and the z/OS Workload Manager. In z/OS, there may be tasks waiting for processing attention, such as transaction programs. The z/OS run time augments the other dispatching modes by debuting non-uniform memory access (NUMA) functionality using HiperDispatch, which dedicates different memory cache to different processors. In a NUMA architecture, processors access local memory (level 2 cache) more quickly than remote cache memory neighboring on another book where access is slower. This can improve throughput for certain types of workloads when data cache is localized to specific processors. This situation is also known as an *affinity node*.

Figure 3-16 shows an overview of how SMP dispatching works.

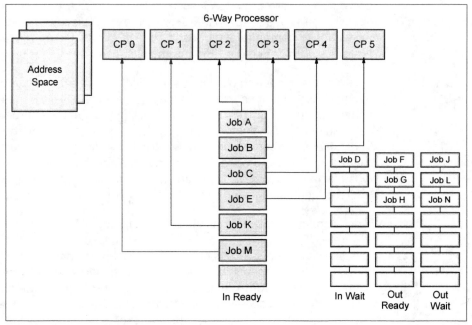

Figure 3-16   How SMP dispatching works

An address space can be in any one of four queues:

▶ IN-READY: In central storage and waiting to be dispatched

▶ IN-WAIT: In central storage, but waiting for some event to complete

▶ OUT-READY: Ready to execute but swapped out

▶ OUT-WAIT: Swapped out and waiting for some event to complete

Only IN-READY work can be selected for dispatching.

3.7.5 Serializing the use of resources

In a multitasking, multiprocessing environment, resource serialization is the technique used to coordinate access to resources that are used by more than one application. Programs that change data need exclusive access to the data. Otherwise, if several programs were to update the same data at the same time, the data could be corrupted (also referred to as a loss of data integrity). Alternately, programs that need only to read data can safely share access to the same data at the same time.

The most common techniques for serializing the use of resources are enqueuing and locking. These techniques allow for orderly access to system resources needed by more than one user in a multiprogramming or multiprocessing environment. In z/OS, enqueuing is managed by the global resource serialization component and locking is managed by various lock manager programs in the supervisor component.

What is global resource serialization

The global resource serialization (GRS) component processes requests for resources from programs running on z/OS. Global resource serialization serializes access to resources to protect their integrity. An installation can connect two or more z/OS systems with channel-to-channel (CTC) adapters to form a GRS complex to serialize access to resources shared among the systems.

When a program requests access to a reusable resource, the access can be requested as exclusive or shared. When global resource serialization grants shared access to a resource, exclusive users cannot obtain access to the resource. Likewise, when global resource serialization grants exclusive access to a resource, all other requestors for the resource wait until the exclusive requestor frees the resource.

What is enqueuing

Enqueuing is the means by which a program running on z/OS requests control of a serially reusable resource. Enqueuing is accomplished by means of the ENQ (enqueue) and DEQ (dequeue) macros, which are available to all programs running on the system. For devices that are shared between multiple z/OS systems, enqueuing is accomplished through the RESERVE and DEQ macros.

On ENQ and RESERVE, a program specifies the names of one or more resources and requests shared or exclusive control of those resources. If the resources are to be modified, the program must request exclusive control; if the resources are not to be modified, the program *should* request shared control, which allows the resource to be shared by other programs that do not require exclusive control. If the resource is not available, the system suspends the requesting program until the resource becomes available. When the program no longer requires control of a resource, it uses the DEQ macro to release it.

What is locking

Through locking, the system serializes the use of system resources by authorized routines and, in a Parallel Sysplex, by processors. A lock is simply a named field in storage that indicates whether a resource is being used and who is using it.

In z/OS, there are two kinds of locks: global locks, for resources related to more than one address space, and local locks, for resources assigned to a particular address space. Global locks are provided for nonreusable or nonsharable routines and various resources.

To use a resource protected by a lock, a routine must first request the lock for that resource. If the lock is unavailable (that is, it is already held by another program or processor), the action taken by the program or processor that requested the lock depends on whether the lock is a *spin lock* or a *suspend lock*:

▶ If a spin lock is unavailable, the requesting processor continues testing the lock until the other processor releases it. As soon as the lock is released, the requesting processor can obtain the lock and control the protected resource. Most global locks are spin locks. The holder of a spin lock should be disabled for most interrupts (if the holder were to be interrupted, it might never be able to gain control to give up the lock).

▶ If a suspend lock is unavailable, the unit of work requesting the lock is delayed until the lock is available. Other work is dispatched on the requesting processor. All local locks are suspend locks.

You might wonder what would happen if two users each request a lock that is held by the other? Would they both wait forever for the other to release the lock first, in a kind of stalemate? In z/OS, such an occurrence would be known as a *deadlock*. Fortunately, the z/OS locking methodology prevents deadlocks.

To avoid deadlocks, locks are arranged in a hierarchy, and a processor or routine can unconditionally request only locks higher in the hierarchy than locks it currently holds. For example, a deadlock could occur if processor 1 held lock A and required lock B, and processor 2 held lock B and required lock A. This situation cannot occur because locks must be acquired in hierarchical sequence. Assume, in this example, that lock A precedes lock B is the hierarchy. Processor 2, then, cannot unconditionally request lock A while holding lock B. It must, instead, release lock B, request lock A, and then request lock B. Because of this hierarchy, a deadlock cannot occur.

z/OS Diagnosis Reference, GA22-7588 includes a table that lists the hierarchy of z/OS locks, along with their descriptions and characteristics.

3.8 Cross-memory services

In the early days of computing, applications and system requirements outgrew the available address space memory. An address space using 24-bit addressing theoretically had access to 16 MB of virtual memory, but only 128 KB of real memory. Address spaces at this time replicated functions, which impacted processing and wasted resources when not used. As demands for this runtime container reached its threshold, IBM added (in MVS/SP V1.3) a feature called *cross memory* to the S/370 architecture. Cross memory introduced a dual-address space (DUAS) architecture, which provided direct access to programs and data in separate address spaces under the control of a new cross-memory authorizing mechanism. This feature contributed to the share-everything design we know today, because address spaces can now share instruction code and data under a controlled environment.

Cross memory allowed subsystems and server-like functions to manage data and control blocks efficiently in private storage. Moving code from common virtual storage to private virtual storage provided virtual storage constraint (VSCR) for the overall system, as well as additional isolation and protection for subsystem control blocks and data. Most of today's operating system functions, subsystems and products use this architecture, such as IMS, DB2, CICS, and WebSphere for z/OS.

In Figure 3-17, Program A (Pgm A) in the Primary Address Space can execute instructions in Program B (Pgm B) contained in a separate or secondary address space. There is no need to duplicate the module and its instructions in the Home Address space; therefore, the Primary Address Space is authorized to execute code residing in another address space. Also, Program C (Pgm C) executing in an address space can access data that resides in memory in a secondary address space. Although not illustrated, data-only address spaces are also called data spaces. They contain byte string structures, but no code.

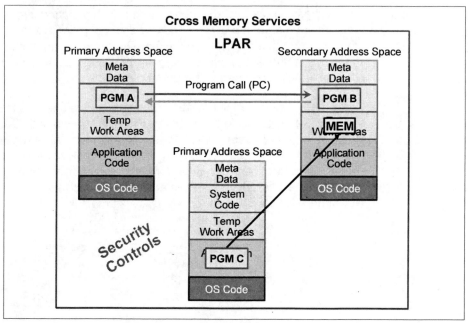

Figure 3-17   Cross-memory functionality

There are special privileged Assembler instructions and macros to implement cross-memory functionality that are inherent in subsystems and products, and are available to system programmers to customize their system's environment.

3.9 Defining characteristics of z/OS

The defining characteristics of z/OS are summarized as follows:

► The use of address spaces in z/OS holds many advantages: Isolation of private areas in different address spaces provides for system security, yet each address space also provides a common area that is accessible to every address space.

- The system is designed to preserve *data integrity*, regardless of how large the user population might be. z/OS prevents users from accessing or changing any objects on the system, including user data, except by the system-provided interfaces that enforce authority rules.

- The system is designed to manage a large number of concurrent batch jobs, with no need for the customer to externally manage workload balancing or integrity problems that might otherwise occur due to simultaneous and conflicting use of a given set of data.

- The security design extends to system functions and simple files. Security can be incorporated into applications, resources, and user profiles.

- This operating environment provides various dispatching modes to address different types of workload behavior and throughput requirements.

- The system allows multiple communications subsystems at the same time, permitting unusual flexibility in running disparate communications-oriented applications (with mixtures of test, production, and fall-back versions of each) at the same time. For example, multiple TCP/IP stacks can be operational at the same time, each with different IP addresses and serving different applications.

- The system provides extensive software recovery levels, making unplanned system restarts rare in a production environment. System interfaces allow application programs to provide their own layers of recovery. These interfaces are seldom used by simple applications; they are normally used by sophisticated applications.

- The system is designed to routinely manage disparate workloads, with automatic balancing of resources to meet production requirements established by the system administrator.

- The system is designed to routinely manage large I/O configurations that might extend to thousands of disk drives, multiple automated tape libraries, many large printers, large networks of terminals, and so on.

- The system is controlled from one or more operator terminals, or from application programming interfaces (APIs) that allow automation of routine operator functions.

- The operator interface is a critical function of z/OS. It provides status information, messages for exception situations, control of job flow, hardware device control, and allows the operator to manage unusual recovery situations.

3.10 Understanding system and product messages

The ability to read and interpret messages is an important skill within any operating system environment. z/OS messages follow a format enabling an experienced technician to quickly identify who wrote the message and why the message was written. Messages provide the ability to access the status of the operating system, optional software products, and applications.

z/OS consists of many components. The base components are the shipped parts of the operating system. Optional software components are not shipped with the base operating system. Optional software components are installed on top of the base operating system. Each component is a collection of modules that write messages. The base components support other optional software components such as transaction processors, database systems, and web application servers. The optional software components are commonly referred to as software products or middleware. The optional software components are available to support processing of data by business applications.

3.10.1 Unique three characters identification components

In z/OS, three unique characters are assigned to each base component of the operating system, and to each optional software component. The module names of a component are prefixed by its uniquely assigned three characters. The messages written by a component modules begin with the same unique three characters.

The same message format is used by both the base components and optional software components with few exceptions. The message format helps isolate and solve problems. The message format is divided into three parts:

► Reply identifier (optional)
► Message identifier
► Message text

Sample message formats follow:

► id CCCnnn   text
► id CCCnnns   text
► id CCCnnnns text
► id CCCnnnnns text
► id CCCSnnns text
► id CCCSSnns text

Where:

- ► (id) "reply identifier" (optional and rarely used): Only present when an operator response is required. Primarily used for operating system components.

- ► The (CCC) component three character "message identifier" prefix uniquely identifies the component the wrote the message.

- ► (nnn,nnnn,nnnnn) is the uniquely assigned "message identifier" number.

- ► (S, SS) subcomponent identifier (optional)

- ► (s) severity level indicator (optional and commonly used)

It is common for a message identifier to have an optional one character severity level suffix. The message identifier severity suffix may include:

A	Action: The operator must perform a specific action.
D	Decision: The operator must choose an alternative.
E	Eventual action or Error: The operator must perform an action when time is available.
I	Information: No operator action is required.
S	Severe error: Severe error messages are used by a system programmer.
W	Wait: Processing stops until the operator performs a required action.

An example of a base component is the JES scheduler services, which is assigned the IEF prefix for its modules and messages. When a message is written by a JES scheduler services module, the message identifier is prefixed with IEF. The JES scheduler services component potentially writes the following message:

```
IEF097I jobname USER userid ASSIGNED
```

Where:

- ► (CCC) is IEF.
- ► (nnn) is 097.
- ► (s) is I.

This example of the JES scheduler services information message (I) can be looked up in a z/OS messages manual (such as *z/OS V1R12.0 MVS System Messages, Vol 1 (ABA-AOM)*, SA22-7631) or at the following address:

```
http://www.ibm.com/systems/z/os/zos/bkserv/lookat/index.html
```

This example message text reads `jobname USER userid ASSIGNED`. Looking up the message identifier (IEF097I) provides additional information. This additional information typically includes:

► Explanation
► System Action (when necessary)
► Operator Response (when necessary)
► Source (component)
► Detecting Module (component module)

Be aware that a few exceptions exist, such as base component Job Entry Subsystem (JES2). JES2 base component messages begin with $HASP.

All skilled z/OS application programmers, administrators, operators, and system programmers learn to become proficient with identifying components involved with a problem that they have encountered, then looking up the messages will provide the additional information they need to help solve theproblem. Repeated experience with attempting to solve a problem is necessary to develop the ability to proficiently read and interpret component messages.

Examples of optional software component message formats

We discuss the z/OS middleware and related software products elsewhere in this book, but they bear mentioning here because these products can provide their own messaging. Consider the following two examples of software product messages:

► DFHPG0001
► DSNE103E

DFH is the 3-character optional software component identifier of a widely used transaction processor, Customer Information Control System (CICS). The *PG* that follows DFH is a 2-character CICS subcomponent identifier for the CICS program manager.

DSN is the 3-character optional software component identifier of a widely used relational database, DB2. The *E* that follows DSN is a 1-character DB2 subcomponent identifier for the DB2 TSO attachment facility.

In the event a problem is encountered with CICS or DB2 where a DFHPG001 or DSNE103E message is written, the respective message provides the guidance you need to resolve the problem.

3.10.2 System completion codes

The system or an application program can issues a completion code when abnormally ending processing by a task, address space, or system module. The completion code indicates the reason for the abnormal end. A completion code can be specified by using the following macros:

- ► ABEND macro
- ► CALLRTM macro
- ► SETRP macro

Abend of a task or address space

The system abnormally ends, or ABENDS, a task if problems are detected by the system or hardware, or an application running on the system. In the following sections, we look at each of these types of errors.

For a system-detected problem

The system abnormally ends a task or address space when the system determines that the task or address space cannot continue processing and produce valid results. For example, a task may incorrectly specify a request for a system service.

Because the system cannot perform the service with incorrect input, the system abnormally ends the task requesting the service. This task is also referred to as a *caller*.

For a hardware-detected problem

The system also abnormally ends a task with a completion code when the system receives control after a hardware-generated interruption that indicates an error in the task. For example, an instruction in an application running in storage key 7 branches to low central storage, which is always in storage key 0. The difference in storage key causes a protection exception. The system recovers from this hardware problem by ending the application's task with an abend X'0C1'. If the application has a recovery routine, the system gives control to the routine; the routine can clean up resources being used by the application and can request a dump.

For an application-detected problem

An application program abnormally ends itself when it determines that it cannot continue processing and produce valid results. For example, an application may be calculating a total by successive additions. After each addition, the application checks the new total against a limit. If the total exceeds the limit, the application issues an ABEND macro to end abnormally and, perhaps, to ask for an ABEND dump. The ABEND macro specifies a user completion code.

Abend of a system service

If a system service represented by a service request block (SRB) experiences a problem, the system gives control to the recovery routine for the service; the routine can issue a SETRP macro to place a system completion code in the system diagnostic work area (SDWA). The system service stops processing. If the service was processing a request from a task, the system abnormally ends the task with the same system completion code. Note that another task can request the system service to do processing.

Format

The format of completion codes is:

► System completion code (or abend code): Three hexadecimal digits
► User completion code: Four decimal digits

3.11 Predictive failure analysis

Soft failures are abnormal yet allowable behaviors that can slowly lead to the degradation of the operating system. To help eliminate soft failures, z/OS has developed Predictive Failure Analysis (PFA). PFA is designed to predict whether a soft failure will occur sometime in the future and to identify the cause while keeping the base operating system components stateless. PFA is intended to detect abnormal behavior early enough to allow you to correct the problem before it affects your business. PFA uses remote checks from IBM Health Checker for z/OS to collect data about your installation. Next, PFA uses machine learning to analyze this historical data to identify abnormal behavior. It warns you by issuing an exception message when a system trend might cause a problem. To help customers correct the problem, it identifies a list of potential issues.

PFA is designed to predict potential problems with z/OS systems. PFA extends availability by going beyond failure detection to predict problems before they occur. PFA provides this support using remote checks from IBM Health Checker for z/OS to collect data about your installation. It uses the data to compare and model system behavior in the future and identifies when a system trend might cause a problem. PFA uses a z/OS UNIX System Services (z/OS UNIX) file system to manage the historical and problem data that it collects.

PFA creates the report output in the following ways:

► In a z/OS UNIX file that stores the list of suspect tasks.

► In an IBM Health Checker for z/OS report that is displayed by z/OS System Display and Search Facility (SDSF) and the message buffer.

► A customer's installation can also set up IBM Health Checker for z/OS to send output to a log.

> **Attention:** The objective of IBM Health Checker for z/OS is to identify potential problems before they impact z/OS availability or, in worst cases, cause outages. It checks the current active z/OS and sysplex settings and definitions for a system and compares the values to those suggested by IBM or defined by customers. It is not meant to be a diagnostic or monitoring tool, but rather a continuously running preventive checker that finds potential problems.

3.12 z/OS and other mainframe operating systems

Much of this book is concerned with teaching you the fundamentals of z/OS, which is the foremost IBM mainframe operating system. We begin discussing z/OS concepts in 3.2, "What is z/OS" on page 92. It is useful for mainframe students, however, to have a working knowledge of other mainframe operating systems. One reason is that a given mainframe computer might run multiple operating systems. For example, the use of z/OS, z/VM, and Linux on the same mainframe is common.

Mainframe operating systems are sophisticated products with substantially different characteristics and purposes, and each could justify a separate book for a detailed introduction. Besides z/OS, four other operating systems dominate mainframe usage: z/VM, z/VSE, Linux on System z, and z/TPF.

3.12.1 z/VM

z/Virtual Machine (z/VM) has two basic components: a *control program* (CP) and a single-user operating system called CMS. As a control program, z/VM is a *hypervisor*, because it runs other operating systems in the virtual machines it creates. Any of the IBM mainframe operating systems such as z/OS, Linux on System z, z/VSE, and z/TPF can be run as *guest systems* in their own virtual machines, and z/VM can run any combination of guest systems.

The control program artificially creates multiple virtual machines from the real hardware resources. To users, it appears as though they have dedicated use of the shared real resources. The shared real resources include printers, disk storage devices, and the CPU. The control program ensures data and application security among the guest systems. The real hardware can be shared among the guests, or dedicated to a single guest for performance reasons. The system programmer allocates the real devices among the guests. For most customers, the use of guest systems avoids the need for larger hardware configurations.

z/VM's other major component is the Conversational Monitor System (CMS). This component of z/VM runs in a virtual machine and provides both an interactive user interface and the general z/VM application programming interface.

3.13 A brief comparison of z/OS and UNIX

What would we discover if we compared z/OS and UNIX? In many cases, we would find that quite a few concepts are mutually understandable to users of either operating system, despite the differences in terminology.

For experienced UNIX users, Table 3-1 provides a small sampling of familiar computing terms and concepts. As a new user of z/OS, many of the z/OS terms will sound unfamiliar to you. As you work through this course, however, the z/OS meanings will be explained and you will find that many elements of UNIX have analogs in z/OS.

Table 3-1   Mapping UNIX to z/OS terms and concepts

Term or concept	UNIX	z/OS
Start the operating system.	Boot the system.	Perform an initial program load (IPL) of the system.
Virtual storage given to each user of the system.	Users get whatever virtual storage they need to reference, within the limits of the hardware and operating system.	Users each get an address space, that is, a range of addresses extending to 2 GB (or even 16 EB) of virtual storage, though some of this storage contains system code that is common for all users.
Data storage.	Files.	Data sets (sometimes called files).
Data format.	Byte orientation; organization of the data is provided by the application.	Record orientation; often an 80-byte record, reflecting the traditional punched card image.

Term or concept	UNIX	z/OS
System configuration data.	The /etc file system controls characteristics.	Parameters in PARMLIB control how the system performs an IPL and how address spaces behave.
Scripting languages.	Shell scripts, Perl, awk, and other languages.	CLISTS (command lists) and REXX execs.
Smallest element that performs work.	A thread. The kernel supports multiple threads.	A task or a service request block (SRB). The z/OS base control program (BCP) supports multiple tasks and SRBs.
A long-running unit of work.	A daemon.	A started task or a long-running job; often this is a subsystem of z/OS.
Order in which the system searches for programs to run.	Programs are loaded from the file system according to the user's PATH environment variable (a list of directories to be searched).	The system searches the following libraries for the program to be loaded: TASKLIB, STEPLIB, JOBLIB, LPALST, and the linklist.
Interactive tools provided by the operating system (not counting the interactive applications that can be added later.)	Users *log in* to systems and execute shell sessions in the shell environment. They can issue the `rlogin` or `telnet` commands to connect to the system. Each user can have many login sessions open at once.	Users *log on* to the system through TSO/E and its panel-driven interface, ISPF. A user ID is limited to having only one TSO/E logon session active at a time. Users can also log in to a z/OS UNIX shell environment using telnet, rlogin, or ssh.
Editing data or code.	Many editors exist, such as vi, ed, sed, and emacs.	ISPF editor.[a]
Source and destination for input and output data.	stdin and stdout.	SYSIN and SYSOUT. SYSUT1 and SYSUT2 are used for utilities. SYSTSIN and SYSTSPRT are used for TSO/E users.
Managing programs.	The **ps** shell command allows users to view processes and threads, and kill jobs with the **kill** command.	SDSF allows users to view and terminate their jobs.

a. There is also a TSO editor, though it is rarely used. For example, when sending email through TSO, the SENDNOTE exec opens a TSO EDIT session to allow the user to compose the email.

A major difference for UNIX users moving to z/OS is the idea that the user is just one of *many* other users. In moving from a UNIX system to the z/OS environment, users typically ask questions such as "Can I have the root password because I need to do...?" or "Would you change this or that and restart the system?" It is important for new z/OS users to understand that potentially thousands of other users are active on the same system, and so the scope of user actions and system restarts in z/OS and z/OS UNIX are carefully controlled to avoid negatively affecting other users and applications.

Under z/OS, there does not exist a single root password or root user. User IDs are external to z/OS UNIX System Services. User IDs are maintained in a security database that is shared with both UNIX and non-UNIX functions in the z/OS system, and possibly even shared with other z/OS systems. Typically, some user IDs have root authority, but these remain individual user IDs with individual passwords. Also, some user IDs do not normally have root authority, but can switch to "root" when circumstances require it.

Both z/OS and UNIX provide APIs to allow in-memory data to be shared between processes. In z/OS, a user can access another user's address spaces directly through *cross-memory services.* Similarly, UNIX has the concept of Shared Memory functions, and these can be used on UNIX without special authority.

z/OS cross-memory services, however, require the issuing program to have special authority, controlled by the authorized program facility (APF). This method allows efficient and secure access to data owned by others, data owned by the user but stored in another address space for convenience, and for rapid and secure communication with services such as transaction managers and database managers.

The z/OS environment is XPG4 branded. XPG4 branding means that products use a common set of UNIX APIs. X/Open branding is the procedure by which a vendor certifies that its product complies with one or more of X/Open's vendor-independent product standards; OpenEdition in MVS V4.2.2 received base branding. In 1996, OpenEdition in MVS/ESA SP Version 5 Release 2 received a full XPG4.2 branding. Branding allows applications that are developed on one branded flavor of UNIX to run unchanged on other branded UNIX systems. It is called branding because it allows the right to use the X/Open Trade Mark.

The z/OS environment is POSIX compliant. The work on Portability Operating Systems Interface (POSIX) started as an effort to standardize UNIX and was performed by a workgroup under the auspices of the Institute of Electrical and Electronics Engineers (IEEE). What they defined was an application programming interface that could be applied not only to UNIX systems but to other operating systems, such as z/OS.

UNIX is not new to the mainframe environment. z/OS UNIX was originally implemented in MVS/ESA V4.3 as OpenEdition and supports the POSIX standards (1003.1, 1003.1a, 1003.1c, and 1003.2) with approximately 300 functions. When OS/390® was renamed to z/OS, the new abbreviation for UNIX System Services became z/OS UNIX.

> **Important:** z/OS UNIX inherits the qualities of service features that are native on the mainframe. This is inclusive of the sophisticated Workload Manager, instrumentation functionality of SMF, and dfStorage Management (dfSMS).

3.14 Additional software products for z/OS

A z/OS system usually contains additional, priced products that are needed to create a practical working system. For example, a production z/OS system usually includes a security manager product and a database manager product. When talking about z/OS, people often assume the inclusion of these additional products. This is normally apparent from the context of a discussion, but it might sometimes be necessary to ask whether a particular function is part of "the base z/OS" or whether it is an add-on product. IBM refers to its own add-on products as *IBM licensed programs*.

Licensed program: An additional, priced software product that is not part of the base z/OS.

With a multitude of independent software vendors (ISVs) offering a large number of products with varying but similar functionality, such as security managers and database managers, the ability to choose from a variety of licensed programs to accomplish a task considerably increases the flexibility of the z/OS operating system and allows the mainframe IT group to tailor the products it runs to meet their company's specific needs.

We will not attempt to list all of the z/OS licensed programs in this text (hundreds exist), but some common choices include:

► Security system

   z/OS provides a framework for customers to add security through the addition of a security management product (the IBM licensed program is Resource Access Control Facility (RACF®)). Non-IBM security system licensed programs are also available.

► Compilers

   z/OS includes an assembler and a C compiler. Other compilers, such as the COBOL compiler and the PL/I compiler, are offered as separate products.

► Relational database

   One example is DB2. Other types of database products, such as hierarchical databases, are also available.

- ► Transaction processing facility

  IBM offers several transaction processing facilities, including:
  - – Customer Information Control System (CICS)
  - – Information Management System (IMS)
  - – IBM WebSphere Application Server for z/OS

- ► Sort program

  Fast, efficient sorting of large amounts of data is highly desirable in batch processing. IBM and other vendors offer sophisticated sorting products.

- ► A large variety of utility programs

  Although not covered in detail in this publication, z/OS provides many system and programmer productivity utilities with samples to enhance and customize your installation's requirements.

  For example, the System Display and Search Facility (SDSF) program that we use extensively in this course to view output from batch jobs is a licensed program. Not every installation purchases SDSF; alternative products are available.

A large number of other products are available from various *independent software vendors* (ISVs).

3.15 Middleware for z/OS

Middleware is typically software between the operating system and a user or user applications. It supplies major functions not provided by the operating system. As commonly used, the term usually applies to major software products such as database managers, transaction monitors, web servers, and so on. *Subsystem* is another term often used for this type of software. These are usually licensed programs, although there are notable exceptions, such as the HTTP Server.

Middleware:
Software that supplies major functions not provided by the operating system.

z/OS is a base for using many middleware products and functions. It is commonplace to run a variety of diverse middleware functions, with multiple instances of some. The routine use of wide-ranging workloads (mixtures of batch, transactions, web serving, database queries and updates, and so on) is characteristic of z/OS.

Typical z/OS middleware includes:

- ► Database systems
- ► Web servers
- ► Message queuing and brokering functions
- ► Transaction managers

- Java virtual machines
- Portal services
- XML processing functions

A middleware product often includes an application programming interface (API). In some cases, applications are written to run completely under the control of this middleware API, while in other cases it is used only for unique purposes.

Some examples of mainframe middleware APIs include:

- The WebSphere suite of products, which provides a complete API that is portable across multiple operating systems. Among these, WebSphere MQ provides cross-platform APIs and inter-platform messaging.

- The DB2 database management product, which provides an API (expressed in the SQL language) that is used with many different languages and applications.

A web server is considered to be middleware and web programming (web pages, CGIs, and so on) is largely coded to the interfaces and standards presented by the web server instead of the interfaces presented by the operating system. Java is another example in which applications are written to run under a Java Virtual Machine (JVM)[21] and are largely independent of the operating system being used.

3.16 The new face of z/OS

IBM z/OS Management Facility (z/OSMF) provides a framework for managing various aspects of a z/OS system through a web browser interface. By streamlining some traditional tasks and automating others, z/OSMF can help simplify some areas of system management and reduce the level of expertise needed for managing a system.

z/OSMF is intended to serve as a single platform for hosting the web-based administrative console functions of IBM server, software, and storage products.

- Because z/OSMF provides system management solutions in a task-oriented, web browser based user interface with integrated user assistance, both new and experienced system programmers can more easily manage the day-to-day operations and administration of the mainframe z/OS systems.

---

[21] A JVM is not related to the virtual machines created by z/VM.

- ► z/OSMF provides a single point of control for:
  - – Performing common system administration tasks
  - – Defining and updating policies that affect system behavior
  - – Performing problem data management.
- ► z/OSMF allows for communication with the z/OS system through a web browser.

Figure 3-18 shows a sample z/OSMF login page.

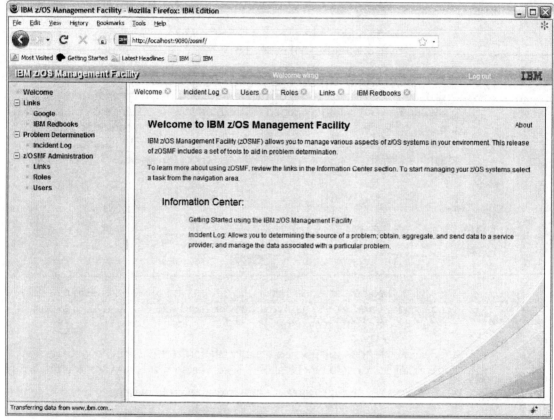

Figure 3-18   Sample z/OSMF login page

Structurally, z/OSMF is a web browser interface that communicates with the z/OSMF application running on the z/OS host system. Depending on the system management task to be performed, z/OSMF interfaces with other z/OS components to offer a simplified interface for performing tasks. These components make up the environment necessary for using the functions available in z/OSMF.

z/OSMF includes guided functions or *tasks* to help with some common system programmer activities, such as the following:

▶ Configure TCP/IP policy-based networking functions on z/OS systems.

▶ Perform problem data management tasks through the Incident Log, which centralizes problem data for your system and simplifies the process of sending diagnostic data to IBM.

▶ Manage z/OS Workload Manager (WLM) service definitions, and provide guidelines for WLM to use when allocating resources. Specifically, you can define, modify, view, copy, import, export, and print WLM service definitions. You can also install a service definition into the WLM couple data set for the sysplex, activate a service policy, and view the status of WLM on each system in the sysplex.

▶ Monitor the performance of the z/OS sysplexes or Linux images in your environment.

▶ Assess the performance of the workloads running on the z/OS sysplexes in your environment.

To learn more about z/OSMF, go to:

http://www.ibm.com/systems/z/os/zos/zosmf/

3.17 Summary

An operating system is a collection of programs that manage the internal workings of a computer system. The operating system taught in this course is z/OS, a widely used mainframe operating system. The z/OS operating system's use of multiprogramming and multiprocessing, and its ability to access and manage enormous amounts of storage and I/O operations, makes it ideally suited for running mainframe workloads.

The concept of virtual storage is central to z/OS. Virtual storage is an illusion created by the architecture, in that the system seems to have more storage than it really has. Virtual storage is created through the use of tables to map virtual storage pages to frames in central storage or slots in auxiliary storage. Only those portions of a program that are needed are actually loaded into central storage. z/OS keeps the inactive pieces of address spaces in auxiliary storage.

z/OS uses address spaces. These spaces contain address ranges of virtual storage. Each user of z/OS gets an address space containing the same range of storage addresses. The use of address spaces in z/OS allows for the isolation of private areas in different address spaces for system security, yet also allows for inter-address space sharing of programs and data through a common area accessible to every address space.

In common usage, the terms central storage, real storage, real memory, and main storage are used interchangeably. Likewise, virtual memory and virtual storage are synonymous.

The amount of central storage needed to support the virtual storage in an address space depends on the working set of the application being used, which varies over time. A user does not automatically have access to all the virtual storage in the address space. Requests to use a range of virtual storage are checked for size limitations and then the necessary paging table entries are constructed to create the requested virtual storage.

Programs running on z/OS and System z mainframes can run with 24-, 31-, or 64-bit addressing (and can switch between these modes if needed). Programs can use a mixture of instructions with 16-bit, 32-bit, or 64-bit operands, and can switch between these if needed.

Mainframe operating systems seldom provide complete operational environments. They depend on licensed programs for middleware and other functions. Many vendors, including IBM, provide middleware and various utility products.

Middleware is a relatively recent term that can embody several concepts at the same time. A common characteristic of middleware is that it provides a programming interface, and applications are written (or partially written) to this interface.

System z has long been an integrated heterogeneous platform. With zEnterprise Blade Extensions, that integration reaches a new level of industry standards providing the capability to run hybrid workloads managed and monitored as a single entity.

Table 3-2 lists the key terms used in this chapter.

Table 3-2 Key terms in this chapter

address space	addressability	auxiliary storage	central storage
control block	dynamic address translation (DAT)	frame	input/output (I/O)
licensed program	middleware	multiprogramming	multiprocessing
page/paging	page stealing	service level agreement (SLA)	slot
swapping	virtual storage	workload manager (WLM)	z/OS
cross memory	system codes	zEnterprise BladeCenter Extension (zBX)	unified resource manager

3.18 Questions for review

To help test your understanding of the material in this chapter, answer the following questions:

1. How does z/OS differ from a single-user operating system? Give two examples.

2. z/OS is designed to take advantage of what mainframe architecture? In what year was it introduced?

3. List the three major types of storage used by z/OS.

4. What is "virtual" about virtual storage?

5. Match the following terms:

   a. Page   ___ auxiliary storage

   b. Frame   ___ virtual storage

   c. Slot   ___ central storage

6. What role does workload management play in a z/OS system?

7. List several defining characteristics of the z/OS operating system.

8. Why are policies a good form of administration in z/OS?

9. List three types of software products that might be added to z/OS to provide a complete system.

10. List several differences and similarities between the z/OS and UNIX operating systems.

11. Which of the following is/are not considered to be middleware in a z/OS system?

    a. Web servers.

    b. Transaction managers.

    c. Database managers.

    d. Auxiliary storage manager.

12. If you received a severity suffix on a console message containing the letter A, what response should you provide?

13. The first three character optional software component identifiers tells you which of the following?

    a. The software component writing the message.

    b. The version of the operating system on which you are running.

    c. The release of the software writing the message.

    d. None of the above.

14. If a system service represented by a service request block (SRB) experiences a problem, which is most correct?

    a. The system gives control to the recovery routine for the service.

    b. The service loops until the operator CANCELs the task.

    c. The system service does not experience any problems.

    d. The Recovery Termination Manager (RTM) is called to end the service.

15. What optional means are used to accelerate certain types of workloads running on System z?

    a. Use of Service Classes within Workload Manager to classify work.

    b. Enabling Specialty Engines to off load specific functions.

    c. Using zEnterprise BladeCenter Extension (zBX) optimizers to speed up certain instruction sets.

    d. All of the above.

3.19 Topics for further discussion

Further exploration of z/OS concepts could include the following areas of discussion:

1. z/OS offers 64-bit addressing. Suppose you want to use this capability to work with a large virtual storage area. You would use the proper programming interface to obtain, say, a 30 GB area of virtual storage and you might write a loop to initialize this area for your application. What are some of the probable side effects of these actions? When is this design practical? What external circumstances need to be considered? What would be different on another platform, such as UNIX?

2. Why might moving programs and data blocks from below the line to above the line be complicated for application owners? How might this be done without breaking compatibility with existing applications?

3. An application program can be written to run in 24-, 31-, or 64-bit addressing mode. How does the programmer select the mode? In a high-level language? In assembler language? You have started using ISPF; what addressing mode is it using?

4. Will more central storage allow a system to run faster? What measurements indicate that more central storage is needed? When is no more central storage needed? What might change this situation?

5. If the current z/OS runs only in z/Architecture mode, why do we mention 24-, 31-, and 64-bit operation? Why mention 32-bit operands?

6. Why bother with allocation for virtual storage? Why not build all the necessary paging tables for all of virtual storage when an address space is first created?

7. Why are licensed programs needed? Why not simply include all of the software with the operating system?

8. What new industry value does zEnterprise bring to z/OS?

4

TSO/E, ISPF, and UNIX: Interactive facilities of z/OS

Objective: In working with the z/OS operating system, you need to know its user interfaces. Chief among these is Time Sharing Option/Extensions (TSO/E) and its menu-driven interface, Interactive System Productivity Facility (ISPF). These programs allow you to log on to the system, run programs, and manipulate data files. Also, you need to know the interactive facilities of the z/OS implementation of UNIX interfaces, known collectively as z/OS UNIX System Services, or z/OS UNIX for short.

After completing this chapter, you will be able to:

- ► Log on to z/OS.
- ► Run programs from the TSO READY prompt.
- ► Navigate through the menu options of ISPF.
- ► Use the ISPF editor to make changes to a data set.
- ► Use the UNIX interfaces on z/OS, including the z/OS UNIX command shell.

Refer to Table 4-2 on page 195 for a list of key terms used in this chapter.

4.1 How do we interact with z/OS

We have mentioned that z/OS is ideal for processing batch jobs, that is, workloads that run in the background with little or no human interaction. However, z/OS is just as much an interactive operating system as it is a batch processing system. By *interactive*, we mean that users (sometimes tens of thousands of them concurrently, in the case of z/OS) can use the system through direct interaction, such as commands and menu style user interfaces.

z/OS provides a number of facilities to allow users to interact directly with the operating system. This chapter provides an overview of each facility:

► "Time Sharing Option/Extensions overview" on page 166 shows how to log on to z/OS and describes the use of a limited set of basic TSO commands that are available as part of the core operating system. Interacting with z/OS in this way is called using TSO in its *native mode*.

► "ISPF overview" on page 172 introduces the ISPF menu system, which is what many people use exclusively to perform work on z/OS. ISPF menus list the functions that are most frequently needed by online users.

► "z/OS UNIX interactive interfaces" on page 188 explores the z/OS UNIX shell and utilities. This facility allows users to write and invoke shell scripts and utilities, and use the shell programming language.

Hands-on exercises are provided at the end of the chapter to help students develop their understanding of these important facilities.

4.2 Time Sharing Option/Extensions overview

Logon:
The procedure used by a user to begin a terminal session.

Time Sharing Option/Extensions (TSO/E) allows users to create an interactive session with the z/OS system. TSO[1] provides a single-user logon capability and a basic command prompt interface to z/OS.

Most users work with TSO through its menu-driven interface, Interactive System Productivity Facility (ISPF). This collection of menus and panels offers a wide range of functions to assist users in working with data files on the system. ISPF users include system programmers, application programmers, administrators, and others who access z/OS. In general, TSO and ISPF make it easier for people with varying levels of experience to interact with the z/OS system.

In a z/OS system, each user is granted a user ID and a password authorized for TSO logon. Logging on to TSO requires a 3270 display device or, more commonly, a TN3270 emulator running on a PC.

---

[1] Most z/OS users refer to TSO/E as simply "TSO," and that is how it is referred to in this book.

3270 emulation:
Using software that enables a client to emulate an IBM 3270 display station or printer, and to use the functions of a host system.

During TSO logon, the system displays the TSO logon screen on the user's 3270 display device or TN3270 emulator. The logon screen serves the same purpose as a Windows logon menu.

z/OS system programmers often modify the particular text layout and information of the TSO logon panel to better suit the needs of the system's users. Therefore, the screen captures shown in this book will likely differ from what you might see on an actual production system.

Figure 4-1 shows a typical example of a TSO logon panel.

```
----------------------------- TSO/E LOGON -----------------------------------


   Enter LOGON parameters below:              RACF LOGON parameters:

  Userid   ===> ZPROF

   Password  ===>                             New Password ===>

   Procedure ===> IKJACCNT                    Group Ident  ===>

   Acct Nmbr ===> ACCNT#

   Size      ===> 860000

   Perform   ===>

   Command   ===>

   Enter an 'S' before each option desired below:
          -Nomail          -Nonotice        -Reconnect         -OIDcard

 PF1/PF13 ==> Help    PF3/PF15 ==> Logoff    PA1 ==> Attention   PA2 ==> Reshow
 You may request specific help information by entering a '?' in any entry field
```

Figure 4-1   Typical TSO/E logon panel

Many of the screen capture examples used in this textbook show program function (PF) key settings. Because it is common practice for z/OS sites to customize the PF key assignments to suit their needs, the key assignments shown in this textbook might not match the PF key settings in use at your site.

A list of the PF key assignments used in this textbook is provided in 4.3.1, "Keyboard mapping used in this book" on page 175.

4.2.1 Data file terms

z/OS files are called *data sets*. Before you can write data into them, space for data sets must be reserved on disk. The user specifies the amount of space and the formatting of it.

The act of creating a file on a mainframe is a somewhat more complicated process than it is on a personal computer (PC). It is not an old technology; there are several good reasons for the differences. One difference is that z/OS traditionally uses what is called a record-oriented file system. In contrast, PC operating systems (Microsoft® Windows, Linux, Mac OS, and so on) uses a byte stream file system.

Record:
A group of related data, words, or fields treated as a unit.

What is the difference? In a byte stream file system, files are just a collection of sequential streams of bits, and there is a special character to tell the computer where a line (or *record*) ends and the next one begins. In a record-oriented file system, files are organized on the disk into separate records. With record-oriented files, you explicitly define the sizes and attributes of your records, so there is no need for a special end line character, which helps conserve system resources. z/OS also supports special byte stream file systems called HFS and zFS; we discuss them in 5.13, "z/OS UNIX file systems" on page 229.

Here are some of the terms used when *allocating* a data set.

Volume serial	A six character name of a disk or tape volume, such as TEST01.
Device type	A model or type of disk device, such as 3390.
Organization	The method of processing a data set, such as sequential.
Record format	The data is stored in chunks called records, of either fixed or variable length.
Record length	The length (number of characters) in each record.
Block size	If records are joined together to save space, this specifies the length of the block in characters.
Extent	An allocation of space to hold the data. When the primary extent is filled, the operating system will automatically allocate more extents, called secondaries.
Space	Disk space is allocated in units called blocks, tracks, or cylinders.

4.2.2 Using TSO commands in native mode

Native mode:
Using TSO
without its
complementary
programs, such
as ISPF.

Most z/OS sites prefer to have the TSO user session automatically switch to the ISPF interface after TSO logon. This section, however, briefly discusses the limited set of basic TSO commands that are available independently of other complementary programs, such as ISPF. Using TSO in this way is called using TSO in its *native mode*.

When a user logs on to TSO, the z/OS system responds by displaying the READY prompt, and waits for input, as shown in Figure 4-2.

```
ICH70001I ZPROF  LAST ACCESS AT 17:12:12 ON THURSDAY, OCTOBER 7,
2004
ZPROF LOGON IN PROGRESS AT 17:12:45 ON OCTOBER 7, 2004
You have no messages or data sets to receive.
READY
```

Figure 4-2   TSO logon READY prompt

The READY prompt accepts simple line commands such as HELP, RENAME, ALLOCATE, and CALL. Figure 4-3 shows an example of an ALLOCATE command that creates a *data set* (a file) on disk.

```
READY
 alloc dataset(zschol.test.cntl) volume(test01) unit(3390) tracks
space(2,1) recfm(f) lrecl(80) dsorg(ps)
READY
listds
 ENTER DATA SET NAME -
zschol.test.cntl
 ZSCHOL.TEST.CNTL
  --RECFM-LRECL-BLKSIZE-DSORG
    F    80    80      PS
 --VOLUMES--
   TEST01
READY
```

Figure 4-3   Allocating a data set from the TSO command line

Native TSO is similar to the interface offered by the native DOS prompt. TSO also includes a basic line mode editor, in contrast to the full screen editor offered by ISPF.

Figure 4-4 is another example of the line commands a user might enter at the READY prompt. Here, the user is entering commands to sort data.

```
READY
ALLOCATE DATASET(AREA.CODES) FILE(SORTIN)    SHR
 READY
ALLOCATE DATASET(*)          FILE(SORTOUT)   SHR
 READY
ALLOCATE DATASET(*)          FILE(SYSOUT)    SHR
 READY
ALLOCATE DATASET(*)          FILE(SYSPRINT)  SHR
 READY
ALLOCATE DATASET(SORT.CNTL)  FILE(SYSIN)     SHR
 READY
CALL 'SYS1.SICELINK(SORT)'

 ICE143I 0 BLOCKSET     SORT  TECHNIQUE SELECTED
 ICE000I 1 - CONTROL STATEMENTS FOR Z/OS DFSORT V1R5
            SORT FIELDS=(1,3,CH,A)
 201  NJ
 202  DC
 203  CT
 204  Manitoba
 205  AL
 206  WA
 207  ME
 208  ID
 ***
```

Figure 4-4   Using native TSO commands to sort data

In this example, the user entered several TSO ALLOCATE commands to assign inputs and outputs to the workstation for the sort program. The user then entered a single CALL command to run the sort program, DFSORT, an optional software product from IBM.

Each ALLOCATE command requires content (specified with the DATASET operand) associated with the following:

- ► SORTIN (in this case, AREA.CODES)
- ► SORTOUT (in this case, *, which means the terminal screen)
- ► SYSOUT
- ► SYSPRINT
- ► SYSIN

After the input and output allocations and the user-entered CALL command complete, the sort program displays the results on the user's screen. As shown in Figure 4-4 on page 170, the SORT FIELDS control statement causes the results to be sorted by area code. For example, NJ (New Jersey) has the lowest number telephone area code, 201.

The native TSO screen control is basic. For example, when a screen fills up with data, three asterisks (***) are displayed to indicate a full screen. Here, you must press the Enter key to clear the screen of data and allow the screen to display the remainder of the data.

4.2.3 Using CLISTs and REXX under TSO

CLIST
A list of commands that is executed as if it were one command.

With native TSO, it is possible to place a list of commands, called a *command list* (CLIST) (pronounced "see list") in a file, and execute the list as though it were one command. When you invoke a CLIST, it issues the TSO/E commands in sequence. CLISTs are used for performing routine tasks; they enable users to work more efficiently with TSO.

For example, suppose that the commands shown in Figure 4-4 on page 170 were grouped in a file called AREA.COMMND. The user could then achieve the same results by using just a single command to execute the CLIST, as follows:

```
EXEC 'CLIST AREA.COMMND'
```

REXX
An interpretive command language used with TSO.

TSO users create CLISTs with the CLIST command language. Another command language used with TSO is called Restructured Extended Executor (REXX). Both CLIST and REXX offer shell script-type processing. These are *interpretive* languages, as opposed to *compiled* languages (although REXX can be compiled as well). This book discusses CLIST and REXX in more detail in Chapter 9, "Using programming languages on z/OS" on page 323.

Some TSO users write functions directly as CLISTs or REXX programs, but these are more commonly implemented as ISPF functions, or by various software products. CLIST programming is unique to z/OS, while the REXX language is used on many platforms.

4.3 ISPF overview

ISPF:
A facility of z/OS that provides access to many of the functions most frequently needed by users.

After logging on to TSO, users typically access the ISPF menu. In fact, many users use ISPF exclusively for performing work on z/OS. ISPF is a full panel application navigated by keyboard. ISPF includes a text editor and browser, and functions for locating and listing files and performing other utility functions. ISPF menus list the functions that are most frequently needed by online users.

Figure 4-5 shows the allocation procedure used to create a data set using ISPF.

```
 Menu   RefList  Utilities  Help
 -------------------------------------------------------------------------------
 Allocate New Data Set
  Command ===>
 Data Set Name  . . . : ZCHOL.TEST.CNTL
 Management class . . .              (Blank for default management class)
  Storage class  . . . .             (Blank for default storage class)
   Volume serial . . . . TEST01      (Blank for system default volume) **
   Device type . . . . .             (Generic unit or device address) **
  Data class . . . . . .             (Blank for default data class)
   Space units . . . . . TRACK       (BLKS, TRKS, CYLS, KB, MB, BYTES
                                      or RECORDS)
   Average record unit               (M, K, or U)
   Primary quantity  . . 2           (In above units)
   Secondary quantity    1           (In above units)
   Directory blocks  . . 0           (Zero for sequential data set) *
   Record format . . . . F
   Record length . . . . 80
   Block size  . . . . .
   Data set name type  :             (LIBRARY, HFS, PDS, or blank)  *
                                     (YY/MM/DD, YYYY/MM/DD
   Expiration date . . .             YY.DDD, YYYY.DDD in Julian form
 Enter "/" to select option          DDDD for retention period in days
    Allocate Multiple Volumes        or blank)

 ( * Specifying LIBRARY may override zero directory block)

 ( ** Only one of these fields may be specified)
  F1=Help F2=Split F3=Exit F7=Backward F8=Forward F9=Swap F10=Actions  F12=Cancel
```

Figure 4-5   Allocating a data set using ISPF panels

Figure 4-6 shows the results of allocating a data set using ISPF panels.

```
Data Set Information
Command ===>

Data Set Name . . . : ZCHOL.TEST.CNTL

General Data                    Current Allocation
 Volume serial . . . : TEST01    Allocated tracks . : 2
 Device type . . . . : 3390      Allocated extents . : 1
 Organization . . . : PS
 Record format . . . : F
 Record length . . . : 80
 Block size . . . . : 80        Current Utilization
 1st extent tracks . : 2         Used tracks . . . . : 0
 Secondary tracks . : 1          Used extents . . . : 0


 Creation date . . . : 2005/01/31
 Referenced date . . : 2005/01/31
 Expiration date . . : ***None***


 F1=Help F2=Split F3=Exit F7=Backward  F8=Forward   F9=Swap
F12=Cancel
```

Figure 4-6   Result of data set allocation using ISPF

Figure 4-7 shows the ISPF menu structure.

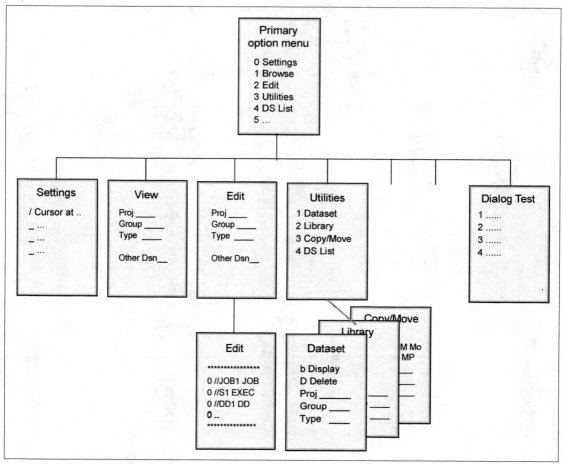

Figure 4-7   ISPF menu structure

To access ISPF under TSO, the user enters a command, such as ISPPDF, from the READY prompt to display the ISPF Primary Option Menu.

Figure 4-8 shows an example of the ISPF Primary Menu.

```
 Menu  Utilities  Compilers  Options  Status  Help
 ------------------------------------------------------------------------------
                            ISPF Primary Option Menu
 Option ===>

 0  Settings      Terminal and user parameters          User ID . : ZPROF
 1  View          Display source data or listings       Time. . . : 17:29
 2  Edit          Create or change source data          Terminal. : 3278
 3  Utilities     Perform utility functions             Screen. . : 1
 4  Foreground    Interactive language processing       Language. : ENGLISH
 5  Batch         Submit job for language processing    Appl ID . : PDF
 6  Command       Enter TSO or Workstation commands     TSO logon : IKJACCT
 7  Dialog Test   Perform dialog testing                TSO prefix: ZPROF
 8  LM Facility   Library administrator functions       System ID : SC04
 9  IBM Products  IBM program development products      MVS acct. : ACCNT#
 10 SCLM          SW Configuration Library Manager      Release . : ISPF 5.2
 11 Workplace     ISPF Object/Action Workplace
 M  More          Additional IBM Products


 Enter X to Terminate using log/list defaults


  F1=Help F2=Split F3=Exit F7=Backward F8=Forward F9=Swap F10=Actions  F12=Cancel
```

Figure 4-8   ISPF Primary Option Menu

4.3.1 Keyboard mapping used in this book

Many of the screen capture examples used in this book show ISPF program
function (PF) key settings at the bottom of the panel. As previously mentioned,
because it is common for z/OS users to customize the PF key assignments to
suit their needs, the key assignments shown in this book might not match the PF
key settings in use on your system. Actual function key settings vary from
customer to customer.

Table 4-1 lists some of the most frequently used PF keys and other keyboard functions and their corresponding keys.

Table 4-1   Keyboard mapping

Function	Key
Enter	Ctrl (right side)
Exit, end, or return	PF3
Help	PF1
PA1 or Attention	Alt-Ins or Esc
PA2	Alt-Home
Cursor movement	Tab or Enter
Clear	Pause
Page up	PF7
Page down	PF8
Scroll left	PF10
Scroll right	PF11
Reset locked keyboard	Ctrl (left side)

The examples in this book use these keyboard settings. For example, directions to press Enter mean that you should press the keyboard's control key (Ctrl) at the lower right. If the keyboard locks up, press the control key at the lower left.

4.3.2 Using PF1-HELP and the ISPF tutorial

From the ISPF Primary Menu, press the PF1 HELP key to display the ISPF tutorial. New users of ISPF should acquaint themselves with the tutorial (Figure 4-9) and with the extensive online help facilities of ISPF.

```
Tutorial -------------------- Table of Contents -------------------- Tutorial

                     ISPF Program Development Facility Tutorial

The following topics are presented in sequence, or may be selected by entering
a selection code in the option field:
      G  General       - General information about ISPF
      0  Settings       - Specify terminal and user parameters
      1  View           - Display source data or output listings
      2  Edit           - Create or change source data
      3  Utilities      - Perform utility functions
      4  Foreground     - Invoke language processors in foreground
      5  Batch          - Submit job for language processing
      6  Command        - Enter TSO command, CLIST, or REXX exec
      7  Dialog Test   - Perform dialog testing
      9  IBM Products - Use additional IBM program development products
      10 SCLM           - Software Configuration and Library Manager
      11 Workplace      - ISPF Object/Action Workplace
      X  Exit           - Terminate ISPF using log and list defaults
      The following topics will be presented only if selected by number:
      A  Appendices    - Dynamic allocation errors and ISPF listing formats
      I  Index          - Alphabetical index of tutorial topics

F1=Help      F2=Split      F3=Exit      F4=Resize    F5=Exhelp    F6=Keyshelp
 F7=PrvTopic  F8=NxtTopic  F9=Swap      F10=PrvPage  F11=NxtPage  F12=Cancel
```

Figure 4-9   ISPF Tutorial main menu

You will most likely only use a fraction of the content found in the entire ISPF tutorial.

Besides the tutorial, you can access online help from any of the ISPF panels. When you invoke help, you can scroll through information. Press the PF1-Help key for explanations of common ISPF entry mistakes, and examples of valid entries. ISPF Help also contains help for the various functions found in the primary option menu.

4.3.3 Using the PA1 key

The PA1 key is an important key for TSO users and every user should know how to find it on the keyboard.

In the early days of 3270 terminals, these terminals had keys labeled PA1, PA2, and PA3. These were called Program Action keys or *PA* keys. In practice, only PA1 is still widely used and it functions as a break key for TSO. In TSO terminology, this is an attention interrupt., that is, pressing the PA1 key will end the current task.

Finding the PA1 key on the keyboard of a 3270 terminal emulator such as TN3270 emulator can be a challenge. A 3270 emulator can be customized to use many different key combinations. On an unmodified x3270 session, the PA1 key is Left Alt-1.

You should learn how to use the PA1 key now, as you will find it useful in the future. If you have a TSO session open, perform the following steps:

1. Go to ISPF option 6. This panel accepts TSO commands.

2. Enter `LISTC LEVEL(SYS1) ALL` on the command line and press Enter. This should produce a panel of output with three asterisks (***) in the last line on the panel. In TSO, the *** indicates that there is more output waiting and you must press Enter to see it (this meaning is consistent in almost all TSO usage).

3. Press Enter for the next panel, and press Enter for the next panel, and so on.

4. Press the PA1 key, using whatever key combination is appropriate for your TN3270 emulator. This should terminate the output.

4.3.4 Navigating through ISPF menus

ISPF includes a text editor and a browser, and functions for locating and listing data sets and performing other utility functions. We have not yet discussed *data sets*, but you need at least a working understanding of data sets to begin the lab exercises in this chapter.

For now, think of a data set as a file used on z/OS to store data or executable code. A data set can have a name up to 44 characters in length, such as ZSCHOLAR.TEST.DATA. Data sets are described in more detail in Chapter 5, "Working with data sets" on page 203.

A data set name is usually segmented, with one or more periods used to create the separate data set *qualifiers* of one to eight characters. The first data set qualifier is the high level qualifier or HLQ. In this example, the HLQ is the ZSCHOLAR portion of the data set name.

z/OS users typically use the ISPF Data Set List utility to work with data sets. To access this utility from the ISPF Primary Option Menu, select Utilities, then select Dslist to display the Data Set List Utility panel, which is shown in Figure 4-10.

```
 Menu   RefList   RefMode   Utilities   Help
 -----------------------------------------------------------------------------
                            Data Set List Utility
 Option ===> _____

     blank Display data set list              P Print data set list
         V Display VTOC information          PV Print VTOC information

 Enter one or both of the parameters below:
    Dsname Level . . .  ZPROF_____
     Volume serial  . .   _____
 Data set list options
     Initial View . . . 1   1. Volume      Enter "/" to select option
                            2. Space       / Confirm Data Set Delete
                            3. Attrib      / Confirm Member Delete
                            4. Total       / Include Additional Qualifiers

 When the data set list is displayed, enter either:
    "/" on the data set list command field for the command prompt pop-up,
    an ISPF line command, the name of a TSO command, CLIST, or REXX exec, or
    "=" to execute the previous command.

  F1=Help F2=Split F3=Exit F7=Backward  F8=Forward   F9=Swap F10=Actions
 F12=Cancel
```

Figure 4-10   Using the Data Set List Utility panel

In the panel, you can use the Dsname Level data entry field to locate and list data sets. To search for one data set in particular, enter the complete (or *fully qualified*) data set name. To search for a range of data sets, such as all data sets sharing a common HLQ, enter only the HLQ in the Dsname Level field.

Qualifiers can be specified fully, partially, or defaulted. At least one qualifier must be partially specified. To search for a portion of a name, specify an asterisk (*) before or after part of a data set name, which causes the utility to return all data sets that match the search criteria. Avoid searching on * alone, because TSO has many places to search in z/OS, so this could take quite a while.

In the majority of ISPF panels, a fully qualified data set name needs to be enclosed in single quotes. Data set names not enclosed in single quotes will, by default, be prefixed with a high level qualifier specified in the TSO PROFILE. This default can be changed by using the PROFILE PREFIX command. In addition, an exception is ISPF option 3.4 DSLIST; do *not* enclose Dsname Level in quotes on this panel.

For example, if you enter *ZPROF* in the Dsname field, the utility lists all data sets with *ZPROF* as a high-level qualifier. The resulting list of data set names (see Figure 4-11) allows the user to edit or browse the contents of any data set in the list.

```
 Menu   Options  View  Utilities  Compilers  Help
 --------------------------------------------------------------------------
 DSLIST - Data Sets Matching ZPROF                          Row 1 of 4
 Command ===>                                     Scroll ===> PAGE

 Command - Enter "/" to select action              Message         Volume
 --------------------------------------------------------------------------
        ZPROF                                                       *ALIAS
        ZPROF.JCL.CNTL                                              EBBER1
        ZPROF.LIB.SOURCE                                            EBBER1
        ZPROF.PROGRAM.CNTL                                          EBBER1
        ZPROF.PROGRAM.LOAD                                          EBBER1
        ZPROF.PROGRAM.SRC                                           EBBER1
 *************************** End of Data Set list ***************************



 F1=Help F2=Split F3=Exit F5=Rfind F7=Up F8=Down F9=Swap F10=Left F11=Right
 F12=Cancel
```

Figure 4-11   Data Set List results for dsname ZPROF

To see all of the possible actions you might take for a given data set, specify a forward slash (/) in the command column to the left of the data set name. ISPF will display a list of possible actions, as shown in Figure 4-12.

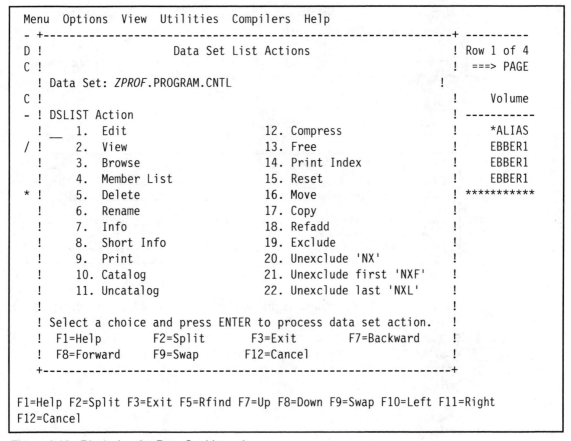

```
 Menu  Options  View  Utilities  Compilers  Help
 - +---------------------------------------------------------------+  ----------
 D !                      Data Set List Actions                    !  Row 1 of 4
 C !                                                                !  ===> PAGE
   ! Data Set: ZPROF.PROGRAM.CNTL                                  !
 C !                                                                !   Volume
 - ! DSLIST Action                                                 !  ----------
   !  __  1.  Edit                 12. Compress                    !    *ALIAS
 / !      2.  View                 13. Free                        !    EBBER1
   !      3.  Browse               14. Print Index                 !    EBBER1
   !      4.  Member List          15. Reset                       !    EBBER1
 * !      5.  Delete               16. Move                        ! ***********
   !      6.  Rename               17. Copy                        !
   !      7.  Info                 18. Refadd                      !
   !      8.  Short Info           19. Exclude                     !
   !      9.  Print                20. Unexclude 'NX'              !
   !     10.  Catalog              21. Unexclude first 'NXF'       !
   !     11.  Uncatalog            22. Unexclude last 'NXL'        !
   !                                                               !
   ! Select a choice and press ENTER to process data set action.  !
   !  F1=Help        F2=Split        F3=Exit        F7=Backward    !
   !  F8=Forward     F9=Swap         F12=Cancel                    !
   +---------------------------------------------------------------+

 F1=Help F2=Split F3=Exit F5=Rfind F7=Up F8=Down F9=Swap F10=Left F11=Right
 F12=Cancel
```

Figure 4-12   Displaying the Data Set List actions

4.3.5 Using the ISPF editor

To edit a data set's contents, enter an e (edit) to the left of the data set name. In a data set, each line of text is known as a *record*.

You can perform the following tasks:

► To view a data set's contents, enter a v (view) as a line command in the column.

► To edit a data set's contents, enter an e (edit) as a line command in the column.

- To edit the contents of a data set, move the cursor to the area of the record to be changed and type over the existing text.

- To find and change text, you can enter commands on the editor command line.

- To insert, copy, delete, or move text, place these commands directly on the line numbers where the action should occur.

To commit your changes, use PF3 or save. To exit the data set without saving your changes, enter Cancel on the edit command line.

Figure 4-13 shows the contents of data set
ZPROF.PROGRAM.CNTL(SORTCNTL) opened in edit mode.

```
  File  Edit  Edit_Settings  Menu  Utilities  Compilers  Test  Help
 -------------------------------------------------------------------------------
  EDIT         ZPROF.PROGRAM.CNTL(SORTCNTL) - 01.00        Columns 00001 00072
  Command ===>                                               Scroll ===> CSR
  ****** **************************** Top of Data ****************************
  000010 SORT FIELDS=(1,3,CH,A)
  ****** **************************** Bottom of Data *************************
```

Figure 4-13   Edit a data set

Take a look at the line numbers, the text area, and the editor command line. Primary command line, line commands placed on the line numbers, and text overtype are three different ways in which you can modify the contents of the data set. Line numbers increment by 10 with the TSO editor so that the programmer can insert nine additional lines between each current line without having to renumber the program.

4.3.6 Using the online help

You can use F1=Help to help you edit data sets. PF1 in edit mode displays the entire editor tutorial (Figure 4-14).

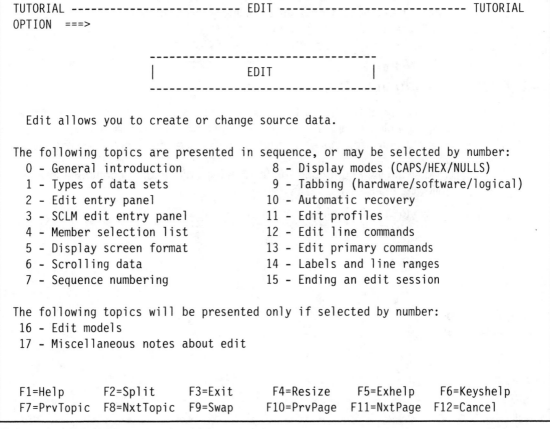

```
TUTORIAL ------------------------- EDIT ---------------------------- TUTORIAL
OPTION  ===>


                    ------------------------------------
                    |                EDIT              |
                    ------------------------------------

   Edit allows you to create or change source data.

The following topics are presented in sequence, or may be selected by number:
   0 - General introduction          8 - Display modes (CAPS/HEX/NULLS)
   1 - Types of data sets            9 - Tabbing (hardware/software/logical)
   2 - Edit entry panel             10 - Automatic recovery
   3 - SCLM edit entry panel        11 - Edit profiles
   4 - Member selection list        12 - Edit line commands
   5 - Display screen format         13 - Edit primary commands
   6 - Scrolling data               14 - Labels and line ranges
   7 - Sequence numbering           15 - Ending an edit session

The following topics will be presented only if selected by number:
 16 - Edit models
 17 - Miscellaneous notes about edit



 F1=Help      F2=Split    F3=Exit     F4=Resize   F5=Exhelp   F6=Keyshelp
 F7=PrvTopic  F8=NxtTopic F9=Swap     F10=PrvPage F11=NxtPage F12=Cancel
```

Figure 4-14   Edit Help panel and tutorial

During the lab, you will edit a data set and use F1=Help to explore the Edit Line Commands and Edit Primary Commands functions. Within the help function, select and review the FIND, CHANGE, and EXCLUDE commands. This lab is important for developing further skills in this course.

A subset of the line commands includes:

i	Insert a line.
Enter key	Press Enter without entering anything to escape insert mode.
i5	Obtain five input lines.
d	Delete a line.

d5	Delete five lines.
dd/dd	Delete a block of lines.
r	Repeat a line.
rr/rr	Repeat a block of lines.
c, then a or b	Copy a line after or before.
c5, then a or b	Copy five lines after or before.
cc/cc, then **a or b**	Copy a block of lines after or before.
m, m5, mm/mm	Move lines.
x	Exclude a line.

4.3.7 Customizing your ISPF settings

The command line for your ISPF session might appear at the bottom of the display, while your instructor's ISPF command line might appear at the top. This is a personal preference, but traditional usage places it at the top of the panel.

If you want your command line to appear at the top of the panel, perform the following steps:

1. Go to the ISPF primary option menu.

2. Select option 0 to display the Settings menu, as shown in Figure 4-15.

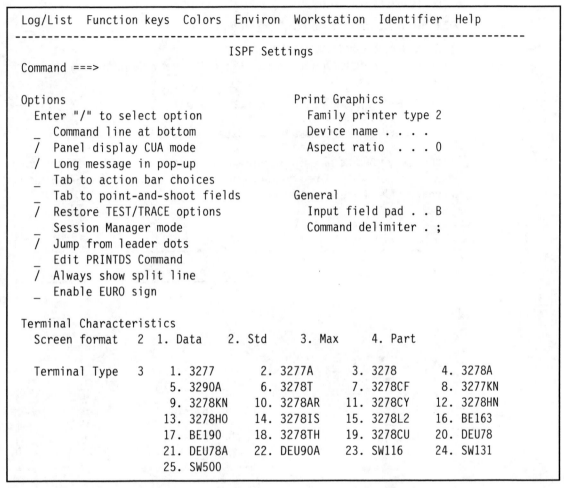

```
Log/List  Function keys  Colors  Environ  Workstation  Identifier  Help
-----------------------------------------------------------------------------
                              ISPF Settings
Command ===>

Options                                Print Graphics
  Enter "/" to select option             Family printer type 2
  _  Command line at bottom              Device name . . . .
  /  Panel display CUA mode              Aspect ratio . . . 0
  /  Long message in pop-up
  _  Tab to action bar choices
  _  Tab to point-and-shoot fields     General
  /  Restore TEST/TRACE options          Input field pad . . B
  _  Session Manager mode                Command delimiter . ;
  /  Jump from leader dots
  _  Edit PRINTDS Command
  /  Always show split line
  _  Enable EURO sign


Terminal Characteristics
  Screen format   2  1. Data    2. Std      3. Max       4. Part

  Terminal Type   3    1. 3277      2. 3277A     3. 3278      4. 3278A
                       5. 3290A     6. 3278T     7. 3278CF    8. 3277KN
                       9. 3278KN   10. 3278AR   11. 3278CY   12. 3278HN
                      13. 3278HO   14. 3278IS   15. 3278L2   16. BE163
                      17. BE190    18. 3278TH   19. 3278CU   20. DEU78
                      21. DEU78A   22. DEU90A   23. SW116    24. SW131
                      25. SW500
```

Figure 4-15   ISPF settings

3. In the list of Options, remove the "/" on the line that says Command line at bottom. Use the Tab or New line key to move the cursor.

While in this menu, you can change some other parameters that you will need later:

► Remove the "/" from Panel display CUA mode.

► Change the Terminal Type to 4. This provides 3270 support for symbols used by the C language.

► Move the cursor to the Log/List option in the top line and press Enter.

- Select 1 (Log Data set defaults).
- Enter Process Option 2 (to delete the data set without printing).
- Press PF3 to exit.

► Move the cursor to the Log/List option again.

- Select 2 (List Data set defaults).
- Enter Process Option 2 to delete the data set without printing.
- PF3 to exit.

► Press PF3 again to exit to the primary menu.

The actions in the bar across the top usually vary from site to site.

Another way to customize ISPF panels is by using the hilite command, as shown in Figure 4-16. This command allows you to tailor various ISPF options to suit the needs of your environment.

```
   File    Languages    Colors    Help
                          Edit Color Settings
Command ===>       (this menu shows up when you type "hilite")_


Language:  1        1.  Automatic        Coloring:    1   1.  Do not color pr
                    2.  Assembler                         2.  Color program
                    3.  BookMaster                        3.  Both IF and DO
                    4.  C                                 4.  DO logic only
                    5.  COBOL                             5.  IF logic only
                    6.  IDL
                    7.  ISPF DTL          Enter "/" to select option
                    8.  ISPF Panel
                    9.  ISPF Skeleton         Parentheses matching
                   10.  JCL               7   Highlight FIND strings
                   11.  Pascal            7   Highlight cursor phrase
                   12.  PL/I
                   13.  REXX              Note: Information from this par
                                          saved in the edit profile.

  F1=Help          F2=Split        F3=Exit          F7=Backward         F8=
  F9=Swap          F10=Actions     F12=Cancel
---------------------------------------------------------------------------
0015                  HIREDATE                         DATE,
0016                  JOB                              CHAR(8),
0017                  EDLEVEL                          SMALLINT,
0018                  SEX                              CHAR(1),
0019                  BIRTHDATE                        DATE,
F1=Help       F2=Split       F3=Exit        F5=Rfind        F6=Rchange
F8=Down       F9=Swap        F10=Left       F11=Right       F12=Cancel
```

Figure 4-16   Using the hilite command

4.3.8 Adding a GUI to ISPF

ISPF is a full panel application that you navigate by using your keyboard. You can, however, download and install a variety of ISPF graphical user interface (GUI) clients to include with a z/OS system. After installing the ISPF GUI client, it is possible to use the mouse.

Figure 4-17 shows an example of an ISPF GUI.

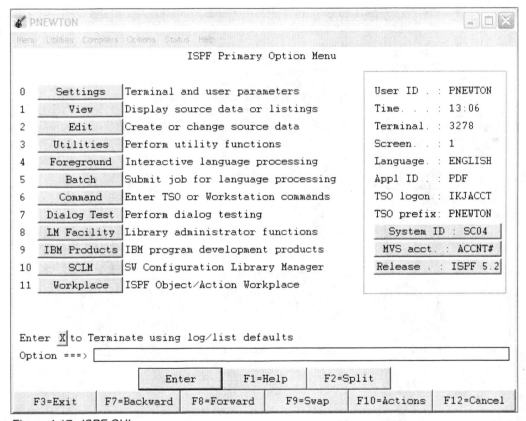

Figure 4-17   ISPF GUI

The drop-down entries at the top of the ISPF panels require you to place the cursor on the selection and press Enter. Move the ISPF GUI client mouse pointer across the drop-down selections to display the respective sub-selections. Also available in the GUI are Enter and PF key boxes.

4.4 z/OS UNIX interactive interfaces

Shell:
A command interpreter for UNIX commands and shell language statements.

The z/OS UNIX shell and utilities provide an interactive interface to z/OS. The shell and utilities can be compared to the TSO function in z/OS.

To perform some command requests, the shell calls other programs, known as *utilities*. The shell can be used to:

▶ Invoke shell scripts and utilities.

▶ Write shell scripts (a named list of shell commands, using the shell programming language).

▶ Run shell scripts and C language programs interactively, in the TSO background or in batch.

Figure 4-18 shows an overview of the shell and utilities.

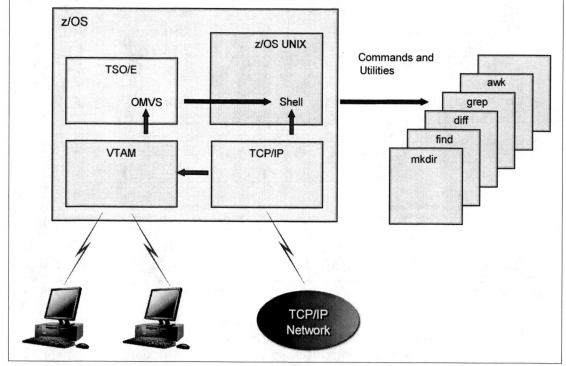

Figure 4-18   Shell and utilities

A user can invoke the z/OS UNIX shell in the following ways:

► From a 3270 display or a workstation running a 3270 emulator

► From a TCP/IP-attached terminal, using the **rlogin** and **telnet** commands

► From a TSO session, using the OMVS command.

As an alternative to invoking the shell directly, a user can use ISHELL by entering the command ISHELL from TSO. ISHELL provides an ISPF panel interface to perform many actions for z/OS UNIX operations.

Figure 4-19 shows an overview of these interactive interfaces, that is, the z/OS UNIX shell and ISHELL. Also, there are some TSO/E commands that support z/OS UNIX, but they are limited to functions such as copying files and creating directories.

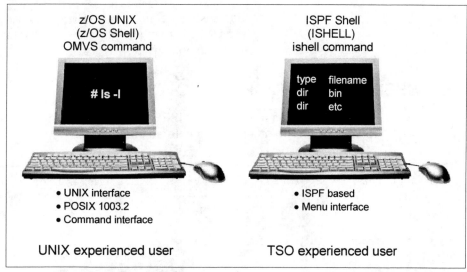

Figure 4-19   z/OS UNIX interactive interfaces

The z/OS UNIX shell is based on the UNIX System V shell and has some of the features from the UNIX Korn shell. The POSIX standard distinguishes between a *command*, which is a directive to the shell to perform a specific task, and a *utility*, which is the name of a program callable by name from the shell. To the user, there is no difference between a command and a utility.

The z/OS UNIX shell provides the environment that has the most functions and capabilities. It supports many of the features of a regular programming language.

You can store a sequence of shell commands in a text file that can be executed. This is called a *shell script*.

The TSO commands used with z/OS UNIX are:

ISHELL The ISHELL command invokes the ISPF panel interface to z/OS UNIX System Services. ISHELL is a good starting point for users familiar with TSO and ISPF who want to use z/OS UNIX. These users can do much of their work with ISHELL, which provides panels for working with the z/OS UNIX file system, including panels for mounting and unmounting file systems and for doing some z/OS UNIX administration.

ISHELL is often good for system programmers, familiar with z/OS, who need to set up UNIX resources for the users.

OMVS The OMVS command is used to invoke the z/OS UNIX shell.

Users whose primary interactive computing environment is a UNIX system should find the z/OS UNIX shell environment familiar.

4.4.1 ISHELL command (ISH)

Figure 4-20 shows the ISHELL or ISPF Shell panel displayed as a result of the ISHELL or ISH command being entered from ISPF Option 6.

```
   File  Directory  Special_file  Tools  File_systems  Options  Setup  Help
   ----------------------------------------------------------------------
                     UNIX System Services ISPF Shell

   Enter a pathname and do one of these:

      - Press Enter.
      - Select an action bar choice.
      - Specify an action code or command on the command line.

   Return to this panel to work with a different pathname.
                                                          More:      +
      /u/rogers_____

      _____
      _____
      _____
```

Figure 4-20 Panel displayed after issuing the ISH command

4.4.2 ISHELL: User files and directories

To search a user's files and directories, enter the following command and then press Enter:

```
/u/userid
```

For example, Figure 4-21 shows the files and directories of the rogers user.

```
                          Directory List

Select one or more files with / or action codes.  If / is used also select an
action from the action bar otherwise your default action will be used.  Select
with S to use your default action.  Cursor select can also be used for quick
navigation.  See help for details.
EUID=0   /u/rogers/
   Type  Perm  Changed-EST5EDT   Owner       ------Size  Filename    Row 1 of 9
_  Dir   700   2002-08-01 10:51  ADMIN            8192   .
_  Dir   555   2003-02-13 11:14  AAAAAAA             0   ..
_  File  755   1996-02-29 18:02  ADMIN             979   .profile
_  File  600   1996-03-01 10:29  ADMIN              29   .sh_history
_  Dir   755   2001-06-25 17:43  AAAAAAA          8192   data
_  File  644   2001-06-26 11:27  AAAAAAA         47848   inventory.export
_  File  700   2002-08-01 10:51  AAAAAAA            16   myfile
_  File  644   2001-06-22 17:53  AAAAAAA         43387   print.export
_  File  644   2001-02-22 18:03  AAAAAAA         84543   Sc.pdf
```

Figure 4-21   Displaying a user's files and directories

From here, you use action codes to perform any of the following actions:

b	Browse a file or directory.
e	Edit a file or directory.
d	Delete a file or directory.
r	Rename a file or directory.
a	Show the attributes of a file or directory.
c	Copy a file or directory.

4.4.3 OMVS command shell session

You use the OMVS command to invoke the z/OS UNIX shell.

The shell is a command processor that you use to:

► Invoke shell commands or utilities that request services from the system.
► Write shell scripts using the shell programming language.
► Run shell scripts and C-language programs interactively (in the foreground), in the background, or in batch.

Shell commands often have options (also known as *flags*) that you can specify, and they usually take an argument, such as the name of a file or directory. The format for specifying the command begins with the command name, then the option or options, and finally the argument, if any.

For example, in Figure 4-22, we show the following command:

ls -al /u/rogers

Where **ls** is the command name, and -al /u/rogers are the options.

```
ROGERS @ SC43:/>ls -al /u/rogers
total 408
drwx------    3 ADMIN    SYS1        8192 Aug  1  2005 .
dr-xr-xr-x   93 AAAAAAA  TTY            0 Feb 13 11:14 ..
-rwxr-xr-x    1 ADMIN    SYS1         979 Feb 29  1996 .profile
-rw-------    1 ADMIN    SYS1          29 Mar  1  1996 .sh_history
-rw-r--r--    1 AAAAAAA  SYS1       84543 Feb 22  2001 Sc.pdf
drwxr-xr-x    2 AAAAAAA  SYS1        8192 Jun 25  2001 data
-rw-r--r--    1 AAAAAAA  SYS1       47848 Jun 26  2001 inventory.export
-rwx------    1 AAAAAAA  SYS1          16 Aug  1  2005 myfile
-rw-r--r--    1 AAAAAAA  SYS1       43387 Jun 22  2001 print.export
```

Figure 4-22   OMVS shell session display after issuing the OMVS command

Path / Path name:
The route through a file system to a specific file.

This command lists the files and directories of the user. If the path name is a file, **ls** displays information about the file according to the requested options. If it is a directory, **ls** displays information about the files and subdirectories therein. You can get information about a directory itself by using the -d option.

If you do not specify any options, **ls** displays only the file names. When **ls** sends output to a pipe or file, it writes one name per line; when it sends output to the terminal, it uses the -C (multi-column) format.

Terminology note: z/OS users tend to use the terms *data set* and *file* synonymously, but not when it comes to z/OS UNIX System Services. With the UNIX support in z/OS, the file system is a data set that contains directories and files, so file has a specific definition. z/OS UNIX files are different from other z/OS data sets because they are byte-oriented rather than record-oriented.

4.4.4 Direct login to the shell

You can log in directly to the z/OS UNIX shell from a system that is connected to z/OS through TCP/IP. Use one of the following methods:

rlogin   You can rlogin (remote log in) to the shell from a system that has rlogin client support. To log in, use the `rlogin` command syntax supported at your site.

telnet   You can telnet into the shell. To log in, use the `telnet` command from your workstation or from another system with telnet client support.

As shown in Figure 4-23, each of these methods requires the inetd daemon to be set up and active on the z/OS system.

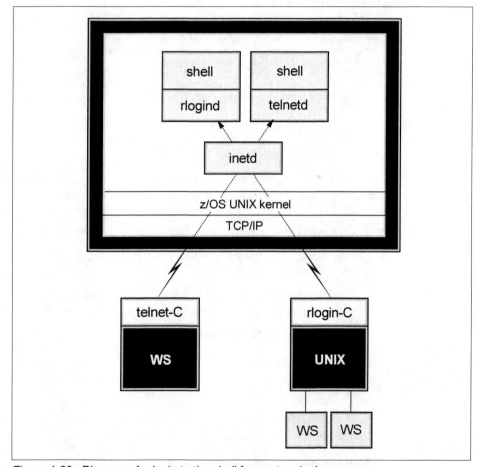

Figure 4-23   Diagram of a login to the shell from a terminal

Figure 4-24 shows the z/OS shell after login through telnet.

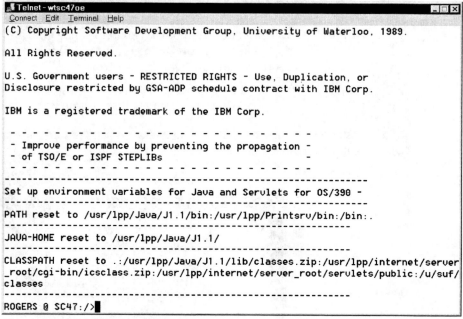

Figure 4-24   Telnet login to the shell panel

There are some differences between the asynchronous terminal support (direct shell login) and the 3270 terminal support (OMVS command):

► You cannot switch to TSO/E. However, you can use the TSO SHELL command to run a TSO/E command from your shell session.

► You cannot use the ISPF editor (this includes the **oedit** command, which invokes ISPF edit).

► You can use the UNIX vi editor, and other interactive utilities that depend on receiving each key stroke, without hitting the Enter key.

► You can use UNIX-style command-line editing.

4.5 Summary

TSO allows users to log on to z/OS and use a limited set of basic commands. This is sometimes called using TSO in its native mode.

ISPF is a menu-driven interface for user interaction with a z/OS system. The ISPF environment is executed from native TSO.

ISPF provides utilities, an editor and ISPF applications to the user. To the extent permitted by various security controls, an ISPF user has full access to most z/OS system functions.

TSO/ISPF should be viewed as a system management interface and a development interface for traditional z/OS programming.

The z/OS UNIX shell and utilities provide a command interface to the z/OS UNIX environment. You can access the shell either by logging on to TSO/E or by using the remote login facilities of TCP/IP (rlogin).

If you use TSO/E, a command called OMVS creates a shell for you. You can work in the shell environment until exiting or temporarily switching back to the TSO/E environment.

Table 4-2 lists the key terms used in this chapter.

Table 4-2   Key terms in this chapter

3270 emulation	command list (CLIST)	ISHELL
ISPF	logon	native mode
OMVS command	path / path name	record
Restructured Extended Executor (REXX)	shell	Time Sharing Option/ Extensions (TSO/E)

4.6 Questions for review

To help test your understanding of the material in this chapter, complete the following questions:

1. If you want more information about a specific ISPF panel or help with a user error, what should be your first action?

2. What makes the ISPF command PFSHOW OFF useful?

3. ISPF is a full-screen interface with a full-screen editor. TSO is a command line interface with only a line editor. The TSO line editor is rarely used. Can you think of a situation that would require the use of the TSO line editor?

4. Can the IBM-provided panels of ISPF be customized?

5. Name the two z/OS UNIX interactive interfaces and explain some of the differences between the two.

4.7 Exercises

The lab exercises in this chapter will help you develop skills in using TSO, ISPF, and the z/OS UNIX command shell. These skills are required for performing lab exercises in the remainder of this text. To perform the lab exercises, each student or team needs a TSO user ID and password (for assistance, see the instructor).

The exercises teach the following skills:

▶ Logging on to z/OS and entering TSO commands

▶ Navigating through the ISPF menu options

▶ Using the ISPF editor

▶ Using SDSF

▶ Opening the z/OS UNIX shell and entering commands

▶ Using the OEDIT and OBROWSE commands

The most commonly used functions, mapped to the keys used, are shown in Table 4-1 on page 176.

4.7.1 Logging on to z/OS and entering TSO commands

Establish a 3270 connection with z/OS using a workstation 3270 emulator and log on with your user ID (we call this *yourid*). From the TSO READY prompt (after you have keyed in =x to exit out of ISPF into native TSO), enter the following commands:

1. PROFILE

   What is the prefix value? Make a note of it; it is your user ID on the system.

2. PROFILE NOPREFIX

   This changes your profile so TSO will not place a prefix at the beginning of your commands. Specifying PROFILE PREFIX (with a value) or NOPREFIX (by itself) tells the system whether to use a value (such as your user ID) to find files in the system. NOPREFIX tells the system not to bother limiting the results to files beginning with your user ID (for example), as it would otherwise do by default.

3. LISTC

   The LISTCAT command (or LISTC, for short) lists the data sets in a particular catalog (we discuss catalogs in Chapter 5, "Working with data sets" on page 203). Your 3270 emulator has a PA1 (attention) key. You can use the PA1 key to end the command output.

When you see the three asterisks (***), it indicates that your screen is filled. Press Enter or PA to continue.

4. PROFILE PREFIX (userid)

   This command specifies that your user ID be prefixed to all non-fully-qualified data set names. This will filter the results of the next command:

5. LISTC

   What is displayed?

6. ISPF (or ISPPDF)

   Enter the ISPF menu-driven interface of TSO.

   On some systems, you also need to select option P to access the main ISPF panel.

4.7.2 Navigating through the ISPF menu options

From the ISPF Primary Option Menu, perform the following steps:

1. Select Utilities, then select Dslist from the Utility Selection panel.

2. Enter SYS1 on the Dsname Level input field and press Enter. What is displayed?

3. Use F8 to page down or forward, F7 to page up or backward, F10 to shift left, and F11 to shift right. Exit with F3.

4. Enter SYS1.PROCLIB on the Dsname Level input field and press Enter. What is displayed?

5. Enter v in the command column to the left of SYS1.PROCLIB. This is a partitioned data set with numerous members. Place an s to the left of any member to select the member for viewing. Press F1. What specific help is provided?

6. Enter =0 on the ISPF command or option line. What is the first option listed in this ISPF Settings panel? Change your settings to place the command line at the bottom of the panel. It is effective on exit from the Settings panel.

7. Enter PFSHOW OFF and then PFSHOW ON. What is the difference? How is this useful?

8. Exit back to the ISPF Primary Option Menu. What value is used to select Utilities?

9. Select Utilities.

10. In the Utilities Selection panel, what value is used to select Dslist? Exit back to the ISPF Primary Option Menu. On the option line, enter the Utilities selection value followed by a period, then enter the Dslist selection value. What panel is displayed?

11. Exit back to the ISPF Primary Option Menu. Place the cursor on the Status entry at the top of the panel and press Enter. Select the Calendar value and press Enter, then select the Session value. What changed?

12. Now set your screen to the original configuration, using the Status drop-down menu and selecting Session.

4.7.3 Using the ISPF editor

From the ISPF Primary Option Menu, perform the following steps:

1. Go to the DSLIST Utility panel and enter *yourid*.JCL in the Dsname Level field. Press Enter.

2. Place e (edit) to the left of *yourid*.JCL. Place s (select) to the left of member EDITTEST. Enter PROFILE on the edit command line, and observe the data that is preceded by the profile and message lines. Read the profile settings and messages, then enter RESET on the command line. What is the result?

3. Enter any string of characters at the end of the first data line, then press Enter. On the command line, enter CAN (cancel). Press Enter to confirm the cancel request. Again, edit EDITTEST in the data set. Were your changes saved?

> **Tip:** As you become more familiar with ISPF, you learn the letters and numbers for some of the commonly used options. Preceding an option with the = key takes you directly to that option, bypassing the menus in between.
>
> You can also go directly to nested options with the = sign. For example, =3.4 takes you directly to a commonly used data set utility menu.

4. Move the cursor to one of the top lines on your display. Press F2. The result is a second ISPF panel. What occurs when F9 is entered repeatedly?

5. Using F9, switch to the ISPF Primary Option Menu, then press F1 to display the ISPF Tutorial panel.

6. From the ISPF Tutorial panel, select Edit, then Edit Line Commands, then Basic Commands. Press Enter to scroll through the basic commands tutorial. As you do so, frequently switch (F9) to the edit session and exercise the commands in EDITTEST. Repeat this same scenario for Move/Copy commands and shifting commands.

7. From the ISPF Tutorial panel, select Edit, then Edit Primary Commands, then FIND/CHANGE/EXCLUDE commands. Press Enter to scroll through the FIND/CHANGE/EXCLUDE commands tutorial. As you do so, frequently switch (F9) to the edit session and exercise the commands in EDITTEST.

8. Enter =X on the ISPF help panel to end the second ISPF panel session. Save and exit the Edit Panel (F3) to return to the ISPF Primary Option Menu.

4.7.4 Using SDSF

From the ISPF Primary Option Menu, locate and select System Display and Search Facility (SDSF), which is a utility that lets you look at output data sets. Select More to find the SDSF option (5), or simply enter =M.5. The ISPF Primary Option Menu typically includes more selections than those listed on the first panel, with instructions about how to display the additional selections.

Perform the following steps:

1. Enter LOG, then shift left (F10), shift right (F11), page up (F7), and page down (F8). Enter TOP, then BOTTOM on the command input line. Enter DOWN 500 and UP 500 on the command input line. You will learn how to read this system log later.

2. Review the SCROLL value to the far left on the command input line:

   Scroll ===> PAGE

   Tab to the SCROLL value. The values for SCROLL can be:

C or CSR	Scroll to where you placed the cursor
P or PAGE	Full page or screen
H or HALF	Half page or half screen

3. You will find the SCROLL value on many ISPF panels, including the editor. You can change this value by overwriting the first letter of the scroll mode over the first letter of the current value. Change the value to CSR, place the cursor on another line in the body of the system log, and press F7. Did it place the line with the cursor at the top?

4. Enter ST (status) on the SDSF command input line, then enter SET DISPLAY ON. Observe the values for Prefix, Best, Owner, and Susanne. To display all of the current values for each, enter * as a filter, for example:

   PREFIX *
   OWNER *
   DEST

   The result should be:

   PREFIX=* DEST=(ALL) OWNER=*

5. Enter DA to display all the active jobs. Enter ST to retrieve the status of all jobs in the input, active, and output queues. Once again, press F7 (page up), F8 (page down), F10 (shift left), and F11 (shift right).

4.7.5 Opening the z/OS UNIX shell and entering commands

From the ISPF Primary Option Menu, select Option 6, then enter the OMVS command. From your home directory, enter the following shell commands:

`id`	Shows your current ID.
`date`	Shows the time and date.
`man date`	Shows the help menu for the **date** command. You can scroll through the panels by pressing Enter. Enter **quit** to exit the panels.
`man man`	Help for the help manual.
`env`	Environment variables for this session.
`type read`	Identifies whether read is a command, a utility, an alias, and so on.
`ls`	Lists a directory.
`ls -1`	Lists the current directory.
`ls -1 /etc.`	Lists the /etc. directory.
`cal`	Displays a calender of the current month.
`cal 2005`	Displays a calender of the year 2005.
`cal 1752`	Display the calender for the year 1752. Is September missing 13 days? [Answer: Yes, all UNIX calendars have 13 days missing from September 1752.]
`exit`	End the OMVS session.

4.7.6 Using the OEDIT and OBROWSE commands

Another way to start the OMVS shell is by entering the TSO OMVS command on any ISPF panel. From your home directory, enter the following shell commands:

`cd /tmp`	This is a directory that you have the authority to update.
`oedit myfile`	This opens the ISPF edit panel and creates a new text file in the current path. Write some text into the editor. Save and exit (F3).
`ls`	Displays the current directory listing in terse mode.
`ls -1`	Displays the current directory listing in verbose mode.

`myfile`	*myfile* can be any file you choose to create.
`obrowse myfile`	Browses the file you just created.
`exit`	Ends the OMVS session.

5

Working with data sets

Objective: In working with the z/OS operating system, you must understand *data sets*, the files that contain programs and data. The characteristics of traditional z/OS data sets differ considerably from the file systems used in UNIX and PC systems. To make matters even more interesting, you can also create UNIX file systems on z/OS, with the common characteristics of UNIX systems.

After completing this chapter, you will be able to:

► Explain what a data set is.

► Describe data set naming conventions and record formats.

► List some access methods for managing data and programs.

► Explain what catalogs and VTOCs are used for.

► Create, delete, and modify data sets.

► Explain the differences between UNIX file systems and z/OS data sets.

► Describe the z/OS UNIX file systems' use of data sets.

Refer to Table 5-1 on page 233 for a list of key terms used in this chapter.

5.1 What is a data set

Nearly all work in the system involves data input or data output. In a mainframe system, the channel subsystem manages the use of I/O devices, such as disks, tapes, and printers, while z/OS associates the data for a given task with a device.

Data set:
A collection of logically related data records, such as a library of macros or a source program.

z/OS manages data by using *data sets*. The term data set refers to a file that contains one or more records. Any named group of records is called a data set. Data sets can hold information such as medical records or insurance records that are used by a program running on the system. Data sets are also used to store information needed by applications or the operating system itself, such as source programs, macro libraries, or system variables or parameters. For data sets that contain readable text, you can print them or display them on a console (many data sets contain load modules or other binary data that is not really printable). Data sets can be *cataloged*, which permits the data set to be referred to by name without specifying where it is stored.

In simplest terms, a *record* is a fixed number of bytes containing data. Often, a record collects related information that we treat as a unit, such as one item in a database or personnel data about one member of a department. The term *field* refers to a specific portion of a record used for a particular category of data, such as an employee's name or department.

The record is the basic unit of information used by a program running on z/OS.[1] The records in a data set can be organized in various ways, depending on how we plan to access the information. If you write an application program that processes things such as personnel data, for example, your program can define a record format for each person's data.

There are many different types of data sets in z/OS, and different methods for accessing them. This chapter discusses three types of data sets: sequential, partitioned, and VSAM data sets.

In a *sequential data set*, records are data items that are stored consecutively. To retrieve the tenth item in the data set, for example, the system must first pass the preceding nine items. Data items that must all be used in sequence, such as the alphabetical list of names in a classroom roster, are best stored in a sequential data set.

A partitioned data set or PDS consists of a *directory* and *members*. The directory holds the address of each member and thus makes it possible for programs or the operating system to access each member directly. Each member, however, consists of sequentially stored records.

---

[1] z/OS UNIX files are different from the typical z/OS data sets because they are byte-oriented rather than record-oriented.

Partitioned data sets are often called *libraries*. Programs are stored as members of partitioned data sets. Generally, the operating system loads the members of a PDS into storage sequentially, but it can access members directly when selecting a program for execution.

In a Virtual Storage Access Method (VSAM) key sequenced data set (KSDS), records are data items that are stored with control information (keys) so that the system can retrieve an item without searching all preceding items in the data set. VSAM KSDS data sets are ideal for data items that are used frequently and in an unpredictable order. We discuss the different types of data sets and the use of catalogs later in this chapter.

A standard reference for information about data sets is *z/OS DFSMS Using Data Sets*, SC26-7410. You can find this and related publications at the z/OS Internet Library website:

```
http://www-03.ibm.com/systems/z/os/zos/bkserv/
```

5.2 Where are data sets stored

z/OS supports many different devices for data storage. Disks or tape are most frequently used for storing data sets on a long-term basis. Disk drives are known as *direct access storage devices* (DASDs) because, although some data sets on them might be stored sequentially, these devices can handle direct access. Tape drives are known as sequential access devices because data sets on tape must be accessed sequentially.

The term *DASD* applies to disks or simulated equivalents of disks. All types of data sets can be stored on DASD (only sequential data sets can be stored on magnetic tape). You use DASD volumes for storing data and executable programs, including the operating system itself, and for temporary working storage. You can use one DASD volume for many different data sets, and reallocate or reuse space on the volume.

To enable the system to locate a specific data set quickly, z/OS includes a data set known as the master catalog that permits access to any of the data sets in the computer system or to other catalogs of data sets. z/OS requires that the master catalog reside on a DASD that is always mounted on a drive that is online to the system. We discuss catalogs further in 5.11, "Catalogs and volume table of contents" on page 222.

5.3 What are access methods

An access method defines the technique that is used to store and retrieve data. Access methods have their own data set structures to organize data, system-provided programs (or *macros*) to define data sets, and utility programs to process data sets.

Access methods are identified primarily by the data set organization. z/OS users, for example, use the basic sequential access method (BSAM) or queued sequential access method (QSAM) with sequential data sets.

There are times when an access method identified with one organization can be used to process a data set organized in a different manner. For example, a sequential data set (not extended-format data set) created using BSAM can be processed by the basic direct access method (BDAM), and vice versa. Another example is UNIX files, which you can process using BSAM, QSAM, basic partitioned access method (BPAM), or virtual storage access method (VSAM).

This text does not describe all of the access methods available on z/OS. Commonly used access methods include the following:

QSAM Queued Sequential Access Method (heavily used)

BSAM Basic Sequential Access Method (for special cases)

BDAM Basic Direct Access Method (becoming obsolete)

BPAM Basic Partitioned Access Method (for libraries)

VSAM Virtual Storage Access Method (used for more complex applications)

5.4 How are DASD volumes used

DASD volumes are used for storing data and executable programs (including the operating system itself), and for temporary working storage. One DASD volume can be used for many different data sets, and space on it can be reallocated and reused.

On a volume, the name of a data set must be unique. A data set can be located by device type, volume serial number, and data set name. This is unlike the file tree of a UNIX system. The basic z/OS file structure is not hierarchical. z/OS data sets have no equivalent to a path name.

Although DASD volumes differ in physical appearance, capacity, and speed, they are similar in data recording, data checking, data format, and programming. The recording surface of each volume is divided into many concentric *tracks*.

The number of tracks and their capacity vary with the device. Each device has an access mechanism that contains read/write heads to transfer data as the recording surface rotates past them.

5.4.1 DASD terminology for UNIX and PC users

The disk and data set characteristics of mainframe hardware and software differ considerably from UNIX and PC systems, and carry their own specialized terminology. Throughout this text, the following terms are used to describe various aspects of storage management on z/OS:

- ▶ *Direct Access Storage Device* (DASD) is another name for a disk drive.
- ▶ A disk drive is also known as a disk volume, a disk pack, or a *Head Disk Assembly* (HDA). We use the term *volume* in this text except when discussing physical characteristics of devices.
- ▶ A disk drive contains cylinders.
- ▶ Cylinders contain tracks.
- ▶ Tracks contain data records and are in Count Key Data (CKD) format.[2]
- ▶ Data blocks are the units of recording on disk.

5.4.2 What are DASD labels

The operating system uses groups of labels to identify DASD volumes and the data sets they contain. Customer application programs generally do not use these labels directly. DASD volumes must use standard labels. Standard labels include a volume label, a data set label for each data set, and optional user labels. A volume label, stored at track 0 of cylinder 0, identifies each DASD volume.

The z/OS system programmer or storage administrator uses the ICKDSF utility program to initialize each DASD volume before it is used on the system. ICKDSF generates the volume label and builds the volume table of contents (VTOC), a structure that contains the data set labels (we discuss VTOCs in 5.11.1, "What is a volume table of contents" on page 222). The system programmer can also use ICKDSF to scan a volume to ensure that it is usable and to reformat all the tracks.

---

[2] Current devices actually use *Extended Count Key Data* (ECKD™) protocols, but we use CKD as a collective name in the text.

5.5 Allocating a data set

To use a data set, you first allocate it (establish a link to it), then access the data using macros for the access method that you have chosen.

The *allocation* of a data set means either or both of two things:

▶ To set aside (create) space for a new data set on a disk.
▶ To establish a logical link between a job step and any data set.

At the end of this chapter, we allocate a data set using ISPF panel option 3.2. Other ways to allocate a data set include the following methods:

Access method services
You can allocate data sets through a multifunction services program called access method services. Access method services include commonly used commands for working with data sets, such as ALLOCATE, ALTER, DELETE, and PRINT.

ALLOCATE
You can use the TSO ALLOCATE command to create data sets. The command actually guides you through the allocation values that you must specify.

ISPF menus
You can use a set of TSO menus called Interactive System Productivity Facility. One menu guides the user through allocation of a data set.

Using JCL
You can use a set of commands called *job control language* to allocate data sets.

5.6 How data sets are named

When you allocate a new data set, you must give the data set a unique name.

HLQ:
The first segment of a multi-segment name.

A data set name can be one name segment, or a series of joined name segments. Each name segment represents a level of qualification. For example, the data set name VERA.LUZ.DATA is composed of three name segments. The first name on the left is called the high-level qualifier (HLQ), and the last name on the right is the lowest-level qualifier (LLQ).

Segments or *qualifiers* are limited to eight characters, the first of which must be alphabetic (A to Z) or *special* (#, @, or $). The remaining seven characters are either alphabetic, numeric (0 - 9), special, or a hyphen (-). Name segments are separated by a period (.).

Including all name segments and periods, the length of the data set name must not exceed 44 characters. Thus, a maximum of 22 name segments can make up a data set name.

For example, the following names are not valid data set names:

► A name with a qualifier that is longer than eight characters (HLQ.ABCDEFGHI.XYZ).

► A name containing two successive periods (HLQ..ABC).

► A name that ends with a period (HLQ.ABC.).

► A name that contains a qualifier that does not start with an alphabetic or special character (HLQ.123.XYZ).

The HLQ for a user's data sets is typically controlled by the security system. There are a number of conventions for the remainder of the name. These are *conventions*, not rules, but are widely used. They include the following items:

► The letters LIB somewhere in the name indicate that the data set is a library. The letters PDS are a lesser-used alternative for this convention.

► The letters CNTL, JCL, or JOB somewhere in the name typically indicate the data set contains JCL (but might not be exclusively devoted to JCL).

► The letters LOAD, LOADLIB, or LINKLIB in the name indicate that the data set contains executables. (A library with z/OS executable modules must be devoted solely to executable modules.)

► The letters PROC, PRC, or PROCLIB indicate a library of JCL procedures.

► Various combinations are used to indicate source code for a specific language, for example COBOL, Assembler, FORTRAN, PL/I, JAVA, C, or C++.

► A portion of a data set name may indicate a specific project, such as PAYROLL.

► Using too many qualifiers is considered poor practice. For example, P390A.A.B.C.D.E.F.G.H.I.J.K.L.M.N.O.P.Q.R.S is a valid data set name (upper case, does not exceed 44 bytes, no special characters) but it is not very meaningful. A good practice is for a data set name to contain three or four qualifiers.

► Again, the periods count toward the 44-character limit.

5.7 Allocating space on DASD volumes through JCL

This section describes allocating a data set as you would using job control language (JCL). We discuss the use of JCL later in this book; this section previews some of the data set space allocation settings you will use later in this book. Besides JCL, other common methods for allocating data sets include the IDCAMS utility program, or using DFSMS to automate the allocation of data sets.

In JCL, you can specify the amount of space required in blocks, records, tracks, or cylinders. When creating a DASD data set, you specify the amount of space needed explicitly through the SPACE parameter, or implicitly by using the information available in a data class.[3] If you begin your data set name with &&, the JCL processor will allocate it as a temporary data set and delete it when the job has completed.

The system can use a data class if SMS is active, even if the data set is not SMS-managed. For system-managed data sets, the system selects the volumes, saving you from having to specify a volume when you allocate a data set.

If you specify your space request by average record length, space allocation is independent of device type. Device independence is especially important to system-managed storage.

5.7.1 Logical records and blocks

A logical record length (LRECL) is a unit of information about a unit of processing (for example, a customer, an account, a payroll employee, and so on). It is the smallest amount of data to be processed, and it is composed of fields that contain information recognized by the processing application.

Logical records, when located on DASD, tape, or optical devices, are grouped within physical records named blocks. BLKSIZE indicates the length of those blocks. Each block of data on a DASD volume has a distinct location and a unique address, thus making it possible to find any block without extensive searching. Logical records can be stored and retrieved either directly or sequentially.

LRECL:
The maximum logical record length. A DCB attribute of a data set.

The maximum length of a logical record (LRECL) is limited by the physical size of the used media.

When the amount of space required is expressed in blocks, you must specify the number and average length of the blocks within the data set.

---
[3] When allocating a data set through DFSMS or the IDCAMS utility program, you can specify space allocations in kilobytes or megabytes, rather than blocks, records, tracks, or cylinders.

Let us take an example of a request for disk storage as follows:

- ▶ Average block length in bytes = 300
- ▶ Primary quantity (number) of blocks = 5000
- ▶ Secondary quantity of blocks, to be allocated if the primary quantity gets filled with data = 100

From this information, the operating system estimates and allocates the amount of disk space required.

5.7.2 Data set extents

Space for a disk data set is assigned in *extents*. An extent is a *contiguous* number of disk drive tracks, cylinders, or blocks. Data sets can increase in extents as they grow. Older types of data sets can have up to 16 extents per volume. Newer types of data sets can have up to 128 extents per volume or 255 extents total on multiple volumes.

Extents are relevant when you are not using PDSEs and have to manage the space yourself, rather than through DFSMS. Here, you want the data set to fit into a single extent to maximize disk performance. Reading or writing contiguous tracks is faster than reading or writing tracks scattered over the disk, as might be the case if tracks were allocated dynamically. But if there is not sufficient contiguous space, a data set goes into extents.

5.8 Data set record formats

Traditional z/OS data sets are *record oriented*. In normal usage, there are no byte stream files such as are found in PC and UNIX systems. (z/OS UNIX has byte stream files, and byte stream functions exist in other specialized areas. These are not considered to be traditional data sets.)

In z/OS, there are no new line (NL) or carriage return and line feed (CR+LF) characters to denote the end of a record. Records are either fixed length or variable length in a given data set. When editing a data set with ISPF, for example, each line is a record.

Traditional z/OS data sets have one of five record formats, as follows:

F (Fixed)   One physical block on disk is one logical record and all the blocks/records are the same size. This format is seldom used.

FB (Fixed Blocked)	Several logical records are combined into one physical block. This can provide efficient space utilization and operation. This format is commonly used for fixed-length records.
V (Variable)	This format has one logical record as one physical block. A variable-length logical record consists of a record descriptor word (RDW) followed by the data. The record descriptor word is a 4 byte field describing the record. The first 2 bytes contain the length of the logical record (including the 4 byte RDW). The length can be from 4 to 32,760 bytes. All bits of the third and fourth bytes must be 0, because other values are used for spanned records. This format is seldom used.
VB (Variable Blocked)	This format places several variable-length logical records (each with an RDW) in one physical block. The software must place an additional Block Descriptor Word (BDW) at the beginning of the block, containing the total length of the block.
U (Undefined)	This format consists of variable-length physical records/blocks with no predefined structure. Although this format may appear attractive for many unusual applications, it is normally used only for executable modules.

We must stress the difference between a block and a record. A block is what is written on disk, while a record is a logical entity.

The terminology here is pervasive throughout z/OS literature. The key terms are:

<table>
<tr><td>

Block Size:
The physical block size written on a disk for F and FB records.

</td><td>

▶ Block Size (BLKSIZE) is the physical block size written on the disk for F and FB records. For V, VB, and U records, it is the maximum physical block size that can be used for the data set.

▶ Logical Record Size (LRECL) is the logical record size (F or FB) or the maximum allowed logical record size (V or VB) for the data set. Format U records have no LRECL.

▶ Record Format (RECFM) is F, FB, V, VB, or U, as just described.

</td></tr>
</table>

These terms are known as data control block (DCB) characteristics, named for the control block where they may be defined in an assembly language program. The user is often expected to specify these parameters when creating a new data set. The type and length of a data set are defined by its record format (RECFM) and logical record length (LRECL). Fixed-length data sets have a RECFM of F, FB, FBS, and so on. Variable-length data sets have a RECFM of V, VB, VBS, and so on.

RECFM:
Record format. One of the characteristics of a data control block.

A data set with RECFM=FB and LRECL=25 is a fixed-length (FB) data set with a record length of 25 bytes (the B is for blocked). For an FB data set, the LRECL tells you the length of each record in the data set; all of the records are the same length. The first data byte of an FB record is in position 1. A record in an FB data set with LRECL=25 might look like this:

```
Positions 1-3:  Country Code = 'USA'
Positions 4-5:  State Code = 'CA'
Positions 6-25: City = 'San Jose' padded with 12 blanks on the right
```

A data set with RECFM=VB and LRECL=25 is a variable-length (VB) data set with a maximum record length of 25 bytes. In a VB data set, the records can have different lengths. The first four bytes of each record contain the RDW, and the first two bytes of the RDW contain the length of that record (in binary). The first data byte of a VB record is in position 5, after the 4 byte RDW in positions 1 - 4. A record in a VB data set with LRECL=25 might look like this:

```
Positions 1-2:   Length in RDW = hex 0011 = decimal 17
Positions 3-4:   Zeros in RDW = hex 0000 = decimal 0
Positions 5-7:   Country Code = 'USA'
Positions 8-9:   State Code =  'CA'
Positions 10-17: City = 'San Jose'
```

Figure 5-1 shows the relationship between records and blocks for each of the five record formats.

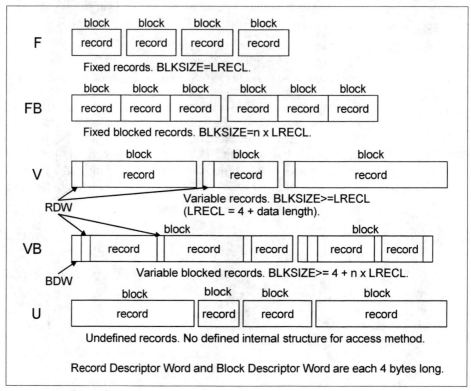

Figure 5-1   Basic record formats

5.9 Types of data sets

There are many different types of data sets in z/OS, and different methods for managing them. This chapter discusses three types:

► Sequential
► Partitioned
► VSAM

These are all used for disk storage; we mention tape data sets briefly as well.

5.9.1 What is a sequential data set

The simplest data structure in a z/OS system is a sequential data set. It consists of one or more records that are stored in physical order and processed in sequence. New records are appended to the end of the data set.

An example of a sequential data set might be an output data set for a line printer or a log file.

A z/OS user defines sequential data sets through job control language (JCL) with a data set organization of PS (DSORG=PS), which stands for physical sequential. In other words, the records in the data set are physically arranged one after another.

This chapter covers mainly disk data sets, but mainframe applications might also use tape data sets for many purposes. Tapes store sequential data sets. Mainframe tape drives have variable-length records (blocks). The maximum block size for routine programming methods is 65 KB. Specialized programming can produce longer blocks. There are a number of tape drive products with different characteristics.

5.9.2 What is a partitioned data set

A *partitioned data set* (PDS) adds a layer of organization to the simple structure of sequential data sets. A PDS is a collection of sequential data sets, called *members*. Each member is like a sequential data set and has a simple name, which can be up to eight characters long.

Member:
A partition of a partitioned data set (PDS) or partitioned data set extended (PDSE).

A PDS also contains a directory. The directory contains an entry for each member in the PDS with a reference (or pointer) to the member. Member names are listed alphabetically in the directory, but members themselves can appear in any order in the library. The directory allows the system to retrieve a particular member in the data set.

A partitioned data set is commonly referred to as a *library*. In z/OS, libraries are used for storing source programs, system and application control parameters, JCL, and executable modules. There are few system data sets that are not libraries.

A PDS loses space whenever a member is updated or added. As a result, z/OS users regularly need to compress a PDS to recover the lost space.

A z/OS user defines a PDS through JCL with a data set organization of PO (DSORG=PO), which stands for partitioned organization.

Library:
A partitioned data set used for storing source programs, parameters, and executable modules.

Why a partitioned data set is structured the way it is

The PDS structure was designed to provide efficient access to libraries of related members, whether they be load modules, program source modules, JCL, or many other types of content.

Many system data sets are also kept in PDS data sets, especially when they consist of many small, related files. For example, the definitions for ISPF panels are kept in PDS data sets.

A primary use of ISPF is to create and manipulate PDS data sets. These data sets typically consist of source code for programs, text for manuals or help screens, or JCL to allocate data sets and run programs.

Advantages of a partitioned data set

A PDS data set offers a simple and efficient way to organize related groups of sequential files. A PDS has the following advantages for z/OS users:

▶ Grouping of related data sets under a single name makes z/OS data management easier. Files stored as members of a PDS can be processed either individually or all the members can be processed as a unit.

▶ Because the space allocated for z/OS data sets always starts at a track boundary on disk, using a PDS is a way to store more than one small data set on a track. This saves you disk space if you have many data sets that are much smaller than a track. A track is 56,664 bytes for a 3390 disk device.

▶ Members of a PDS can be used as sequential data sets, and they can be appended (or *concatenated*) to sequential data sets.

▶ Multiple PDS data sets can be concatenated to form large libraries.

▶ PDS data sets are easy to create with JCL or ISPF; they are easy to manipulate with ISPF utilities or TSO commands.

Disadvantages of a partitioned data set

PDS data sets are simple, flexible, and widely used. However, some aspects of the PDS design affect both performance and the efficient use of disk storage, as follows:

▶ Wasted space

When a member in a PDS is replaced, the new data area is written to a new section within the storage allocated to the PDS. When a member is deleted, its pointer is deleted too, so there is no mechanism to reuse its space. This wasted space is often called *gas* and must be periodically removed by reorganizing the PDS, for example, by using the IEBCOPY utility to compress it.

- Limited directory size

  The size of a PDS directory is set at allocation time. As the data set grows, it can acquire more space in units of the amount you specified as its secondary space. These extra units are called *secondary extents*.

  However, you can only store a fixed number of member entries in the PDS directory because its size is fixed when the data set is allocated. If you need to store more entries than there is space, you have to allocate a new PDS with more directory blocks and copy the members from the old data set into it. This means that when you allocate a PDS, you must calculate the amount of directory space you need.

- Lengthy directory searches

  As mentioned earlier, an entry in a PDS directory consists of a name and a pointer to the location of the member. Entries are stored in alphabetical order of the member names. Inserting an entry near the front of a large directory can cause a large amount of I/O activity, as all the entries behind the new one are moved along to make room for it.

  Entries are also searched sequentially in alphabetical order. If the directory is large and the members small, it might take longer to search the directory than to retrieve the member when its location is found.

5.9.3 What is a partitioned data set extended

A partitioned data set extended (PDSE) consists of a directory and zero or more members, just like a PDS. It can be created with JCL, TSO/E, and ISPF, just like a PDS, and can be processed with the same access methods. PDSE data sets are stored only on DASD, not on tape.

PDS / PDSE:
A z/OS library containing members, such as source programs.

The directory can expand automatically as needed, up to the addressing limit of 522,236 members. It also has an index, which provides a fast search for member names. Space from deleted or moved members is automatically reused for new members, so you do not have to compress a PDSE to remove wasted space. Each member of a PDSE can have up to 15,728,639 records. A PDSE can have a maximum of 123 extents, but it cannot extend beyond one volume. When a directory of a PDSE is in use, it is kept in processor storage for fast access.

PDSE data sets can be used in place of nearly all PDS data sets that are used to store data. But the PDSE format is not intended as a PDS replacement. When a PDSE is used to store load modules, it stores them in structures called *program objects*.

Partitioned data set extended versus partitioned data set extended

In many ways, a PDSE is similar to a PDS. Each member name can be eight bytes long. For accessing a PDS directory or member, most PDSE interfaces are indistinguishable from PDS interfaces. PDS and PDSE data sets are processed using the same access methods (BSAM, QSAM, and BPAM). And, in case you were wondering, within a given PDS or PDSE, the members must use the same access method.

However, PDSE data sets have a different internal format, which gives them increased usability. You can use a PDSE in place of a PDS to store data or programs. In a PDS, you store programs as *load modules.* In a PDSE, you store programs as program objects. If you want to store a load module in a PDSE, you must first convert it into a program object (using the IEBCOPY utility).

PDSE data sets have several features that can improve user productivity and system performance. The main advantage of using a PDSE over a PDS is that a PDSE automatically reuses space within the data set without the need for anyone to periodically run a utility to reorganize it.

Also, the size of a PDS directory is fixed regardless of the number of members in it, while the size of a PDSE directory is flexible and expands to fit the members stored in it.

Further, the system reclaims space automatically whenever a member is deleted or replaced, and returns it to the pool of space available for allocation to other members of the same PDSE. The space can be reused without having to do an IEBCOPY compress.

Other advantages of PDSE data sets are:

► PDSE members can be shared. This makes it easier to maintain the integrity of the PDSE when modifying separate members of the PDSE at the same time.

► Reduced directory search time. The PDSE directory, which is indexed, is searched using that index. The PDS directory, which is organized alphabetically, is searched sequentially. The system might cache in storage directories of frequently used PDSE data sets.

► Creation of multiple members at the same time. For example, you can open two DCBs to the same PDSE and write two members at the same time.

► PDSE data sets contain up to 123 extents. An extent is a continuous area of space on a DASD storage volume, occupied by or reserved for a specific data set.

► When written to DASD, logical records are extracted from the user's blocks and reblocked. When read, records in a PDSE are reblocked into the block size specified in the DCB. The block size used for the reblocking can differ from the original block size.

5.9.4 When a data set runs out of space

As mentioned earlier, when you allocate a data set, you reserve a certain amount of space in units of blocks, tracks, or cylinders on a storage disk. If you use up that space, the system displays the message SYSTEM ABEND 'OD37,' or possibly B37 or E37.

We have not discussed abnormal ends or abends in this text, but this problem is something you will have to deal with if it occurs. If you are in an edit session, you will not be able to exit the session until you resolve the problem.

Among the things you can do to resolve a space shortage abend are:

► If the data set is a PDS, you can compress it by performing the following steps:

  a. Split (PF 2) the panel and select UTILITIES (option 3).

  b. Select LIBRARIES (option 1) on the Utility Selection Menu.

  c. Specify the name of the data set and enter C on the option line.

  d. When the data set is compressed, you should see the message COMPRESS SUCCESSFUL.

  e. You can then swap (PF 9) to the edit session and save the new material.

► Allocate a larger data set and copy into it by performing the following steps:

  a. Split (PF 2) the panel and select UTILITIES (option 3), then DATASET (option 2) from the other side of the split.

  b. Specify the name of the data set that received the abend to display its characteristics.

  c. Allocate another data set with more space.

  d. Select MOVE/COPY (option 3) on the Utility Selection Menu to copy members from the old data set to the new larger data set.

  e. Browse (option 1) the new data set to make sure everything was copied correctly.

  f. Swap (PF 9) back to the abending edit session, enter CC on the top line of input and the bottom line of input, enter CREATE on the command line, and press the Enter key.

g. Enter the new, larger data set name and a member name to receive the copied information.

h. You see the abending edit session again. Enter CAN on the command line. Press the RETURN key (PF 4) key to exit the edit session.

i. Select DATASET (option 2) from the Utility Selection Menu to delete the old data set.

j. Rename the new data set to the old name.

▶ Cancel the new material entered in the edit session by entering CAN on the command line. You should then be able to exit without abending; however, all information that was not previously saved is lost.

5.10 What is Virtual Storage Access Method

The term Virtual Storage Access Method (VSAM) applies to both a data set type and the access method used to manage various user data types. As an access method, VSAM provides much more complex functions than other disk access methods. VSAM keeps disk records in a unique format that is not understandable by other access methods.

VSAM:
An access method for direct or sequential processing of fixed length and variable length records.

VSAM is used primarily for applications. It is not used for source programs, JCL, or executable modules. VSAM files cannot be routinely displayed or edited with ISPF.

You can use VSAM to organize records into four types of data sets: key-sequenced, entry-sequenced, linear, or relative record. The primary difference among these types of data sets is the way their records are stored and accessed.

VSAM data sets are briefly described as follows:

▶ Key Sequence Data Set (KSDS)

This is the most common use for VSAM. Each record has one or more key fields and a record can be retrieved (or inserted) by key value. This provides random access to data. Records are of variable length.

▶ Entry Sequence Data Set (ESDS)

This form of VSAM keeps records in sequential order. Records can be accessed sequentially. It is used by IMS, DB2, and z/OS UNIX.

▶ Relative Record Data Set (RRDS)

This VSAM format allows retrieval of records by number: record 1, record 2, and so on. This provides random access and assumes the application program has a way to derive the desired record numbers.

▶ Linear Data Set (LDS)

This is, in effect, a byte-stream data set and is the only form of a byte-stream data set in traditional z/OS files (as opposed to z/OS UNIX files). A number of z/OS system functions use this format heavily, but it is rarely used by application programs.

There are several additional methods of accessing data in VSAM that are not listed here. Most applications use VSAM for keyed data.

VSAM works with a logical data area known as a control interval (CI), which is shown in Figure 5-2. The default CI size is 4 KB, but it can be up to 32 KB. The CI contains data records, unused space, record descriptor fields (RDFs), and a CI descriptor field.

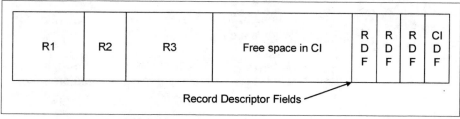

Figure 5-2 Simple VSAM control interval

Multiple CIs are placed in a control area (CA). A VSAM data set consists of control areas and index records. One form of index record is the sequence set, which is the lowest-level index pointing to a control interval.

VSAM data is always variable-length and records are automatically blocked in control intervals. The RECFM attributes (F, FB, V, VB, and U) do not apply to VSAM, nor does the BLKSIZE attribute. You can use the Access Method Services (AMS) utility to define and delete VSAM structures, such as files and indexes. Example 5-1 shows an example.

Example 5-1 Defining a VSAM KSDS using AMS

```
DEFINE CLUSTER -
(NAME(VWX.MYDATA) -
VOLUMES(VSER02) -
RECORDS(1000 500)) -
 DATA -
(NAME(VWX.KSDATA) -
 KEYS(15 0) -
RECORDSIZE(250 250) -
BUFFERSPACE(25000) ) -
INDEX -
```

```
(NAME(VWX.KSINDEX) -
CATALOG (UCAT1)
```

There are many details of VSAM processing that are not included in this brief
description. Most processing is handled transparently by VSAM; the application
program merely retrieves, updates, deletes or adds records based on key
values.

5.11 Catalogs and volume table of contents

z/OS uses a catalog and a volume table of contents (VTOC) on each DASD to
manage the storage and placement of data sets; these are described in the
sections that follow:

▶ 5.11.1, "What is a volume table of contents" on page 222
▶ 5.11.2, "What is a catalog" on page 223

z/OS also makes it possible to group data sets based on historically related data,
as described in 5.11.3, "What is a generation data group" on page 226.

5.11.1 What is a volume table of contents

z/OS requires a particular format for disks, which is shown in Figure 5-3.

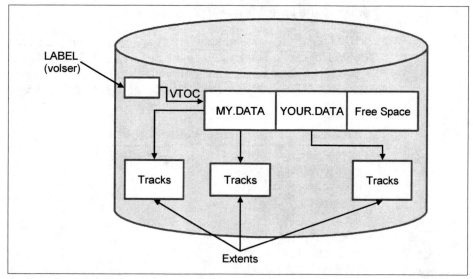

Figure 5-3   Disk label, VTOC, and extents

Record 1 on the first track of the first cylinder provides the label for the disk. It contains the 6-character volume serial number (volser) and a pointer to the *volume table of contents* (VTOC), which can be located anywhere on the disk.

VTOC:
A structure that contains the data set labels.

The VTOC lists the data sets that reside on its volume, along with information about the location and size of each data set, and other data set attributes. A standard z/OS utility program, ICKDSF, is used to create the label and VTOC.

When a disk volume is initialized with ICKDSF, the owner can specify the location and size of the VTOC. The size can be quite variable, ranging from a few tracks to perhaps 100 tracks, depending on the expected use of the volume. More data sets on the disk volume require more space in the VTOC.

The VTOC also has entries for all the free space on the volume. Allocating space for a data set causes system routines to examine the free space records, update them, and create a new VTOC entry. Data sets are always an integral number of tracks (or cylinders) and start at the beginning of a track (or cylinder).

You can also create a VTOC with an index. The VTOC index is actually a data set with the name SYS1.VTOCIX.*volser,* which has entries arranged alphabetically by data set name with pointers to the VTOC entries. It also has bitmaps of the free space on the volume. A VTOC index allows the user to find the data set much faster.

5.11.2 What is a catalog

A catalog describes data set attributes and indicates the volumes on which a data set is located. When a data set is cataloged, it can be referred to by name without the user needing to specify where the data set is stored. Data sets can be cataloged, uncataloged, or recataloged. All system-managed DASD data sets are cataloged automatically in a catalog. Cataloging of data sets on magnetic tape is not required, but it can simplify users' jobs.

In z/OS, the master catalog and user catalogs store the locations of data sets. Both disk and tape data sets can be cataloged.

To find a data set that you have requested, z/OS must know three pieces of information:

- ► Data set name
- ► Volume name

Catalog:
Describes data set attributes, including where the data set is located.

- ► Unit (the volume device type, such as a 3390 disk or 3590 tape)

You can specify all three values on ISPF panels or in JCL. However, the unit device type and the volume are often not relevant to an user or application program.

A system catalog is used to store and retrieve the UNIT and VOLUME location of a data set. In its most basic form, a catalog can provide the unit device type and volume name for any data set that is cataloged. A system catalog provides a simple look up function. With this facility, the user need only provide a data set name.

Master catalogs and user catalogs

A z/OS system always has at least one master catalog. If it had a single catalog, this catalog would be the master catalog and the location entries for all data sets would be stored in it. A single catalog, however, would be not be efficient or flexible, so a typical z/OS system uses a master catalog and numerous *user catalogs* connected to it, as shown in Figure 5-4 on page 225. The master catalog usually stores only the name of the user catalogs.

A user catalog is a data set used to locate the DASD volume in which the requested data set is stored. User application data sets are cataloged in this type of catalog. An alias is a special entry in the master catalog pointing to a user catalog that coincides with the high level qualifier (HLQ) of a data set name. The alias is used to find the user catalog in which the data set location information exists. The data set with this HLQ is cataloged in that user catalog.

In Figure 5-4 on page 225, the data set name of the master catalog is SYSTEM.MASTER.CATALOG. This master catalog stores the full data set name and location of all data sets with a SYS1 prefix, such as SYS1.A1. Two HLQ (alias) entries were defined to the master catalog, IBMUSER and USER. The statement that defined IBMUSER included the data set name of the user catalog containing all the fully qualified IBMUSER data sets with their respective location. The same is true for USER HLQ (alias).

When SYS1.A1 is requested, the master catalog returns the location information, volume (WRK001) and unit (3390), to the requestor. When IBMUSER.A1 is requested, the master catalog redirects the request to USERCAT.IBM, then USERCAT.IBM returns the location information to the requestor.

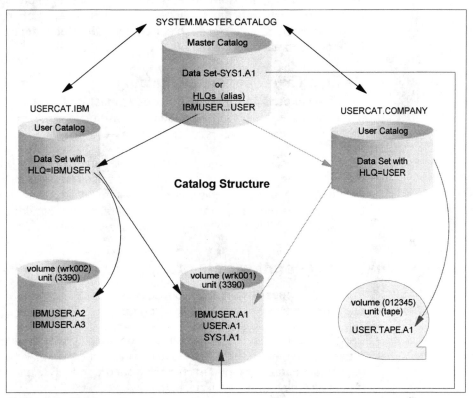

Figure 5-4   Catalog concept

Take, as a further example, the following DEFINE statements:

```
DEFINE  ALIAS ( NAME ( IBMUSER ) RELATE ( USERCAT.IBM ) )
DEFINE  ALIAS ( NAME ( USER ) RELATE ( USERCAT.COMPANY ) )
```

These statements are used to place IBMUSER and USER alias names in the master catalog with the name of the user catalog that will store the fully qualified data set names and location information. If IBMUSER.A1 is cataloged, a JCL statement to allocate it to the job would be:

```
//INPUT DD DSN=IBMUSER.A1,DISP=SHR
```

If IBMUSER.A1 is not cataloged, a JCL statement to allocate it to the job would be:

```
//INPUT DD DSN=IBMUSER.A1,DISP=SHR,VOL=SER=WRK001,UNIT=3390
```

As a general rule, all user data sets in a z/OS installation are cataloged. Uncataloged data sets are rarely needed and their use is often related to recovery problems or installation of new software. Data sets created through ISPF are automatically cataloged.

Using an alternate master catalog

So, what happens if an installation loses its master catalog, or the master catalog somehow becomes corrupted? Such an occurrence would pose a serious problem and require swift recovery actions.

To prevent this situation, most system programmers define a backup for the master catalog. The system programmer specifies this alternate master catalog during system startup. In this case, the system programmer should keep the alternate on a volume separate from that of the master catalog (to protect against a situation in which the volume becomes unavailable).

5.11.3 What is a generation data group

In z/OS, it is possible to catalog successive updates or generations of related data. They are called generation data groups (GDGs).

Each data set within a GDG is called a generation or generation data set (GDS). A generation data group (GDG) is a collection of historically related non-VSAM data sets that are arranged in chronological order, that is, each data set is historically related to the others in the group.

Within a GDG, the generations can have like or unlike DCB attributes and data set organizations. If the attributes and organizations of all generations in a group are identical, the generations can be retrieved together as a single data set.

There are advantages to grouping related data sets. For example:

▶ All of the data sets in the group can be referred to by a common name.

▶ The operating system is able to keep the generations in chronological order.

▶ Outdated or obsolete generations can be automatically deleted by the operating system.

Generation data sets have sequentially ordered absolute and relative names that represent their age. The operating system's catalog management routines use the absolute generation name. Older data sets have smaller absolute numbers. The relative name is a signed integer used to refer to the latest (0), the next to the latest (-1), and so on, generation.

For example, the data set name LAB.PAYROLL(0) refers to the most recent data set of the group, LAB.PAYROLL(-1) refers to the second most recent data set, and so on. The relative number can also be used to catalog a new generation (+1). A generation data group (GDG) base is allocated in a catalog before the generation data sets are cataloged. Each GDG is represented by a GDG base entry.

For new non-system-managed data sets, if you do not specify a volume and the data set is not opened, the system does not catalog the data set. New system-managed data sets are always cataloged when allocated, with the volume assigned from a storage group.

5.12 Role of DFSMS in managing space

In a z/OS system, space management involves the allocation, placement, monitoring, migration, backup, recall, recovery, and deletion of data sets. These activities can be done either manually or through the use of automated processes. When data management is automated, the operating system determines object placement and automatically manages data set backup, movement, space, and security. A typical z/OS production system includes both manual and automated processes for managing data sets.

Depending on how a z/OS system and its storage devices are configured, a user or program can directly control many aspects of data set usage, and in the early days of the operating system, users were required to do so. Increasingly, however, z/OS customers rely on installation-specified settings for data and resource management, and space management products, such as DFSMS, to automate the use of storage for data sets.

Data management includes these main tasks:

► Sets aside (allocates) space on DASD volumes.

► Automatically retrieves cataloged data sets by name.

► Mounts magnetic tape volumes in the drive.

► Establishes a logical connection between the application program and the medium.

► Controls access to data.

► Transfers data between the application program and the medium.

The primary means of managing space in z/OS is through the DFSMS component of the operating system. DFSMS performs the essential data, storage, program, and device management functions of the system. DFSMS is a set of products, and one of these products, DSFMSdfp, is required for running z/OS. DFSMS, together with hardware products and installation-specific settings for data and resource management, provides system-managed storage in a z/OS environment.

The heart of DFSMS is the Storage Management Subsystem (SMS). Using SMS, the system programmer or storage administrator defines policies that automate the management of storage and hardware devices. These policies describe data allocation characteristics, performance and availability goals, backup and retention requirements, and storage requirements for the system. SMS governs these policies for the system, and the Interactive Storage Management Facility (ISMF) provides the user interface for defining and maintaining the policies.

SMS:
Storage
Management
Subsystem.

The data sets allocated through SMS are called system-managed data sets or SMS-managed data sets. When you allocate or define a data set to use SMS, you specify the data set requirements through a data class, a storage class, and a management class. Typically, you do not need to specify these classes, because a storage administrator has set up automatic class selection (ACS) routines to determine which classes are used for a given data set.

DFSMS provides a set of constructs, user interfaces, and routines (using the DFSMS products) to help the storage administrator. The core logic of DFSMS, such as the ACS routines, ISMF code, and constructs, resides in DFSMSdfp. DFSMShsm and DFSMSdss are involved in the management class construct. With DFSMS, the z/OS system programmer or storage administrator can define performance goals and data availability requirements, create model data definitions for typical data sets, and automate data backup. DFSMS can automatically assign, based on installation policy, those services and data definition attributes to data sets when they are created. IBM storage management-related products determine data placement, manage data backup, control space usage, and provide data security.

5.13 z/OS UNIX file systems

Think of a UNIX file system as a container that holds part of the entire UNIX directory tree. Unlike a traditional z/OS library, a UNIX file system is hierarchical and byte-oriented. To find a file in a UNIX file system, you search one or more directories (Figure 5-5). There is no concept of a z/OS catalog that points directly to a file.

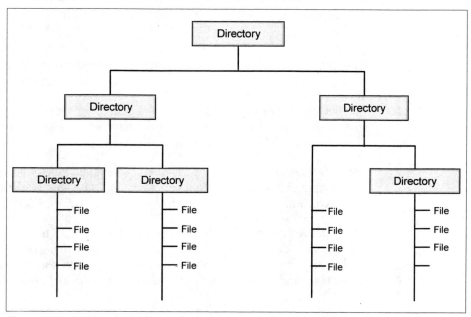

Figure 5-5   A hierarchical file system structure

z/OS UNIX System Services (z/OS UNIX) allows z/OS users to create UNIX file systems and file system directory trees on z/OS, and to access UNIX files on z/OS and other systems. In z/OS, a UNIX file system is mounted over an empty directory by the system programmer (or a user with mount authority).

You can use the following file system types with z/OS UNIX:

▶ System z File System (zFS), which is a file system that stores files in VSAM linear data sets.

▶ Hierarchical file system (HFS), a mountable file system, which is being phased out by zFS.

▶ z/OS Network File System (z/OS NFS), which allows a z/OS system to access a remote UNIX (z/OS or non-z/OS) file system over TCP/IP, as though it were part of the local z/OS directory tree.

► Temporary file system (TFS), which is a temporary, in-memory physical file system that supports in-storage mountable file systems.

As with other UNIX file systems, a path name identifies a file and consists of directory names and a file name. A fully qualified file name, which consists of the name of each directory in the path to a file plus the file name itself, can be up to 1023 bytes long.

The path name is constructed of individual directory names and a file name separated by the forward-slash character, for example:

`/dir1/dir2/dir3/MyFile`

Like UNIX, z/OS UNIX is case-sensitive for file and directory names. For example, in the same directory, the file MYFILE is a different file than MyFile.

The files in a hierarchical file system are sequential files, and are accessed as byte streams. A record concept does not exist with these files other than the structure defined by an application.

The zFS data set that contains the UNIX file system is a z/OS data set type (a VSAM linear data set). zFS data sets and z/OS data sets can reside on the same DASD volume. z/OS provides commands for managing zFS space utilization.

The integration of the zFS file system with existing z/OS file system management services provides automated file system management capabilities that might not be available on other UNIX platforms. This integration allows file owners to spend less time on tasks such as backup and restore of entire file systems.

5.13.1 z/OS data sets versus file system files

Many elements of UNIX have analogs in the z/OS operating system. Consider, for example, that the organization of a user catalog is analogous to a user directory (`/u/ibmuser`) in the file system.

In z/OS, the user prefix assigned to z/OS data sets points to a user catalog. Typically, one user owns all the data sets whose names begin with his user prefix. For example, the data sets belonging to the TSO/E user ID IBMUSER all begin with the high-level qualifier (prefix) IBMUSER. There could be different data sets named IBMUSER.C, IBMUSER.C.OTHER, and IBMUSER.TEST.

In the UNIX file system, ibmuser would have a user directory named /u/ibmuser. Under that directory, there could be a subdirectory named /u/ibmuser/c, and /u/ibmuser/c/pgma would point to the pgma file (see Figure 5-6).

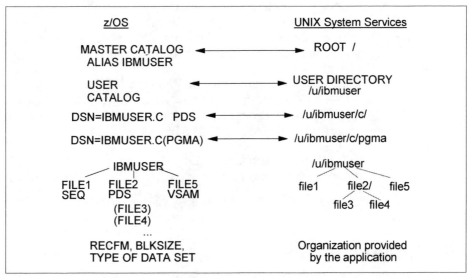

Figure 5-6   Comparison of z/OS data sets and file system files

Of the various types of z/OS data sets, a partitioned data set (PDS) is most like a user directory in the file system. In a partitioned data set, such as IBMUSER.C, you could have members (files) PGMA, PGMB, and so on. For example, you might have IBMUSER.C(PGMA) and IBMUSER.C(PGMB). Along the same lines, a subdirectory such as /u/ibmuser/c can hold many files, such as pgma, pgmb, and so on.

All data written to a hierarchical file system can be read by all programs as soon as it is written. Data is written to a disk when a program issues an **fsync()**.

5.14 Working with a zFS file system

The z/OS Distributed File Service (DFS) System z File System (zFS) is a z/OS UNIX System Services (z/OS UNIX) file system that can be used in addition to the hierarchical file system (HFS). zFS file systems contain files and directories that can be accessed with z/OS UNIX application programming interfaces (APIs). These file systems can support access control lists (ACLs). zFS file systems can be mounted into the z/OS UNIX hierarchy along with other local (or remote) file system types (for example, HFS, TFS, AUTOMNT, and NFS).

The Distributed File Service server message block (SMB) provides a server that makes z/OS UNIX files and data sets available to SMB clients. The data sets supported include sequential data sets (on DASD), PDS and PDSE, and VSAM data sets. The data set support is usually referred to as record file system (RFS) support. The SMB protocol is supported through the use of TCP/IP on z/OS. This communication protocol allows clients to access shared directory paths and shared printers. Personal computer (PC) clients in the network can use the file and print sharing functions that are included in their operating systems.

Supported SMB clients include Windows XP Professional, Windows Terminal Server on Windows 2000 server, Windows Terminal Server on Windows 2003, and Linux. At the same time, these files can be shared with local z/OS UNIX applications and with DCE DFS clients.

Using DFS is described in *z/OS DFS Administration*, SC24-5989. You can find this and related publications at the z/OS Internet Library website:

```
http://www-03.ibm.com/systems/z/os/zos/bkserv/
```

5.15 Summary

A data set is a collection of logically related data; it can be a source program, a library of programs, or a file of data records used by a processing program. Data set *records* are the basic unit of information used by a processing program.

Users must define the amount of space to be allocated for a data set (before it is used), or these allocations must be automated through the use of DFSMS. With DFSMS, the z/OS system programmer or storage administrator can define performance goals and data availability requirements, create model data definitions for typical data sets, and automate data backup. DFSMS can automatically assign, based on installation policy, those services and data definition attributes to data sets when they are created. Other storage management-related products can be used to determine data placement, manage data backup, control space usage, and provide data security.

Almost all z/OS data processing is record-oriented. Byte-stream files are not present in traditional processing, although they are a standard part of z/OS UNIX. z/OS records and physical blocks follow one of several well-defined formats. Most data sets have DCB attributes that include the record format (RECFM—F, FB, V, VB, U), the maximum logical record length (LRECL), and the maximum block size (BLKSIZE).

z/OS libraries are known as partitioned data sets (PDS or PDSE) and contain members. Source programs, system and application control parameters, JCL, and executable modules are almost always contained in libraries.

Virtual storage access method (VSAM) is an access method that provides much more complex functions than other disk access methods. VSAM is primarily for applications and cannot be edited with ISPF.

z/OS data sets have names with a maximum of 44 uppercase characters, divided by periods into qualifiers with a maximum of 8 bytes per qualifier name. The high-level qualifier (HLQ) may be fixed by system security controls, but the rest of a data set name is assigned by the user. A number of conventions exist for these names.

An existing data set can be located when the data set name, volume, and device type are known. These requirements can be shortened to knowing only the data set name if the data set is cataloged. The system catalog is a single logical function, although its data may be spread across the master catalog and many user catalogs. In practice, almost all disk data sets are cataloged. One side effect of this is that all (cataloged) data sets must have unique names.

A file in the UNIX file system can be either a text file or a binary file. In a text file, each line of text is separated by a new line delimiter. A binary file consists of sequences of binary words (byte stream), and no record concept other than the structure defined by an application exists. An application reading the file is responsible for interpreting the format of the data. z/OS treats an entire UNIX file system hierarchy as a collection of data sets. Each data set is a mountable file system.

Table 5-1 lists the key terms used in this chapter.

Table 5-1   Key terms in this chapter

block size	catalog	data set
high-level qualifier or HLQ	library	logical record length (LRECL)
member	PDS / PDSE	record format (RECFM)
system-managed storage	Virtual Storage Access Method (VSAM)	VTOC

5.16 Questions for review

To help test your understanding of the material in this chapter, complete the following questions:

1. What is a data set? What types of data sets are used on z/OS?
2. Why are unique data set names needed by z/OS?
3. Why is a PDS used?
4. Do application programs use libraries? Why or why not?
5. What determines the largest file a traditional UNIX system can use? Is there an equivalent limit for z/OS?
6. Do you see any patterns in temporary data set names?
7. What special characters are used to identify a temporary data set in a JCL stream?
8. The data set information provided by ISPF 3.4 is helpful. Why not display all the information on the basic data set list panel?
9. We created a source library in one of the exercises and specified fixed-length 80-byte records. Why?
10. The disk volume used for class exercises is *WORK02*. Can you allocate a data set on other volumes? On any volume?
11. What information about a data set is stored in a catalog? What DD operands would be required if a data set were not in the catalog?
12. What is the difference between the master catalog and a user catalog?

5.17 Exercises

The lab exercises in this chapter help you develop skills in working with data sets using ISPF. These skills are required for performing lab exercises in the remainder of this book.

To perform the lab exercises, you or your team require a TSO user ID and password (for assistance, see the instructor).

The exercises teach the following skills:

- ► Exploring ISPF Option 3.4
- ► Allocating a data set with ISPF 3.2
- ► Copying a source library
- ► Working with data set members

- ► Listing a data set and other ISPF 3.4 options
- ► Performing a catalog search

> **Tip:** The 3270 Enter key and the PC Enter key can be confused with each other. Most 3270 emulators permit the user to assign these functions to any key on the keyboard, and we assume that the 3270 Enter function is assigned to the right Ctrl key. Some z/OS users, however, prefer to have the large PC Enter key perform the 3270 Enter function and have Shift-Enter (or the numeric Enter key) perform the 3270 New Line function.

5.17.1 Exploring ISPF Option 3.4

One of the most useful ISPF panels is Option 3.4. You can access this option by, in the ISPF primary option menu, selecting Option 3 (Utilities) and then Option 4 (Dslist, for data set list). This sequence can be abbreviated by entering 3.4 in the primary menu, or =3.4 from any panel.

Many ISPF users work almost exclusively within the 3.4 panels. We cover some of the 3.4 functions here and others in subsequent exercises in this text. be careful when working with 3.4 options; they can affect changes on an individual or system-wide basis.

z/OS users typically use ISPF Option 3.4 to check the data sets on a DASD volume or examine the characteristics of a particular data set. Users might need to know:

- ► What data sets are on this volume.
- ► How many different data set types are on the volume.
- ► What are the DCB characteristics of a particular file.

Let us answer these questions using WORK02 as a sample volume, or another volume as specified by your instructor. Perform the following steps:

1. In the 3.4 panel, enter WORK02 in the Volume Serial field. Do not enter anything on the Option==> line or in the Dsname Level field.

2. Use PF8 and PF7 to scroll through the data set list that is produced.

3. Use PF11 and PF10 to scroll sideways to display more information. This is not really scrolling in this case; the additional information is obtained only when PF11 or PF10 is used.

   The first PF11 display provides tracks, percent used, XT, and device type. The XT value is the number of *extents* used to obtain the total tracks shown. The ISPF utility functions can determine the amount of space actually used for some data sets, and this is shown as a percentage when possible.

The next PF11 display shows the DCB characteristics: DSORG, RECFM, LRECL, and BLKSIZE. The data set organization (DSORG) types are:

PS	Sequential data set (QSAM and BSAM)
PO	Partitioned data set
VS	VSAM data set
blank	Unknown organization (or no data exists)

RECFM, LRECL, and BLKSIZE should be familiar. In some cases, usually when a standard access method is not used or when no data has been written, these parameters cannot be determined. VSAM data sets have no direct equivalent for these parameters and are shown as question marks.

Look at another volume for which a larger range of characteristics can be observed. The instructor can supply volume serial numbers. Another way to find such a volume is to use option 3.2 to find where SYS1.PARMLIB resides, then examine that volume.

5.17.2 Allocating a data set with ISPF 3.2

ISPF provides a convenient method for allocating data sets. In this exercise, you create a new library that you can use later in the course for storing program source data. The new data sets should be placed on the WORK02 volume and should be named *yourid*.LIB.SOURCE (where yourid is your student user ID).

For this exercise, assume that 10 tracks of primary space and 5 tracks for secondary extents is sufficient, and that 10 directory blocks is sufficient. Furthermore, we know we want to store 80-byte fixed-length records in the library. Perform the following steps:

1. Start at the ISPF primary menu.

2. Go to option 3.2, or go to option 3 (Utilities) and then go to option 2 (Data Set).

3. Type the letter A in the Option ==> field, but do not press Enter yet.

4. Type the name of the new data set in the Data Set Name field, but do not press Enter yet. The name can be with single quotes (for example, '*yourid*.LIB.SOURCE') or without quotes (LIB.SOURCE) so that TSO/ISPF automatically uses the current TSO user ID as the HLQ.

5. Enter WORK02 in the Volume Serial field and press Enter.

6. Complete the indicated fields and press Enter:
   - Space Units = TRKS
   - Primary quantity = 10
   - Secondary quantity = 5
   - Directory blocks = 10

- Record format = FB
- Record length = 80
- Block size = 0 (this tells z/OS to select an optimum value)
- Data set type = PDS

This should allocate a new PDS on WORK02. Check the upper right corner, where the following message appears:

```
Menu RefList Utilities Help
------------------------------------------------------------------------
Data Set Utility Data set allocated
Option ===>
A Allocate new data set C Catalog data set
.....
```

5.17.3 Copying a source library

A number of source programs are needed for exercises in ZPROF.ZSCHOLAR.LIB.SOURCE on WORK02. There are several ways to copy data sets (including libraries). Perform the following steps:

1. Go to ISPF option 3.3 (Utilities, Move/Copy).

2. On the first panel:

   a. Type C in the Option==> field.

   b. Type 'ZPROF.ZSCHOLAR.LIB.SOURCE' in the Data Set Name field. The single quotes are needed in this case.

   c. The Volume Serial is not needed because the data set is cataloged.

   d. Press Enter.

3. On the second panel:

   a. Type 'yourid.LIB.SOURCE' in the Data Set Name field and press Enter. If this PDS does not exist, type 1 to inherit the attributes of the source library. This should produce a panel listing all the members in the input library:

   b. Type S before every member name and then press Enter.

   This action copies all the indicated members from the source library to the target library. We could have specified 'ZPROF.ZSCHOLAR.LIB.SOURCE(*)' for the input data set; this would automatically copy all the members. This is one of the few cases where *wild cards* are used with z/OS data set names.

4. Create another library and move several members from LIB.SOURCE into the new library. Name the library 'yourid.MOVE.SOURCE'. Verify that the moved members are in the new library and no longer in the old one. Copy those members back into the LIB library. Verify that they exist in both libraries.

5. Rename a member in the MOVE library. Rename the MOVE library to `'yourid.TEST.SOURCE'`.

5.17.4 Working with data set members

There are several ways to add a new member to a library. We want to create a new member named TEST2 to the library that we previously edited. Perform the following steps:

1. From the ISPF primary menu, use option 2.

2. Enter the name of your library without specifying a member name, for example, *yourid*.JCL. This provides a list of member names already in the library.

3. Verify that member EDITTEST has the same contents you used earlier:

   a. If necessary, scroll so you can see member name EDITTEST.

   b. Move the cursor to the left of this line.

   c. Type S and press Enter.

   d. Look at your earlier work to assure yourself it is unchanged.

   e. Press PF3 to exit ("back out of") member EDITTEST. You will see the library member name list again.

4. Enter S TEST2 on the command line at the top of the panel and press Enter. (S TEST2 can be read as "select TEST2.") This creates member TEST2 and places the panel in input mode.

5. Enter a few lines of anything, using the commands and functions we discussed earlier.

6. Press PF3 to save TEST2 and exit from it.

7. Press PF3 again to exit from the ISPF Edit function.

Hereafter, we simply say "Enter xxx" when editing something or using other ISPF functions. This means (1) type xxx, and (2) press the Enter key. The New Line key (which has Enter printed on it) is used only to position the cursor on the panel.

5.17.5 Listing a data set and other ISPF 3.4 options

Go to the ISPF 3.4 panel. Enter *yourid* in the Dsname Level field and press Enter. This should list all the cataloged data sets in the system with the indicated HLQ. An alternative is to leave the Dsname Level field blank and enter WORK02 in the Volume Serial field; this lists all the data sets on the indicated volume. (If both fields are used, the list will contain only the cataloged data sets with a matching HLQ that appear on the specified volume.)

A number of functions can be invoked by entering the appropriate letter before a data set name. For example, position the cursor before one of the data set names and press PF1 (Help). The Help panel lists all the line commands that can be used from the data set name list of the 3.4 panel. Do not experiment with these commands without understanding their functions. Not all of these functions are relevant to this class. The relevant commands are:

E	Edit the data set.
B	Browse the data set.
D	Delete the data set.
R	Rename the data set.
Z	Compress a PDS library to recover lost space.
C	Catalog the data set.
U	Uncatalog the data set.

When a member list is displayed (as when a library is edited or browsed), several line commands are available:

S	Select this member for editing or browsing.
R	Rename the member.
D	Delete the member.

5.17.6 Performing a catalog search

The ISPF 3.4 option can be used for catalog searches on partial names. Use PF1 Help to learn more about this important function by performing the following steps:

1. Select option 3.4.

2. Press PF1 for help and select Display a data set list. Press Enter to scroll through the information panels.

3. Select Specifying the DSNAME LEVEL. Press Enter to scroll through the information panels.

4. Press PF3 to exit from the Help function.

Notice that the 3.4 DSNAME LEVEL field does not use quotes and the current TSO/E user ID is not automatically used as a prefix for names in this field. This is one of the few exceptions to the general rule for specifying data set names in TSO.

6

Using Job Control Language and System Display and Search Facility

Objective: As a technical professional in the world of mainframe computing, you need to know Job Control Language (JCL), the language that tells z/OS which resources are needed to process a batch job or start a system task.

After completing this chapter, you will be able to:

► Explain how JCL works with the system, JCL coding techniques, and a few of the more important statements and keywords.

► Create a simple job and submit it for execution.

► Check the output of your job through the System Display and Search Facility (SDSF).

Refer to Table 6-1 on page 263 for a list of key terms used in this chapter.

6.1 What is Job Control Language

Job Control Language (JCL) is used to tell the system what program to execute, followed by a description of program inputs and outputs. It is possible to *submit* JCL for batch processing or *start* a JCL procedure (PROC), which is considered a started task. The details of JCL can be complicated, but the general concepts are quite simple. Also, a small subset of JCL accounts for at least 90% of what is actually used. This chapter discusses selected JCL options.

JCL:
Tells the system what program to execute and defines its inputs and outputs.

While application programmers need some knowledge of JCL, the production control analyst responsible must be *highly* proficient with JCL, to create, monitor, correct, and rerun the company's daily batch workload.

There are three basic JCL statements:

JOB Provides a name (jobname) to the system for this batch workload. It can optionally include accounting information and a few job-wide parameters.

EXEC Provides the name of a program to execute. There can be multiple EXEC statements in a job. Each EXEC statement within the same job is a *job step*.

DD The Data Definition provides inputs and outputs to the execution program on the EXEC statement. This statement links a data set or other I/O device or function to a ddname coded in the program. DD statements are associated with a particular job step.

Figure 6-1 shows the basic JCL coding syntax.

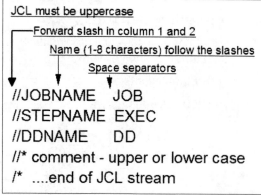

Figure 6-1   Basic JCL coding syntax

Example 6-1 shows some sample JCL.

Example 6-1   JCL example

```
//MYJOB     JOB 1
//MYSORT    EXEC PGM=SORT
//SORTIN    DD DISP=SHR,DSN=ZPROF.AREA.CODES
//SORTOUT   DD SYSOUT=*
//SYSOUT    DD SYSOUT=*
//SYSIN     DD *
  SORT FIELDS=(1,3,CH,A)
/*
```

In Chapter 4, "TSO/E, ISPF, and UNIX: Interactive facilities of z/OS" on page 165, we executed the same routine from the TSO READY prompt. Each JCL DD statement is equivalent to the TSO ALLOCATE command. Both are used to associate a z/OS data set with a *ddname*, which is recognized by the program as an input or output. The difference in method of execution is that TSO executes the sort in the foreground while JCL is used to execute the sort in the background.

When submitted for execution:

MYJOB	A jobname the system associates with this workload.
MYSORT	The stepname, which instructs the system to execute the SORT program.
SORTIN	On the DD statement, this is the ddname. The SORTIN ddname is coded in the SORT program as a program input. The data set name (DSN) on this DD statement is *ZPROF*.AREA.CODES. The data set can be shared (DISP=SHR) with other system processes. The data content of *ZPROF*.AREA.CODES is SORT program input.
SORTOUT	This ddname is the SORT program output.
SYSOUT	SYSOUT=* specifies sending system output messages to the Job Entry Subsystem (JES) print output area. It is possible to send the output to a data set.
SYSIN	DD * is another input statement. It specifies that what follows is data or control statements. In this case, it is the sort instruction telling the SORT program which fields of the SORTIN data records are to be sorted.

We use *JCL statements* in this text; some z/OS users use the older term *JCL card*, even though JCL resides in storage rather than punched cards.

6.2 JOB, EXEC, and DD parameters

The JOB, EXEC and DD statements have many parameters to allow the user to specify instructions and information. Describing them all would fill an entire book (refer to *z/OS MVS JCL Reference*, SA22-7597 for more information).

This section provides only a brief description of a few of the more commonly used parameters for the JOB, EXEC, and DD statements.

6.2.1 JOB parameters

JOB statement: JCL that identifies the job and the user who submits it.

The JOB statement `//MYJOB JOB 1` has the job name MYJOB. The 1 is an accounting field that can be subject to system exits that might be used for charging system users.

Some common JOB statement parameters include:

REGION=	Requests specific memory resources to be allocated to the job.
NOTIFY=	Sends notification of job completion to a particular user, such as the submitter of the job.
USER=	Specifies that the job will assume the authority of the user ID specified.
TYPRUN=	Delays or holds the job from running. It will be released later.
CLASS=	Directs a JCL statement to execute on a particular input queue.
MSGCLASS=	Directs job output to a particular output queue.
MSGLEVEL=	Controls the number of system messages to be received.

Here is an example of a JOB statement:

```
//MYJOB JOB 1,NOTIFY=&SYSUID,REGION=6M
```

6.2.2 EXEC parameters

EXEC statement: JCL that gives the name of a program to be executed.

The EXEC JCL statement `//MYSTEP EXEC` has a *stepname* of MYSTEP. Following the EXEC is either PGM=(executable program name) or a JCL procedure name. When a JCL PROC is present, then the parameters will be the variable substitutions required by the JCL PROC.

Common parameters found in the `EXEC PGM=` statement are:

PARM=   Parameters known by and passed to the program.

COND=   Boolean logic for controlling execution of other EXEC steps in this job. `IF`, `THEN`, `ELSE` JCL statements exist that are superior to using COND; however, lots of old JCL may exist in production environments using this statement.

TIME=   Imposes a time limit.

Here is an example of a EXEC statement:

```
//MYSTEP EXEC PGM=SORT
```

6.2.3 DD parameters

DD statement: Specifies inputs and outputs for the program in the EXEC statement.

The DD JCL statement `//MYDATA DD` has a ddname of MYDATA. The DD or Data Definition statement has significantly more parameters than the JOB or EXEC statements. The DD JCL statement can be involved with many aspects of defining or describing attributes of the program inputs or outputs. Some common DD statement parameters are:

DSN=   The name of the data set; this can include creation of temporary or new data sets or a reference back to the data set name.

DISP=   Data set disposition, such as whether the data set needs to be created or already exists, and whether the data set can be shared by more than one job. See 6.3, "Data set disposition and the DISP parameter" on page 246 for more information about this important parameter.

SPACE=   Amount of disk storage requested for a new data set.

SYSOUT=   Defines a print location (and the output queue or data set).

VOL=SER=   Volume name, disk name, or tape name.

UNIT=   System disk, tape, special device type, or esoteric (local name).

DEST=   Routes output to a remote destination.

DCB=   The data set control block parameter has numerous subparameters. The most common subparameters are:

    LRECL=   Logical record length, which is the number of bytes/characters in each record.

RECFM=	The record format, which can be fixed, blocked, variable, and so on.
BLOCKSIZE=	Stores records in a block of this size, typically a multiple of LRECL. A value of 0 will let the system pick the best value.
DSORG=	This is the data set organization, which can be sequential, partitioned, and so on.
LABEL=	The tape label expected (No Label or Standard Label followed by data set location). A tape can store multiple data sets; each data set on the tape is in a file position. The first data set on tape is file 1.
DUMMY	Results in a null input or throwing away data written to this ddname.
*	Input data or control statements follow. This is a method of passing data to a program from the JCL stream.
*,DLM=	Everything following this statement is data input (even //) until the two alphanumeric or special characters specified are encountered in column 1.

6.3 Data set disposition and the DISP parameter

All JCL parameters are important, but the DISP function is perhaps the most important one for DD statements. Among its other uses, the DISP parameter advises the system about the data set enqueuing needed for this job to prevent conflicting usage of the data set by other jobs.

The complete parameter has these fields:

```
DISP=(status,normal end,abnormal end)
DISP=(status,normal end)
DISP=status
```

Where status can be NEW, OLD, SHR, or MOD:

NEW	Indicates that a new data set will be created. This job has exclusive access to the data set while it is running. The data set must not already exist on the same volume as the new data set or be in a system or user catalog.
OLD	Indicates that the data set already exists and that this job will have exclusive access to it while it is running.

SHR	Indicates that the data set already exists and that several concurrent jobs can share access while they are running. All the concurrent jobs must specify SHR.
MOD	Indicates that the data set already exists and the current job must have exclusive access while it is running. If the current job opens the data set for output, the output will be appended to the current end of the data set.

Job step:
The JCL statements that request and control execution of a program and that specify the resources needed to run the program.

The *normal end* parameter indicates what to do with the data set (the *disposition*) if the current job step ends normally. Likewise, the abnormal end parameter indicates what to do with the data set if the current job step abnormally ends.

The options are the same for both parameters:

DELETE	Delete (and uncatalog) the data set at the end of the job step.
KEEP	Keep (but not catalog) the data set at the end of the job step.
CATLG	Keep and catalog the data set at the end of the job step.
UNCATLG	Keep the data set but uncatalog it at the end of the job step.
PASS	Allow a later job step to specify a final disposition.

The default disposition parameters (for normal and abnormal end) are to leave the data set as it was before the job step started. (We discussed catalogs in 5.11.2, "What is a catalog" on page 223.)

You might wonder, what would happen if you specified DISP=NEW for a data set that already exists? Very little, actually! To guard against the inadvertent erasure of files, z/OS rejects a DISP=NEW request for an existing data set. You get a JCL error message instead of a new data set.

6.3.1 Creating new data sets

If the DISP parameter for a data set is NEW, you must provide more information, including:

- ► A data set name.
- ► The type of device for the data set.
- ► A volser if it is a disk or labeled tape.
- ► If a disk is used, the amount of space to be allocated for the primary extent must be specified.

- ▶ If it is a partitioned data set, the size of the directory must be specified.

- ▶ Optionally, DCB parameters can be specified. Alternately, the program that will write the data set can provide these parameters.

The DISP and data set names have already been described. Briefly, the other parameters are:

Volser
The format for this in a DD statement is VOL=SER=*xxxxxx*, where xxxxxx is the volser. The VOL parameter can specify other details, which is the reason for the format.

Device type
There are a number of ways to do this, but UNIT=*xxxx* is the most common statement. The xxxx can be an IBM device type (such as 3390), or a specific device address (such as 300), or an *esoteric name* defined by the installation (such as SYSDA). Typically, you code SYSDA to tell the system to choose any available disk volume from a pool of available devices.

Member name
Remember that a library (or partitioned data set (PDS)) member can be treated as a data set by many applications and utilities. The format DSNAME=*ZPROF*.LIB.CNTL(TEST) is used to reference a specific member. If the application or utility program is expecting a sequential data set, then either a sequential data set or a member of a library must be specified. A whole library name (without a specific member name) can be used only if the program/utility is expecting a library name.

SPACE

The SPACE DD parameter is required for allocating data sets on DASD. It identifies the space required for your data set. Before a data set can be created on disk, the system must know how much space the data set requires and how the space is to be measured.

There are a number of different formats and variations for this. Common examples are:

SPACE=(TRK,10)   Ten tracks with no secondary extents

SPACE=(TRK,(10,5))   Ten tracks for the primary, five tracks for each secondary extent

SPACE=(CYL,5)   Can use CYL (cylinders) instead of TRK

SPACE=(TRK,(10,5,8))   PDS with eight directory blocks

SPACE=(1000,(50000,10000)) Primary 50000 records @ 1000 bytes each

In the basic case, SPACE has two parameters. These are the unit of measurement and the amount of space. The unit of measure can be tracks, cylinders, or the average block size.[1]

The amount of space typically has up to three subparameters:

▶ The first parameter is the primary extent size, expressed in terms of the unit of measure. The system attempts to obtain a single extent (contiguous space) with this much space. If the system cannot obtain this space in less than five extents (on a single volume) before the job starts, the job is failed.

▶ The second parameter, if used, is the size of each secondary extent. The system does not obtain this much space before the job starts and does not guarantee that this space is available. The system obtains secondary extents dynamically, while the job is executing. In the basic examples shown here, the secondary extents are on the same volume as the primary extent.

▶ The third parameter, if it exists, indicates that a partitioned data set (library) is being created. This is the only indication that a PDS is being created instead of another type of data set. The numeric value is the number of directory blocks (255 bytes each) that are assigned for the PDS directory. (Another JCL parameter is needed to create a PDSE instead of a PDS.)

If the space parameter contains more than one subparameter, the whole space parameter must be inclosed in parentheses.

6.4 Continuation and concatenation

Concatenation: A single ddname can have multiple DD statements (input data sets).

As a consequence of the limitations of the number of characters that could be contained in single 80-column punched cards used in earlier systems, z/OS introduced the concepts of continuation and concatenation. Therefore, z/OS retained these conventions to minimize the impact on previous applications and operations.

Continuation of JCL syntax involves a comma at the end of the last complete parameter. The next JCL line would include // followed by at least one space, and then the additional parameters. JCL parameter syntax on a continuation line must begin on or before column sixteen and should not extend beyond column 72.[2]

---

[1] The unit of measure can also be KB and MB, but these are not as commonly used.
[2] Columns 73 through 80 are reserved for card sequence numbers.

Note the following example JCL statement:

```
//JOBCARD JOB 1,REGION=8M,NOTIFY=ZPROF
```

The JCL statement above would have the same result as the following continuation JCL:

```
//JOBCARD JOB 1,
//         REGION=8M,
//         NOTIFY=ZPROF
```

An important feature of DD statements is the fact that a single ddname can have multiple DD statements. This is called *concatenation*.

The following JCL indicates that data sets are concatenated:

```
//DATAIN DD DISP=OLD,DSN=MY.INPUT1
//       DD DISP=OLD,DSN=MY.INPUT2
//       DD DISP=SHR,DSN=YOUR.DATA
```

Concatenation applies only to input data sets. The data sets are automatically processed in sequence. In our example, when the application program reads to the end of MY.INPUT1, the system automatically opens MY.INPUT2 and starts reading it. The application program is not aware that it is now reading a second data set. This continues until the last data in the concatenation is read; at that point, the application receives an end-of-file indication.

6.5 Why z/OS uses symbolic file names

z/OS normally uses symbolic file names,[3] and this is another defining characteristic of this operating system. It applies a naming redirection between a data set-related name used in a program and the actual data set used during execution of that program.

---

[3] This function applies to normal traditional processing. Some languages, such as C, have defined interfaces that bypass this function.

Figure 6-2 shows an example of symbolic file names.

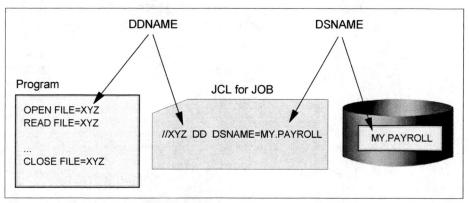

Figure 6-2   DDNAME and DSNAME

Symbolic file name:
A naming redirection between a data set-related name used in a program and the actual data set used during execution of that program.

In Figure 6-2, we have a program, in some arbitrary language, that needs to open and read a data set.[4] When the program is written, the name XYZ is arbitrarily selected to reference the data set. The program can be compiled and stored as an executable. When someone wants to run the executable program, a JCL statement must be supplied that relates the name XYZ to an actual data set name. This JCL statement is a DD statement. The symbolic name used in the program is a DDNAME and the real name of the data set is a DSNAME.

The program can be used to process different input data sets simply by changing the DSNAME in the JCL. This capability becomes significant for large commercial applications that might use dozens of data sets in a single execution of the program. A payroll program for a large corporation is a good example.

---

[4] The pseudo-program uses the term *file*, as is common in most computer languages.

A payroll program can be an exceptionally complex application that might use hundreds of data sets. The same program might be used for different divisions in the corporation by running it with different JCL, as shown in Figure 6-3. Likewise, it can be tested against special test data sets by using a different set of JCL.

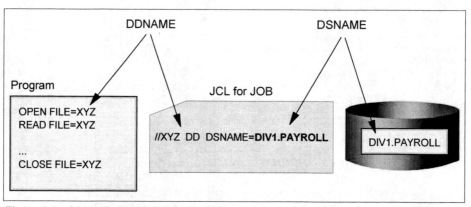

Figure 6-3   Symbolic file name: Same program, but another data set

The firm could use the same company-wide payroll application program for different divisions and only change a single parameter in the JCL card (DD DSN=DIV1.PAYROLL). The parameter value DIV1.PAYROLL causes the program to access the data set for Division 1. This example demonstrates the power and flexibility afforded by JCL and symbolic file names.

This DDNAME--JCL--DSNAME processing applies to all traditional z/OS work, although it might not always be apparent. For example, when ISPF is used to edit a data set, ISPF builds the internal equivalent of a DD statement and then opens the requested data set with the DD statement. The ISPF user does not see this processing; it takes place "transparently."[5]

---

[5] Here, we are temporarily ignoring some of the operational characteristics of the z/OS UNIX interfaces of z/OS; the discussion applies to traditional z/OS usage.

6.6 Reserved DDNAMES

A programmer can select *almost* any name for a DD name, but using a meaningful name (within the eight character limit) is recommended.

There are a few reserved DD names that a programmer cannot use (all of these are optional DD statements):

```
//JOBLIB DD ...
//STEPLIB DD ...
//JOBCAT DD ...
//STEPCAT DD ...
//SYSABEND DD ...
//SYSUDUMP DD ...
//SYSMDUMP DD ...
//CEEDUMP DD ...
```

A JOBLIB DD statement, placed just after a JOB statement, specifies a library that should be searched first for the programs executed by this job. A STEPLIB DD statement, placed just after an EXEC statement, specifies a library that should be searched first for the program executed by the EXEC statement. A STEPLIB overrides a JOBLIB if both are used.

JOBCAT and STEPCAT are used to specify private catalogs, but these are rarely used (the most recent z/OS releases no longer support private catalogs). Nevertheless, these DD names should be treated as reserved names.

The SYSABEND, SYSUDUMP, SYSMDUMP, and CEEDUMP DD statements are used for various types of memory dumps that are generated when a program abnormally ends (ABENDs.)

6.7 JCL procedures (PROCs)

PROC:
A procedure library member that contains part (usually the fixed part) of the JCL for a given task.

Some programs and tasks require a larger amount of JCL than a user can easily enter. JCL for these functions can be kept in procedure libraries. A procedure library member contains *part* of the JCL for a given task (usually the fixed, unchanging part of JCL). The user of the procedure supplies the variable part of the JCL for a specific job. In other words, a JCL procedure is like a macro.

Such a procedure is sometimes known as a *cataloged procedure*. A cataloged procedure is not related to the system catalog; rather, the name is a carryover from another operating system.

Example 6-2 shows an example of a JCL procedure (PROC).

Example 6-2   Example JCL procedure

```
//MYPROC     PROC
//MYSORT     EXEC PGM=SORT
//SORTIN     DD DISP=SHR,DSN=&SORTDSN
//SORTOUT    DD SYSOUT=*
//SYSOUT     DD SYSOUT=*
//           PEND
```

Much of this JCL should be recognizable now. JCL functions presented here include:

▶ PROC and PEND statements are unique to procedures. They are used to identify the beginning and end of the JCL procedure.

▶ PROC is preceded by a label or name; the name defined in Example 6-2 is MYPROC.

▶ JCL variable substitution is the reason JCL PROCs are used. &SORTDSN is the only variable in Example 6-2.

In Example 6-3, we include the inline procedure in Example 6-2 in our job stream.

Example 6-3   Sample inline procedure

```
//MYJOB      JOB 1
//*-------------------------------*
//MYPROC     PROC
//MYSORT     EXEC PGM=SORT
//SORTIN     DD DISP=SHR,DSN=&SORTDSN
//SORTOUT    DD SYSOUT=*
//SYSOUT     DD SYSOUT=*
//           PEND
//*-------------------------------*
//STEP1      EXEC MYPROC,SORTDSN=ZPROF.AREA.CODES
//SYSIN      DD *
  SORT FIELDS=(1,3,CH,A)
```

When MYJOB is submitted, the JCL from Example 6-2 is effectively substituted for EXEC MYPROC. The value for &SORTDSN must be provided.

SORTDSN and its value were placed on a separate line, a continuation of the EXEC statement. Notice the comma after MYPROC.

`//SYSIN DD *` followed by the SORT control statement will be appended to the substituted JCL.

6.7.1 JCL PROC statement override

When an entire JCL PROC statement needs to be replaced, then a JCL PROC override statement can be used. An override statement has the following form:

`//stepname.ddname DD ...`

Example 6-4 shows an example of overriding the `SORTOUT` DD statement in `MYPROC`. Here, `SORTOUT` is directed to a newly created sequential data set.

Example 6-4   Sample procedure with statement override

```
//MYJOB     JOB 1
//*-------------------------------*
//MYPROC     PROC
//MYSORT     EXEC PGM=SORT
//SORTIN     DD DISP=SHR,DSN=&SORTDSN
//SORTOUT    DD SYSOUT=*
//SYSOUT     DD SYSOUT=*
//          PEND
//*-------------------------------*
//STEP1      EXEC MYPROC,SORTDSN=ZPROF.AREA.CODES
//MYSORT.SORTOUT DD DSN=ZPROF.MYSORT.OUTPUT,
//           DISP=(NEW,CATLG),SPACE=(CYL,(1,1)),
//           UNIT=SYSDA,VOL=SER=SHARED,
//           DCB=(LRECL=20,BLKSIZE=0,RECFM=FB,DSORG=PS)
//SYSIN      DD *
  SORT FIELDS=(1,3,CH,A)
```

6.7.2 How a job is submitted for batch processing

Using UNIX and AIX as an analogy, a UNIX process can be processed in the background by appending an ampersand (&) to the end of a command or script. Pressing Enter then submits the work as a background process.

In z/OS terminology, work (a job) is submitted for batch processing. Batch processing is a rough equivalent to UNIX background processing. The job runs independently of the interactive session. The term batch is used because it is a large collection of jobs that can be queued, waiting their turn to be executed when the needed resources are available.

Commands to submit jobs might take any of the following forms:

ISPF editor command line SUBmit and press Enter.

ISPF command shell SUBmit 'USER.JCL', where the data set is sequential.

ISPF command line TSO SUBmit 'USER.JCL', where the data set is sequential.

ISPF command line TSO SUBmit 'USER.JCL(MYJOB)', where the data set is a library or partitioned data set containing member MYJOB.

TSO command line SUBmit 'USER.JCL'

Figure 6-4 shows three different points at which you can enter the SUBMIT command.

```
ISPF EDIT command line:

  EDIT ---- userid.SORT.JCL ----------------------LINE 00000000 COL 001 080
  COMMAND ===> SUBMIT                                       SCROLL ===> CSR
  ***************************** TOP OF DATA *****************************
  //userid  JOB 'accounting data',
                      .
                      .
                      .


TSO/E command line:

  ---------------------- TSO COMMAND PROCESSOR -------------------------
  ENTER TSO COMMAND OR CLIST BELOW:


  ===> SUBMIT 'userid.SORT.JCL'




  ENTER SESSION MANAGER MODE ===> NO     (YES or NO)


After READY mode message:

     .
     .
     .
    READY
   SUBMIT 'userid.SORT.JCL'
```

Figure 6-4 Several ways to submit a JCL stream for processing

6.8 Understanding SDSF

After submitting a job, it is common to use the *System Display and Search Facility* (SDSF) to review the output for successful completion or review and correct JCL errors. SDSF allows you to display printed output held in the JES spool area. Much of the printed output sent to JES by batch jobs (and other jobs) is never actually printed. Instead it is inspected using SDSF and deleted or used as needed.

SDSF provides a number of additional functions, including:

SDSF:
Displays printed output held in the JES spool area for inspection.

► Viewing the system log and searching for any literal string

► Entering system commands (in earlier versions of the operating system, only the operator could enter commands)

► Controlling job processing (hold, release, cancel, and purge jobs)

► Monitoring jobs while they are being processed

► Displaying job output before deciding to print it

► Controlling the order in which jobs are processed

► Controlling the order in which output is printed

► Controlling printers and initiators

Figure 6-5 shows the SDSF primary option menu.

```
  Display  Filter  View  Print  Options  Help
 ---------------------------------------------------------------------------
 ISFPCU41----------------  SDSF PRIMARY OPTION MENU  --------------------------
 COMMAND INPUT ===> _                                    SCROLL ===> PAGE

 DA      Active users                 INIT   Initiators
 I       Input queue                  PR     Printers
 O       Output queue                 PUN    Punches
 H       Held output queue            RDR    Readers
 ST      Status of jobx               LINE   Lines
                                      NODE   Nodes
 LOG     System log                   SO     Spool offload
 SR      System requests              SP     Spool volumes
 MAS     Members in the MAS
 JC      Job classes                  ULOG   User session log
 SE      Scheduling environments
 RES     WLM resources
 ENC     Enclaves
 PS      Processes

 END     Exit SDSF

 Licensed Materials - Property of IBM

 5694-A01 (C) Copyright IBM Corp. 1981, 2002. All rights reserved.
 US Government Users Restricted Rights - Use, duplication or
 disclosure restricted by GSA ADP Schedule Contract with IBM Corp.


  F1=HELP        F2=SPLIT       F3=END         F4=RETURN     F5=IFIND       F6=BOOK
  F7=UP          F8=DOWN        F9=SWAP        F10=LEFT      F11=RIGHT      F12=RETRIEVE
```

Figure 6-5   SDSF primary option menu

SDSF uses a hierarchy of online panels to guide users through its functions, as shown in Figure 6-6.

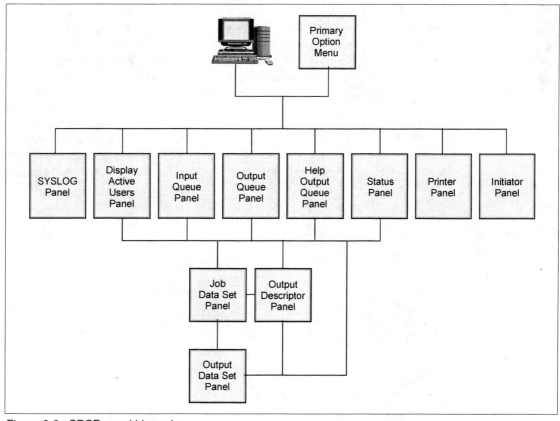

Figure 6-6 SDSF panel hierarchy

You can see the JES output data sets created during the execution of your batch job. They are saved on the JES spool data set.

You can see the JES data sets in any of the following queues:

I	Input
DA	Execution queue
O	Output queue
H	Held queue
ST	Status queue

For output and held queues, you cannot see those JES data sets you requested to be automatically purged by setting a MSGCLASS sysout class that has been defined to not save output. Also, depending on the MSGCLASS you chose for the JOB card, the sysouts can be either in the output queue or in the held queue.

Jobname:
The name by which a job is known to the system (JCL statement).

Screen 1 in Figure 6-7 displays a list of the jobs we submitted and whose output we directed to the held (Class T) queue, as identified in the MSGCLASS=T parameter on the job card. In our case, only one job has been submitted and executed. Therefore, we only have one job on the held queue. Entering a ? command in the NP column displays the output files generated by job 7359.

Screen 2 in Figure 6-7 displays three ddnames: the JES2 messages log file, the JES2 JCL file, and the JES2 system messages file. This option is useful when you are seeing jobs with many files directed to SYSOUT and you want to display one associated with a specific step. You issue an S in the NP column to select a file you want.

Screen 1

```
  Display  Filter  View  Print  Options  Help
-----------------------------------------------------------------------
SDSF HELD OUTPUT DISPLAY ALL CLASSES   LINES 44        LINE 1-1 (1)
COMMAND INPUT ===>                                     SCROLL ===> PAGE
PREFIX=*  DEST=(ALL)  OWNER=*   SYSNAME=
NP   JOBNAME  JobID    Owner    Prty C ODisp Dest          Tot-Rec  Tot-
?_   MIRIAM2  JOB26044 MIRIAM    144 T HOLD  LOCAL              44
```

Screen 2

```
  Display  Filter  View  Print  Options  Help
-----------------------------------------------------------------------
SDSF JOB DATA SET DISPLAY - JOB MIRIAM2  (JOB26044)    LINE 1-3 (3)
COMMAND INPUT ===> _                                   SCROLL ===> PAGE
PREFIX=*  DEST=(ALL)  OWNER=*   SYSNAME=
NP   DDNAME    StepName ProcStep DSID Owner    C Dest       Rec-Cnt Page
     JESMSGLG  JES2               2 MIRIAM    T LOCAL           20
     JESJCL    JES2               3 MIRIAM    T LOCAL           12
     JESYSMSG  JES2               4 MIRIAM    T LOCAL           12
```

Figure 6-7   SDSF viewing the JES2 Output files

To see all files, instead of a ?, type S in the NP column; the JES2 job log is displayed similar to the one shown in Example 6-5.

Example 6-5   JES2 job log

```
J E S 2   J O B   L O G   --   S Y S T E M   S C 6 4   --   N O D E

13.19.24 JOB26044 ---- WEDNESDAY, 27 AUG 2003 ----
13.19.24 JOB26044  IRR010I  USERID MIRIAM   IS ASSIGNED TO THIS JOB.
13.19.24 JOB26044  ICH70001I MIRIAM   LAST ACCESS AT 13:18:53 ON WEDNESDAY, AUGU
13.19.24 JOB26044  $HASP373 MIRIAM2  STARTED - INIT 1   - CLASS A - SYS SC64
13.19.24 JOB26044  IEF403I MIRIAM2 - STARTED - ASID=0027 - SC64
13.19.24 JOB26044  -                                        --TIMINGS (MINS.)--
13.19.24 JOB26044  -JOBNAME  STEPNAME PROCSTEP   RC   EXCP    CPU    SRB  CLOCK
13.19.24 JOB26044  -MIRIAM2           STEP1      00      9    .00    .00    .00
13.19.24 JOB26044  IEF404I MIRIAM2 - ENDED - ASID=0027 - SC64
13.19.24 JOB26044  -MIRIAM2  ENDED.  NAME-MIRIAM            TOTAL CPU TIME=
13.19.24 JOB26044  $HASP395 MIRIAM2  ENDED
------ JES2 JOB STATISTICS ------
  27 AUG 2003 JOB EXECUTION DATE
          11 CARDS READ
          44 SYSOUT PRINT RECORDS
           0 SYSOUT PUNCH RECORDS
           3 SYSOUT SPOOL KBYTES
        0.00 MINUTES EXECUTION TIME
         1 //MIRIAM2 JOB 19,MIRIAM,NOTIFY=&SYSUID,MSGCLASS=T,
        // MSGLEVEL=(1,1),CLASS=A
        IEFC653I SUBSTITUTION JCL - 19,MIRIAM,NOTIFY=MIRIAM,MSGCLASS=T,MSGLEVE
         2 //STEP1 EXEC PGM=IEFBR14
        //*-------------------------------------------------*
//* THIS IS AN EXAMPLE OF A NEW DATA SET ALLOCATION
        //*-------------------------------------------------*
         3 //NEWDD DD   DSN=MIRIAM.IEFBR14.TEST1.NEWDD,
        //           DISP=(NEW,CATLG,DELETE),UNIT=SYSDA,
        //           SPACE=(CYL,(10,10,45)),LRECL=80,BLKSIZE=3120
         4 //SYSPRINT  DD  SYSOUT=T
        /*
ICH70001I MIRIAM   LAST ACCESS AT 13:18:53 ON WEDNESDAY, AUGUST 27, 2003
IEF236I ALLOC. FOR MIRIAM2 STEP1
IGD100I 390D ALLOCATED TO DDNAME NEWDD   DATACLAS (         )
IEF237I JES2 ALLOCATED TO SYSPRINT
IEF142I MIRIAM2 STEP1 - STEP WAS EXECUTED - COND CODE 0000
IEF285I   MIRIAM.IEFBR14.TEST1.NEWDD                 CATALOGED
IEF285I   VOL SER NOS= SBOX38.
IEF285I   MIRIAM.MIRIAM2.JOB26044.D0000101.?         SYSOUT
IEF373I STEP/STEP1  /START 2003239.1319
IEF374I STEP/STEP1  /STOP 2003239.1319 CPU   0MIN 00.00SEC SRB   0MIN 00.00S
IEF375I  JOB/MIRIAM2 /START 2003239.1319
IEF376I  JOB/MIRIAM2 /STOP 2003239.1319 CPU   0MIN 00.00SEC SRB   0MIN 00.00S
```

6.9 Utilities

z/OS includes a number of programs called *utilities*, which are useful in batch processing. These programs provide many small, obvious, and useful functions. A basic set of system-provided utilities is described in Appendix C, "Utility programs" on page 649.

Customer sites often add their own customer-written utility programs (although most users refrain from naming them utilities) and many of these are widely shared by the user community. Independent software vendors also provide many similar products (for a fee).

6.10 System libraries

z/OS has many standard system libraries. A brief description of several libraries is appropriate here. The traditional libraries include:

▶ SYS1.PROCLIB: This library contains JCL procedures distributed with z/OS. In practice, there are many other JCL procedure libraries (supplied with various program products) concatenated with it.

▶ SYS1.PARMLIB: This library contains control parameters for z/OS and for some program products. In practice, there may be other libraries concatenated with it.

▶ SYS1.LINKLIB: This library contains many of the basic execution modules of the system. In practice, it is one of a large number of execution libraries that are concatenated.

▶ SYS1.LPALIB: This library contains system execution modules that are loaded into the link pack area when the system is initialized. There may be several other libraries concatenated with it. Programs stored here are available to other address spaces.

▶ SYS1.NUCLEUS: This library contains the basic supervisor ("kernel") modules of z/OS.

▶ SYS1.SVCLIB: This library contains user-written routines (appendages) to the operating system routines known as supervisor calls (SVCs).

These libraries are in standard PDS format and are found on the system disk volumes. They are discussed in more detail in 16.3.1, "z/OS system libraries" on page 533.

6.11 Summary

Basic JCL contains three types of statements: JOB, EXEC, and DD. A job can contain several EXEC statements (*steps*) and each step might have several DD statements. JCL provides a wide range of parameters and controls; only a basic subset is described here.

A batch job uses ddnames to access data sets. A JCL DD statement connects the ddname to a specific data set (DS name) for one execution of the program. A program can access different groups of data sets (in different jobs) by changing the JCL for each job.

The DISP parameters of DD statements help to prevent unwanted simultaneous access to data sets. This is important for general system operation. The DISP parameter is not a security control; it helps manage the integrity of data sets. New data sets can be created through JCL by using the DISP=NEW parameter and specifying the desired amount of space and the desired volume.

System users are expected to write simple JCL, but normally use JCL procedures for more complex jobs. A cataloged procedure is written once and can then be used by many users. z/OS supplies many JCL procedures, and locally-written ones can be added easily. A user must understand how to override or extend statements in a JCL procedure to supply the parameters (usually DD statements) needed for a specific job.

Table 6-1 lists the key terms used in this chapter.

Table 6-1   Key terms used in this chapter

concatenation	DD statement	EXEC statement
job control language (JCL)	JOB statement	job step
jobname	PROC	SDSF
symbolic file name	system library	utility

6.12 Questions for review

To help test your understanding of the material in this chapter, answer the following review questions:

1. In the procedure fragment and job in 6.7, "JCL procedures (PROCs)" on page 253, where is the COBOL source code? What is the likely output data set for the application? What is the likely input data set? How would we code the JCL for a SYSOUT data set for the application?

2. We have three DD statements:

```
//DD1   DD   UNIT=3480,...
//DD2   DD   UNIT=0560,...
//DD3   DD   UNIT=560,...
```

What do these numbers mean? How do we know this?

3. JCL can be submitted or started. What is the difference?

4. Explain the relationship between a data set name, a DD name, and the file name within a program.

5. Which JCL statement (JOB, EXEC, or DD) has the most parameters? Why?

6. What is the difference between JCL and a JCL PROC? What is the benefit of using a JCL PROC?

7. To override a JCL PROC statement in the JCL stream executing the PROC, what PROC names must be known? What is the order of the names on the JCL override statement?

8. When a JCL job has multiple EXEC statements, what is the type of name associated with each EXEC statement?

6.13 Topics for further discussion

This material is intended to be discussed in class, and these discussions should be regarded as part of the basic course text:

1. Why has the advent of database systems potentially changed the need for large numbers of DD statements?

2. The first positional parameter of a JOB statement is an accounting field. How important is accounting for mainframe usage? Why?

6.14 Exercises

The lab exercises in this chapter help you develop skills for creating batch jobs and submitting them for execution on z/OS. These skills are required for performing lab exercises in the remainder of this text.

To perform the lab exercises, you or your team requires a TSO user ID and password (for assistance, see the instructor).

The exercises teach the following tasks:

- ► Creating a simple job
- ► Using ISPF in split screen mode
- ► Manipulating text in ISPF
- ► Submitting a job and checking the results
- ► Creating a PDS member
- ► Copying a PDS member

6.14.1 Creating a simple job

Perform the following steps:

1. From ISPF, navigate to the Data Set List Utility panel and enter *yourid*.JCL in the Dsname Level field (described in an earlier exercise).

2. Enter e (edit) to the left (in the command column) of *yourid*.JCL. Enter s (select) to the left of member JCLTEST. Enter RESet on the editor command line.

3. Notice that only a single JCL line is in the data set, that is, EXEC PGM=IEFBR14. This is a system utility that does not request any input or output and is designed to complete with a successful return code (0). Enter SUBMIT or SUB on the command line and press Enter.

4. Enter 1 in response to the following message:

   IKJ56700A ENTER JOBNAME CHARACTER(S) -

   The result will be the following message:

   IKJ56250I JOB *yourid*1(JOB00037) SUBMITTED

   Whenever you see three asterisks (***), it means there is more data to see. Press Enter to continue.

   When the job finishes, you should see the following message:

   $HASP165 *yourid*1 ENDED AT SYS1 MAXCC=0 CN(INTERNAL)

5. Add (insert) a new first line in your file that will hold a JOB statement. The JOB statement must precede the EXEC statement. (Hint: Replicate (r) the single EXEC statement, then overwrite the EXEC statement with your JOB statement.)   This JOB statement should read:

   //*yourid*A JOB 1

   Replace yourid with your team user ID, leave the A, then submit this JCL and press PF3 to save the file and exit the editor.

6. From the ISPF Primary Option Menu, find SDSF (described in 7.9.5, "Using SDSF" on page 294). You can use the split screen function for a new screen session, giving you one session for the DSLIST and the other for SDSF.

7. In the SDSF menu, enter `PREFIX yourid*`, then enter `ST` (Status Panel). Both jobs that you submitted should be listed. Place `S` (select) to the left of either job, then page up and down to view the messages produced from the execution. Press PF3 to exit.

8. Edit JCLTEST again, and insert the following lines at the bottom:

```
//CREATE DD DSN=yourid.MYTEST,DISP=(NEW,CATLG),
// UNIT=SYSDA,SPACE=(TRK,1)
```

9. Submit the content of JCLTEST created above, press PF3 (save and exit edit), then view the output of this job using SDSF. Notice that you have two jobs with the same jobname. The jobname with the highest JOBID number is the last one that was run.

   a. What was the condition code? If it was greater than 0, page down to the bottom of the output listing to locate the JCL error message. Correct the JCLTEST and resubmit. Repeat until `cond code=0000` is received.

   b. Navigate to the Data Set List Utility panel (`=3.4`) and enter *yourid*.MYTEST in the DSNAME level field. What volume was used to store the data set?

   c. Enter `DEL` / in the numbered left (command) column of the data set to delete the data set. A confirmation message may appear asking you to confirm that you want to delete the data set.

   d. We just learned that batch execution of program IEFBR14, which requires no inputs or outputs, returns a condition code 0 (success) if there were no JCL errors. Although IEFBR14 does no I/O, JCL instructions are read and executed by the system. This program is useful for creating (DISP=NEW) and deleting (DISP=(OLD,DELETE)) data sets on a DD statement.

10. From any ISPF panel, enter the following command in the Command Field `==>`:

```
TSO SUBMIT JCL(JCLERROR)
```

   Your user ID is the prefix (high-level qualifier) of data set JCL containing member JCLERROR.

   a. You will be prompted to enter a suffix character for a generated job card. Take note of the jobname and job number from the submit messages.

   b. Use SDSF and select the job output. Page down to the bottom. Do you see the JCL error? What are the incorrect and correct JCL DD operands? Correct the JCL error located in *yourid*.JCL(JCLERROR). Resubmit JCLERROR to validate your correction.

11. From any ISPF panel, enter `TSO SUBMIT JCL(SORT)`. Your user ID is the assumed prefix of data set JCL containing member SORT.

   a. You will be prompted to enter a suffix character for a generated job card. Take note of the jobname and job number from the submit messages.

b. Use SDSF and place a ? to the left of the job name. The individual listing from the job will be displayed. Place s (select) to the left of SORTOUT to view the sort output, then press PF3 to return. Select JESJCL. Notice the "job statement generated message" and the "substitution JCL" messages.

12. Purge some (or all) unnecessary job output. From SDSF, place a p (purge) to the left of any job that you would like to purge from the JES output queue.

13. From the ISPF panel, enter TSO SUBMIT JCL(SORT) and review the output.

14. From the ISPF panel, enter TSO SUBMIT JCL(SORTPROC) and review the output. You may not see the output in the SDSF ST panel, because the jobname is not starting with *yourid*. To see all output, enter PRE *, then OWNER *yourid* to see only the jobs that are owned by you.

15. What JCL differences exist between SORT and SORTPROC? In both JCL streams, the SYSIN DD statement references the sort control statement. Where is the sort control statement located?

> **Tip:** All JCL references to &SYSUID are replaced with the user ID that submitted the job.

16. Edit the partitioned data set member containing the SORT control statement. Change FIELD=(1,3,CH,A) to FIELD=(6,20,CH,A). Press PF3 and then from the ISPF panel enter TSO SUBMIT JCL(SORT). Review the job's output using SDSF. Was this sorted by code or area?

17. From the ISPF panel, enter TSO LISTC ALL. By default, this command will list all catalog entries for data sets beginning with *yourid*. The system catalog will return the data set names, the name of the catalog storing the detailed information, the volume location, and a devtype number that equates to specific values for JCL UNIT= operand. LISTC is an abbreviation for LISTCAT.

6.14.2 Using ISPF in split screen mode

As discussed earlier, most ISPF users favor a split screen. This is easily accomplished by performing the following steps:

1. Move the cursor to the bottom (or top) line.

2. Press PF2 to split the screen.

3. Press PF9 to switch between the two screens.

4. Press PF3 (perhaps several times) to exit from one of the splits. The screen need not be split at the top or bottom. The split line can be positioned on any line by using PF2. More than two screens can be used.

Try using these ISPF commands:

```
START
SWAP LIST          -
SWAP <screen number.>
```

6.14.3 Manipulating text in ISPF

After logging on to TSO/E and activating ISPF, look at the primary option menu and perform the following steps:

1. Enter each option and write down its purpose and function. Each team should prepare a brief summary for one of the 12 functions on the ISPF panel (items 0-11). Note that z/OS installations often heavily customize the ISPF panels to suit their needs.

2. Create a test member in a partitioned data set. Enter some lines of information, then experiment with the commands below. Use PF1 if you need help.

i	Insert a line.
Enter key	Press Enter without entering anything to escape insert mode.
i5	Obtain five input lines.
d	Delete a line.
d5	Delete five lines.
dd/dd	Delete a block of lines (place a DD on the first line of the block and another DD on the last line of the block).
r	Repeat (or replicate) a line.
rr/rr	Repeat (replicate) a block of lines (where an RR marks the first line of the block and another RR marks the last line).
c along with a or b	Copy a line after or before another line.
c5 along with a or b	Copy five lines after or before another line.
cc/cc along with a or b	Copy a block of lines after or before another line.
m, m5, mm/mm	Move line(s).
x, x5, xx/xx	Exclude lines.
s	Redisplay (show) the lines you excluded.
(	Shift right columns.
)	Shift left columns.

| < | Shift left data. |
| > | Shift right data. |

6.14.4 Submitting a job and checking the results

Edit member COBOL1 in the *yourid*.LIB.SOURCE library and inspect the COBOL program. There is no JCL with it. Now edit member COBOL1 in *yourid*.JCL.[6] Inspect the JCL carefully. It uses a JCL procedure to compile and run a COBOL program.[7] Perform the following steps:

1. Change the job name to *yourid* plus additional characters.

2. Change the NOTIFY parameter to your user ID.

3. Add TYPRUN=SCAN to your job card.

4. Type SUB on the ISPF command line to submit the job.

5. Split your ISPF screen and go to SDSF on the new screen (you might have this already from an earlier exercise).

6. In SDSF, go to the ST (Status) display and look for your job name.

   You may need to enter a PRE or OWNER command on the SDSF command line to see any job names. (A previous user may have issued a prefix command to see only certain job names.)

7. Type S beside your job name to see all of the printed output:
   – Messages from JES2
   – Messages from the initiator
   – Messages from the COBOL compiler
   – Messages from the binder
   – Output from the COBOL program

8. Remove TYPRUN=SCAN when you are ready to run your job.

9. Use PF3 to "move up" a level and type ? beside your job name to display another output format.

   The instructor can tell you the purposes of the various JES2 and initiator messages.

10. Resubmit the job with MSGLEVEL=(1,1) in the JOB statement.

11. Resubmit the job with MSGLEVEL=(0,0) in the JOB statement.

The MSGLEVEL parameter controls the number of initiator messages that are produced.

---

[6] The matching member names (COBOL1) are not required; however, they are convenient.

[7] This is not exactly the COBOL procedure we discussed earlier. Details of these procedures sometimes change from release to release of the operating system.

6.14.5 Creating a PDS member

There are several ways to create a new PDS member. Try each of the following, using your own user ID. In the following steps, TEST3, TEST4, TEST5, and TEST6 represent new member names. Enter a few lines of text in each case. Using the ISPF edit panel, perform the following steps:

1. Go to the ISPF primary menu.
2. Go to option 2 (Edit).
3. In the Data Set Name line, enter JCL(TEST3) (no quotes).
4. Enter a few text lines and press PF3 to save the new member.

A new member can be created while viewing the member list in edit mode by performing the following steps:

1. Use option 3.4 (or option 2) to edit *yourid*.JCL.
2. While viewing the member list, enter S TEST4 in the command line.
3. Enter a few text lines and press PF3 to save the new member.

A new member can be created while editing an existing member by performing the following steps:

1. Edit *yourid*.JCL(TEST1) or any other existing member.
2. Select a block of lines by entering cc (in the line command area) in the first and last lines of the block.
3. Enter CREATE TEST5 on the command line, which creates the TEST5 member in the current library.

A new member can be created with JCL. Enter the following JCL in *yourid*.JCL(TEST5) or any other convenient location:

```
//yourid1 JOB 1,JOE,MSGCLASS=X
//STEP1 EXEC PGM=IEBGENER
//SYSIN DD DUMMY
//SYSPRINT DD SYSOUT=*
//SYSUT2 DD DISP=OLD,DSN= yourid.JCL(TEST6)
//SYSUT1 DD *
This is some text to put in the member
More text
/*
```

Save the member. It will be used later.

6.14.6 Copying a PDS member

There are many ways to copy a library member. An earlier exercise used the ISPF 3.3 panel function to copy all the members of a library. The same function can be used to copy one or more members.

While editing a library member, we can copy another member of the library into it by performing the following steps:

1. Edit a library member.

2. Mark a line in this member with a (after) or b (before) to indicate where the other member should be copied.

3. Enter COPY *xxx* on the command line, where *xxx* is the name of another member in the current data set.

We can copy a member from another data set (or a sequential data set) by performing the following steps:

1. Edit a member or sequential data set.

2. Mark a line with A (after) or B (before) to indicate where to insert the new material.

3. Enter COPY on the command line to display the Edit/View-Copy panel.

4. Enter the full sequential data set name (with single quotes, if necessary) or a full library name (including member name) in the Data Set Name field.

7

Batch processing and the job entry subsystem

Objective: As a mainframe professional, you need to understand the ways in which the system processes your company's core applications, such as payroll. Such workloads are usually performed through *batch processing,* which involves executing one or more *batch jobs* in a sequential flow.

Further, you need to understand how the *job entry subsystem* (JES) enables batch processing. JES helps z/OS receive jobs, schedule them for processing, and determine how job output is processed.

After completing this chapter, you will be able to:

► Give an overview of batch processing and how work is initiated and managed in the system.
► Explain how JES governs the flow of work through a z/OS system.

Refer to Table 7-1 on page 291 for a list of key terms used in this chapter.

7.1 What is batch processing

The term *batch job* originated in the days when punched cards contained the directions for a computer to follow when running one or more programs. Multiple card decks representing multiple jobs would often be stacked on top of one another in the hopper of a card reader, and be run in batches.

As a historical note, Herman Hollerith (1860-1929) created the punched card in 1890 while he worked as a statistician for the United States Census Bureau. To help tabulate results for the 1890 U.S. census, Hollerith designed a paper card with 80 columns and 12 rows; he made it equal to the size of a U.S. dollar bill of that time. To represent a series of data values, he punched holes into the card at the appropriate row/column intersections. Hollerith also designed an electromechanical device to "read" the holes in the card, and the resulting electrical signal was sorted and tabulated by a computing device. (Mr. Hollerith later founded the Computing Tabulating Recording Company, which eventually became IBM.)

Today, jobs that can run without user interaction, or can be scheduled to run as resources permit, are called batch jobs. A program that reads a large file and generates a report, for example, is considered to be a batch job.

Batch job:
A program that can be executed with minimal human interaction, typically executed at a scheduled time.

There is no direct counterpart to z/OS batch processing in PC or UNIX systems. Batch processing is for those frequently used programs that can be executed with minimal human interaction. They are typically executed at a scheduled time or on an as-needed basis. Perhaps the closest comparison is with processes run by an AT or CRON command in UNIX, although the differences are significant. You might also consider batch processing as being somewhat analogous to the printer queue as it is typically managed on an Intel-based operating system. Users submit jobs to be printed, and the print jobs wait to be processed until each is selected by priority from a queue of work called a print spool.

To enable the processing of a batch job, z/OS professionals use job control language (JCL) to tell z/OS which programs are to be executed and which files will be needed by the executing programs. As we learned in Chapter 6, "Using Job Control Language and System Display and Search Facility" on page 241, JCL allows the user to describe certain attributes of a batch job to z/OS, such as:

► Who you are (the submitter of the batch job)
► What program to run
► Where input and output are located
► When a job is to run

After the user submits the job to the system, there is normally no further human interaction with the job until it is complete.

7.2 What is a job entry subsystem

z/OS uses a *job entry subsystem* (JES) to receive jobs into the operating system, to schedule them for processing by z/OS, and to control their output processing. JES is the component of the operating system that provides supplementary job management, data management, and task management functions, such as scheduling, control of job flow, and the reading and writing of input and output streams on auxiliary storage devices, concurrently with job execution (a process called *spooling*).

JES:
A collection of programs that handles the batch workload on z/OS.

z/OS manages work as tasks and subtasks. Both transactions and batch jobs are associated with an internal task queue that is managed on a priority basis. JES is a component of z/OS that works on the front end of program execution to prepare work to be executed. JES is also active on the back end of program execution to help clean up after work is performed. This includes managing the printing of output generated by active programs.

More specifically, JES manages the input and output job queues and data.

For example, JES handles the following aspects of batch processing for z/OS:

- ▶ Receiving jobs into the operating system
- ▶ Scheduling them for processing by z/OS
- ▶ Controlling their output processing

z/OS has two versions of job entry systems: JES2 and JES3. Of these, JES2 is the most common by far and is the JES used in examples in this text. JES2 and JES3 have many functions and features, but their most basic functions are as follows:

- ▶ Accept jobs submitted in various ways:
    - – From ISPF through the SUBMIT command
    - – Over a network
    - – From a running program, which can submit other jobs through the JES internal reader
    - – From a card reader (very rare!)

Spooling:
The reading and writing (by JES) of input and output streams on auxiliary storage devices concurrently with job execution.

- ▶ Queue jobs waiting to be executed. Multiple queues can be defined for various purposes.
- ▶ Queue jobs for an *initiator,* which is a system program that requests the next job in the appropriate queue.
- ▶ Accept printed output from a job while it is running and queue the output.
- ▶ Optionally, send output to a printer, or save it on *spool* for PSF, InfoPrint, or another output manager to retrieve.

JES uses one or more disk data sets for *spooling*, which is the process of reading and writing input and output streams on auxiliary storage devices, concurrently with job execution, in a format convenient for later processing or output operations. (*Spool* is an acronym that stands for *simultaneous peripheral operations online*).

JES combines multiple spool data sets (if present) into a single conceptual data set. The internal format is not in a standard access-method format and is not written or read directly by applications. Input jobs and printed output from many jobs are stored in the single (conceptual) spool data set. In a small z/OS system, the spool data sets might be a few hundred cylinders of disk space; in a large installation, they might be many complete volumes of disk space.

The basic elements of batch processing are shown in Figure 7-1.

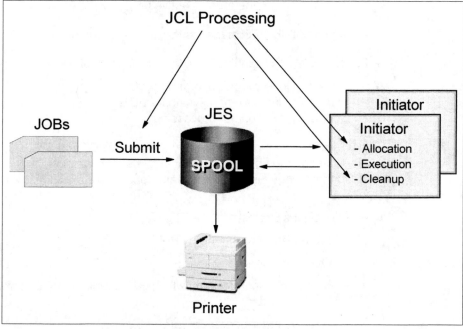

Figure 7-1   Basic batch flow

Initiator:
The part of the operating system that reads and processes operation control language statements from the system input device.

The *initiator* is an integral part of z/OS that reads, interprets, and executes the JCL. It is normally running in several address spaces (as *multiple initiators*). An initiator manages the running of batch jobs, one at a time, in the same address space. If ten initiators are active (in ten address spaces), then ten batch jobs can run at the same time. JES does some JCL processing, but the initiator does the key JCL work.

The jobs in Figure 7-1 on page 276 represent JCL and perhaps data intermixed with the JCL. Source code input for a compiler is an example of data (the source statements) that might be intermixed with JCL. Another example is an accounting job that prepares the weekly payroll for different divisions of a firm (presumably, the payroll application program is the same for all divisions, but the input and master summary files may differ).

The diagram represents the jobs as punched cards (using the conventional symbol for punched cards) although real punched card input is rare now. Typically, a job consists of card images (80-byte fixed-length records) in a member of a partitioned data set.

7.3 What does an initiator do

To run multiple jobs asynchronously, the system must perform a number of functions:

- ▶ Select jobs from the input queues (JES does this).
- ▶ Ensure that multiple jobs (including TSO users and other interactive applications) do not conflict in data set usage.
- ▶ Ensure that single-user devices, such as tape drives, are allocated correctly.
- ▶ Find the executable programs requested for the job.
- ▶ Clean up after the job ends and then request the next job.

Most of this work is done by the initiator, based on JCL information for each job. The most complex function is to ensure there are no conflicts due to data set utilization. For example, if two jobs try to write in the same data set at the same time (or one reads while the other writes), there is a conflict.[1] This event would normally result in corrupted data. The primary purpose of JCL is to tell an initiator what is needed for the job.

The prevention of conflicting data set usage is critical to z/OS and is one of the defining characteristics of the operating system. When the JCL is properly constructed, the prevention of conflicts is automatic. For example, if job A and job B must both write to a particular data set, the system (through the initiator) does not permit both jobs to run at the same time. Instead, whichever job starts first causes an initiator attempting to run the other job to wait until the first job completes.

---

[1] There are cases where such usage is correct and JCL can be constructed for these cases. In the case of simple batch jobs, such conflicts are normally unacceptable.

7.4 Job and output management with job entry subsystem and initiators

Let us look at how JES and the z/OS initiators work together to process batch jobs, using two scenarios.

7.4.1 Batch job scenario 1

Imagine that you are a z/OS application programmer developing a program for non-skilled users. Your program is supposed to read a couple of files, write to another couple of files, and produce a printed report. This program will run as a batch job on z/OS.

What sorts of functions are needed in the operating system to fulfill the requirements of your program? How will your program access those functions?

First, you need a sort of special language to inform the operating system about your needs. On z/OS, this is the job control language (JCL). The use of JCL is covered in detail in Chapter 6, "Using Job Control Language and System Display and Search Facility" on page 241, but for now assume that JCL provides the means for you to request resources and services from the operating system for a batch job.

Specifications and requests you might make for a batch job include the functions you need to compile and execute the program, and allocate storage for the program to use as it runs.

With JCL, you can specify the following items:

▶ Who you are (important for security reasons).

▶ Which resources (programs, files, and memory) and services are needed from the system to process your program. You might, for example, need to do the following:

    – Load the compiler code in memory.

    – Make your source code accessible to the compiler, that is, when the compiler asks for a read, your source statements are brought to the compiler memory.

    – Allocate some amount of memory to accommodate the compiler code, I/O buffers, and working areas.

    – Make an output disk data set accessible to the compiler to receive the object code, which is usually referred to as the *object deck* (OBJ).

    – Make a print file accessible to the compiler, where it will tell you your eventual mistakes.

- Conditionally, have z/OS load the newly created object deck into memory (but skip this step if the compilation failed).
- Allocate some amount of memory for your program to use.
- Make all the input and output files accessible to your program.
- Make a printer for eventual messages accessible to your program.

In turn, you require the operating system to:

▶ Convert JCL to control blocks that describe the required resources.

▶ Allocate the required resources (programs, memory, and files).

▶ Schedule the execution on a timely basis, for example, your program only runs if the compilation succeeds.

▶ Free the resources when the program is done.

The parts of z/OS that perform these tasks are JES and a batch initiator program.

Think of JES as the manager of the jobs waiting in a queue. It manages the priority of the set of jobs and their associated input data and output results. The initiator uses the statements on the JCL cards to specify the resources required of each individual job after it has been released (dispatched) by JES.

Procedure: A set of JCL statements.

Your JCL as described is called a *job*, which in this case is formed by two sequential steps: compilation and execution. The steps in a job are always executed sequentially. The job must be submitted to JES to be executed. To make your task easier, z/OS provides a set of procedures in a data set called SYS1.PROCLIB. A procedure is a set of JCL statements that are ready to be executed.

Example 7-1 shows a JCL procedure that can compile, link-edit, and execute a program (these steps are described in Chapter 8, "Designing and developing applications for z/OS" on page 299). The first step identifies the COBOL compiler, as declared in //COBOL EXEC PGM=IGYCRCTL. The statement //SYSLIN DD describes the output of the compiler (the object deck).

The object deck is the input for the second step, which performs link-editing (through program IEWL). Link-editing is needed to resolve external references and *bring in* or *link* the previously developed common routines (a type of code re-use).

In the third step, the program is executed.

Example 7-1   Procedure to compile, link-edit, and execute programs

```
000010 //IGYWCLG PROC LNGPRFX='IGY.V3R2M0',SYSLBLK=3200,
000020 //              LIBPRFX='CEE',GOPGM=GO
```

```
000030 //*
000040 //******************************************************************
000050 //*                                                              *
000060 //*   Enterprise COBOL for z/OS and OS/390                       *
000070 //*                  Version 3 Release 2 Modification 0           *
000080 //*                                                              *
000090 //*   LICENSED MATERIALS - PROPERTY OF IBM.                      *
000100 //*                                                              *
000110 //*   5655-G53 5648-A25 (C) COPYRIGHT IBM CORP. 1991, 2002       *
000120 //*   ALL RIGHTS RESERVED                                        *
000130 //*                                                              *
000140 //*   US GOVERNMENT USERS RESTRICTED RIGHTS - USE,               *
000150 //*   DUPLICATION OR DISCLOSURE RESTRICTED BY GSA                *
000160 //*   ADP SCHEDULE CONTRACT WITH IBM CORP.                       *
000170 //*                                                              *
000180 //******************************************************************
000190 //*
000300 //COBOL   EXEC PGM=IGYCRCTL,REGION=2048K
000310 //STEPLIB  DD   DSNAME=&LNGPRFX..SIGYCOMP,
000320 //              DISP=SHR
000330 //SYSPRINT DD   SYSOUT=*
000340 //SYSLIN   DD   DSNAME=&&LOADSET,UNIT=SYSDA,
000350 //              DISP=(MOD,PASS),SPACE=(TRK,(3,3)),
000360 //              DCB=(BLKSIZE=&SYSLBLK)
000370 //SYSUT1   DD   UNIT=SYSDA,SPACE=(CYL,(1,1))
000440 //LKED    EXEC PGM=HEWL,COND=(8,LT,COBOL),REGION=1024K
000450 //SYSLIB   DD   DSNAME=&LIBPRFX..SCEELKED,
000460 //              DISP=SHR
000470 //SYSPRINT DD   SYSOUT=*
000480 //SYSLIN   DD   DSNAME=&&LOADSET,DISP=(OLD,DELETE)
000490 //         DD   DDNAME=SYSIN
000500 //SYSLMOD  DD   DSNAME=&&GOSET(&GOPGM),SPACE=(TRK,(10,10,1)),
000510 //              UNIT=SYSDA,DISP=(MOD,PASS)
000520 //SYSUT1   DD   UNIT=SYSDA,SPACE=(TRK,(10,10))
000530 //GO      EXEC PGM=*.LKED.SYSLMOD,COND=((8,LT,COBOL),(4,LT,LKED)),
000540 //              REGION=2048K
000550 //STEPLIB  DD   DSNAME=&LIBPRFX..SCEERUN,
000560 //              DISP=SHR
000570 //SYSPRINT DD   SYSOUT=*
000580 //CEEDUMP  DD   SYSOUT=*
000590 //SYSUDUMP DD   SYSOUT=*
```

To invoke a procedure, you can write some simple JCL, as shown in Example 7-2. In this example, we added other DD statements, such as:

```
//COBOL.SYSIN DD *
```

It contains the COBOL source code.

Example 7-2   COBOL program

```
000001 //COBOL1 JOB (POK,999),MGELINSKI,MSGLEVEL=(1,1),MSGCLASS=X,
000002 //   CLASS=A,NOTIFY=&SYSUID
000003 /*JOBPARM SYSAFF=*
000004 // JCLLIB   ORDER=(IGY.SIGYPROC)
000005 //*
000006 //RUNIVP EXEC IGYWCLG,PARM.COBOL=RENT,REGION=1400K,
000007 //             PARM.LKED='LIST,XREF,LET,MAP'
000008 //COBOL.STEPLIB DD DSN=IGY.SIGYCOMP,
000009 //             DISP=SHR
000010 //COBOL.SYSIN DD *
000011       IDENTIFICATION DIVISION.
000012       PROGRAM-ID.    CALLIVP1.
000013       AUTHOR.         STUDENT PROGRAMMER.
000014       INSTALLATION.  MY UNIVERSITY
000015       DATE-WRITTEN.  JUL 27, 2004.
000016       DATE-COMPILED.
000017       /
000018       ENVIRONMENT DIVISION.
000019       CONFIGURATION SECTION.
000020       SOURCE-COMPUTER.  IBM-390.
000021       OBJECT-COMPUTER.  IBM-390.
000022
000023       PROCEDURE DIVISION.
000024          DISPLAY "***** HELLO WORLD *****" UPON CONSOLE.
000025          STOP RUN.
000026
000027 //GO.SYSOUT DD SYSOUT=*
000028 //
```

During the execution of a step, the program is controlled by z/OS, not by JES (Figure 7-2). Also, a spooling function is needed at this point in the process.

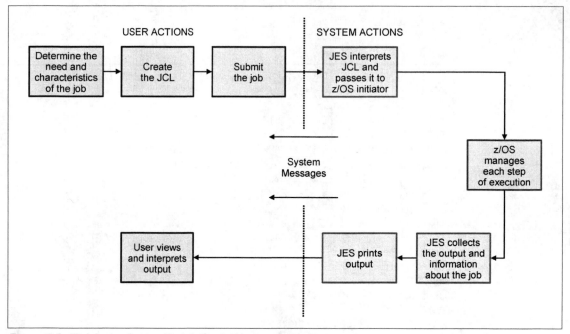

Figure 7-2   Related actions with Job Control Language

Spooling is the means by which the system manipulates its work, including:

► Using storage on *direct access storage devices* (DASDs) as buffer storage to reduce processing delays when transferring data between peripheral equipment and a program to be run.

► Reading and writing input and output streams on an intermediate device for later processing or output.

► Performing an operation, such as printing while the computer is busy with other work.

There are two sorts of spooling: input and output. Both improve the performance of the program reading the input and writing the output.

To implement input spooling in JCL, you declare `// DD *`, which defines one file whose content records are in JCL between the `// DD *` statement and the `/*` statements. All the logical records must have 80 characters. In this case, this file is read and stored in a specific JES2 spool area (a huge JES file on disk), as shown in Figure 7-3.

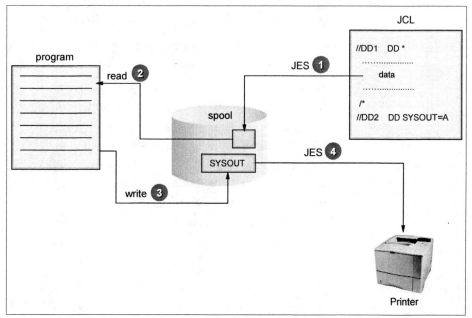

Figure 7-3   Spooling

Later, when the program is executed and asks to read this data, JES2 picks up the records in the spool and delivers them to the program (at disk speed).

To implement output spooling in JCL, you specify the keyword `SYSOUT` on the DD statement. `SYSOUT` defines an empty file in the spool, allocated with logical records of 132 characters in a printed format (EBCDIC/ASCII/UNICODE). This file is allocated by JES when interpreting a DD card with the `SYSOUT` keyword, and used later for the step program. Generally, after the end of the job, this file is printed by a JES function.

7.4.2 Batch job scenario 2

Suppose now that you want to make a backup of one master file and then update the master file with records read in from another file (the *update* file). If so, you need a job with two steps. In Step 1, your job reads the master file and writes it to tape. In Step 2, another program (which can be written in COBOL) is executed to read a record from the update file and searches for its match in the master file.

The program updates the existing record (if it finds a match) or adds a new record if needed.

In this scenario, what kind of functions are needed in the operating system to meet your requirements?

Build a job with two steps that specify the following:

► Who you are.

► What resources are needed by the job, such as the following:

  – Load the backup program (that you already have compiled).

  – How much memory the system needs to allocate to accommodate the backup program, I/O buffers, and working areas.

  – Make an output tape data set accessible to the backup program to receive the backup, a copy, and the master file data set itself.

  – At program end, indicate to the operating system that now your update program needs to be loaded into memory (however, this should not be done if the backup program failed).

  – Make the update file and master file accessible to the update program.

  – Make a printer for eventual messages accessible to your program.

Your JCL must have two steps, the first one indicating the resources for the backup program, and the second for the update program (Figure 7-4).

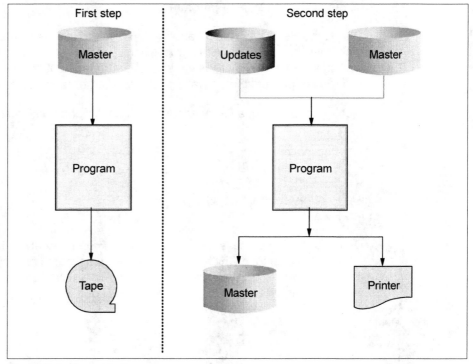

Figure 7-4   Scenario 2

Logically, the second step will not be executed if the first one fails for any reason. The second step will have a // DD SYSOUT statement to indicate the need for output spooling.

The jobs are only allowed to start when there are enough resources available. In this way, the system is made more efficient: JES manages jobs before and after running the program, and the base control program manages jobs during processing.

Two types of job entry subsystems are offered with z/OS: JES2 and JES3. This section discusses JES2. For a brief comparison of JES2 and JES3, see 7.6, "JES2 compared to JES3" on page 289.

7.5 Job flow through the system

Let us look in more detail at how a job is processed through the combination of JES and a batch initiator program.

During the life of a job, JES2 and the base control program of z/OS control different phases of the overall processing. The job queues contain jobs that are waiting to run, currently running, waiting for their output to be produced, having their output produced, and waiting to be purged from the system.

Generally speaking, a job goes through the following phases:

- ▶ Input
- ▶ Conversion
- ▶ Processing
- ▶ Output
- ▶ Print/punch (hard copy)
- ▶ Purge

Checkpoint:
A point at which information about the status of a job and the system can be recorded so that the job step can be started later.

During batch job processing, numerous *checkpoints* occur. A checkpoint is a point in processing at which information about the status of a job and the system can be recorded (in a file called a *checkpoint data set*). Checkpoints allow the job step to be restarted later if it ends abnormally due to an error.

Figure 7-5 shows the different phases of a job during batch processing.

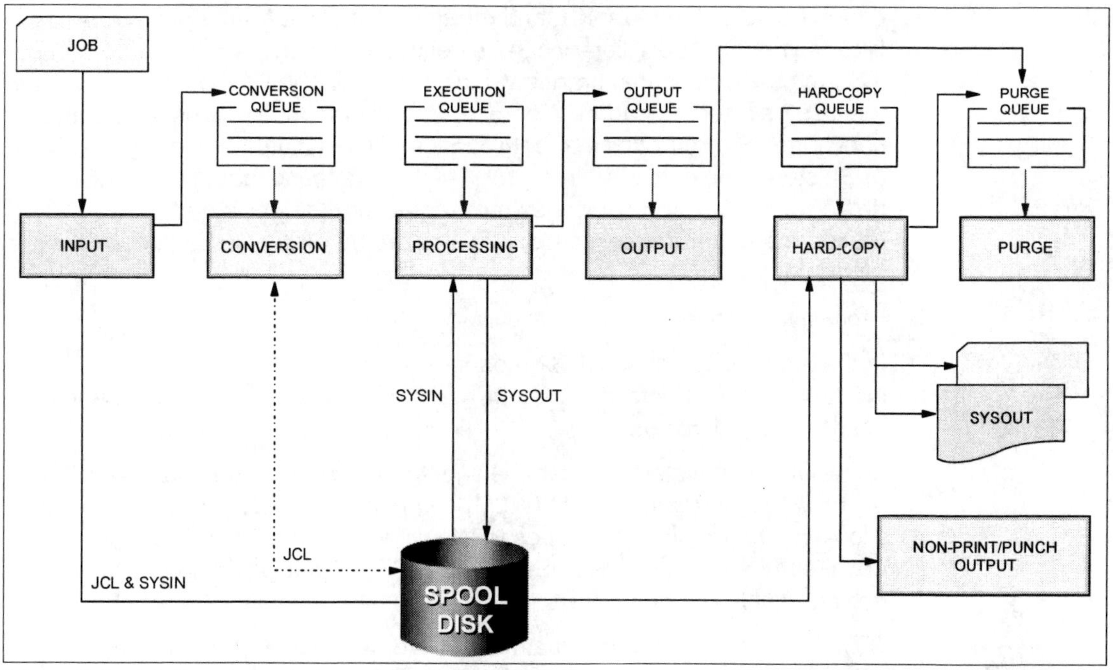

Figure 7-5   Job flow through the system

Where:

1. Input phase

    JES2 accepts jobs, in the form of an input stream, from input devices, from other programs through internal readers, and from other nodes in a job entry network.

    The internal reader is a program that other programs can use to submit jobs, control statements, and commands to JES2. Any job running in z/OS can use an internal reader to pass an input stream to JES2. JES2 can receive multiple jobs simultaneously through multiple internal readers.

    The system programmer defines internal readers to be used to process all batch jobs other than *started tasks* (STCs) and TSO requests.

    JES2 reads the input stream and assigns a job identifier to each JOB JCL statement. JES2 places the job's JCL, optional JES2 control statements, and SYSIN data onto DASD data sets called *spool data sets*. JES2 then selects jobs from the spool data sets for processing and subsequent running.

2. Conversion phase

   JES2 uses a converter program to analyze a job's JCL statements. The converter takes the job's JCL and merges it with JCL from a procedure library. The procedure library can be defined in the JCLLIB JCL statement, or system/user procedure libraries can be defined in the PROCxx DD statement of the JES2 startup procedure. Then, JES2 converts the composite JCL into converter/interpreter text that both JES2 and the initiator can recognize. Next, JES2 stores the converter/interpreter text on the spool data set. If JES2 detects any JCL errors, it issues messages, and the job is queued for output processing rather than execution. If there are no errors, JES2 queues the job for execution.

3. Processing phase

   In the processing phase, JES2 responds to requests for jobs from the initiators. JES2 selects jobs that are waiting to run from a job queue and sends them to initiators.

   An initiator is a system program belonging to z/OS, but controlled by JES or by the workload management (WLM) component of z/OS, which starts a job allocating the required resources to allow it to compete with other jobs that are already running (WLM is discussed in 3.5, "What is workload management" on page 126).

   JES2 initiators are initiators that are started by the operator or by JES2 automatically when the system initializes. They are defined to JES2 through JES2 initialization statements. The installation associates each initiator with one or more job classes to obtain an efficient use of available system resources. Initiators select jobs whose classes match the initiator-assigned class, obeying the priority of the queued jobs.

   WLM initiators are started by the system automatically based on performance goals, relative importance of the batch workload, and the capacity of the system to do more work. The initiators select jobs based on their service class and the order they were made available for execution. Jobs are routed to WLM initiators through a JOBCLASS JES2 initialization statement.

4. Output phase

SYSOUT: Specifies the destination for the output from the jobsystem-produced output.

   JES2 controls all SYSOUT processing. SYSOUT is system-produced output, that is, all output produced by, or for, a job. This output includes system messages that must be printed, as well as data sets requested by the user that must be printed or punched. After a job finishes, JES2 analyzes the characteristics of the job's output in terms of its output class and device setup requirements; then JES2 groups data sets with similar characteristics. JES2 queues the output for print or punch processing.

5. Hardcopy phase

   JES2 selects output for processing from the output queues by output class, route code, priority, and other criteria. The output queue can have output that can be processed locally or at a remote location. After processing all the output for a particular job, JES2 puts the job on the purge queue.

6. Purge phase

   When all processing for a job completes, JES2 releases the spool space assigned to the job, making the space available for allocation to subsequent jobs. JES2 then issues a message to the operator indicating that the job has been purged from the system.

7.6 JES2 compared to JES3

As mentioned earlier, IBM provides two kinds of job entry subsystems: JES2 and JES3. In many cases, JES2 and JES3 perform similar functions: They read jobs into the system, convert them to internal machine-readable form, select them for processing, process their output, and purge them from the system.

In a mainframe installation that has only one processor, JES3 provides tape setup, dependent job control, and deadline scheduling for users of the system, while JES2 in the same system would require its users to manage these activities through other means. In an installation with a multi-processor configuration, there are noticeable differences between the two, mainly in how JES2 exercises independent control over its job processing functions, that is, within the configuration, each JES2 processor controls its own job input, job scheduling, and job output processing. Most installations use JES2, as do the examples in this text.

Figure 7-6 lists some differences between JES2 and JES3.

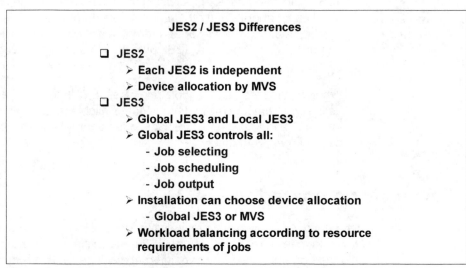

Figure 7-6   JES2/JES3 differences

In cases where multiple z/OS systems are clustered (a *sysplex*), it is possible to configure JES2 to share spool and checkpoint data sets with other JES2 systems in the same sysplex. This configuration is called Multi-Access Spool (MAS). In contrast, JES3 exercises centralized control over its processing functions through a single global JES3 processor. This global processor provides all job selection, scheduling, and device allocation functions for all of the other JES3 systems.

7.7 Summary

Batch processing is the most fundamental function of z/OS. Many batch jobs are run in parallel and JCL is used to control the operation of each job. Correct use of JCL parameters (especially the DISP parameter in DD statements) allows parallel, asynchronous execution of jobs that may need access to the same data sets.

An initiator is a system program that processes JCL, sets up the necessary environment on an address space, and runs a batch job in the same address space. Multiple initiators (each in an address space) permit the parallel execution of batch jobs.

A goal of an operating system is to process work while making the best use of system resources. To achieve this goal, resource management is needed during key phases to do the following:

► Before job processing, reserve input and output resources for jobs.

► During job processing, manage spooled SYSIN and SYSOUT data.

► After job processing, free all resources used by the completed jobs, making the resources available to other jobs.

z/OS shares with JES the management of jobs and resources. JES receives jobs into the system, schedules them for processing by z/OS, and controls their output processing. JES is the manager of the jobs waiting in a queue. It manages the priority of the jobs and their associated input data and output results. The initiator uses the statements in the JCL records to specify the resources required of each individual job after it is released (dispatched) by JES.

IBM provides two kinds of job entry subsystems: JES2 and JES3. In many cases, JES2 and JES3 perform similar functions.

During the life of a job, both JES and the z/OS base control program control different phases of the overall processing. Jobs are managed in queues: jobs that are waiting to run (conversion queue), currently running (execution queue), waiting for their output to be produced (output queue), having their output produced (hard-copy queue), and waiting to be purged from the system (purge queue).

Table 7-1 lists the key terms used in this chapter.

Table 7-1   Key terms used in this chapter

batch job	checkpoint	initiator
job entry subsystem (JES)	procedure	purge
spooling	SYSIN	SYSOUT

7.8 Questions for review

To help test your understanding of the material in this chapter, answer the following questions:

1. What is batch processing?

2. Why does z/OS need a JES?

3. During the life of a job, what types of processing does JES2 typically perform?

4. What does the acronym *spool* stand for?

5. What are some of the jobs performed by an initiator?

7.9 Exercises

These exercises cover the following topics:

► Learning about system volumes

► Using a utility program in a job

► Examining the TSO logon JCL

► Exploring the master catalog

► Using SDSF

► Using TSO REXX and ISPF

7.9.1 Learning about system volumes

Use the ISPF functions to explore several system volumes. The following are of interest:

► Examine the naming of VSAM data sets. Note the words DATA and INDEX as the last qualifier.

► Find the spool area. This may involve a guess based on the data set name. How large is it?

► Find the basic system libraries, such as SYS1.PROCLIB and so on. Look at the member names.

► Consider the ISPF statistics field that is displayed in a member list. How does it differ for source libraries and execution libraries?

7.9.2 Using a utility program in a job

z/OS has a utility program named IEBGENER to copy data. It uses four DD statements:

► `SYSIN` for control statements. We can code `DD DUMMY` for this statement, because we do not have any control statements for this job.

► `SYSPRINT` for messages from the program. Use `SYSOUT=X` for this lab.

► `SYSUT1` for the input data.

► `SYSUT2` for the output data.

The basic function of the program is to copy the data set pointed to by SYSUT1 to the data set pointed to by SYSUT2. Both must be sequential data sets or members of a library.

The program automatically obtains the data control block (DCB) attributes from the input data set and applies them to the output data set. Write the JCL for a job to list the *yourid*.JCL(TEST1) member to SYSOUT=X.

7.9.3 Examining the TSO logon JCL

The password panel of the TSO logon process contains the name of the JCL procedure used to create a TSO session. There are several procedures with different characteristics.

Look at the ISPFPROC procedure. The instructor can help find the correct library for ISPFPROC.

► What is the name of the basic TSO program that is executed?

► Why are there so many DD statements? Notice the concatenation.

Look for IKJACCNT procedure. This is a minimal TSO logon procedure.

7.9.4 Exploring the master catalog

Go to ISPF option 6 and perform the following steps:

1. Use a LISTC LEVEL(SYS1) command for a basic listing of all the SYS1 data sets in the master catalog.

   Note that they are either NONVASM or CLUSTER (and associated DATA and INDEX entries). The CLUSTERs are for VSAM data sets.

2. Use the PA1 key to end the listing (for help, see 3.3.3, "Using the PA1 key" on page 3-14).

3. Use a LISTC LEVEL(SYS1) ALL command for a more extended listing.

   Note the VOLSER and device type data for the NONVSAM data sets. This is the basic information in the catalog.

4. Use LISTC LEVEL(xxx) to view one of the ALIAS levels and note that it comes from a user catalog.

> **Note:** If you enter the profile command with NOPREFIX, it produces a system-wide display when you enter the commands LISTC and LISTC ALL. These commands allow you to see all of the entries in the master catalog, including ALIAS entries.

7.9.5 Using SDSF

From the ISPF Primary Option Menu, locate and select the System Display and Search Facility (SDSF). This utility allows you to display output data sets. The ISPF Primary Option Menu typically includes more selections than those listed on first panel, with instructions about how to display the additional selections.

Return to 6.14.1, "Creating a simple job" on page 265 and repeat the steps through Step 5 if needed. This will provide a job listing for these exercises.

SDSF Exercise 1

While viewing the output listing, assume that you want to save it permanently to a data set for later viewing. At the command input line, enter PRINT D. A window prompts you to enter a data set name in which to save it. You can use an already existing data set or create a new one.

For this example, create a new data set by entering yourid.cobol.list. In the disposition field, enter NEW. Press Enter to return to the previous panel. Note that the top right of the panel displays PRINT OPENED. This means you can now print the listing. On the command input, enter PRINT. Displayed at the top right of the panel will be the number of lines printed (xxx LINES PRINTED). This means the listing has now been placed in the data set that you created. On the command line, enter PRINT CLOSE. At the top right of the panel, you should now see PRINT CLOSED.

Now let us look at the data set you created, *yourid*.cobol.list, and view the listing. Go to =3.4 and enter your user ID. A listing of all your data sets should appear. Locate *yourid*.cobol.list and enter a B next to it in the command area. You should see the listing exactly as it appeared when you were using SDSF. You can now return to SDSF ST and purge (P) your listing, because you now have a permanent copy.

Return to the main SDSF panel and enter LOG to display a log of all activity in the system. Here, you can see much the information that the Operations Staff might see. For example, at the bottom of the list, you might see the outstanding Reply messages to which an operator can reply.

/R xx,/DISP TRAN ALL

Scroll to the bottom to see results. Note that operator commands from the SDSF LOG command must be preceded by a forward slash (/) so that it is recognized as a system command.

Now, enter M in the command input and press F7; this will display the top of the log. Type F and your user ID to display the first entry associated with your user ID. Most likely this will be when you logged onto TSO. Next, enter F *youridX*, where X represents one of the jobs you submitted above. Here you should see your job being received into the JES2 internal reader, and following that a few lines indicating the status of your job as it runs. Perhaps you might see a JCL error, or *youridX* started | ended.

SDSF Exercise 2

This exercise uses the Print functions above. Save the log into a data set exactly as you did in the Print exercise.

SDSF Exercise 3

In this exercise, you enter operator commands from the Log panel. Enter the following at the command input line and look at the resulting displays:

/D A,L	This lists all active jobs in the system.
/D U,,,A80,24	This lists currently online DASD VOLUMES.
/V A88,OFFLINE	Scroll to the bottom to see results (M F8).
/D U,,,A88,2	Check its Status; note that VOLSER is not displayed for offline volumes. While a volume is offline, you can run utilities such as ICKDSF, which allows you to format a volume.
/V A88,ONLINE	Scroll to the bottom and see the results.
/D U,,,A88,2	Check its status; VOLSER is now displayed.
/C U=*yourid*	Cancels a job (your TSO session in this case).
Logon yourid	Log back onto your ID.

7.9.6 Using TSO REXX and ISPF

In the data set USER.CLIST, there is a REXX program called ITSODSN. This program can be run by entering the following at any ISPF command input line:

```
TSO ITSODSN
```

You will be prompted to enter the name of the data set that you want to create. You do not need to enter *yourid*, as TSO will add it to the name if your prefix is active. It will give you a choice of two types of data sets, sequential or partitioned, and asks you what volume you want to store the data set on. It will then allocate the data set with your user ID appended to it. Go to =3.4, locate the data set, and examine it with an S option to be sure it is what you want.

REXX Exercise 1

In the REXX program, you find several characteristics of the data set that have been coded for you, for example, LRECL and BLKSIZE. Modify the program so that the user is prompted to enter any data set characteristics that they want to enter. You may also change the program in any other way that you like. Make a backup copy of the program before you begin.

REXX Exercise 2

REXX under TSO and batch can directly address other subsystems, as you have already seen in this program when it directly allocates a data set using a TSO command enclosed in quotes. Another way of executing functions outside of REXX is through a host command environment. A few examples of host command environments are:

TSO	Time Sharing Option
MVS	For REXX running in a non-TSO environment
ISPEXEC	Access to the ISPF environment under TSO

Modify the REXX program so that after the data set is allocated, REXX opens the data set by using the ISPF Edit command, enters some data, exits with PF3, and then uses =3.4 to examine your data set. Remember that if the data set is partitioned (PO), you have to open a member. You can use whatever you want as a member name in the format *yourid.name(membername)*.

> **Hints:**
> - It is easier to use the second format of the host command environment above.
> - Notice the use of the REXX "if then else" logic and the "do end" within the logic.
> - Use the ADDRESS ISPEXEC "edit DATASET(....)" command.

Part 2

Application programming on z/OS

In this part, we introduce the tools and utilities for developing a simple program to run on z/OS. The chapters that follow guide the student through the process of application design, choosing a programming language, and using a runtime environment.

8

Designing and developing applications for z/OS

Objective: As your company's newest z/OS application designer or programmer, you will be asked to design and write new programs, or modify existing programs, to meet your company's business goals. Such an undertaking requires that you fully understand the various user requirements for your application and know which z/OS system services to use.

This chapter provides a brief review of the common design, code, and test cycle for a new application. Much of this information is applicable to all computing platforms in general, not just mainframes.

After completing this chapter, you will be able to:

► Describe the roles of the application designer and application programmer.
► List the major considerations for designing an application for z/OS.
► Describe the advantages and disadvantages of batch versus online for an application.
► Briefly describe the process for testing a new application on z/OS.
► List three advantages for using z/OS as the host for a new application.

Refer to Table 8-3 on page 320 for a list of key terms used in this chapter.

8.1 Application designers and programmers

The tasks of *designing* an application and *developing* one are distinct enough to treat each one in a separate book. In larger z/OS sites, separate departments might be used to carry out each task. This chapter provides an overview of these job roles and shows how each skill fits into the overall view of a typical application development life cycle on z/OS.

The application designer is responsible for determining the best programming solution for an important business requirement. The success of any design depends in part on the designer's knowledge of the business itself, awareness of other roles in the mainframe organization, such as programming and database design, and understanding of the business's hardware and software. In short, the designer must have a global view of the entire project.

Another role involved in this process is the business systems analyst. This person is responsible for working with users in a particular department (accounting, sales, production control, manufacturing, and so on) to identify business needs for the application. Like the application designer, the business systems analyst requires a broad understanding of the organization's business goals, and the capabilities of the information system.

Application:
A set of files that make up software for the user.

The application designer gathers requirements from business systems analysts and users. The designer also determines which IT resources will be available to support the application. The application designer then writes the design specifications for the application programmers to implement.

The application programmer is responsible for developing and maintaining application programs, that is, the programmer builds, tests, and delivers the application programs that run on the mainframe for the users. Based on the application designer's specifications, the programmer constructs an application program using a variety of tools. The build process includes many iterations of code changes and compiles, application builds, and unit testing.

During the development process, the designer and programmer must interact with other roles in the enterprise. The programmer, for example, often works on a team of other programmers who are building code for related application modules.

When the application modules are completed, they are passed through a testing process that can include functional, integration, and system tests. Following this testing process, the application programs must be acceptance-tested by the user community to determine whether the code actually accomplishes what the users desire.

Besides creating new application code, the programmer is responsible for maintaining and enhancing the company's existing mainframe applications. In fact, this is frequently the primary job for many application programmers for the mainframe today. While many mainframe installations still create new programs with COBOL or PL/I, languages such as Java have become popular for building new applications on the mainframe, just as on distributed platforms.

8.2 Designing an application for z/OS

During the early design phases, the application designer makes decisions regarding the characteristics of the application. These decisions are based on many criteria, which must be gathered and examined in detail to arrive at a solution that is acceptable to the user. The decisions are not independent of each other, in that one decision will have an impact on others and all decisions made take into account the scope of the project and its constraints.

Design:
The task of determining the best programming solution for a given business requirement.

Designing an application to run on z/OS shares many of the steps followed for designing an application to run on other platforms, including the distributed environment. z/OS, however, introduces some special considerations. This chapter provides some examples of the decisions that the z/OS application designer makes during the design process for a given application. The list is not meant to be exhaustive, but rather to give you an idea of the process involved:

► "Designing for z/OS: Batch or online" on page 302
► "Designing for z/OS: Data sources and access methods" on page 302
► "Designing for z/OS: Availability and workload requirements" on page 302
► "Designing for z/OS: Exception handling" on page 303

Beyond these decisions, other factors that might influence the design of a z/OS application might include the choice of one or more programming languages and development environments. Other considerations discussed in this chapter include the following:

► Using mainframe character sets in "Using the EBCDIC character set" on page 310.

► Using an interactive development environment (IDE) in "Using application development tools" on page 315.

We discuss differences between the various programming languages in Chapter 9, "Using programming languages on z/OS" on page 323.

Keep in mind that the best designs are those that start with the end result in mind. We must know what it is that we are striving for before we start to design.

8.2.1 Designing for z/OS: Batch or online

When designing an application for z/OS and the mainframe, a key consideration is whether the application runs as a batch program or an online program. In some cases, the decision is obvious, but most applications can be designed to fit either paradigm. How, then, does the designer decide which approach to use?

Reasons for using batch or online:

► Reasons for using batch

   – Data is stored on tape.
   – Transactions are submitted for overnight processing.
   – The user does not require online access to data.

► Reasons for using online:

   – The user requires online access to data.
   – High response time requirements.

8.2.2 Designing for z/OS: Data sources and access methods

Here, the designer's considerations typically include the following:

► What data must be stored?

► How will the data be accessed? This includes a choice of access method.

► Are the requests ad hoc or predictable?

► Will we choose PDS, VSAM, or a database management system (DBMS), such as IMS or DB2?

8.2.3 Designing for z/OS: Availability and workload requirements

For an application that will run on z/OS, the designer must be able to answer the following questions:

► What is the quantity of data to store and access?

► Is there a need to share the data?

► What are the response time requirements?

► What are the cost constraints of the project?

► How many users will access the application at once?

► What is the availability requirement of the application (24x7, 8:00 a.m. to 5:00 p.m. on weekdays, and so on)?

8.2.4 Designing for z/OS: Exception handling

Are there any unusual conditions that might occur? If so, we need to incorporate these in our design to prevent failures in the final application. We cannot always assume, for example, that input will always be entered as expected.

8.3 Application development life cycle: An overview

An application is a collection of programs that satisfies certain specific requirements (resolves certain problems). The solution could reside on any platform or combination of platforms, from a hardware or operating system point of view.

As with other operating systems, application development on z/OS is usually composed of the following phases:

► Design phase

  – Gather user, hardware and software requirements.

  – Perform analysis.

  – Develop the design in its various iterations:

    • High-level design

    • Detailed design

  – Hand over the design to application programmers.

Develop
Build, test, and deliver an application program.

► Code and test the application.

► Perform user tests.

  The user tests application for functionality and usability.

► Perform system tests:

  – Perform integration test (test application with other programs to verify that all programs continue to function as expected).

  – Perform performance (volume) test using production data.

► Go to production and hand off to operations.

  Ensure that all documentation is in place (user training and operation procedures).

► Maintenance phase: Ongoing day-to-day changes and enhancements to application.

Figure 8-1 shows the process flow of the various phases of the application development life cycle.

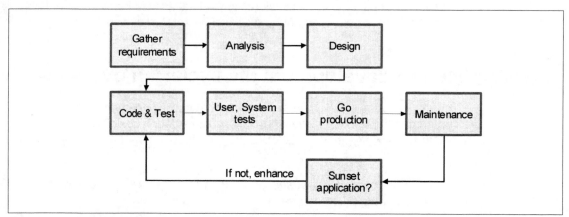

Figure 8-1   Application development life cycle

Figure 8-2 shows the design phase up to the point of starting development. After all of the requirements have been gathered, analyzed, verified, and a design has been produced, we are ready to pass on the programming requirements to the application programmers.

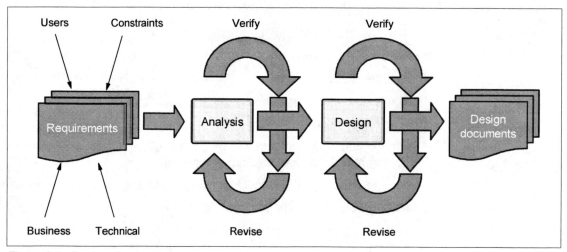

Figure 8-2   Design phase

The programmers take the design documents (programming requirements) and then proceed with the iterative process of coding, testing, revising, and testing again, as shown in Figure 8-3.

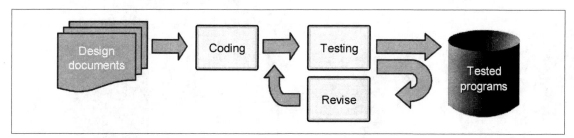

Figure 8-3   Development phase

After the programs have been tested by the programmers, they will be part of a series of formal user and system tests. These tests are used to verify usability and functionality from a user point of view, as well as to verify the functions of the application within a larger framework (Figure 8-4).

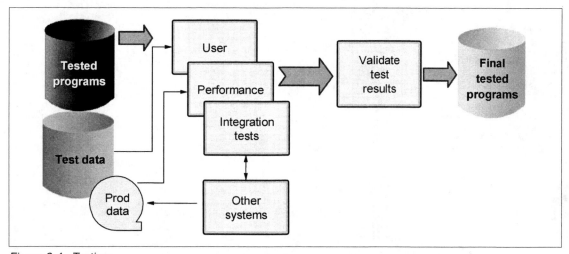

Figure 8-4   Testing

The final phase in the development life cycle is to go to production and enter a steady state. As a prerequisite to going to production, the development team needs to provide documentation. This usually consists of user training and operational procedures. The user training familiarizes the users with the new application. The operational procedures documentation enables operations to take over responsibility for running the application on an ongoing basis.

In production, the changes and enhancements are handled by a group (possibly the same programming group) that performs the maintenance. At this point in the life cycle of the application, changes are tightly controlled and must be rigorously tested before being implemented into production (Figure 8-5).

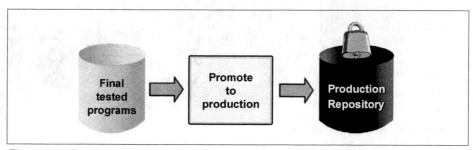

Figure 8-5   Production

As mentioned before, to meet user requirements or solve problems, an application solution might be designed to reside on any platform or a combination of platforms. As shown in Figure 8-6, our specific application can be located in any of the three environments: Internet, enterprise network, or central site. The operating system must provide access to any of these environments.

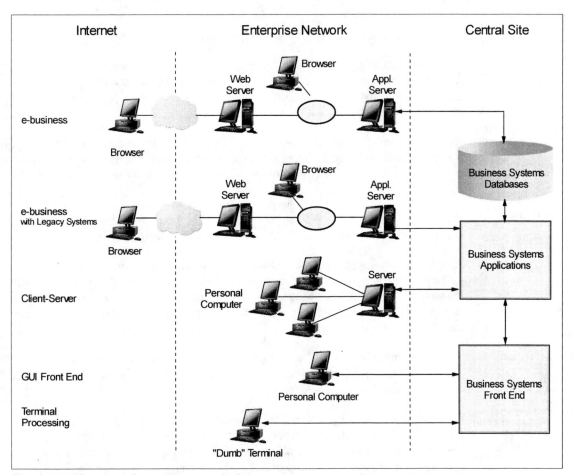

Figure 8-6   Growing infrastructure complexity

To begin the design process, we must first assess what we need to accomplish. Based on the constraints of the project, we determine how and with what we accomplish the goals of the project. To do so, we conduct interviews with the users (those requesting the solution to a problem) and the other stakeholders.

The results of these interviews should inform every subsequent stage of the life cycle of the application project. At certain stages of the project, we again call upon the users to verify that we have understood their requirements and that our solution meets their requirements. At these milestones of the project, we also ask the users to sign off on what we have done, so that we can proceed to the next step of the project.

8.3.1 Gathering requirements for the design

When designing applications, there are many ways to classify the requirements: functional requirements, non-functional requirements, emerging requirements, system requirements, process requirements, constraints on the development and on the operation, to name a few.

Computer applications operate on data, which needs to be accessed from either a local or remote location. The applications manipulate the data, performing some kind of processing on it, and then present the results to whomever was asking for in the first place.

This simple description involves many processes and many operations that have many different requirements, from computers to software products.

Although each application design is a separate case and can have many unique requirements, some of these are common to all applications that are part of the same system. Not only because they are part of the same set of applications that comprise a given information system, but also because they are part of the same installation, which is connected to the same external systems.

Platform:
Often refers to an operating system, implying both the OS and the hardware (environment).

One of the problems faced by systems as a whole is that components are spread across different machines, different platforms, and so on, each one performing its work in a *server farm* environment.

An important advantage to the IBM System z approach is that applications can be maintained using tools that reside on the mainframe. Some of these mainframe tools make it possible to have different platforms sharing resources and data in a coordinated and secure way according to workload or priority.

Here is a list of the various types of requirements for an application. The list is not exclusive; some items already include others.

- ► Accessibility
- ► Recoverability
- ► Serviceability
- ► Availability
- ► Security
- ► Connectivity

- ► Performance objectives
- ► Resource management
- ► Usability
- ► Frequency of data backup
- ► Portability
- ► Web services
- ► Changeability
- ► Inter-communicability
- ► Failure prevention and fault analysis

8.4 Developing an application on the mainframe

After the analysis has been completed and the decisions have been made, the process passes on to the application programmer. The programmer must adhere to the specifications of the designer. However, given that the designer is probably not a programmer, there may be changes required because of programming limitations. But at this point in the project, we are not talking about design changes, merely changes in the way the program does what the designer specified it should do.

The development process is iterative, usually working at the module level. A programmer will usually follow this process:

1. Code a module.

2. Test a module for functionality.

3. Make corrections to the module.

4. Repeat from step 2 until successful.

After testing has been completed on a module, it is signed off and effectively frozen to ensure that if changes are made to it later, it will be tested again. When sufficient modules have been coded and tested, they can be tested together in tests of ever-increasing complexity.

This process is repeated until all of the modules have been coded and tested. Although the process diagram shows testing only after development has been completed, testing is continuously occurring during the development phase.

8.4.1 Using the EBCDIC character set

z/OS data sets are commonly encoded in the Extended Binary Coded Decimal Interchange (EBCDIC) character set. This is an 8-bit character set that was developed before 8-bit ASCII (American Standard Code for Information Interchange) became commonly used. Most z/OS UNIX files are also encoded in EBCDIC. Some exceptions, for compatibility with ASCII platforms, include IBM WebSphere and some Java files.

Most systems that you are familiar with use ASCII. You need to be aware of the difference in encoding schemes when moving data from ASCII-based systems to EBCDIC-encoded systems. Generally, the conversion is handled internally, for example, when text is sent from a 3270 emulator running on a PC to a TSO session. However, when transferring programs, the characters must not normally be translated and a binary transfer must be specified. Occasionally, even when transferring text, there are problems with certain characters, such as the OR sign (|) or the logical *not*, and the programmer must look at the actual value of the translated character.

A listing of EBCDIC and ASCII bit assignments is presented in Appendix D, "EBCDIC - ASCII table" on page 661 and might be useful for this discussion. ASCII and EBCDIC are both 8-bit character sets. The difference is the way they assign bits for specific characters. Table 8-1 shows a few examples.

Table 8-1   EBCDIC and ASCII bit assignments

Character	EBCDIC	ASCII
A	11000001 (x'C1')	01000001 (x'41')
B	11000010 (x'C2')	01000010 (x'42')
a	10000001 (x'81')	01100001 (x'61')
1	11110001 (x'F1')	00110001 (x'31')
space	01000000 (x'40')	00100000 (x'20')

Although the ASCII arrangement might seem more logical, the huge amount of existing data in EBCDIC and the large number of programs that are sensitive to the character set make it impractical to convert all existing data and programs to ASCII.

A character set has a collating sequence, corresponding to the binary value of the character bits. For example, A has a lower value than B in both ASCII and EBCDIC. The collating sequence is important for sorting and for almost any program that scans and manipulates character strings.

Table 8-2 shows the general collating sequence for common characters in the two character sets.

Table 8-2   Collating sequence for common characters in EBCDIC and ASCII

Value range	EBCDIC	ASCII
Lowest values	space	space
	punctuation	punctuation
	lower case	numbers
	upper case	upper case
Highest value	numbers	lower case

For example, "a" is less than "A" in EBCDIC, but "a" is greater than "A" in ASCII. Numeric characters are less than any alphabetic letter in ASCII, but are greater than any letter in EBCDIC. A-Z and a-z are two contiguous sequences in ASCII. In EBCDIC there are gaps between some letters. If we subtract A from Z in ASCII we have 25. If we subtract A from Z in EBCDIC, we have 40 (due to the gaps in binary values between some letters).

Converting simple character strings between ASCII and EBCDIC is trivial. The situation is more difficult if the character being converted is not present in the standard character set of the target code. A good example is a logical *not* symbol that is used in a major mainframe programming language (PL/I); there is no corresponding character in the ASCII set. Likewise, some ASCII characters used for C programming were not present in the original EBCDIC character set, although these were later added to EBCDIC. There is still some confusion about the cent sign (¢) and the hat symbol (^), and a few more obscure symbols.

Mainframes also use several versions of double-byte character sets (DBCS), mostly for Asian languages. The same character sets are used by some PC programs.

Traditional mainframe programming does not use special characters to terminate fields. In particular, nulls and new line characters (or carriage return and line feed (CR/LF) character pairs) are not used. There is no concept of a *binary* versus a *text* file. Bytes can be interpreted as EBCDIC or ASCII or something else if programmed properly. If such files are sent to a mainframe printer, it attempts to interpret them as EBCDIC characters because the printer is sensitive to the character set. The z/OS web server routinely stores ASCII files because the data will be interpreted by a PC browser program that expects ASCII data. Providing that no one attempts to print the ASCII files on a mainframe printer (or display them on a 3270), the system does not care what character set is being used.

8.4.2 Unicode on the mainframe

Unicode, an industry standard, is an 8- or 16-bit character set intended to represent text and symbols in all modern languages and I/T protocols. Mainframes (using EBCDIC for single-byte characters), PCs, and various RISC systems use the same Unicode assignments.

Unicode is maintained by the Unicode Consortium. More information about the Unicode Consortium can be found at:

http://www.unicode.org/

There is increasing use of Unicode in mainframe applications. The latest System z mainframes include a number of unique hardware instructions for Unicode. Unicode usage on mainframes is primarily in Java and COBOL. However, z/OS middleware products are also beginning to use Unicode.

8.4.3 Interfaces for z/OS application programmers

When operating systems are developed to meet the needs of the computing marketplace, applications are written to run on those operating systems. Over the years, many applications have been developed that run on z/OS and, more recently, UNIX. To accommodate customers with UNIX applications, z/OS contains a full UNIX operating system in addition to its traditional z/OS interfaces. The z/OS implementation of UNIX interfaces is known collectively as z/OS UNIX System Services, or z/OS UNIX for short.

The most common interface for z/OS developers is TSO/E and its panel-driven interface, ISPF, using a 3270 terminal. Generally, developers use 3270 terminal emulators running on personal computers, rather than actual 3270 terminals. Emulators can provide developers with auxiliary functions, such as multiple sessions, and uploading and downloading code and data from the PC. TSO/E and other z/OS user interfaces are described in Chapter 4, "TSO/E, ISPF, and UNIX: Interactive facilities of z/OS" on page 165.

Program development on z/OS typically involves the use of a line editor to manipulate source code files, the use of batch jobs for compilation, and a variety of mechanisms for testing the code. Interactive debuggers, based on 3270 terminal functions, are available for common languages. This chapter introduces the tools and utilities for developing a simple program to run on z/OS.

Development using only the z/OS UNIX portion of z/OS can be through telnet sessions (from which the vi editor is available), through 3270 and TSO/E using other editors, or through X Window System sessions from personal computers running X servers. The X server interfaces are less commonly used.

Alternate methods of application development are also available. Integrated development environments (IDEs) that offer syntax highlighting, code analysis and understanding, and source code re-factoring capabilities can be used for Java and COBOL language source code.

See Figure 8-7 for an example of one of these IDEs.

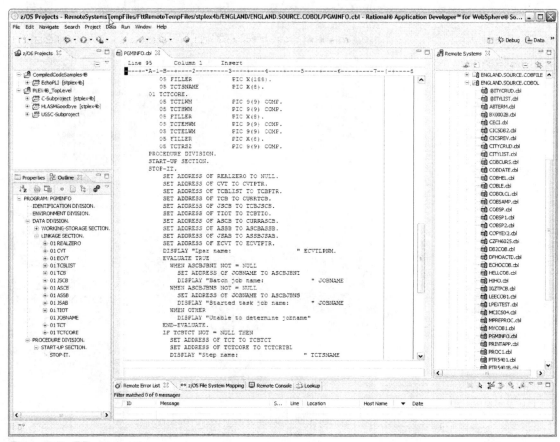

Figure 8-7   RDz page

IBM Rational® development tools support integration with both mainframe file systems (data sets and files) and source configuration management (SCM) systems. This allows application programmers to develop mainframe applications seamlessly with applications running on other systems using sophisticated tools.

This book discusses the use of online applications and middleware products in Part 3, "Online workloads for z/OS" on page 399, which includes topics on network communications, database management, and web serving.

8.4.4 Using application development tools

Producing well-tested code requires the use of tools on the mainframe. The primary tool for the programmer is the ISPF editor.

When developing traditional, procedural programs in languages such as COBOL and PL/I, the programmer often logs on to the mainframe and uses an IDE or the ISPF editor to modify the code, compile it, and run it. The programmer uses a common repository (such as the IBM Software Configuration Library Manager (SCLM)) to store code that is under development. The repository allows the programmer check code in or out, and ensures that programmers do not interfere with each others' work. SCLM is included with ISPF as an option from the main menu.

Executable:
A program file ready to run in a particular environment.

For purposes of simplicity, the source code could be stored and maintained in a partitioned data set (PDS or PDSE). However, using a PDS does not provide change control or prevent multiple updates to the same version of code in the way that SCLM would. So, wherever we have written "checking out" or "saving" to SCLM, assume that you could substitute this with "edit a PDS member" or "save a PDS member."

When the source code changes are complete, the programmer submits a JCL file to compile the source code, bind the application modules, and create an executable for testing. The programmer conducts "unit tests" of the functionality of the program. The programmer uses job monitoring and viewing tools to track the running programs, view the output, and make appropriate corrections to source code or other objects. Sometimes, a program will create a "dump" of memory when a failure occurs. The programmer can also use tools to interrogate the dump output and to sift through executing code to identify the failure points.

Some mainframe application programmers have now switched to the use of IDE tools to accelerate the edit/compile/test process. IDEs allow application programmers to edit, test, and debug source code on a workstation instead of directly on the mainframe system. The use of an IDE is particularly useful for building "hybrid" applications that employ host-based programs or transactional systems, but also contain a web browser-like user interface.

After the components are developed and tested, the application programmer packages them into the appropriate deployment format and passes them to the team that coordinates production code deployments.

Application enablement services available on z/OS include:

► Language Environment®
► C/C++ IBM Open Class® Library
► DCE Application Support1
► Encina Toolkit Executive2

- C/C++ with Debug Tool
- GDDM-PGF
- GDDM-REXX
- HLASM Toolkit
- Traditional languages, such as COBOL, PL/I, and Fortran

8.4.5 Conducting a debugging session

The application programmer conducts a "unit test" to test the functionality of a particular module being developed. The programmer uses job monitoring and viewing software, such as SDSF (described in 6.8, "Understanding SDSF" on page 257), to track the running compile jobs, view the compiler output, and verify the results of the unit tests. If necessary, the programmer makes the appropriate corrections to source code or other objects.

Sometimes, a program will create a "dump" of memory when a failure occurs. When this happens, a z/OS application programmer might use tools such as IBM Debug Tool and IBM Fault Analyzer to interrogate the dump output and to trace through executing code to find the failure or misbehaving code.

A typical development session follows these steps:

1. Log on to z/OS.
2. Enter ISPF and open/check out source code from the SCLM repository (or PDS).
3. Edit the source code to make the necessary modifications.
4. Submit JCL to build the application and do a test run.
5. Switch to SDSF to view the running job status.
6. View the job output in SDSF to check for errors.
7. View the dump output to find bugs.[1]
8. Re-run the compile/link/go job and view the status.
9. Check the validity of the job output.
10. Save the source code in SCLM (or PDS).

---

[1] The origin of the term "programming bug" is often attributed to US Navy Lieutenant Grace Murray Hopper in 1945. As the story goes, Lt. Hopper was testing the Mark II Aiken Relay Calculator at Harvard University. One day, a program that worked previously mysteriously failed. Upon inspection, the operator found that a moth was trapped between the circuit relay points and had created a short circuit (early calculators occupied many square feet, and consisted of tens of thousands of vacuum tubes). The September 9, 1945 log included both the moth and the entry: "First actual case of a bug being found", and that they had "debugged the machine".

Some mainframe application programmers have now switched to the use of IDE tools to accelerate the edit/compile/test process. IDE tools such as IBM Rational Developer for z/OS are used to edit source code using the LPEX editor and to run either local compiles "off-platform" for syntax checking or remote compiles directly on the host system, and to perform debugging on the host with a GUI debugger.

Transaction: An activity or request that updates master files for orders, changes, additions, and so on.

The use of the IDE is particularly useful if hybrid applications are being built that employ host-based programs in COBOL or transaction systems such as CICS and IMS, but also contain a web browser-like user interface. The IDE provides a unified development environment to build both the online transaction processing (OLTP) components in a high-level language and the HTML front-end user interface components. After the components are developed and tested, they are packaged into the appropriate deployment format and passed to the team that coordinates production code deployments.

Besides new application code, the application programmer is responsible for the maintenance and enhancement of existing mainframe applications. In fact, this is the primary job for many high-level language programmers on the mainframe today. While most z/OS customers are still creating new programs with COBOL or PL/I, languages such as Java have become popular for building new applications on the mainframe, just as on distributed platforms.

However, for those of us interested in the traditional languages, there is still widespread development of programs on the mainframe in high-level languages such as COBOL and PL/I. There are hundreds of thousands of programs in production on mainframe systems around the world, and these programs are critical to the day-to-day business of the corporations that use them. COBOL and other high-level language programmers are needed to maintain existing code and make updates and modifications to those programs.

Also, many corporations continue to build new application logic in COBOL and other traditional languages, and IBM continues to enhance the high-level language compilers to include new functions and features that allow these languages to continue to use newer technologies and data formats.

8.4.6 Performing a system test

The difference between the testing done at this stage and the testing done during the development phase is that we are now testing the application as a whole, as well as in conjunction with other applications. We also carry out tests that can only be done after the application coding has been completed because we need to know how the whole application performs, and not just a portion of it.

The tests performed during this phase are:

▶ User testing: Testing the application for functionality and usability.

▶ Integration testing: The new application is tested together with other applications to see if they interface as expected.

▶ Performance or stress testing: The application is tested using copies of actual production data (or at least production data volume) to see how well the application performs when there is high demand.

The results of the user and integration tests need to be verified to ensure that they are satisfactory. In addition, the performance of the application must match the requirements. Any issues coming out of these tests need to be addressed before going into production. The number of issues encountered during the testing phase are a good indication of how well we did our design work.

8.5 Going into production on the mainframe

The act of "going into production" is not simply turning on a switch to make the application production-ready. It is much more complicated than that. And from one project to the next, the way in which a program goes into production can change. In some cases, where we have an existing system that we are replacing, we might decide to run in parallel for a period of time prior to switching over to the new application. In this case, we run both the old and the new systems against the same data and then compare the results. If after a certain period of time we are satisfied with the results, we switch to the new application. If we discover problems, we can correct them and continue the parallel run until there are not any new problems.

In other cases, we are dealing with a new system, and we might just have a cut-over day when we start using it. Even in the case of a new system, we are usually replacing some form of system, even if it is a manual system, so we could still do a parallel test if we want.

Whichever method is used to go into production, there are still all of the loose ends that need to be taken care of before we hand the system over to Operations. One of the tasks is to provide documentation for the system, and procedures for running and using it. We need to train everyone who interacts with the system.

When all of the documentation and training has been done, we can hand over responsibility for the running of the application to Operations and responsibility for maintaining the application to the Maintenance group. In some cases, the Development group also maintains applications.

At this point, the application development life cycle reaches a steady state and we enter the maintenance phase of the application. From this point onward, we only apply enhancements and day-to-day changes to the application. Because the application now falls under a change control process, all changes require testing according to the process for change control, before they are accepted into production. In this way, a stable, running application is ensured for users.

8.6 Summary

This chapter describes the roles of the application designer and application programmer. The discussion is intended to highlight the types of decisions that are involved in designing and developing an application to run in the mainframe environment. This is not to say that the process is much different on other platforms, but some of the questions and conclusions can be different.

This chapter then describes the life cycle of designing and developing an application to run on z/OS. The process begins with the requirement gathering phase, in which the application designer analyzes user requirements to see how best to satisfy them. There might be many ways to arrive at a given solution; the object of the analysis and design phases is to ensure that the optimal solution is chosen. Here, "optimal" does not mean "quickest," although time is an issue in any project. Instead, optimal refers to the best overall solution, with regard to user requirements and problem analysis.

The EBCDIC character set is different from the ASCII character set. On a character-by-character basis, translation between these two character sets is trivial. When collating sequences are considered, the differences are more significant and converting programs from one character set to the other can be trivial or it can be quite complex. The EBCDIC character set became an established standard before the current 8-bit ASCII character set had significant use.

At the end of the design phase, the programmer's role takes over. The programmer must now translate the application design into error-free program code. Throughout the development phase, the programmer tests the code as each module is added to the whole. The programmer must correct any logic problems that are detected and add the updated modules to the completed suite of tested programs.

An application rarely exists in isolation. Rather, an application is usually part of a larger set of applications, where the output from one application is the input to the next application. To verify that a new application does not cause problems when incorporated into the larger set of applications, the application programmer conducts a system test or integration test.

These tests are themselves designed, and many test results are verified, by the actual application users. If any problems are found during system test, they must be resolved and the test repeated before the process can proceed to the next step.

Following a successful system test, the application is ready to go into production. This phase is sometimes referred to as promoting an application. Once promoted, the application code is now more closely controlled. A business would not want to introduce a change into a working system without being sure of its reliability. At most z/OS sites, strict rules govern the promotion of applications (or modules within an application) to prevent untested code from contaminating a "pure" system.

At this point in the life cycle of an application, it has reached a steady state. The changes that will be made to a production application are enhancements, functional changes (for example, tax laws change, so payroll programs need to change), or corrections.

Table 8-3 lists the key terms used in this chapter.

Table 8-3   Key terms used in this chapter

application	ASCII	database
design	develop	EBCDIC
executable	platform	transaction

8.7 Questions for review

To help test your understanding of the material in this chapter, answer the following review questions:

1. What are the differences between an application designer and an application programmer? Which role must have a global view of the entire project?

2. In which phase of the application development life cycle does the designer conduct interviews?

3. What is the reason for using a repository to manage source code?

4. What are the phases in an application development life cycle? State briefly what happens in each phase.

5. If you were a designer on a specific project and the time line for getting the new application into production was short, what decisions might you make to reduce the overall time line of the project?

6. As part of your system testing phase, you do a performance test on the application. Why would you use production data to do this test?

7. Give some possible reasons for deciding to use batch for an application versus online.

8. Why not store all documents in ASCII format, so they would not have to be converted from EBCDIC?

9

Using programming languages on z/OS

Objective: As your company's newest z/OS application programmer, you need to know which programming languages are supported on z/OS, and how to determine which is best for a given set of requirements.

After completing this chapter, you will be able to:

- ▶ List several common programming languages for the mainframe.
- ▶ Explain the differences between a compiled language and an interpreted language.
- ▶ Create a simple CLIST or REXX program.
- ▶ Choose an appropriate data file organization for an online application.
- ▶ Compare the advantages of a high level language to those of the Assembler language.
- ▶ Explain the relationship between a data set name, a DD name, and the file name within a program.
- ▶ Explain how the use of z/OS Language Environment affects the decisions made by the application designer.

Refer to Table 9-1 on page 361 for a list of key terms used in this chapter.

9.1 Overview of programming languages

A computer language is the way that a human communicates with a computer. It is needed because a computer works only with its machine language (bits and bytes). This is slow and cumbersome for humans to use. Therefore, we write programs in a computer language, which then gets converted into machine language for the computer to process.

There are many computer languages, and they have been evolving from machine language into a more natural way of writing. Some languages have been adapted to the kind of application that they intended to solve and to the kind of approach used in the design. The word *generation* has been used to indicate this evolution.

Programming language:
The means by which a human communicates with a computer.

A classification of computer languages follows:

1. Machine language, the first generation, is direct machine code.

2. Assembler, the second generation, uses mnemonics to produce the instructions to be translated later into machine language by an assembly program, such as Assembler language.

3. Procedural languages, the third generation, also known as high-level languages (HLL), such as Pascal, FORTRAN, Algol, COBOL, PL/I, Basic, and C. The coded program, called a source program, has to be translated through a compilation step.

Generation:
Stages in the evolution of computer languages.

4. Non-procedural languages, the fourth generation, also known as 4GL, is used for predefined functions in applications for databases, report generators, queries, such as RPG, CSP, and QMF™.

5. Visual Programming languages that use a mouse and icons, such as VisualBasic and VisualC++.

6. Hypertext Markup Language, which are used for writing World Wide Web documents.

7. Object-oriented language, OO technology, such as Smalltalk, Java, and C++.

8. Other languages, for example, 3D applications.

Each computer language evolved separately, driven by the creation of and adaptation to new standards. In the following sections, we describe several of the most widely used computer languages supported by z/OS:

- ▶ "Using Assembler language on z/OS" on page 326
- ▶ "Using COBOL on z/OS" on page 328
- ▶ "Using PL/I on z/OS" on page 338
- ▶ "Using C/C++ on z/OS" on page 342
- ▶ "Using Java on z/OS" on page 343

- ► "Using CLIST language on z/OS" on page 345
- ► "Using REXX on z/OS" on page 347

In addition, we can add the use of shell script and Perl in the z/OS UNIX System Services environment to this list.

For the computer languages under discussion, we have listed their evolution and classified them. There are:

- ► Procedural and non-procedural
- ► Compiled and interpreted
- ► Machine-dependent and non-machine-dependent

Assembler language programs are *machine-dependent*, because the language is a symbolic version of the machine's language on which the program is running. Assembler language instructions can differ from one machine to another, so an Assembler language program written for one machine might not be portable to another. Rather, it would most likely need to be rewritten to use the instruction set of the other machine. A program written in a high-level language (HLL) would run on other platforms, but it would need to be recompiled into the machine language of the target platform.

Most of the HLLs that we touch upon in this chapter are *procedural languages*. This type is well-suited to writing structured programs. The *non-procedural languages*, such as SQL and RPG, are more suited for special purposes, such as report generation.

Most HLLs are compiled into machine language, but some are interpreted. Those that are compiled result in machine code that is efficient for repeated executions. Interpreted languages must be parsed, interpreted, and executed each time that the program is run. The trade-off for using interpreted languages is a decrease in programmer time, but an increase in machine resources.

The advantages of compiled and interpreted languages are further explored in 9.11, "Compiled versus interpreted languages" on page 350.

9.2 Choosing a programming language for z/OS

In developing a program to run on z/OS, your choice of a programming language might be determined by the following considerations:

- ► What type of application?
- ► What are the response time requirements?
- ► What are the budget constraints for development and ongoing support?
- ► What are the time constraints of the project?
- ► Do we need to write some of the subroutines in different languages because of the strengths of a particular language versus the overall language of choice?
- ► Do we use a compiled or an interpreted language?

The sections that follow look at considerations for several languages commonly supported on the mainframe.

9.3 Using Assembler language on z/OS

Assembler: A compiler for Assembler language programs.

Assembler language is a symbolic programming language that can be used to code instructions instead of coding in machine language. It is the symbolic programming language that is closest to the machine language in form and content. Therefore, Assembler language is an excellent candidate for writing programs in which:

- ► You need control of your program, down to the byte or bit level.
- ► You must write subroutines[1] for functions that are not provided by other symbolic programming languages, such as COBOL, FORTRAN, or PL/I.

Assembler language is made up of statements that represent either instructions or comments. The instruction statements are the working part of the language, and they are divided into the following three groups:

- ► A *machine instruction* is the symbolic representation of a machine language instruction or instruction sets, such as:
  - IBM Enterprise Systems Architecture/390 (ESA/390)
  - IBM z/Architecture

  It is called a machine instruction because the assembler translates it into the machine language code that the computer can execute.

---

[1] Subroutines are programs that are invoked frequently by other programs and by definition should be written with performance in mind. Assembler language is a good choice for writing a subroutine.

▶ An *assembler instruction* is a request to the assembler to do certain operations during the assembly of a source module, for example, defining data constants, reserving storage areas, and defining the end of the source module.

▶ A *macro instruction* or *macro* is a request to the assembler program to process a predefined sequence of instructions called a *macro definition*. From this definition, the assembler generates machine and assembler instructions, which it then processes as though they were part of the original input in the source module.

Compiler:
Software that converts a set of high-level language statements into a lower-level representation.

The assembler produces a program listing containing information that was generated during the various phases of the assembly process.[2] It is really a compiler for Assembler language programs.

The assembler also produces information for other processors, such as a *binder* (or *linker*, for earlier releases of the operating system). Before the computer can execute your program, the object code (called an *object deck* or simply OBJ) has to be run through another process to resolve the addresses where instructions and data will be located. This process is called *linkage-editing* (or *link-editing*, for short) and is performed by the binder.

Binder:
Binds (link-edits) object decks into load modules.

The binder or linkage editor (for more details, see 10.3.7, "How a linkage editor is used" on page 378) uses information in the object decks to combine them into load modules. At program fetch time, the load module produced by the binder is loaded into virtual storage. After the program is loaded, it can be run.

Load module:
Produced by the linkage editor from object modules; it is ready to be loaded and run.

---

[2] A program listing does not contain *all* of the information that is generated during the assembly process. To capture all of the information that could possibly be in the listing (and more), the z/OS programmer can specify an assembler option called ADATA to have the assembler produce a SYSADATA file as output. The SYSADATA file is not human-readable; its contents are in a form that is designed for a tool to process. The use of a SYSADATA file is simpler for tools to process than the older custom of extracting similar data through "listing scrapers".

Figure 9-1 shows these steps.

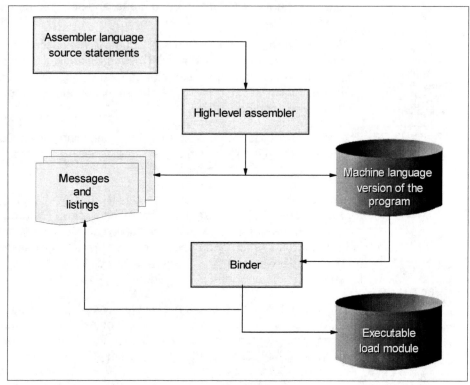

Figure 9-1   Assembler source to executable module

You can find more information about using Assembler language on z/OS in *HLASM General Information*, GC26-4943 and *HLASM Language Reference*, SC26-4940. These books are available on the web at:

```
http://www-947.ibm.com/support/entry/portal/Documentation
```

9.4 Using COBOL on z/OS

Common Business-Oriented Language (COBOL) is a programming language similar to English that is widely used to develop business-oriented applications in the area of commercial data processing. COBOL has become a generic term for computer programming in this kind of computer language. However, as used in this chapter, COBOL refers to the product IBM Enterprise COBOL for z/OS and OS/390.

In addition to the traditional characteristics provided by the COBOL language, this version of COBOL is capable, through COBOL functions, of integrating COBOL applications into web-oriented business processes. With the capabilities of this release, application developers can perform the following functions:

Debugging:
Debugging means locating the errors in the source code (the program logic).

▶ Use new debugging functions in Debug Tool.

▶ Enable interoperability with Java when an application runs in an IMS Java-dependent region

▶ Simplify the componentization of COBOL programs and enable interoperability with Java components across distributed applications

▶ Promote the exchange and usage of data in standardized formats including XML and Unicode

Using Enterprise COBOL for z/OS and OS/390, COBOL and Java applications can interoperate in the e-business world.

The COBOL compiler produces a program listing containing all the information that it generated during the compilation. The compiler also produces information for other processors, such as the binder.

Before the computer can execute your program, the object deck has to be run through another process to resolve the addresses where instructions and data will be located. This process is called *linkage edition* and is performed by the binder.

The binder uses information in the object decks to combine them into load modules (these are further discussed in 10.3.7, "How a linkage editor is used" on page 378). At program fetch time, the load module produced by the binder is loaded into virtual storage. When the program is loaded, it can then be run.

Figure 9-2 illustrates the process of translating the COBOL source language statements into an executable load module. This process is similar to that of Assembler language programs. In fact, this same process is used for all of the HLLs that are compiled.

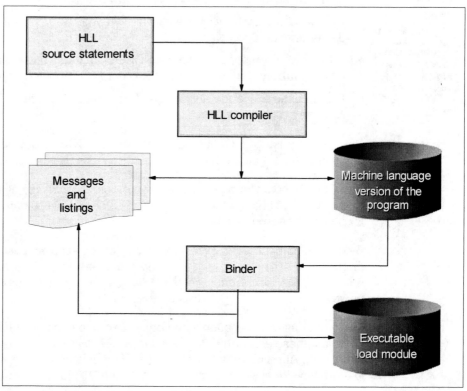

Figure 9-2   HLL source to executable module

9.4.1 COBOL program format

With the exception of the COPY and REPLACE statements and the end program marker, the statements, entries, paragraphs, and sections of a COBOL source program are grouped into the following four divisions:

▶ IDENTIFICATION DIVISION, which identifies the program with a name and, if you want, gives other identifying information.

▶ ENVIRONMENT DIVISION, where you describe the aspects of your program that depend on the computing environment.

- DATA DIVISION, where the characteristics of your data are defined in one of the following sections in the DATA DIVISION:
  - FILE SECTION: Defines data used in input-output operations.
  - LINKAGE SECTION: Describes data from another program.

  When defining data developed for internal processing:

  - WORKING-STORAGE SECTION: Has storage statically allocated and remain for the life of the run unit.
  - LOCAL-STORAGE SECTION: Has storage allocated each time a program is called and de-allocated when the program ends.
  - LINKAGE SECTION: Describes data from another program.
- PROCEDURE DIVISION, where the instructions related to the manipulation of data and interfaces with other procedures are specified.

  The PROCEDURE DIVISION of a program is divided into sections and paragraphs, which contain sentences and statements, as described here:

  - Section: A logical subdivision of your processing logic. A section has a section header and is optionally followed by one or more paragraphs. A section can be the subject of a PERFORM statement. One type of section is for declaratives.

    Declaratives are a set of one or more special purpose sections, written at the beginning of the PROCEDURE DIVISION, the first of which is preceded by the key word DECLARATIVES and the last of which is followed by the key word END DECLARATIVES.

  - Paragraph: A subdivision of a section, procedure, or program. A paragraph can be the subject of a statement.
  - Sentence: A series of one or more COBOL statements ending with a period.
  - Statement: Performs a defined step of COBOL processing, such as adding two numbers.
  - Phrase: A subdivision of a statement.

Examples of COBOL divisions

Example 9-1 and Example 9-2 shows examples of IDENTIFICATION DIVISION and ENVIRONMENT DIVISION, respectively.

Example 9-1   IDENTIFICATION DIVISION

```
IDENTIFICATION DIVISION.
Program-ID. Helloprog.
Author. A. Programmer.
Installation.  Computing Laboratories.
Date-Written.  08/21/2002.
```

Example 9-2   ENVIRONMENT DIVISION

```
ENVIRONMENT DIVISION.
CONFIGURATION SECTION.
SOURCE-COMPUTER. computer-name.
OBJECT-COMPUTER. computer-name.
SPECIAL-NAMES.
  special-names-entries.
INPUT-OUTPUT SECTION.
FILE-CONTROL.
    SELECT [OPTIONAL] file-name-1
        ASSIGN TO system-name [FOR MULTIPLE {REEL | UNIT}]
        [ .... .
I-O-CONTROL.
    SAME [RECORD] AREA FOR file-name-1 ... file-name-n.
```

Example of input-output coding

Example 9-3 shows an example of input-output coding.

Example 9-3   Input and output files in FILE-CONTROL

```
IDENTIFICATION DIVISION.
. . .
ENVIRONMENT DIVISION.
INPUT-OUTPUT SECTION.
FILE-CONTROL.
    SELECT filename ASSIGN TO assignment-name
    ORGANIZATION IS org ACCESS MODE IS access
    FILE STATUS IS file-status
. . .
DATA DIVISION.
FILE SECTION.
FD  filename
01  recordname
    nn . . . fieldlength & type
```

```
        nn . . . fieldlength & type
    . . .
    WORKING-STORAGE SECTION
    01 file-status  PICTURE 99.
    . . .
    PROCEDURE DIVISION.
        . . .
        OPEN iomode filename
        . . .
        READ filename
        . . .
        WRITE recordname
        . . .
        CLOSE filename
        . . .
        STOP RUN.
```

Where:

► `org` indicates the organization, which can be SEQUENTIAL, LINE SEQUENTIAL, INDEXED, or RELATIVE.

► `access` indicates the access mode, which can be SEQUENTIAL, RANDOM, or DYNAMIC.

► `iomode` is for INPUT or OUTPUT mode. If you are only reading from a file, use INPUT. If you are only writing to it, use OUTPUT or EXTEND. If you are both reading and writing, ise I-O, except for organization LINE SEQUENTIAL.

► Other values like `filename`, `recordname`, `fieldname` (nn in the example), `fieldlength` and `type` are also specified.

9.4.2 COBOL relationship between JCL and program files

Example 9-4 shows the relationship between JCL statements and the files in a COBOL program. By not referring to physical locations of data files in a program, we achieve device independence, that is, we can change where the data resides and what it is called without having to change the program. We would only need to change the JCL.

Example 9-4   COBOL relationship between JCL and program files

```
//MYJOB    JOB
//STEP1    EXEC IGYWCLG
...
    INPUT-OUTPUT SECTION.
    FILE-CONTROL.
```

```
      SELECT INPUT1 ASSIGN TO INPUTDSN .....
      SELECT DISKOUT ASSIGN TO OUTFILE ...
  FILE SECTION.
    FD INPUT1
       BLOCK CONTAINS...
       DATA RECORD IS INPUT-RECORD
    01 INPUT-RECORD
...
    FD DISKOUT
       DATA RECORD IS OUTPUT-RECORD
    01 OUTPUT-RECORD
...
/*
//GO.INPUTDSN DD DSN=MY.INPUT,DISP=SHR
//GO.OUTFILE DD DSN=MY.OUTPUT,DISP=OLD
```

Example 9-4 on page 333 shows a COBOL compile, link, and go job stream, listing the file program statements and the JCL statements to which they refer.

The COBOL SELECT statements create the links between the DDNAMEs INPUTDSN and OUTFILE, and the COBOL FDs INPUT1 and OUTPUT1, respectively. The COBOL FDs are associated with group items INPUT-RECORD and OUTPUT-RECORD.

The DD cards INPUTDSN and OUTFILE are related to the data sets MY.INPUT and MY.OUTPUT, respectively. The end result of this linkage in our example is that records read from the file INPUT1 will be read from the physical data set MY.INPUT and records written to the file OUTFILE will be written to the physical data set MY.OUTPUT. The program is completely independent of the location of the data and the name of the data sets.

Figure 9-3 shows the relationship between the physical data set, the JCL, and the program for Example 9-4 on page 333.

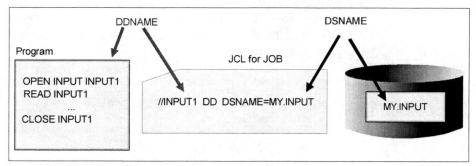

Figure 9-3   Relationship between JCL, program, and data set

Again, because the program does not make any reference to the physical data set, we would not need to recompile the program if the name of the data set or its location were to change.

9.4.3 Running COBOL programs under UNIX

To run COBOL programs in the UNIX environment, you must compile them with the Enterprise COBOL or the COBOL for OS/390 and VM compiler. They must be reentrant, so use the compiler and binder option RENT.

9.4.4 Communicating with Java methods

To achieve inter-language interoperability with Java, you must follow certain rules and guidelines for:

- ▶ Using services in the Java Native Interface (JNI)
- ▶ Coding data types
- ▶ Compiling your COBOL programs

You can invoke methods that are written in Java from COBOL programs, and you can invoke methods that are written in COBOL from Java programs. For basic Java object capabilities, you can use COBOL object-oriented language. For additional Java capabilities, you can call JNI services.

Because Java programs might be multi-threaded and use asynchronous signals, compile your COBOL programs with the THREAD option.

9.4.5 Creating a DLL or a DLL application

A dynamic link library (DLL) is a file that contains executable code and data that is bound to a program at run time. The code and data in a DLL can be shared by several applications simultaneously. Creating a DLL or a DLL application is similar to creating a regular COBOL application. It involves writing, compiling, and linking your source code.

Special considerations when writing a DLL or a DLL application include:

► Determining how the parts of the load module or the application relate to each other or to other DLLs

► Deciding what linking or calling mechanisms to use

Depending on whether you want a DLL load module or a load module that references a separate DLL, you need to use slightly different compiler and binder options.

9.4.6 Structuring OO applications

You can structure applications that use object-oriented (OO) COBOL syntax in one of three ways. An OO application can begin with:

► A COBOL program, which can have any name.

► A Java class definition that contains a method called *main*. You can run the application with the Java command, specifying the name of the class that contains main and zero or more strings as command-line arguments.

► A COBOL class definition that contains a factory method called *main*. You can run the application with the Java command, specifying the name of the class that contains main and zero or more strings as command-line arguments.

For more information about using COBOL on z/OS, see *Enterprise COBOL for z/OS and OS/390 V3R2 Language Reference*, SC27-1408 and *Enterprise COBOL for z/OS and OS/390 V3R2 Programming Guide*, SC27-1412. These books are available on the web at:

```
http://www-947.ibm.com/support/entry/portal/Documentation
```

9.5 HLL relationship between JCL and program files

In 9.4.2, "COBOL relationship between JCL and program files" on page 333, we learned how to isolate a COBOL program from changes in data set name and data set location. The technique of referring to physical files by a symbolic file name is not restricted to COBOL; it is used by all HLLs and even in Assembler language. See Example 9-5 for a generic HLL example of a program that references data sets through symbolic file names.

Example 9-5   HLL relationship between JCL and program files

```
//MYJOB     JOB
//STEP1     EXEC CLG
...
   OPEN FILE=INPUT1
   OPEN FILE=OUTPUT1
   READ FILE=INPUT1
...
   WRITE FILE=OUTPUT1
...
   CLOSE FILE=INPUT1
   CLOSE FILE=OUTPUT1
/*
//GO.INPUT1  DD DSN=MY.INPUT,DISP=SHR
//GO.OUTPUT1 DD DSN=MY.OUTPUT,DISP=OLD
```

Isolating your program from changes to data set name and location is the normal objective. However, there could be cases when a program needs to access a specific data set at a specific location on a direct access storage device (DASD). This can be accomplished in Assembler language and even in some HLLs.

The practice of "hardcoding" data set names or other such information in a program is not usually considered a good programming practice. Values that are hardcoded in a program are subject to change and therefore require that the program be recompiled each time a value changed. Externalizing these values from programs, as with the case of referring to data sets within a program by a symbolic name, is a more effective practice that allows the program to continue working even if the data set name changes.

For a more detailed explanation about using a symbolic name to refer to a file, refer to 6.5, "Why z/OS uses symbolic file names" on page 250.

9.6 Using PL/I on z/OS

Programming Language/I (PL/I, pronounced "P-L one"), is a full-function, general-purpose, high-level programming language suitable for the development of:

► Commercial applications
► Engineering/scientific applications
► Many other applications

The process of compiling a PL/I source program and then link-editing the object deck into a load module is basically the same as it is for COBOL. See Figure 9-2 on page 330, 10.3.7, "How a linkage editor is used" on page 378 and Figure 9-3 on page 335 for more details.

The relationship between JCL and program files is the same for PL/I as it is for COBOL and other HLLs. See Figure 9-3 on page 335 and Example 9-5 on page 337 for more details.

9.6.1 PL/I program structure

Variable:
Holds data assigned to it until a new value is assigned.

PL/I is a block-structured language, consisting of packages, procedures, statements, expressions, and built-in functions, as shown in Figure 9-4 on page 339.

PL/I programs are made up of blocks. A *block* can be either a subroutine, or just a group of statements. A PL/I block allows you to produce highly modular applications, because blocks can contain declarations that define variable names and storage classes. Thus, you can restrict the scope of a variable to a single block or a group of blocks, or you can make it known throughout the compilation unit or a load module.

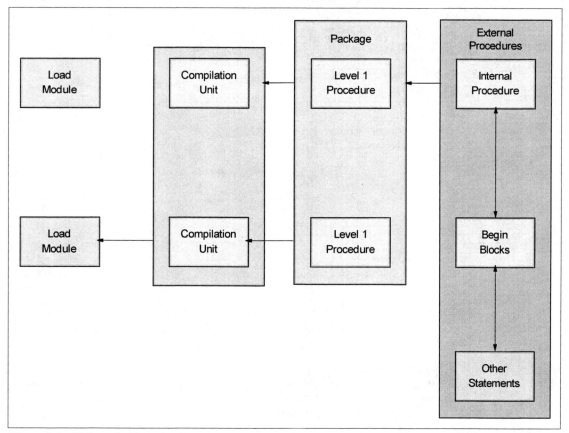

Figure 9-4   PL/I application structure

A PL/I application consists of one or more separately loadable entities, known as a *load modules*. Each load module can consist of one or more separately compiled entities, known as *compilation units*. Unless otherwise stated, a *program* refers to a PL/I application or a compilation unit.

A compilation unit is a PL/I package or an external procedure. Each package can contain zero or more procedures, some or all of which can be exported. A PL/I external or internal procedure contains zero or more blocks.

A PL/I block is either a PROCEDURE or a begin block, any of which contains zero or more statements or zero or more blocks. A procedure is a sequence of statements delimited by a procedure statement and a corresponding end statement, as shown in Example 9-6. A procedure can be a main procedure, a subroutine, or a function.

Example 9-6   A procedure block

```
A: procedure;
      statement-1
      statement-2

      .


      .


      .

      statement-n
      end Name;
```

A begin *block* is a sequence of statements delimited by a begin statement and a corresponding end statement, as shown in Example 9-7. A program is terminated when the main procedure is terminated.

Example 9-7   Begin block

```
B:  begin;
      statement-1
      statement-2

      .


      .

      statement-n
      end B;
```

9.6.2 Preprocessors

The PL/I compiler allows you to select one or more of the integrated preprocessors required by your program. You can select the include preprocessor, the macro preprocessor, the SQL preprocessor, or the CICS preprocessor, and you can select the order in which you would like them to be called.

Preprocessor:
Software that performs some preliminary processing on the input before it is processed by the main program.

Each preprocessor supports a number of options to allow you to tailor the processing to your needs:

► Include preprocessor

This preprocessor allows you to incorporate external source files into your programs by using include directives other than the PL/I directive %INCLUDE (the %INCLUDE directive is used to incorporate external text into the source program).

► Macro preprocessor

Macros allow you to write commonly used PL/I code in a way that hides implementation details and the data that is manipulated, and exposes only the operations. In contrast to a generalized subroutine, macros allow generation of only the code that is needed for each individual use.

► SQL preprocessor

In general, the coding for your PL/I program will be the same whether or not you want it to access a DB2 database. However, to retrieve, update, insert, and delete DB2 data and use other DB2 services, you must use SQL statements. You can use dynamic and static EXEC SQL statements in PL/I applications.

To communicate with DB2, you need to perform the following tasks:

– Code any SQL statements you need, delimiting them with EXEC SQL.
– Use the DB2 precompiler or compile using the PL/I PP(SQL()) compiler option.

Before you can take advantage of EXEC SQL support, you must have authority to access a DB2 system.

Note that the PL/I SQL preprocessor currently does not support DBCS.

► CICS preprocessor

You can use EXEC CICS statements in PL/I applications that run as transactions under CICS.

For more information about using PL/I on z/OS, see the IBM publications *Enterprise PL/I for z/OS V3R3 Language Reference*, SC27-1460 and *Enterprise PL/I for z/OS V3R3 Programming Guide*, SC27-1457. These books are available on the web at:

```
http://www-947.ibm.com/support/entry/portal/Documentation
```

9.6.3 Using the SAX parser

The PL/I compiler provides an interface called PLISAXx (x = A or B) that provides you with basic XML capability. The support includes a high-speed XML parser, which allows programs to accept inbound XML messages, check them for being well-formed, and transform their contents to PL/I data structures.

The XML support does not provide XML generation, which must be accomplished by using PL/I program logic. The XML support has no special environmental requirements. It executes in all the principal runtime environments, including CICS, IMS, and MQ Series, as well as z/OS batch and TSO.

9.7 Using C/C++ on z/OS

C is a programming language designed for a wide variety of programming purposes, including:

► System-level code
► Text processing
► Graphics

The C language contains a concise set of statements with functionality added through its library. This division enables C to be both flexible and efficient. An additional benefit is that the language is highly consistent across different systems.

The process of compiling a C source program and then link-editing the object deck into a load module is basically the same as it is for COBOL. See Figure 9-2 on page 330, 10.3.7, "How a linkage editor is used" on page 378, and Figure 9-3 on page 335 to review this process. The relationship between JCL and program files is the same for PL/I as it is for COBOL and other HLLs. See Figure 9-3 on page 335 and Example 9-5 on page 337 for more information.

For more information about using C and C++ on z/OS, refer to *C/C++ Language Reference*, SC09-4764 and *C/C++ Programming Guide*, SC09-4765. These books are available on the web at:

```
http://www-947.ibm.com/support/entry/portal/Documentation
```

9.8 Using Java on z/OS

Java is an object-oriented programming language developed by Sun Microsystems Inc. Java can be used for developing traditional mainframe commercial applications and Internet and intranet applications that use standard interfaces.

Java is an increasingly popular programming language used for many applications across multiple operating systems. IBM is a major supporter and user of Java across all of the IBM computing platforms, including z/OS. The z/OS Java products provide the same, full function Java APIs as on all other IBM platforms. In addition, the z/OS Java licensed programs have been enhanced to allow Java access to z/OS unique file systems. Programming languages such as Enterprise COBOL and Enterprise PL/I in z/OS provide interfaces to programs written in Java. These languages provide a set of interfaces or facilities for interacting with programs written in Java, as explained for COBOL in 9.4.4, "Communicating with Java methods" on page 335 and for PL/I in 9.6.3, "Using the SAX parser" on page 342.

The various Java Software Development Kit (SDK) licensed programs for z/OS help application developers use the Java APIs for z/OS, write or run applications across multiple platforms, or use Java to access data that resides on the mainframe. Some of these products allow Java applications to run in only a 31-bit addressing environment. However, with 64-bit SDKs for z/OS, pure Java applications that were previously storage-constrained by 31-bit addressing can execute in a 64-bit environment. Also, some mainframes support a special processor for running Java applications called the System z Application Assist Processor (zAAP). Programs can be run interactively through z/OS UNIX or in batch.

9.8.1 IBM SDK products for z/OS

As with Java SDKs for other IBM platforms, z/OS Java SDK licensed programs are supplied for industry standard APIs. The z/OS SDK products are independent of each other and can be ordered and serviced separately.

At the time of the writing of this book, the following Java SDKs are available for z/OS:

▶ The Java SDK 1.3.1 product called IBM Developer Kit for OS/390, Java 2 Technology Edition works on z/OS as well as the older OS/390. This is a 31-bit product. Many z/OS customers have moved (or *migrated*) their Java applications to the latest versions of Java.

- IBM SDK for z/OS, Java 2 Technology Edition, Version 1.4 is the IBM 31-bit port of the Sun Microsystems Java Software Development Kit (SDK) to the z/OS platform and is certified as a fully compliant Java product. IBM has successfully executed the Java Certification Kit (JCK) 1.4 provided by Sun Microsystems, Inc.

- IBM SDK for z/OS, Java 2 Technology Edition, Version 1.4 runs on z/OS Version 1 Release 4 or later, or z/OS.e Version 1 Release 4 or later. It provides a Java execution environment equivalent to that available on any other server platform.

- IBM 64-bit SDK for z/OS, Java 2 Technology Edition, Version 1.4 allows Java applications to execute in a 64-bit environment. It runs on z/OS Version 1 Release 6 or later. As with the 31-bit product, this product allows usage of the Java SDK1.4 APIs.

IBM provides more information about its Java SDK products for z/OS on the web at:

`http://www-03.ibm.com/systems/z/os/zos/tools/java/`

9.8.2 Using the Java Native Interface

The Java Native Interface (JNI) is the Java interface to native programming languages and is part of the Java Development Kits. If the standard Java APIs do not have the functionality you need, the JNI allows Java code that runs within a Java Virtual Machine (JVM) to operate with applications and libraries written in other languages, such as PL/I. In addition, the Invocation API allows you to embed a Java Virtual Machine into your native PL/I applications.

Java is a fairly complete programming language; however, there are situations in which you want to call a program written in another programming language. You would do this from Java with a method call to a native language, known as a *native method*. Programming through the JNI lets you use native methods to do many different operations. A native method can:

- Use Java objects in the same way that a Java method uses these objects.

- Create Java objects, including arrays and strings, and then inspect and use these objects to perform its tasks.

- Inspect and use objects created by Java application code.

- Update Java objects that it created or were passed to it; these updated objects can then be made available to the Java application.

Lastly, native methods can also easily call already-existing Java methods, capitalizing on the functionality already incorporated in the Java programming framework. In this way, both the native language side and the Java side of an application can create, update, and access Java objects, and then share these objects between them.

9.9 Using CLIST language on z/OS

The CLIST language is an interpreted language. Like programs in other high-level interpreted languages, CLISTs are easy to write and test. You do not compile or link-edit them. To test a CLIST, you simply run it and correct any errors that might occur until the program runs without error.

The CLIST and REXX languages are the two command languages available from TSO/E. The CLIST language enables you to work more efficiently with TSO/E.

The term CLIST (pronounced "see list") stands for *command list*; it is called this because the most basic CLISTs are lists of TSO/E commands. When you invoke such a CLIST, it issues the TSO/E commands in sequence.

The CLIST programming language is used for:

► Performing routine tasks (such as entering TSO/E commands)

► Invoking other CLISTs

► Invoking applications written in other languages

► ISPF applications (such as displaying panels and controlling application flow)

9.9.1 Types of CLISTs

A CLIST can perform a wide range of tasks, but most fall into one of three general categories:

► CLISTs that perform routine tasks

► CLISTs that are structured applications

► CLISTs that manage applications written in other languages

These are described in this section.

CLISTs that perform routine tasks

As a user of TSO/E, you probably perform certain tasks on a regular basis. These tasks might involve entering TSO/E commands to check on the status of data sets, to allocate data sets for particular programs, or to print files.

You can write CLISTs that significantly reduce the amount of time that you have to spend on these routine tasks. By grouping all the instructions required to perform a task in a CLIST, you reduce the time, number of keystrokes, and errors involved in performing the task and increase your productivity. A CLIST can consist of TSO/E commands only or a combination of TSO/E commands and CLIST statements.

CLISTs that are structured applications

The CLIST language includes the basic tools you need to write complete, structured applications. Any CLIST can invoke another CLIST, which is referred to as a *nested* CLIST. CLISTs can also contain separate routines called *sub-procedures*. Nested CLISTs and sub-procedures let you separate your CLISTs into logical units and put common functions in a single location. Specific CLIST statements let you:

► Define common data for sub-procedures and nested CLISTs.

► Restrict data to certain sub-procedures and CLISTs.

► Pass specific data to a sub-procedure or nested CLIST.

For interactive applications, CLISTs can issue ISPF commands to display full-screen panels. Conversely, ISPF panels can invoke CLISTs, based on input that a user types on the panel.

CLISTs that manage applications written in other languages

Suppose you have access to applications written in other programming languages, but the interfaces to these applications might not be easy to use or remember. Rather than write new applications, you can write CLISTs that provide easy-to-use interfaces between the user and such applications.

A CLIST can send messages to, and receive messages from, the terminal to determine what the user wants to do. Then, based on this information, the CLIST can set up the environment and issue the commands required to invoke the program that performs the requested tasks.

9.9.2 Executing CLISTs

To execute a CLIST, use the EXEC command. From an ISPF command line, type TS0 at the beginning of the command. In TSO/E EDIT or TEST mode, use the EXEC subcommand as you would use the EXEC command. (CLISTs executed under EDIT or TEST can issue only EDIT or TEST subcommands and CLIST statements, but you can use the END subcommand in a CLIST to end EDIT or TEST mode and allow the CLIST to issue TSO/E commands.)

9.9.3 Other uses for the CLIST language

Besides issuing TSO/E commands, CLISTs can perform more complex programming tasks. The CLIST language includes the programming tools you need to write extensive, structured applications. CLISTs can perform any number of complex tasks, from displaying a series of full-screen panels to managing programs written in other languages.

CLIST language features include:

► An extensive set of arithmetic and logical operators for processing numeric data

► String-handling functions for processing character data

► CLIST statements that let you structure your programs, perform I/O, define and modify variables, and handle errors and attention interrupts

9.10 Using REXX on z/OS

The Restructured Extended Executor (REXX) language is a procedural language that allows programs and algorithms to be written in a clear and structural way. It is an interpreted and compiled language. An interpreted language is different from other programming languages, such as COBOL, because it is not necessary to compile a REXX command list before executing it. However, you can choose to compile a REXX command list before executing it to reduce processing time.

The REXX programming language is typically used for:

► Performing routine tasks, such as entering TSO/E commands

► Invoking other REXX execs

► Invoking applications written in other languages

► ISPF applications (displaying panels and controlling application flow)

► One-time quick solutions to problems

- System programming

- Wherever we can use another HLL compiled language

REXX is also used in the Java environment, for example, a dialect of REXX called NetRexx works seamlessly with Java. NetRexx programs can use any Java classes directly, and can be used for writing any Java class. This brings Java security and performance to REXX programs, and REXX arithmetic and simplicity to Java. Thus, a single language, NetRexx, can be used for both scripting and application development.

The structure of a REXX program is simple. It provides a conventional selection of control constructs. For example, these include IF... THEN... ELSE... for simple conditional processing, SELECT... WHEN... OTHERWISE... END for selecting from a number of alternatives, and several varieties of DO... END for grouping and repetitions. No GOTO instruction is included, but a SIGNAL instruction is provided for abnormal transfer of control such as error exits and computed branching.

The relationship between JCL and program files is the same for REXX as it is for COBOL and other HLLs. See Figure 9-3 on page 335 and Example 9-5 on page 337 for more details.

9.10.1 Compiling and executing REXX command lists

A REXX program compiled under z/OS can run under z/VM. Similarly, a REXX program compiled under z/VM can run under z/OS. A REXX program compiled under z/OS or z/VM can run under z/VSE if REXX/VSE is installed.

The process of compiling a REXX source program and then link-editing the object deck into a load module is basically the same as it is for COBOL. See Figure 9-2 on page 330, 10.3.7, "How a linkage editor is used" on page 378 and Figure 9-3 on page 335 to see this process.

There are three main components of the REXX language when using a compiler:

- IBM Compiler for REXX on System z. The Compiler translates REXX source programs into compiled programs.

- IBM Library for REXX on System z. The Library contains routines that are called by compiled programs at run time.

- Alternate Library. The Alternate Library contains a language processor that transforms the compiled programs and runs them with the interpreter. It can be used by z/OS and z/VM users who do not have the IBM Library for REXX on System z to run compiled programs.

The Compiler and Library run on z/OS systems with TSO/E, and under CMS on z/VM systems. The IBM Library for REXX in REXX/VSE runs under z/VSE.

The Compiler can produce output in the following forms:

- Compiled EXECs

  These behave exactly like interpreted REXX programs. They are invoked the same way by the system's EXEC handler, and the search sequence is the same. The easiest way of replacing interpreted programs with compiled programs is by producing compiled EXECs. Users need not know whether the REXX programs they use are compiled EXECs or interpretable programs. Compiled EXECs can be sent to z/VSE to be run there.

- Object decks under z/OS or TEXT files under z/VM.

- A TEXT file is an object code file whose external references have not been resolved (this term is used on z/VM only). These must be transformed into executable form (load modules) before they can be used. Load modules and MODULE files are invoked the same way as load modules derived from other compilers, and the same search sequence applies. However, the search sequence is different from that of interpreted REXX programs and compiled EXECs. These load modules can be used as commands and as parts of REXX function packages. Object decks or MODULE files can be sent to z/VSE to build phases.

- IEXEC output

  This output contains the expanded source of the REXX program being compiled. Expanded means that the main program and all the parts included at compilation time by means of the %INCLUDE directive are contained in the IEXEC output. Only the text within the specified margins is contained in the IEXEC output. Note, however, that the default setting of MARGINS includes the entire text in the input records.

You can find more information about REXX in the following publications:

- *The REXX Language*, 2nd Ed., ZB35-5100
- *z/OS TSO/E REXX Reference*, SA22-7790
- *z/OS Using REXX and z/OS UNIX System Services*, SA22-7806
- *Creating Java Applications using NetRexx*, SG24-2216

Also, visit the following website for more information:

`http://www.ibm.com/software/awdtools/REXX/language/REXXlinks.html`

9.11 Compiled versus interpreted languages

During the design of an application, you might need to decide whether to use a compiled language or an interpreted language for the application source code. Both types of languages have their strengths and weaknesses. Usually, the decision to use an interpreted language is based on time restrictions on development or for ease of future changes to the program. A trade-off is made when using an interpreted language. You trade speed of development for higher execution costs. Because each line of an interpreted program must be translated each time it is executed, there is a higher impact. Thus, an interpreted language is generally more suited to ad hoc requests than predefined requests.

9.11.1 Advantages of compiled languages

Assembler, COBOL, PL/I, C/C++ are all translated by running the source code through a compiler. This results in efficient code that can be executed any number of times. The impact of the translation is incurred just once, when the source is compiled; thereafter, it need only be loaded and executed.

Interpreted languages, in contrast, must be parsed, interpreted, and executed each time the program is run, thereby greatly adding to the cost of running the program. For this reason, interpreted programs are usually less efficient than compiled programs.

Some programming languages, such as REXX and Java, can be either interpreted or compiled.

9.11.2 Advantages of interpreted languages

In "9.11.1, "Advantages of compiled languages" on page 350", we discussed the reasons for using languages that are compiled. In "9.9, "Using CLIST language on z/OS" on page 345" and "9.10, "Using REXX on z/OS" on page 347", we discussed the strong points of interpreted languages. There is no simple answer as to which language is "better"; it depends on the application. Even within an application, we could use many different languages. For example, one of the strengths of a language such as CLIST is that it is easy to code, test, and change. However, it is not efficient. The trade-off is machine resources for programmer time.

Keeping this situation in mind, we can see that it would make sense to use a compiled language for the intensive parts of an application (heavy resource usage), whereas interfaces (invoking the application) and less-intensive parts could be written in an interpreted language. An interpreted language might also be suited for ad hoc requests or even for prototyping an application.

One of the jobs of a designer is to weigh the strengths and weaknesses of each language and then decide which part of an application is best served by a particular language.

9.12 What is z/OS Language Environment

As we mentioned in Chapter 8, "Designing and developing applications for z/OS" on page 299, an *application* is a collection of one or more programs cooperating to achieve particular objectives, such as inventory control or payroll. The goals of application development include modularizing and sharing code, and developing applications on a workstation-based front end.

On z/OS, the Language Environment product provides a common environment for all conforming high-level language (HLL) products. An HLL is a programming language above the level of Assembler language and below that of program generators and query languages. z/OS Language Environment establishes a common language development and execution environment for application programmers on z/OS. Whereas functions were previously provided in individual language products, Language Environment eliminates the need to maintain separate language libraries.

In the past, programming languages had a limited ability to call each other and behave consistently across different operating systems. This characteristic constrained programs that wanted to use several languages in an application. Programming languages had different rules for implementing data structures and condition handling, and for interfacing with system services and library routines.

With Language Environment, and its ability to call one language from another, z/OS application programmers can use the functions and features in each language.

9.12.1 How Language Environment is used

Language Environment establishes a common runtime environment for all participating HLLs. It combines essential runtime services, such as routines for runtime message handling, condition handling, and storage management. These services are available through a set of interfaces that are consistent across programming languages. The application program can either call these interfaces directly, or use language-specific services that call the interfaces.

With Language Environment, you can use one runtime environment for your applications, regardless of the application's programming language or system resource needs.

Figure 9-5 shows the components in the Language Environment, including:

► Basic routines that support starting and stopping programs, allocating storage, communicating with programs written in different languages, and indicating and handling conditions.

► Common library services, such as math or date and time services, that are commonly needed by programs running on the system. These functions are supported through a library of callable services.

► Language-specific portions of the runtime library.

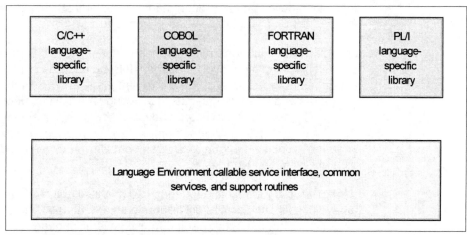

Figure 9-5   z/OS Language Environment components

Language Environment is the prerequisite runtime environment for applications generated with the following IBM compiler products:

► z/OS C/C++
► C/C++ Compiler for z/OS
► AD/Cycle® C/370™ Compiler
► VisualAge® for Java, Enterprise Edition for OS/390
► Enterprise COBOL for z/OS and OS/390
► COBOL for z/OS
► Enterprise PL/I for z/OS and OS/390
► PL/I for MVS and VM (formerly AD/Cycle PL/I for MVS and VM)
► VS FORTRAN and FORTRAN IV (in compatibility mode)

In many cases, you can run compiled code generated from the previous versions of the above compilers. A set of assembler macros is also provided to allow assembler routines to run with Language Environment.

9.12.2 A closer look at Language Environment

The language-specific portions of Language Environment provide language interfaces and specific services that are supported for each individual language, and that can be called through a common callable interface. In this section, we discuss some of these interfaces and services in more detail.

Figure 9-6 shows a common runtime environment established through Language Environment.

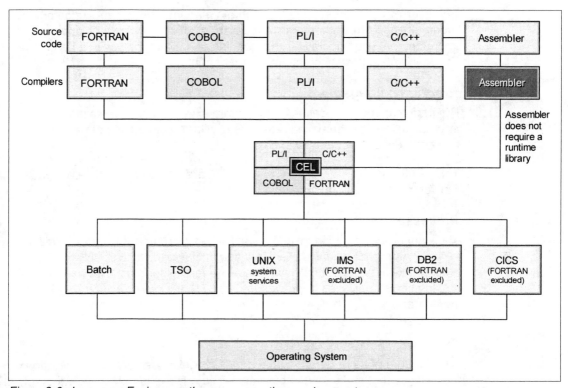

Figure 9-6   Language Environment's common runtime environment

The Language Environment architecture is built from models for the following services:

► Program management
► Condition handling
► Message services
► Storage management

Program management model

The Language Environment program management model provides a framework within which an application runs. It is the foundation for all of the component models (condition handling, runtime message handling, and storage management) that comprise the Language Environment architecture.

The program management model defines the effects of programming language semantics in mixed-language applications, and integrates transaction processing and multithreading.

Some terms used to describe the program management model are common programming terms; other terms are described differently in other languages. It is important that you understand the meaning of the terminology in a Language Environment context as compared to other contexts.

Program management

Program management defines the program execution constructs of an application, and the semantics associated with the integration of various management components of such constructs.

Three entities, *process, enclave,* and *thread,* are at the core of the Language Environment program management model.

Processes

The highest level component of the Language Environment program model is the *process*. A process consists of at least one enclave and is logically separate from other processes. Language Environment generally does not allow language file sharing across enclaves or provide the ability to access collections of externally stored data.

Enclaves

A key feature of the program management model is the *enclave*, a collection of the routines that make up an application. The enclave is the equivalent of any of the following:

- ► A run unit, in COBOL
- ► A program, consisting of a main C function and its sub-functions, in C and C++
- ► A main procedure and all of its subroutines, in PL/I
- ► A program and its subroutines, in Fortran

In Language Environment, environment is normally a reference to the runtime environment of HLLs at the enclave level. The enclave consists of one main routine and zero or more subroutines. The main routine is the first to execute in an enclave; all subsequent routines are named as subroutines.

Threads

Each enclave consists of at least one *thread*, the basic instance of a particular routine. A thread is created during enclave initialization with its own runtime stack, which keeps track of the thread's execution, as well as a unique instruction counter, registers, and condition-handling mechanisms. Each thread represents an independent instance of a routine running under an enclave's resources.

Figure 9-7 illustrates the full Language Environment program model, with its multiple processes, enclaves, and threads. Each process is within its own address space. An enclave consists of one main routine, with any number of subroutines.

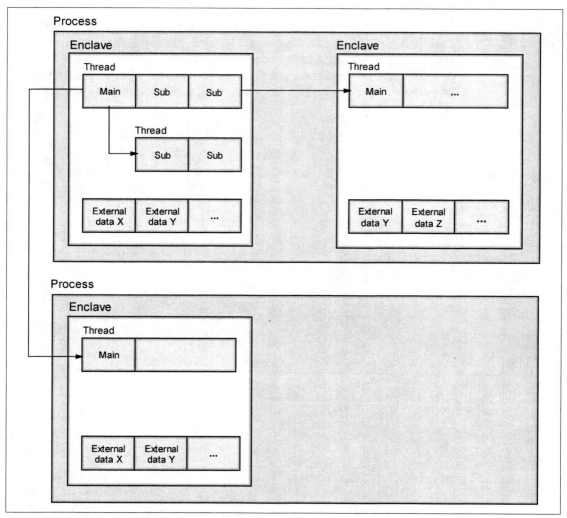

Figure 9-7   Full Language Environment program model

The threads can create enclaves, which can create more threads, and so on.

Condition-handling model

For single-language and mixed-language applications, the Language Environment runtime library provides a consistent and predictable condition-handling facility. It does not replace current HLL condition handling, but instead allows each language to respond to its own unique environment and to a mixed-language environment.

Language Environment condition management gives you the flexibility to respond directly to conditions by providing callable services to signal conditions and to interrogate information about those conditions. It also provides functions for error diagnosis, reporting, and recovery.

Message-handling model and multilingual computing

A set of common message handling services that create and send runtime informational and diagnostic messages is provided by Language Environment.

With the message handling services, you can use the condition token that is returned from a callable service or from some other signaled condition, format it into a message, and deliver it to a defined output device or to a buffer.

Multilingual computing callable services allow you to set a national language that affects the language of the error messages and the names of the day, week, and month. It also allows you to change the country setting, which affects the default date format, time format, currency symbol, decimal separator character, and thousands separator.

Storage management model

Common storage management services are provided for all Language Environment-conforming programming languages; Language Environment controls stack and heap storage used at run time. It allows single-language and mixed-language applications to access a central set of storage management facilities, and offers a multiple-heap storage model to languages that do not now provide one. The common storage model removes the need for each language to maintain a unique storage manager, and avoids the incompatibilities between different storage mechanisms.

9.12.3 Running your program with Language Environment

After compiling your program, you can perform the following actions:

► Link-edit and run an existing object deck and accept the default Language Environment runtime options

► Link-edit and run an existing object deck and specify new Language Environment runtime options

► Call a Language Environment service

Accepting the default runtime options

To run an existing object deck under batch and accept all of the default Language Environment runtime options, you can use a Language Environment-provided link-edit and run cataloged procedure called CEEWLG (cataloged procedures were discussed in 6.7, "JCL procedures (PROCs)" on page 253). The CEEWLG procedure identifies the Language Environment libraries that your object deck needs to link-edit and run.

Runtime library services

The Language Environment libraries are located in data sets identified with a high-level qualifier specific to the installation. For example, SCEERUN contains the runtime library routines needed during execution of applications written in C/C++, PL/I, COBOL, and Fortran. SCEERUN2 contains the runtime library routines needed during execution of applications written in C/C++ and COBOL.

Applications that require the runtime library provided by Language Environment can access the SCEERUN and SCEERUN2 data sets using one or both of these methods:

► LNKLST
► STEPLIB

> **Important:** Language Environment library routines are divided into two categories: resident routines and dynamic routines. The resident routines are linked with the application and include such things as initialization and termination routines and pointers to callable services. The dynamic routines are not part of the application and are dynamically loaded during run time.

There are certain considerations that you must be aware of before link-editing and running applications under Language Environment.

Language Environment callable services

COBOL application developers will find Language Environment's consistent condition handling services especially useful. For all languages, the same condition handling occurs with common math services, as well as the date and time services.

Language Environment callable services are divided into the following groups:

- ► Communicating conditions services
- ► Condition handling services
- ► Date and time services
- ► Dynamic storage services
- ► General callable services
- ► Initialization and termination services
- ► Locale callable services
- ► Math services
- ► Message handling services
- ► Multilingual computing services

The callable services are more fully described in *z/OS Language Environment Programming Reference*, SA22-7562.

Language Environment calling conventions

Language Environment services can be invoked by HLL library routines, other Language Environment services, and user-written HLL calls. In many cases, services are invoked by HLL library routines as a result of a user-specified function. Here are examples of the invocation of a callable math service from three of the languages we have described in this chapter. Also, look at the referenced examples in 9.9.3, "Other uses for the CLIST language" on page 347.

Example 9-8 shows how a COBOL program invokes the math callable services CEESDLG1 for log base 10.

Example 9-8 Sample invocation of a math callable service from a COBOL program

```
        77   ARG1RL   COMP-2.
        77   FBCODE   PIC X(12).
        77   RESLTRL COMP-2.
             CALL "CEESDLG1" USING ARG1RL , FBCODE ,
             RESLTRL.
```

9.13 Summary

This chapter outlines the many decisions you might need to make when you design and develop an application to run on z/OS. Selecting a programming language to use is one important step in the design phase of an application. The application designer must be aware of the strengths and the weaknesses of each language to make the best choice, based on the particular requirements of the application.

A critical factor in choosing a language is determining which one is used the most at a given installation. If COBOL is used for most of the applications in an installation, it will likely be the language of choice for the installation's new applications as well.

Understand that even when a choice for the primary language is made, however, it does not mean that you are locked into that choice for all programs within the application. There might be a case for using multiple languages, for example, to take advantage of the strengths of a particular language for only certain parts of the application. Here, it might be best to write frequently invoked subroutines in the Assembler language to make the application as efficient as possible, even when the rest of the application is written in COBOL or another high-level language.

Many z/OS sites maintain a library of subroutines that are shared across the business. The library might include, for example, date conversion routines. As long as these subroutines are written using standard linkage conventions, they can be called from other languages, regardless of the language in which the subroutines are written.

Each language has its inherent strengths, and designers should exploit these strengths. If a given application merits the added complication of writing it in multiple languages, the designer should take advantage of the particular features of each language. Keep in mind, however, that when it is time to update the application, other people must be able to program these languages as well. This is a cardinal rule of programming. The original programmer might be long gone, but the application will live on and on.

Thus, complexity in design must always be weighed against ease of maintenance.

Table 9-1 lists the key terms used in this chapter.

Table 9-1 Key terms used in this chapter

assembler	binder	compiler
debugging	dynamic link library	generation
I/O (input/output)	interpreter	load modules
preprocessor	programming language	variable

9.14 Questions for review

To help test your understanding of the material in this chapter, complete the following questions:

1. Why might a program be written in Assembler language?

2. Do companies continue to enhance the compilers for COBOL and PL/I?

3. Why are CLIST and REXX called interpreted languages?

4. What are the main areas of suitability for CLISTs and REXX?

5. Which interpreted language can also be compiled?

6. Is the use of Language Environment mandatory in z/OS application development?

7. Which of the data file organizations are appropriate for online applications? Which are appropriate for batch applications?

8. What is an HLL? What are some of the advantages of writing in an HLL versus Assembler language?

9. Assume that PROG1 program is run using the JCL below:

```
//job     JOB
//STEP010  EXEC PGM=PROG1
//STEPLIB  DD DSN=MY.PROGLIB,DISP=SHR
//INPUT1   DD DSN=A.B.C,DISP=SHR
//OUTPUT1  DD DSN=X.Y.Z,DISP=SHR
```

If the INPUT1 DD card were changed to use the data set A1.B1.C1, would we be able to use the same program to process it? Assume that the new data set has the same characteristics as the old data set.

9.15 Topics for further discussion

Here are topics for further discussion:

1. If performance is a consideration, should you write a program in a compiled language or an interpreted language?

2. If you have to develop a transaction system, which of the following is your best choice?

   a. COBOL or PL/I on CICS
   b. C/C++ on CICS
   c. A combination of the above

3. Which language would you use to write an application that calculated premiums on an insurance policy? Assume that this application will be invoked by many other applications.

4. Can a COBOL program call an Assembler language program? Why would you want to have this capability?

10

Compiling and link-editing a program on z/OS

Objective: As your company's newest z/OS application programmer, you will be asked to create new programs to run on z/OS. Doing so will require you to know how to compile, link, and execute a program.

After completing this chapter, you will be able to:

► Explain the purpose of a compiler.

► Compile a source program.

► Explain the difference between the linkage editor and the binder.

► Create executable code from a compiled program.

► Explain the difference between an object deck and a load module.

► Run a program on z/OS.

Refer to Table 10-1 on page 390 for a list of key terms used in this chapter.

10.1 Source, object, and load modules

A program can be divided into logical units that perform specific functions. A logical unit of code that performs a function or several related functions is a *module*. Separate functions should be programmed into separate modules, a process called *modular programming*. Each module can be written in the symbolic language that best suits the function to be performed.

Source module:
The input to a language translator (compiler).

Each module is assembled or compiled by one of the language translators. The input to a language translator is a *source module*; the output from a language translator is an *object deck*. Before an object deck can be executed, it must be processed by the binder (or the linkage editor). The output of the binder is a *load module;* see Figure 10-1.

Object deck:
The output from a language translator.

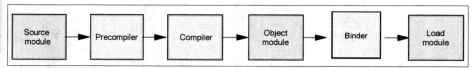

Figure 10-1 Source, object, and load modules

Depending on the status of the module, whether it is a source, object, or load, it can be stored in a library. A library is a partitioned data set (PDS) or a partitioned data set extended (PDSE) on direct access storage. PDSs and PDSEs are divided into partitions called members. In a library, each member contains a program or part of a program.

10.2 What are source libraries

Source programs (or *source code*) are a set of statements written in a computer language, as discussed in Chapter 9, "Using programming languages on z/OS" on page 323. Source programs, after they are error-free, are stored in a partitioned data set known as a *source library*. Source libraries contain the source code to be submitted for a compilation process, or to be retrieved for modification by an application programmer.

Copybook:
A shared library in which programmers store commonly used program segments.

A *copybook* is a source library containing pre-written text. It is used to copy text into a source program, at compile time, as a shortcut to avoid having to code the same set of statements over and over again. It is usually a shared library in which programmers store commonly used program segments to be later included into their source programs. It should not be confused with a subroutine or a program. A copybook member is just text; it might not be actual programming language statements.

A *subroutine* is a commonly-called routine that performs a predefined function. The purpose behind a copybook member and a subroutine are essentially the same, that is, to avoid having to code something that has previously been done. However, a subroutine is a small program (compiled, link-edited, and executable) that is called and returns a result, based on the information that it was passed. A copybook member is just text that will be included in a source program on its way to becoming an executable program. The term copybook is a COBOL term, but the same concept is used in most programming languages.

If you use copybooks in the program that you are compiling, you can retrieve them from the source library by supplying a DD statement for SYSLIB or other libraries that you specify in COPY statements. In Example 10-1, we insert the text in member INPUTRCD from the library DEPT88.BOBS.COBLIB into the source program that is to be compiled.

Example 10-1   Copybook in COBOL source code

```
//COBOL.SYSLIB  DD   DISP=SHR,DSN=DEPT88.BOBS.COBLIB
//SYSIN    DD  *
      IDENTIFICATION DIVISION.
   . . .
      COPY INPUTRCD
   . . .
```

Libraries must reside on direct access storage devices (DASDs). They cannot be in a hierarchical file system (HFS) when you compile using JCL or under TSO.

10.3 Compiling programs on z/OS

Linkage editor: Converts object decks into executable load modules.

The function of a compiler is to translate source code into an object deck, which must then be processed by a binder (or a linkage editor) before it is executed. During the compilation of a source module, the compiler assigns relative addresses to all instructions, data elements, and labels, starting from zero.

The addresses are in the form of a base address plus a displacement. This allows programs to be relocated, that is, they do not have to be loaded into the same location in storage each time that they are executed. (See 10.4, "Creating load modules for executable programs" on page 383 for more information about relocatable programs.) Any references to external programs or subroutines are left as unresolved. These references will either be resolved when the object deck is linked, or dynamically resolved when the program is executed.

To compile programs on z/OS, you can use a batch job, or you can compile under TSO/E through commands, CLISTs, or ISPF panels. For C programs, you can compile in a z/OS UNIX shell by using the **c89** command. For COBOL programs, you can compile in a z/OS UNIX shell by using the **cob2** command.

For compiling through a batch job, z/OS includes a set of cataloged procedures that can help you avoid some of the JCL coding you would otherwise need to do. If none of the cataloged procedures meet your needs, you need to write all of the JCL for the compilation.

As part of the compilation step, you need to define the data sets needed for the compilation and specify any compiler options necessary for your program and the desired output.

The data set (library) that contains your source code is specified on the SYSIN DD statement, as shown in Example 10-2.

Example 10-2   SYSIN DD statement for the source code

```
//SYSIN     DD   DSNAME=dsname,
//               DISP=SHR
```

You can place your source code directly in the input stream. If you do so, use this SYSIN DD statement:

```
//SYSIN     DD   *
```

When you use the DD * convention, the source code must follow the statement. If another job step follows the compilation, the EXEC statement for that step follows the /* statement or the last source statement.

10.3.1 What is a precompiler

Some compilers have a precompile or preprocessor to process statements that are not part of the computer programming language. If your source program contains EXEC CICS statements or EXEC SQL statements, then it must first be pre-processed to convert these statements into COBOL, PL/I, or Assembler language statements, depending on the language in which your program is written.

10.3.2 Compiling with cataloged procedures

The simplest way to compile your program under z/OS is by using a batch job with a *cataloged procedure*. A cataloged procedure is a set of job control statements placed in a partitioned data set (PDS) called the procedure library (PROCLIB). z/OS comes with a procedure library called SYS1.PROCLIB.

Cataloged procedure
A set of job control statements in a PDS called a procedure library.

This system library is discussed more thoroughly in 16.3.7, "SYS1.PROCLIB" on page 538. A simple way to look at the use of cataloged procedures is to think of them as copybooks. Instead of source statements, however, cataloged procedures contain JCL statements. You do not need to code a JCL statement to tell the system where to find them because they are located in a system library that automatically gets searched when you execute JCL that references a procedure.

You need to include the following information in the JCL for compilation:

▶ Job description

▶ Execution statement to invoke the compiler

▶ Definitions for the data sets needed but not supplied by the procedure

COBOL compiling procedure

The JCL in Example 10-3 executes the IGYWC procedure, which is a single-step procedure for compiling a source program. It produces an object deck that will be stored in the SYSLIN data set, as we can see in Example 10-4.

Example 10-3   Basic JCL for compiling a COBOL source program inline

```
//COMP JOB
//COMPILE EXEC IGYWC
//SYSIN DD *
IDENTIFICATION DIVISION (source program)
.
.
.
/*
//
```

Example 10-4   Procedure IGYWC: COBOL compile

```
//IGYWC   PROC   LNGPRFX='IGY.V3R2M0',SYSLBLK=3200
//*
//*   COMPILE A COBOL PROGRAM
//*
//*   PARAMETER   DEFAULT VALUE
//*    SYSLBLK    3200
//*    LNGPRFX    IGY.V3R2M0
//*
//*   CALLER MUST SUPPLY //COBOL.SYSIN DD . . .
//*
//COBOL   EXEC PGM=IGYCRCTL,REGION=2048K
//STEPLIB  DD  DSNAME=&LNGPRFX..SIGYCOMP,
```

```
//              DISP=SHR
//SYSPRINT DD  SYSOUT=*
//SYSLIN   DD  DSNAME=&&LOADSET,UNIT=SYSDA,
//              DISP=(MOD,PASS),SPACE=(TRK,(3,3)),
//              DCB=(BLKSIZE=&SYSLBLK)
//SYSUT1   DD  UNIT=SYSDA,SPACE=(CYL,(1,1))
//SYSUT2   DD  UNIT=SYSDA,SPACE=(CYL,(1,1))
//SYSUT3   DD  UNIT=SYSDA,SPACE=(CYL,(1,1))
//SYSUT4   DD  UNIT=SYSDA,SPACE=(CYL,(1,1))
//SYSUT5   DD  UNIT=SYSDA,SPACE=(CYL,(1,1))
//SYSUT6   DD  UNIT=SYSDA,SPACE=(CYL,(1,1))
//SYSUT7   DD  UNIT=SYSDA,SPACE=(CYL,(1,1))
```

The SYSIN DD statement indicates the location of the source program. In this case, the asterisk (*) indicates that it is in the same input stream.

For PL/I programs, in addition to the replacement of the source program, the compile EXEC statement should be replaced by the following statement:

```
//compile EXEC IBMZC
```

The statements shown in Example 10-4 on page 367 make up the IGYWC cataloged procedure used in Example 10-3 on page 367. As mentioned previously, the result of the compilation process, the compiled program, is placed in the data set identified on the SYSLIN DD statement.

COBOL pre-processor and compiling and linking procedure

The JCL in Example 10-5 executes the DFHEITVL procedure, which is a three-step procedure for pre-processing a COBOL source program, compiling the output from the pre-processing step, and then linking it into a load library. The first step produces pre-processed source code in the SYSPUNCH temporary data sets, with any CICS calls expanded into COBOL language statements. The second step takes this temporary data set as input and produces an object deck that is stored in the SYSLIN temporary data set, as shown in Example 10-6 on page 369. The third step takes the SYSLIN temporary data set as input, as well as any other modules that might need to be included, and creates a load module in the data set referenced by the SYSLMOD DD statement.

Example 10-5   Pre-processing, compiling, and linking a COBOL source program inline

```
//PPCOMLNK   JOB
//PPCL       EXEC DFHEITVL,PROGLIB='MY.LOADLIB'
//TRN.SYSIN     DD *
  IDENTIFICATION DIVISION (source program)
    EXEC CICS ...
  ...
```

```
    EXEC CICS ...
...
//LKED.SYSIN DD *
   NAME PROG1(R)
/*
```

Example 10-6   Procedure DFHEITVL: COBOL preprocessor, compile, and link

```
//DFHEITVL PROC SUFFIX=1$,          Suffix for translator module
//*
//* This procedure has been changed since CICS/ESA Version 3
//*
//* Parameter INDEX2 has been removed
//*
//       INDEX='CICSTS12.CICS', Qualifier(s) for CICS libraries
//       PROGLIB=&INDEX..SDFHLOAD,   Name of output library
//       DSCTLIB=&INDEX..SDFHCOB,    Name of private macro/DSECT lib
//       COMPHLQ='SYS1',             Qualifier(s) for COBOL compiler
//       OUTC=A,                     Class for print output
//       REG=2M,                     Region size for all steps
//       LNKPARM='LIST,XREF',        Link edit parameters
//       STUB='DFHEILIC',            Link edit INCLUDE for DFHECI
//       LIB='SDFHCOB',              Library
//       WORK=SYSDA                  Unit for work data sets
//*       This procedure contains 4 steps
//*       1.   Exec the COBOL translator
//*            (using the supplied suffix 1$)
//*       2.   Exec the vs COBOL II compiler
//*       3.   Reblock &LIB(&STUB) for use by the linkedit step
//*       4.   Linkedit the output into data set &PROGLIB
//*
//*       The following JCL should be used
//*       to execute this procedure
//*
//*       //APPLPROG EXEC DFHEITVL
//*       //TRN.SYSIN  DD *
//*           .
//*           . Application program
//*           .
//*       /*
//*       //LKED.SYSIN DD *
//*           NAME anyname(R)
//*       /*
//*
//* Where   anyname   is the name of your application program.
```

```
//*         (Refer to the system definition guide for full details,
//*         including what to do if your program contains calls to
//*         the common programming interface.)
//*
//TRN      EXEC PGM=DFHECP&SUFFIX,
//              PARM='COBOL2',
//              REGION=&REG
//STEPLIB  DD DSN=&INDEX..SDFHLOAD,DISP=SHR
//SYSPRINT DD SYSOUT=&OUTC
//SYSPUNCH DD DSN=&&SYSCIN,
//              DISP=(,PASS),UNIT=&WORK,
//              DCB=BLKSIZE=400,
//              SPACE=(400,(400,100))
//*
//COB      EXEC PGM=IGYCRCTL,REGION=&REG,
//              PARM='NODYNAM,LIB,OBJECT,RENT,RES,APOST,MAP,XREF'
//STEPLIB  DD DSN=&COMPHLQ..COB2COMP,DISP=SHR
//SYSLIB   DD DSN=&DSCTLIB,DISP=SHR
//         DD DSN=&INDEX..SDFHCOB,DISP=SHR
//         DD DSN=&INDEX..SDFHMAC,DISP=SHR
//         DD DSN=&INDEX..SDFHSAMP,DISP=SHR
//SYSPRINT DD SYSOUT=&OUTC
//SYSIN    DD DSN=&&SYSCIN,DISP=(OLD,DELETE)
//SYSLIN   DD DSN=&&LOADSET,DISP=(MOD,PASS),
//              UNIT=&WORK,SPACE=(80,(250,100))
//SYSUT1   DD UNIT=&WORK,SPACE=(460,(350,100))
//SYSUT2   DD UNIT=&WORK,SPACE=(460,(350,100))
//SYSUT3   DD UNIT=&WORK,SPACE=(460,(350,100))
//SYSUT4   DD UNIT=&WORK,SPACE=(460,(350,100))
//SYSUT5   DD UNIT=&WORK,SPACE=(460,(350,100))
//SYSUT6   DD UNIT=&WORK,SPACE=(460,(350,100))
//SYSUT7   DD UNIT=&WORK,SPACE=(460,(350,100))
//*
//COPYLINK EXEC PGM=IEBGENER,COND=(7,LT,COB)
//SYSUT1   DD DSN=&INDEX..&LIB(&STUB),DISP=SHR
//SYSUT2   DD DSN=&&COPYLINK,DISP=(NEW,PASS),
//              DCB=(LRECL=80,BLKSIZE=400,RECFM=FB),
//              UNIT=&WORK,SPACE=(400,(20,20))
//SYSPRINT DD SYSOUT=&OUTC
//SYSIN    DD DUMMY
//*
//LKED     EXEC PGM=IEWL,REGION=&REG,
//              PARM='&LNKPARM',COND=(5,LT,COB)
//SYSLIB   DD DSN=&INDEX..SDFHLOAD,DISP=SHR
//         DD DSN=&COMPHLQ..COB2CICS,DISP=SHR
```

```
//          DD DSN=&COMPHLQ..COB2LIB,DISP=SHR
//SYSLMOD    DD DSN=&PROGLIB,DISP=SHR
//SYSUT1     DD UNIT=&WORK,DCB=BLKSIZE=1024,
//             SPACE=(1024,(200,20))
//SYSPRINT   DD SYSOUT=&OUTC
//SYSLIN     DD DSN=&&COPYLINK,DISP=(OLD,DELETE)
//           DD DSN=&&LOADSET,DISP=(OLD,DELETE)
//           DD DDNAME=SYSIN
```

In Example 10-5 on page 368, you can see that the JCL is a bit more complicated than in the simple compile job (Example 10-3 on page 367). After we go from one step to multiple steps, we must tell the system which step we are referring to when we supply JCL overrides.

Looking at the JCL in Example 10-6 on page 369, we see that the first step (each step is an EXEC statement, and the step name is the name on the same line as the EXEC statement) is named TRN, so we must qualify the SYSIN DD statement with TRN to ensure that it will be used in the TRN step.

Similarly, the fourth step is called LKED, so we must qualify the SYSIN DD statement with LKED in order for it to apply to the LKED step. See 6.7.1, "JCL PROC statement override" on page 255 for more information about overriding a cataloged procedure.

The end result of running the JCL in Example 10-5 on page 368 (assuming that there are no errors) should be to pre-process and compile our inline source program, link-edit the object deck, and then store the load module called PROG1 in the data set MY.LOADLIB.

The statements shown in Example 10-6 on page 369 make up the DFHEITVL cataloged procedure used in Example 10-5 on page 368. As with the other compile and link procedures, the result of the preprocessor, compile, and link steps, which is the load module, is placed in the data set identified on the SYSLMOD DD statement.

COBOL compiling and linking procedure

The JCL in Example 10-7 executes the IGYWCL procedure, which is a two-step procedure for compiling a source program and linking it into a load library. The first step produces an object deck that is stored in the SYSLIN temporary data set, as shown in Example 10-8. The second step takes the SYSLIN temporary data set as input, as well as any other modules that might need to be included, and creates a load module in the data set referenced by the SYSLMOD DD statement.

The end result of running the JCL in Example 10-7 (assuming that there are no errors) should be to compile our inline source program, link-edit the object deck, and then store the load module called PROG1 in the data set MY.LOADLIB.

Example 10-7   Basic JCL for compiling and linking a COBOL source program inline

```
//COMLNK   JOB
//CL       EXEC IGYWCL
//COBOL.SYSIN    DD *
  IDENTIFICATION DIVISION (source program)
  .
  .
  .
/*
//LKED.SYSLMOD DD DSN=MY.LOADLIB(PROG1),DISP=OLD
```

The statements shown in Example 10-8 make up the IGYWCL cataloged procedure used in Example 10-7. As mentioned previously, the result of the compile and link steps, which is the load module, is placed in the data set identified on the SYSLMOD DD statement.

Example 10-8   Procedure IGYWCL: COBOL compiling and linking

```
//IGYWCL PROC   LNGPRFX='IGY.V2R1M0',SYSLBLK=3200,
//             LIBPRFX='CEE',
//             PGMLIB='&&GOSET',GOPGM=GO
//*
//*   COMPILE AND LINK EDIT A COBOL PROGRAM
//*
//*   PARAMETER   DEFAULT VALUE
//*    LNGPRFX    IGY.V2R1M0
//*    SYSLBLK    3200
//*    LIBPRFX    CEE
//*    PGMLIB     &&GOSET          DATA SET NAME FOR LOAD MODULE
//*    GOPGM      GO               MEMBER NAME FOR LOAD MODULE
//*
```

```
//*   CALLER MUST SUPPLY //COBOL.SYSIN DD ...
//*
//COBOL  EXEC PGM=IGYCRCTL,REGION=2048K
//STEPLIB  DD  DSNAME=&LNGPRFX..SIGYCOMP,
//             DISP=SHR
//SYSPRINT DD  SYSOUT=*
//SYSLIN   DD  DSNAME=&&LOADSET,UNIT=VIO,
//             DISP=(MOD,PASS),SPACE=(TRK,(3,3)),
//             DCB=(BLKSIZE=&SYSLBLK)
//SYSUT1   DD  UNIT=VIO,SPACE=(CYL,(1,1))
//SYSUT2   DD  UNIT=VIO,SPACE=(CYL,(1,1))
//SYSUT3   DD  UNIT=VIO,SPACE=(CYL,(1,1))
//SYSUT4   DD  UNIT=VIO,SPACE=(CYL,(1,1))
//SYSUT5   DD  UNIT=VIO,SPACE=(CYL,(1,1))
//SYSUT6   DD  UNIT=VIO,SPACE=(CYL,(1,1))
//SYSUT7   DD  UNIT=VIO,SPACE=(CYL,(1,1))
//LKED   EXEC PGM=HEWL,COND=(8,LT,COBOL),REGION=1024K
//SYSLIB   DD  DSNAME=&LIBPRFX..SCEELKED,
//             DISP=SHR
//SYSPRINT DD  SYSOUT=*
//SYSLIN   DD  DSNAME=&&LOADSET,DISP=(OLD,DELETE)
//         DD  DDNAME=SYSIN
//SYSLMOD  DD  DSNAME=&PGMLIB(&GOPGM),
//             SPACE=(TRK,(10,10,1)),
//             UNIT=VIO,DISP=(MOD,PASS)
//SYSUT1   DD  UNIT=VIO,SPACE=(TRK,(10,10))
```

COBOL compiling, linking, and go procedure

The JCL in Example 10-9 executes the IGYWCLG procedure, which is a three-step procedure for compiling a source program, linking it into a load library, and then executing the load module. The first two steps are the same as those in the compile and link example (Example 10-7 on page 372). However, whereas in Example 10-7 on page 372 we override the SYSLMOD DD statement to permanently save the load module, in Example 10-9, we do not need to save it to execute it. That is why the override to the SYSLMOD DD statement in Example 10-9 is enclosed in square brackets, to indicate that it is optional.

Example 10-9   Compiling, linking and executing a COBOL source program inline

```
//CLGO    JOB
//CLG     EXEC IGYWCLG
//COBOL.SYSIN    DD *
  IDENTIFICATION DIVISION (source program)
  .
```

```
     .
     .
     .
/*
[//LKED.SYSLMOD DD DSN=MY.LOADLIB(PROG1),DISP=OLD]
```

If it is coded, then the load module PROG1 will be permanently saved in
MY.LOADLIB. If it is not coded, then the load module will be saved in a
temporary data set and deleted after the GO step.

In Example 10-9 on page 373, you can see that the JCL is similar to the JCL
used in the simple compile job (Example 10-3 on page 367). Looking at the JCL
in Example 10-10, the only difference between it and the JCL in Example 10-8 on
page 372 is that we have added the GO step. The end result of running the JCL
in Example 10-9 on page 373 (assuming that there are no errors) should be to
compile our inline source program, link-edit the object deck, store the load
module (either temporarily or permanently), and then execute the load module.

The statements shown in Example 10-10 make up the IGYWCLG cataloged
procedure used in Example 10-9 on page 373.

Example 10-10   Procedure IGYWCLG: COBOL compile, link, and go

```
//IGYWCLG PROC LNGPRFX='IGY.V2R1M0',SYSLBLK=3200,
//             LIBPRFX='CEE',GOPGM=GO
//*
//*   COMPILE, LINK EDIT AND RUN A COBOL PROGRAM
//*
//*   PARAMETER  DEFAULT VALUE     USAGE
//*    LNGPRFX   IGY.V2R1M0
//*    SYSLBLK   3200
//*    LIBPRFX   CEE
//*    GOPGM     GO
//*
//*   CALLER MUST SUPPLY //COBOL.SYSIN DD ...
//*
//COBOL  EXEC PGM=IGYCRCTL,REGION=2048K
//STEPLIB  DD  DSNAME=&LNGPRFX..SIGYCOMP,
//             DISP=SHR
//SYSPRINT DD  SYSOUT=*
//SYSLIN   DD  DSNAME=&&LOADSET,UNIT=VIO,
//             DISP=(MOD,PASS),SPACE=(TRK,(3,3)),
//             DCB=(BLKSIZE=&SYSLBLK)
//SYSUT1   DD  UNIT=VIO,SPACE=(CYL,(1,1))
//SYSUT2   DD  UNIT=VIO,SPACE=(CYL,(1,1))
//SYSUT3   DD  UNIT=VIO,SPACE=(CYL,(1,1))
```

```
//SYSUT4    DD   UNIT=VIO,SPACE=(CYL,(1,1))
//SYSUT5    DD   UNIT=VIO,SPACE=(CYL,(1,1))
//SYSUT6    DD   UNIT=VIO,SPACE=(CYL,(1,1))
//SYSUT7    DD   UNIT=VIO,SPACE=(CYL,(1,1))
//LKED    EXEC PGM=HEWL,COND=(8,LT,COBOL),REGION=1024K
//SYSLIB    DD   DSNAME=&LIBPRFX..SCEELKED,
//               DISP=SHR
//SYSPRINT  DD   SYSOUT=*
//SYSLIN    DD   DSNAME=&&LOADSET,DISP=(OLD,DELETE)
//          DD   DDNAME=SYSIN
//SYSLMOD   DD   DSNAME=&&GOSET(&GOPGM),SPACE=(TRK,(10,10,1)),
//               UNIT=VIO,DISP=(MOD,PASS)
//SYSUT1    DD   UNIT=VIO,SPACE=(TRK,(10,10))
//GO      EXEC PGM=*.LKED.SYSLMOD,COND=((8,LT,COBOL),(4,LT,LKED)),
//               REGION=2048K
//STEPLIB   DD   DSNAME=&LIBPRFX..SCEERUN,
//               DISP=SHR
//SYSPRINT  DD   SYSOUT=*
//CEEDUMP   DD   SYSOUT=*
//SYSUDUMP  DD   SYSOUT=*
```

10.3.3 Compiling object-oriented (OO) applications

If you use a batch job or TSO/E to compile an OO COBOL program or class
definition, the generated object deck is written, as usual, to the data set that you
identify with the SYSLIN or SYSPUNCH ddname.

If the COBOL program or class definition uses the JNI[1] environment structure to
access JNI callable services, copy the JNI.cpy file from the HFS to a PDS or
PDSE member called JNI, identify that library with a SYSLIB DD statement, and
use a COPY statement of the form COPY JNI in the COBOL source program.

As shown in Example 10-11, use the SYSJAVA ddname to write the generated
Java source file to a file in the HFS.

Example 10-11   SYSJAVA ddname for a Java source file

```
//SYSJAVA DD PATH='/u/userid/java/Classname.java',
//            PATHOPTS=(OWRONLY,OCREAT,OTRUNC),
//            PATHMODE=SIRWXU,
//            FILEDATA=TEXT
```

---

[1] The Java Native Interface (JNI) is the Java interface to native programming languages and is part of
the Java Development Kits. By writing programs that use the JNI, you ensure that your code is
portable across many platforms.

10.3.4 What is an object deck

An *object deck* is a collection of one or more compilation units produced by an assembler, compiler, or other language translator, and used as input to the binder (or linkage editor).

An object deck is in relocatable format with machine code that is not executable. A load module is also relocatable, but with executable machine code. A load module is in a format that can be loaded into virtual storage and relocated by the program manager, a program that prepares load modules for execution by loading them at specific storage locations.

Object decks and load modules share the same logical structure consisting of:

► Control dictionaries, containing information to resolve symbolic cross-references between control sections of different modules, and to relocate address constants

► Text, containing the instructions and data of the program

► An end-of-module indication, which is an END statement in an object deck, or an end-of-module indicator in a load module

Object decks are stored in a partitioned data set identified by the SYSLIN or SYSPUNCH DD statement, which is input to the next linkage edition process.

10.3.5 What is an object library

You can use an object library to store object decks. The object decks to be link-edited are retrieved from the object library and transformed into an executable or loadable program.

When using the OBJECT compiler option, you can store the object deck on disk as a traditional data set, as an UNIX file, or on tape. The DISP parameter of the SYSLIN DD statement indicates whether the object deck is to be:

► Passed to the binder (or linkage editor) after compile (DISP=PASS)

► Cataloged in an existent object library (DISP=OLD)

► Kept (DISP=KEEP)

► Added to a new object library, which is cataloged at the end of the step (DISP=CATLG)

An object deck can be the primary input to the binder by specifying its data set name and member name on the `SYSLIN DD` statement. In the following example, the member named TAXCOMP in the object library USER.LIBROUT is the primary input. USER.LIBROUT is a cataloged partitioned data set:

```
//SYSLIN     DD     DSNAME=USER.LIBROUT(TAXCOMP),DISP=SHR
```

The library member is processed as though it were a sequential data set.

10.3.6 How program management works

Although program management components provide many services, they are used primarily to convert object decks into executable programs, store them in program libraries, and load them into virtual storage for execution.

You can use the program management binder and loader to perform these tasks. These components can also be used in conjunction with the linkage editor. A load module produced by the linkage editor can be accepted as input by the binder, or can be loaded into storage for execution by the program management loader. The linkage editor can also process load modules produced by the binder.

Figure 10-2 shows how the program management components work together, and how each one is used to prepare an executable program. We have already discussed some of these components (source modules and object decks), so now we take a look at the rest of them.

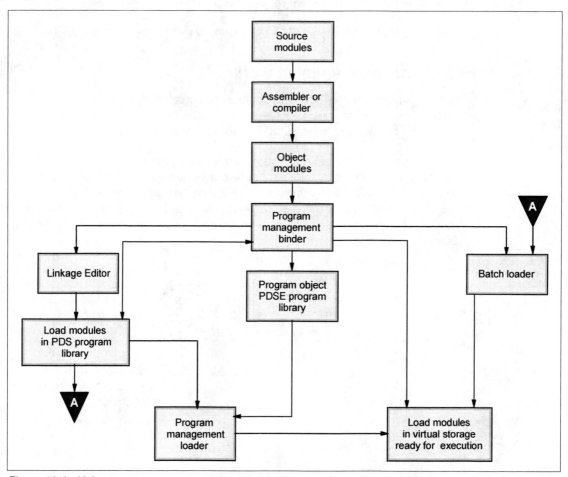

Figure 10-2   Using program management components to create and load programs

10.3.7 How a linkage editor is used

Linkage editor processing follows the source program assembly or compilation of any problem program. The *linkage editor* is both a processing program and a service program used in association with the language translators.

Linkage editor and loader processing programs prepare the output of language translators for execution. The linkage editor prepares a load module that will be brought into storage for execution by the program manager.

The linkage editor accepts two major types of input:

- Primary input, consisting of object decks and linkage editor control statements.

- Additional user-specified input, which can contain either object decks and control statements, or load modules. This input is either specified by you as input, or is incorporated automatically by the linkage editor from a call library.

Output of the linkage editor consists of two types:

- A load module placed in a library (a partitioned data set) as a named member.

- Diagnostic output produced as a sequential data set.

The loader prepares the executable program in storage and passes control to it directly.

10.3.8 How a load module is created

When processing object decks and load modules, the linkage editor assigns consecutive relative virtual storage addresses to control sections, and resolves references between control sections. Object decks produced by several different language translators can be used to form one load module.

An output load module is composed of all input object decks and input load modules processed by the linkage editor. The control dictionaries of an output module are, therefore, a composite of all the control dictionaries in the linkage editor input. The control dictionaries of a load module are called the composite external symbol dictionary (CESD) and the relocation dictionary (RLD). The load module also contains the text from each input module, and an end-of-module indicator.

Figure 10-3 shows the process of compiling two source programs: PROGA and PROGB. PROGA is a COBOL program and PROGB is an Assembler language program. PROGA calls PROGB. In this figure, we see that after compilation, the reference to PROGB in PROGA is an unresolved reference. The process of link-editing the two object decks resolves the reference so that when PROGA is executed, the call to PROGB will work correctly. PROGB will be transferred, it will execute, and control will return to PROGA, after the point where PROGB was called.

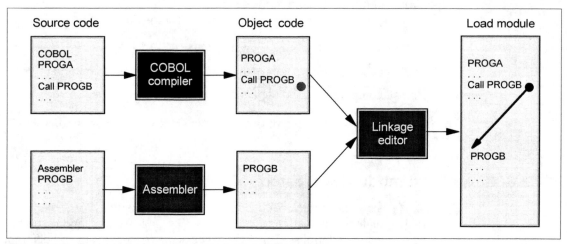

Figure 10-3   Resolving references during load module creation

Using the binder

The *binder* provided with z/OS performs all of the functions of the linkage editor. The binder link-edits (combines and edits) the individual object decks, load modules, and program objects that make up an application and produces a single program object or load module that you can load for execution. When a member of a program library is needed, the loader brings it into virtual storage and prepares it for execution.

You can use the binder to:

▶ Convert an object deck or load module into a program object and store it in a partitioned data set extended (PDSE) program library, or in a z/OS UNIX file.

▶ Convert an object deck or program object into a load module and store it in a partitioned data set (PDS) program library. This is equivalent to what the linkage editor does with object decks and load modules.

▶ Convert object decks or load modules, or program objects, into an executable program in virtual storage and execute the program. This is equivalent to what the batch loader does with object decks and load modules.

The binder processes object decks, load modules and program objects, link-editing or binding multiple modules into a single load module or program object. Control statements specify how to combine the input into one or more load modules or program objects with contiguous virtual storage addresses. Each object deck can be processed separately by the binder, so that only the modules that have been modified need to be recompiled or reassembled. The binder can create programs in 24-bit, 31-bit, and 64-bit addressing modes.

You assign an addressing mode (AMODE) to indicate which hardware addressing mode is active when the program executes. Addressing modes are:

▶ 24, which indicates that 24-bit addressing must be in effect.

▶ 31, which indicates that 31-bit addressing must be in effect.

▶ 64, which indicates that 64-bit addressing must be in effect.

▶ ANY, which indicates that 24-bit, 31-bit, or 64-bit addressing can be in effect.

▶ MIN, which requests that the binder assign an AMODE value to the program module.

The binder selects the most restrictive AMODE of all control sections in the input to the program module. An AMODE value of 24 is the *most* restrictive; an AMODE value of ANY is the *least* restrictive.

All of the services of the linkage editor can be performed by the binder. For more information about the layout of an address and which areas of the address space are addressable by 24 bits, 31 bits and 64 bits, see 3.4.9, "A brief history of virtual storage and 64-bit addressability" on page 117.

Binder and linkage editor

The binder relaxes or eliminates many restrictions of the linkage editor. The binder removes the linkage editor's limit of 64 aliases, allowing a load module or program object to have as many aliases as desired. The binder accepts any system-supported block size for the primary (SYSLIN) input data set, eliminating the linkage editor's maximum block size limit of 3200 bytes. The binder also does not restrict the number of external names, whereas the linkage editor sets a limit of 32767 names.

The prelinker provided with z/OS Language Environment is another facility for combining object decks into a single object deck. Following a pre-link, you can link-edit the object deck into a load module (which is stored in a PDS), or bind it into a load module or a program object (which is stored in a PDS, PDSE, or zFS file). With the binder, however, z/OS application programmers no longer need to pre-link, because the binder handles all of the functionality of the pre-linker. Whether you use the binder or linkage editor is a matter of preference. The binder is the latest way to create your load module.

The primary input, required for every binder job step, is defined on a DD statement with the ddname SYSLIN. Primary input can be:

- A sequential data set
- A member of a partitioned data set (PDS)
- A member of a partitioned data set extended (PDSE)
- Concatenated sequential data sets, or members of partitioned data sets or PDSEs, or a combination
- A z/OS UNIX file

The primary data set can contain object decks, control statements, load modules and program objects. All modules and control statements are processed sequentially, and their order determines the order of binder processing. The order of the sections after processing, however, might not match the input sequence.

Binder example

Example 10-12 shows a job that can be used to link-edit an object deck. The output from the LKED step will be placed in a private library identified by the SYSLMOD DD. The input is passed from a previous job step to a binder job step in the same job (for example, the output from the compiler is direct input to the binder).

Example 10-12 Binder JCL example

```
//LKED     EXEC PGM=IEWL,PARM='XREF,LIST', IEWL is IEWBLINK alias
//              REGION=2M,COND=(5,LT,prior-step)
//*
//*       Define secondary input
//*
//SYSLIB   DD  DSN=language.library,DISP=SHR          optional
//PRIVLIB  DD  DSN=private.include.library,DISP=SHR optional
//SYSUT1   DD  UNIT=SYSDA,SPACE=(CYL,(1,1))           ignored
//*
//*       Define output module library
//*
//SYSLMOD  DD  DSN=program.library,DISP=SHR           required
//SYSPRINT DD  SYSOUT=*                               required
//SYSTERM  DD  SYSOUT=*                               optional
//*
//*       Define primary input
//*
//SYSLIN   DD  DSN=&&OBJECT,DISP=(MOD,PASS)           required
//         DD  * inline control statements
```

```
            INCLUDE  PRIVLIB(membername)
            NAME     modname(R)
/*
```

An explanation of the JCL statements follows:

EXEC	Binds a program module and stores it in a program library. Alternative names for IEWBLINK are IEWL, LINKEDIT, EWL, and HEWLH096. The PARM field option requests a cross-reference table and a module map to be produced on the diagnostic output data set.
SYSUT1	Defines a temporary direct access data set to be used as the intermediate data set.
SYSLMOD	Defines a temporary data set to be used as the output module library.
SYSPRINT	Defines the diagnostic output data set, which is assigned to output class A.
SYSLIN	Defines the primary input data set, &&OBJECT, which contains the input object deck; this data set was passed from a previous job step and is e passed at the end of this job step.
INCLUDE	Specifies sequential data sets, library members, or z/OS UNIX files that will be sources of additional input for the binder (in this case, a member of the private library PRIVLIB).
NAME	Specifies the name of the program module created from the preceding input modules, and serves as a delimiter for input to the program module. (R) indicates that this program module replaces an identically named module in the output module library.

10.4 Creating load modules for executable programs

Relocatable:
The load module can be located at any address in virtual storage.

A *load module* is an executable program stored in a partitioned data set program library. Creating a load module to execute only requires that you use a batch loader or program management loader. Creating a load module that can be stored in a program library requires that you use the binder or linkage editor. In all cases, the load module is relocatable, which means that it can be located at any address in virtual storage within the confines of the residency mode (RMODE).

After a program is loaded, control is passed to it, with a value in the base register. This gives the program its starting address, where it was loaded, so that all addresses can be resolved as the sum of the base plus the offset. Relocatable programs allow an identical copy of a program to be loaded in many different address spaces, each being loaded at a different starting address. See 10.3, "Compiling programs on z/OS" on page 365 for further discussion about relocatable programs.

10.4.1 Batch loader

The *batch loader* combines the basic editing and loading services (which can also be provided by the linkage editor and program manager) into one job step. The batch loader accepts object decks and load modules, and loads them into virtual storage for execution. Unlike the binder and linkage editor, the batch loader does not produce load modules that can be stored in program libraries. The batch loader prepares the executable program in storage and passes control to it directly.

Batch loader processing is performed in a load step, which is equivalent to the link-edit and go steps of the binder or linkage editor. The batch loader can be used for both compile-load and load jobs. It can include modules from a call library (SYSLIB), the link pack area (LPA), or both. Like the other program management components, the batch loader supports addressing and residence mode attributes in the 24-bit, 31-bit, and 64-bit addressing modes. The batch loader program is reentrant and therefore can reside in the resident link pack area.

In more recent releases of z/OS, the binder replaces the batch loader.

10.4.2 Program management loader

The program management loader increases the services of the program manager component by adding support for loading program objects. The loader reads both program objects and load modules into virtual storage and prepares them for execution. It resolves any address constants in the program to point to the appropriate areas in virtual storage, and supports the 24-bit, 31-bit, and 64-bit addressing modes.

In processing object and load modules, the linkage editor assigns consecutive relative virtual storage addresses to control sections and resolves references between control sections. Object decks produced by several different language translators can be used to form one load module.

In Example 10-13, we have a compile, link-edit, and execute job, in this case for an assembler program.

Example 10-13 Compiling, link-editing, and executing JCL

```
//USUAL      JOB   A2317P,'COMPLGO'
//ASM        EXEC  PGM=IEV90,REGION=256K,  EXECUTES ASSEMBLER
//                 PARM=(OBJECT,NODECK,'LINECOUNT=50')
//SYSPRINT   DD    SYSOUT=*,DCB=BLKSIZE=3509  PRINT THE ASSEMBLY LISTING
//SYSPUNCH   DD    SYSOUT=B PUNCH THE ASSEMBLY LISTING
//SYSLIB     DD    DSNAME=SYS1.MACLIB,DISP=SHR THE MACRO LIBRARY
//SYSUT1     DD    DSNAME=&&SYSUT1,UNIT=SYSDA,   A WORK DATA SET
//                 SPACE=(CYL,(10,1))
//SYSLIN     DD    DSNAME=&&OBJECT,UNIT=SYSDA, THE OUTPUT OBJECT DECK
//                 SPACE=(TRK,(10,2)),DCB=BLKSIZE=3120,DISP=(,PASS)
//SYSIN      DD    *                           inline SOURCE CODE
                   .
                   .
                   code
                   .
/*
//LKED       EXEC  PGM=HEWL,                    EXECUTES LINKAGE EDITOR
//                 PARM='XREF,LIST,LET',COND=(8,LE,ASM)
//SYSPRINT   DD    SYSOUT=*                     LINKEDIT MAP PRINTOUT
//SYSLIN     DD    DSNAME=&&OBJECT,DISP=(OLD,DELETE) INPUT OBJECT DECK
//SYSUT1     DD    DSNAME=&&SYSUT1,UNIT=SYSDA,   A WORK DATA SET
//                 SPACE=(CYL,(10,1))
//SYSLMOD    DD    DSNAME=&&LOADMOD,UNIT=SYSDA,   THE OUTPUT LOAD MODULE
//                 DISP=(MOD,PASS),SPACE=(1024,(50,20,1))
//GO         EXEC  PGM=*.LKED.SYSLMOD,TIME=(,30), EXECUTES THE PROGRAM
//                 COND=((8,LE,ASM),(8,LE,LKED))
//SYSUDUMP   DD    SYSOUT=*                     IF FAILS, DUMP LISTING
//SYSPRINT   DD    SYSOUT=*,                    OUTPUT LISTING
//                 DCB=(RECFM=FBA,LRECL=121)
//OUTPUT     DD    SYSOUT=A,                    PROGRAM DATA OUTPUT
//                 DCB=(LRECL=100,BLKSIZE=3000,RECFM=FBA)
//INPUT      DD    *                            PROGRAM DATA INPUT
                   .
                   .
                   data
                   .
/*
//
```

Notes:

► In the ASM step (compile), `SYSIN DD` is used for the inline source code and `SYSLIN DD` is used for the output object deck.

► In the LKED (linkage-edition) step, the `SYSLIN DD` is used for the input object deck and the `SYSLMOD DD` is used for the output load module.

► In the GO step (execute the program), the `EXEC JCL` statement states that it will execute a program identified in the `SYSLMOD DD` statement of the previous step.

► This example does not use a cataloged procedure, as the COBOL examples did; instead, all of the JCL has been coded inline. We could have used an existing JCL procedure, or coded one and then only supplied the overrides, such as the INPUT DD statement.

10.4.3 What is a load library

A *load library* contains programs ready to be executed. A load library can be any of the following:

► System library
► Private library
► Temporary library

System library

Unless a job or step specifies a private library, the system searches for a program in the system libraries when you use the following code:

```
//stepname  EXEC  PGM=program-name
```

The system looks in the libraries for a member with a name or alias that is the same as the specified program-name. The most-used system library is SYS1.LINKLIB, which contains executable programs that have been processed by the linkage editor. For more information about system libraries, see 16.3.1, "z/OS system libraries" on page 533.

Private library

Each executable, user-written program is a member of a private library. To tell the system that a program is in a private library, the DD statement defining that library can be coded in one of the following ways:

- ▸ By using a DD statement with the ddname JOBLIB after the JOB statement, and before the first EXEC statement in the job

- ▸ If the library is going to be used in only one step, by using a DD statement with the ddname STEPLIB in the step

To execute a program from a private library, use the following code:

```
//stepname   EXEC   PGM=program-name
```

When you use JOBLIB or STEPLIB, the system searches for the program to be executed in the library defined by the JOBLIB or STEPLIB DD statement before searching in the system libraries.

If an earlier DD statement in the job defines the program as a member of a private library, refer to that DD statement to execute the program:

```
//stepname   EXEC   PGM=*.stepname.ddname
```

Private libraries are particularly useful for programs that are used too seldom to be needed in a system library. For example, programs that prepare quarterly sales tax reports are good candidates for a private library.

Temporary library

Temporary libraries are partitioned data sets created to store a program until it is used in a later step of the *same* job. A temporary library is created and deleted within a job.

When testing a newly written program, a temporary library is particularly useful for storing the load module from the linkage editor until it is executed by a later job step. Because the module will not be needed by other jobs until it is fully tested, it should not be stored in a private library or a system library. In Example 10-13 on page 385, the LKED step creates a temporary library called &&LOADMOD on the SYSLMOD DD statement. In the GO step, we refer back to the same temporary data set by using the following code:

```
//GO        EXEC   PGM=*.LKED.SYSLMOD,....
```

10.5 Overview of compilation to execution

In Figure 10-4, we can see the relationship between the object decks and the load module stored in a load library and then loaded into central memory for execution.

We start with two programs, A and B, which are compiled into two object decks. The two object decks are linked into one load module call MYPROG, which is stored in a load library on direct access storage. The load module MYPROG is then loaded into central storage by the program management loader, and control is transferred to it to for execution.

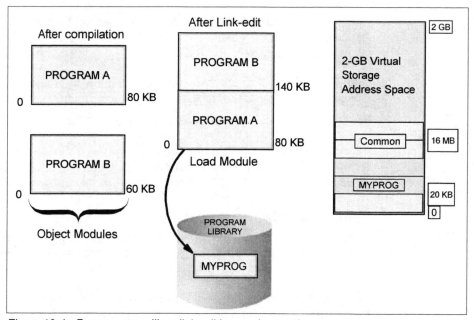

Figure 10-4   Program compiling, link-editing, and execution

10.6 Using procedures

To save time and prevent errors, you can prepare sets of job control statements and place them in a partitioned data set (PDS) or partitioned data set extended (PDSE), known as a *procedure library*. This can be used, for example, to compile, assemble, link-edit, and execute a program, as shown in Example 10-13 on page 385. For a more in-depth discussion about JCL procedures, see 6.7, "JCL procedures (PROCs)" on page 253.

A procedure library is a library that contains procedures. A set of job control statements in the system procedure library, SYS1.PROCLIB (or an installation-defined procedure library), is called a *cataloged procedure*. (SYS1.PROCLIB is shown in 6.10, "System libraries" on page 262.)

To test a procedure before storing it in a procedure library, add the procedure to the input stream and execute it; a procedure in the input stream is called an *inline procedure*. The maximum number of inline procedures you can code in any job is 15. To test a procedure in the input stream, it must end with a procedure end (PEND) statement. The PEND statement signals the end of the PROC. This is only required when the procedure is coded inline. In a procedure library, you do not require a PEND statement.

An inline procedure must appear in the same job before the EXEC statement that calls it.

Three symbolic parameters are defined in the cataloged procedure shown in Example 10-14; they are &STATUS, &LIBRARY, and &NUMBER. Values are assigned to the symbolic parameters on the PROC statement. These values are used if the procedure is called but no values are assigned to the symbolic parameters on the calling EXEC statement.

Example 10-14   Sample definition of a procedure

```
//DEF      PROC   STATUS=OLD,LIBRARY=SYSLIB,NUMBER=777777
//NOTIFY   EXEC   PGM=ACCUM
//DD1      DD     DSNAME=MGMT,DISP=(&STATUS,KEEP),UNIT=3400-6,
//                VOLUME=SER=888888
//DD2      DD     DSNAME=&LIBRARY,DISP=(OLD,KEEP),UNIT=3390,
//                VOLUME=SER=&NUMBER
```

In Example 10-15, we test the procedure called DEF. Note that the procedure is delineated by the PROC and PEND statements. The EXEC statement that follows the procedure DEF references the procedure to be invoked. In this case, because the name DEF matches a procedure that was previously coded inline, the system uses the procedure inline and will not search any further.

Example 10-15   Testing a procedure inline

```
//TESTJOB  JOB  ....
//DEF      PROC   STATUS=OLD,LIBRARY=SYSLIB,NUMBER=777777
//NOTIFY   EXEC   PGM=ACCUM
//DD1      DD     DSNAME=MGMT,DISP=(&STATUS,KEEP),UNIT=3400-6,
//                VOLUME=SER=888888
//DD2      DD     DSNAME=&LIBRARY,DISP=(OLD,KEEP),UNIT=3390,
//                VOLUME=SER=&NUMBER
```

```
//        PEND
//*
//TESTPROC EXEC DEF
//
```

10.7 Summary

This chapter describes the process for translating a source program into an
executable load module and executing the load module. The basic steps for this
translation are to compile and link-edit, although there might be a third step to
pre-process the source prior to compiling it. The pre-processing step would be
required if your source program issues CICS command language calls or SQL
calls. The output of the pre-processing step is then fed into the compile step.

The purpose of the compile step is to validate and translate source code into
relocatable machine language, in the form of object code. Although the object
code is machine language, it is not yet executable. It must be processed by a
linkage editor, binder, or loader before it can be executed.

The linkage editor, binder, and loader take as input object code and other load
modules, and then produce an executable load module and, in the case of the
loader, execute it. This process resolves any unresolved references within the
object code and ensures that everything that is required for this program to
execute is included within the final load module. The load module is now ready
for execution.

To execute a load module, it must be loaded into central storage. The binder or
program manager service loads the module into storage and then transfers
control to it to begin execution. Part of transferring control to the module is to
supply it with the address of the start of the program in storage. Because the
program's instructions and data are addressed using a base address and a
displacement from the base, this starting address gives addressability to the
instructions and data within the limits of the range of displacement.[2]

Table 10-1 lists the key terms used in this chapter.

Table 10-1   Key terms used in this chapter

binder	copybook	linkage editor
load module	object deck	object-oriented code

---
[2] The maximum displacement for each base register is 4096 (4 KB). Any program bigger than 4 KB
must have more than one base register to have addressability to the entire program.

procedure	procedure library .	program library
relocatable	source module	

10.8 Questions for review

To help test your understanding of the material in this chapter, answer the following questions:

1. What steps are needed to be able to execute a source program?
2. How can I modify an object deck? A load module?
3. How many different types of load libraries can the system have?
4. What is a procedure library, and what is it used for?
5. What is the difference between the linkage editor and the binder?
6. How are copybooks and cataloged procedure libraries similar?
7. What is the purpose of a compiler? What are the inputs and outputs?
8. What does relocatable mean?
9. What is the difference between an object deck and a load module?
10. What is the SYSLMOD DD statement used for?
11. Why is a PEND statement required in an inline PROC and not in a cataloged PROC?

10.9 Exercises

The lab exercises in this chapter help you develop skills in preparing programs to run on z/OS. These skills are required for performing lab exercises in the remainder of this text.

To perform the lab exercises, you or your team require a TSO user ID and password (for assistance, see the instructor).

The exercises teach the following procedures:

► "Exercise: Compiling and linking a program" on page 392
► "Exercise: Executing a program" on page 394

10.9.1 Exercise: Compiling and linking a program

In this section, use at least two programming languages to compile and link a program using the following JCL data set:

yourid.LANG.CNTL(*language*)

Where *language* is either ASM, ASMLE, C, C2, COBOL, COBOL2, PL1, or PL12.

Do this exercise before attempting the exercise in 10.9.2, "Exercise: Executing a program" on page 394. The results of successfully running each job in this exercise is creating the load modules that will be executed in the next exercise.

Note: The JCL needs to be modified to specify the high-level qualifier (HLQ) of the student submitting the jobs. In addition, any jobs referring to Language Environment data sets might also need to be modified. See the comment boxes for more information.

To submit the jobs, enter SUBMIT on the ISPF command line. After the job completes, you need to use SDSF to view the output of the job.

Perform the following steps:

1. Submit the following data set to compile and link a complex Assembler language program:

   yourid.LANG.CNTL(ASMLE)

   Note: The student might need to modify the JCL for data sets beginning with CEE. Ask your system programmer what the high-level qualifier (HLQ) is for the Language Environment data sets. The JCL that might need to be changed is highlighted here:

   ```
   //C.SYSLIB    DD DSN=SYS1.MACLIB,DISP=SHR
   //            DD DSN=CEE.SCEEMAC,DISP=SHR
   //C.SYSIN     DD DSN=ZUSER##.LANG.SOURCE(ASMLE),DISP=SHR
   //L.SYSLMOD   DD DSN=ZUSER##.LANG.LOAD(ASMLE),DISP=SHR
   //L.SYSLIB    DD DSN=CEE.SCEELKED,DISP=SHR
   //            DD DSN=CEE.SCEELKEX,DISP=SHR
   ```

2. Submit the following data set to compile and link a simple Assembler language program:

   yourid.LANG.CNTL(ASM)

3. Submit the following data set to compile and link a complex C language program:

yourid.LANG.CNTL(C)

> **Note:** The student might need to modify the JCL for data sets beginning with CEE and CBC. Ask your system programmer what the high-level qualifiers (HLQs) are for the Language Environment and C language data sets. The JCL that might need to be changed is highlighted here:

```
//STEP1 EXEC PROC=EDCCB,LIBPRFX=CEE,LNGPRFX=CBC,
//    INFILE='ZUSER##.LANG.SOURCE(C)',
//    OUTFILE='ZUSER##.LANG.LOAD(C),DISP=SHR'
```

4. Submit the following data set to compile and link a simple C language program:

yourid.LANG.CNTL(C2)

> **Note:** The student might need to modify the JCL for data sets beginning with CEE and CBC. Ask your system programmer what the high-level qualifiers (HLQs) are for the Language Environment and C language data sets. The JCL that might need to be changed is highlighted here:

```
//STEP1 EXEC PROC=EDCCB,LIBPRFX=CEE,LNGPRFX=CBC,
//    INFILE='ZUSER##.LANG.SOURCE(C2)',
//    OUTFILE='ZUSER##.LANG.LOAD(C2),DISP=SHR'
```

5. Submit the following data set to compile and link a complex COBOL language program:

yourid.LANG.CNTL(COBOL)

> **Note:** The student might need to modify the JCL for data sets beginning with CEE. Ask your system programmer what the high-level qualifier (HLQ) is for the Language Environment data sets. The JCL that might need to be changed is highlighted here:

```
//SYSIN        DD DSN=ZUSER##.LANG.SOURCE(COBOL),DISP=SHR
//COBOL.SYSLIB DD DSN=CEE.SCEESAMP,DISP=SHR
//LKED.SYSLMOD DD DSN=ZUSER##.LANG.LOAD(COBOL),DISP=SHR
```

6. Submit the following data set to compile and link a simple COBOL language program:

yourid.LANG.CNTL(COBOL2)

7. Submit the following data set to compile and link a complex PL/I language program:

   yourid`.LANG.CNTL(PL1)`

   > **Note:** The student might need to modify the JCL for data sets beginning with CEE. Ask your system programmer what the high-level qualifier (HLQ) is for the Language Environment data sets. The JCL that might need to be changed is highlighted here:
   >
   > ```
   > //SYSIN       DD DSN=ZUSER##.LANG.SOURCE(PL1),DISP=SHR
   > //PLI.SYSLIB  DD DSN=CEE.SCEESAMP,DISP=SHR
   > //BIND.SYSLMOD DD DSN=ZUSER##.LANG.LOAD(PL1),DISP=SHR
   > ```

8. Submit the following data set to compile and link a simple PL/I language program:

   yourid`.LANG.CNTL(PL12)`

10.9.2 Exercise: Executing a program

Do not attempt to run any of the following jobs if you have not successfully completed the exercise in 10.9.1, "Exercise: Compiling and linking a program" on page 392, because they will end in errors.

The following exercise contains actions to execute, for each language sample, the load module that was previously stored when a compile and link job was run. For the interpreted languages, you execute the source members directly from:

yourid`.LANG.SOURCE(`*language*`)`

Where *language* is either of CLIST or REXX.

Note: The JCL needs to be modified to specify the HLQ of the student submitting the jobs. To submit the jobs, enter SUBMIT on the ISPF command line. After the job completes, you need to use SDSF to view the output of the job.

In order for these jobs to run successfully, the student must have completed the compile and link jobs in 10.9.1, "Exercise: Compiling and linking a program" on page 392 to create the load modules in *ZPROF*.LANG.LOAD.

If these jobs did not run successfully, then the student could receive errors in the job log in SDSF similar to the following output:

```
CSV003I REQUESTED MODULE ASM        NOT FOUND
CSV028I ABEND806-04  JOBNAME=ZPROF2     STEPNAME=STEP1
IEA995I SYMPTOM DUMP OUTPUT  238
SYSTEM COMPLETION CODE=806  REASON CODE=00000004
```

The module name, JOBNAME, and STEPNAME vary, according to which job had been submitted.

Perform the following steps:

1. Submit the following data set to execute a complex Assembler language program:

   `yourid.LANG.CNTL(USEASMLE)`

   This example accesses z/OS Language Environment and prints the following message:

   ```
   IN THE MAIN ROUTINE
   ```

2. Submit the following data set to execute a simple Assembler language program:

   `yourid.LANG.CNTL(USEASM)`

   This example sets the return code to 15 and exits.

3. Submit the following data set to execute a complex C language program:

   `yourid.LANG.CNTL(USEC)`

   This example prints out the local date and time.

4. Submit the following data set to execute a simple C language program:

   `yourid.LANG.CNTL(USEC2)`

   This example prints out the message `Hello World`.

5. Submit the following data set to execute a complex COBOL language program:

   yourid.LANG.CNTL(USECOBOL)

   This example prints out the local date and time.

6. Submit the following data set to execute a simple COBOL language program:

   yourid.LANG.CNTL(USECOBO2)

   This example prints out the message HELLO WORLD.

7. Submit the following data set to execute a complex PL/I language program:

   yourid.LANG.CNTL(USEPL1)

   This example prints out the local date and time.

8. Submit the following data set to execute a simple PL/I language program:

   yourid.LANG.CNTL(USEPL12)

   This example prints out the message HELLO WORLD.

9. Execute the following complex CLIST language program:

   yourid.LANG.SOURCE(CLIST)

   This example prompts the user for a high-level qualifier (HLQ) and then produces a formatted catalog listing for that HLQ.

   On the ISPF command line, enter:

   TSO EX '*yourid*.LANG.SOURCE(CLIST)'

   When prompted, enter the HLQ *yourid*.

10. Execute the following simple CLIST language program:

    yourid.LANG.SOURCE(CLIST2)

    This example prints out the message HELLO WORLD.

    On the ISPF command line, enter:

    TSO EX '*yourid*.LANG.SOURCE(CLIST2)'

11. Execute the following complex REXX language program:

    yourid.LANG.SOURCE(REXX)

    This example prompts the user for a high-level qualifier (HLQ) and then produces a formatted catalog listing for that HLQ.

    On the ISPF command line, enter:

    TSO EX '*yourid*.LANG.SOURCE(REXX)'

    When prompted, enter the HLQ *yourid*.

12. Execute the following simple REXX language program:

    yourid.LANG.SOURCE(REXX2)

    This example prints out the message HELLO WORLD.

    On the ISPF command line, enter:

    TSO EX '*yourid*.LANG.SOURCE(REXX2)'

Part 3

Online workloads for z/OS

In this part, we examine the major categories of online or *interactive* workloads performed on z/OS, such as transaction processing, database management, and web serving. The chapters that follow guide the student through discussions of network communications and several popular middleware products, including IBM DB2, CICS, and IBM WebSphere.

11

Transaction management systems on z/OS

Objective: To expand your knowledge of mainframe workloads, you must understand the role of mainframes in today's online world. This chapter introduces concepts and terminology for transactional processing, and presents an overview of the major types of system software used to process online workloads on the mainframe. In this chapter, we focus on two of the most widely used transaction management products for z/OS: CICS and IMS.

After completing this chapter, you will be able to:

▶ Describe the role of large systems in a typical online business.

▶ List the attributes common to most transaction systems.

▶ Explain the role of CICS in online transaction processing.

▶ Describe CICS programs, CICS transactions, and CICS tasks.

▶ Explain what conversational and pseudo-conversational programming is.

▶ Explain CICS and web enabling.

▶ Discuss the IMS components.

Refer to Table 11-1 on page 430 for a list of key terms used in this chapter.

11.1 Online processing on the mainframe

In earlier chapters, we discussed the possibilities of batch processing, but those are not the only applications running on z/OS and the mainframe. Online applications also run on z/OS, as we show in this chapter. We also describe what online, or interactive, applications are and discuss their common elements in the mainframe environment.

We examine databases, which are a common way of storing application data. Databases make development easier, especially in the case of a relational database management system (RDBMS), by removing the burden from the programmer organizing and managing the data. Later in this chapter, we discuss several widely used transaction management systems for mainframe-based enterprises.

We begin with the example of a travel agency with a requirement common to many mainframe customers: Provide customers with more immediate access to services and use the benefits of Internet-based commerce.

11.2 Example of global online processing: The new big picture

A big travel agency has relied on a mainframe-based batch system for many years. Over the years, the agency's customers have enjoyed excellent service, and the agency has continuously improved its systems.

When the business began, their IT staff designed some applications to support the agency's internal and external processes: Employee information, customer information, contacts with car rental companies, hotels all over the world, scheduled flights of airlines, and so on. At first these application were updated periodically by batch processing.

This kind of data is not static, however, and has become increasingly prone to frequent change. Because prices, for example, change frequently, it has become more difficult over time to maintain current information. The agency's customers want their information *now* and that is not always possible through fixed intervals of batch updates (consider the time difference between Asia, Europe, and America).

If these workloads are done through traditional mainframe batch jobs, it means a certain time lapse between the reception of the change and the actual update. The agency needs a way to update small amounts of data provided in bits and pieces. by phone, fax, or email, the instant that changes occur (Figure 11-1).

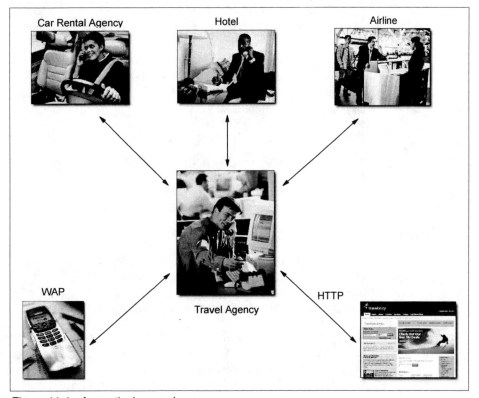

Figure 11-1   A practical example

Therefore, the agency IT staff created some new applications. Because changes need to be immediately provided to the applications's users, the new applications are transactional in nature. The applications are called transaction or interactive applications, because changes in the system data are effective immediately.

The travel agency contacted its suppliers to see what could be done. They needed a way to let their computers talk to each other. Some of the airlines were also working on mainframes, others were not, and everybody wanted to keep their own applications.

Eventually, they found a solution that made communicating easy: you could just ask a question and some seconds later get the result.

More innovations were required because the customers also evolved. Personal computer became ubiquitous, so they want to see travel possibilities over the Internet. Some customers also use their mobile computers as a wireless access point (WAP).

11.3 Transaction systems for the mainframe

Transactions occur in everyday life, for example, when you exchange money for goods and services or do a search on the Internet. A transaction is an exchange, usually a request and response, that occurs as a routine event in running the day-to-day operations of an organization.

Transactions have the following characteristics:

► A small amount of data is processed and transferred per transaction.
► There are a large numbers of users.
► They are executed in large numbers.

11.3.1 What are transaction programs

A business transaction is a self-contained business deal. Some transactions involve a short conversation (for example, an address change). Others involve multiple actions that take place over an extended period (for example, the booking of a trip, including car, hotel, and airline tickets).

A single transaction might consist of many application programs that carry out the processing needed. Large-scale transaction systems (such as the IBM CICS product) rely on the *multitasking* and *multithreading* capabilities of z/OS to allow more than one task to be processed at the same time, with each task saving its specific variable data and keeping track of the instructions each user is executing.

Multitasking is essential in any environment in which thousands of users can be logged on at the same time. When a multitasking transaction system receives a request to run a transaction, it can start a new task that is associated with *one instance* of the execution of the transaction, that is, one execution of a transaction, with a particular set of data, usually on behalf of a particular user at a particular terminal. You might also consider a task to be analogous to a UNIX thread. When the transaction completes, the task is ended.

Multithreading: A single copy of an application can be processed by several transactions concurrently.

Multithreading allows a single copy of an application program to be processed by several transactions concurrently. Multithreading requires that all transactional application programs be reentrant; that is, they must be serially reusable between entry and exit points.

Among programming languages, reentrance is ensured by a *fresh* copy of working storage section being obtained each time the program is invoked.

11.3.2 What is a transaction system

Figure 11-2 shows the main characteristics of a transaction system. Before the advent of the Internet, a transaction system served hundreds or thousands of *terminals* with dozens or hundreds of transactions per second. This workload was rather predictable both in transaction rate and mix of transactions.

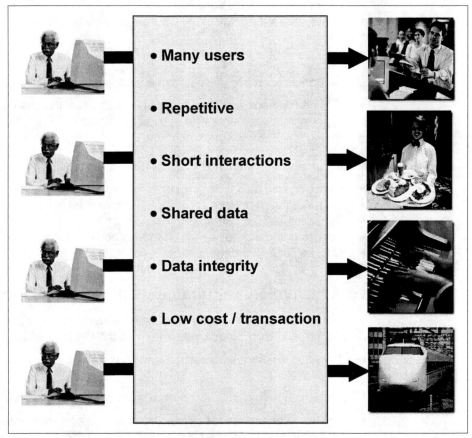

- **Many users**

- **Repetitive**

- **Short interactions**

- **Shared data**

- **Data integrity**

- **Low cost / transaction**

Figure 11-2   Characteristics of a transaction system

Transaction systems must be able to support a high number of concurrent users and transaction types.

Transaction:
A unit of work performed by one or more transaction programs, involving a specific set of input data and initiating a specific process or job.

One of the main characteristics of a transaction or online system is that the interactions between the user and the system are brief. Most transactions are executed in short time periods; one second, in some cases. The user will perform a complete business transaction through short interactions, with immediate response time required for each interaction. These are mission-critical applications; therefore, continuous availability, high performance, and data protection and integrity are required.

Online transaction processing (OLTP) is transaction processing that occurs interactively. It requires:

- Immediate response time
- Continuous availability of the transaction interface to the user
- Security
- Data integrity

Online transactions are familiar to many people. Some examples include:

- ATM transactions, such as deposits, withdrawals, inquiries, and transfers
- Supermarket payments with debit or credit cards
- Buying merchandise over the Internet

In fact, an online system has many of the characteristics of an operating system:

- Managing and dispatching tasks
- Controlling user access authority to system resources
- Managing the use of memory
- Managing and controlling simultaneous access to data files
- Providing device independence

11.3.3 What are the typical requirements of a transaction system

In a transaction system, transactions must comply with four primary requirements known jointly by the mnemonic A-C-I-D or ACID:

- *A*tomicity: The processes performed by the transaction are done as a whole or not at all.

- *C*onsistency: The transaction must work only with consistent information.

- *I*solation: The processes coming from two or more transactions must be isolated from one another.

- *D*urability: The changes made by the transaction must be permanent.

Usually, transactions are initiated by an user who interacts with the transaction system through a terminal. In the past, transaction systems supported only terminals and devices connected through a teleprocessing network. Today, transaction systems can serve requests submitted in any of the following ways:

- ► Web page
- ► Remote workstation program
- ► Application in another transaction system
- ► Triggered automatically at a predefined time
- ► Web service and web 2.0 requests
- ► Arrival of asynchronous messages

11.3.4 What is commit and roll back

In transaction systems, *commit and roll back* refers to the set of actions used to ensure that an application program either makes *all* changes to the resources represented by a single unit of recovery (UR), or makes *no* changes at all. The two-phase commit protocol provides commit and rollback. It verifies that either all changes or no changes are applied even if one of the elements (such as the application, the system, or the resource manager) fails. The protocol allows for restart and recovery processing to take place after system or subsystem failure.

The two-phase commit protocol is initiated when the application is ready to commit or back out its changes. At this point, the coordinating recovery manager, also called the *sync point manager,* gives each resource manager participating in the unit of recovery an opportunity to vote on whether its part of the UR is in a consistent state and can be committed. If all participants vote YES, the recovery manager instructs all the resource managers to commit the changes. If any of the participants vote NO, the recovery manager instructs them to back out the changes. This process is usually represented as two phases.

In phase 1, the application program issues the sync point or rollback request to the sync point coordinator. The coordinator issues a PREPARE command to send the initial sync point flow to all the UR agent resource managers. In response to the PREPARE command, each resource manager involved in the transaction replies to the sync point coordinator stating whether it is ready to commit or not.

When the sync point coordinator receives all the responses back from all its agents, phase 2 is initiated. In this phase, the sync point coordinator issues the commit or rollback command based on the previous responses. If any of the agents responded with a negative response, the sync point initiator causes *all* of the sync point agents to roll back their changes.

The instant when the coordinator records the fact that it is going to tell all the resource managers to either commit or roll back is known as the *atomic instant.*

Regardless of any failures after that time, the coordinator assumes that all changes will either be committed or rolled back. A sync point coordinator usually logs the decision at this point. If any of the participants abnormally end (*abend*) after the atomic instant, the abending resource manager must work with the sync point coordinator, when it restarts, to complete any commits or rollbacks that were in process at the time of the abend.

On z/OS, the primary sync point coordinator is called the Resource Recovery Services (RRS). Also, the IBM transaction manager product, CICS, includes its own built-in sync point coordinator.

During the first phase of the protocol, the agents do not know whether the sync point coordinator will commit or roll back the changes. This time is known as the *in-doubt* period. The UR is described as having a particular state depending on what stage it is at in the two-phase commit process:

► Before a UR makes any changes to a resource, it is described as being *in-reset*.

► While the UR is requesting changes to resources, it is described as being *in-flight*.

► After a commit request has been made (Phase 1), it is described as being *in-prepare*.

► After the sync point manager has made a decision to commit (phase 2 of the two-phase commit process), it is *in-commit*.

► If the sync point manager decides to back out, it is *in-backout*.

Figure 11-3 illustrates the two-phase commit.

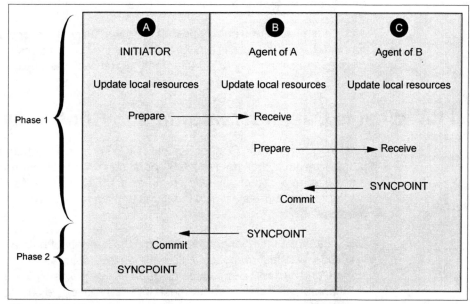

Figure 11-3 Two-phase commit

Most widely used transaction management systems on z/OS, such as CICS or IMS, support two-phase commit protocols. CICS, for example, supports full two-phase commit in transactions with IMS and the DB2 database management system, and supports two-phase commit across distributed CICS systems.

There are many restrictions imposed on application developers attempting to develop new applications that require updates in many different resource managers, perhaps across a number of systems. Many of these new applications use technologies such as DB2 stored procedures and Enterprise Java Beans, and use client attachment facilities of CICS or IMS that do not support two-phase commit. If any of these resource managers are used by an application to update resources, it is not possible to have a global coordinator for the sync point.

The lack of a global sync point coordinator might influence an application design for the following reasons:

► The application is not capable of having complex and distributed transactions if not all of the resource managers are participating in the two-phase commit protocol.

► The application cannot be designed as a single application (or unit of recovery) across multiple systems (except for CICS).

The application programmer would have to program around these limitations. For example, the programmer could limit the choice of where to put the business data to ensure that all the data could be committed in a single unit of recovery.

Also, these limitations could affect the recoverability of the protected resources or their integrity in case of a failure of one of the components, because resource managers have no way to either commit or roll back the updates.

11.4 What is Customer Information Control System

Customer Information Control System (CICS) is a general-purpose transaction processing subsystem for the z/OS operating system. CICS provides services for running an application online, by request, at the same time as many other users are submitting requests to run the same applications, using the same files and programs.

CICS manages the sharing of resources, the integrity of data and prioritization of execution, with fast response. CICS authorizes users, allocates resources (real storage and cycles), and passes on database requests by the application to the appropriate database manager (such as DB2). We could say that CICS acts like, and performs many of the same functions, as the z/OS operating system.

A *CICS application* is a collection of related programs that together perform a business operation, such as processing a travel request or preparing a company payroll. CICS applications execute under CICS control, using CICS services and interfaces to access programs and files.

CICS applications are traditionally run by submitting a transaction request. Execution of the transaction consists of running one or more application programs that implement the required function. In CICS documentation, you might find CICS application programs that are simply called "programs," and sometimes the term "transaction" is used to refer to the processing done by the application programs.

CICS applications can also take the form of Enterprise Java Beans. You can discover more about this form of programming in Java Applications in CICS in the CICS Information Center, found at:

```
http://www-01.ibm.com/support/docview.wss?uid=swg21200934
```

11.4.1 CICS in a z/OS system

In a z/OS system, CICS provides a layer of function for managing transactions, while the operating system continues to be the final interface with the computer hardware. CICS essentially separates a particular kind of application program (namely, online applications) from others in the system, and handles these programs itself.

When an application program accesses a terminal or any device, for example, it does not communicate directly with it. The program issues commands to communicate with CICS, which communicates with the needed access methods of the operating system. Finally, the access method communicates with the terminal or device.

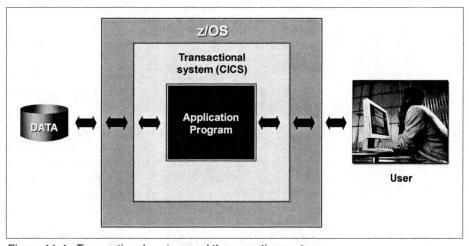

Figure 11-4   Transactional system and the operating system

A z/OS system might have multiple copies of CICS running at one time. Each CICS starts as a separate z/OS address space. CICS provides an option called multi-region operation (MRO), which enables the separation of different CICS functions into different CICS regions (address spaces), so a specific CICS address space (or more) might handle the terminal control and be named the terminal owning region (TOR). Other possibilities include application-owning regions (AORs) for applications and file-owning regions (FORs) for files.

11.4.2 CICS programs, transactions, and tasks

CICS allows you to keep your application logic separate from your application resources. To develop and run CICS applications, you need to understand the relationship between CICS programs, transactions, and tasks. These terms are used throughout CICS publications and appear in many commands:

► Transaction

A transaction is a piece of processing initiated by a single request. This is often from an user terminal, but might also be made from a web page, from a remote workstation program, from a web service or atom feed request, as a result of the arrival of an asynchronous message, or triggered automatically at a predefined time. The *CICS Internet Guide*, SC34-6007, *CICS Web Services Guide*, SC34-6458, and *CICS External Interfaces Guide*, SC34-6006 describe different ways of running CICS transactions.

A CICS transaction is given a 4-character name, which is defined in the program control table (PCT).

► Application program

A single transaction consists of one or more *application programs* that, when run, carry out the processing needed.

However, the term *transaction* is used in CICS to mean both a single event and all other transactions of the same type. You describe each transaction type to CICS with a *transaction resource definition*. This definition gives the transaction type a name (the transaction identifier (TRANSID)) and tells CICS several things about the work to be done, such as what program to invoke first and what kind of authentication is required throughout the execution of the transaction.

You run a transaction by submitting its TRANSID to CICS. CICS uses the information recorded in the TRANSACTION definition to establish the correct execution environment, and starts the first program.

► Unit of work

Unit of work:
A transaction; also, a complete operation that is recoverable.

The term transaction is now used extensively in the IT industry to describe a unit of recovery or what CICS calls a *unit of work*. This is typically a complete operation that is recoverable; it can be committed or backed out entirely as a result of a programmed command or system failure. In many cases, the scope of a CICS transaction is also a single unit of work, but you should be aware of the difference in meaning when reading non-CICS publications.

► Task

You also see the word *task* used extensively in CICS publications. This word also has a specific meaning in CICS. When CICS receives a request to run a transaction, it starts a new task that is associated with this one instance of the execution of the transaction, that is, one execution of a transaction, with a particular set of data, usually on behalf of a particular user at a particular terminal. You can also consider it analogous to a *thread*. When the transaction completes, the task is terminated.

11.4.3 Using programming languages

You can use COBOL, OO COBOL, C, C++, Java, PL/I, or Assembler language to write CICS application programs to run on z/OS. Most of the processing logic is expressed in standard language statements, but you use CICS commands, or the Java and C++ class libraries, to request CICS services.

Most of the time, you use the CICS command level programming interface, EXEC CICS. This is the case for COBOL, OO COBOL, C, C++, PL/I, and assembler programs. These commands are defined in detail in the *CICS Application Programming Reference*, SC34-6434.

Programming in Java with the JCICS class library is described in the Java Applications in CICS component of the CICS Information Center.

Programming in C++ with the CICS C++ classes is described in *CICS C++ OO Class Libraries*, SC34-6437.

11.4.4 Conversational and pseudo-conversational programming

Conversational transaction:
A program that conducts a conversation with a user.

In CICS, when the programs being executed enter into a conversation with the user, it is called a *conversational transaction* (Figure 11-5). A non-conversational transaction (Figure 11-6 on page 415), by contrast, processes one input, responds, and ends (disappears). It never pauses to read a second input from the terminal, so there is no real conversation.

There is a technique in CICS called pseudo-conversational processing, in which a series of non-conversational transactions gives the appearance (to the user) of a single conversational transaction. No transaction exists while the user waits for input; CICS takes care of reading the input when the user gets around to sending it. Figure 11-5 and Figure 11-6 on page 415 show different types of conversational transactions using an example of a record update in a banking account.

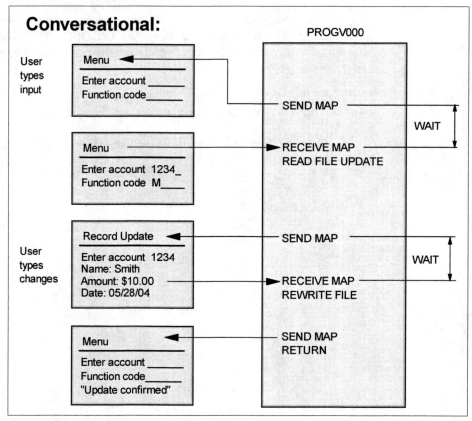

Figure 11-5   Example of a conversational transaction

In a conversational transaction, programs hold resources while waiting to receive data. In a pseudo-conversational transaction, no resources are held during these waits (Figure 11-6).

More information about these topics can be found in *CICS Transaction Server for z/OS - CICS Application Programming Guide*, SC34-6231.

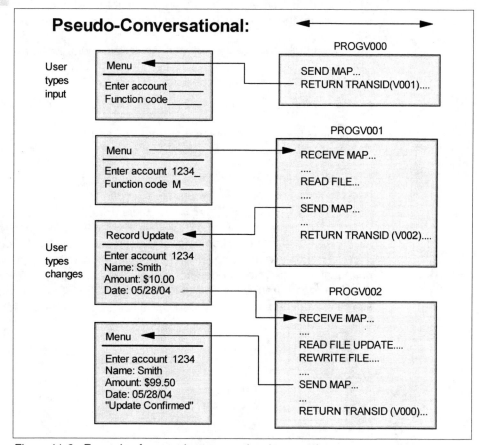

Figure 11-6   Example of a pseudo-conversational transaction

11.4.5 CICS programming commands

The general format of a CICS command is EXECUTE CICS (or EXEC CICS) followed by the name of the command and possibly one or more options.

You can write many application programs using the CICS command-level interface without any knowledge of, or reference to, the fields in the CICS control blocks and storage areas. However, you might need to get information that is valid outside the local environment of your application program.

When you need a CICS system service, for example, when reading a record from a file, you just include a CICS command in your code. In COBOL, for example, CICS commands appear as follows:

```
EXEC CICS function option option ... END-EXEC.
```

function is the action you want to perform. Reading a file is READ, writing to a terminal is SEND, and so on.

option is a specification that is associated with the function. Options are expressed as keywords. For example, the options for the READ command include FILE, RIDFLD, UPDATE, and others. FILE tells CICS which file you want to read, and is always followed by a value indicating or pointing to the file name. RIDFLD (record identification field, that is, the key) tells CICS which record and likewise needs a value. The UPDATE option simply means that you intend to change the record, and it does not take any value. So, to read with intent to modify a record from a file known to CICS as ACCTFIL, and using a key that we stored in working storage as ACCTC, we issued the command shown in Example 11-1.

Example 11-1   CICS command example

```
EXEC CICS
   READ FILE('ACCTFIL')
        RIDFLD(ACCTC) UPDATE ...
END-EXEC.
```

You can use the ADDRESS and ASSIGN commands to access such information. For programming information about these commands, see *CICS Transaction Server for z/OS - CICS System Programming Reference*, SC34-6233. When using the ADDRESS and ASSIGN commands, various fields can be read but should not be set or used in any other way. This means that you should not use any of the CICS fields as arguments in CICS commands, because these fields may be altered by the EXEC interface modules.

11.4.6 How a CICS transaction flows

To begin an online session with CICS, users usually begin by "signing on," which is the process that identifies them to CICS. Signing on to CICS gives users the authority to invoke certain transactions. When signed on, users invoke the particular transaction they intend to use. A CICS transaction is usually identified by a 1- to 4-character transaction identifier or TRANSID, which is defined in a table that names the initial program to be used for processing the transaction.

Application programs are stored in a library on a direct access storage device (DASD) attached to the processor. They can be loaded when the system is started, or simply loaded as required. If a program is in storage and is not being used, CICS can release the space for other purposes. When the program is next needed, CICS loads a fresh copy of it from the library.

In the time it takes to process one transaction, the system may receive messages from several terminals. For each message, CICS loads the application program (if it is not already loaded), and starts a task to execute it. Thus, multiple CICS tasks can be running concurrently.

Multithreading is a technique that allows a single copy of an application program to be processed by several transactions concurrently. For example, one transaction may begin to execute an application program (a traveller requests information). While this happens, another transaction may then execute the same copy of the application program (another traveller requests information). Compare this with *single-threading*, which is the execution of a program to completion; processing of the program by one transaction is completed before another transaction can use it. Multithreading requires that all CICS application programs be quasi-reentrant, that is, they must be serially reusable between entry and exit points. CICS application programs using the CICS commands obey this rule automatically.

CICS maintains a separate thread of control for each task. When, for example, one task is waiting to read a disk file, or to get a response from a terminal, CICS is able to give control to another task. Tasks are managed by the CICS *task control* program.

CICS manages both multitasking and requests from the tasks themselves for services (of the operating system or of CICS itself). This allows CICS processing to continue while a task is waiting for the operating system to complete a request on its behalf. Each transaction that is being managed by CICS is given control of the processor when that transaction has the highest priority of those that are ready to run.

While it runs, your application program requests various CICS facilities to handle message transmissions between it and the terminal, and to handle any necessary file or database accesses. When the application is complete, CICS returns the terminal to a standby state. Figure 11-7, Figure 11-8 on page 419, and Figure 11-9 on page 419 help you understand what goes on.

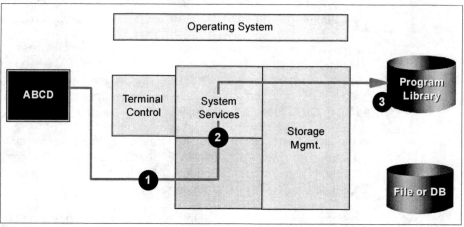

Figure 11-7   CICS transaction flow (Part 1)

The flow of control during a transaction (code ABCD) is shown by the sequence of numbers 1 to 8. (We are only using this transaction to show some of the stages than can be involved.) The meanings of the eight stages are as follows:

1. *Terminal control* accepts characters ABCD, entered at the terminal, and puts them into working storage.

2. *System services* interpret the transaction code ABCD as a call for an application program called ABCD00. If the terminal operator has authority to invoke this program, it is either found already in storage or loaded into storage.

3. Modules are brought from the *program library* into working storage.

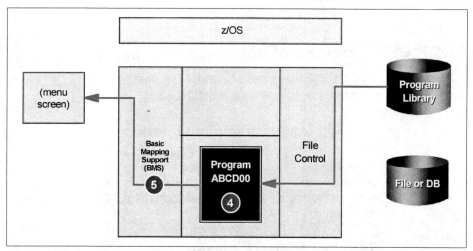

Figure 11-8   CICS transaction flow (Part 2)

4. A *task* is created. Program ABCD00 is given control on its behalf.

5. ABCD00 invokes *Basic Mapping Support* (BMS) and terminal control to send a menu to the terminal, allowing the user to specify precisely what information is needed.

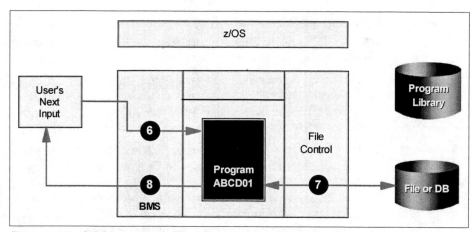

Figure 11-9   CICS transaction flow (Part 3)

6. BMS and terminal control also handle the user's next input, returning it to ABCD01 (the program designated by ABDC00 to handle the next response from the terminal), which then invokes file control.

7. *File control* reads the appropriate file for the invocation the terminal user has requested.

8. Finally, ABCD01 invokes BMS and terminal control to format the retrieved data and present it on the terminal.

11.4.7 CICS services for application programs

CICS applications execute under CICS control, using CICS services and interfaces to access programs and files.

Application programming interface

You use the *application programming interface* (API) to access CICS services from the application program. You write a CICS program in much the same way as you write any other program. Most of the processed logic is expressed in standard language elements, but you can use CICS commands to request CICS services.

Terminal control services

These services allow a CICS application program to communicate with terminal devices. Through these services, information may be sent to a terminal panel and the user input may be retrieved from it. It is not easy to deal with *terminal control services* in a direct way. Basic Mapping Support (BMS) lets you communicate with a terminal with a higher language level. It formats your data, and you do not need to know the details of the data stream.

File and database control services

We may differentiate the following two different CICS data management services:

1. *CICS file control* offers you access to data sets that are managed by either the Virtual Storage Access Method (VSAM) or the Basic Direct Access Method (BDAM). CICS file control lets you read, update, add, and browse data in VSAM and BDAM data sets and delete data from VSAM data sets.

2. *Database control* lets you access DL/I and DB2 databases. Although CICS has two programming interfaces to DL/I, we recommend that you use the higher-level EXEC DL/I interface. CICS has one interface to DB2, the EXEC SQL interface, which offers powerful statements for manipulating sets of tables, thus relieving the application program of record-by-record (or segment-by-segment, in the case of DL/I) processing.

Other CICS services

Other CICS services include:

▶ *Task control* can be used to control the execution of a task. You may suspend a task or schedule the use of a resource by a task by making it serially reusable. Also, the priority assigned to a task may be changed.

- *Program control* governs the flow of control between application programs in a CICS system. The name of the application referred to in a program control command must have been defined as a program to CICS. You can use program control commands to link one of your application programs to another, and transfer control from one application program to another, with no return to the requesting program.

- *Temporary Storage (TS)* and *Transient Data (TD) control*. The CICS temporary storage control facility provides the application programmer with the ability to store data in temporary storage queues, either in main storage or in auxiliary storage on a direct-access storage device, or, in the case of temporary storage, the Coupling Facility. The CICS transient data control facility provides a generalized queuing facility to queue (or store) data for subsequent or external processing.

- *Interval control* services provide functions that are related to time. Using interval control commands, you can start a task at a specified time or after a specified interval, delay the processing of a task, and request notification when a specified time has expired, among other actions.

- *Storage control* controls requests for main storage to provide intermediate work areas and other main storage needed to process a transaction. CICS makes working storage available with each program automatically, without any request from the application program, and provides other facilities for intermediate storage both within and among tasks. In addition to the working storage provided automatically by CICS, however, you can use other CICS commands to get and release main storage.

- *Dump and trace control*. The dump control provides a transaction dump when an abnormal termination occurs during the execution of an application program. CICS trace is a debugging aid for application programmers that produces trace entries of the sequence of CICS operations.

11.4.8 Program control

A transaction (task) may execute several programs in the course of completing its work.

The program definition contains one entry for every program used by any application in the CICS system. Each entry holds, among other things, the language in which the program is written. The transaction definition has an entry for every transaction identifier in the system, and the important information kept about each transaction is the identifier and the name of the first program to be executed on behalf of the transaction.

You can see how these two sets of definitions, transaction and program, work in concert:

► The user types in a transaction identifier at the terminal (or the previous transaction determined it).

► CICS looks up this identifier in the list of installed transaction definitions.

► This tells CICS which program to invoke first.

► CICS looks up this program in the list of installed transaction definitions, finds out where it is, and loads it (if it is not already in the main storage).

► CICS builds the control blocks necessary for this particular combination of transaction and terminal, using information from both sets of definitions. For programs in command-level COBOL, this includes making a private copy of working storage for this particular execution of the program.

► CICS passes control to the program, which begins running using the control blocks for this terminal. This program may pass control to any other program in the list of installed program definitions, if necessary, in the course of completing the transaction.

There are two CICS commands for passing control from one program to another. One is the LINK command, which is similar to a CALL statement in COBOL. The other is the XCTL (transfer control) command, which has no COBOL counterpart. When one program links another, the first program stays in main storage. When the second (linked-to) program finishes and gives up control, the first program resumes at the point after the LINK. The linked-to program is considered to be operating at one logical level lower than the program that does the linking.

In contrast, when one program transfers control to another, the first program is considered terminated, and the second operates at the same level as the first. When the second program finishes, control is returned not to the first program, but to whatever program last issued a LINK command.

Some people like to think of CICS itself as the highest program level in this process, with the first program in the transaction as the next level down, and so on. Figure 11-10 illustrates this concept.

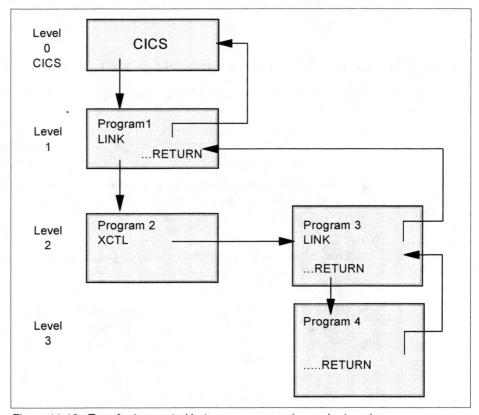

Figure 11-10   Transferring control between programs (normal returns)

The LINK command looks like the following code:

```
EXEC CICS LINK PROGRAM(pgmname)
     COMMAREA(commarea) LENGTH(length) END-EXEC.
```

Where pgmname is the name of the program to which you want to link. Commarea is the name of the area containing the data to be passed or the area to which results are to be returned. The COMMAREA interface is also an option to invoke CICS programs.

A sound principle of CICS application design is to separate the presentation logic from the business logic; communication between the programs is achieved by using the LINK command and data is passed between such programs in the COMMAREA. Such a modular design provides not only a separation of functions, but also much greater flexibility for the web enablement of existing applications using new presentation methods.

11.4.9 Customer Information Control System programming roadmap

Typical steps for developing a CICS application that uses the EXEC CICS command level programming interface are as follows:

1. Design the application, identifying the CICS resources and services you will use. See Part 1, "Writing CICS Applications", of *CICS Transaction Server for z/OS - CICS Application Programming Guide*, SC34-6231.

2. Write the program in the language of your choice, including EXEC CICS commands to request CICS services. See *CICS Transaction Server for z/OS - CICS System Programming Reference*, SC34-6233 for a list of CICS commands.

   One of the needed components for online transactions is the panel definition, that is, the layout of what is displayed on the panel (such as a web page); in CICS we call this a *map*.

3. Depending on the compiler, you might only need to compile the program and install it in CICS, or you might need to define translator options for the program and then translate and compile your program. See *CICS Application Programming Guide* for more details.

4. Define your program and related transactions to CICS with PROGRAM resource definitions and TRANSACTION resource definitions, as described in *CICS Resource Definition Guide*, SC34-6430.

5. Define any CICS resources that your program uses, such as files, queues, or terminals.

6. Make the resources known to CICS using the CEDA INSTALL command described in *CICS Resource Definition Guide*.

11.4.10 Our online example

Referring back to our travel agency example in 11.2, "Example of global online processing: The new big picture" on page 402, examples of CICS transactions might be:

► Adding, updating, or deleting employee information
► Adding, updating, or deleting available cars by rental company
► Getting the number of available cars by rental company

- Updating prices of rental cars
- Adding, updating, or deleting regular flights by airline
- Getting the number of sold tickets by airline or by destination

Figure 11-11 shows how a user can calculate the average salary by department. The department is entered by the user and the transaction calculates the average salary.

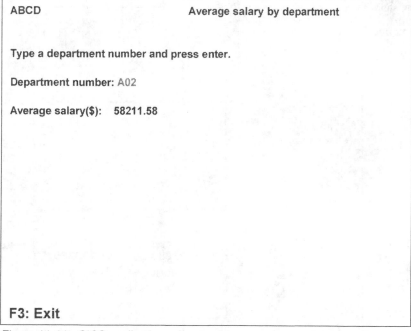

ABCD   Average salary by department

Type a department number and press enter.

Department number: A02

Average salary($):   58211.58

F3: Exit

Figure 11-11   CICS application user panel

Notice that you can add PF key definitions to the user screens in your CICS applications.

11.5 What is Information Management System

Created in 1969 as Information Management System/360, IMS is both a transaction manager and a database manager for z/OS. IMS consists of three components: the Transaction Manager (TM), the Database Manager (DB), and a set of system services that provide common services to the other two components (Figure 11-12).

IMS:
An IBM product that supports hierarchical databases, data communication, translation processing, and database backout and recovery.

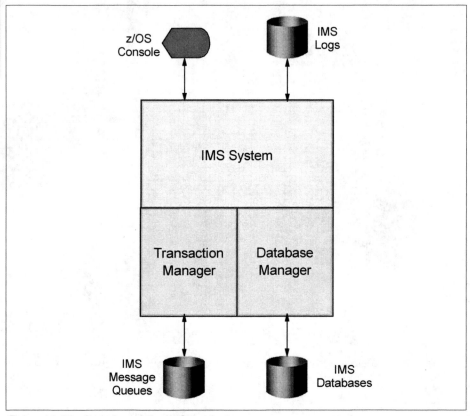

Figure 11-12   Overview of the IMS product

As IMS developed over the years, new interfaces were added to meet new business requirements. It is now possible to access IMS resources using a number of interfaces to the IMS components.

In this chapter, we look at the transaction manager functions of IMS; we discuss the database functions more thoroughly in Chapter 12, "Database management systems on z/OS" on page 433.

You write an IMS program in much the same way you write any other program. You can use COBOL, OO COBOL, C, C++, Java, PL/I, or Assembler language to write IMS application programs. More information about programming in Java can be found in *IMS Java Guide and Reference*, SC18-7821.

IMS Transaction Manager

The IMS Transaction Manager provides users of a network with access to applications running under IMS. The users can be people at terminals or workstations, or they can be other application programs either on the same z/OS system, on other z/OS systems, or on non-z/OS platforms.

A transaction is a setup of input data that triggers the execution of a specific business application program. The message is destined for an application program, and the return of any results is considered one transaction.

IMS Database Manager

The IMS Database Manager component of IMS provides a central point of control and access for the data that is processed by IMS applications. It supports databases using the IMS hierarchical database model and provides access to these databases from applications running under the IMS Transaction Manager, the CICS transaction monitor (now known as Transaction Server for z/OS), and z/OS batch jobs.

The Database Manager component provides facilities for securing (backup/recovery) and maintaining the databases. It allows multiple tasks (batch or online) to access and update the data, while retaining the integrity of that data. It also provides facilities for tuning the databases by reorganizing and restructuring them. IMS databases are organized internally using a number of IMS database organization access methods. The database data is stored on disk storage using the normal operating system access methods.

We look at the Database Manager component of IMS in more detail in Chapter 12, "Database management systems on z/OS" on page 433.

IMS System Services

There are a number of functions that are common to both the Database Manager and Transaction Manager:

- ▶ Restart and recovery of the IMS subsystems following failures

- ▶ Security: Controlling access to IMS resources

- ▶ Managing the application programs: Dispatching work, loading application programs, and providing locking services

- ▶ Providing diagnostic and performance information

▶ Providing facilities for the operation of the IMS subsystems

▶ Providing an interface to other z/OS subsystems with which IMS applications interface

11.5.1 IMS in a z/OS system

IMS runs on System z and earlier forms of the S/390 architecture or compatible mainframes, and on z/OS and earlier forms of the operating system. An IMS subsystem runs in several address spaces in a z/OS system. There is one controlling address space and several dependent address spaces providing IMS services and running IMS application programs.

For historical reasons, some documents describing IMS use the term *region* to describe a z/OS address space, for example, IMS Control Region. In this book, we use the term region whenever this is in common usage. You can take the term region as being the same as a z/OS address space.

To make the best use of the unique strengths of z/OS, IMS performs the following tasks:

▶ Runs in multiple address spaces. IMS subsystems (except for IMS/DB batch applications and utilities) normally consist of a control region address space, dependent address spaces providing system services, and dependent address spaces for application programs.

▶ Runs multiple tasks in each address space. IMS, particularly in the control regions, creates multiple z/OS subtasks for the various functions to be performed. This allows other IMS subtasks to be dispatched by z/OS while one IMS subtask is waiting for system services.

▶ Uses z/OS cross-memory services to communicate between the various address spaces making up an IMS subsystem. It also uses the z/OS Common System Area (CSA) to store IMS control blocks that are frequently accessed by the IMS address spaces, thus minimizing the impact of using multiple address spaces.

▶ Uses the z/OS subsystem feature. IMS dynamically registers itself as a z/OS subsystem. It uses this facility to detect when dependent address spaces fail, and prevent cancellation of dependent address spaces (and to interact with other subsystems such as DB2 and WebSphere MQ).

▶ Can make use of a z/OS sysplex. Multiple IMS subsystems can run on the z/OS systems making up the sysplex and access the same IMS databases.

11.5.2 IMS Transaction Manager messages

The network inputs and outputs to IMS Transaction Manager take the form of messages that are input and output to and from IMS and the physical terminals or application programs in the network. These messages are processed asynchronously (that is, IMS will not always send a reply immediately, or indeed ever, when it receives a message, and unsolicited messages may also be sent from IMS).

The messages can be of four types:

► Transactions: Data in these messages is passed to IMS application programs for processing.

► Messages to go to other logical destinations, such as network terminals.

► Commands for IMS to process.

► Messages for the IMS APPC feature to process. Because IMS uses an asynchronous protocol for messages, but APPC uses synchronous protocols (that is, it always expects a reply when a message is sent), the IMS TM interface for APPC has to perform special processing to accommodate this situation.

If IMS is not able to process an input message immediately, or cannot send an output message immediately, the message is stored on a message queue external to the IMS system. IMS will not normally delete the message from the message queue until it has received confirmation that an application has processed the message, or it has reached its destination.

11.6 Summary

In this chapter, we learned that transaction applications keep changing, depending on the needs of the organization, its customers, and suppliers. At other times, changes are implemented through new technologies, but the dependable, solid application remains unchanged. Interaction with the computer happens online through the help of a transaction manager. Many transaction managers and database managers exist, but their principles are the same.

CICS is a transactional processing subsystem, which means that it runs applications on your behalf online, by request, at the same time that many other users may be submitting requests to run the same applications, using the same files and programs. CICS manages the sharing of resources, integrity of data, and prioritization of execution, with fast response.

CICS applications are traditionally run by submitting a *transaction* request. Execution of the transaction consists of running one or more *application programs* that implement the required function.

You write a CICS program in much the same way as you write any other program. You can use COBOL, C, C++, Java, PL/I, or Assembler language to write CICS application programs. Most of the processing logic is expressed in standard language statements, but you also use *CICS commands*. The CICS commands are grouped according to their function, terminal interaction, access to files, or program linking. Most of the CICS resources may be defined and altered online through CICS-supplied transactions. Other supplied transactions allow you to monitor the CICS system. The continued growth of the Internet has caused many corporations to consider the best ways to make their existing systems available to users on the Internet. A brief overview of the different technologies available for *web enablement* of CICS applications has been shown.

Information Management System (IMS) consists of three components: the Transaction Manager (TM), the Database Manager (DB), and a set of system services that provide common services to the other two components. You write an IMS program in much the same way you write any other program. You can use COBOL, OO COBOL, C, C++, Java, PL/I, or assembler language to write IMS application programs.

Table 11-1 lists the key terms used in this chapter.

Table 11-1   Key terms used in this chapter

basic mapping support (BMS)	CICS command	CICS TS
conversational	IMS TM	Information Management System (IMS)
Internal Resource Lock Manager (IRLM)	multi-threading	pseudo-conversational
region	transaction	unit of work

11.7 Questions for review

To help test your understanding of the material in this chapter, answer the following questions:

1. What might be some typical online transactions that you perform frequently?

2. Why are multitasking and multithreading important to online transaction processing?

3. What are some common characteristics of an online transaction system?

4. Explain two-phase commit.

5. Describe the main phases in the CICS programming road map.

6. How might the meaning of "business transaction" differ from "CICS transaction"?

7. How do you define resources in CICS?

8. What are the major components of IMS, and what are their tasks?

9. What are the four types of IMS messages?

11.8 Exercise: Create a CICS program

In this exercise, we create an CICIS program. During this exercise, you might find it helpful to consult *CICS Transaction Server for z/OS - CICS Application Programming Guide*, SC34-6231.

11.8.1 Analyze and update the class program

When we analyze and update the class program, consider the following actions:

▶ Think of a possible use for the COMMAREA.

Consider passing data between programs called with LINK or XCTL. A generic program for error processing may be developed; all the invocations to it may be done by passing the required error data through the COMMAREA. Also, the COMMAREA option of the return command is designed for passing data between successive transactions in a pseudo-conversational sequence.

The state of a resource may be passed by the first transaction through COMMAREA to be compared to its current state by the second transaction. It may be necessary to know if this state has changed since the last interaction before allowing an update. In web applications, the business logic in a CICS application can be invoked by using the COMMAREA interface.

▶ Several simple updates to the class program transaction may be done quite easily:

– Include one additional output field in the panel. The maximum value of employee commissions could be an example.

A new field has to be defined in the map source. Perhaps some literals have to be changed. Assemble the map and generate the new copy file. Modify the program to have another column in the SQL statement and move its content after retrieval to the corresponding new output field in the map. Execute the preparation job for the user program. New copies for program and map are required in the CICS session.

 – Create a transaction that could be like a main menu; one of the options would start the current program.

Only two variable fields are required in the map for this transaction: the option field and the message line. Only one option has to be initially included, the one for the current ABCD transaction. The same mapset may be used to include the new map. The ABCD transaction has to be modified to do the RETURN TRANSID to the new transaction. Only the following resources have to be added to the CICS system: the new transaction and programs (user program and map).

 – Learn about the CICS HANDLE CONDITION statement and discover where it may be used.

Try to add error control to the RECEIVE CICS command. The MAPFAIL condition occurs when no usable data is transmitted from the terminal after a RECEIVE command.

Business transaction

Analyze a typical business transaction. Think of different CICS programs and transactions that could be needed to accomplish this task. Draw a diagram to show the flow of the process.

The example that is developed in *CICS Application Programming Primer*, SC33-0674 could be appropriate. A department store with credit customers keeps a master file of its customers' accounts. The application performs the following actions:

► Displays customer account records
► Adds new account records
► Modifies or deletes existing account records
► Prints a single copy of a customer account record
► Accesses records by name

12

Database management systems on z/OS

Objective: You need a good working understanding of the major types of system software used to process online workloads on the mainframe. In this chapter, we focus on two of the most widely used database management system (DBMS) products for z/OS: DB2 and IMS DB.

After completing this chapter, you will be able to:

- ▶ Explain how databases are used in a typical online business.
- ▶ Describe two models for network connectivity for large systems.
- ▶ Explain the role of DB2 in online transaction processing.
- ▶ List common DB2 data structures.
- ▶ Compose simple SQL queries to run on z/OS.
- ▶ Give an overview of application programming with DB2.
- ▶ Explain what the IMS components are.
- ▶ Describe the structure of the IMS DB subsystem.

Refer to Table 12-2 on page 468 for a list of key terms used in this chapter.

433

12.1 Database management systems for the mainframe

This section gives an overview of basic database (DB) concepts, what they are used for, and what the advantages are. There are many databases, but here we limit the scope to the two types that are used most on mainframes: hierarchical and relational databases.

12.2 What is a database

A database provides for the storing and control of business data. It is independent from (but not separate from the processing requirements of) one or more applications. If properly designed and implemented, the database should provide a single consistent view of the business data, so that it can be centrally controlled and managed.

One way of describing a logical view of this collection of data is to use an entity relationship model. The database records details (attributes) of particular items (entities) and the relationships between the different types of entities. For example, for the stock control area of an application, you would have Parts, Purchase Orders, Customers, and Customer Orders (entities). Each entity would have attributes; the Part would have a Part No, Name, Unit Price, Unit Quantity, and so on.

These entities would also have relationships between them, for example, a customer would be related to orders placed, which would be related to the part that had been ordered, and so on.

Figure 12-1 illustrates an entity relationship model.

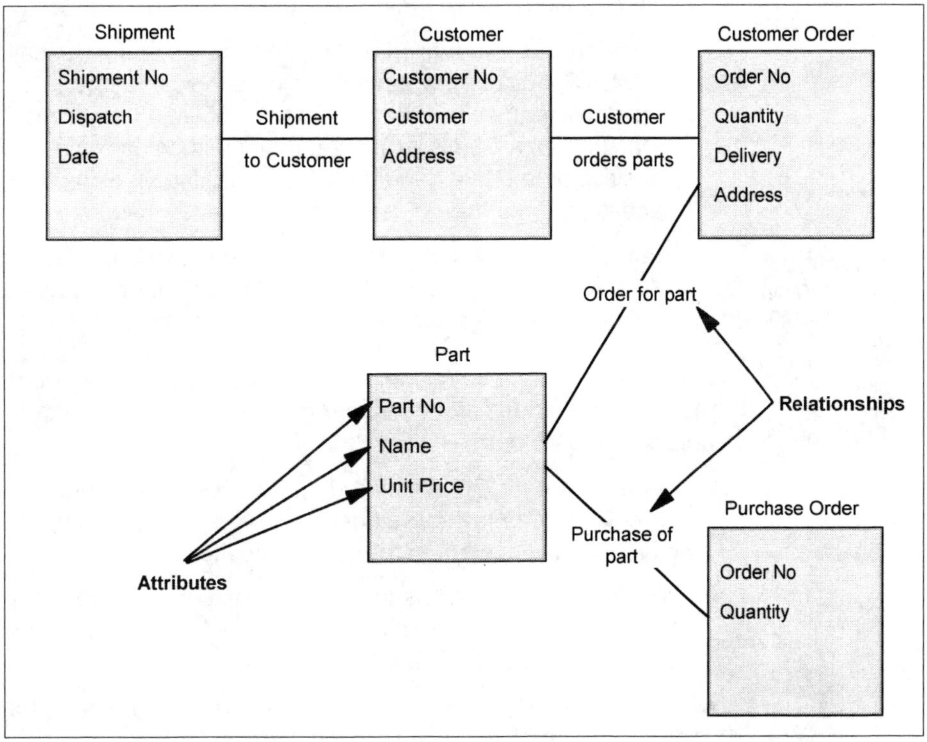

Figure 12-1   Entities, attributes, and relationships

A database management system (DBMS), such as the IMS Database Manager
(IMS/DB) component or the DB2 product, provides a method for storing and
using the business data in the database.

12.3 Why use a database

DBMS:
A database
management
system, which
provides a
method of
storing and
using data in a
database.

When computer systems were first developed, the data was stored on individual
files that were unique to an application or even a small part of an individual
application. But a properly designed and implemented DBMS provides many
advantages over a flat file PDS system:

► It reduces the application programming effort.

► It manages more efficiently the creation and modification of, and access to,
data than a non-DBMS system. As you know, if new data elements need to
be added to a file, then all applications that use that file must be rewritten,
even those that do not use the new data element.

This situation does not need to occur happen when using a DBMS. Although many programmers have resorted to "tricks" to minimize this application programming rewrite task, it still requires effort.

► It provides a greater level of data security and confidentiality than a flat file system. Specifically, when accessing a logical record in a flat file, the application can see *all* data elements, including any confidential or privileged data. To minimize this exposure, many customers have resorted to putting sensitive data into a separately managed file, and linking the two as necessary. This may cause data consistency issues.

Segment:
Any partition, reserved area, partial component, or piece of a larger structure.

With a DBMS, the sensitive data can be isolated in a separate segment (in IMS/DB) or View (in DB2) that prevents unauthorized applications from seeing it. But these data elements are an integral part of the logical record!

However, the same details might be stored in several different places, for example, the details of a customer might be in both the ordering and invoicing application. This causes a number of problems:

► Because the details are stored and processed independently, details that are supposed to be the same (for example, a customer's name and address) might be inconsistent in the various applications.

► When common data has to be changed, it must be changed in several places, causing a high workload. If any copies of the data are missed, it results in the problems detailed in the previous point.

► There is no central point of control for the data to ensure that it is secure, both from loss and from unauthorized access.

► The duplication of the data wastes space on storage media.

The use of a database management system such as IMS/DB or DB2 to implement the database also provides additional advantages. The DBMS:

► Allows multiple tasks to access and update the data simultaneously, while preserving database integrity. This is particularly important where large numbers of users are accessing the data through an online application.

► Provides facilities for the application to update multiple database records and ensures that the application data in the various records remains consistent even if an application failure occurs.

► Is able to put confidential or sensitive data in a separate segment (in IMS) or table (in DB2). In contrast, in a PDS or VSAM flat file, the application program gets access to every data element in the logical record. Some of these elements might contain data that should be restricted.

► Provides utilities that control and implement backup and recovery of the data, preventing loss of vital business data.

- Provides utilities to monitor and tune access to the data.

- Is able to change the structure of the logical record (by adding or moving data fields). Such changes usually requires that every application that accesses the VSAM or PDS file must be reassembled or recompiled, even if it does not need the added or changed fields. A properly designed data base insulates the application programmer from such changes.

Keep in mind, however, that the use of a database and database management system will not, in itself, produce the advantages detailed here. It also requires the proper design and administration of the databases, and development of the applications.

12.4 Who is the database administrator

Database administrators (DBAs) are primarily responsible for specific databases in the subsystem. In some companies, DBAs are given the special group authorization, SYSADM, which gives them the ability to do almost everything in the DB2 subsystem, and gives them jurisdiction over all the databases in the subsystem. In other companies, a DBA's authority is limited to individual databases.

The DBA creates the hierarchy of data objects, beginning with the database, then table spaces, tables, and any indexes or views that are required. This person also sets up the referential integrity definitions and any necessary constraints.

The DBA essentially implements the physical database design. Part of this involves having to do space calculations and determining how large to make the physical data sets for the table spaces and index spaces, and assigning storage groups (also called *storgroups*).

There are many tools that can assist the DBA in these tasks. DB2, for example, provides the Administration Tool and the DB2 Estimator. If objects increase in size, the DBA is able to alter certain objects to make changes.

The DBA can be responsible for granting authorizations to the database objects, although sometimes there is a special security administration group that does this task.

The centralization of data and control of access to this data is inherent to a database management system. One of the advantages of this centralization is the availability of consistent data to more than one application. As a consequence, this dictates tighter control of that data and its usage.

Responsibility for an accurate implementation of control lies with the DBA. Indeed, to gain the full benefits of using a centralized database, you must have a central point of control for it. Because the actual implementation of the DBA function is dependent on a company's organization, we limit ourselves to a discussion of the roles and responsibilities of a DBA. The group fulfilling the DBA role needs experience in both application and systems programming.

In a typical installation, the DBA is responsible for:

► Providing the standards for, and the administration of, databases and their use

► Guiding, reviewing, and approving the design of new databases

► Determining the rules of access to the data and monitoring its security

► Ensuring database integrity and availability, and monitoring the necessary activities for reorganization backup and recovery

► Approving the operation of new programs with existing production databases, based on results of testing with test data

In general, the DBA is responsible for the maintenance of current information about the data in the database. Initially, this responsibility might be carried out using a manual approach. But it can be expected to grow to a scope and complexity sufficient to justify, or necessitate, the use of a data dictionary program.

The DBA is not responsible for the actual content of databases. This is the responsibility of the user. Rather, the DBA enforces procedures for accurate, complete, and timely update of the databases.

12.5 How is a database designed

The process of database design, in its simplest form, can be described as the structuring of the data elements for the various applications, in such an order that:

► Each data element is readily available by the various applications, now and in the foreseeable future.

► The data elements are efficiently stored.

► Controlled access is enforced for those data elements with specific security requirements.

A number of different models for databases have been developed over the years (such as hierarchical, relational, or object) so that there is no consistent vocabulary for describing the concepts involved.

12.5.1 Entities

A database contains information about entities. An *entity* is something that:

▶ Can be uniquely defined.

▶ We may collect substantial information about, now or in the future.

In practice, this definition is limited to the context of the applications and business under consideration. Examples of entities are parts, projects, orders, customers, trucks, and so on. It should be clear that defining entities is a major step in the database design process. The information we store in databases about entities is described by data attributes.

12.5.2 Data attributes

A *data attribute* is a unit of information that specifies a fact about an entity. For example, suppose the entity is a part. Name=Washer, Color=Green, and Weight=143 are three facts about that part. Thus, these are three data attributes.

A data attribute has a name and a value. A data attribute name tells the kind of fact being recorded; the value is the fact itself. In this example, Name, Color, and Weight are data attribute names, while Washer, Green and 143 are values. A value must be associated with a name to have a meaning.

An *occurrence* is the value of a data attribute for a particular entity. An attribute is always dependent on an entity. It has no meaning by itself. Depending on its usage, an entity can be described by one single data attribute, or more. Ideally, an entity should be uniquely defined by one single data attribute, for example, the order number of an order. Such a data attribute is called the *key* of the entity. The key serves as the identification of a particular entity occurrence, and is a special attribute of the entity. Keys are not always unique. Entities with equal key values are called *synonyms*.

For example, the full name of a person is generally not a unique identification. In such cases, we have to rely on other attributes, such as full address, birthday, or an arbitrary sequence number. A more common method is to define a new attribute that serves as the unique key, for example, employee number.

12.5.3 Entity relationships

The entities identified will also have connections between them, called *relationships*. For example, an order might be for a number of parts. Again, these relationships only have meaning within the context of the application and business.

These relationships can be one-to-one (that is, one occurrence of an entity relates to a single occurrence of another entity), one-to-many (one occurrence of an entity relates to many occurrences of another entity), or many-to-many (many occurrences of one entity have a relationship with many occurrences of another entity).

Relationships can also be *recursive*, that is, an entity can have a relationship with other occurrences of the same entity. For example, a part, say a fastener, might consist of several other parts: bolt, nut, and washer.

12.5.4 Application functions

Data itself is not the ultimate goal of a database management system. It is the application processing performed on the data that is important. The best way to represent that processing is to take the smallest application unit representing a user interacting with the database, for example, one single order or one part's inventory status. In the following sections, we call this an *application function*.

Functions are processed by application programs. In a batch system, large numbers of functions are accumulated into a single program (that is, all orders of a day), then processed against the database with a single scheduling of the desired application program. In the online system, just one or two functions may be grouped together into a single program to provide one iteration with a user.

Although functions are always distinguishable, even in batch, some people prefer to talk about programs rather than functions. But a clear understanding of functions is mandatory for good design, especially in a DB environment. After you have identified the functional requirements of the application, you can decide how to best implement them as programs using CICS or IMS. The function is, in some way, the individual use of the application by a particular user. As such, it is the focal point of the DB system.

12.5.5 Access paths

Each function bears in its input some kind of identification with respect to the entities used (for example, the part number when accessing a parts database). These are referred to as the *access paths* of that function. In general, functions require random access, although for performance reasons sequential access is sometimes used. This is particularly true if the functions are in batches, and if they are numerous relative to the database size, or if information is needed from most database records. For efficient random access, each access path should use the entities key.

12.6 What is a database management system

A database management system (or DBMS) is essentially nothing more than a computerized data-keeping system. Users of the system are given facilities to perform several kinds of operations on such a system for either manipulation of the data in the database or the management of the database structure itself. Database Management Systems (DBMSs) are categorized according to their data structures or types.

There are several types of databases that can be used on a mainframe to use z/OS: inverted list, hierarchical, network, or relational.

Mainframe sites tend to use a hierarchical model when the data *structure* (not data values) of the data needed for an application is relatively static. For example, a Bill of Material (BOM) database structure always has a high level assembly part number, and several levels of components with subcomponents. The structure usually has a component forecast, cost, and pricing data, and so on. The structure of the data for a BOM application rarely changes, and new data elements (not values) are rarely identified. An application normally starts at the top with the assembly part number, and goes down to the detail components.

Root:
The top level of a hierarchy.

Both database systems offer the benefits listed in 12.3, "Why use a database" on page 435. RDBMS has the additional, significant advantage over the hierarchical DB of being non-navigational. By *navigational*, we mean that in a hierarchical database, the application programmer must know the structure of the database. The program must contain specific logic to navigate from the root segment to the desired child segments containing the desired attributes or elements. The program must still access the intervening segments, even though they are not needed.

The remainder of this section discusses the relational database structure.

12.6.1 What structures exist in a relational database

Relational databases include the following structures:

► Database

  A database is a logical grouping of data. It contains a set of related table spaces and index spaces. Typically, a database contains all the data that is associated with one application or with a group of related applications. You could have a payroll database or an inventory database, for example.

► Table

A table is a logical structure made up of rows and columns. Rows have no fixed order, so if you retrieve data you might need to sort the data. The order of the columns is the order specified when the table was created by the database administrator. At the intersection of every column and row is a specific data item called a value, or, more precisely, an atomic value. A table is named with a high-level qualifier of the owner's user ID followed by the table name, for example TEST.DEPT or PROD.DEPT. There are three types of tables:

– A base table that is created and holds persistent data
– A temporary table that stores intermediate query results
– A results table that is returned when you query tables

Table 12-1 shows an example of a DB2 table.

Table 12-1 Example of a DB2 table (department table)

DEPTNO	DEPTNAME	MGRNO	ADMRDEPT
A00	SPIFFY COMPUTER SERVICE DIV.	000010	A00
B01	PLANNING	000020	A00
C01	INFORMATION CENTER	000030	A00
D01	DEVELOPMENT CENTER		A00
E01	SUPPORT SERVICES	000050	A00
D11	MANUFACTURING SYSTEMS	000060	D01
D21	ADMINISTRATION SYSTEMS	000070	D01
E11	OPERATIONS	000090	E01
E21	SOFTWARE SUPPORT	000100	E01

In this table, we use:

– Columns: The ordered set of columns are DEPTNO, DEPTNAME, MGRNO, and ADMRDEPT. All the data in a given column must be of the same data type.

– Rows: Each row contains data for a single department.

– Values: At the intersection of a column and row is a *value*. For example, PLANNING is the value of the DEPTNAME column in the row for department B01.

► Indexes

An index is an ordered set of pointers to rows of a table. Unlike the rows of a table that are not in a specific order, an index must always be maintained in order by DB2. An index is used for two purposes:

– For performance, to retrieve data values more quickly

– For uniqueness

By creating an index for an employee's name, you can retrieve data more quickly for that employee than by scanning the entire table. Also, by creating a unique index for an employee number, DB2 enforces the uniqueness of each value. A unique index is the only way DB2 can enforce uniqueness.

Creating an index automatically creates the *index space*, the data set that contains the index.

► Keys

A key is one or more columns that are identified as such in the creation of a table or index, or in the definition of referential integrity.

– Primary key

A table can only have one primary key because it defines the entity. There are two requirements for a primary key:

i. It must have a value, that is, it cannot be null.

ii. It must be unique, that is, it must have a unique index defined on it.

– Unique key

We already know that a primary key must be unique, but it is possible to have more than one unique key in a table. In our EMP table example (see "Employee table" on page 646), the employee number is defined as the primary key and is therefore unique. If we also had a social security value in our table, hopefully that value would be unique. To guarantee this setup, you could create a unique index on the social security column.

– Foreign key

A foreign key is a key that is specified in a referential integrity constraint to make its existence dependent on a primary or unique key (parent key) in another table.

The example given is that of an employee's work department number relating to the primary key defined on the department number in the DEPT table. This constraint is part of the definition of the table.

12.7 What is DB2

The general concepts of a relational database management system (RDBMS) are discussed in Chapter 11, "Transaction management systems on z/OS" on page 401. Most table examples in this chapter can be found in Appendix B, "DB2 sample tables" on page 643. These tables, such as EMP and DEPT, are part of the Sample Database that comes with the DB2 product on all platforms. We are using Version 8 in the screen captures. Therefore, the owner of our tables is DSN8810.

The elements that DB2 manages can be divided into two categories: data structures that are used to organize user data, and system structures that are controlled by DB2. Data structures can be further broken down into *basic structures* and *schema structures*. Schema structures are fairly new objects that were introduced on the mainframe for compatibility within the DB2 family. A *schema* is a logical grouping of these new objects.

12.7.1 Data structures in DB2

Earlier in this chapter, we discussed most of the basic structures common to DBRMs. Now, let us look at several structures that are specific to DB2.

Views

View:
A way of looking at the data in a table to control who can see what.

A *view* is an alternative way of looking at the data in one or more tables. It is like an overlay that you would put over a transparency to only allow people to see certain aspects of the base transparency. For example, you can create a view on the department table to only let users have access to one particular department to update salary information. You do not want them to see the salaries in other departments. You create a view of the table that only lets the users see one department, and they use the view like a table. Thus, a view is used for security reasons. Most companies will not allow users to access their tables directly, but instead use a view to accomplish this task. The users get access through the view. A view can also be used to simplify a complex query for less experienced users.

Table space

A table is just a logical construct. It is kept in an actual physical data set called a *table space*. Table spaces are storage structures and can contain one or more tables. A table space is named using the database name followed by the table space name, such as PAYROLL.ACCNT_RECV. There are three types of table spaces: simple, segmented, and partitioned. For more detailed information, see *DB2 UDB for z/OS: SQL Reference,* SC18-7426.

DB2 uses VSAM data sets. Each segment is a VSAM data set.

Index space

An *index space* is another storage structure that contains a single index. In fact, when you create an index, DB2 automatically defines an index space for you.

Storage groups

A *storage group* consists of a set of volumes on disks (DASD) that hold the data sets in which tables and indexes are actually stored.

Figure 12-2 gives an overview of the data structures in DB2.

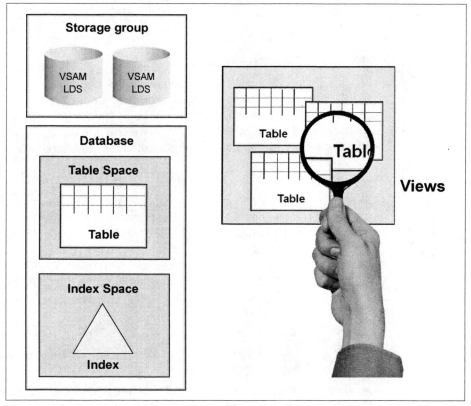

Figure 12-2   Hierarchy of the objects in a DB2 subsystem

12.7.2 Schema structures

In this section, we discuss the various DB2 schema structures

User-defined Data Type

A User-defined Data Type (UDT) is a way for users to define their own data types above and beyond the usual character and numeric data types. However, UDTs are based upon the already existing DB2 data types. If you deal in international currencies, you would most likely want to differentiate the various types of monies. With a UDT definition, you could define the EURO, based on the decimal data type, as a distinct data type in addition to YEN or US_DOLLAR. As a result, you could not add a YEN to a EURO because they are distinct data types.

User-defined Function

A User-defined Function (UDF) can be simply defined on an already existing DB2 function, such as rounding or averaging, or can be more complex and written as an application program that could be accessed by an SQL statement. In our international currency example, we could use a UDF to convert one currency value to another to perform arithmetic functions.

Trigger

A *trigger* defines a set of actions that are executed when an insert, update, or delete operation occurs on a specific table. For example, let us say that every time you insert an employee into your EMP table, you also want to add one to an employee count that you keep in a company statistics table. You can define a trigger that will be "fired" when you do an insert into EMP. This firing will automatically add one to the appropriate column in the COMPANY_STATS table.

Large Object

An Large Object (LOB) is a data type used by DB2 to manage unstructured data. There are three types of LOBs:

► Binary Large Objects (BLOBs): These are used for photographs and pictures, audio and sound clips, and video clips.

► Character Large Objects (CLOBs): These are used for large text documents.

► Double Byte Character Large Objects (DBCLOBs): These are used for storing large text documents written in languages that require double-byte characters, such as kanji.

LOBs are stored in special auxiliary tables that use a special LOB table space. In your EMP base table, text material such as a resume can be included for employees. Because this is a large amount of data, it is contained in its own table. A column in the EMP table, defined as a CLOB, would have a pointer to this special LOB auxiliary table that is stored in an LOB table space. Each column defined as an LOB would have its own associative auxiliary table and LOB table space.

Stored procedure

A *stored procedure* is a user-written application program that typically is stored and run on the server (but it can be run for local purposes as well). Stored procedures were specifically designed for the client/server environment where the client would only have to make one call to the server, which would then run the stored procedure to access DB2 data and return the results. This eliminates the need to make several network calls to run several individual queries against the database, which can be expensive.

You can think of a stored procedure as being somewhat like a subroutine that can be called to perform a set of related functions. It is an application program, but is defined to DB2 and managed by the DB2 subsystem.

System structures

In this section, we discuss the various DB2 system structures.

Catalog and directory

DB2 itself maintains a set of tables that contain metadata or data about all the DB2 objects in the subsystem. The *catalog* keeps information about all the objects, such as the tables, views, indexes, table spaces, and so on, while the *directory* keeps information about the application programs. The catalog can be queried to see the object information; the directory cannot.

When you create a user table, DB2 automatically records the table name, creator, its table space, and database in the catalog and puts this information in the catalog table called SYSIBM.SYSTABLES. All the columns defined in the table are automatically recorded in the SYSIBM.SYSCOLUMNS table.

In addition, to record that the owner of the table has authorization on the table, a row is automatically inserted into SYSIBM.SYSTABAUTH. Any indexes created on the table would be recorded in the SYSIBM.SYSINDEXES table.

Buffer pools

Buffer pools are areas of virtual storage in which DB2 temporarily stores pages of table spaces or indexes. They act as a cache area between DB2 and the physical disk storage device where the data resides. A data page is retrieved from disk and placed in a buffer pool page. If the needed data is already in a buffer, expensive I/O access to the disk can be avoided.

Active and archive logs

DB2 records all data changes and other significant events in a *log*. This information is used to recover data in the event of a failure, or DB2 can roll the changes back to a previous point in time. DB2 writes each log record to a data set called the *active log*.

When the active log is full, DB2 copies the contents to a disk or tape data set called the *archive log*. A bootstrap data set keeps track of these active and archive logs. DB2 uses this information in recovery scenarios, for system restarts, or for any activity that requires reading the log. A bootstrap data set allows for point-in-time recovery.

12.7.3 DB2 address spaces

DB2 is a multi-address space subsystem requiring a minimum of three address spaces:

▶ System services
▶ Database services
▶ Lock manager services (IRLM)

In addition, Distributed Data Facility (DDF) is used to communicate with other DB2 Subsystems. Figure 12-3 shows these address spaces.

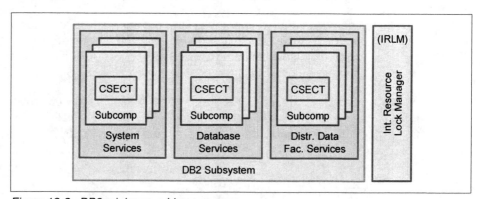

Figure 12-3   DB2 minimum address spaces

12.7.4 Using DB2 utilities

On z/OS, the DBA maintains database objects through a set of utilities and programs, which are submitted using JCL jobs. Usually, a company will have a data set library for these jobs that DBAs copy and use. However, there are tools that will generate the JCL, such as the Administration Tool and the Utility option on the DB2I panel.

The utilities help the DBAs do their jobs. You could divide the utilities into the following categories:

► Data Organization utilities

After tables are created, the DBA uses the LOAD utility to populate them, with the ability to compress large amounts of data. There is also the UNLOAD utility or the DSNTIAUL assembler program that can allows the DBA move or copy data from one subsystem to another.

It is possible to keep the data in a certain order by using the REORG utility. Subsequent insertions and loads can disturb this order, and the DBA must schedule subsequent REORGs based on reports from the RUNSTATS utility, which provides statistics and performance information. You can even run RUNSTATS against the system catalogs.

► Backup and Recovery utilities

It is vital that a DBA take image copies of the data and the indexes with the COPY utility to recover data. A DBA can make a full copy or an incremental copy (only for data). Because recovery can only be done to a full copy, the MERGECOPY utility is used to merge incremental copies with a full one. The RECOVER utility can recover back to an image copy for a point-in-time recovery. More often, it is used to recover to an image copy, and then information from the logs, which record all data changes, is applied to recover forward to a current time. If there is not an image copy, an index can be recreated with REBUILD INDEX.

► Data consistency utilities

One of the important data consistency utilities is the CHECK utility, which can be used to check and help correct referential integrity and constraint inconsistencies, especially after an additional population or after a recovery.

A typical use of utilities is to run RUNSTATS, then EXPLAIN, and then RUNSTATS again.

12.7.5 Using DB2 commands

Both the system administrator and the DBA use DB2 commands to monitor the subsystem. The DB2I panel and the Administration Tool provide you with the means to easily enter these commands. The -DISPLAY DATABASE command displays the status of all table spaces and index spaces within a database. For example, without an image copy, your table can be put in a *copy pending* status, requiring that you run the COPY utility. There are several other display commands, such as DISPLAY UTILITY for the status of a utility job, or you can display buffer pool, thread, and log information.

There are also DSN commands that you can issue from a TSO session or batch job. However, these can be more simply entered using the options from the DB2I panel: BIND, DCLGEN, RUN, and so on. (In some shops, DBAs are responsible for binds, although these are usually done by programmers as part of the compile job.)

12.8 What is SQL

Structured Query Language (SQL) is a high-level language that is used to specify what information a user needs without having to know how to retrieve it. The database is responsible for developing the access path needed to retrieve the data. SQL works at a set level, meaning that it is designed to retrieve one or more rows. Essentially, it is used on one or more tables and returns the result as a results table.

SQL has three categories based on the functionality involved:

▶ DML: Data manipulation language, which is used to read and modify data

▶ DDL: Data definition language, which is used to define, change, or drop DB2 objects

▶ DCL: Data control language, which used to grant and revoke authorizations

Several tools can be used to enter and execute SQL statements. Here we focus on SQL Processing Using File Input (SPUFI). SPUFI is part of the DB2 Interactive (DB2I) menu panel, which is a selection from your ISPF panel when DB2 is installed. (This, of course, depends on how you set up your system's menu panels.)

SPUFI is most commonly used by database administrators. It allows you to write and save one or more SQL statements at a time. DBAs use it to grant or revoke authorizations, and sometimes it is used to create objects when they need to be created immediately. SPUFI is also often used by developers to test their queries, which ensures that the query returns exactly what they want.

Another tool that you might encounter on the mainframe is the Query Management Facility™ (QMF), which allows you to enter and save just one SQL statement at a time. QMF's main strength is its reporting facility.[1] It enables you to design flexible and reusable report formats, including graphs. In addition, it provides a Prompted Query capability that helps users unfamiliar with SQL to build simple SQL statements. Another tool is the Administration Tool, which has SPUFI capabilities and a query building facility.

Figure 12-4 shows how SQL is entered using SPUFI. It is the first selection on the DB2I panel. Note that the name of this DB2 subsystem is DB8H.

```
                           DB2I PRIMARY OPTION MENU              SSID: DB8H
COMMAND ===> 1_

Select one of the following DB2 functions and press ENTER.

   1    SPUFI                    (Process SQL statements)
   2    DCLGEN                   (Generate SQL and source language declarations)
   3    PROGRAM PREPARATION      (Prepare a DB2 application program to run)
   4    PRECOMPILE               (Invoke DB2 precompiler)
   5    BIND/REBIND/FREE         (BIND, REBIND, or FREE plans or packages)
   6    RUN                      (RUN an SQL program)
   7    DB2 COMMANDS             (Issue DB2 commands)
   8    UTILITIES                (Invoke DB2 utilities)
   D    DB2I DEFAULTS            (Set global parameters)
   X    EXIT                     (Leave DB2I)






   F1=HELP        F2=SPLIT      F3=END        F4=RETURN      F5=RFIND      F6=RCHANGE
   F7=UP          F8=DOWN       F9=SWAP       F10=LEFT       F11=RIGHT     F12=RETRIEVE
```

Figure 12-4   Entering SQL using SPUFI

SPUFI uses file input and output, so it is necessary to have two data sets pre-allocated:

► The first, which can be named ZPROF.SPUFI.CNTL, is typically a partitioned data set to keep or save your queries as members. A sequential data set would write over your SQL.

► The output file, which can be named ZPROF.SPUFI.OUTPUT, must be sequential, which means your output is written over for the next query. If you want to save it, you must rename the file, using the ISPF menu edit facilities.

---

[1] QMF includes a governor function to cap the amount of CPU that might be consumed by a poorly constructed or runaway query.

In Figure 12-5 you can see how the SPUFI data sets are assigned.

```
                         SPUFI                        SSID: DB8H
   ===>


   Enter the input data set name:      (Can be sequential or partitioned)
    1  DATA SET NAME ... ===> 'ZPROF.SPUFI.CNTL(dept)'
    2  VOLUME SERIAL ... ===>           (Enter if not cataloged)
    3  DATA SET PASSWORD ===>           (Enter if password protected)


   Enter the output data set name:     (Must be a sequential data set)
    4  DATA SET NAME ... ===> 'ZPROF.SPUFI.OUTPUT'


   Specify processing options:
    5  CHANGE DEFAULTS.. ===> NO        (Y/N - Display SPUFI defaults panel?)
    6  EDIT INPUT ...... ===> YES       (Y/N - Enter SQL statements?)
    7  EXECUTE ......... ===> YES       (Y/N - Execute SQL statements?)
    8  AUTOCOMMIT ...... ===> YES       (Y/N - Commit after successful run?)
    9  BROWSE OUTPUT.... ===> YES       (Y/N - Browse output data set?)


   For remote SQL processing:
   10  CONNECT LOCATION  ===>



    F1=HELP       F2=SPLIT      F3=END     F4=RETURN    F5=RFIND     F6=RCHANGE
    F7=UP         F8=DOWN       F9=SWAP    F10=LEFT     F11=RIGHT    F12=RETRIEVE
```

Figure 12-5   Assigning SPUFI data sets

Notice option 5, which you can change to YES temporarily to see the default
values. One value you might want to change is the maximum number of rows
retrieved.

With option 5 set to NO, if you press the Enter key, SPUFI will open the input file,
ZPROF.SPUFI.CNTL(DEPT), so that you may enter or edit an SQL statement.
When you enter recov on in the command and press Enter, the warning at the
top of the panel will disappear. This option is part of the profile mentioned earlier
in this book.

The panel is shown in Figure 12-6.

```
   File   Edit   Edit_Settings   Menu   Utilities   Compilers   Test   Help
 ─────────────────────────────────────────────────────────────────────────────
 EDIT        ZPROF.SPUFI.CNTL(DEPT) - 01.00            Columns 00001 00072
 Command ===>                                           Scroll ===> PAGE
 ****** *************************** Top of Data *******************************
 ......  Select deptno
 ......     from dsn8810.dept_
 ......
 ......
 ......
 ......
 ......
 ......
 ......
 ......
 ......
 ......
 ......
 ......
 ......
 ......
 ......
 ......

 F1=Help      F2=Split     F3=Exit      F5=Rfind     F6=Rchange    F7=Up
 F8=Down      F9=Swap      F10=Left     F11=Right    F12=Cancel
```

Figure 12-6   Editing the input file

If your profile is set to CAPS ON, the SQL statement you have just entered will normally change to capital letters at the Enter prompt, but you do not need to use this setting in our example.

Notice that DSN8810.DEPT is the table name. This is the qualified name of the table, because we want to use the sample tables, which are created by the DSN8810 user.

If you enter just one SQL statement, you do not need to use the SQL terminator, which is a semi-colon (;), because it is specified in the defaults (but you can change it if necessary using option 5 of the previous panel). However, if you enter more than one SQL statement, you need to use a semicolon at the end of each statement to indicate that you have more than one.

At this point, you need to go back to the first panel of SPUFI by pressing the F3 key. The panel shown in Figure 12-7 opens.

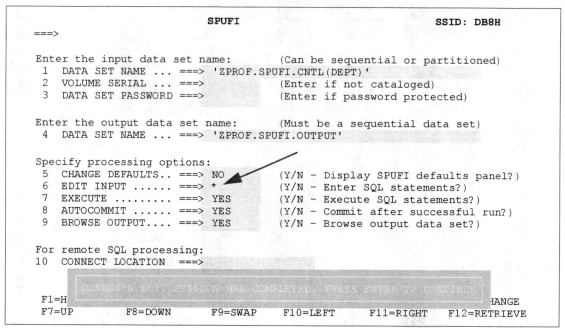

```
                            SPUFI                              SSID: DB8H
  ===>

  Enter the input data set name:        (Can be sequential or partitioned)
   1   DATA SET NAME ... ===> 'ZPROF.SPUFI.CNTL(DEPT)'
   2   VOLUME SERIAL ... ===>            (Enter if not cataloged)
   3   DATA SET PASSWORD ===>            (Enter if password protected)

  Enter the output data set name:       (Must be a sequential data set)
   4   DATA SET NAME ... ===> 'ZPROF.SPUFI.OUTPUT'

  Specify processing options:
   5   CHANGE DEFAULTS.. ===> NO         (Y/N - Display SPUFI defaults panel?)
   6   EDIT INPUT ...... ===> *          (Y/N - Enter SQL statements?)
   7   EXECUTE ......... ===> YES        (Y/N - Execute SQL statements?)
   8   AUTOCOMMIT ...... ===> YES        (Y/N - Commit after successful run?)
   9   BROWSE OUTPUT.... ===> YES        (Y/N - Browse output data set?)

  For remote SQL processing:
  10   CONNECT LOCATION  ===>

           DSNE808A EDIT SESSION HAS COMPLETED. PRESS ENTER TO CONTINUE

   F1=H                                                              HANGE
   F7=UP        F8=DOWN        F9=SWAP     F10=LEFT     F11=RIGHT   F12=RETRIEVE
```

Figure 12-7   Returning to the first SPUFI panel

Notice that there is an asterisk (*) for option 6 because you just finished editing your SQL. At this point, if you press Enter, you will execute your SQL statement and the output file will automatically open, because BROWSE OUTPUT is set to YES. The first part of the output is shown in Figure 12-8.

```
   Menu   Utilities   Compilers   Help

 BROWSE      ZPROF.SPUFI.OUTPUT                       Line 00000000 Col 001 080
 Command ===>                                                  Scroll ===> PAGE
 ******************************** Top of Data *********************************
 ----------+----------+----------+----------+----------+----------+----------+
 select deptno                                                        00010000
   from dsn8810.dept                                                  00020000
 ----------+----------+----------+----------+----------+----------+----------+
 DEPTNO
 ----------+----------+----------+----------+----------+----------+----------+
 A00
 B01
 C01
 D01
 D11
 D21
 E01
 E11
 E21
 F22
 G22

    F1=Help      F2=Split   F3=Exit    F5=Rfind    F7=Up     F8=Down    F9=Swap
    F10=Left    F11=Right  F12=Cancel
```

Figure 12-8   First part of the SPUFI query results

To get to the second (and in this case, final) panel, press F8, and you will see Figure 12-9.

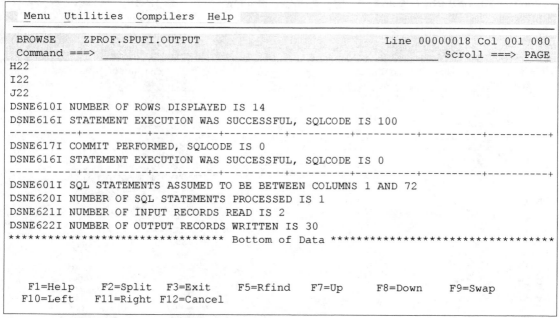

```
   Menu   Utilities   Compilers   Help
 ─────────────────────────────────────────────────────────────────────────────
   BROWSE      ZPROF.SPUFI.OUTPUT                    Line 00000018 Col 001 080
   Command ===>                                              Scroll ===> PAGE
 H22
 I22
 J22
 DSNE610I NUMBER OF ROWS DISPLAYED IS 14
 DSNE616I STATEMENT EXECUTION WAS SUCCESSFUL, SQLCODE IS 100
 ----------+---------+---------+---------+---------+---------+---------+---------+
 DSNE617I COMMIT PERFORMED, SQLCODE IS 0
 DSNE616I STATEMENT EXECUTION WAS SUCCESSFUL, SQLCODE IS 0
 ----------+---------+---------+---------+---------+---------+---------+---------+
 DSNE601I SQL STATEMENTS ASSUMED TO BE BETWEEN COLUMNS 1 AND 72
 DSNE620I NUMBER OF SQL STATEMENTS PROCESSED IS 1
 DSNE621I NUMBER OF INPUT RECORDS READ IS 2
 DSNE622I NUMBER OF OUTPUT RECORDS WRITTEN IS 30
 ******************************* Bottom of Data ********************************


    F1=Help     F2=Split   F3=Exit    F5=Rfind    F7=Up     F8=Down    F9=Swap
    F10=Left    F11=Right  F12=Cancel
```

Figure 12-9   Second part of the SPUFI query results

Notice that you have a result table with just one column. This is what was specified in SELECT, but only in DEPTNO. We have retrieved the DEPTNO from all the (14) rows in the table. There are a few messages. One gives the number of rows retrieved. Another indicates that SQLCODE (an SQL return code indicating success or not) is 100, which means end of file, so there are no more results to show.

For more information about SQL, see *DB2 UDB for z/OS: SQL Reference*, SC18-7426. You can find this and other related publications at the z/OS Internet Library website:

```
http://www-03.ibm.com/systems/z/os/zos/bkserv/
```

12.9 Application programming for DB2

SQL is not a full programming language, but it is necessary for accessing and manipulating data in a DB2 database. It is a 4GL nonprocedural language that was developed in the mid-1970s to use with DB2. SQL can either be used dynamically with an interpretive program such as SPUFI, or it can be embedded and compiled or assembled in a host language.

So how do you write an application program that accesses DB2 data? To perform this task, SQL is embedded in the source code of a programming language, such as Java, Smalltalk, REXX, C, C++, COBOL, Fortran, PL/I, or high-level Assembler. There are two categories of SQL statements that can be used in a program: static and dynamic.

► Static

SQL refers to complete SQL statements that are written in the source code. In the program preparation process, DB2 develops access paths for the statements, and these are recorded in DB2. The SQL never changes from one run to another, and the same determined access paths are used without DB2 having to create them again, a process that can impact processing. (All SQL statements must have an access path.)

► Dynamic

SQL refers to SQL statements that are only partially or totally unknown when the program is written. Only when the program runs does DB2 know what the statements are and is able to determine the appropriate access paths. These statements are not recorded because the statements can change from one run to another. An example of this is SPUFI. SPUFI is actually an application program that accepts dynamic SQL statements. These statements are the SQL statements that you enter in the input file. Each time you use SPUFI, the SQL can change, so special SQL preparation statements are embedded in the application to handle this change.

We now concentrate on static SQL to understand the processes involved when using DB2. We also want to add that it may seem complex, but each action has a good reason for being there.

12.9.1 DB2 program preparation: The flow

The traditional program preparation process, compile and linkedit, must have some additional steps to prepare SQL, because compilers do not recognize SQL. These steps, including compile and linkedit, can be done through the DB2I panel, although the whole process is usually done in one JCL job stream except for DCLGEN. Figure 12-10 gives an overview of this process.

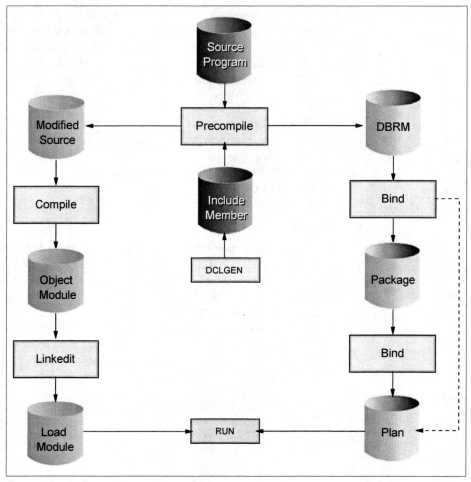

Figure 12-10   Program preparation flow

DCLGEN

DCLGEN allows you to automatically generate your source definitions for the DB2 objects that will be used in your program. This is set up in a member of a DCLGEN library that can optionally be included in your source program. If you do not include it, you must manually code the definitions. The DB2 database administrator usually creates them, based on the company's rules. During this phase, you need a running DB2 system, because the definitions are taken from the DB2 catalog.

PRECOMPILE

Because compilers cannot handle SQL, the precompile step comments out the SQL statements and leaves behind a CALL statement to DB2. This action passes some parameters such as host variable addresses (to place data into), statement numbers, and a modified time stamp called a *consistency token* (but often referred to as the time stamp). During this phase, you do not need a running DB2 system; everything is done without accessing DB2.

The precompiler identifies the SQL by using special beginning and ending flags that must be included for each SQL statement. The beginning flag, EXEC SQL, is the same for all programming languages. The ending flag differs: COBOL uses END-EXEC. (period), while C and other languages use a semi-colon. Here is a COBOL example:

```
EXEC SQL
    SELECT EMPNO, LASTNAME
      INTO :EMPNO, :LASTNAME
      FROM EMP
END-EXEC.
```

In this example, EMPNO and LASTNAME are retrieved into host variables, which are preceded by a colon. Host variables (HVs) are variables defined in the "host" language (COBOL, PL/I, and so on), the language that embeds the SQL. During the DCLGEN phase, a set of these variables are also defined. The HV name here is the same as the column name, which is not a requirement; it can be any name that has a data type compatible with the columns data type.

After the precompile, our program is divided into two parts:

▶ The modified source code, which is the original source code, were the SQL is commented out and replaced by CALLs.

▶ The database request module (DBRM), which is usually a member of a PDS library and contains the SQL statements of the program.

The modified source code is passed on to the compiler to be compiled and link-edited to create an executable load module, just like any program that does not contain SQL.

You can embed any type of SQL into your program, such as DML, DDL, and DCL, as long as the authorization rules are respected.

BIND

BIND can be thought of as the DB2 equivalent compile process for the DBRM. BIND does three things:

► Checks your syntax for errors.

► Checks authorization.

► Most importantly, it determines the access paths for your statements. DB2 has a component called the *optimizer*, which assesses all the different ways that your data can be accessed, such as scanning an entire table, using an index, which index, and so on. It weighs the costs of each and picks the least. It is referred to as a cost-based optimizer (as opposed to a rule-based optimizer).

The SQL with its access path (and the consistency token/time stamp) is stored as a package in a DB2 directory. Other information, such as package information and the actual SQL, is stored in the catalog. The bind creates the executable SQL code for one application in a package. Now DB2 has all the information it needs to get to the requested data for this program.

Programs often call subroutines, which also contain SQL calls. Each of these subroutines then also has a package. You need to group all DB2 information together. Therefore, we need another step: another bind, but this time to create a *plan*.

Even if you are not using a subroutine, you still need to create a plan. The plan might contain more information than just your program information. This is a common practice: The plan contains all packages of one project and every run uses the same plan.

To be complete, we need to add the DBRMs there were originally bound straight into the plan (they are called instream DBRMs). However, if there is one small change to one of the programs, you need to rebind the whole plan. The same needs to be done when an index is added.

During this binding process, DB2 updates its directory and catalog. Updating means preventing other people from updating (the data is locked for them), so it is nearly impossible to perform other actions against DB2. To avoid this constraint, packages were introduced. Now you only need to rebind the one package, so the duration of the update is short, and the impact on other users is almost zero. There are still plans around with instream DBRMs, although most companies choose to convert them into packages.

Plans are unique to the mainframe environment. Other platforms do not use them.

RUN

When you execute your application program, the load module is loaded into main storage. When an SQL statement is encountered, the CALL to DB2, which replaced the SQL statement, passes its parameters to DB2. One of those parameters is the consistency token. This token, or time stamp, is also in the package. The packages in the specified plan of DB2 are then searched for the corresponding time stamp, and the appropriate package is loaded and executed. So, for the run, you need to specify the plan name as a parameter.

One last note: The result of an SQL statement is usually a result set (more than one row). An application program can only deal with one record, or row, at a time. There is a special construction added to DB2, called a *cursor* (essentially a pointer), which allows you, in your embedded SQL, to fetch, update, or delete one row at a time, from your result set.

To learn more, see *DB2 UDB for z/OS: Application Programming and SQL Guide,* SC18-7415.

12.10 Functions of the IMS Database Manager

A database management system (DBMS) provides facilities for business application transactions or processes to access stored information. The role of a DBMS is to provide the following functions:

▶ Allow access to the data for multiple users from a single copy of the data.

▶ Control concurrent access to the data so as to maintain integrity for all updates.

▶ Minimize hardware device and operating system access method dependencies.

▶ Reduce data redundancy by maintaining only one copy of the data.

12.11 Structure of the IMS Database Manager subsystem

The IMS Database Manager provides a central point for the control and access to application data. IMS provides a full set of utility programs to provide all these functions within the IMS product. This section describes the various types of z/OS address spaces and their relationships with each other. The core of an IMS subsystem is the *control region*, running in one z/OS address space. This has a number of dependent address spaces running in other regions that provide additional services to the control region, or in which the IMS application programs run.

In addition to the control region, some applications and utilities used with IMS run in separate batch address spaces. These are separate from an IMS subsystem and its control region, and have no connection with it.

For historical reasons, some documents describing IMS use the term region to describe a z/OS address space, for example, IMS Control Region. In this course, we use the term *region* wherever this is in common usage. You can take the term region as being the same as a z/OS address space.

Figure 12-11 illustrates the IMS DB/DC subsystem. If you want more details, we refer you to *An Introduction to IMS* by Meltz, et al.

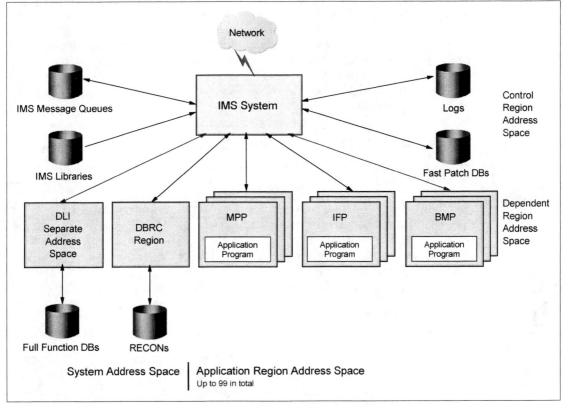

Figure 12-11 Structure of the IMS DB/DC subsystem

12.11.1 The IMS hierarchical database model

IMS uses a hierarchical model as the basic method for storing data, which is a pragmatic way of storing the data and implementing the relationships between the various types of entities.

In this model, the individual entity types are implemented as segments in a hierarchical structure. The hierarchical structure is determined by the designer of the database, based on the relationships between the entities and the access paths required by the applications.

Note that in the IMS program product itself, the term database is used slightly differently from its use in other DBMSs. In IMS, a database is commonly used to describe the implementation of one hierarchy, so that an application would normally access a large number of IMS databases. Compared to the relational model, an IMS database is approximately equivalent to a table.

DL/I allows a wide variety of data structures. The maximum number of segment types is 255 per hierarchical data structure. A maximum of 15 segment levels can be defined in a hierarchical data structure. There is no restriction on the number of occurrences of each segment type, except as imposed by physical access method limits.

Sequence to access the segments

The sequence of traversing the hierarchy is top to bottom, left to right, front to back (for twins).

Segment code numbers do not take twins into account and sequential processing of a database record is in a hierarchical sequence. All segments of a database record are included, so the twins have a place in hierarchical sequences. Segments may contain sequence fields that determine the order in which they are stored and processed.

The hierarchical data structure in Figure 12-12 describes the data of one database record as seen by the application program. It does not represent the physical storage of the data. The physical storage is of no concern to the application program.

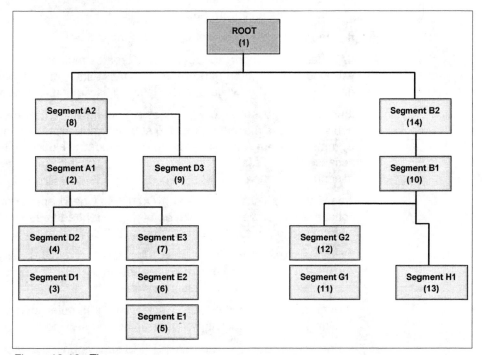

Figure 12-12   The sequence

The basic building element of a hierarchical data structure is the parent/child relationship between segments of data, also illustrated in Figure 12-12.

12.11.2 IMS use of z/OS services

IMS is designed to make the best use of the features of the z/OS operating system. This usage includes:

► It runs in multiple address spaces.

  IMS subsystems (except for IMS/DB batch applications and utilities) normally consist of a control region address space, dependent address spaces providing system services, and dependent address spaces for application programs.

Running in multiple address spaces has the following advantages:

- It maximizes CPU usage when running on a multiple-processor CPC.
- Address spaces can be dispatched in parallel on different CPUs.
- It isolates the application programs from the IMS systems code, and reduces outages from application failures.

▶ It runs multiple tasks in each address space.

IMS, particularly in the control regions, creates multiple z/OS subtasks for the various functions to be performed. This task allows other IMS subtasks to be dispatched by z/OS while one IMS subtask is waiting for system services.

▶ It uses z/OS cross-memory services to communicate between the various address spaces making up an IMS subsystem. It also uses the z/OS Common System Area (CSA) to store IMS control blocks that are frequently accessed by the address spaces making up the IMS subsystem. This action minimizes the impact of running in multiple address spaces.

▶ It uses the z/OS subsystem feature to detect when dependent address spaces fail, to prevent cancellation of dependent address spaces, and to interact with other subsystems such as DB2 and WebSphere MQ.

▶ It can make use of a z/OS sysplex (discussed later in this text). Multiple IMS subsystems can run on the z/OS systems making up the sysplex and access the same IMS databases. This provides:

- Increased availability: z/OS systems and IMS subsystems can be switched in and out without interrupting the service.
- Increased capacity: The multiple IMS subsystems can process far greater volumes.

12.11.3 Evolution of IMS

Initially, all IMS/DB online applications used IMS/TM as the interface to the database. However, with the growing popularity of DB2, many customers began to develop online applications using DB2 as a database, next to their existing good applications. That is why you see a lot of mixed environments in the real world.

12.11.4 Our online example

Looking back to our travel agent example in Chapter 11, "Transaction management systems on z/OS" on page 401, examples of IMS transactions could be in the part of the airline company:

▶ Some of the batches may be updated daily, such as the payments executed by travel agents and other customers.

▶ Other batches may be reminders that are sent to the travel agents and other customers to make some payments.

▶ Checking whether reservations are made (and paid) can be an online application.

▶ Checking whether there are available seats.

12.12 Summary

Data can be stored in a flat file, but this usually results in a great amount of duplication, which may result in inconsistent data. Therefore, it is better to create central databases, which can be accessed (for reading and changing) from various places. The handling of consistency, security, and so on, is done by the database management system; the users and developers do not need to worry about it.

The relational database is the predominant approach to data organization in today's business world. IBM DB2 implements such relational principles as primary keys, referential integrity, a language to access the database (SQL), nulls, and normalized design. In a relational database, the most fundamental structure is the table with columns and rows.

There is a hierarchical dependency to the basic objects in DB2. The table structure can have indexes and views created on it. If a table is removed, these objects also get removed. Tables are contained in a physical data set called the table space, which is associated with a database that is a logical grouping of table spaces. Newer schema objects in DB2 include UDTs, UDFs, LOBs, triggers, and stored procedures.

DB2 also has system structures that help manage the subsystem. The catalog and directory keep metadata about all the objects in the RDBMS. Buffer pools are used to hold pages of data from disk storage for faster retrieval; the active or archive logs and the BSDS are a way for DB2 to record all the changes made to the data for recovery purposes.

The only way to access the data in DB2 databases is with SQL. It is not a full programming language, and it works at the set level, using a result table when it manipulates data. SQL has three categories based on functionality: DML, DDL, and DCL. On the mainframe, SPUFI is a tool used to enter SQL statements.

Some special steps are needed to use SQL in application programs because traditional 3GL compilers do not recognize SQL. The precompiler comments out SQL statements in a program, copies them to a DBRM with a consistency token, and replaces them with calls to DB2. The modified source code is then compiled and link-edited. The DBRM performs a BIND process that determines the access path and stores this executable SQL code in a package. Packages are then logically associated with a plan. When run, the call to DB2 in the load module passes its consistency token to DB2 to be matched to its twin in the appropriate plan to execute the SQL.

SQL can handle both static and dynamic statements, and EXPLAIN can be used to discover what access path the optimizer chose for the SQL.

The EXPLAIN statement defines an access path for a query to improve its performance. EXPLAIN statements are especially useful for multi-table and multi-access database queries.

Table 12-2 lists the key terms used in this chapter.

Table 12-2   Key terms used in this chapter

database administrator (DBA)	Data Language/Interface (DL/I)	DBMS
EXPLAIN	full-function database	modified source
multitasking	multithreading	SPUFI
SQL	SYSADM	view

12.13 Questions for review

To help test your understanding of the material in this chapter, answer the following questions:

1. What DB2 objects define a physical storage area? Does a table?

2. What are some of the problems with the following SQL statement:

```
SELECT *
FROM PAYROLL;
```

3. What category of SQL would you use to define objects to DB2?

4. How does the precompiler find an SQL statement in a program?

5. How is a load module put back together using the SQL statements?

6. How could you discover what access path the optimizer chooses? What process creates this path?

7. What is a stored procedure?

8. What are some of the responsibilities of a system administrator?

9. What are some of the responsibilities of a database administrator (DBA)?

10. What are some of the ways that security is handled by DB2?

11. What is the database structure of IMS-DB? Describe it.

12.14 Exercise 1: Use SPUFI in a COBOL program

You need a connection to DB2 to perform this exercise.

12.14.1 Step 1: Creating files

Before you start the DB2 exercise, you need to create two more PDSs:

► ZUSER##.DB2.INCLUDE, where you store your DCLGENs
► ZUSER##.DB2.DBRM, where you store your DBRMs

You can use ZUSER##.LANG.CNTL as base.

Furthermore, you also need a ZUSER##.SPUFI.OUTPUT file, which should be a flat file of record format VB, with a record length of 4092 and block length of 4096.

12.14.2 Step 2: DCLGEN

DCLGEN is an easy way to generate COBOL definition statements for the DB2 information that you use in an application program. These statements can then be included in the source program.

Perform the following steps:

1. From the DB2I (DB2 Interactive) menu, choose D for DB2I Defaults (Figure 12-13) and press Enter.

```
                          DB2I PRIMARY OPTION MENU                SSID: DB8H
COMMAND ===> D_

Select one of the following DB2 functions and press ENTER.

   1   SPUFI                   (Process SQL statements)
   2   DCLGEN                  (Generate SQL and source language declarations)
   3   PROGRAM PREPARATION     (Prepare a DB2 application program to run)
   4   PRECOMPILE              (Invoke DB2 precompiler)
   5   BIND/REBIND/FREE        (BIND, REBIND, or FREE plans or packages)
   6   RUN                     (RUN an SQL program)
   7   DB2 COMMANDS            (Issue DB2 commands)
   8   UTILITIES               (Invoke DB2 utilities)
   D   DB2I DEFAULTS           (Set global parameters)
   X   EXIT                    (Leave DB2I)




   F1=HELP       F2=SPLIT      F3=END       F4=RETURN     F5=RFIND      F6=RCHANGE
   F7=UP         F8=DOWN       F9=SWAP      F10=LEFT      F11=RIGHT     F12=RETRIEVE
```

Figure 12-13   DB2I menu

2. On the DB2I Defaults Panel 1, specify IBMCOB for option 3 Application
   Language (Figure 12-14).

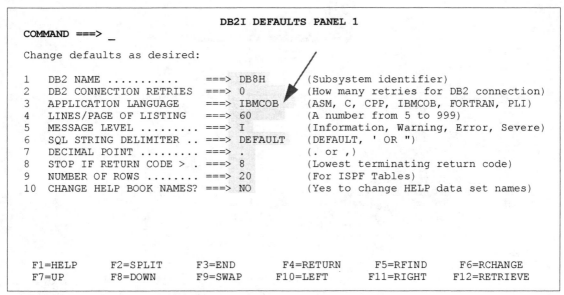

```
                        DB2I DEFAULTS PANEL 1
COMMAND ===> _

Change defaults as desired:

1    DB2 NAME ..........      ===> DB8H        (Subsystem identifier)
2    DB2 CONNECTION RETRIES  ===> 0           (How many retries for DB2 connection)
3    APPLICATION LANGUAGE    ===> IBMCOB      (ASM, C, CPP, IBMCOB, FORTRAN, PLI)
4    LINES/PAGE OF LISTING   ===> 60          (A number from 5 to 999)
5    MESSAGE LEVEL ........  ===> I           (Information, Warning, Error, Severe)
6    SQL STRING DELIMITER .. ===> DEFAULT     (DEFAULT, ' OR ")
7    DECIMAL POINT ......... ===> .           (. or ,)
8    STOP IF RETURN CODE > . ===> 8           (Lowest terminating return code)
9    NUMBER OF ROWS ........ ===> 20          (For ISPF Tables)
10   CHANGE HELP BOOK NAMES? ===> NO          (Yes to change HELP data set names)




   F1=HELP      F2=SPLIT     F3=END      F4=RETURN     F5=RFIND     F6=RCHANGE
   F7=UP        F8=DOWN      F9=SWAP     F10=LEFT      F11=RIGHT    F12=RETRIEVE
```

Figure 12-14   DB2I DEFAULTS PANEL 1

3. Press Enter, and on DB2I Defaults Panel 2, specify DEFAULT for the COBOL string delimiter under option 2 and G for the DBCS symbol for DCLGEN for option 3. Press Enter (Figure 12-15).

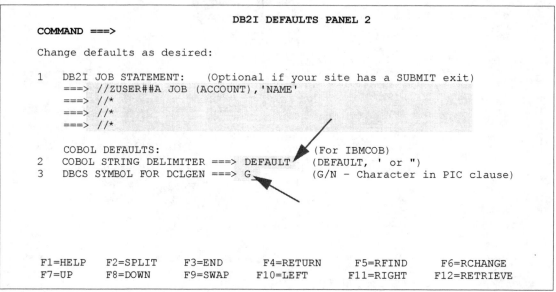

```
                              DB2I DEFAULTS PANEL 2
COMMAND ===>

Change defaults as desired:

1   DB2I JOB STATEMENT:    (Optional if your site has a SUBMIT exit)
    ===> //ZUSER##A JOB (ACCOUNT),'NAME'
    ===> //*
    ===> //*
    ===> //*

    COBOL DEFAULTS:                              (For IBMCOB)
2   COBOL STRING DELIMITER ===> DEFAULT         (DEFAULT, ' or ")
3   DBCS SYMBOL FOR DCLGEN ===> G               (G/N - Character in PIC clause)




  F1=HELP    F2=SPLIT    F3=END     F4=RETURN    F5=RFIND     F6=RCHANGE
  F7=UP      F8=DOWN     F9=SWAP    F10=LEFT     F11=RIGHT    F12=RETRIEVE
```

Figure 12-15 DB2I DEFAULT PANEL 2

This action confirms that you have the correct language.

4. After pressing Enter, you are on the main DB2I panel (Figure 12-13 on page 470); select option 2, DCLGEN.

You need to have a destination data set already allocated to hold your DCLGEN definition (ZUSER##.DB2.INCLUDE); it should be created for you. If you do not have one, go to the ISPF menu and create a PDS file.

5. As shown in Figure 12-16, you need to specify the table, the table owner, your PDS file, and the action ADD. The resulting message should be:

```
EXECUTION COMPLETE, MEMBER DCLEMP ADDED
***
```

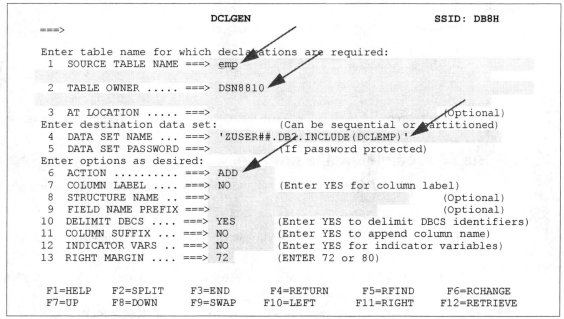

```
                            DCLGEN                        SSID: DB8H
   ===>

   Enter table name for which declarations are required:
    1    SOURCE TABLE NAME ===> emp

    2    TABLE OWNER ..... ===> DSN8810

    3    AT LOCATION ..... ===>                          (Optional)
   Enter destination data set:         (Can be sequential or partitioned)
    4    DATA SET NAME ... ===> 'ZUSER##.DB2.INCLUDE(DCLEMP)'
    5    DATA SET PASSWORD ===>         (If password protected)
   Enter options as desired:
    6    ACTION .......... ===> ADD
    7    COLUMN LABEL .... ===> NO      (Enter YES for column label)
    8    STRUCTURE NAME .. ===>                          (Optional)
    9    FIELD NAME PREFIX ===>                          (Optional)
   10    DELIMIT DBCS .... ===> YES     (Enter YES to delimit DBCS identifiers)
   11    COLUMN SUFFIX ... ===> NO      (Enter YES to append column name)
   12    INDICATOR VARS .. ===> NO      (Enter YES for indicator variables)
   13    RIGHT MARGIN .... ===> 72      (ENTER 72 or 80)


   F1=HELP    F2=SPLIT    F3=END     F4=RETURN    F5=RFIND    F6=RCHANGE
   F7=UP      F8=DOWN     F9=SWAP    F10=LEFT     F11=RIGHT   F12=RETRIEVE
```

Figure 12-16   DCLGEN

If the definition of the table changes, you must also change DCLGEN and use REPLACE.

12.14.3 Step 3: Testing your SQL

Go to SPUFI and test SPUFI.CNTL PDS. In that PDS, find the SELECT member. This is the SQL statement you use in your program. The where-clause is not there, so that you can see all the results you can obtain. It also gives you the opportunity to know what departments are available in the table.

For more complex queries, this is common practice. As an application developer, you must execute the right SQL.

12.14.4 Step 4: Creating the program

Here, you can create a program or use the program that is supplied for you in LANG.SOURCE(COBDB2). This sample program calculates the average salary for one department. You specify the department and obtain the result. To end the program, enter 999.

To modify this program, add the following information:

▸ Your variables (include the member you have created in 12.14.1, "Step 1: Creating files" on page 469).

▸ Specify the SQL delimiters for COBOL.

If you search for "???", you will find the locations where you add the information.

12.14.5 Step 5: Completing the program

Edit the LANG.CNTL(COBDB2) job and make the changes at the top of the job.

Perform the following steps:

1. Step PC: This is the DB2 precompile.lit splits your source into two parts: the DBRM and the modified source.

2. Steps COB, PLKED and LKED: These steps perform the compile and linking of your modified source.

3. Step BIND: This step perform the binding of the package and the plan.

   If you needed to change your program, which bind could be left out? Feel free to change the program. Instead of the average, you can ask the minimum or maximum salary within a department (then you just need to change the SQL).

4. Step Run: This step runs the program in batch for two departments: A00 and D21.

12.14.6 Step 6: Running the program from TSO

Instead of running your program in batch, try running it from the TSO READY prompt. To do so, you must allocate both files to your session (this must be done before you run the job).

Enter the following lines and press Enter after each line:

```
TSO alloc da(*) f(sysprint) reuse
tso alloc da(*) f(sysin) reuse
```

Return to your DB2I panel. Select option 6 RUN. Here, you enter the file name and the plan name (Figure 12-17).

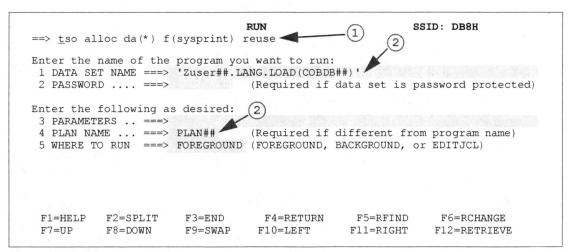

Figure 12-17   Ready to execute

Figure 12-18 shows the execution of the program.

```
 ENTER WORKDEPT OR 999 TO STOP...
A01
  *** THIS WORKDEPT DOES NOT EXIST ***

 ENTER WORKDEPT OR 999 TO STOP...
A00
  WORKDEPT AVERAGE SALARY
  A00        40850.00

 ENTER WORKDEPT OR 999 TO STOP...
D21
  WORKDEPT AVERAGE SALARY
  D21        25668.57

 ENTER WORKDEPT OR 999 TO STOP...
D11
  WORKDEPT AVERAGE SALARY
  D11        25147.27

 ENTER WORKDEPT OR 999 TO STOP...
999
  *** _
```

Figure 12-18   The execution of the program

z/OS HTTP Server

Objective: As a mainframe professional, you need to know how to deploy a web application on z/OS and how to enable z/OS for serving web-based workloads.

After completing this chapter, you will be able to:

► List the three server modes.

► Explain static and dynamic web pages.

► List at least two functions from each of the groups: basic, security, and caching.

Refer to Table 13-1 on page 490 for a list of key terms used in this chapter.

13.1 Introduction to web-based workloads on z/OS

As enterprises move many of their applications to the World Wide Web, mainframe organizations face the complexity of enabling and managing new web-based workloads in addition to more traditional workloads, such as batch processing.

The next chapters show how middleware products are used to supply the key functions needed to enable z/OS for processing web-based workloads:

► Chapter 13, "z/OS HTTP Server" on page 477
► Chapter 14, "IBM WebSphere Application Server on z/OS" on page 493
► Chapter 15, "Messaging and queuing" on page 513

These chapters use IBM products in the examples, but many such middleware products exist in the marketplace today.

13.2 What is z/OS HTTP Server

z/OS HTTP Server serves static and dynamic web pages. HTTP Server has the same capabilities as any other web server, but it also has some features that are z/OS-specific. You can run HTTP Server in any of three modes, with each offering advantages for handling web-based workloads:

Stand-alone server This mode is typically used for HTTP Server-only implementations (simple websites). Its main role is to provide a limited exposure to the Internet.

Scalable server This mode is typically used for interactive websites, where the traffic volume increases or declines dynamically. It is intended for a more sophisticated environment, in which servlets and JSPs are invoked.

Multiple servers This mode uses a combination of stand-alone and scalable servers to improve scalability and security throughout the system. For example, a stand-alone server could be used as a gateway to scalable servers, and the gateway could verify the user authentication of all requests, and reroute requests to the other servers.

13.2.1 Serving static web pages on z/OS

With a web server on z/OS, such as HTTP Server, the serving of static web pages is similar to web servers on other platforms. The user sends an HTTP request to HTTP Server to obtain a specific file. HTTP Server retrieves the file from its file repository and sends it to the user, along with information about the file (such as mime type and size) in the HTTP header.

HTTP Server has a major difference from other web servers, however. Because z/OS systems encode files in EBCDIC, the documents on z/OS must first be converted to the ASCII format typically used on the Internet (binary documents such as pictures need not be converted). HTTP Server performs these conversions, thus saving the programmer from performing this step. However, the programmer must use FTP to load documents on the server, that is, the programmer specifies ASCII as the FTP transport format to have the file converted from EBCDIC. For binary transfers, the file is not converted.

13.2.2 Serving dynamic web pages on z/OS

Dynamic web pages are an essential part of web-based commerce. Every kind of interaction and personalization requires dynamic content. When a user completes a form on a website, for example, the data in the form must be processed, and feedback must be sent to the user.

Two approaches for serving dynamic web pages on z/OS are:

► Using CGI for dynamic web pages
► Using the plug-in interface

Using CGI for dynamic web pages

One way to provide dynamic web pages is through the Common Gateway Interface (CGI), which is part of the HTTP protocol. CGI is a standard way for a web server to pass a web user's HTTP request to an application. CGI generates the output and passes it back to HTTP Server, which sends it back to the user in an HTTP response (Figure 13-1).

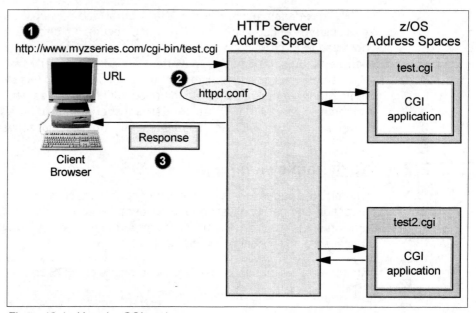

Figure 13-1   How the CGI works

CGI is not limited to returning only HTML pages; the application can also create plain text documents, XML documents, pictures, PDF documents, and so on. The MIME type must reflect the content of the HTTP response.

CGI has one major disadvantage, which is that each HTTP request requires a separate address space. This causes a lack of efficiency when there are many requests at a time. To avoid this problem, FastCGI[1] was created. Basically, the HTTP Server FastCGI plug-in is a program that manages multiple CGI requests in a single address space, which saves many program instructions for each request. FastCGI is a way to combine the advantages of normal CGI programming with some of the performance benefits you get by using the Go Webserver Application Programming Interface (GWAPI) interface.

---

[1] http://www.fastcgi.com/drupal/

Note: The Go Webserver Application Programming Interface (GWAPI) is an interface to the HTTP Server that allows you to extend the server's base functions. You can write extensions to do customized processing, such as:

► Enhance the basic authentication or replace it with a site-specific process

► Add error handling routines to track problems or produce alerts about serious conditions .

► Detect and track information that comes in from the requesting client, such as server referrals and user agent code

By default, FastCGI support in the web server is disabled. More information about HTTP Server plug-ins is provided in "Using the plug-in interface" on page 481.

Using the plug-in interface

Another way of providing dynamic content is by using the plug-in interface of HTTP Server, which allows one of several products to interface with HTTP Server. Here, for example, are some ways in which HTTP Server can pass control to IBM WebSphere:

► WebSphere plug-in, using the same address space

Figure 13-2 shows a simple configuration in which no J2EE server is needed. This servlet can connect to CICS or IMS, or to DB2 through Java Database Connectivity (JDBC). However, coding business logic inside servlets is not recommended.

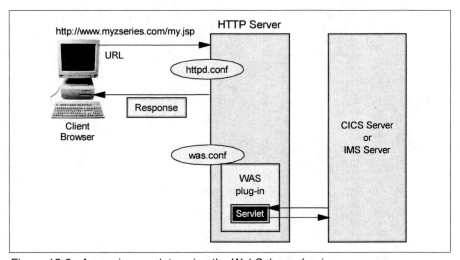

Figure 13-2   Accessing servlets using the WebSphere plug-in

▶ Web container inside HTTP Server, using a separate Enhanced JavaBean (EJB) container

Figure 13-3 shows a more usable configuration in which the servlets run in a different address space than the EJBs, so the EJBs are invoked from remote calls. The EJBs then obtain information from other servers.

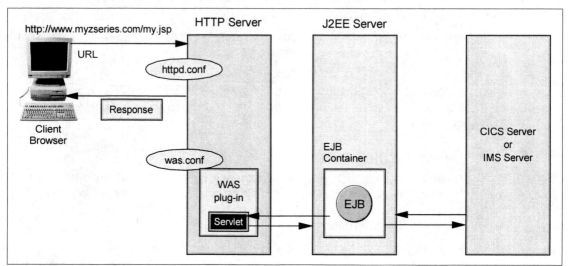

Figure 13-3   Accessing EJBs from a WebSphere plug-in

► Separate J2EE server with both web container and EJB container

In addition to running your servlets locally within the WebSphere plug-in, you can also use the WebSphere plug-in to run servlets remotely in a web container, as shown in Figure 13-4. This allows you to localize your servlets and EJBs to the same z/OS address space, so that no remote EJB calls are required.

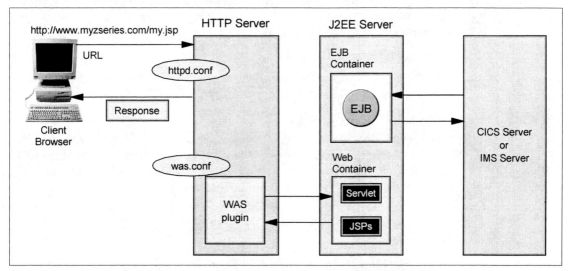

Figure 13-4   Accessing servlets in a web container using the WebSphere plug-in

If you are using IBM WebSphere Application Server, HTTP Server might not be needed, yet there are several ways in which HTTP Server can interact with WebSphere Application Server. These possibilities are mentioned here.

13.3 HTTP Server capabilities

HTTP Server provides capabilities similar to other web servers, but with some functions specific to z/OS as well. The z/OS-specific functions can be grouped as follows:

► Basic functions
► Security functions
► File caching

13.3.1 Basic functions

- EBCDIC/ASCII file access

  The server accesses files and converts them, if needed, from EBCDIC to ASCII encoding.

- Performance and usage monitoring

  As part of the z/OS features, HTTP Server can produce system management facilities (SMF[2]) records that the system programmer can retrieve later to do performance and usage analysis.

- Tracing and logging

  HTTP Server comes with a complete set of logging, tracing, and reporting capabilities that allow you to keep track of every HTTP request.

- Server Side Include (SSI)

  Server Side Include allows you to insert information into documents (static or dynamic) that the server sends to the clients. This could be a variable (such as the "Last modified" date), the output of a program, or the content of another file. Enabling this function, but not using it, can have a serious performance impact.

- Simple Network Management Protocol (SNMP) Management Information Base (MIB)

  HTTP Server provides an SNMP MIB and SNMP subagent, so you can use any SNMP-capable network management system to monitor your server's health, throughput, and activity. It can then notify you if your specified threshold values are exceeded.

- Cookies support

  Because HTTP is a stateless protocol, a state can be added by using cookies, which store information on the client's side. This support is useful for multiple web pages, for example, to achieve customized documents or for banner rotation.

- Multi-Format Processing

  This feature is used to personalize web pages. The browser sends header information along with the request, including the *accept header*. This information includes the language of the user. HTTP Server can make use of the contents of the accept header to select the appropriate document to return to the client.

---

[2] SMF is an optional feature of z/OS that provides you with the means for gathering and recording information that can be used to evaluate system usage for accounting, chargeback, and performance tuning.

▶ Persistent connections

Using this HTTP/1.1-specific feature, not every request has to establish a new connection. Persistent connections stay "alive" for a certain amount of time to enable the use of a given connection to another request.

▶ Virtual hosts

Virtual hosts allow you to run one web server while making it appear to clients as though you are running several. This is achieved by using different DNS names for the same IP or different IP addresses bound to the same HTTP Server.

13.3.2 Security functions

▶ Thread level security

An independent security environment can be set for each thread running under HTTP Server, which basically means that every client connecting to the server will have its own security environment.

▶ HTTPS/SSL support

HTTP Server has full support for the Secure Socket Layer (SSL) protocol. HTTPS uses SSL as a sublayer under the regular HTTP layer to encrypt and decrypt HTTP requests and HTTP responses. HTTPS uses port 443 for serving instead of HTTP port 80.

▶ LDAP support

The Lightweight Data Access Protocol (LDAP) specifies a simplified way to retrieve information from an X.500-compliant directory in an asynchronous, client/server type of protocol.

▶ Certificate authentication

As part of the SSL support, HTTP Server can use certificate authentication and act as a certificate authority.

▶ Proxy support

HTTP Server can act as a proxy server. You cannot, however, use the Fast Response Cache Accelerator (FRCA).

13.3.3 File caching

Performance can be significantly increased by using any of the following file caching (buffering) possibilities:

- ► HTTP Server caching HFS files
- ► HTTP Server caching z/OS data sets
- ► z/OS UNIX caching HFS files
- ► Fast Response Cache Accelerator (FRCA)

13.3.4 Plug-in code

The WebSphere HTTP Server plug-in is code that runs inside various web servers: IBM HTTP Server, Apache, IIS, and Sun Java System. Requests are passed over to the plug-in, where they are handled based on a configuration file.

The plug-in is code supplied with WebSphere that runs inside various HTTP servers. Those HTTP servers may be the IBM HTTP Server on z/OS. As workload comes into the HTTP Server, directives in the HTTP Server's configuration file (`httpd.conf`) are used to make a decision: Is the work request coming in something the HTTP Server handles or is it something this is passed to the plug-in itself?

Once inside the plug-in, the logic that acts upon the request is determined by the plug-in's configuration file, not the HTTP Server's configuration file. That configuration file is, by default, called the `plugin-cfg.xml` file. Information about which of the application servers the request goes to is defined in this file. This file is something that is created by WebSphere Application Server and does not necessarily need modifying, although you have the flexibility to do so.

In general, plug-ins provide functionality extensions for HTTP Server. Figure 13-5 shows one example of its use, although there are many different plug-ins that can be configured to assist in the customization of your web environment. Another popular plug-in is the Lightweight Directory Access Protocol Server (LDAP) used for security authentication.

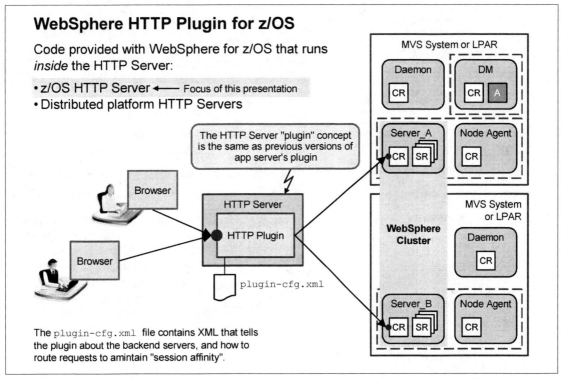

Figure 13-5   Example of a plug-in

13.3.5 HTTP proxy servers

In today's networking environment, there is great demand for fast Internet access. Using a proxy cache improves the response time for your Internet users,

The HTTP Server includes the proxy, caching, and filtering features of IBM Web Traffic Express. With these features, your server can act as a proxy, and retrieve Internet data from multiple servers. With the optional caching features, you can manage its caching functions to optimize server performance and minimize user response time.

Proxy server terminology

Here is a list of the terminology used with proxy servers:

Proxy server
A server that accepts requests from clients (usually browsers, but possibly servers) and forwards these requests to servers. The proxy server can cache files that it receives from destination servers. The proxy server can then return these cached files to clients on subsequent requests, without requesting the files from the destination servers again.

Origin server
The web server that holds the original copy of the resource.

Content server
Another term for the origin server.

Destination server
Another term for the origin server.

Firewall
A functional unit that protects and controls the connection of one network to other networks. The firewall prevents unwanted or unauthorized communication traffic from entering the protected network and allows only selected communication traffic to leave the protected network. The firewall can contain a proxy server.

Socks server
A circuit-level proxy server that establishes a connection from a client to an application, and then forwards the data in both directions without further interference. This activity is not a function of web proxy servers, but special purpose hardware and software.

Forward proxy server
A proxy server configuration that requires users to define the proxy server in the users' browsers. An organization for a specific group of people usually sets up this type of proxy to handle requests on behalf of those people.

Reverse proxy server	A proxy server configuration that is transparent to users because the users do not configure their browsers to point to the proxy.
Hidden proxy server	Another term for reverse proxy server.
Secure Sockets Layer (SSL) tunneling	A proxy server forwards an SSL request to a destination server without decrypting the request. The tunneling proxy server only understands the destination server address and port number. The proxy server does not need SSL configured. Only the destination server needs to support SSL and decrypt requests. HTTPS requests come into the proxy server non-SSL port, which is port 80 by default. The proxy server redirects the requests to the destination server SSL port, usually set to 443. The SSL tunneling proxy server must have the CONNECT method set on the Enable directive. Most filtering by the proxy server becomes impossible when using tunneling. For example, virus screening is not possible. Filtering based on the URL or header fields also becomes impossible because the proxy server with SSL tunneling enabled does not decrypt this information. SSL tunneling only works for a forward proxy.

For a reverse proxy, you can implement an alternative to SSL tunneling. In this case, the SSL connection only occurs between the browser and the proxy server. The connection between the proxy server and the origin server is non-SSL. The reverse proxy decrypts the information and passes it to the origin server. Use this implementation when the origin server lacks SSL capability and needs the proxy server to provide secure connections across the Internet or an intranet.

13.4 Summary

z/OS provides HTTP Server for both static and dynamic web pages. HTTP Server supports the WebSphere plug-in (which handles EJB containers and J2EE), and security and file caching. These features make it easier to work with dynamic web pages.

Table 13-1 lists the key terms used in this chapter.

Table 13-1   Key terms used in this chapter

CGI	dynamic	FRCA
HTTP	J2EE	LDAP
proxy	SSL	static

13.5 Questions for review

To help test your understanding of the material in this chapter, answer the following questions:

1. List the three server modes.
2. Explain static and dynamic web pages.
3. List at least two functions from each of the three groups: basic, security, and caching.

13.6 Exercises

Use the ISHELL or OMVS shell for this exercise. Also, you will need to know:

▶ The location of the HTTP Server configuration file `httpd.conf`
▶ The IP address or the name of the HTTP Server

Perform each of the following steps and answer the questions:

1. Browse the `httpd.conf` file of the HTTP Server product installed on z/OS. In which directory are the web documents stored (F "URL translation rules")? Also, which port should be used (F "Port directive")?

2. From a web browser window, display the class HTTP Server. How is WebSphere plugged into this HTTP Server (F "WebSphere")?

3. Use OEDIT to create an HTML document in the web documents folder. Name it *yourid*test.html. Here is an example:

```
<!doctype html public "//W3//Comment//EN">
<html>
<head>
<META content="text/html; charset=iso-8859-1">
<title> This is a simple HTML Exercise</title>
</head>
<body bgcolor="#FFFFFF">
<p>Hello World
</body>
</html>
```

4. Open a web browser and go to your HTML document, for example:

   `http://www.`*yourserver*`.com/`*yourid*`test.html`

   What needs to be done to install your own CGI?

5. Examine the `httpd.conf` file. Is the HTCounter CGI option "Date and Time" enabled? If so, change *yourid*text.html and add the following line to the body section:

   `<img src="/cgi-bin/datetime?Timebase=Local">`

   Save the file. What has changed?

14

IBM WebSphere Application Server on z/OS

Objective: As a mainframe professional, you need to know how to deploy a web application on z/OS. You also need to know how to enable z/OS for processing web-based workloads.

After completing this chapter, you will be able to:

- ► List the six qualities of the J2EE Application model.
- ► Describe the infrastructure design of the WebSphere Application Server
- ► Give three reasons for running WebSphere Application Server under z/OS.
- ► Name three connectors to CICS, DB2, and IMS.

Refer to Table 14-1 on page 511 for a list of key terms used in this chapter.

14.1 What is WebSphere Application Server for z/OS

As enterprises move many of their applications to the web, mainframe organizations face the complexity of enabling and managing new web-based workloads in addition to more traditional workloads, such as batch processing.

WebSphere Application Server is a comprehensive, sophisticated, Java 2 Enterprise Edition (J2EE) and web services technology-based application system. WebSphere Application Server on z/OS is a J2EE implementation conforming to the current Software Development Kit (SDK) specification supporting applications at an API level. As mentioned, it is a Java Application deployment and runtime environment built on open standards-based technology supporting all major functions, such as servlets, Java server pages (JSPs), and Enterprise Java Beans (EJBs), including the latest technology integration of services and interfaces.

The application server run time is highly integrated with all inherent features and services offered on z/OS. The application server can interact with all major subsystems on the operating system, including DB2, CICS, and IMS. It has extensive attributes for security, performance, scalability, and recovery. The application server also uses sophisticated administration and tooling functions, thus providing seamless integration into any data center or server environment.

WebSphere Application Server is an e-business application deployment environment. It is built on open standards-based technology, such as CORBA, HTML, HTTP, IIOP, and J2EE-compliant Java technology standards for servlets, Java Server Pages (JSP) technology, and Enterprise Java Beans (EJB), and it supports all Java APIs needed for J2EE compliance.

> **Attention:** Using z/OS as the underlying operating system for WebSphere Application Server does not mean rebuilding your non z/OS processes for administration, operation, and development, or that your administration staff needs to learn a new product.
>
> The WebSphere API's are the same, while the z/OS operating systems offers additional capabilities that simplifies things and provides high availability, disaster recovery, performance settings, and management options.

An essential concept running on z/OS is that the WebSphere Application Server on distributed platforms is based on a single process model. This means that the entire application server runs in a single process, which contains the Java Virtual Machine (JVM). If this process crashes for some reason, all applications that are deployed to this application server will be unavailable unless the application server is clustered.

With WebSphere Application Server for z/OS, a logical application server can consist of multiple JVMs, each executing in a different address space. These address spaces are called servant regions (SR), each containing one JVM. If a servant region abends, another servant region can take over the incoming requests in an multiple-servant environment.

In fact, each logical application server on z/OS has cluster capabilities through the use of multiple servants. These mini-clusters benefit from cluster advantages, such as availability and scalability without the processing impact of a real cluster. This is a key differentiator from distributed platforms.

Important: With regard to administration, WebSphere Application Server for z/OS uses the same concepts as distributed environments to create and manage application servers. However, each application server is consists of multiple address spaces that represent a single logical application server.

At minimum, one application server consists of one control region (CR) and one servant region (SR) (Figure 14-1). Additional servant regions can be added statically by defining a minimum amount of servant regions. Defining a maximum amount of servants, that is, higher than the minimum amount, allows the z/OS Workload Manager (WLM) to add more servants dynamically according to the demand of the workload. In practice, the amount of servant regions is limited by the physical memory available on the system.

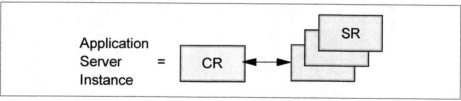

Figure 14-1   An application server instance

The main responsibility of the control region is to handle the incoming connections from the clients and dispatch the requests to the WLM queues that are contained in the control region (Figure 14-2). Each WLM queue represents a service class defined to the WebSphere application runtime. Refer to 3.5, "What is workload management" on page 126 for more information.

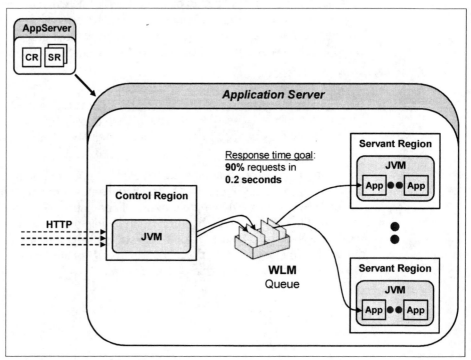

Figure 14-2   Architecture of a single application server

Attention: The z/OS Workload Manager (WLM) allows you to prioritize work requests on a transaction granularity, compared to server granularity on a distributed environments. Therefore, a service class will be assigned to each work request. For example, you can define a service class in WLM that has the goal to complete 90% of the requests within 0.2 seconds. The WLM tries to achieve this goal with all available resources. If the response times of the user transactions do not meet the defined goals, the WLM starts additional servant regions to process the incoming work requests.

The application server on z/OS supports two types of configurations: Base and Network Deployment. Each configuration uses essentially the same architectural hierarchy, composed of *servers*, *nodes* and *cells*. However, cells and nodes play an important role only in the Network Deployment configuration.

14.2 Servers

A server is the primary runtime component; this is where your application actually executes. The server provides containers and services that specialize in enabling the execution of specific Java application components. Each application server runs in its own Java Virtual Machine (JVM).

Depending on the configuration, servers might work separately or in combination, as follows:

▶ In a Base configuration, each application server functions as a separate entity. There is no workload distribution or common administration among the application servers.

A base or stand-alone application server provides the necessary capabilities to run J2EE compliant applications. A stand-alone application server is a good starting point for development and test teams. It can also be used for proof of concept or light-weight applications that do not require extended system resources.

▶ In a Network Deployment configuration, multiple application servers are maintained from a central administration point.

The Network Deployment runtime configuration is appropriate for J2EE Production applications providing failover and clustering functionality for workload balancing to ensure high availability.

There is a special type of application server called a Java Message Service (JMS) Server, which is message oriented middleware (MOM). Messaging is covered in Chapter 15, "Messaging and queuing" on page 513.

14.3 Nodes (and node agents)

A node is a logical grouping of WebSphere-managed server processes that share common configuration and operational control. A node is generally associated with one physical installation of the application server.

As you move up to the more advanced application server configurations, the concepts of configuring multiple nodes from one common administration server and workload distribution among nodes are introduced. In these centralized management configurations, each node has a node agent that works with a Deployment Manager to manage administration processes.

14.4 Cells

A cell is a grouping of nodes into a single administrative domain. In the Base configuration, a cell contains one node. That node may have multiple servers, but the configuration files for each server are stored and maintained individually (XML-based).

With the Network Deployment configuration, a cell can consist of multiple nodes, all administered from a single point. The configuration and application files for all nodes in the cell are centralized into a cell master configuration repository. This centralized repository is managed by the deployment manager process and synchronized with local copies held on each of the nodes.

Figure 14-3 shows both Base and Network Deployment cell configurations.

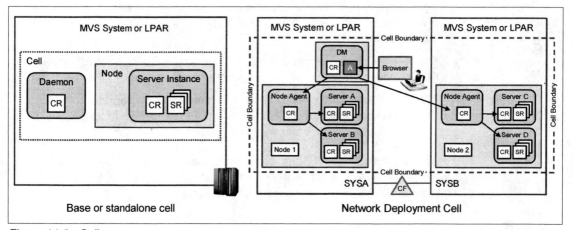

Figure 14-3   Cells

The administration interface for a Base application server is contained within an enterprise archive file (EAR) physically within the server itself. The Network Deployment offering has its administration contained in a separate interface outside of the server(s) run time, because this component is not part of the operational components and can be quiesced when not in use to save resources.

Attention: A cell provides an administration boundary and a node is a collection of servers grouped together for the purpose of administration.

In the address spaces used for the application server, there is the concept of *containers*, which provide runtime separation between the various elements that execute. A single container, known as an EJB container, is used to run Enterprise Java Beans. Another container, known as the web container, is used to execute web-related elements, such as HTML, GIF files, servlets, and Java server pages (JSPs). Together, they make up the application server run time within the JVM.

> **Important:** A daemon server (DM) is always required with either configuration. The daemon is another special single-CR server. It is not an application server: no applications can be installed into it. The daemon routes client requests to the appropriate server. To perform this task, it has to know which servers are active and know the applications that are on them. The daemon returns a token to the client that can be used to access the application in the selected server, which allows requests to be routed to a server based upon availability.

14.5 J2EE application model on z/OS

The J2EE Application Model on z/OS is exactly the same as on other platforms, and it follows the SDK specification, exhibiting the following qualities:

- Functional: Satisfies user requirements.
- Reliable: Performs under changing conditions.
- Usable: Enables easy access to application functions.
- Efficient: Uses system resources wisely.
- Maintainable: Can be modified easily.
- Portable: Can be moved from one environment to another.

WebSphere Application Server on z/OS supports four major models of application design: web-based computing, integrated enterprise computing, multithreading distributed business computing, and service-oriented computing. All these design models focus on separating the application logic from the underlying infrastructure, that is, the physical topology and explicit access to the information system are distinct from the programming model for the application.

The J2EE programming model supported by WebSphere Application Server for z/OS makes it easier to build applications for new business requirements because it separates the details from the underlying infrastructure. It provides for the deployment of the component and service-oriented programming model offered by J2EE.

14.6 Running WebSphere Application Server on z/OS

WebSphere Application Server runs as a standard subsystem on z/OS. Therefore, it inherits all the characteristics of mainframe qualities and functionality that accompany that platform, such as its unique capacity for running hundreds of heterogeneous workloads concurrently, and meeting service level objectives defined by the user.

14.6.1 Consolidation of workloads

As discussed in previous chapters, a mainframe can be used to consolidate workloads from many individual servers. Therefore, if there is a large administration impact or concern about the physical capacity of many individual servers, the mainframe can take on the role of a single server environment managing those workloads. It can present a single view of administration, performance, and recovery for applications that harness the mainframe's services during execution.

Several application servers can easily be migrated into one logical partition of a mainframe's resources, thus providing ease of management and monitoring (logical partitions (LPARs) are discussed in Chapter 2, "Mainframe hardware systems and high availability" on page 45). Consolidation also allows for instrumentation and metric gathering, resulting in easier capacity analysis.

14.6.2 WebSphere for z/OS security

The combination of zSeries hardware- and software-based security, along with incorporated J2EE security, offers significant defense against possible intrusions. The product security is a layered architecture built on top of the operating system platform, the Java Virtual Machine (JVM), and Java2 security.

WebSphere Application Server for z/OS integrates infrastructure and mechanisms to protect sensitive J2EE resources and administrative resources, addressing the enterprise from an end-to-end security perspective based on industry standards.

The open architecture possesses secure connectivity and interoperability with all mainframe Enterprise Information Systems, which includes:

- ► CICS Transaction Server (TS)
- ► DB2
- ► Lotus® Domino®
- ► IBM Directory

WebSphere Application Server integrates with RACF and WebSEAL Secure Proxy (Trusted Association Interceptor), providing a unified, policy-based, and permission-based model for securing all web resources and Enterprise Java Bean components, as defined in the J2EE specification.

14.6.3 Continuous availability

WebSphere for z/OS uses the IBM System z platform's internal error detection and correction internal capabilities. WebSphere for z/OS has recovery termination management that detects, isolates, corrects, and recovers from software errors. WebSphere for z/OS can differentiate and prioritize work based on service level agreements. It offers clustering capability and the ability to make nondisruptive changes to software components, such as resource managers.

In a critical application, WebSphere for z/OS can implement a failure management facility of z/OS called automatic restart manager (ARM). This facility can detect application failures, and restart servers when failures occur. WebSphere uses ARM to recover application servers (servants). Each application server running on a z/OS system is registered with an ARM restart group.

WebSphere for z/OS can implement a feature called *clustering*. Clustering technology is used extensively in high availability solutions involving WebSphere, as shown in Figure 14-4.

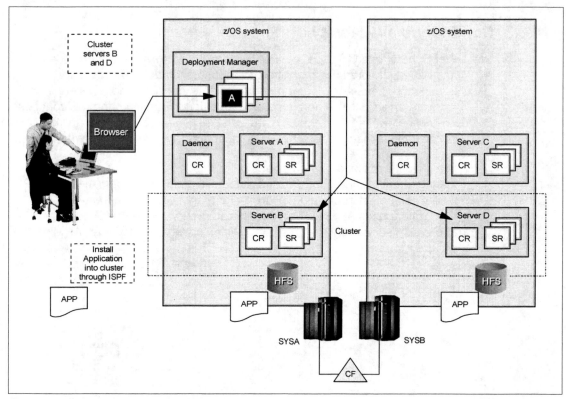

Figure 14-4   Clustering of servers in a cell

A cluster consists of multiple copies of the same component with the expectation that at least one of the copies will be available to service a request. In general, the cluster works as a unit where there is some collaboration among the individual copies to ensure that the request can be directed toward a copy that is capable of servicing the request.

Designers of a high availability solution participate in establishing a service level as they determine the number and placement of individual members of clusters. WebSphere for z/OS provides management for some of the clusters needed to create the desired service level. Greater service levels of availability can be obtained as WebSphere clusters are supplemented with additional cluster technologies.

A WebSphere Application Server cluster is composed of individual cluster members, with each member containing the same set of applications. In front of a WebSphere Application Server cluster is a workload distributor, which routes the work to individual members.

Clusters can be vertical within an LPAR (that is, two or more members residing in a z/OS system) or they can be placed horizontally across LPARs to obtain the highest availability in the event an LPAR containing a member has an outage.

A workload in this case can still be taken on from the remaining cluster members. Also within these two configurations, it is possible to have a hybrid in which the cluster is composed of vertical and horizontal members (Figure 14-5).

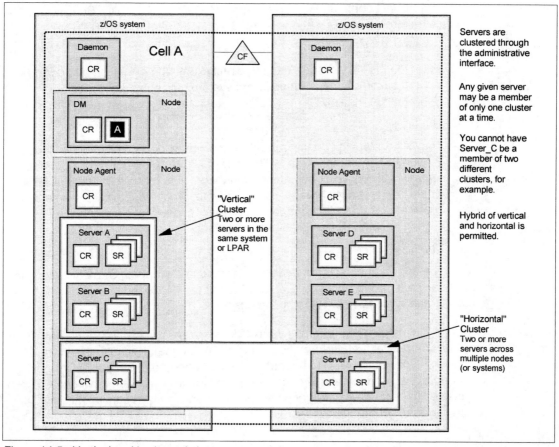

Figure 14-5   Vertical and horizontal clusters

You might wonder when to use vertical clustering as opposed to horizontal clustering. You might use vertical clustering to check the dispatching efficiency of a single system. In a vertical cluster, the servers compete with each other for resources.

14.6.4 Performance

Performance is highly dependent on application design and coding, regardless of the power of the runtime platform; a badly written application will perform just as poorly on z/OS as it would on another platform.

WebSphere Application Server for z/OS uses mainframe qualities in hardware, and software characteristics incorporating Workload Management schemes, dynamic LPAR configuration, and Parallel Sysplex functionality. Specifically, it uses the three distinct functions of z/OS workload management (WLM):

▶ Routing

  WLM routing services are used to direct clients to servers on a specific system based on measuring current system utilization, known as the Performance Index (PI).

▶ Queuing

  The WLM queuing service is used to dispatch work requests from a Controller Region to one or more Server Regions. It is possible for a Work Manager to register with WLM as a Queuing Manager, which tells WLM that this server would like to use WLM-managed queues to direct work to other servers, which allows WLM to manage server spaces to achieve the specified performance goals established for the work.

▶ Prioritize

  The application server provides for starting and stopping Server Regions to set work priority, which allows WLM to manage application server instances to achieve goals specified by the business.

WLM maintains a performance index (PI) for each service class period to measure how actual performance varies from the goal. Because there are several types of goals, WLM needs some way of comparing how well or poorly work in one service class is doing compared to other work. A service class (SC) is used to describe a group of work within a workload with equivalent performance characteristics.

14.7 Application server configuration on z/OS

An application server configuration on z/OS includes the following:

► Base server node
► Network Deployment Manager

14.7.1 Base server node

The base application server node is the simplest operating structure in the
Application Server for z/OS. It consists of an application server and a daemon
server (one node and one cell), as shown in Figure 14-6. All of the configuration
files and definitions are kept in the HFS directory structure created for this base
application server. The daemon server is a special server with one controller
region. The system architecture of WebSphere for z/OS calls for one daemon
server per cell per system or LPAR.

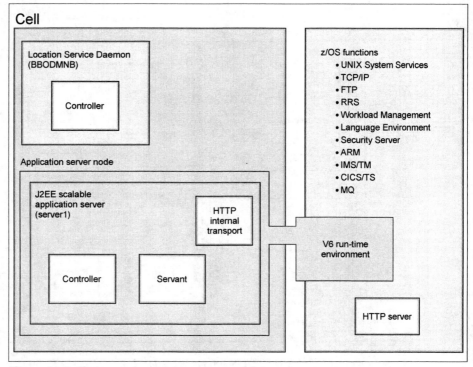

Figure 14-6   Base server node

Each base application server node contains administration for its own cell domain and a separate repository for its configuration. Therefore, you can have many base application servers, each isolated from the others, having their own administration policy for their specific business needs.

14.7.2 Network Deployment Manager

Network Deployment Manager (Figure 14-7) is an extension to the base application server. It allows the system to administer multiple application servers from one centralized location. Here, application servers are attached to nodes, and multiple nodes belong to a cell. With the Deployment Manager, horizontally and vertically scaled systems, as well as distributed applications, can be easily administered.

The Network Deployment Manager also manages the repositories on each node, performing such tasks as creating, maintaining, and removing the repositories. The system uses an extract and modify method to update the configuration.

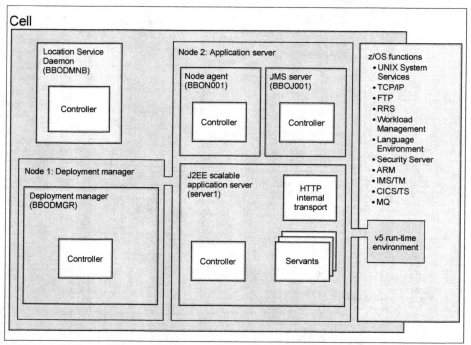

Figure 14-7   Network Deployment Manager

14.8 Connectors for Enterprise Information Systems

The ability of applications to interface with resources outside of the application server process and to use those resources efficiently has always been an important requirement. Equally important is the ability for vendors to plug in their own solutions for connecting to and using their resources.

An application might require access to many types of resources, which may or may not be located in the same machine as the application. Therefore, access to a resource begins with a connection that is a pathway from an application to a resource, which might be another transaction manager or database manager.

Java program access to a broad range of back-end resources is performed through a resource adapter. This is a system-level software driver that plugs into an application server and enables a Java application to connect to various back-end resources.

The following considerations are common to all connections:

► Creating a connection can be expensive. Setting up a connection can take a long time when compared to the amount of time the connection is actually used.

► Connections must be secure. This is often a joint effort between the application and the server working with the resource.

► Connections must perform well. Performance can be critical to the success of an application, and it is a function of the application's overall performance.

► Connections must be monitorable and have good diagnostics. The quality of the diagnostics for a connection depends on the information regarding the status of the server and the resource.

► Methods for connecting to and working with a resource. Different database architectures require different means for access from an application server.

► Quality of service, which becomes a factor when accessing resources outside of the application server. The application might require the ACID (Atomicity, Consistency, Isolation, and Durability) properties that can be obtained when using data in managing a transaction.

Enterprise resources are often older resources that were developed over time by a business and are external to the application server process. Each type of resource has its own connection protocol and proprietary set of interfaces to the resource. Therefore, the resource has to be adapted for it to be accessible from a JVM process contained in an application server.

WebSphere Application Server has facilities to interface with other z/OS subsystems, such as CICS, DB2, and IMS, which is done through a resource adapter and a connector. Accessing back-end Enterprise Information Systems (EIS) extends the functionality of the application server into existing business functions, providing enhanced capabilities.

The J2EE Connector Architecture (JCA) defines the contracts between the application, the connector, and the application server where the application is deployed. The application has a component called the *resource adapter*. This is contained within the application code handling the interface to the connector that the application developer creates.

From a programming perspective, this means that programmers can use a single unified interface to obtain data from the EIS. The resource adapter will sort out the different elements and provide a programming model that is independent of the actual EIS behavior and communication requirements.

Figure 14-8 shows an example of a basic architecture of a connector to an EIS.

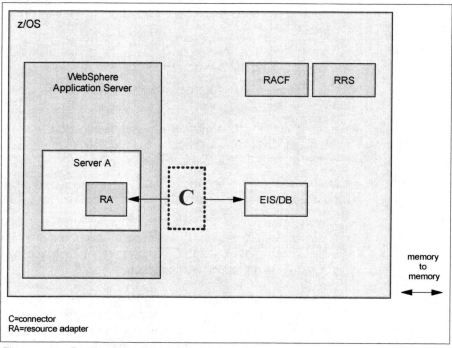

Figure 14-8   Basic architecture of a connector to an EIS

14.8.1 z/OS connectors

WebSphere for z/OS provides the following *connectors* to allow web applications on z/OS to interface with the mainframe middleware products CICS, IMS, and DB2:

- ► CICS Transaction Gateway
- ► IMS Connect
- ► DB2 Java Database Connectivity

CICS Transaction Gateway

Customer Information Control System (CICS) uses the CICS Transaction Gateway (CTG) to connect from the application server to CICS. CTG provides the interface between Java and CICS application transactions. It is a set of client and server software components incorporating the services and facilities that re needed to access CICS from the application server. CTG uses special APIs and protocols in servlets or EJBs to request services and functions of the CICS Transaction Manager.

IMS Connect

IMS Connect is the connector TCP/IP server that enables an application server client to exchange messages with IMS Open Transaction Manager Access (OTMA). This server provides communication links between TCP/IP clients and IMS databases. It supports multiple TCP/IP clients accessing multiple databases. To protect information that is transferred through TCP/IP, IMS Connect provides Secure Sockets Layer (SSL) support.

IMS Connect can also perform router functions between application server clients and local option clients with databases and IMSplex resources. Request messages received from TCP/IP clients using TCP/IP connections, or local option clients using the z/OS Program Call (PC), are passed to a database through cross-system Coupling Facility (XCF) sessions. IMS Connect receives response messages from the database and then passes them back to the originating TCP/IP or local option clients.

IMS Connect supports TCP/IP clients communicating with socket calls, but it can also support any TCP/IP client that communicates with a different input data stream format. User-written message exits can execute in the IMS Connect address space to convert the z/OS installation's message format to OTMA message format before IMS Connect sends the message to IMS. The user-written message exits also convert OTMA message format to the installation's message format before sending a message back to IMS Connect. IMS Connect then sends output to the client.

DB2 Java Database Connectivity

The Java Database Connectivity (JDBC) is an application programming interface (API) that the Java programming language uses to access different forms of tabular data, as well as some hierarchical systems, such as IMS. JDBC specifications were developed by Sun Microsystems together with relational database providers, such as Oracle and IBM, to ensure portability of Java applications across database platforms.

This interface does not necessarily fall into the category of "connector" because there is no separate address space required for its implementation. The interface is a Java construct that looks like a Java class, but does not provide an implementation of its methods. For JDBC, the actual implementation of the JDBC interface is provided by the database vendor as a "driver". This provides portability because all access using the JDBC is through standard calls with standard parameters. Thus, an application can be coded with little regard to the database being used, because all of the platform-dependent code is stored in the JDBC drivers.

As a result, JDBC must be flexible with regard to what functionality it does and does not provide, solely based on the fact that different database systems have different levels of functionality. JDBC drivers provide the physical code that implements the objects, methods, and data types defined in the specification. JDBC standards define four types of drivers, numbered 1 through 4. The distinction between them is based on how the driver is physically implemented and how it communicates with the database.

z/OS supports only Type 2 and Type 4 drivers, as follows:

► Type 2

   The JDBC API calls platform- and database-specific code to access the database. This is the most common driver type used, and offers the best performance. However, because the driver code is platform-specific, a different version has to be coded (by the database vendor) for each platform.

► Type 4

   A Type 4 driver is fully written in Java, and accesses the target database directly using the protocol of the database itself. (In the case of DB2, this is DRDA.) Because the driver is fully written in Java, it can be ported to any platform that supports that DBMS protocol without change, thus allowing applications to also use it across platforms without change.

   A Java application, running under WebSphere Application Server, talks to the (Universal) Type 4 JDBC driver that supports two-phase commit, and the driver talks directly to the remote database server through DRDA. The Universal Type 4 driver implements DRDA Application Requester functionality.

To access DB2 on z/OS, IBM provides a Type 2 driver and a driver that combines Type 2 and Type 4 JDBC implementations. In general, JDBC Type 2 connectivity is used for Java programs that run on the same z/OS system with the target DB2 subsystem. JDBC Type 4 connectivity is used for Java programs that run on a z/OS system other than that of the target DB2 subsystem.

14.9 Summary

WebSphere Application Server is a comprehensive, sophisticated, Java 2 Enterprise Edition (J2EE) and web services technology-based application system. We have seen how to deploy a web application on z/OS, as well as how to enable z/OS for processing web-based workloads. The application server on z/OS supports two types of configurations: Base and Network Deployment. Each configuration uses essentially the same architectural hierarchy, composed of servers, nodes, and cells. However, cells and nodes play an important role only in the Network Deployment configuration. An application might require access to many types of resources, which may or may not be located in the same machine as the application. Therefore, access to a resource begins with a connection that is a pathway from an application to a resource, which might be another transaction manager or database manager

Table 14-1 lists the key terms used in this chapter.

Table 14-1   Key terms used in this chapter

cell	cluster	CGI
CS	EIS	J2EE
JMX	node	SR

14.10 Questions for review

To help test your understanding of the material in this chapter, answer the following questions:

1. List the six qualities of the J2EE Application model.

2. List three reasons for running WebSphere Application Server under z/OS.

3. Name three connectors.

4. What is a major difference between HTTP Server and WebSphere Application Server for z/OS?

5. What are some features of WebSphere Application Server that contribute to continuous availability?

15

Messaging and queuing

Objective: As a mainframe professional, you need to understand messaging and queuing. These functions are needed for communication between heterogeneous applications and platforms.

After completing this chapter, you will be able to:

- ▸ Explain why messaging and queuing is used.
- ▸ Describe the asynchronous flow of messages.
- ▸ Explain the function of a queue manager.
- ▸ List three z/OS-related adapters.

Refer to Table 15-1 on page 524 for a list of key terms used in this chapter.

15.1 What WebSphere MQ is

Most large organizations today have IT systems that come from various manufacturers, which often makes it difficult to share communications and data across systems. Many of these organizations also need to communicate and share data electronically with suppliers and customers, who might have other disparate systems. It would be handy to have a message handling tool that could receive data from one type of system and send that data to another type.

IBM WebSphere MQ facilitates application integration by passing messages between applications and web services. It is used on more than 35 hardware platforms and for point-to-point messaging from Java, C, C++, and COBOL applications. Three-quarters of enterprises that buy inter-application messaging systems buy WebSphere MQ. In the largest installation, billions of messages a day are transmitted.

When data held on different databases on different systems must be kept synchronized, there are few protocols to coordinate updates, deletions, and so on. Mixed environments are difficult to keep aligned; complex programming is often required to integrate them.

Message queues, and the software that manages them, such as IBM WebSphere MQ for z/OS, enable program-to-program communication. In the context of online applications, *messaging* and *queuing* can be understood as follows:

▶ Messaging means that programs communicate by sending each other messages (data) rather than by calling each other directly.

▶ Queuing means that the messages are placed on queues in storage, so that programs can run independently of each other, at different speeds and times, in different locations, and without having a logical connection between them.

15.2 Synchronous communication

Figure 15-1 shows the basic mechanism of program-to-program communication using a synchronous communication model.

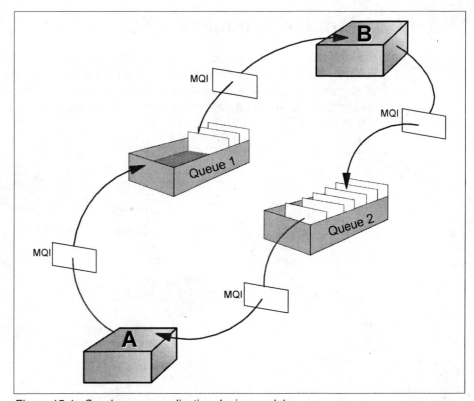

Figure 15-1   Synchronous application design model

Program A prepares a message and puts it on Queue 1. Program B gets the message from Queue 1 and processes it. Both Program A and Program B use an application programming interface (API) to put messages on a queue and get messages from a queue. The WebSphere MQ API is called the Message Queue Interface (MQI).

When Program A puts a message on Queue 1, Program B might not be running. The queue stores the message safely until Program B starts and is ready to get the message. Likewise, when Program B gets the message from Queue 1, Program A might no longer be running. Using this model, there is no requirement for two programs communicating with each other to be executing at the same time.

There is clearly a design issue, however, about how long Program A should wait before continuing with other processing. This design might be desirable in some situations, but when the wait is too long, it is not so desirable any more. Asynchronous communication is designed to handle those situations.

15.3 Asynchronous communication

Using the asynchronous model, Program A puts messages on Queue 1 for Program B to process, but it is Program C, acting asynchronously to Program A, which gets the replies from Queue 2 and processes them. Typically, Program A and Program C would be part of the same application. You can see the flow of this activity in Figure 15-2.

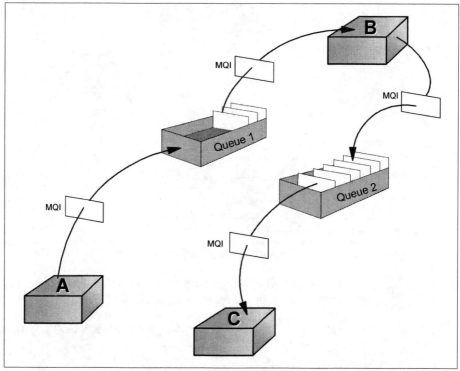

Figure 15-2   Asynchronous application design model

The asynchronous model is natural for WebSphere MQ. Program A can continue to put messages on Queue 1 and is not blocked by having to wait for a reply to each message. It can continue to put messages on Queue 1 even if Program B fails. If so, Queue 1 stores the messages safely until Program B is restarted.

In a variation of the asynchronous model, Program A could put a sequence of messages on Queue 1, optionally continue with some other processing, and then return to get and process the replies itself. This property of WebSphere MQ, in which communicating applications do not have to be active at the same time, is known as *time independence*.

15.4 Message types

WebSphere MQ uses four types of messages:

Datagram   A message for which no response is expected.

ich a reply is requested.

st message.

escribes an event, such as the
error or a confirmation of the arrival of a

15.   ueue manager

sages sent by programs. They are
ue manager.

n a queue, the queue manager ensures

he receiving application

be delivered to a queue owned by another
n as the assured delivery property of

15

s and manages queues is called a queue
g services for applications, ensures that
ue, routes messages to other queue
through a common programming interface
(MQI).

The queue manager can retain messages for future processing in the event of application or system outages. Messages are retained in a queue until a successful completion response is received through the MQI.

There are similarities between queue managers and database managers. Queue managers own and control queues similar to the way that database managers own and control their data storage objects. They provide a programming interface to access data, and also provide security, authorization, recovery, and administrative facilities.

There are also important differences, however. Databases are designed to provide long-time data storage with sophisticated search mechanisms, whereas queues are not designed for this function. A message on a queue generally indicates that a business process is incomplete; it might represent an unsatisfied request, an unprocessed reply, or an unread report. Figure 15-4 on page 521 shows the flow of activity in queue managers and database managers.

15.5.2 Types of message queues

Several types of message queues exist. In this book, the most relevant are the following:

► Local queue

A queue is local if it is owned by the queue manager to which the application program is connected. It is used to store messages for programs that use the same queue manager. The application program does not have to run on the same machine as the queue manager.

► Remote queue

A queue is remote if it is owned by a different queue manager. A remote queue is not a real queue; it is only the *definition* of a remote queue to the local queue manager. Programs cannot read messages from remote queues. Remote queues are associated with a transmission queue.

► Transmission queue

This local queue has a special purpose: it is used as an intermediate step when sending messages to queues that are owned by a different queue manager. Transmission queues are transparent to the application, that is, they are used internally by the queue manager channel initiator.

► Initiation queue

This is a local queue to which the queue manager writes (transparently to the programmer) a trigger message when certain conditions are met on another local queue, for example, when a message is put into an empty message queue or in a transmission queue.

Two WebSphere MQ applications monitor initiation queues and read trigger messages, the trigger monitor, and the channel initiator. The *trigger monitor* can start applications, depending on the message. The *channel initiator* starts the transmission between queue managers.

▶ Dead-letter queue

A queue manager (QM) must be able to handle situations when it cannot deliver a message, for example:

– The destination queue is full.
– The destination queue does not exist.
– The message puts have been inhibited on the destination queue.
– The sender is not authorized to use the destination queue.
– The message is too large.

When one of these conditions occurs, the message is written to the dead-letter queue. This queue is defined when the queue manager is created, and each QM should have one. It is used as a repository for all messages that cannot be delivered.

15.6 What is a channel

A *channel* is a logical communication link. The conversational style of program-to-program communication requires the existence of a communications connection between each pair of communicating applications. Channels shield applications from the underlying communications protocols.

WebSphere MQ uses two kinds of channels:

▶ Message channel

A message channel connects two queue managers through message channel agents (MCAs). A message channel is unidirectional, composed of two message channel agents (a sender and a receiver) and a communication protocol. An MCA transfers messages from a transmission queue to a communication link, and from a communication link to a target queue. For bidirectional communication, it is necessary to define a *pair* of channels, consisting of a sender and a receiver.

▶ MQI channel

An MQI channel connects a WebSphere MQ client to a queue manager. Clients do not have a queue manager of their own. An MQI channel is bidirectional.

In WebSphere MQ for z/OS, all channels run inside a separate process from the queue manager, called the Channel Initiator (CHINIT).

15.7 How transactional integrity is ensured

A business might require two or more distributed databases to be maintained in step. WebSphere MQ offers a solution involving multiple units of work acting asynchronously, as shown in Figure 15-3.

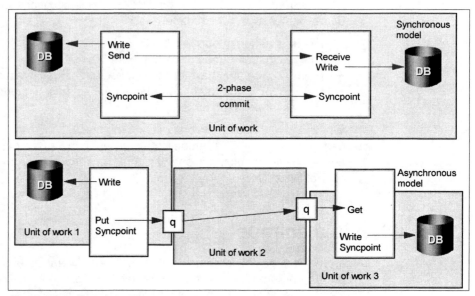

Figure 15-3   Data integrity

The top half of Figure 15-3 shows a two-phase commit structure, while the WebSphere MQ solution is shown in the lower half, as follows:

► The first application writes to a database, places a message on a queue, and issues a sync point to commit the changes to the two resources. The message contains data that is to be used to update a second database on a separate system. Because the queue is a remote queue, the message goes no further than the transmission queue within this unit of work. When the unit of work is committed, the message becomes available for retrieval by the sending MCA.

► In the second unit of work, the sending MCA gets the message from the transmission queue and sends it to the receiving MCA on the system with the second database, and the receiving MCA places the message on the destination queue. This is performed reliably because of the assured delivery property of WebSphere MQ. When this unit of work is committed, the message becomes available for retrieval by the second application.

▶ In the third unit of work, the second application gets the message from the destination queue and updates the database using the data contained in the message.

It is the transactional integrity of units of work 1 and 3, and the once and once only, assured delivery property of WebSphere MQ used in unit of work 2, which ensures the integrity of the complete business transaction. If the business transaction is a more complex one, many units of work may be involved.

15.8 Example of messaging and queuing

Now let us return to the earlier example of a travel agency to see how messaging facilities play a role in booking a vacation. Assume that the travel agent must reserve a flight, a hotel room, and a rental car. All of these reservations must succeed before the overall business transaction can be considered complete (Figure 15-4).

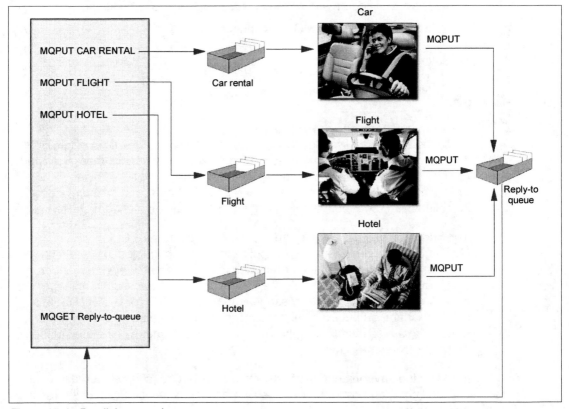

Figure 15-4 Parallel processing

With a message queue manager such as WebSphere MQ, the application can send several requests at once; it need not wait for a reply to one request before sending the next. A message is placed on each of three queues, serving the flight reservations application, the hotel reservations application, and the car rental application. Each application can then perform its respective task in parallel with the other two and place a reply message on the reply-to queue. The agent's application waits for these replies and produces a consolidated answer for the travel agent.

Designing the system in this way can improve the overall response time. Although the application might normally process the replies only when they have all been received, the program logic may also specify what to do when only a partial set of replies is received within a given period of time.

15.9 Interfacing with CICS, IMS, batch, or TSO/E

WebSphere MQ is available for a variety of platforms. WebSphere MQ for z/OS includes several adapters to provide messaging and queuing support for:

- ▶ CICS: The WebSphere MQ-CICS bridge
- ▶ IMS: The WebSphere MQ-IMS bridge
- ▶ Batch or TSO/E

15.9.1 Bridges

A common pattern is to drive transactions based on the content of messages. While the adapters described in 15.9, "Interfacing with CICS, IMS, batch, or TSO/E" on page 522 allow transactions to be written to retrieve messages and operate on them, there is often a requirement to drive unaltered older transactions using message data passed in an MQ message. MQ provides so-called *bridges* for both the IMS and CICS transaction manager environments.

The bridge provides a gateway from a queue to the transaction manager. Messages put to the queue by an application are constructed to contain header information that describes the transaction to be run and the environment on which to run it. The bridge starts the transaction in the transaction manager and passes the remainder of the message to that transaction for processing. In a similar manner, output from the transaction is intercepted by the bridge and turned into a message that is placed on the ReplyToQueue nominated in the original request message.

In the bridge environment, the transaction does not need to be altered to contain any MQI calls, and need not even be aware that it is being driven as the result of an MQ message.

15.10 Sysplex support

Within a sysplex, a group of WebSphere MQ for z/OS queue managers can be grouped into a Queue Sharing Group (QSG). The QSG provides a common point of administration and control. Queue managers within the QSG are able to share a common set of definitions of MQ resources. However, the real power of the QSG is that queue managers are all able to access a set of shared queues.

Shared queues are based on list structures defined in one or more Coupling Facility structures. Queue managers in the QSG can concurrently store and retrieve messages from the same shared queue, which leads to high availability of the messages held on shared queues, as the queue and messages stored there can be used even in the event of failure or planned outage of other queue managers or LPARs. The shared queue model is highly scalable, as processing is distributed across the sysplex; message rates in excess of 10,000 persistent messages per second on a single shared queue have been measured.

When viewed from the network, a QSG provides "shared channels" to move messages between shared (or private) queues and the network; these can be started in a workload balanced fashion on any queue manager. Inbound channel connections can use a network distribution mechanism such as sysplex distributor to workload balance both message and MCI channels across the queue sharing group.

By using sysplex technologies, the QSG presents a messaging and queuing service with unparalleled qualities of service, which often lies at the heart of an enterprise application infrastructure.

15.11 Java Message Service

Java Message Service (JMS) is an industry standard Java application programming interface (API), which is an integral part of the Java Platform Enterprise Edition (renamed from J2EE). WebSphere MQ provides classes for JMS, which allow applications written to the JMS standard to use the capabilities of the WebSphere MQ messaging service. These classes are provided as an integral part of the IBM Java Platform Enterprise Edition application server, WebSphere Application Server.

Java is an attractive application development language, as programming skills are widely available. An application written to the JMS specification is independent of the JMS messaging provider and is portable between platforms and messaging providers.

Of particular interest in WebSphere Application Server is the capability to deploy Message Driven Beans (MDBs). An MDB is a mechanism for driving EJBs on the arrival of an asynchronous message in such a way that the message content is presented as input to an EJB. In this context, the MQ classes for JMS allow an MQ message to be presented as a JMS message to an MDB, which can drive appropriate business logic. Often, such an MDB performs a database query or update and sends a response, again using the JMS API, with the entire processing being encapsulated in a transaction.

15.12 Summary

In an online application environment, messaging and queuing enables communication between applications on different platforms. IBM WebSphere MQ for z/OS is an example of software that manages messaging and queuing in the mainframe and other environments. With messaging, programs communicate through messages, rather than by calling each other directly. With queuing, messages are retained on queues in storage, so that programs can run independently of each other (asynchronously).

Here are some of the functional benefits of WebSphere MQ:

► A common application programming interface, the MQI, which is consistent across the supported platforms.

► Data transfer data with assured delivery. Messages are not lost, even if a system fails. There is not duplicate delivery of messages.

► Asynchronous communication, that is, communicating applications need not be active at the same time.

► Message-driven processing as a style of application design. An application is divided into discrete functional modules that can run on different systems, be scheduled at different times, or act in parallel.

► Application programming is made faster when the programmer is shielded from the complexities of the network.

Table 15-1 lists the key terms used in this chapter.

Table 15-1 Key terms used in this chapter

asynchronous application	channel	dead-letter queue
local queue	message-driven	MQI
QM	remote queue	sync point

15.13 Questions for review

To help test your understanding of the material in this chapter, answer the following questions:

1. Why is messaging and queuing needed for communication between heterogeneous applications and platforms?

2. Describe the asynchronous flow of messages.

3. Explain the function of a queue manager.

4. List three z/OS-related adapters.

5. What is the purpose of MQI?

6. For what is a dead-letter queue used?

Part 4

System programming on z/OS

In this part, we reveal the inner workings of z/OS through discussions of system libraries, security, and procedures for starting (performing an IPL) and stopping a z/OS system. This part also includes chapters about hardware details and virtualization, and the clustering of multiple z/OS systems in a sysplex.

16

Overview of system programming

Objective: As a z/OS system programmer, you need to know how z/OS works.

After completing this chapter, you will be able to:

► Discuss the responsibilities of a z/OS system programmer.

► Explain system libraries, their use, and methods for managing their content.

► List the different types of operator consoles.

► Describe the process of performing an IPL of a system.

Refer to Table 16-1 on page 563 for a list of key terms used in this chapter.

16.1 The role of the system programmer

The system programmer is responsible for managing the mainframe hardware configuration, and installing, customizing, and maintaining the mainframe operating system. Installations need to ensure that their system and its services are available and operating to meet service level agreements. Installations with 24/7 operations need to plan for minimal disruption of their operation activities.

In this chapter, we examine several areas of interest for the would-be z/OS system programmer. Although this text cannot cover every aspect of system programming, it is important to learn that the job of the z/OS system programmer is complex and requires skills in many aspects of the system, such as:

- Device I/O configurations
- Processor configurations
- Console definitions
- System libraries where the software is placed
- System data sets and their placement
- Customization parameters that are used to define your z/OS configuration
- Security administration

As shown in Figure 16-1, the role of system programmer usually includes some degree of involvement in all of the following aspects of system operation:

- ► Customizing the system
- ► Managing system performance
- ► Configuring I/O devices
- ► Following a process of change control
- ► Configuring consoles
- ► Initializing the system

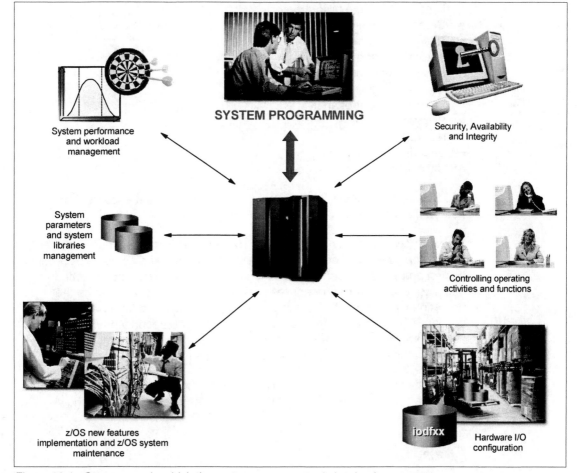

Figure 16-1   Some areas in which the system programmer is involved

16.2 What is meant by separation of duties

In a large z/OS installation, there is usually a "separation of duties" both among members of the system programming staff, and between the system programming department and other departments in the IT organization.

A typical z/OS installation includes the following roles and more:

- ► z/OS system programmer
- ► CICS system programmer
- ► Database system programmer
- ► Database administrator
- ► Network system programmer
- ► Automation specialist
- ► Security manager
- ► Hardware manager
- ► Production control analyst
- ► System operator
- ► Network operator
- ► Security administrator
- ► Service manager

In part, the separation of duties is an audit requirement; it ensures that one person does not have too much power on a system.

When a new application is added to a system, for example, a number of tasks need to be performed before the application can be used by users. A production control analyst is needed to add batch applications into the batch scheduling package, add the new procedures to a procedure library, and set up the operational procedures. The system programmer is needed to perform tasks concerned with the system itself, such as setting up security privileges and adding programs to system libraries. The programmer is also involved with setting up any automation for the new application.

On a test system, however, a single person might have to perform all the roles, including being the operator, and this is often the best way to learn how everything works.

16.3 Customizing the system

This section describes the following topics:

- ► System libraries where the software is located
- ► System data sets and their placement
- ► I/O device configuration
- ► Console definitions
- ► Customization parameters used to define the z/OS configuration
- ► z/OS implementation and maintenance

16.3.1 z/OS system libraries

As can be seen in Figure 16-2, different types of data exist in a system.

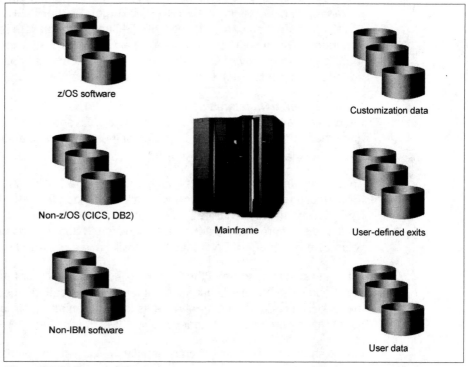

z/OS software

Customization data

Non-z/OS (CICS, DB2)

Mainframe

User-defined exits

Non-IBM software

User data

Figure 16-2   Types of data

First, there is the z/OS software supplied by IBM. It is usually installed onto a series of disk volumes known as the system residence volumes (SYSRES).

Much of the flexibility of z/OS is built on these SYSRES sets. They make it possible to apply maintenance to a new set that is cloned from the production set while the current set is running production work. A short outage can then be taken to perform an IPL from the new set (and the maintenance has been implemented). Also, the change can be backed out by performing an IPL from the old set.

Fixes to z/OS are managed with a product called System Modification Program/Extended (SMP/E). Indirect cataloging using system symbols is used so that a particular library is cataloged as being on, for example, SYSRES volume 2, and the name of that volume is resolved by the system at IPL time from the system symbols. Symbols are discussed in 16.3.11, "What system symbols are" on page 543.

Another group of volumes are the non-z/OS and non-IBM software volumes. These volumes may be combined into one group. The majority of non-z/OS software is not usually on the SYSRES volumes, as the SYSRES sets are usually managed as one entity by SMP/E. The other software is then managed separately. These volumes do not form part of the SYSRES sets, and therefore there is only one copy of each library. As many volumes as required can be added to this group, each with an individual disk name.

Customization data refers to items such as SYS1.PARMLIB, SYS1.PROCLIB, the master catalog, the IODF, page data sets, JES spools, the /etc directory, and other items essential to the running of the system. It is also where SMP/E data is stored to manage the software.

These data sets are not always located on separate DASD volumes from IBM-supplied z/OS software; some installations place the PARMLIB and PROCLIB on the first SYSRES pack, others place them on the master catalog pack or elsewhere. This is a matter of choice and depends on how the SYSRES volumes are managed. Each installation will have a preferred method.

On many systems, some of the IBM-supplied defaults are not appropriate, so they need to be modified. User exits and user modifications (usermods) are made to IBM code so that it behaves as the installation requires. The modifications are usually managed using SMP/E.

Finally, there is *user data*, which is usually the largest pool of disk volumes. This is not part of the system libraries, but is presented here for completeness. It contains production, test, and user data. It is often split into pools and managed by System Managed Storage (SMS), which can target data to appropriately managed volumes. For example, production data can be placed on volumes that are backed up daily, whereas user data may only be captured weekly and may be migrated to tape after a short period of inactivity to free up the disk volumes for further data.

z/OS has many standard system libraries, such as: SYS1.PARMLIB, SYS1.LINKLIB, SYS1.LPALIB, SYS1.PROCLIB, and SYS1.NUCLEUS. Some of these are related to IPL processing, while others are related to the search order of invoked programs or to system security, as described here:

▶ SYS1.PARMLIB contains control parameters for the whole system.

▶ SYS1.LINKLIB has many execution modules of the system.

▶ SYS1.LPALIB contains the system execution modules that are loaded into the link pack area when the system initializes.

▶ SYS1.PROCLIB contains JCL procedures distributed with z/OS.

▶ SYS1.NUCLEUS has the basic supervisor modules of the system.

▶ SYS1.SVCLIB has the supervisor call routines.

16.3.2 SYS1.PARMLIB

SYS1.PARMLIB is a required partitioned data set that contains IBM-supplied and installation-created members. It must reside on a direct access volume, which can be the system residence volume. PARMLIB is an important data set in a z/OS operating system, and can be thought of as performing a function similar to /etc on a UNIX system.

The purpose of the PARMLIB is to provide many initialization parameters in a pre-specified form in a single data set, and thus minimize the need for the operator to enter parameters.

All parameters and members of the SYS1.PARMLIB data set are described in *z/OS MVS Initialization and Tuning Reference, SA22-7592*. Some of the most important PARMLIB members are discussed in this section.

16.3.3 Link pack area

The link pack area (LPA) is a section of the common area of an address space. It exists below the system queue area (SQA) and consists of the pageable link pack area (PLPA), then the fixed link pack area (FLPA), if one exists, and finally the modified link pack area (MLPA).

LPA modules are loaded in common storage, and shared by all address spaces in the system. Because these modules are reentrant and are not self-modifying, each can be used by a number of tasks in any number of address spaces at the same time. Modules found in LPA do not need to be brought into virtual storage because they are already in virtual storage.

Modules placed anywhere in the LPA are always in virtual storage, and modules placed in FLPA are also always in central storage. LPA modules must be referenced often to prevent their pages from being stolen. When a page in LPA (other than in FLPA) is not continually referenced by multiple address spaces, it tends to be stolen.

16.3.4 Pageable link pack area

The PLPA is an area of common storage that is loaded at IPL time (when a cold start is done and the CLPA option is specified). This area contains read-only system programs, along with any read-only reentrant user programs selected by an installation that can be shared among users of the system. The PLPA and extended PLPA contain all members of SYS1.LPALIB and other libraries that are specified in the active LPALSTxx through the LPA parameter in IEASYSxx or from the operator's console at system initialization (this would override the PARMLIB specification).

You may use one or more LPALSTxx members in SYS1.PARMLIB to concatenate your installation's program library data sets to SYS1.LPALIB. You can also use the LPALSTxx member to add your installation's read-only reenterable user programs to the pageable link pack area (PLPA). The system uses this concatenation, which is referred to as the *LPALST concatenation*, to build the PLPA during the nucleus initializing process. SYS1.LPALIB must reside in a direct access volume, which can be the system residence volume.

Figure 16-3 shows an example of the LPALSTxx member.

```
   File  Edit  Edit_Settings  Menu  Utilities  Compilers  Test  Help
--------------------------------------------------------------------------------
EDIT       SYS1.PARMLIB(LPALST7B) - 01.03          Columns 00001 00072
Command ===>                                   Scroll ===> CSR
****** ***************************** Top of Data *****************************
000200 SYS1.LPALIB,
000220 SYS1.SERBLPA,
000300 ISF.SISFLPA,
000500 ING.SINGMOD3,
000600 NETVIEW.SCNMLPA1,
000700 SDF2.V1R4M0.SDGILPA,
000800 REXX.SEAGLPA,
001000 SYS1.SIATLPA,
001100 EOY.SEOYLPA,
001200 SYS1.SBDTLPA,
001300 CEE.SCEELPA,
001400 ISP.SISPLPA,
001600 SYS1.SORTLPA,
001700 SYS1.SICELPA,
001800 EUV.SEUVLPA,
001900 TCPIP.SEZALPA,
002000 EQAW.SEQALPA,
002001 IDI.SIDIALPA,
002002 IDI.SIDILPA1,
002003 DWW.SDWWLPA(SBOX20),
002010 SYS1.SDWWDLPA,
002020 DVG.NFTP230.SDVGLPA,
002200 CICSTS22.CICS.SDFHLPA(SBOXD3)
****** ***************************** Bottom of Data *****************************
```

Figure 16-3   Example of the LPALST PARMLIB member

16.3.5 Fixed link pack area

The FLPA is loaded at IPL time, with the modules listed in the active IEAFIXxx member of SYS1.PARMLIB. This area should be used only for modules that significantly increase performance when they are fixed rather than pageable. The best candidates for the FLPA are modules that are infrequently used, but are needed for fast response.

Modules from the LPALST concatenation, the linklist concatenation, SYS1.MIGLIB, and SYS1.SVCLIB can be included in the FLPA. FLPA is selected through specification of the FIX parameter in IEASYSxx, which is appended to IEAFIX to form the IEAFIXxx PARMLIB member, or from the operator's console at system initialization.

Figure 16-4 shows an IEAFIX PARMLIB member; part of the modules for FLPA belong to the SYS1.LPALIB library.

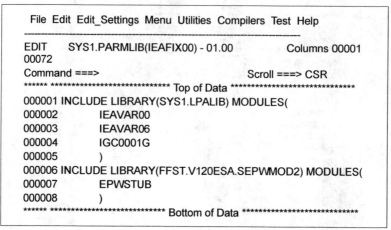

```
    File  Edit  Edit_Settings  Menu  Utilities  Compilers  Test  Help
-----------------------------------------------------------------------
EDIT      SYS1.PARMLIB(IEAFIX00) - 01.00              Columns 00001
00072
Command ===>                                      Scroll ===> CSR
****** ***************************** Top of Data *****************************
000001 INCLUDE LIBRARY(SYS1.LPALIB) MODULES(
000002          IEAVAR00
000003          IEAVAR06
000004          IGC0001G
000005          )
000006 INCLUDE LIBRARY(FFST.V120ESA.SEPWMOD2) MODULES(
000007          EPWSTUB
000008          )
****** ***************************** Bottom of Data **************************
```

Figure 16-4   The IEAFIX PARMLIB member

16.3.6 Modified link pack area

The MLPA can be used to contain reenterable routines from APF-authorized libraries (see 18.7.1, "Authorized programs" on page 603) that are to be part of the pageable extension to the link pack area during the current IPL. Note that the MLPA exists only for the duration of an IPL. Therefore, if an MLPA is desired, the modules in the MLPA must be specified for each IPL (including quick start and warm start IPLs). When the system searches for a routine, the MLPA is searched before the PLPA. The MLPA can be used at IPL time to temporarily modify or update the PLPA with new or replacement modules.

16.3.7 SYS1.PROCLIB

SYS1.PROCLIB is a required partitioned data set that contains the JCL procedures used to perform certain system functions. The JCL can be for system tasks or for processing program tasks invoked by the operator or the programmer.

16.3.8 The master scheduler subsystem

The *master scheduler subsystem* is used to establish communication between the operating system and the primary job entry subsystem, which can be JES2 or JES3. When you start z/OS, master initialization routines initialize system services, such as the system log and communication task, and start the master scheduler address space, which becomes address space number one (ASID=1).

Then, the master scheduler may start the job entry subsystem (JES2 or JES3). JES is the primary job entry subsystem. On many production systems, JES is not started immediately; instead, the automation package starts all tasks in a controlled sequence. Then other defined subsystems are started. All subsystems are defined in the PARMLIB library, member IEFSSNxx. These subsystems are *secondary subsystems*.

An initial MSTJCL00 load module can be found in the SYS1.LINKLIB library. If modifications are required, the recommended procedure is to create an MSTJCLxx member in the PARMLIB data set. The suffix is specified by the MSTRJCL parameter in the IEASYSxx member of PARMLIB. The MSTJCLxx member is commonly called the *master JCL*. It contains data definition (DD) statements for all system input and output data sets that are needed to do the communication between the operating system and JES.

Example 16-1 shows a sample MSTJCLxx member.

Example 16-1 Sample master JCL

```
File   Edit   Edit_Settings   Menu   Utilities   Compilers   Test   Help
---------------------------------------------------------------------------
EDIT        SYS1.PARMLIB(MSTJCL00) - 01.07              Columns 00001 00072
Command ===>                                            Scroll ===> CSR
****** *************************** Top of Data ******************************
000100 //MSTRJCL  JOB MSGLEVEL=(1,1),TIME=1440
000200 //         EXEC PGM=IEEMB860,DPRTY=(15,15)
000300 //STCINRDR DD SYSOUT=(A,INTRDR)
000400 //TSOINRDR DD SYSOUT=(A,INTRDR)
000500 //IEFPDSI  DD DSN=SYS1.PROCLIB,DISP=SHR
000600 //         DD DSN=CPAC.PROCLIB,DISP=SHR
000700 //         DD DSN=SYS1.IBM.PROCLIB,DISP=SHR
000800 //IEFJOBS  DD DSN=SYS1.STCJOBS,DISP=SHR
000900 //SYSUADS  DD DSN=SYS1.UADS,DISP=SHR
****** *************************** Bottom of Data ***************************
```

When the master scheduler has to process the start of a started task, the system determines whether the START command refers to a procedure or to a job. If the IEFJOBS DD exists in the MSTJCLxx member, the system searches the IEFJOBS DD concatenation for the member requested in the START command.

If there is no member by that name in the IEFJOBS concatenation, or if the IEFJOBS concatenation does not exist, the system searches the IEFPDSI DD for the member requested in the START command. If a member is found, the system examines the first record for a valid JOB statement and, if one exists, uses the member as the JCL source for the started task. If the member does not have a valid JOB statement in its first record, the system assumes that the source JCL is a procedure and creates JCL to invoke the procedure.

After the JCL source has been created (or found), the system processes the JCL. As shipped, MSTJCL00 contains an IEFPDSI DD statement that defines the data set that contains procedure source JCL for started tasks. Normally this data set is SYS1.PROCLIB; it may be a concatenation. For useful work to be performed, SYS1.PROCLIB must at least contain the procedure for the primary JES, as shown in the next section.

16.3.9 A job procedure library

SYS1.PROCLIB contains the JES2 cataloged procedure. This procedure defines the job-related procedure libraries, as shown in Example 16-2.

Example 16-2 How to specify procedure libraries in the JES2 procedure

```
//PROC00 DD DSN=SYS1.PROCLIB,DISP=SHR
//       DD  DSN=SYS3.PROD.PROCLIB,DISP=SHR
//PROC01 DD DSN=SYS1.PROC2,DISP=SHR
...
//PROC99 DD DSN=SYS1.LASTPROC,DISP=SHR
...
```

Many installations have long lists of procedure libraries in the JES procedure. This is because JCLLIB is a relatively recent innovation.

Care should be taken about the number of users who can delete these libraries because JES will not start if one is missing. Normally a library that is in use cannot be deleted, but JES does not hold these libraries although it uses them all the time.

You can override the default specification by specifying this statement:

```
/*JOBPARM PROCLIB=
```

After the name of the procedure library, you code the name of the DD statement in the JES2 procedure that points to the library to be used. For example, in Example 16-2 on page 540, let us assume that you run a job in class A and that class has a default PROCLIB specification on PROC00. If you want to use a procedure that resides in SYS1.LASTPROC, you need to include this statement in the JCL:

```
/*JOBPARM PROCLIB=PROC99
```

Another way to specify a procedure library is to use the JCLLIB JCL statement. This statement allows you to code and use procedures without using system procedure libraries. The system searches the libraries in the order in which you specify them on the JCLLIB statement, prior to searching any unspecified default system procedure libraries.

Example 16-3 shows the use of the JCLLIB statement.

Example 16-3   Sample JCLLIB statement

```
//MYJOB  JOB
//MYLIBS JCLLIB   ORDER=(MY.PROCLIB.JCL,SECOND.PROCLIB.JCL)
//S1     EXEC PROC=MYPROC1
...
```

Assuming that the system default procedure library includes SYS1.PROCLIB only, the system searches the libraries for procedure MYPROC1 in the following order:

1. MY.PROCLIB.JCL
2. SECOND.PROCLIB.JCL
3. SYS1.PROCLIB

16.3.10 Search order for programs

When a program is requested through a system service (like LINK, LOAD, XCTL, or ATTACH) using default options, the system searches for it in the following sequence:

1. Job pack area (JPA)

   A program in JPA has already been loaded in the requesting address space. If the copy in JPA can be used, it will be used. Otherwise, the system either searches for a new copy or defers the request until the copy in JPA becomes available. (For example, the system defers a request until a previous caller is finished before reusing a serially-reusable module that is already in JPA.)

2. TASKLIB

   A program can allocate one or more data sets to a TASKLIB concatenation. Modules loaded by unauthorized tasks that are found in TASKLIB must be brought into private area virtual storage before they can run. Modules that have previously been loaded in common area virtual storage (LPA modules or those loaded by an authorized program into CSA) must be loaded into common area virtual storage before they can run.

3. STEPLIB or JOBLIB

   These are specific DD names that can be used to allocate data sets to be searched ahead of the default system search order for programs. Data sets can be allocated to both the STEPLIB and JOBLIB concatenations in JCL or by a program using dynamic allocation. However, only one or the other will be searched for modules. If both STEPLIB and JOBLIB are allocated for a particular jobstep, the system searches STEPLIB and ignores JOBLIB.

   Any data sets concatenated to STEPLIB or JOBLIB will be searched after any TASKLIB but before LPA. Modules found in STEPLIB or JOBLIB must be brought into private area virtual storage before they can run. Modules that have previously been loaded in common area virtual storage (LPA modules or those loaded by an authorized program into CSA) must be loaded into common area virtual storage before they can run.

4. LPA, which is searched in this order:

   a. Dynamic LPA modules, as specified in PROGxx members

   b. Fixed LPA (FLPA) modules, as specified in IEAFIXxx members

   c. Modified LPA (MLPA) modules, as specified in IEALPAxx members

   d. Pageable LPA (PLPA) modules, loaded from libraries specified in LPALSTxx or PROGxx

   LPA modules are loaded in common storage, shared by all address spaces in the system. Because these modules are reentrant and are not self-modifying, each can be used by any number of tasks in any number of address spaces at the same time. Modules found in LPA do not need to be brought into virtual storage, because they are already in virtual storage.

5. Libraries in the linklist, as specified in PROGxx and LNKLSTxx

   By default, the linklist begins with SYS1.LINKLIB, SYS1.MIGLIB, and SYS1.CSSLIB. However, you can change this order using SYSLIB in PROGxx and add other libraries to the linklist concatenation. The system must bring modules found in the linklist into private area virtual storage before the programs can run.

The default search order can be changed by specifying certain options on the macros used to call programs. The parameters that affect the search order the system will use are EP, EPLOC, DE, DCB, and TASKLIB. For more information about these parameters, see the section "The search for the load module" in Chapter 4, " Program management", in *z/OS MVS Programming: Assembler Services Guide*, SA22-7605. Some IBM subsystems (notably CICS and IMS) and applications (such as ISPF) use these facilities to establish other search orders for programs.

16.3.11 What system symbols are

System symbols are elements that allow different z/OS systems to share PARMLIB definitions while retaining unique values in those definitions. System symbols act like variables in a program; they can take on different values, based on the input to the program. When you specify a system symbol in a shared PARMLIB definition, the system symbol acts as a "placeholder". Each system that shares the definition replaces the system symbol with a unique value during initialization.

Each system symbol has a name (which begins with an ampersand (&) and optionally ends with a period (.)) and a substitution text, which is the character string that the system substitutes for a symbol each time it appears.

There are two types of system symbols:

Dynamic   The substitution text can change at any point in an IPL.

Static   The substitution text is defined at system initialization and remains fixed for the life of an IPL.

Some symbols are reserved for system use. You can display the symbols in your system by entering the D SYMBOLS command. Example 16-4 shows the result of entering this command.

Example 16-4   Partial output of the D SYMBOLS command (some lines removed)

```
HQX7708 ----------------- SDSF PRIMARY OPTION MENU  --
COMMAND INPUT ===> -D SYMBOLS
  IEA007I STATIC SYSTEM SYMBOL VALUES
          &SYSALVL.  = "2"
          &SYSCLONE. = "70"
          &SYSNAME.  = "SC70"
          &SYSPLEX.  = "SANDBOX"
          &SYSR1.    = "Z17RC1"
          &ALLCLST1. = "CANCEL"
          &CMDLIST1. = "70,00"
          &COMMDSN1. = "COMMON"
```

```
&DB2.       = "V8"
&DCEPROC1.  = "."
&DFHSMCMD.  = "00"
&DFHSMHST.  = "6"
&DFHSMPRI.  = "NO"
&DFSPROC1.  = "."
&DLIB1.     = "Z17DL1"
&DLIB2.     = "Z17DL2"
&DLIB3.     = "Z17DL3"
&DLIB4.     = "Z17DL4"
&IEFSSNXX.  = "R7"
&IFAPRDXX.  = "4A"
```

The IEASYMxx PARMLIB member provides a single place to specify system parameters for each system in a multisystem environment. IEASYMxx contains statements that define static system symbols and specify IEASYSxx PARMLIB members that contain system parameters (the SYSPARM statement).

Example 16-5 shows an IEASYMxx PARMLIB member.

Example 16-5   Partial IEASYMxx PARMLIB member (some lines removed)

```
SYSDEF          SYSCLONE(&SYSNAME(3:2))
                  SYMDEF(&SYSR2='&SYSR1(1:5).2')
                  SYMDEF(&SYSR3='&SYSR1(1:5).3')
                  SYMDEF(&DLIB1='&SYSR1(1:3).DL1')
                  SYMDEF(&DLIB2='&SYSR1(1:3).DL2')
                  SYMDEF(&DLIB3='&SYSR1(1:3).DL3')
                  SYMDEF(&DLIB4='&SYSR1(1:3).DL4')
                  SYMDEF(&ALLCLST1='CANCEL')
                  SYMDEF(&CMDLIST1='&SYSCLONE.,00')
                  SYMDEF(&COMMDSN1='COMMON')
                  SYMDEF(&DFHSMCMD='00')
                  SYMDEF(&IFAPRDXX='00')
                  SYMDEF(&DCEPROC1='.')
                  SYMDEF(&DFSPROC1='.')
SYSDEF          HWNAME(SCZP901)
                LPARNAME(A13)
                SYSNAME(SC70)
                SYSPARM(R3,70)
                SYMDEF(&IFAPRDXX='4A')
                SYMDEF(&DFHSMHST='6')
                SYMDEF(&DFHSMPRI='NO')
                SYMDEF(&DB2='V8')
```

In the example, the &SYSNAME variable has the value specified by the SYSNAME keyword (SC70 in this case). Because each system in a sysplex has a unique name, we can use &SYSNAME in the specification of system-unique resources, where permitted. As an example, we could specify the name of an SMF data set as SYS1.&SYSNAME..MAN1, with a substitution resulting in the name SYS1.SC70.MAN1 when running on SC70.

You can use variables to construct the values of other variables. In Example 16-5 on page 544, we see &SYSCLONE taking on the value of &SYSNAME beginning at position 3 for a length of 2. Here, &SYSCLONE will have a value of 70. Similarly, we see &SYSR2 constructed from the first five positions of &SYSR1 with a suffix of 2. Where is &SYSR1 defined? &SYSR1 is system-defined with the VOLSER of the IPL volume. If you refer back to Example 16-4 on page 543, you see the values of &SYSR1 and &SYSR2.

We also see here the definition of a global variable defined to all systems (&IFAPRDXX with a value of 00) and its redefinition for SC70 to a value of 4A.

System symbols are used in cases where multiple z/OS systems share a single PARMLIB. Here, the use of symbols allows individual members to be used with symbolic substitution, as opposed to having each system require a unique member. The LOADxx member specifies the IEASYMxx member that the system is to use.

16.4 Managing system performance

The task of "tuning" a system is an iterative and continuous process, and it is the discipline that most directly impacts all users of system resources in an enterprise. The z/OS Workload Management (WLM) component, which we discussed in 3.5, "What is workload management" on page 126, is an important part of this process and includes initial tuning and selecting appropriate parameters for various system components and subsystems.

After the system is operational and criteria have been established for the selection of jobs for execution through job classes and priorities, WLM controls the distribution of available resources according to the parameters specified by the installation.

WLM, however, can only deal with available resources. If these are inadequate to meet the needs of the installation, even optimal distribution may not be the answer; other areas of the system should be examined to determine the possibility of increasing available resources.

When requirements for the system increase and it becomes necessary to shift priorities or acquire additional resources (such as a larger processor, more storage, or more terminals), the system programmer needs to modify WLM parameters to reflect changed conditions.

16.5 Configuring I/O devices

The I/O configurations to the operating system (software) and the channel subsystem (hardware) must be defined. The Hardware Configuration Definition (HCD) component of z/OS consolidates the hardware and software I/O configuration processes under a single interactive user interface. The output of HCD is an I/O definition file (IODF), which contains I/O configuration data. An IODF is used to define multiple hardware and software configurations to the z/OS operating system.

When a new IODF is activated, HCD defines the I/O configuration to the channel subsystem and the operating system. Using the HCD activate function or the z/OS ACTIVATE operator command, changes can be made in the current configuration without having to perform an initial program load (IPL) of the software or a power-on reset (POR) of the hardware. Making changes while the system is running is known as *dynamic configuration* or *dynamic reconfiguration*.

16.6 Following a process of change control

Data center management is typically held accountable to Service Level Agreements (SLAs), often through a specialist team of service managers. Change control mechanics and practices in a data center are implemented to ensure that SLAs are met.

The implementation of any change must be under the control of the Operations staff. When a change is introduced into a production environment that results in problems or instability, the Operations staff is responsible for observing, reporting, and then managing the activities required to correct the problem or back out the change.

Although system programmers normally originate and implement their own changes, sometimes changes are based on a request through the change management system. Any instructions for Operations or other groups would be in the change record, and the approval of each group is required.

Implementing business application changes would normally be handled by a production control analyst. Application changes normally reside in test libraries, and an official request (with audit trail) results in the programs in the test libraries being promoted to the production environment.

Procedures involved in the change must be circulated to all interested parties. When all parties consider the change description to be complete, then it is considered for implementation and either scheduled, deferred, or possibly rejected.

The factors that need to be considered when planning a change are:

► The benefits that will result from the change
► What will happen if the change is not done
► The resources required to implement the change
► The relative importance of the change request compared to others
► Any interdependency of change requests

All change involves risk. One of the advantages of the mainframe is the high availability that it offers. All change must therefore be carefully controlled and managed. A high proportion of any system programmer's time is involved in the planning and risk assessment of change. One of the most important aspects of change is how to reverse it and go back to the previous state.

16.6.1 Risk assessment

It is common practice for data center management to have a weekly change control meeting to discuss, approve, or reject changes. These changes might be for applications, a system, a network, hardware, or power.

An important part of any change is *risk assessment,* in which the change is considered and evaluated from the point of view of risk to the system. Low risk changes may be permitted during the day, while higher risk changes would be scheduled for an outage slot.

It is also common practice for a data center to have periods of low and high risk, which influences decisions. For example, if the system runs credit authorizations, then the periods around major public holidays are usually extremely busy and may cause a change freeze. Also, annual sales are extremely busy periods in retailing and may cause changes to be rejected.

IT organizations achieve their goals through disciplined change management processes and policy enforcement. These goals include:

► High service availability
► Increased security
► Audit readiness
► Cost savings

16.6.2 Change control record system

A *change control record system* is typically in place to allow for the requesting, tracking, and approval of changes. It is usually the partner of a *problem management system*. For example, if a production system has a serious problem on a Monday morning, then one of the first actions is to examine the changes that were implemented over the weekend to determine if these have any bearing on the problem.

These records also show that the system is under control, which is often necessary to prove to auditors, especially in the heavily regulated financial services sector. The Sarbanes-Oxley Act of 2002 in the United States, which addresses corporate governance, has established the need for an effective internal control system. Demonstrating strong change management and problem management in IT services is part of compliance with this measure. Additionally, the 8th Directive on Company Law in the European Union, which is under discussion at the time of writing, will address similar areas to Sarbanes-Oxley.

For these reasons, and at a bare minimum, before any change is implemented there should be a set of controlled documents defined, which are known as *change request forms*. These should include the following:

► Who: The department, group, or person that requires the change, who is responsible for implementing the change, completing the successful test, and responsible for backout if required. Also, who will "sign off" the change as successful.

► What: The affected systems or services (for example, email, file service, domain, and so on). Include as much detail as possible. Ideally, complete instructions should be included so that the change could be performed by someone else in an emergency.

► When: The start date and time and estimated duration of the change. There are often three dates: requested, scheduled, and actual.

► Where: The scope of change, and the business units, buildings, departments or groups affected or required to assist with the change.

► How: The implementation plan and a plan for backing off the changes, if the need arises.

- Priority: High, medium, low, business as usual, emergency, or dated (for example, a clock change).

- Risk: High, medium, low.

- Impact: What will happen if the change is implemented, what will happen if it is not, what other systems may be affected, and what will happen if something unexpected occurs.

16.6.3 Production control

Production control usually involves a specialized staff to manage batch scheduling, using a tool such as IBM Tivoli® Workload Scheduler to build and manage a complex batch schedule. This work might involve daily and weekly backups running at particular points within a complex sequence of application suites. Databases and online services might also be taken down and brought back up as part of the schedule. While making such changes, production control often needs to accommodate public holidays and other special events, such as (in the case of a retail sales business) a winter sale.

Production control is also responsible for taking a programmer's latest program and releasing it to production. This task typically involves moving the source code to a secure production library, recompiling the code to produce a production load module, and placing that module in a production load library. JCL is copied and updated to production standards and placed in the appropriate procedure libraries, and application suites added to the job scheduler.

There might also be an interaction with the system programmer if a new library needs to be added to the linklist, or authorized.

16.7 Configuring consoles

Operating z/OS involves managing hardware such as processors and peripheral devices (including the consoles where your operators do their work), and software, such as the z/OS operating control system, the job entry subsystem, subsystems (such as NetView®) that can control automated operations, and all the applications that run on z/OS.

The operation of a z/OS system involves the following items:

- Message and command processing that forms the basis of operator interaction with z/OS and the basis of z/OS automation

- Console operations, or how operators interact with z/OS to monitor or control the hardware and software

Planning z/OS operations for a system must take into account how operators use consoles to do their work and how to manage messages and commands. The system programmer needs to ensure that operators receive the necessary messages at their consoles to perform their tasks, and select the proper messages for suppression, automation, or other kinds of message processing.

In terms of z/OS operations, how the installation establishes console recovery or whether an operator must perform an IPL a system to change processing options are important planning considerations.

Because messages are also the basis for automated operations, the system programmer needs to understand message processing to plan z/OS automation.

As more installations make use of multisystem environments, the need to coordinate the operating activities of those systems becomes crucial. Even for single z/OS systems, an installation needs to think about controlling communication between functional areas.

In both single and multisystem environments, the commands that operators can enter from consoles can be a security concern that requires careful coordination. As a planner, the system programmer needs to make sure that the right people are doing the right tasks when they interact with z/OS.

A *console configuration* consists of the various consoles that operators use to communicate with z/OS. Your installation first defines the I/O devices it can use as consoles through the Hardware Configuration Definition (HCD), an interactive interface on the host that allows the system programmer to define the hardware configuration for both the channel subsystem and operating system.

Hardware Configuration Manager (HCM) is the graphical user interface to HCD. HCM interacts with HCD in a client/server relationship (that is, HCM runs on a workstation and HCD runs on the host). The host systems require an internal model of their connections to devices, but it can be more convenient and efficient for the system programmer to maintain (and supplement) that model in a visual form. HCM maintains the configuration data as a diagram in a file on the workstation in sync with the IODF on the host. Although it is possible to use HCD directly for hardware configuration tasks, many customers prefer to use HCM exclusively, because of its graphical interface.

In addition to HCD, after the devices have been defined, z/OS is told which devices to use as consoles by specifying the appropriate device numbers in the CONSOLxx PARMLIB member.

Generally, operators on a z/OS system receive messages and enter commands on MCS and SMCS consoles. They can use other consoles (such as NetView consoles) to interact with z/OS, but here we describe the MCS, SMCS, and EMCS consoles as they are commonly used at z/OS sites:

► *Multiple Console Support (MCS) consoles* are devices that are locally attached to a z/OS system and provide the basic communication between operators and z/OS. MCS consoles are attached to control devices that do *not* support systems network architecture or SNA protocols.

► *SNA Multiple Console Support (SMCS) consoles* are devices that do not have to be locally attached to a z/OS system and provide the basic communication between operators and z/OS. SMCS consoles use z/OS Communications Server to provide communication between operators and z/OS, instead of direct I/O to the console device.

► *Extended Multiple Console Support (EMCS) consoles* are devices (other than MCS or SMCS consoles) from which operators or programs can enter commands and receive messages. Defining EMCS consoles as part of the console configuration allows the system programmer to extend the number of consoles beyond the MCS console limit, which is 99 for each z/OS system in a sysplex.

The system programmer defines these consoles in a configuration according to their functions. Important messages that require action can be directed to the operator, who can act by entering commands on the console. Another console can act as a monitor to display messages to an operator working in a functional area like a tape pool library, or to display messages about printers at your installation.

Figure 16-5 shows a console configuration for a z/OS system that also includes the system console, an SMCS console, NetView, and TSO/E.

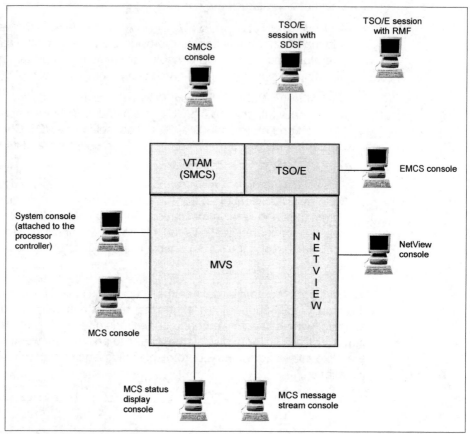

Figure 16-5   Sample console configuration for a z/OS system

The *system console* function is provided as part of the Hardware Management Console (HMC). An operator can use the system console to start z/OS and other system software, and during recovery situations when other consoles are unavailable.

In addition to MCS and SMCS consoles, the z/OS system shown in Figure 16-5 has a NetView console defined to it. NetView works with system messages and command lists to help automate z/OS operator tasks. Many system operations can be controlled from a NetView console.

Users can monitor many z/OS system functions from TSO/E terminals. Using the System Display and Search Facility (SDSF) and the Resource Measurement Facility™ (RMF™), TSO/E users can monitor z/OS and respond to workload balancing and performance problems. An authorized TSO/E user can also initiate an extended MCS console session to interact with z/OS.

The MCS consoles shown in Figure 16-5 on page 552 are:

- An MCS console from which an operator can view messages and enter z/OS commands. This console is in full capability mode because it can receive messages and accept commands. An operator can control the operations for the z/OS system from an MCS or SMCS console.

- An MCS status display console

  An operator can view system status information from DEVSERV, DISPLAY, TRACK, or CONFIG commands. However, because this is a status display console, an operator cannot enter commands from the console. An operator on a full capability console can enter these commands and route the output to a status display console for viewing.

- An MCS message-stream console

  A message-stream console can display system messages. An operator can view messages routed to this console. However, because this is a message-stream console, an operator cannot enter commands from here. Routing codes and message level information for the console are defined so that the system can direct relevant messages to the console screen for display. Thus, an operator who is responsible for a functional area such as a tape pool library, for example, can view MOUNT messages.

In many installations, this proliferation of panels has been replaced by operator workstations that combine many of these panels onto one windowed display. Generally, the hardware console is separate, but most other terminals are combined. The systems are managed by alerts for exception conditions from the automation product.

The IBM Open Systems Adapter-Express Integrated Console Controller (OSA-ICC) is the modern way to connect consoles. OSA-ICC uses TCP/IP connections over Ethernet LAN to attach to personal computers as consoles through a TN3270 connection (telnet).

16.8 Initializing the system

An initial program load (IPL) is the act of loading a copy of the operating system from disk into the processor's real storage and executing it.

z/OS systems are designed to run continuously with many months between reloads, allowing important production workloads to be continuously available. Change is the usual reason for a reload, and the level of change on a system dictates the reload schedule. For example:

- A test system may have an IPL performed daily or even more often.
- A high-availability banking system may only be reloaded once a year, or even less frequently, to refresh the software levels.
- Outside influences may often be the cause of IPLs, such as the need to test and maintain the power systems in the machine room.
- Sometimes badly behaved software uses up system resources that can only be replenished by an IPL, but this sort of behavior is normally the subject of investigation and correction.

Many of the changes that required an IPL in the past can now be done dynamically. Examples of these tasks are:

- Adding a library to the linklist for a subsystem, for example, CICS
- Adding modules to LPA

An IPL of z/OS is performed using the Hardware Management Console (HMC). You need to supply the following information to perform an IPL of z/OS:

- The device address of the IPL volume
- The LOADxx member that contains pointers to system parameters
- The IODF data set that contains the configuration information
- The device address of the IODF volume

16.8.1 Initialization process

The system initialization process (Figure 16-6) prepares the system control program and its environment to do work for the installation. This process essentially consists of:

► System and storage initialization, including the creation of system component address spaces

► Master scheduler initialization and subsystem initialization

When the system is initialized and the job entry subsystem is active, the installation can submit jobs for processing by using the START, LOGON, or MOUNT command.

The initialization process begins when the system programmer selects the LOAD function at the Hardware Management Console (HMC). z/OS locates all usable central storage that is online and available, and begins creating the various system areas.

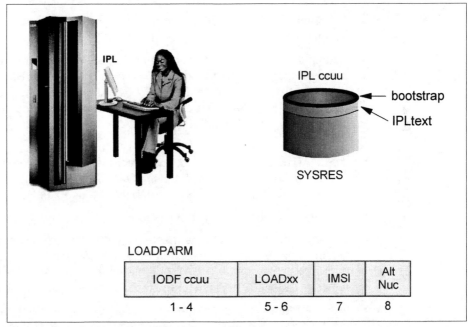

Figure 16-6   Performing an IPL of the machine

Not all disks attached to a CPU have loadable code on them. A disk that does is generally referred to as an "IPLable" disk, and more specifically as the SYSRES volume.

IPLable disks contain a bootstrap module at cylinder 0 track 0. At IPL, this bootstrap is loaded into storage at real address zero and control is passed to it. The bootstrap then reads the IPL control program IEAIPL00 (also known as IPL text) and passes control to it. This in turn starts the more complex task of loading the operating system and executing it.

After the bootstrap is loaded and control is passed to IEAIPL00, IEAIPL00 prepares an environment suitable for starting the programs and modules that make up the operating system by performing the following steps:

1. It clears central storage to zeros before defining storage areas for the master scheduler.

2. It locates the SYS1.NUCLEUS data set on the SYSRES volume and loads a series of programs from it (known as IPL Resource Initialization Modules (IRIMs)).

3. These IRIMs begin creating the normal operating system environment of control blocks and subsystems.

Some of the more significant tasks performed by the IRIMs are as follows:

▶ Read the LOADPARM information entered on the hardware console at the time the IPL command was executed.

▶ Search the volume specified in the LOADPARM member for the IODF data set. IRIM first attempts to locate LOADxx in SYS0.IPLPARM. If this is unsuccessful, it will look for SYS1.IPLPARM, and so on, up to and including SYS9.IPLPARM. If at this point it still has not been located, the search continues in SYS1.PARMLIB. (If LOADxx cannot be located, the system loads a wait state.)

▶ If a LOADxx member is found, it is opened and information, including the nucleus suffix (unless overridden in LOADPARM), the master catalog name, and the suffix of the IEASYSxx member to be used, is read from it.

▶ Load the operating system's nucleus.

▶ Initialize virtual storage in the master scheduler address space for the System Queue Area (SQA), the Extended SQA (ESQA), the Local SQA (LSQA), and the Prefixed Save Area (PSA). At the end of the IPL sequence, the PSA replaces IEAIPL00 at real storage location zero, where it will then stay.

▶ Initialize real storage management, including the segment table for the master scheduler, segment table entries for common storage areas, and the page frame table.

The last of the IRIMs then loads the first part of the Nucleus Initialization Program (NIP), which invokes the Resource Initialization Modules (RIMs), one of the earliest of which starts communications with the NIP console defined in the IODF.

The system continues the initialization process, interpreting and acting on the system parameters that were specified. NIP carries out the following major initialization functions:

▶ Expands the SQA and the extended SQA by the amounts specified on the SQA system parameter.

▶ Creates the pageable link pack area (PLPA) and the extended PLPA for a cold start IPL, or resets tables to match an existing PLPA and extended PLPA for a quick start or a warm start IPL. For more information about quick starts and warm starts, see *z/OS MVS Initialization and Tuning Reference, SA22-7592.*

▶ Loads modules into the fixed link pack area (FLPA) or the extended FLPA. Note that NIP carries out this function only if the FIX system parameter is specified.

▶ Loads modules into the modified link pack area (MLPA) and the extended MLPA. Note that NIP carries out this function only if the MLPA system parameter is specified.

▶ Allocates virtual storage for the common service area (CSA) and the extended CSA. The amount of storage allocated depends on the values specified on the CSA system parameter at IPL.

▶ Page-protects the NUCMAP, PLPA and extended PLPA, MLPA and extended MLPA, FLPA and extended FLPA, and portions of the nucleus.

An installation can override page protection of the MLPA and FLPA by specifying NOPROT on the MLPA and FIX system parameters.

IEASYSnn, a member of PARMLIB, contains parameters and pointers that control the direction that the IPL takes (Example 16-6).

Example 16-6   Partial listing of IEASYS00 member

```
--------------------------------------------------------------------------
File  Edit  Edit_Settings  Menu  Utilities  Compilers  Test  Help
--------------------------------------------------------------------------
EDIT      SYS1.PARMLIB(IEASYS00) - 01.68             Columns 00001 00072
Command ===>                                            Scroll ===> CSR
****** *************************** Top of Data ****************************
000001 ALLOC=00,
000002 APG=07,
000003 CLOCK=00,
```

```
000004 CLPA,
000005 CMB=(UNITR,COMM,GRAPH,CHRDR),
000006 CMD=(&CMDLIST1.),
000007 CON=00,
000008 COUPLE=00,  WAS FK
000009 CSA=(2M,128M),
000010 DEVSUP=00,
000011 DIAG=00,
000012 DUMP=DASD,
000013 FIX=00,
000014 GRS=STAR,
000015 GRSCNF=ML,
000016 GRSRNL=02,
000017 IOS=00,
000018 LNKAUTH=LNKLST,
000019 LOGCLS=L,
000020 LOGLMT=999999,
000021 LOGREC=SYS1.&SYSNAME..LOGREC,
000022 LPA=(00,L),
000023 MAXUSER=1000,
000024 MSTRJCL=00,
000025 NSYSLX=250,
000026 OMVS=&OMVSPARM.,
----------------------------------------------------------------------------------------------
```

To see information about how the IPL of your system was performed, you can issue the D IPLINFO command (Example 16-7).

Example 16-7   Output of the D IPLINFO command

```
D IPLINFO
IEE254I  11.11.35 IPLINFO DISPLAY 906
 SYSTEM IPLED AT 10.53.04 ON 08/15/2005
 RELEASE z/OS 01.07.00    LICENSE = z/OS
 USED LOADS8 IN SYS0.IPLPARM ON C730
 ARCHLVL = 2   MTLSHARE = N
 IEASYM LIST = XX
 IEASYS LIST = (R3,65) (OP)
 IODF DEVICE C730
 IPL DEVICE 8603 VOLUME Z17RC1
```

System address space creation

In addition to initializing system areas, z/OS establishes system component address spaces. It establishes an address space for the master scheduler and other system address spaces for various subsystems and system components. Some of the component address spaces are *MASTER*, ALLOCAS, APPC, CATALOG, and so on.

Master scheduler initialization

Master scheduler initialization routines initialize system services, such as the system log and communications task, and start the master scheduler itself. They also start the creation of the system address space for the job entry subsystem (JES2 or JES3), and then start the job entry subsystem.

Subsystem initialization

Subsystem initialization is the process of readying a subsystem for use in the system. IEFSSNxx members of SYS1.PARMLIB contain the definitions for the primary subsystems, such as JES2 or JES3, and the secondary subsystems, such as NetView and DB2. For detailed information about the data contained in IEFSSNxx members for secondary systems, refer to the installation manual for the specific system.

During system initialization, the defined subsystems are initialized. You should define the primary subsystem (JES) first because other subsystems, such as DB2, require the services of the primary subsystem in their initialization routines. Problems can occur if subsystems that use the subsystem affinity service in their initialization routines are initialized before the primary subsystem. After the primary JES is initialized, the subsystems are initialized in the order in which the IEFSSNxx PARMLIB members are specified by the SSN parameter. For example, for SSN=(aa,bb), PARMLIB member IEFSSNaa would be processed before IEFSSNbb.

START/LOGON/MOUNT processing

After the system is initialized and the job entry subsystem is active, jobs can be submitted for processing. When a job is activated through START (for batch jobs), LOGON (for time-sharing jobs), or MOUNT, a new address space is allocated. Note that before LOGON, the operator must have started VTAM and TSO, which have their own address spaces.

Figure 16-7 shows some of the important system address spaces and VTAM, CICS, TSO, a TSO user, and a batch initiator. Each address space has 2 GB of virtual storage by default, whether the system is running in 31-bit or 64-bit mode.

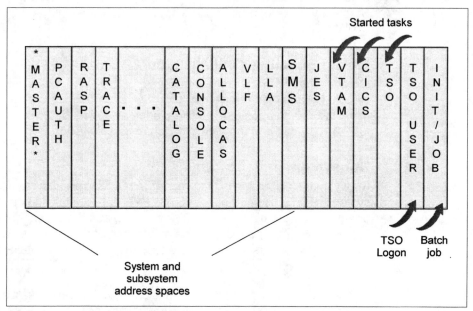

Figure 16-7 Virtual storage layout for multiple address spaces

Recall that each address space is mapped as shown in Figure 3-13 on page 123. The private areas are available only to that address space, but common areas are available to all.

During initialization of a z/OS system, the operator uses the system console or hardware management console, which is connected to the support element. From the system console, the operator initializes the system control program during the Nucleus Initialization Program (NIP) stage.

During the NIP stage, the system might prompt the operator to provide system parameters that control the operation of z/OS. The system also issues informational messages that inform the operator about the stages of the initialization process.

16.8.2 IPL types

Several types of IPL exist, and are described as follows:

► Cold start

An IPL that loads (or reloads) the PLPA and clears the VIO data set pages. The first IPL after system installation is always a cold start because the PLPA is initially loaded. Subsequent IPLs are cold starts when the PLPA is reloaded, either to alter its contents or to restore its contents if they were lost. This is usually done when changes have been made to the LPA (for example, when a new SYSRES containing maintenance is being loaded).

► Quick start

An IPL that does not reload the PLPA, but clears the VIO data set pages. (The system resets the page and segment tables to match the last-created PLPA.) This is usually done when there have been no changes to LPA, but VIO must be refreshed. This prevents the warm start of jobs that were using VIO data sets.

► Warm start

An IPL that does not reload the PLPA, and preserves journaled VIO data set pages. This IPL allows jobs that were running at the time of the IPL to restart with their journaled VIO data sets.

> **Note:** VIO is a method of using memory to store small temporary data sets for rapid access. However, unlike a RAM disk on a PC, these are actually backed up to disk and so can be used as a restart point. Obviously, there should not be too much data stored in this way, so the size is restricted.

Often, the preferred approach is to do a cold start IPL (specifying CLPA). The other options can be used, but extreme care must be taken to avoid unexpected change or backout of changes. A warm start could be used when you have long-running jobs which you want to restart after IPL, but an alternative approach is to break down those jobs into smaller pieces that pass real data sets rather than use VIO. Modern disk controllers with large cache memory have reduced the need for VIO data to be kept for long periods.

Also, do not confuse a cold start IPL (CLPA would normally be used rather than the term "cold start") with a JES cold start. Cold starting JES is something that is done extremely rarely, if ever, on a production system, and totally destroys the existing data in JES.

16.8.3 Shutting down the system

To shut down the system, each task must be closed in turn, in the correct order. On modern systems, this is the task of the automation package. Shutting down the system usually requires a single command. This command shuts down most tasks except for the Automation task itself. The Automation task is closed manually, and then any commands needed to remove the system from a sysplex or serialization ring are issued.

16.9 Summary

The role of the z/OS system programmer is to install, customize, and maintain the operating system.

The system programmer must understand the following areas (and more):

- ► System customization
- ► Workload management
- ► System performance
- ► I/O device configuration
- ► Operations

To maximize the performance of the task of retrieving modules, the z/OS operating system has been designed to maintain in memory those modules that are needed for fast response to the operating system, as well as for critical applications. Link pack area (LPA), linklist, and authorized libraries are the cornerstones of the fetching process.

We also discussed the system programmer's role in configuring consoles and setting up message-based automation.

We discussed the following topics regarding a system start, or IPL:

- ► IPL and the initialization process
- ► Types of IPLs: cold start, quick start, and warm start
- ► Reasons for performing an IPL

Table 16-1 lists the key terms used in this chapter.

Table 16-1   Key terms used in this chapter

HCD	IODF	IPL
linklist	LOADPARM	LPA
nucleus	PARMLIB	PROCLIB
PSA	SMP/E	SQA
SYSRES	system symbols	WTOR

16.10 Questions for review

To help test your understanding of the material in this chapter, answer the following questions:

1. In Example 16-2 on page 540, assume that the class assigned to a certain job has a default PROCLIB concatenation of PROC00. The job needs a procedure that resides in SYS1.OTHERPRO. What can be done to accomplish this task? Which procedure libraries would be searched if nothing were done?

2. Why are console operations often automated?

3. Why does a message and command structure lend itself to automation?

4. Why are system reloads necessary?

5. What are the three types of reloads and how do they differ?

16.11 Topics for further discussion

Here are topics for further discussion:

1. One reason the mainframe is considered secure is because it does not permit "plug-in" devices; only devices defined by the system programmer can be connected and used. In your opinion, is this correct?

2. Compare the search path in 16.3.10, "Search order for programs" on page 541 to the search paths used in other operating systems.

3. Discuss the following statement in relation to z/OS and other operating systems you are familiar with: The main goal of a system programmer is to avoid system reloads.

16.12 Exercises

Here are some exercises you can perform:

1. Discover which IEASYSxx members were used in the current IPL. Did the operator specify the suffix of an alternate IEASYSxx?

2. Did the operator specify any parameter in response to the SPECIFY SYSTEM PARAMETERS message? If the answer is Y, find the related PARMLIB members for that parameter and obtain the parameter value that would be active if that operator response hadn't occurred.

3. Perform the following tasks:

   a. On your system, discover the IPL device address and the IPL Volume. Go to SDSF, enter ULOG, and then /D IPLINFO.

   b. What is the IODF device address?

   c. What is the LOADxx member that was used for IPL? What is the data set that contains this LOADxx member?

   d. Browse this member; what is the name of the system catalog used by the system?

   e. What is the name of the IODF data set currently used? Enter /D IOS,CONFIG.

   f. The system parameters can come from a number of PARMLIB data sets. Enter /D PARMLIB. What are the PARMLIB data sets used by your system?

17

Using System Modification Program/Extended

Objective: As a z/OS system programmer, it is your responsibility to ensure that all software products and their modifications are properly installed on the system. You have to ensure that all products are installed at the proper level so that the elements of the system can work together. At first, this task might not sound too difficult, but as the complexity of the software configuration increases, so does the task of monitoring all the elements of the system.

System Modification Program/Extended (SMP/E) is the primary means of installing and updating the software in a z/OS system. SMP/E consolidates installation data, allows more flexibility in selecting changes to be installed, provides a dialog interface, and supports dynamic allocation of data sets.

After completing this chapter, you will be able to explain:

► What SMP/E is.

► What system modifications are.

► The data sets used by SMP/E.

► How SMP/E can help you install and maintain products, and monitor changes to products.

565

Refer to Table 17-1 on page 594 for a list of key terms used in this chapter.

17.1 What is SMP/E

SMP/E is the z/OS tool for managing the installation of software products on a z/OS system and for tracking modifications to those products. SMP/E controls these changes at the component level by:

► Selecting the proper levels of code to be installed from a large number of potential changes.

► Calling system utility programs to install the changes.

► Keeping records of the installed changes by providing a facility to enable you to inquire about the status of your software and to reverse changes if necessary.

All code and its modifications are located in the SMP/E database called the *consolidated software inventory* (CSI), which is composed of one or more virtual storage access method (VSAM) data sets.

SMP/E can be run either using batch jobs or using dialogs under Interactive System Productivity Facility/Program Development Facility (ISPF/PDF). With SMP/E dialogs, you can interactively query the SMP/E database and create and submit jobs to process SMP/E commands. We discuss the basic commands for working with SMP/E in 17.11, "Working with SMP/E" on page 581.

A standard reference for information about SMP/E is the *SMP/E User's Guide*, SA22-7773. You can find this and related publications at the z/OS Internet Library website:

http://www-03.ibm.com/systems/z/os/zos/bkserv/

17.2 The SMP/E view of the system

A z/OS system might appear to be one big block of code that drives the CPU. Actually, z/OS is a complex system comprising many different smaller blocks of code. Each of those smaller blocks of code perform a specific function within the system (Figure 17-1).

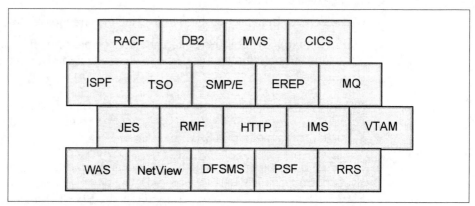

Figure 17-1   SMP/E view of the system

For example, some of the functions that can appear in a z/OS system include:

- Base Control Program (BCP)
- CICS
- DFSMS
- HTTP Server
- ISPF
- JES2 or JES3
- Open Systems Adapter/Support Facility (OSA/SF)
- Resource Measurement Facility (RMF)
- System Display and Search Facility (SDSF)
- SMP/E
- Time Sharing Option/Extensions (TSO/E)
- WebSphere MQ
- z/OS UNIX System Services (z/OS UNIX)

Each system function is composed of one or more load modules. In a z/OS environment, a load module represents the basic unit of machine-readable, executable code. Load modules are created by combining one or more object modules and processing them with a link-edit utility. The link-editing of modules is a process that resolves external references and addresses. The functions on your system, therefore, are one or more object modules that have been combined and link-edited.

To see where the object module comes from, look at the example in Figure 17-2.

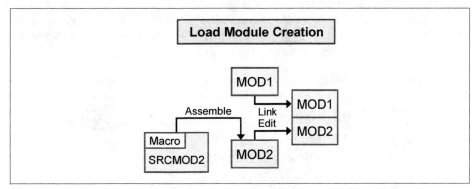

Figure 17-2   Load module creation

Most of the time, object modules are part of a product. In this example, the object module, MOD1 is part of the product. Other times, you might need to assemble the source code sent to you by product packagers to create the object module. You can modify the source code and then assemble it to produce an object module. In the example, SRCMOD2 is source code that you assemble to create object module MOD2. When assembled, you link-edit object module MOD2 with object module MOD1 to form the load module LMOD1.

In addition to object modules and source code, most products distribute many other parts, such as macros, help-panels, CLISTs, and other z/OS library members. These modules, macros, and other types of data and code are the basic building blocks of your system. All of these building blocks are called *elements*.

Elements are associated with, and depend upon, other products or services that may be installed on the same z/OS system. They describe the relationship the software has with other products or services that may be installed on the same z/OS system.

17.3 Changing the elements of the system

Over time, you need to change the software on your z/OS system. These changes may be necessary to improve the usability or reliability of a product. You might want to add some new functions to your system, upgrade some of the elements of your system, or modify some elements for a variety of reasons. Software, whether it is a product or service, consists of elements, such as macros, modules, source, and other types of data (such as CLISTs or sample procedures).

17.3.1 What is a SYSMOD

SYSMOD:
The input data to SMP/E that defines the introduction, replacement, or updating of elements in z/OS.

SMP/E can install a large variety of system updates, provided they are packaged as a system modification (SYSMOD). A SYSMOD is the actual package of elements and control information that SMP/E needs to install and track system modifications.

SYSMODs are composed of a combination of elements and control information. They are composed of two parts, as follows:

► Modification control statements (MCSs), designated by ++ as the first two characters, that tell SMP/E:

  – What elements are being updated or replaced

  – How the SYSMOD relates to product software and other SYSMODs

  – Other specific installation information

► Modification text, which is the object modules, macros, and other elements supplied by the SYSMOD

17.3.2 Types of SYSMODS

There are four different categories of SYSMODs, each supporting a task you might want to perform:

FUNCTION
This type of SYSMOD introduces a new product, a new version or release of a product, or updated functions for an existing product into the system.

PTF
A *program temporary fix* (PTF) is an IBM-supplied correction for a reported problem. They are meant to be installed in all environments. PTFs may be used as preventive service to avoid certain known problems that may have not yet appeared on your system, or they may be used as corrective service to fix problems you have already encountered. The installation of a PTF must always be preceded by that of a function SYSMOD, and often other PTFs as well.

APAR
An *authorized program analysis report* (APAR) is a temporary fix designed to correct or bypass a problem for the first reporter of the problem. An APAR might not be applicable to your environment. The installation of an APAR must always be preceded by that of a function SYSMOD, and sometimes of a particular PTF. An APAR is designed to be installed on a particular preventive-service level of an element.

USERMOD　　　　　This type of SYSMOD is created by you, either to change IBM code or to add independent functions to the system. The installation of a USERMOD must always be preceded by that of a function SYSMOD, sometimes certain PTFs, APAR fixes, or other USERMODs.

SMP/E keeps track of the functional and service levels of each element and uses this SYSMOD hierarchy to determine such things as which functional and service levels of an element should be installed and the correct order for installing updates for elements.

17.4 Introducing an element into the system

One way you can modify your system is to introduce new elements into that system. To accomplish this task using SMP/E, you can install a function SYSMOD. The function SYSMOD introduces a new product, a new version or release of a product, or updated functions for an existing product into the system. All other types of SYSMODs are dependent upon the function SYSMOD, because they are all modifications of the elements originally introduced by the function SYSMOD.

When we refer to installing a function SYSMOD, we are referring to the placement of all the product's elements in the system data sets, or libraries. Examples of these libraries are SYS1.LPALIB, SYS1.MIGLIB, and SYS1.SVCLIB.

Figure 17-3 shows the process of creating executable code in the production system libraries.

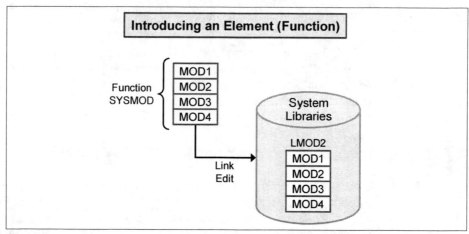

Figure 17-3   Introducing an element

In Figure 17-3, the installation of a function SYSMOD link-edits object modules MOD1, MOD2, MOD3, and MOD4 to create load module LMOD2. The executable code created in load module LMOD2 is installed in the system libraries through the installation of the function SYSMOD.

There are two types of function SYSMODs:

▶ A *base* function SYSMOD adds or replaces an entire system function. Examples of base functions are SMP/E and JES2.

▶ A *dependent* function SYSMOD provides an addition to an existing system function. It is called dependent because its installation depends upon a base function already being installed. Examples of dependent functions are the language features for SMP/E.

Both base function SYSMODs and dependent function SYSMODs are used to introduce new elements into the system. Example 17-1 shows an example of a simple function SYSMOD that introduces four elements.

Example 17-1   Example of a simple function SYSMOD

```
++FUNCTION(FUN0001)/* SYSMOD type and identifier.*/.
++VER(Z038)/* For an OS/390 system*/.
++MOD(MOD1)RELFILE(1)/* Introduce this module*/.
   DISTLIB(AOSFB)/* in this distribution library*/.
++MOD(MOD2)RELFILE(1)/* Introduce this module/*
   DISTLIB(AOSFB)/* in this distribution library.*/.
```

```
++MOD(MOD3)RELFILE(1)/* Introduce this module*/.
   DISTLIB(AOSFB)/* in this distribution library.*/.
++MOD(MOD4)RELFILE(1)/* Introduce this module*/.
   DISTLIB(AOSFB)/* in this distribution library.*/.
```

17.5 Preventing or fixing problems with an element

When a problem with a software element is discovered, IBM supplies its customers with a tested fix for that problem. This fix comes in the form of a program temporary fix (PTF). Although you may not have experienced the problem the PTF is intended to prevent, it is wise to install the PTF on your system. The PTF SYSMOD is used to install the PTF, thereby preventing the occurrence of that problem on your system.

Usually, PTFs are designed to replace or update one or more complete elements of a system function.

Let us look at Figure 17-4.

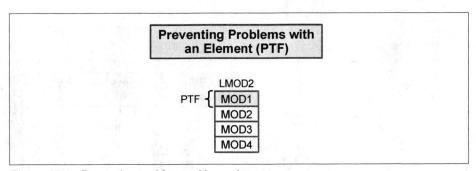

Figure 17-4   Preventing problems with an element

In Figure 17-4, we see a previously installed load module, LMOD2. If we want to replace the element MOD1, we should install a PTF SYSMOD that contains the module MOD1. That PTF SYSMOD replaces the element in error with the corrected element. As part of the installation of the PTF SYSMOD, SMP/E relinks LMOD2 to include the new and corrected version of MOD1.

Example 17-2 shows an example of a simple PTF SYSMOD.

Example 17-2   Example of a simple PTF SYSMOD

```
++PTF(PTF0001)/* SYSMOD type and identifier.*/.
++VER(Z038)FMID(FUN0001)/* Apply to this product.*/.
++MOD(MOD1)/* Replace this module*/.
```

```
        DISTLIB(AOSFB)/* in this distribution library*/.
    ...
    ... object code for module
    ...
```

PTF SYSMODs are always dependent upon the installation of a function
SYSMOD. In some cases, some PTF SYSMODs may also be dependent upon
the installation of other PTF SYSMODs. These dependencies are called
prerequisites. We discuss a typical PTF prerequisite in 17.8, "Keeping track of the
elements of the system" on page 577.

17.6 Fixing problems with an element

APAR:
A temporary
correction of a
defect in an
IBM system
control
program or
licensed
program that
affects a
specific user.

You might sometimes find it is necessary to correct a serious problem that
occurs on your system before a PTF is ready for distribution. In this situation,
IBM supplies you with an authorized program analysis report (APAR). An APAR
is a fix designed to quickly correct a specific area of an element or replace an
element in error. You install an APAR SYSMOD to implement a fix, thereby
updating the incorrect element.

In Figure 17-5, the shaded section shows an area of MOD2 containing an error.

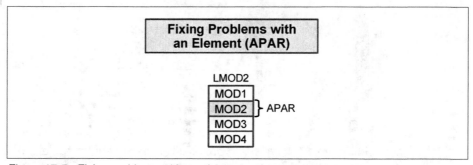

Figure 17-5   Fixing problems with an element

The processing of the APAR SYSMOD provides a modification for object module
MOD2. During the installation of the APAR SYSMOD, MOD2 is updated (and
corrected) in load module LMOD2.

Example 17-3 shows an example of a simple APAR SYSMOD.

Example 17-3   Example of a simple APAR SYSMOD

```
++APAR(APAR001)/* SYSMOD type and identifier.*/.
++VER(Z038)FMID(FUN0001)/* Apply to this product.*/.
```

```
    PRE(UZ00004)/* at this service level.*/.
++ZAP(MOD2)/* Update this module/*
    DISTLIB(AOSFB)/* in this distribution library.*/.
...
... zap control statements
...
```

The APAR SYSMOD always has the installation of a function SYSMOD as a
prerequisite, and can also be dependent upon the installation of other PTF or
APAR SYSMODs.

17.7 Customizing an element: USERMOD SYSMOD

If you need a product to perform differently from the way it was designed, you
might want to customize that element of your system. IBM provides you with
certain modules that allow you to tailor IBM code to meet your specific needs.
After making the desired changes, you add these modules to your system by
installing a USERMOD SYSMOD. This SYSMOD can be used to replace or
update an element, or to introduce a totally new user-written element into the
system. In either case, the USERMOD SYSMOD is built by you either to change
IBM code or to add your own code to the system.

In Figure 17-6, MOD3 has been updated through the installation of a USERMOD
SYSMOD.

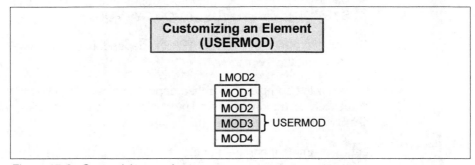

Figure 17-6   Customizing an element

Example 17-4 shows an example of a simple USERMOD SYSMOD.

Example 17-4   Example of a simple USERMOD SYSMOD

```
++USERMOD(USRMOD1)/* SYSMOD type and identifier.*/.
++VER(Z038)FMID(FUN0001)/* Apply to this product*/.
   PRE(UZ00004)/* at this service level.*/.
++SRCUPD(JESMOD3)/* Update this source module/*
   DISTLIB(AOSFB)/* in this distribution library.*/.
...
... update control statements
...
```

The prerequisites for USERMOD SYSMODs are the installation of a function SYSMOD, and possibly the installation of other PTF, APAR, or USERMOD SYSMODs.

17.7.1 SYSMOD prerequisites and corequisites

As you have learned, PTF, APAR, and USERMOD SYSMODs all have the function SYSMOD as a prerequisite. In addition to their dependencies on the function SYSMOD:

▶ PTF SYSMODs might be dependent upon other PTF SYSMODs.

▶ APAR SYSMODs might be dependent upon PTF SYSMODs and other APAR SYSMODs.

▶ USERMOD SYSMODs might be dependent upon PTF SYSMODs, APAR SYSMODs, and other USERMOD SYSMODs.

Sometimes a PTF or even an APAR is dependent upon other PTF SYSMODs that are called *corequisites*.

Consider the complexity of these dependencies. When you multiply that complexity by hundreds of load modules in dozens of libraries, the need for a tool like SMP/E becomes apparent.

Let us examine the impact of these dependencies on the maintenance of software in a z/OS environment.

17.8 Keeping track of the elements of the system

The importance of keeping track of system elements and their modifications becomes readily apparent when we examine the z/OS maintenance process. Often, a PTF contains multiple element replacements.

In the example shown in Figure 17-7, PTF1 contains replacements for two modules, MOD1 and MOD2. Although load module LMOD2 contains four modules, only two of those modules are being replaced.

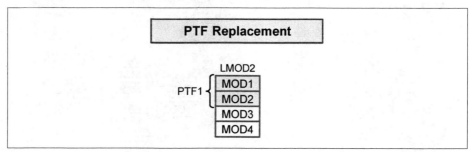

Figure 17-7   PTF replacement

But what happens if a second PTF replaces some of the code in a module that was replaced by PTF1? Let us look at Figure 17-8.

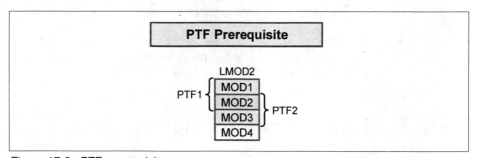

Figure 17-8   PTF prerequisite

In this example, PTF2 contains replacements for MOD2 and MOD3. For MOD1, MOD2, and MOD3 to interface successfully, PTF1 must be installed before PTF2, because MOD3 supplied in PTF2 may depend on the PTF1 version of MOD1 to be present. It is this dependency that constitutes a prerequisite. SYSMOD prerequisites are identified in the modification control statements (MCS) part of the SYSMOD package we discussed in 17.3, "Changing the elements of the system" on page 569.

In addition to tracking prerequisites, there is another important reason to track system elements. The same module is often part of many different load modules. Let us take a look at the example in Figure 17-9.

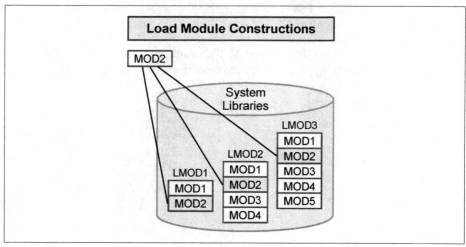

Figure 17-9   Load module constructions

In Figure 17-9, the same MOD2 module is present in LMOD1, LMOD2, and LMOD3. When a PTF is introduced that replaces the element MOD2, that module must be replaced in all the load modules in which it exists. Therefore, it is imperative that we keep track of all load modules and the modules they contain.

You can now appreciate how complicated the tracking of system elements and their modification levels can become. Let us take a brief look at how we implement the tracking capabilities of SMP/E.

17.9 Tracking and controlling requisites

To track and control elements successfully, all elements and their modifications and updates must be clearly identified to SMP/E. SMP/E relies on modification identifiers to accomplish this task. There are three modification identifiers associated with each element:

► *Function Modification Identifiers* (FMIDs) identify the function SYSMOD that introduces the element into the system.

► *Replacement Modification Identifiers* (RMIDs) identify the last SYSMOD (in most cases a PTF SYSMOD) to replace an element.

► *Update Modification Identifiers* (UMIDs) identify the SYSMOD that updates the element since it was last replaced.

SMP/E uses these modification identifiers to track all SYSMODs installed on your system, which ensures that they are installed in the proper sequence. Now that we realize the need for element tracking and know the types of things SMP/E tracks, let us look at how SMP/E performs its tracking function.

17.10 How does SMP/E work

Let us review our discussion about how functions are installed into the system. We begin with elements, such as modules, macros, and source code. These elements are then processed by utilities, such as an assembler or link-editor, to create load modules. The load modules contain the machine-readable, executable code.

Your production system in a z/OS environment consists of the z/OS operating system and all the code needed to do your everyday work. Where are all these items kept, and how are they organized? Let us discuss that in the following sections.

17.10.1 The distribution and target libraries

To properly perform its processing, SMP/E must maintain a great deal of information about the structure, content, and modification status of the software it manages. Think of all the information SMP/E has to maintain as though it were all the information contained in the public library.

In a public library, you see bookshelves filled with books and a card catalog with drawers containing a card for each book in the library. These cards contain information, such as the title, author, publishing dates, type of book, and a pointer to the actual book on the shelf.

In the SMP/E environment, there are two distinct types of "bookshelves." They are referred to as the *distribution libraries* and the *target libraries*. In much the same way the bookshelves in the public library hold the library books, the distribution and target libraries hold the elements of the system.

Distribution libraries contain all the elements, such as modules and macros, that are used as input for running your system. One important use of the distribution libraries is for backup. Should a serious error occur with an element on the production system, the element can be replaced by a stable level found in the distribution libraries.

Target libraries contain the executable code that is needed to run the system.

17.10.2 The consolidated software inventory

As you think of the analogy of the public library, you can see that there is one important piece of that picture that we have not yet considered. In the public library, there is a card catalog to help you find the book or piece of information for which you are looking. SMP/E provides the same type of tracking mechanism in the form of the *consolidated software inventory* (CSI).

CSI:
The SMP/E data set that contains information about the structure of a user's system.

The CSI data sets contain all the information SMP/E needs to track the distribution and target libraries. As the card catalog contains a card for each book in the library, the CSI contains an entry for each element in its libraries. The CSI entries contain the element name, type, history, how the element was introduced into the system, and a pointer to the element in the distribution and target libraries. The CSI does not contain the element itself, but rather a description of the element it represents.

Let us see exactly how these entries are arranged in the CSI.

The SMP/E zones

The cards in the public library card catalog are arranged alphabetically by the author's last name, and by the topic and title of the book. In the CSI, entries for the elements in the distribution and target libraries are grouped according to their installation status, that is, entries representing elements found in the distribution libraries are contained in the distribution zone. Entries representing elements found in the target libraries are contained in the target zone. Both of these zones serve the same purpose as the drawers of the public library card catalog.

In addition to the distribution and target zones, the SMP/E CSI also contains a global zone. Figure 17-10 shows the relationship between SMPE zones and libraries.

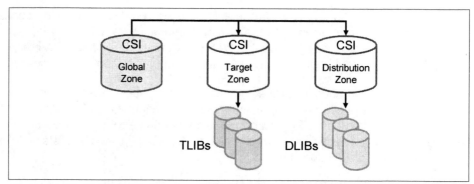

Figure 17-10   Relationship between SMP/E zones and libraries

The global zone contains:

▶ Entries needed to identify and describe each target and distribution zone to SMP/E

▶ Information about SMP/E processing options

▶ Status information for all SYSMODs SMP/E has begun to process

▶ Exception data for SYSMODs requiring special handling or that are in error

In SMP/E, when we speak of exception data, we are usually referring to HOLDDATA. HOLDDATA is often supplied for a product to indicate a specified SYSMOD should be held from installation. Reasons for holding a SYSMOD can be:

▶ A PTF is in error and should not be installed until the error is corrected (ERROR HOLD).

▶ Certain system actions may be required before SYSMOD installation (SYSTEM HOLD).

▶ The user may want to perform some actions before installing the SYSMOD (USER HOLD).

Now you can see how all the elements of the system fit together, and how they can be installed, modified, and tracked using SMP/E.

17.11 Working with SMP/E

Now that you are familiar with SMP/E and what it can do, you are probably wondering what you need to know to get started using SMP/E. The SMP/E process is performed by three simple basic commands: RECEIVE, APPLY, and ACCCEPT. Let us take a look at these commands.

17.11.1 Using the RECEIVE command

The RECEIVE command allows you to take a SYSMOD that is outside of SMP/E and stage it into the SMP/E library domain, which begins to construct the CSI entries that describe them. This allows them to be queried for input into later processes. More recently, the source can be downloaded from a website, although usually it comes from a tape or even third-party vendor media.

This process's role accomplishes several tasks (Figure 17-11):

- ▶ Constructing entries in the Global Zone for describing the SYSMOD.
- ▶ Ensuring the SYSMOD is valid, such as the syntax for modification control statements (MCS) associated to the products installed in the CSI.
- ▶ Installing the SYSMOD into the libraries. An example is the PTF temporary store library.
- ▶ Assessing the HOLDDATA to ensure errors are not introduced.

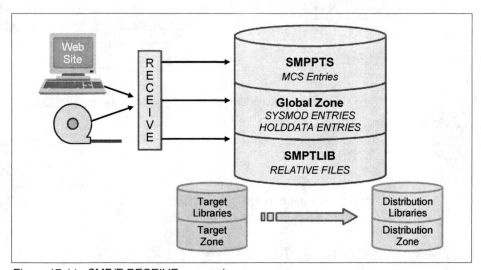

Figure 17-11   SMP/E RECEIVE processing

During the RECEIVE processing, the MCS for each SYSMOD is copied to an SMP/E temporary storage area called the SMPPTS data set containing the inline element replacement or update for that SYSMOD. There are also RELFILEs that package the elements in relative files that are separate from MCSs, which are mostly used by function SYSMODs. Relative files are stored in another temporary storage area called SMPTLIB data sets.

SMP/E updates the global zone with information about the SYSMODs that it has received.

In the course of maintaining the system, you need to install service and process the related HOLDDATA. For example, assume that IBM has supplied you with a service tape (such as a CBPDO or ESO tape) and you want to install it on the system. The first step is to receive the SYSMODs and HOLDDATA that are contained on the tape by entering these commands:

```
SET BDY(GLOBAL).
RECEIVE.
```

Doing so causes SMP/E to receive all the SYSMODs and HOLDDATA on the tape.

Examples of RECEIVE commands

To receive only HOLDDATA that might require special handling or that is in error, use this command:

```
SET BDY(GLOBAL).
RECEIVE HOLDDATA.
```

To receive only SYSMODs for installation into the global zone, use this command:

```
SET BDY(GLOBAL).
RECEIVE SYSMODS.
```

To receive all SYSMODs, including HOLDDATA, for a specific product (for example, WebSphere Application Server), use a command like the following:

```
SET BDY(GLOBAL).
RECEIVE FORFMID(H28W500).
```

17.11.2 Using the APPLY command

The APPLY command specifies which of the received SYSMODs are to be selected for installation in the target libraries (TLIBs). SMP/E also ensures that all other required SYSMODs (prerequisites) have been installed or are being installed concurrently and in the proper sequence. The source of the elements is the SMPTLIB data sets, the SMPPTS data set, or indirect libraries, depending on how it was packaged. This phase of the SMP/E process entails the following:

► Executing the appropriate utility to install the SYSMOD into the target library, depending on the type of input text supplied and target module being changed.

► Ensuring that the relationship of the new SYSMOD with other SYSMODs in the target zone is correct.

► The CSI is modified displaying the updated modules.

The APPLY command updates the system libraries and should be carefully used on a live production system. We recommend that you initially use a copy of the production target libraries and zones.

The target zone reflects the content of the target libraries. Therefore, after the utility is completed and the zone updated, it accurately reflects the status of those libraries.

The APPLY processing (Figure 17-12) is where the target zone is accurately updated:

▶ All SYSMOD entries in the Global Zone are updated to reflect that the SYSMOD has been applied to the target zone.

▶ The target zone accurately reflects each SYSMOD entry applied. Element entries (such as MOD and LMOD) are also created in the target zone.

▶ BACKUP entries are created in the SMPSCDS data set so the SYSMOD can be restored, if at all necessary.

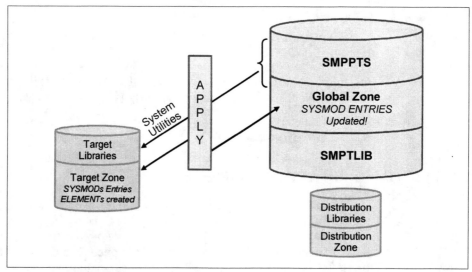

Figure 17-12   SMP/E APPLY processing

Similar to the RECEIVE process, the APPLY command has many different operands for flexibility to select SYSMODs you would like to see for installation in the target libraries, and provides an assortment of output. The directives used instruct SMP/E what you want installed.

To install only PTF SYSMODs, enter a command such as the following one:

```
SET BDY(ZOSTGT1).
APPLY PTFS.
```

To select PTF SYSMODs, you name them in the directives, for example:

```
SET BDY(ZOSTGT1).
APPLY SELECT(UZ00001, UZ00002).
```

Sometimes, you might want to install only corrective fixes (APARs) or user modifications (USERMODs) into the target library, for example:

```
SET BDY(ZOSTGT1).
APPLY APARS
USERMODS.
```

At other times, you might want to update a selected product from a distribution tape:

```
SET BDY(ZOSTGT1).
APPLY PTFS
FORFMID(H28W500).
```

or

```
SET BDY (ZOSTGT1).
APPLY FORFMID(H28W500).
```

In the previous two examples, SMP/E applies all applicable PTFs for the FMID. Unless you specify otherwise, PTFs are the default SYSMOD type.

Using APPLY CHECK

There might be times when you want to see which SYSMODs are included before you actually install them. You can perform this task by including the CHECK operand with commands such as the following ones:

```
SET BDY(MVSTGT1).
APPLY PTFS
APARS
FORFMID(HOP1)
GROUPEXTEND CHECK.
```

When these commands complete, you can check the SYSMOD status report to see which SYSMODs would have been installed if you had not specified the CHECK operand. If you are satisfied with the results of this trial run, you can enter the commands again, without the CHECK operand, to actually install the SYSMODs.

17.11.3 Using the ACCEPT command

When a SYSMOD is installed into its target library, and you have tested it, you then accept the change through the ACCEPT command. This step takes the selected SYSMODs and installs them into the associated distribution libraries.

On the ACCEPT command, you specify operands to indicate which of the received SYSMODs are to be selected for installation. During this phase, SMP/E also ensures that the correct functional level of each element is selected.

The ACCEPT command performs the following tasks (Figure 17-13):

▶ Updates CSI entries with the targeted elements in the distribution zone.

▶ Rebuilds or creates the targeted elements in the distribution libraries using the content of the SYSMOD as input.

▶ Verifies the target zone CSI entries for the affected modules and SYSMODs, ensuring that they are consistent with the library content.

▶ Performs housekeeping of obsolete or expired elements. ACCEPT processing deletes the global zone CSI entries, PTS members, and SMPTLIBs for those SYSMODs affected. For example, ACCEPT deletes the global zone SYSMOD entries and MCS statements in the SMPPTS data set for those SYSMODs that have been accepted into the distribution zone.

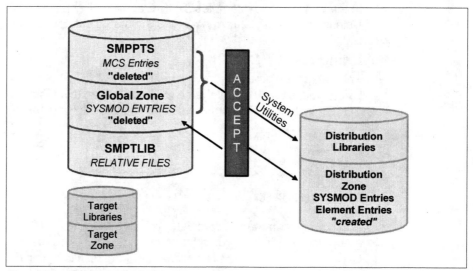

Figure 17-13   SMP/E ACCEPT processing

As a further option, you can skip having SMP/E clean up the global zone cleanup. If so, SMP/E saves this information.

There is a "stop" ACCEPT processing that SMP/E provides so you can ensure that all prerequisites are satisfied before the installation of the SYSMODs. This is a check for you to see what will happen (assist you in detecting problems) without actually modifying the distribution libraries.

> **Important:** Should the SYSMOD be in error, do not ACCEPT it. Use the RESTORE process, which takes the modules updated by the selected SYSMOD and rebuilds the copies in the target libraries using the specific modules in the distribution libraries as input. Also, RESTORE updates the target zone CSI entries to reflect the removal of the SYSMOD. When ACCEPT processing is completed, there is *no way* it can be backed out, therefore the changes are permanent.

After applying the SYSMODs into the target zone, you can then tell SMP/E to install only the eligible PTF SYSMODs into the distribution zone:

```
SET BDY(ZOSDLB1).
ACCEPT PTFS.
```

To install PTF SYSMODS, select the particular ones:

```
SET BDY(ZOSDLB1).
ACCEPT SELECT(UZ00001,UZ00002).
```

There are situations where you may want to update a particular product with all SYSMODs:

```
SET BDY(ZOSDLB1).
ACCEPT PTFS
FORFMID(H28W500).
```

or

```
SET BDY(ZOSDLB1).
ACCEPT FORFMID(H28W500).
```

> **Note:** In the two cases above, SMP/E accepts all applicable PTFs for the product whose FMID is H28W500 (located in the distribution zone ZOSDLB1).

ACCEPTING prerequisite SYSMODs

When installing a SYSMOD, you may not know whether it has prerequisites (sometimes, an ERROR SYSMOD is held). In these situations, you can direct SMP/E to check whether an equivalent (or superseding) SYSMOD is available by specifying the GROUPEXTEND operand:

```
SET BDY(ZOSDLB1).
ACCEPT PTFS
FORFMID(H28W500)
GROUPEXTEND.
```

> **Note:** If SMP/E cannot find a required SYSMOD, it looks for and uses a SYSMOD that supersedes the required one.

A good way to see which SYSMODs are included before you actually install them is by using the CHECK operand:

```
SET BDY(ZOSTGT1).
ACCEPT PTFS
FORMFMID(H28W500)
GROUPEXTEND
CHECK.
```

ACCEPT reporting

When this last phase is completed, the following reports will assist you in assessing the results:

► SYSMOD Status Report: Provides a summary of the processing that took place for each SYSMOD, based on the operands you specified on the ACCEPT command.

► Element Summary Report: Provides a detailed look at each element affected by the ACCEPT processing and in which libraries they reside.

► Causer SYSMOD Summary Report: Provides a list of SYSMODs that caused other SYSMODs to fail and describes the errors that must be fixed to be successfully processed.

► File Allocation Report: Provides a list of the data sets used for the ACCEPT processing and supplies information about these data sets.

17.11.4 Other SMP/E facilities

All the information located in the global zone (Figure 17-14), combined with the information found in the target and distribution zones, make up the data that SMP/E requires to install and track the system's software, which is often a great deal of data. You can display this information by using the following SMP/E facilities:

► The LIST command creates a hardcopy that lists information about the system.

► The REPORT command checks, compares, and generates a hardcopy of the information about zone content.

► QUERY dialogs through ISPF.

► The SMP/E CSI API, which can be used to write application programs to query the content of the system.

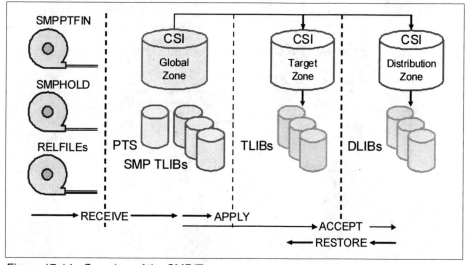

Figure 17-14   Overview of the SMP/E process

Example 17-5 shows the JCL used to create CSI data sets to hold the SMP zones.

Example 17-5   Example of a CSI VSAM cluster definition

```
//DEFINE JOB'accounting info',MSGLEVEL=(1,1)
//STEP01 EXECPGM=IDCAMS
//CSIVOL DD UNIT=3380,VOL=SER=volid1,DISP-SHR
//SYSPRINTDDSYSOUT=A
//SYSIN  DD *
```

```
      DEFINE CLUSTER(-
              NAME(SMPE.SMPCSI.CSI)-
              FREESPACE(10 5)-
              KEYS(24 0)-
              RECORDSIZE(24 143)-
              SHAREOPTIONS(2 3)-
      VOLUMES(volid1)-
          )              -
        DATA(            -
              NAME(SMPE.SMPCSI.CSI.DATA)-
              CONTROLINTERVALSIZE(4096)-
              CYLINDERS(250 20)-
        INDEX(           -
              NAME(SMPE.SMPCSI.CSI.INDEX)-
              CYLINDERS(5 3)-
          )
      CATALOG(user.catalog)
    /*
```

Example 17-6 shows the JCL used to run an SMP job in batch mode.

Example 17-6   SMP batch job example

```
//SMPJOB JOB'accounting info',MSGLEVEL=(1,1)
//SMPSTEPEXEC SMPPROC
//SMPPTFINDD...points to the file or data set that contains
//*           the SYSMODs to be received
//SMPHOLDDD ...points to the file or data set that contains
//*           the HOLDDATA to be received
//SMPTLIBDD UNIT=3380,VOL=SER=TLIB01
//SMPCNTLDD *
SET BDY(GLOBAL)/* Set to global zone */.
RECEIVESYSMOD/* receive SYSMODS and*/
   HOLDDATA/* HOLDDATA*/
   SOURCEID(MYPTFS)/* Assign a source ID*/
      /* */.
LISTMCS/* List the cover letters*/
   SOURCEID(MYPTFS)/* for the SYSMODs*/
      /* */.
SETBDY(TARGET1)/* Set to target zone*/.
APPLYSOURCEID(MYPTFS)/* Apply the SYSMODS*/
      /* */.
LISTLOG/* List the target zone log*/.
/*
```

17.12 Data sets used by SMP/E

Let us review our discussion about how SMP/E stores information about the system.

When SMP/E processes SYSMODs, it installs the elements in the appropriate libraries and updates its own records of the processing it has done. SMP/E installs program elements into two types of libraries:

▶ Target libraries contain the executable code needed to run your system (for example, the libraries from which you run your production system or your test system).

▶ Distribution libraries (DLIBs) contain the master copy of each element for a system. They are used as input to the SMP/E GENERATE command or the system generation process to build target libraries for a new system. They are also used by SMP/E for backup when elements in the target libraries have to be replaced or updated.

To install elements in these libraries, SMP/E uses a database made up of several types of data sets:

▶ SMPCSI (CSI) data sets are VSAM data sets used to control the installation process and record the results of processing. A CSI can be divided into multiple partitions through the VSAM key structure. Each partition is referred to as a *zone*.

There are three types of zones:

− A single *global zone* is used to record information about SYSMODs that have been received into the SMPPTS data set. The global zone also contains information enabling SMP/E to access the other two types of zones, information about system utilities that SMP/E calls to install elements from SYSMODs, and information allowing you to tailor SMP/E processing.

− One or more *target zones* are used to record information about the status and structure of the operating system (or target) libraries. Each target zone also points to the related distribution zone, which can be used during APPLY, RESTORE, and LINK processing when SMP/E is processing a SYSMOD and needs to check the level of the elements in the distribution libraries.

− One or more *distribution zones* are used to record information about the status and structure of the distribution libraries (DLIBs). Each DLIB zone also points to the related target zone, which is used when SMP/E is accepting a SYSMOD and needs to check if the SYSMOD has already been applied.

There can be more than one zone in an SMPCSI data set (in fact, there can be up to 32766 zones per data set). For example, an SMPCSI data set can contain a global zone, several target zones, and several distribution zones. The zones can also be in separate SMPCSI data sets. One SMPCSI data set can contain just the global zone, a second SMPCSI data set the target zones, and a third SMPCSI data set the distribution zones.

► An SMPPTS (PTS) data set is a data set for temporary storage of SYSMODs waiting to be installed. The PTS is used strictly as a storage data set for SYSMODs. The RECEIVE command stores SYSMODs directly on the PTS without any modifications of SMP/E information. The PTS is related to the global zone in that both data sets contain information about the received SYSMODs. Only one PTS can be used for a given global zone. Therefore, you can look at the global zone and the PTS as a pair of data sets that must be processed (for example, deleted, saved, or modified) concurrently.

► The SMPSCDS (SCDS) data set contains backup copies of target zone entries modified during APPLY processing. Therefore, each SCDS is directly related to a specific target zone, and each target zone must have its own SCDS.

SMP/E also uses the following data sets:

► The SMPMTS (MTS) data set is a library in which SMP/E stores copies of macros during installation when no other target macro library is identified. Therefore, the MTS is related to a specific target zone, and each target zone must have its own MTS data set.

► The SMPSTS (STS) data set is a library in which SMP/E stores copies of the source during installation when no other target source library is identified. Therefore, the STS is related to a specific target zone, and each target zone must have its own STS data set.

► The SMPLTS (LTS) data set is a library that maintains the base version of a load module. The load module in this library specifies a SYSLIB allocation to implicitly include modules. Therefore, the LTS is related to a specific target zone, and each target zone must have its own LTS data set.

► Other utility and work data sets.

SMP/E uses information in the CSI data sets to select proper element levels for installation, to determine which libraries should contain which elements, and to identify which system utilities should be called for the installation.

System programmers can also use the CSI data sets to obtain the latest information about the structure, content, and status of the system. SMP/E provides this information in reports, listings, and dialogs to help you:

► Investigate function and service levels

► Understand intersections and relationships of SYSMODs (either installed or waiting to be installed)

► Build job streams for SMP/E processing

17.13 Summary

As a z/OS system programmer, it is your responsibility to ensure that all software products and their modifications are properly installed on the system. On z/OS, the primary means for managing changes to the system software is through SMP/E.

SMP/E can be run either using batch jobs or using dialogs under the Interactive System Productivity Facility/Program Development Facility (ISPF/PDF). With SMP/E dialogs, you can interactively query the SMP/E database and create and submit jobs to process SMP/E commands.

Software installed by SMP/E must be packaged as system modifications (SYSMODs), which combine the updated element with control information. This information describes the elements and any relationships the software has with other products or service that may also be installed on the same system.

The SMP/E JCL and commands are used frequently by a large enterprise z/OS system programmer; however, SMP/E MCS instructions will rarely be coded by the same system programmer. The product and SYSMOD packaging include the necessary MCS statements.

A critical responsibility of the system programmer is to work with IBM defect support when a problem surfaces in z/OS or optional IBM products. Problem resolution requires the system programmer to receive and apply fixes to the enterprise system.

Table 17-1 lists the key terms used in this chapter.

Table 17-1   Key terms used in this chapter

authorized program analysis report (APAR)	consolidated service (software?) inventory (CSI)	distribution library (DLIB)
distribution zone	global zone	program temporary fix (PTF)
SYSMOD	target library	target zone

17.14 Questions for review

To help test your understanding of the material in this chapter, answer the following questions:

1. What purpose does SMP/E serve in a z/OS system?

2. What are the two types of function SYSMODs? How are they different?

3. What kind of information is stored in the CSI data set?

4. What is the difference between an APAR and a PTF?

5. Fill in the blank: In SMP/E, you use the _____ command to install selected SYSMODs into their associated distribution libraries.

17.15 Topics for further discussion

Here are topics for further discussion:

► What is the importance of an orderly change management process in a large systems enterprise?

► How do installation and maintenance provide the basis for high availability in the z/OS environment?

18

Security on z/OS

Objective: In working with z/OS, you need to understand the importance of security and the facilities used by z/OS to implement it. An installation's data and application programs are among its most valuable resources. They must be protected from unauthorized access both internally (employees) and externally (customers, business partners, and hackers).

After completing this chapter, you will be able to:

- ► Explain security and integrity concepts.
- ► Explain RACF and its interface with the operating system.
- ► Authorize a program.
- ► Discuss integrity concepts.
- ► Explain the importance of change control.
- ► Explain the concept of risk assessment.

Refer to Table 18-1 on page 607 for a list of key terms used in this chapter.

18.1 Why security is important

Over time, it has become much easier to create and access computerized information. No longer is system access limited to a handful of highly skilled programmers. Information can now be created and accessed by almost anyone who takes a little time to become familiar with the newer, easier-to-use, high-level inquiry languages.

More and more people are becoming increasingly dependent on computer systems and the information they store in these systems. As general computer literacy and the number of people using computers has increased, the need for data security has taken on a new measure of importance. No longer can the installation depend on keeping data secure simply because no one knows how to access the data.

Furthermore, making data secure not only means making confidential information inaccessible to those who should not see it, it also means preventing the inadvertent destruction of files by people who may not even know that they are improperly manipulating data.

An operating system is said to have system integrity when it is designed, implemented, and maintained to protect itself against unauthorized access, and does so to the extent that security controls specified for that system cannot be compromised. Specifically for z/OS, this means that there must be no way for any unauthorized program, using any system interface, defined or undefined, to perform the following tasks:

- ▶ Obtain control in an authorized state
- ▶ Bypass store or fetch protection
- ▶ Bypass password checking

18.2 Security facilities of z/OS

In the following sections, we cover the facilities of z/OS that provide its high level of security and integrity.

Data about customers is a valuable resource that could be sold to competitors. So the aim of any security policy is to provide users with only their required level of access and to deny non-authorized users access. This is one reason why auditors prefer that users or groups are granted specific access, rather than using universal access facilities. The traditional focus of mainframe security was to focus on stopping unauthorized people from logging on to the system, and then ensuring that users were only allowed access to data on a need-to-know basis.

As mainframes have become Internet servers, however, additional security has been required. There are outside threats such as hackers, viruses, and Trojan horses; the Security Server includes tools to deal with these threats.

However, the main threat to company data has always been from within the company itself. An employee within a company has a much better chance of obtaining data than someone outside. A well-thought-out security policy is always the first line of defense.

Furthermore, z/OS provides a number of integrity features to minimize intentional or accidental damage from other programs. Many installations run several copies of z/OS and often do not permit general TSO/ISPF users to access the production systems. z/OS security controls can protect the production environment if they are properly configured and prevent a TSO/ISPF user (either maliciously or accidentally) from impacting important production work.

18.3 Security roles

In the past, it was the system programmer who, working with management, decided the overall security policy and procedures. Today, companies are seeking higher levels of security, so they appoint a separate security manager. The system programmer might not have direct responsibility for security, other than advising the security manager about new products. Separation of duties is necessary to prevent any one individual from having uncontrolled access to the system.

A system administrator assigns user IDs and initial passwords and ensures that the passwords are non-trivial, random, and frequently changed. Because the user IDs and passwords are so critically important, special care must be taken to protect the files that contain them.

18.4 The IBM Security Server

Many installations use a package called the IBM Security Server, which is commonly referred to by the name of its most well-known component, Resource Access Control Facility (RACF).

z/OS security provisions include:

► Controlling the access of users (user ID and password) to the system
► Restricting the functions that an authorized user can perform on the systems' data files and programs

For students who would like to learn more about the tools available to a z/OS security administrator, here is a list of the security components of z/OS that are collectively known as the Security Server:

► DCE Security Server

This server provides a fully functional OSF DCE 1.1 level security server that runs on z/OS.

► Lightweight Directory Access Protocol (LDAP) Server

This server is based on a client/server model that provides client access to an LDAP server. An LDAP directory provides an easy way to maintain directory information in a central location for storage, update, retrieval, and exchange.

► z/OS Firewall Technologies

This program is an IPv4 network security firewall program for z/OS. In essence, the z/OS firewall consists of traditional firewall functions and support for virtual private networks.

The inclusion of a firewall means that the mainframe can be connected directly to the Internet if required without any intervening hardware and can provide the required levels of security to protect vital company data. With the VPN technology, securely encrypted tunnels can be established through the Internet from a client to the mainframe.

► Network Authentication Service for z/OS

This service provides Kerberos security services without requiring that you purchase or use a middleware product such as Distributed Computing Environment (DCE).

► Enterprise Identity Mapping (EIM)

This program offers a new approach to enabling inexpensive solutions that allows you to easily manage multiple user registries and user identities in an enterprise.

► PKI Services

This program allows you to establish a public key infrastructure and serve as a certificate authority for your internal and external users, issuing and administering digital certificates in accordance with your own organization's policies.

► Resource Access Control Facility (RACF)

This is the primary component of the z/OS Security Server; it works closely with z/OS to protect vital resources.

The topic of security can be a whole course by itself. In this book, we introduce you to the RACF component and show how its features are used to implement z/OS security.

18.4.1 Resource Access Control Facility

Access, in a computer-based environment, means the ability to do something with a computer resource (for example, use, change, or view something). Access control is the method by which this ability is explicitly enabled or restricted. Computer-based access controls are called *logical access controls*. These are protection mechanisms that limit users' access to information to only what is appropriate for them.

Logical access controls are often built into the operating system, or may be part of the logic of application programs or major utilities, such as database management systems. They may also be implemented in add-on security packages that are installed into an operating system; such packages are available for a variety of systems, including PCs and mainframes. Additionally, logical access controls may be present in specialized components that regulate communications between computers and networks.

Resource Access Control Facility (RACF) is an add-on software product that provides basic security for a mainframe system. There are other security software packages, such as ACF2 or Top Secret, both from Computer Associates.

RACF protects resources by granting access only to authorized users of the protected resources. RACF retains information about users, resources, and access authorities in special structures called *profiles* in its database, and it refers to these profiles when deciding which users should be permitted access to protected system resources.

To accomplish its goals, RACF gives you the ability to:

► Identify and authenticate users.

► Authorize users to access protected resources.

► Log and report various attempts of unauthorized access to protected resources.

► Control the means of access to resources.

► Allow applications to use the RACF macros.

Figure 18-1 offers a simple view of RACF functions.

RACF uses a user ID and a system-encrypted password to perform its user identification and verification. The user ID identifies the person to the system as a RACF user. The password verifies the user's identity. Often, exits are used to enforce a password policy, such as a minimum length, lack of repeating characters or adjacent keyboard letters, and also the use of numerics and letters. Popular words such as "password" or the use of the user ID are often banned.

The other important policy is the frequency of password change. If a user ID has not been used for a long time, it may be revoked and special action is needed to use it again. When someone leaves a company, there should be a special procedure that ensures that the user IDs are deleted from the system.

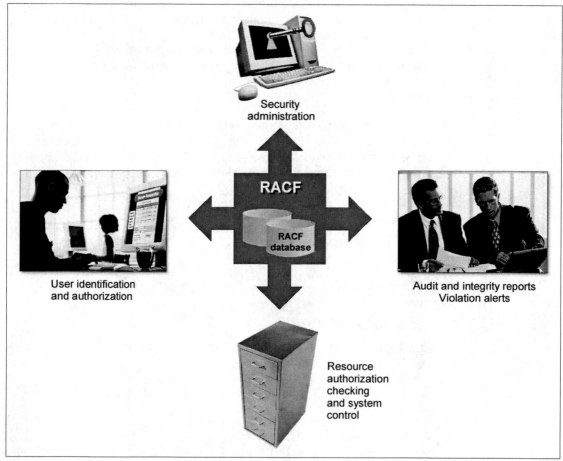

Figure 18-1   Overview of RACF functions

18.4.2 System authorization facility

The system authorization facility (SAF) is part of the z/OS operating system and provides the interfaces to the callable services provided to perform authentication, authorization, and logging.

SAF does not require any other product as a prerequisite, but overall system security functions are greatly enhanced and complemented if it is used concurrently with RACF. The key element in SAF is the SAF router. This router is always present, even when RACF is not present.

The SAF router provides a common focal point for all products providing resource control. This focal point encourages the use of common control functions shared across products and across systems. The resource managing components and subsystems call the z/OS router as part of certain decision-making functions in their processing, such as access-control checking and authorization-related checking. These functions are called *control points*.

The system authorization facility (SAF) conditionally directs control to RACF (if RACF is present), or to a user-supplied processing routine, or both, when receiving a request from a resource manager.

18.5 Security administration

Data security is the protection of data from accidental or deliberate unauthorized disclosure, modification, or destruction. Based on this definition, it is apparent that all data-processing installations have at least potential security or control problems. Users have found, from past experience, that data security measures can have a significant impact on operations in terms of both administrative tasks and demands made on the user.

RACF gives the user defined with the SPECIAL attribute (the security administrator) many responsibilities both at the system level and at the group level. The security administrator is the focal point for planning security in the installation and needs to:

► Determine which RACF functions to use.

► Identify the level of RACF protection.

► Identify which data RACF is to protect.

► Identify administrative structures and users.

18.5.1 RACF Remote Sharing Facility

The RACF Remote Sharing Facility (RRSF) allows you to administer and maintain RACF databases that are distributed throughout the enterprise. It provides improvements in system performance, system management, system availability, and usability. RRSF helps to ensure that data integrity is kept across system or network failures and delays. It lets you know when key events have occurred and returns output to view at your convenience.

18.5.2 RACF with middleware

Major subsystems such as CICS and DB2 use the facilities of RACF to protect transactions and files. Much of the work to configure RACF profiles for these subsystems is done by the CICS and DB2 system programmers. So there is a need for people in these roles to have a useful understanding of RACF and how it relates to the software they manage.

18.6 Operator console security

We can look at one example of how z/OS security affects system functions by discussing the operator consoles. Console security means controlling which commands operators can enter on their consoles to monitor and control z/OS. How you define command authorities for your consoles, or control logon for operators, enables you to plan the operations security of your z/OS system or sysplex. In a sysplex, because an operator on one system can enter commands that affect the processing on another system, your security measures become more complicated and you need to plan accordingly.

For multiple console support (MCS) consoles, you can use the following keywords to control whether operators can enter commands from a console:

▶ The AUTH keyword on the CONSOLE statement of CONSOLxx

▶ The LOGON keyword of the DEFAULT statement and RACF commands and profiles.

For extended MCS consoles, you can control what an authorized SDSF or TSO/E user can do during a console session. Because an extended MCS console can be associated with a TSO/E user ID and not a physical console, you might want to use RACF to limit not only the z/OS commands a user can enter, but from which TSO/E terminals the user can enter the commands.

18.7 Integrity

There are many features and facilities in z/OS specifically designed to protect one program from affecting another, either intentionally or accidentally. This is why z/OS is known for program integrity and security.

This section discusses:

▸ The authorized program facility (APF)

▸ Storage protection

▸ Cross-memory communication

18.7.1 Authorized programs

z/OS contains a feature called the authorized program facility (APF) to allow selected programs to access sensitive system functions. APF was designed to avoid integrity exposures. The installation identifies which libraries contain those special functions or programs. Those libraries are then called APF libraries.

An APF-authorized program can do virtually anything that it wants. It is essentially an extension of the operating system. It can put itself into the supervisor state or a system key. It can modify system control blocks. It can execute privileged instructions (while in the supervisor state). It can turn off logging to cover its tracks. Clearly, this authorization must be given out sparingly and monitored carefully.

You can use APF to identify system or user programs that can use sensitive system functions. For example, APF:

▸ Restricts the use of sensitive system supervisor call (SVC) routines (and sensitive user SVC routines, if you need them) to APF-authorized programs.

▸ Allows the system to fetch all modules in an authorized job step task only from authorized libraries, to prevent programs from counterfeiting a module in the module flow of an authorized job step task.

Many system functions, such as supervisor calls (SVCs) or special paths through SVCs, are sensitive. Access to these functions must be restricted to only authorized programs to avoid compromising the security and integrity of the system.

The system considers a task authorized when the executing program has the following characteristics:

▶ It runs in supervisor state (bit 15 of the program status word (PSW) is zero). We discussed the PSW in Chapter 3, "z/OS overview" on page 91.

▶ It runs with PSW key 0 to 7 (bits 8 through 11 of the PSW contain a value in the range 0 to 7).

▶ All previous programs executed in the same task were APF programs.

Libraries that contain authorized programs are known as authorized libraries. APF-authorized programs must reside in one of the following authorized libraries:

▶ SYS1.LINKLIB
▶ SYS1.SVCLIB
▶ SYS1.LPALIB
▶ Authorized libraries specified by your installation

18.7.2 Storage protection

Mainframe hardware has a *storage protection* function. It is normally used to prevent unauthorized alteration of storage. It can also be used to prevent unauthorized reading of storage areas, although z/OS protects only small areas of storage this way. Storage protection works on 4 KB pages. It deals only with real memory, not virtual memory. When a page of virtual memory is copied from disk to a free page in main storage, z/OS also sets an appropriate storage protection key in that page of main storage.

Storage protection was much more significant before multiple address spaces came into use. When multiple users and jobs were in a single address space (or in real memory in the days before virtual memory), protecting a user's memory from corruption (or inappropriate data peeking) was critical. With z/OS, the primary protection for each user's memory is the isolation provided by multiple address spaces.

Storage protection keys cannot be altered by application programs. There is no way, using the storage protection function, for a normal application program (that is, not an *authorized program*) to protect part of its virtual memory from other parts of the application in the same address space.

An additional storage protection bit (for each 4 KB page of real memory) is the *page protection* bit. This prevents even system routines (running in key 0, which can normally store anywhere) from storing in the page. This bit is typically used to protect LPA pages from accidental damage by system routines.

18.7.3 Cross-memory communication

With proper page table management by the operating system, users and applications in different address spaces are completely isolated from each other. One exception to this isolation is the common area. Another exception is *cross-memory communication.*

With proper setup by the operating system, it is possible for a program in one standard address space to communicate with programs in other address spaces. A number of cross-memory capabilities are possible, but two are commonly used:

▸ The ability to call a program that resides in a different address space

▸ The ability to access (fetch, store) virtual memory in another address space

The first case uses the *program call* (PC) instruction. After the proper setup has been completed by z/OS, only a single hardware instruction is needed to call a program in another address space. A common example of this involves DB2, the major IBM database product. Various parts of DB2 occupy up to four address spaces. Users of DB2 may be TSO users, batch jobs, and other middleware (such as a web server). When these users issue SQL instructions for DB2, the SQL interface in the application uses a program call to obtain services from the DB2 address spaces.

Cross-memory programming can be rather complex and must be coordinated with z/OS security controls. In practice, almost all cross-memory usage is in major middleware products and is rarely directly used by typical application programs.

Routine application programming seldom ventures into this area. Both the mainframe hardware architecture and internal z/OS design protect these functions from improper use and there have been no significant security or integrity concerns related to the cross-memory capabilities.

18.7.4 z/OS firewall technologies

The traditional firewall functions act as a blockade between your intranet (a secure, internal private network) and another (non-secure) network or the Internet. The purpose of a firewall is to prevent unwanted or unauthorized communication into or out of the secure network. The firewall has two jobs:

▸ It lets users in your own network use authorized resources from the outside network without compromising your network's data and other resources.

▸ It keeps users who are outside your network from coming in to compromise or attack your network.

There are several ways a firewall can protect your network. A firewall can provide screening services that deny or grant access based on such things as user name, host name, and TCP/IP protocol. A firewall can also provide a variety of services that let authorized users through while keeping unauthorized users out, and at the same time ensure that all communications between your network and the Internet appear to end at the firewall, denying the outside world to see the structure of your network.

18.8 Summary

Making data secure does not mean just making confidential information inaccessible to those who should not see it; it means preventing the inadvertent destruction of files by people who may not even know that they are improperly manipulating data. Without better awareness of good data security practices, technology evolution could result in a higher likelihood of unauthorized persons accessing, modifying, or destroying data, either inadvertently or deliberately. The Security Server is a set of features in z/OS that provides security implementation.

The system authorization facility (SAF) is part of the z/OS operating system and provides the interfaces to the callable services provided to perform authentication, authorization, and logging.

The Resource Access Control Facility (RACF) is a component of the Security Server for z/OS and controls access to all protected z/OS resources. RACF protects resources by granting access only to authorized users of the protected resources and retains information about the users, resources, and access authorities in specific profiles.

RACF provides the tools and databases to allow z/OS licensed programs such as TSO, CICS, and DB2, to check and verify a user's access level and thus permit or deny the use of data sets, transactions, or database views.

RACF enables the organization to define individuals and groups who use the system RACF protects. For example, for a secretary in the organization, a security administrator uses RACF to define a user profile that defines the secretary's user ID, initial password, and other information.

To accomplish its goals, RACF gives you the ability to:

- ► Identify and authenticate users.
- ► Authorize users to access the protected resources.
- ► Log and report attempts of unauthorized access to protected resources.
- ► Control the means of access to resources.

The operation of a z/OS system involves the following tasks:

- ► Console operations, or how operators interact with z/OS to monitor or control the hardware and software

- ► Message and command processing that forms the basis of operator interaction with z/OS and the basis of z/OS automation

Operating z/OS involves managing hardware such as processors and peripheral devices, and software such as the z/OS operating control system, the job entry subsystem, and all the applications that run on z/OS.

When implementing console security, the installation can control which commands operators can enter on their consoles to monitor and control z/OS. Basically, the customization is made in RACF and in the CONSOLxx member in PARMLIB.

Table 18-1 lists the key terms used in this chapter.

Table 18-1   Key terms used in this chapter

authorized libraries	authorized program facility (APF)	encryption
firewall	hacker	page protection bit
password	Resource Access Control Facility (RACF)	security policy
separation of duties	system integrity	user ID

18.9 Questions for review

To help test your understanding of the material in this chapter, answer the following questions:

1. Is the following statement true or false?

   Access information in the resource profiles can be set only at the group level. This means that it is impossible for a single user to have the update attribute to a specific data set if the RACF group to which the user is connected has only the read attribute.

2. In the following situation, what occurs with the program if no authorized SVC or special functions are invoked?

   a. There is one program link-edited with AC=0.
   b. The program runs from an APF-authorized library.

3. In the following example, what are the possible problems of a program executing from a library called SYS1.LINKLIB located in the volume MPRES2?

```
D PROG,APF,ENTRY=1
CSV450I 05.24.55 PROG,APF DISPLAY 979
FORMAT=DYNAMIC
ENTRY VOLUME DSNAME
    1  MPRES1 SYS1.LINKLIB?
```

18.10 Topics for further discussion

Here are topics for further discussion:

1. On other platforms, how do you protect data sets or files? Is there a way to prevent the execution of a specific application?

2. RACF enables you to assign the group administrator attribute to users. Using this function, it is possible to implement a decentralized administration. Discuss the pros and cons.

18.11 Exercises

Here are some exercises you can perform:

1. Try to log on to TSO after changing the initial logon procedure IKJACCNT to IKJACCN1. The expected message is:

```
IKJ56483I THE PROCEDURE NAME IKJACCN1 HAS NOT BEEN AUTHORIZED FOR
THIS USERID
```

2. Using your TSO user ID (now with your default logon procedure IKJACCNT), try to delete the data set *ZPROF*.JCL.NOT.DELETE, which is set up by the standard jobs in the supplied JCL. This is a protected data set and you can only read its content.

3. Execute the next sample JCL to obtain a DSMON utility report with the current RACF group tree structure (available in the sample JCL as member DSMON):

```
//DSMONRPT JOB (POK,999),'DSMONREPORT',MSGLEVEL=(1,1),MSGCLASS=X,
// CLASS=A,NOTIFY=&SYSUID
/*JOBPARM SYSAFF=*
//*
//* NOTE:
//* REMEMBER THAT ICHDSM00 MUST BE RUN BY A USER WITH AUDITOR
ATTRIBUTE
```

```
//*
//STEPNAME EXEC PGM=ICHDSM00
//SYSPRINT DD SYSOUT=A
//SYSUT2   DD SYSOUT=A
//SYSIN    DD *
 FUNCTION RACGRP
/*
```

4. Verify that the SYS1.LINKLIB library is an APF-authorized library:

   - Using the DISPLAY APF command to display the entire APF list.

   - Using the ENTRY= operand in the DISPLAY APF command.

   - Using the DSNAME= operand in the DISPLAY APF command. Verify the entry number in the command display result in the syslog.

5. The following JCL example can be used to invoke the ADRDSSU utility and issue a WTOR message in the console. The WTOR command lets you write an ADR112A message to the system console. The ADR112A message requests that the operator perform an action, and then issue a reply. You can use WTOR, for example, to request that the operator mount a required volume or quiesce a database before your DFSMSdss job continues to process (available in the sample JCL as member ADRDSSU):

```
//WTORTEST JOB (POK,999),'USER',MSGLEVEL=(1,1),MSGCLASS=X,
// CLASS=A,NOTIFY=&SYSUID
//          EXEC PGM=ADRDSSU
//SYSPRINT DD   SYSOUT=*
//SYSIN    DD   *
 WTOR 'TEST'
/*
```

DFSMSdss assigns the following routing code to the WTOR message:

```
1 Primary operator action
```

DFSMSdss assigns the following descriptor code to the WTOR message:

```
2 Immediate action required.
```

In the SDSF main panel, choose the SR option (system requests) and reply with any response you want.

19

Network communications on z/OS

Objective: In working with z/OS network communications, you need to interact with TCP/IP and SNA networks.

In this chapter, you learn:

► How various communication network models compare with each other.

► The software components of the z/OS Communications Server product.

► How the SNA subarea and APPN network topology compare.

► How the IP network can be used to transport data between SNA applications.

► Commonly used TCP/IP and Virtual Telecommunication Access Method (VTAM) commands.

Refer to Table 19-1 on page 630 for a list of key terms used in this chapter.

19.1 Communications in z/OS

Network communication has both software and hardware aspects, and a separation of software and hardware communications duties is common in large enterprises. A skilled network expert, however, needs to understand both aspects. This chapter provides a brief overview of communications software on the mainframe.

As a system programmer, the network professional must bring a thorough understanding of z/OS communications software to any project that involves working with the company's network. While network hardware technicians have specific skills and tools for supporting the physical network, their expertise often does not extend to the z/OS communications software. When a nationwide retail chain opens a new store, the z/OS system programmers and network hardware technicians must coordinate their efforts to open the new store.

z/OS includes a fully featured communications server with multiprotocol networking (Figure 19-1). This chapter begins with an overview of the available networking technologies on z/OS and then discusses the main operational aspects of the operating system's communications server in 19.3, "z/OS Communications Server" on page 616.

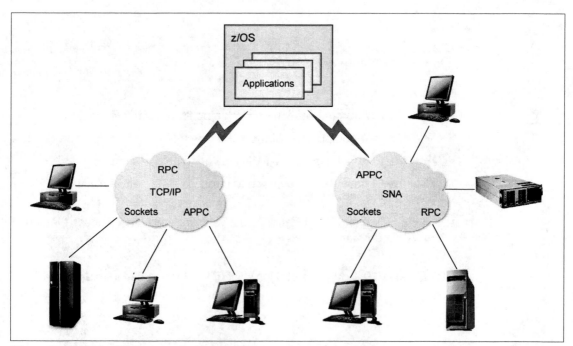

Figure 19-1 IBM z/OS Communications Server

19.2 Brief history of data networks

Established in 1969, Transmission Control Protocol/Internet Protocol (TCP/IP) is actually five years older than System Network Architecture (SNA). However, SNA was immediately made available to the public, while TCP/IP was limited at first to military and research institutions, for use in the interconnected networks that formed the precursors to the Internet.

In addition, SNA was designed to include network management controls not originally in TCP/IP through the Synchronous Data Link Control (SDLC) protocol. In the 1980s, SNA was widely implemented by large corporations because it allowed their IT organizations to extend central computing capability worldwide with reasonable response times and reliability. For example, widespread use of SNA allowed the retail industry to offer new company credit card accounts to customers at the point-of-sale.

In 1983, TCP/IP entered the public domain in Berkeley BSD UNIX. TCP/IP maturity, applications, and acceptance advanced through an open standards committee, the Internet Engineering Task Force (IETF), using the Request Ford Comment (RFC) mechanism.

The term *internet* is used as a generic term for a TCP/IP network and should not be confused with the *Internet*, which consists of the large international backbone networks connecting all TCP/IP hosts that have links to the Internet backbone.

TCP/IP was designed for interconnected networks (an internet) and seemed to be easier to set up, while SNA design was hierarchical with the "centralized" mainframe being at the top of the hierarchy. The SNA design included network management, data flow control, and the ability to assign "class of service" priorities to specific data workloads.

Communication between autonomous SNA networks became available in 1983. Before that, SNA networks could not talk to each other easily. The ability of independent SNA networks to share business application and network resources is called SNA Network Interconnect (SNI).

19.2.1 SNA and TCP/IP on z/OS

SNA was developed by IBM. SNA enabled corporations to communicate with its locations around the country. To perform this task, SNA included products such as Virtual Telecommunication Access Method (VTAM), Network Control Program (NCP), terminal controllers, and the SDLC protocol. What TCP/IP and the Internet were to the public in the 1990s, SNA was to large enterprises in the 1980s.

TCP/IP is an industry-standard, nonproprietary set of communications protocols that provides reliable end-to-end connections between applications over interconnected networks of different types. TCP/IP was widely embraced when the Internet came of age because it permitted access to remote data and processing for a relatively small cost. TCP/IP and the Internet resulted in a proliferation of small computers and communications equipment for chat, email, conducting business, and downloading and uploading data.

Large SNA enterprises have recognized the increased business potential of expanding the reach of SNA-hosted data and applications to this proliferation of small computers and communications equipment in customers' homes, small offices, and so on.

19.2.2 Layered network models

TCP/IP and SNA are both layered network models. Each can indirectly map to the international Open Systems Interconnect (OSI) network model (Figure 19-2).

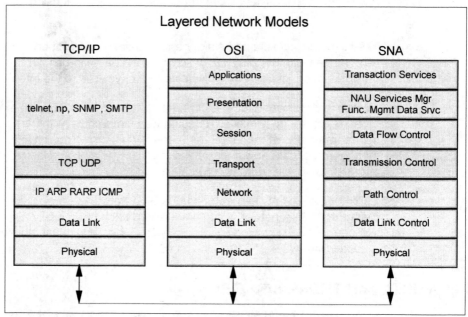

Figure 19-2   Open Systems Interconnect (OSI) network model

The OSI network model depicts the organization of the individual elements of technology involved with end-to-end data communication. As shown in Figure 19-2 on page 614, the OSI network model provides some common ground for both SNA and TCP/IP. Although neither technology maps directly into the OSI network model (TCP/IP and SNA existed before the OSI network model was formalized), common ground still exists due to the defined model layers.

The OSI network model is divided into seven layers. OSI layer 7 (Application) indirectly maps into the top layers of the SNA and TCP/IP stacks. OSI layer 1 (Physical) and layer 2 (Data Link) map into the bottom layers of SNA and TCP/IP stacks.

In one typical scenario, two geographically separated endpoint software applications are connected at each end by a layered network model. Data is sent by one endpoint application and received by the other endpoint application. The applications can reside on large mainframes, PCs, point-of-sale (POS) devices, ATMs, terminals, or printer controllers. Endpoints in SNA are called logical units (LUs), while endpoints in IP are called application ports (ports for short).

Consider how this model might be used in the network communications for a large chain of grocery stores. Each time a customer pays for groceries at one of the many point-of-sale (POS) locations in a grocery store, the layered network model is used twice:

▶ The POS application resides at the top of the local layered network stack.

▶ The application that records details of the sale and authorizes completion resides at the top of a remote layer network stack.

The local network stack might run on a non-mainframe system with attached POS devices, while the remote network stack would quite often run on a mainframe, to handle transactions received from all of the store locations. Method of payment, purchases, store location, and time are recorded by mainframe applications, and authorization to print a sales receipt is returned back through both layered network stacks to complete the sale.

This transactional model is commonly known as a request/server or client/server relationship.

19.2.3 Network reliability and availability

What if the network or attached mainframe for our example grocery store chain were to somehow become unavailable? Most POS systems in use today include the ability to accumulate transactions in an intelligent store POS controller or small store processor. When the outage is corrected, the accumulated transactions can then be sent in bulk to the mainframe.

In the previous example, the recovery of transactions would be essential to preventing bookkeeping and inventory problems at the store and in the chain's central office. The cumulative effect of unaddressed, inaccurate records could easily destroy a business. Therefore, reliability, availability and serviceability (RAS) are just as important in the design of a network as they are in the mainframe itself.

19.2.4 Factors contributing to the continued use of SNA

SNA is stable, trusted, and relied upon for mission-critical business applications worldwide. A significant amount of the world's corporate data is handled by z/OS-resident SNA applications.[1] A distinctive strength of SNA is that it is connection-oriented with many timers and control mechanisms to ensure reliable delivery of data.

Mainframe IT organizations are often reluctant and skeptical about moving away from SNA, despite the allure of TCP/IP and web-based commerce. This reluctance is often justified. Rewriting stable, well-tuned business applications to change from SNA program interfaces to TCP/IP sockets can be costly and time consuming.

Many businesses choose to use web-enabling technologies to make the vast amount of centralized data available to the TCP/IP-based web environment, while maintaining the SNA APIs. This "best of both worlds" approach ensures that SNA and VTAM will be around well into the foreseeable future.

19.3 z/OS Communications Server

z/OS includes the z/OS Communications Server, which is an integrated set of software components that enable network communications for applications running on z/OS. z/OS Communications Server provides the data transportation corridor between the external network and the business applications running on z/OS.

z/OS Communications Server provides a set of communications protocols that support peer-to-peer connectivity functions for both local and wide-area networks, including the most popular wide area network, the Internet. z/OS Communications Server also provides performance enhancements that can benefit a variety of TCP/IP applications; it also includes a number of commonly used applications.

---

[1] SNA applications running on z/OS are also known as VTAM applications.

z/OS Communications Server includes a number of sophisticated products and functions. The major services are:

▶ IP, using Transmission Control Protocol/Internet Protocol (TCP/IP)

▶ Systems Network Architecture (SNA), using Virtual Telecommunication Access Method (VTAM)

The Communications Storage Manager (CSM) component provides a shared I/O buffer for data flow. The CSM function allows authorized host applications to share data without having to physically move the data.

z/OS Communications Server, with its combination of TCP/IP and SNA functions, is implemented on a number of platforms besides z/OS, such as AIX, Microsoft Windows, and Linux. As a result, z/OS application programmers can use technological advancements in communications (information access, electronic commerce, and collaboration) across distinctly different operating systems.

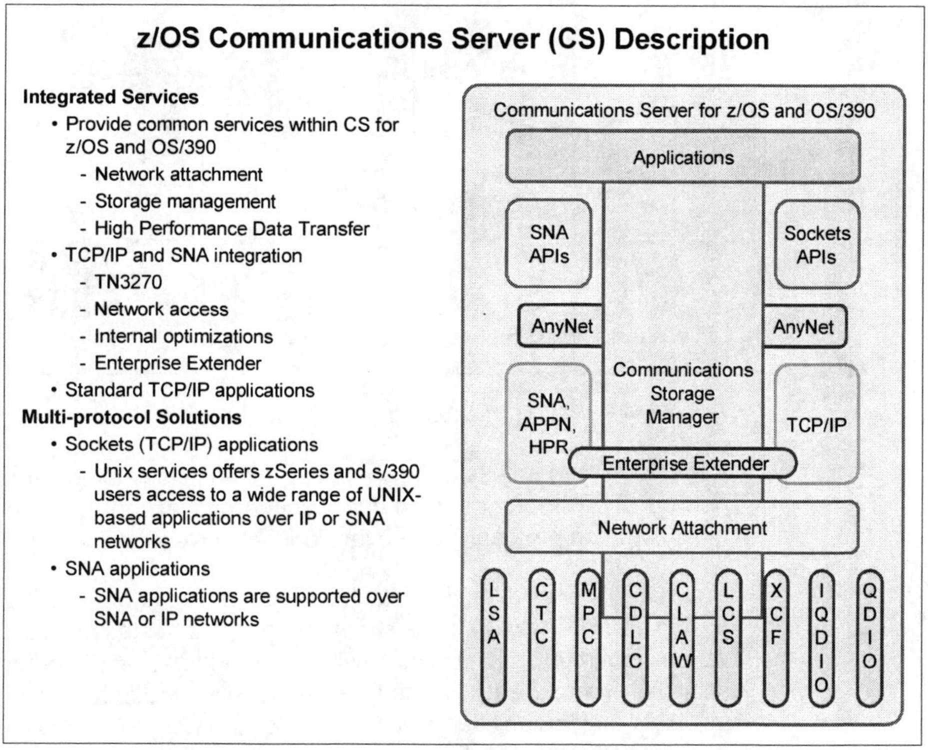

Figure 19-3   The z/OS Communications Server

19.4 TCP/IP overview

TCP/IP is the general term used to describe the suite of protocols that form the basis for the Internet. It was first included in the UNIX system offered by the University of California at Berkeley, and is now delivered with essentially all network-capable computers in the world. Figure 19-4 gives an overview of TCP/IP.

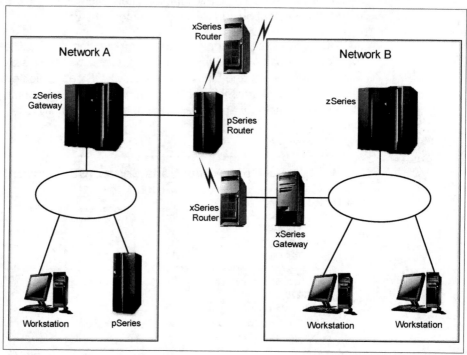

Figure 19-4   TCP/IP introduction

All systems, regardless of size, appear the same to other systems in the TCP/IP network. TCP/IP can be used over Local Area Network (LAN) hardware using most common protocols, and over Wide Area Networks (WANs).

In a TCP/IP network environment, a machine that is running TCP/IP is called a *host*. A TCP/IP network consists of one or more hosts linked together through various communication links. Any host can address all the other hosts directly to establish communication. The links between networks are invisible to an application communicating with a host. It does not matter whether an application is a older CICS application using MVS services or a newly downloaded application using the UNIX component. System administrators may have to choose which components and programming interfaces to use. But to the application, the components used are transparent.

19.4.1 Using commands to monitor TCP/IP

z/OS supports TCP/IP commands found in other operating systems, such as:

► NETSTAT
► PING
► TRACERTE
► NSLOOKUP

You can enter these commands from an authorized TSO session from:

► The TSO Ready prompt
► The ISPF command shell
► Any ISPF command line by prefixing the command with TSO
► Batch programs

Example 19-1 shows the results you might see when entering NETSTAT commands from the TSO Ready prompt.

Example 19-1   Sample NETSTAT output

```
**** NETSTAT ROUTE output ****
MVS TCP/IP NETSTAT CS V1R5        TCPIP Name: TCPIP         21:38:18
Destination     Gateway          Flags    Refcnt   Interface
-----------     -------          -----    ------   ---------
Default         5.12.6.92        UGS      000001   OSA2380LNK
5.12.6.0        0.0.0.0          US       000000   OSA2380LNK
5.12.6.66       0.0.0.0          UH       000000   OSA2380LNK
5.12.6.67       0.0.0.0          UH       000000   STAVIPA1LNK
15.1.100.0      0.0.0.0          US       000000   IQDIOLNK0A016443
15.1.100.4      0.0.0.0          UHS      000000   IQDIOLNK0A016443
15.1.100.42     0.0.0.0          UHS      000000   IQDIOLNK0A016443

**** NETSTAT BYTE output ****
MVS TCP/IP NETSTAT CS V1R5        TCPIP Name: TCPIP         21:41:18
User Id  Conn   Local Socket        Foreign Socket        State
-------  ----   ------------        --------------        -----
DASU8G25 000048BF 0.0.0.0..523      0.0.0.0..0            Listen
D8G2DIST 00000072 0.0.0.0..38062    0.0.0.0..0            Listen
D8G2DIST 00000031 0.0.0.0..38060    0.0.0.0..0            Listen
FTPMVS1  00000022 5.12.6.66..21     0.0.0.0..0            Listen
FTPOE1   00000024 5.12.6.67..21     0.0.0.0..0            Listen
INETD4   00000083 0.0.0.0..7        0.0.0.0..0            Listen
INETD4   00000081 0.0.0.0..19       0.0.0.0..0            Listen
```

19.4.2 Using console commands to manage TCP/IP

You can use the DISPLAY TCPIP and VARY TCPIP commands to manage the network and TCP/IP applications on z/OS.

These commands include additional options, such as the following:

► The DISPLAY TCPIP command can be used to display information about the following items:
  - NETSTAT report output for a TCP/IP stack
  - Information about OMPROUTE, a dynamic routing daemon
  - The TCP/IP stack's storage utilization
  - The TCP/IP stack's sysplex status
  - The TN3270 server information

► The VARY TCPIP command includes options to:
  - Drop specific socket connections
  - Start or stop communication devices
  - Set up packet and socket tracing
  - Purge ARP or neighbor cache entries
  - Change the TCP/IP stack's sysplex status
  - Control the TN3270 server
  - Alter the TCP/IP network configuration

For more information about the IP commands, see *z/OS Communications Server IP System Administrators Commands*, SC31-8781.

19.4.3 Using virtual Internet protocol addresses for availability and load balancing

TCP/IP on z/OS allows network administrators to define *virtual Internet protocol addresses* (VIPAs). A VIPA address is managed by the low level communications protocol inherent in z/OS. Such an address can be automatically mapped to more than one z/OS system at the same time. It can be dynamically transferred from one z/OS system to another. It can be dynamically transferred from one IP application to another, even if the application exists on another z/OS host. All of this is transparent to the network and most applications.

Furthermore, a VIPA address can be associated with all physical adapters on a z/OS host. There is effectively no limit to the number of physical adapters a z/OS host can support.

At the same time, VIPA addresses can work in conjunction with the workload management services of z/OS to move inbound IP connections to a z/OS host that has the largest amount of available system resources.

19.4.4 TN3270: The gateway to z/OS

When z/OS hosts existed in a SNA-only environment, dedicated terminal controllers and "dumb" (non-programmable) terminals were the cornerstone of communicating with z/OS. The data protocol used to communicate between the dumb terminal and z/OS is called the 3270 data stream (we discuss this topic more thoroughly in 19.5.6, "Background: 3270 data stream" on page 628). As TCP/IP became a world standard, the 3270 data stream was adapted for use on a TCP/IP network. By blending 3270 with the existing telnet standard, the Telnet 3270 standard emerged. Today, TN3270 has been further refined into TN3270 Enhanced, or TN3270E. This standard is defined in RFC 2355.

To communicate with z/OS using TN3270[2], a client such as Personal Communications is run on the workstation. This client establishes a TN3270 session using TCP. On the z/OS side, a TN3270 server converts the TN3270 protocol to SNA protocol and the connection to an application is completed using VTAM. The completion of the SNA portion is done by the TN3270 server acquiring a Logical Unit (LU) on behalf of the TN3270 client. Then, an LU-LU session is established between the TN3270 server and the target application. We discuss LU-LU sessions in greater detail in 19.5, "VTAM overview" on page 621.

19.5 VTAM overview

In z/OS, VTAM provides the SNA layer network communication stack to transport data between applications and the user. VTAM manages the SNA-defined resources, establishes sessions between these resources, and tracks session activity.

VTAM performs a number of tasks in a network, for example:

► It monitors and controls the activation and connection of resources.

► It establishes connections and manages the flow and pacing of sessions.

► It provides application programming interfaces (for example, an APPC API for LU 6.2 programming) that allow access to the network by user-written application programs and IBM-provided subsystems.

► It provides interactive terminal support for the Time Sharing Option (TSO).

► It provides support for both locally and remotely attached resources.

z/OS runs only one VTAM address space. Each application that uses VTAM, such as CICS/TS, requires a VTAM definition. The application and VTAM use this definition to establish connections to other applications or users.

---

[2] Effectively all clients today run TN3270E, but the term TN3270 is used to describe either protocol.

Each endpoint of an SNA session is known as a logical unit (LU). An LU is a device or program by which an user (application program, a terminal operator, or an input/output mechanism) gains access to the SNA network. VTAM-established sessions are known as LU-to-LU sessions. In an SNA network, CICS/TS, for example, is considered an LU and typically has many sessions with other LUs, such as displays, printers, POS devices, and other remote CICS/TS regions. Each LU is assigned a unique network addressable unit (NAU) to facilitate communication.

A physical unit (PU) controls one or more LUs. A PU is not literally a physical device in the network. Rather, it is a portion of a device (usually programming or circuitry, or both) that performs control functions for the device in which it is located and, in some cases, for other devices that are attached to the PU-containing device.

A PU exists in each node of an SNA network to manage and monitor the resources (such as attached links and adjacent link stations) of the node.

The PU exists either within the device or within an attached controlling device. VTAM must activate the PU before it can activate and own each LU attached to the PU.

Even the mainframe is a type of PU, with attached LUs of which CICS/TS is an example. There are three types of PUs:

▶ PU Type 5 is in the mainframe.

▶ PU Type 4 is a wide area network communication controller.

▶ PU Type 2 is a peripheral communication controller. PU Type 2s can be directly attached to the mainframe or to a PU Type 4.

Figure 19-5 gives an overview of VTAM.

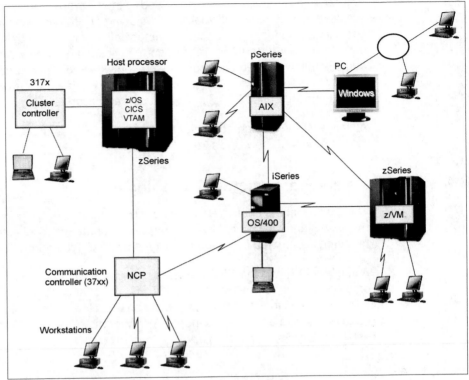

Figure 19-5   VTAM overview: The SNA environment

19.5.1 Network topologies supported by VTAM

Although TCP/IP is by far the most common way to communicate over a network with a z/OS host, some environments still use native SNA, and many environments now carry (encapsulate) SNA traffic over UDP/IP. The hierarchical design of SNA serves the centralized data processing needs of large enterprises. At the top of this hierarchy is VTAM. VTAM serves the following types of network topologies:

► Subarea
► Advanced Peer-to-Peer Networking (APPN)
► Subarea/APPN mixed

The part of VTAM that manages a subarea topology is called the System Services Control Point (SSCP). The part of VTAM that manages APPN topology is called the Control Point (CP).

VTAM subarea networks predate APPN. In many large enterprises, migration of subarea networks to an APPN topology is a desired technical objective. If Enterprise Extender (EE) is also added to the network, additional functions are available, including TCP/IP packet enveloping of SNA application data. This consolidates older SNA-specific communication equipment by redirecting SNA data flows through existing TCP/IP communication networks. Also, VTAM administration and required coordination between communication hardware and software personnel can be significantly reduced with a pure APPN topology as a result of its increased flexibility over subarea networks.

All three VTAM configuration types (subarea, APPN, and mixed subarea/APPN) exist throughout the world's large enterprises.

19.5.2 What is a subarea network topology

The distinguishing characteristics of a VTAM subarea network include the ownership and sharing of SNA resources. A subarea is a collection of SNA resources controlled by a single PU Type 5 or PU Type 4 node.

A single VTAM and the SNA resources it owns is called a *domain*. A cross-domain resource manager (CDRM) allows for communication between VTAM domains in the SNA network. When an LU requests a session to be established with an LU in a separate VTAM domain, the VTAMs cooperate to establish a *cross-domain session*.

Figure 19-6 shows a pure VTAM subarea network. This diagram might, for example, be representative of a business that is based in New York City with a large presence in Los Angeles, and a later expansion into Chicago. Figure 19-6 includes three VTAM domains and six subareas. The Chicago subarea then becomes part of the domain of its controlling VTAM.

In general, full migration from the older subarea topology to an APPN topology is a desired technical objective due to opportunities to use a newer IP network infrastructure and the cost reduction associated with elimination of older SNA network equipment. It also simplifies VTAM network management through more dynamic capabilities.

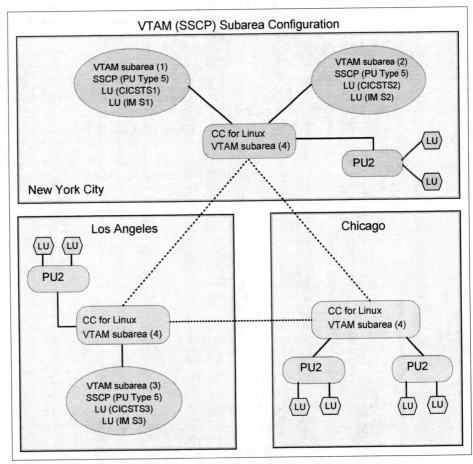

Figure 19-6   A pure VTAM subarea network

19.5.3 Advanced Peer-to-Peer Networking network topology

Advanced Peer-to-Peer Networking (APPN) is a type of data communications support that routes data in a network between two or more systems that do not need to be directly connected.

APPN topology does not have a subarea number or have exclusive ownership of the SNA resources. Each APPN-participating VTAM is included in a geographically dispersed collection of shared SNA resources, eliminating the need for a cross-domain resource manager to establish sessions.

APPN includes a high-performance routing (HPR) method of sending SNA application data through existing TCP/IP network equipment. APPN includes a function called Enterprise Extender (EE), sometimes referred to as HPR/IP. EE ensures that SNA applications can be served by state-of-the-art IP networking technology.

HPR is not limited exclusively to SNA/APPN over TCP/IP networks. Rather, HPR is the APPN function that provides high-performance delivery of data through an APPN network, combined with the high-availability feature of dynamic rerouting of sessions around failures in the network. But HPR is supported over most types of APPN connections (not just APPN over TCP/IP). Enterprise Extender (EE) is the APPN/HPR function that allows SNA sessions and other APPN functions (like HPR) to work over a TCP/IP network (instead of a native SNA network).

Assume that the company shown in Figure 19-6 on page 625 later migrates from the subarea network topology to the APPN topology. Figure 19-7 shows the same company after migration.

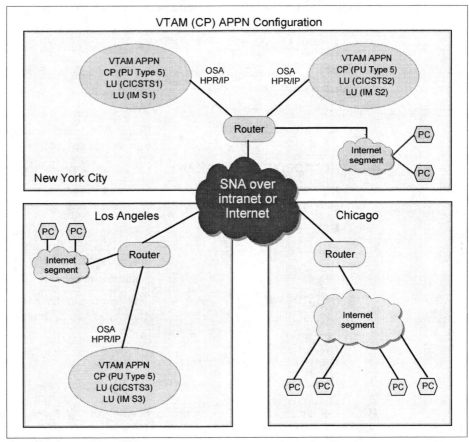

Figure 19-7   APPN topology

19.5.4 Summary of VTAM topologies

VTAM can be a subarea SSCP, an APPN CP, or both SSCP and CP serving a mixed network. The newer APPN topology is a desired architecture because of its ability to directly participate with existing IP infrastructures.

The original subarea SSCP VTAMs naturally evolves into a mixed subarea SSCP and APPN CP to take advantage of EE HPR/IP function, which reduces the cost of network-attached SNA communication equipment. This evolution will most likely lead to subsequent decisions to migrate all remaining subareas to APPN topology to reduce network complexity.

19.5.5 Using commands to monitor VTAM

The following list is a small sampling of VTAM commands used to gather information about a VTAM environment.

▶ List the status of VTAM resources with DISPLAY(D NET,) commands, for example:

D NET,VTAMOPTS	Displays VTAM startup options.
D NET,CSM[,OWNERID=ALL]	Displays communication storage usage.
D NET,APPLS	Displays the status of defined applications (ACBs).
D NET,MAJNODES	Displays the status of all major nodes that have been activated by VTAM.
D NET,TOPO,LIST=SUMMARY	Displays the APPN topology information.
D NET,CPCP	Displays the status of APPN CP-CP sessions.
D NET,SESSIONS	Displays the status of subarea SSCP-SSCP sessions, LU-LU sessions (including CP-CP sessions), SSCP-LU sessions, and SSCP-PU sessions.
D NET,CDRMS	Displays the status of subarea cross domain resource managers.
D NET,EXIT	Displays the status of VTAM exit routines.

▶ Activate/Deactivate VTAM resources with VARY (V NET,) commands.

▶ Alter the VTAM environment with the MODIFY (F VTAM,) commands.

z/OS system programmers use products such as IBM Tivoli NetView to monitor and report on the status of VTAM resources.

For more information about VTAM commands, see *z/OS Communications Server SNA Operations*, SC31-8779.

19.5.6 Background: 3270 data stream

What HTML is to a web application and browser, the 3270 data stream is to an SNA application and device in an LU-LU session. Specialized commands are embedded in the data of panel devices and printers. The 3270 data stream is data with these embedded instructions and data field descriptors. The 3270 data stream commands are created and read by SNA applications, such as Physical Unit (PU) controllers managing the displays, printers, and TN3270 emulators available in AIX and PC operating systems.

One of the most notable advantages of the 3270 data stream is that a full panel of data entries and corrections is sent to the receiving SNA application when the Enter key or PF key is pressed.

The 3270 data stream includes column and row addresses of data fields, along with data descriptors, such as color, protected panel areas, and unprotected panel areas.

When an SNA application sends data to a panel, it includes column/row location placement of individual data fields, descriptors of the data fields, and the panel position of the cursor. The 3270 data stream ability to permit completion of data entry before sending to the SNA applications saves the CPU from unnecessary interruptions. Conversely, every key stroke of a VT100 vi session requires CPU attention. When the key stroke CNTRL-G is entered at a VT100 display, something needs to understand this key stroke so that the status line can be displayed.

The SNA 3270 data stream is critical to the success of the SNA network ability to centrally manage many thousands of geographically dispersed display panels and printers.

19.6 Summary

Enterprise networks can be designed, customized, operated, and supported using combined features and functions of both SNA and TCP/IP network layers using z/OS Communications Server on z/OS, AIX, Windows, Linux, and Linux on System z.

A significant number of large enterprises use 3270 and SNA applications and have no need to rewrite the business application APIs. As a result, VTAM continues to be supported while integrating it with technologies such as APPN, HPR, and EE. In addition, TCP/IP uses VTAM for memory management, device communication (all IP devices go through VTAM), and TN3270 sessions.

Enterprises can, for selected SNA workloads, use z/OS Communications Server products to replace some of the old SNA infrastructure components, such as the IBM 3725/45 (NCP) communication controller hardware or other channel-attached SNA controllers.

Table 19-1 lists the key terms used in this chapter.

Table 19-1   Key terms used in this chapter

APPN	communications server	Internet
Internet segment	LU	LU-to-LU
NCP	OSI	PU
SDLC	SNA	stack
subarea	TCP/IP	VTAM

19.7 Questions for review

To help test your understanding of the material in this chapter, answer the following questions:

1. What components are common between the SNA and TCP/IP network layers?

2. Is the majority of the world's corporate data served by z/OS SNA applications?

3. Does a business need to rewrite SNA business applications to web-enable the application?

4. What is the difference between an SNA subarea network and APPN topology?

5. Why is APPN topology more desirable than a SNA subarea network?

6. What do HTML and a 3270 data stream have in common?

7. What is common about an IP address and an SNA "network addressable unit" (NAU)?

8. What z/OS Communications Server resources are shared by TCP/IP and VTAM?

9. What z/OS Communications Server component provides a shared I/O data buffer area to both TCP/IP and VTAM?

19.8 Demonstrations and exercises

Here are some demonstrations and exercises you can perform:

1. From SDSF, enter the TCP/IP command /D TCPIP,,NETSTAT,HOME and from ISPF enter TSO NETSTAT HOME.

   Is the output from each command the same? What is the home IP address or addresses of this z/OS system?

2. From SDSF, enter the VTAM command /D NET,CSM.

   - How much space TOTAL ALL SOURCES is INUSE?
   - How much space TOTAL ALL SOURCES is FREE?
   - How much space TOTAL ALL SOURCES is AVAILABLE?

3. From SDSF, enter the following VTAM commands:

   ```
   /D NET,APPLS
   /D NET,MAJNODES
   /D NET,TOPO,LIST=SUMMARY
   /D NET,CPCP
   /D NET,SESSIONS
   /D NET,SESSIONS,LIST=ALL
   /D NET,TSOUSER,ID=yourid
   ```

   Write down your IP address ___.___.___.___

   Briefly describe how the output of this command could be useful.

4. From ISPF, start the z/OS UNIX shell with TSO OMVS.

   - Enter netstat -h.
     Does this command produce the same information as in Exercise 1?

   - Note that you can use the TCP/IP commands from the z/OS UNIX shell as well (prefix o).

   - Enter ping your.ip.addr.ess.

   - Enter traceroute your.ip.addr.ess.

   - Exit the z/OS UNIX shell (exit).

A

A brief look at IBM mainframe history

This appendix discusses the development of the IBM mainframe from 1964 to the present, as shown in Figure A-1.

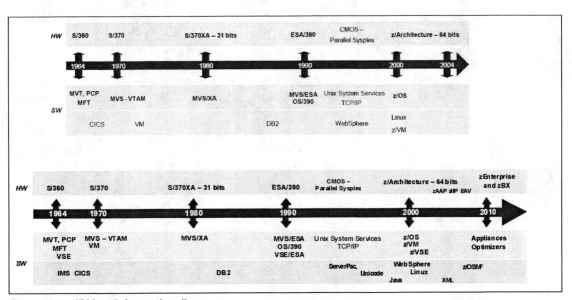

Figure A-1   IBM mainframe time line

633

On April 7, 1964, IBM introduced System/360 (S/360), a family of five increasingly powerful computers that ran the same operating system and could use the same 44 peripheral devices (Figure A-2). Introduced with S/360 were the I/O subsystem concept (namely defining processors to transfer data between memory and I/O devices) and parallel channels (channels to transmit data in parallel to I/O devices).

Figure A-2   S/360 Model 40

For the first time, companies could run mission-critical applications for business on a highly secure platform.

In 1968, IBM introduced Customer Information Control System (CICS). It allowed workplace personnel to enter, update, and retrieve data online. To date, CICS remains one of the industry's most popular transaction monitors.

In 1969, Apollo 11's successful landing on the moon was supported by several System 360s, Information Management System (IMS) 360, and IBM software.

In the summer of 1970, IBM announced a family of machines named System/370 (S/370) that had an enhanced instruction set (Figure A-3). These machines were capable of using more than one processor in the same system (initially two), sharing the memory. Through the 1970s, the machines got bigger and faster, and multiprocessor systems became common. The 370 Model 145 was the first computer with fully integrated monolithic memory (circuits in which all of the same elements (resistors, capacitors, and diodes) are fabricated on a single slice of silicon) and 128-bit bipolar chips. More than 1,400 microscopic circuit elements were etched onto each one-eighth-inch-square chip.

Figure A-3   S/370 Model 165

Able to run System/360 programs, thus easing the upgrade burden for customers, System/370 was also one of the first lines of computers to include "virtual memory" technology. This is a technique developed to expand the capabilities of the computer by using space on the hard drive to accommodate the memory requirements of software.

1980 saw the introduction of the 3081 processor (Figure A-4). The 3081 offered a two-fold increase in internal performance from the previous mainframe processor, the 3033. It also featured Thermal Conduction Modules (TCMs) that significantly reduce space, cooling, and power requirements.

Figure A-4   3081 processor complex

Around 1982, addresses were extended from 24 bits to 31 bits (370XA).

In 1984, IBM announced a 1 Mb Silicon and Aluminum Metal Oxide Semiconductor (SAMOS) chip. Although "mega" means million, the chip actually holds 1,048,576 bits of information in a space smaller than a child's fingernail.

In 1988, extensions were added to support multiple address spaces. In that year, using the mainframe, customers could deploy the DB2 database beyond "decision support systems" and into core transactional processing, driving reductions in CPU costs and dramatic improvements in concurrency.

In this period, IBM introduced the logical partition (LP) concept, which makes it possible to logically partition a mainframe into several independent processors sharing the same hardware.

Some industry pundits, however, did not think the mainframe would survive the early 1990s. They predicted that the rapid growth in personal computers and small servers would render "Big Iron" (industry jargon for mainframe) obsolete. But IBM believed that serious, security-rich, industrial-strength computing would always be in demand, so it introduced System/390 (S/390) (Figure A-5). IBM stuck with the mainframe, but reinvented it from the inside, infusing it with an entirely new technology core and reducing its price.

Figure A-5   S/390 G5 and G6

IBM introduced the concepts of *system clustering* and *data sharing*, and announced S/390 Parallel Sysplex, which made high levels of system availability possible.

Complementary Metal Oxide Semiconductor (CMOS)-based processors were introduced into the mainframe environment, replacing the bipolar technology and setting the new direction for modern mainframe technology. CMOS chips required less power than chips using just one type of transistor.

In the same decade, IBM introduced the parallel channel through Enterprise System Connectivity (ESCON) and began the integration of the network adapter to the mainframe through the Open System Adapter (OSA).

In 1998, IBM introduced a new module capable of surpassing the 1,000 MIPS barrier, making it one of the world's most powerful mainframes. Also in this period, the concept of logical partition was extended to support 15 partitions.

Capacity Upgrade on Demand (CUoD) debuted on S/390 in 1999. CUoD provides extra processors as spare capacity that can be "turned on" as dictated by business needs. It provides a critical tool that can help companies better manage spikes in demand and handle unpredictable changes.

Still in 1999, IBM introduced the first enterprise server to use the IBM innovative copper chip technology. The synergy helped extend customers' ability to handle millions of e-business workload transactions and large-scale Enterprise Resource Planning applications. A new concept arose at that time, that is, the possibility to increase the machines' capacity without stopping them.

FICON, a new fiber optic channel, was introduced and provides up to eight times the capacity of ESCON channels. Also in 1999, Linux appeared on S/390 for the first time.

In October 2000, IBM announced the first generation of the IBM eServer zSeries mainframes. The z/Architecture is an extension of ESA/390 and supports 64-bit addressing. Dynamic channel management was also introduced, as well as specialized cryptographic capability. The mainframe became "open" and capable of executing Linux; special processors (IFLs) were developed.

IBM eServer zSeries z900 was launched in 2000 and was the first IBM server "designed from the ground up for e-business" (Figure A-6).

Figure A-6   z900

The z900 was followed by the IBM eServer zSeries z990 (Figure A-7). The z990 reached 9000 MIPS; the increased scalability was further supported by the increase in the number of logical partitions available from 15 to 30 LPARs. There is still a 256-channel limit per operating system image, but z990 can have 1024 channels distributed in four Logical Channel SubSystems (LCSSs). The current model also offers IFL, a special processor for Linux to manage clustering, and zAAP to process Java.

Figure A-7   z990

zSeries is based on the 64-bit z/Architecture, which is designed to reduce memory and storage bottlenecks and which can automatically direct resources to priority workloads through Intelligent Resource Director (IRD). IRD is a key feature of the z/Architecture. Together, Parallel Sysplex technology and IRD are designed to provide the flexibility and responsiveness required by on demand business workloads.

The z990 provides a multibook system structure that supports the configuration of one to four *books*. Each book is composed of a Multiple Chip Module (MCM) with 12 processors, of which eight can be configured as standard processors; memory cards that can support up to 64 GB of memory per book and high performance Self-Timed Interconnects. The maximum number of processors available on a z990 is 32.

To support the highly scalable multibook system design, the Channel SubSystem (CSS) has been enhanced with Logical Channel SubSystems (LCSSs), which offers the capability to install up to 1024 ESCON channels across three I/O cages. With Spanned Channel support, HiperSockets™, ICB, ISC-3, OSA-Express, and FICON Express can be shared across LCSSs for additional flexibility.

High-speed interconnects for TCP/IP communication, known as HiperSockets, allow TCP/IP traffic to travel among partitions and virtual servers at memory speed, rather than network speed.

The latest generation of mainframes, the IBM System z9® 109 (z9-109) is the next step in the evolution of the IBM mainframe family (Figure A-8). It uses the z/Architecture and instruction set (with some extensions) of the z900 and z990 servers. (This architecture, formerly known as ESAME Architecture, is commonly known as 64-bit architecture, although it provides much more than 64-bit capability.) The physical appearance of the z9-109 server and z990 servers is similar. However, in addition to extending zSeries technology, the z9-109 server delivers enhancements in the areas of performance, scalability, availability, security, and virtualization.

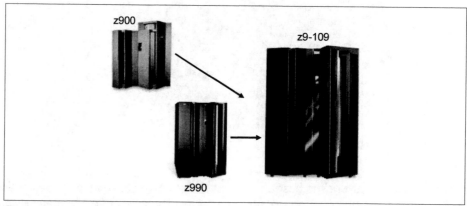

Figure A-8   z9-109

Examples of further mainframe evolution in the z9-109 include:

► A modular multi-book design that supports one to four books and up to 54 processor units (customer-usable PUs) per server

► Full 64-bit real and virtual storage support, and any logical partition can be defined for 31-bit or 64-bit addressability

► Up to 512 GB of system memory

► Up to 60 logical partitions

In previous generations of mainframes, the number of I/O devices in a system was limited by the number of channels, the number of control units on each channel, and the number of devices on each channel. The addressing structure was also a limitation. The fixed three-byte addresses (one byte each for channel, control unit, and device) of early systems evolved into four-byte device numbers, allowing up to almost 64 KB device addresses.

The z9-109 server continues this growth by providing Multiple Subchannel Sets (MSS), allowing up to almost 128 KB device addresses.

Channel performance has evolved from parallel channels to ESCON channels to FICON channels. The z9-109 server continues such growth by providing a significantly higher-performance option for channel programming.

Server workloads have been partly offloaded into segregated processors, such as system assist processors, ICFs, IFLs, and zAAPs. The z9-109 server enhances the management of these workloads by providing separate pools for PR/SM handling of shared ICFs, IFPs, and zAAPs.

Basic "real" systems evolved into virtual systems and this evolution has extended to systems, processors, memory, I/O devices, LAN interfaces, and so on. The z9-109 server continues this direction with new instructions that improve the performance of virtual machine QDIO operations. This is done by creating a pass through architecture designed to reduce host programming impact, avoiding the stopping of guest processing when adapter interruptions are present.

Recent mainframe generations have extended the instruction set to include instructions more compatible with other platforms (such as binary floating point), instructions to better implement popular languages (such as the string-handling instructions for C/C++), instructions to improve register usage (such as the relative and immediate instructions, and the long-displacement instructions), and so on. The z9-109 server continues this expansion with new and changed instructions.

Cryptographic hardware assistance has been available in many forms on earlier systems, and with much more emphasis in more recent servers. The z9-109 server continues the evolution of cryptographic hardware processing by extending the functions of the basic cryptographic instructions and by consolidating the options (secure coprocessor and accelerator) in a single feature. The two options can be individually defined to the feature.

Transparent hardware recovery has been a keystone in mainframe design and has evolved in many directions. The z9-109 server continues this evolution by extending such transparent recovery functions to include the paths from I/O cages to system memory.

Concurrent maintenance is a major design goal for modern mainframes and often involves balancing a design between replicated components and more integration onto chips and MCMs. The z9-109 server allows for a single book, in a multi-book configuration, to be concurrently removed and reinstalled during an upgrade or repair.

DB2 sample tables

Most of the examples in Chapter 12, "Database management systems on z/OS" on page 433refer to the tables in this appendix. As a group, the tables include information that describes employees and departments and make up a sample application that illustrates most of the features of DB2.

Department table

The department table (DEPT) describes each department in the enterprise, identifies its manager, and shows the department to which it reports. The table resides in table space DSN8D81A.DSN8S81D and is created by using the following code:

```
CREATE TABLE DSN8810.DEPT
        (DEPTNO    CHAR(3)        NOT NULL,
         DEPTNAME  VARCHAR(36)    NOT NULL,
         MGRNO     CHAR(6)                 ,
         ADMRDEPT  CHAR(3)        NOT NULL,
         LOCATION  CHAR(16)                ,
         PRIMARY KEY (DEPTNO)             )
 IN DSN8D81A,DSN8S81D
 CCSID EBCDIC;
```

Because the table is self-referencing, and also is part of a cycle of dependencies, its foreign keys must be added later with these statements:

```
ALTER TABLE DSN8810.DEPT
        FOREIGN KEY RDD (ADMRDEPT) REFERENCES DSN8810.DEPT
               ON DELETE CASCADE;

ALTER TABLE DSN8810.DEPT
        FOREIGN KEY RDE (MGRNO) REFERENCES DSN8810.EMP
               ON DELETE SET NULL;
```

Table B-1 shows the content of the department table.

Table B-1   Content of the department table

Column	Column name	Description
1	DEPTNO	Department ID (the primary key).
2	DEPTNAME	A name describing the general activities of the department.
3	MGRNO	Employee number (EMPNO) of the department manager.
4	ADMRDEPT	ID of the department to which this department reports. The department at the highest level reports to itself.
5	LOCATION	The remote location name.

Table B-2 shows the indexes on the department table.

Table B-2   Indexes on the department table

Name	On column	Type of index
DSN8810.XDEPT1	DEPTNO	Primary and ascending
DSN8810.XDEPT2	MGRNO	Ascending
DSN8810.XDEPT3	ADMRDEPT	Ascending

Table B-3 shows additional content of the department table.

Table B-3   Additional content of the department table

DEPTNO	DEPTNAME	MGRNO	ARMRDEPT	LOCATION
A00	SPIFFY COMPUTER SERVICE DIV.	000010	A00	---------------
B01	PLANNING	000020	A00	---------------
C01	INFORMATION CENTER	000030	A00	---------------
D01	DEVELOPMENT CENTER	----------	A00	---------------
E01	SUPPORT SERVICES	000050	A00	---------------
D11	MANUFACTURING SYSTEMS	000060	D01	---------------
D21	ADMINISTRATION SYSTEMS	000070	D01	---------------
E11	OPERATIONS	000090	E01	---------------
E21	SOFTWARE SUPPORT	000100	E01	---------------
F22	BRANCH OFFICE F2	----------	E01	---------------
G22	BRANCH OFFICE G2	----------	E01	---------------
H22	BRANCH OFFICE H2	----------	E01	---------------
I22	BRANCH OFFICE I2	----------	E01	---------------
J22	BRANCH OFFICE J2	----------	E01	---------------

Relationship to other tables

The table is self-referencing; the value of the administering department must be a department ID. The table is a parent table of:

► The employee table, through a foreign key on column WORKDEPT.

► The project table, through a foreign key on column DEPTNO. It is a dependent of the employee table, through its foreign key on column MGRNO.

Employee table

The employee table (EMP) identifies all employees by an employee number and lists basic personnel information. The table resides in the partitioned table space DSN8D81A.DSN8S81E. Because it has a foreign key referencing DEPT, that table and the index on its primary key must be created first. Then EMP is created by using the following code:

```
CREATE TABLE DSN8810.EMP
     (EMPNO     CHAR(6)                              NOT NULL,
      FIRSTNME  VARCHAR(12)                          NOT NULL,
      MIDINIT   CHAR(1)                              NOT NULL,
      LASTNAME  VARCHAR(15)                          NOT NULL,
      WORKDEPT  CHAR(3)                                      ,
      PHONENO   CHAR(4)            CONSTRAINT NUMBER CHECK
      (PHONENO >= '0000' AND
       PHONENO <= '9999')                                   ,
      HIREDATE  DATE                                         ,
      DOB       CHAR(8)                                      ,
      EDLEVEL   SMALLINT                                     ,
      SEX       CHAR(1)                                      ,
      BIRTHDATE DATE                                         ,
      SALARY    DECIMAL(9,2)                                 ,
      BONUS     DECIMAL(9,2)                                 ,
      COMM      DECIMAL(9,2)                                 ,
      PRIMARY KEY (EMPNO)                                    ,
      FOREIGN KEY RED (WORKDEPT) REFERENCES DSN8810.DEPT
                  ON DELETE SET NULL                        )
EDITPROC  DSN8EAE1
IN DSN8D81A.DSN8S81E
CCSID EBCDIC;
```

Table B-4 shows the columns of the employee table.

Table B-4   Columns of the employee table

Column	Column name	Description
1	EMPNO	Employee number (the primary key)
2	FIRSTNME	First name of employee
3	MIDINIT	Middle initial of employee
4	LASTNAME	Last name of employee
5	WORKDEPT	ID of department in which the employee works
6	PHONENO	Employee telephone number
7	HIREDATE	Date of hire
8	JOB	Job held by the employee
9	EDLEVEL	Number of years of formal education
10	SEX	Sex of the employee (M or F)
11	BIRTHDATE	Date of birth
12	SALARY	Yearly salary in dollars
13	BONUS	Yearly bonus in dollars
14	COMM	Yearly commission in dollars

Table B-5 shows the indexes of the employee table.

Table B-5   Indexes of the employee table

Name	On column	Type of index
DSN8810.XEMP1	EMPNO	Primary, partitioned, ascending
DSN8810.XEMP2	WORKDEPT	Ascending

Relationship to other tables

The table is a parent table of:

► The department table, through a foreign key on column MGRNO.

► The project table, through a foreign key on column RESPEMP. It is a dependent of the department table, through its foreign key on column WORKDEPT.

C

Utility programs

There is no specific definition of what constitutes a z/OS utility program, but common usage includes only a few z/OS-provided programs as *utilities*. The UNIX community, by contrast, considers many of the standard commands as utilities. This includes compilers, backup programs, filters, and many other types of programs. To the z/OS community, these are *applications* or *programs*, not utilities.[1] The difference is simply one of terminology, but it can be confusing to new z/OS users.

z/OS utilities are batch programs (although they can be used in the TSO foreground with the appropriate ALLOC commands) and they tend to have similar JCL requirements. These utilities include DD statements for SYSPRINT, SYSIN, SYSUT1, and SYSUT2. Most z/OS users are familiar with IEFBR14, IEBGENER, and IEBCOPY. VSAM users must be familiar with IDCAMS.

Considering the wide-ranging functions and abilities of z/OS, there are only a small number of system-provided utilities, which has resulted in a large number of customer-written utility programs (although most users refrain from naming them utilities), and many of them are widely shared by the user community. Independent software vendors also provide many similar products (for a fee). Some of these can be categorized as utilities; of these, some compete with IBM utilities, while many others provide functions not included with the IBM-provided utilities.

---

[1] z/OS UNIX uses the common UNIX terminology for utilities.

649

Most of the basic and system utilities described here are described in *z/OS DFSMSdfp Utilities*, SC26-7414. This appendix is intended to provide a summary of what is available and to provide simple examples of the most basic utility functions.

Basic utilities

A few utility programs (using the traditional terminology) are widely used in batch jobs. They are described in some detail here.

IEFBR14

The only function of this program is to provide a zero (0) completion code. It is used as a safe vehicle to "execute JCL." The notion of executing JCL is incorrect terminology, but it conveys the idea well. For example, consider the following job:

```
//OGDEN1 JOB 1,BILL,MSGCLASS=X
// EXEC PGM=IEFBR14
//A DD DSN=OGDEN.LIB.CNTL,DISP=(NEW,CATLG),VOL=SER=WORK02,
//         UNIT=3390,SPACE=(CYL,(3,1,25)
//B DD DSN=OGDEN.OLD.DATA,DISP=(OLD,DELETE)
```

This is a useful job, although the program that is executed (IEFBR14) does nothing. While preparing to run the job, the initiator allocates OGDEN.LIB.CNTL and keeps the data set when the job ends. It also deletes OGDEN.OLD.DATA at the end of the job. The DD names A and B have no meaning and are used because the syntax of a DD statement requires a DD name.

The same functions to create one data set and delete another could be performed through ISPF, for example, but these actions might be needed as part of a larger sequence of batch jobs.

> **Note:** The name IEFBR14 is interesting. One IBM group writing early OS/360 code used the prefix IEF for all their modules. In assembly language, BR means Branch to the address in a Register. Branching to the address in general register 14 is the standard way to end a program. While not an especially clever name, practically all dedicated z/OS users remember IEFBR14 easily.

IEFBR14 is not a utility in the sense that it is not included in *z/OS DFSMSdfp Utilities*, SC26-7414. However, there is no other practical category for this useful program, so we have arbitrarily placed it in the utility category.

IEBGENER

The IEBGENER utility copies one sequential data set to another. (Remember that a member of a partitioned data set can be used as a sequential data set.) It can also do some filtering of the data, change LRECL and BLKSIZE, generate records, and several other functions. However, the most common use is to simply copy data sets. A typical job could be the following one:

```
//OGDEN2 JOB 1,BILL,MSGCLASS=X
//   PGM=IEBGENER
//SYSIN DD DUMMY
//SYSPRINT DD SYSOUT=X
//SYSUT1 DD DISP=SHR,DSN=BILL.SEQ.DATA
//SYSUT2 DD DISP=(NEW,CATLG),DSN=BILL.COPY.DATA,UNIT=3390,
//   VOL=SER=WORK02,SPACE=(TRK,3,3))
```

IEBGENER requires four DD statements with the DD names indicated in the example. The SYSIN DD statement is used to read control parameters; for simple uses, no control parameters are needed, and a DD DUMMY can be used. The SYSPRINT statement is for messages from IEBGENER. The SYSUT1 statement is for input and the SYSUT2 statement is for output. This example reads an existing data set and copies it to a new data set.

If the output data set is new and if no DCB parameters are specified, IEBGENER copies the DCB parameters from the input data set. (The DCB parameters include LRECL, RECFM, and BLKSIZE, as described in 5.8, "Data set record formats" on page 211.)

Another common example is something like the following example:

```
//OGDEN2 JOB 1,BILL,MSGCLASS=X
//   PGM=IEBGENER
//SYSIN DD DUMMY
//SYSPRINT DD SYSOUT=X
//SYSUT2 DD DISP=OLD,DSN=BILL.TEST.DATA
//SYSUT1 DD *
   This is in-stream data. It can be as long
   as you like. It appears to an application as
   LRECL=80, RECFM=F, BLKSIZE=80. You would
   want to have the SYSUT2 data set allocated with
   a better blocksize.
/*
```

This example assumes BILL.TEST.DATA has already been created. This job overwrites it with the data in the SYSUT1 input stream. Because the output data set already exists, IEBGENER uses its existing DCB attributes.

IEBGENER is the most basic copy or list program supplied with z/OS. It has been present since the first release of OS/360.

IEBCOPY

This utility is commonly used for several purposes:

▶ To copy selected (or all) members from one partitioned data set to another.

▶ To copy a partitioned data set into a unique sequential format known as an *unloaded* partitioned data set. As a sequential data set, it can be written on tape, sent by FTP,[2] or manipulated as a simple sequential data set.

▶ To read an unloaded partitioned data set (which is a sequential file) and recreate the original partitioned data set. Optionally, only selected members might be used.

▶ To *compress* partitioned data sets (in place) to recover lost space.

Most z/OS software products are distributed as unloaded partitioned data sets. The ISPF copy options (option 3.3, among others) uses IEBCOPY "under the covers." Moving a PDS or PDSE from one volume to another is easily done with IEBCOPY. If there is a need to manipulate partitioned data sets in batch jobs, IEBCOPY is probably used. Equivalent manipulation under TSO (using ISPF) uses IEBCOPY indirectly.

A simple IEBCOPY job might be the following one:

```
//OGDEN5 JOB 1,BILL,MSGCLASS=X
// EXEC PGM=IEBCOPY
//SYSPRINT DD SYSOUT=*
//SYSIN DD DUMMY
//SYSUT1 DD DISP=SHR,DSN=OGDEN.LIB.SOURCE
//SYSUT2 DD DISP=(NEW,KEEP),UNIT=TAPE,DSN=OGDENS.SOURCE,
//          VOL=SER=123456
```

This job unloads OGDEN.LIB.SOURCE (which we assume is a partitioned data set) and write it on tape. (The name TAPE is assumed to be an *esoteric name* that the local installation associates with tape drives.) By default, IEBCOPY copies from SYSUT1 to SYSUT2. Notice that the data set name on tape is not the same as the data set name used as input (the same name could be used, but there is no requirement to do so). The following job could be used to restore the PDS on another volume:

```
//JOE6 JOB 1,JOE,MSGCLASS=X
// EXEC PGM=IEBCOPY
```

---

[2] The output data set is normally V or VB, and there are additional considerations about sending V or VB data sets through FTP.

```
//SYSPRINT DD SYSOUT=*
//SYSIN DD DUMMY
//SYSUT1 DD DISP=OLD,UNIT=TAPE,DSN=OGDENS.SOURCE,
//            VOL=SER=123456
//SYSUT2 DD DISP=(NEW,CATLG),DSN=P390Z.LIB.PGMS,UNIT=3390,
//            SPACE=(TRK,(10,10,20)),VOL=SER=333333
```
In this example IEBCOPY will detect that the input data set is an unloaded partitioned data set. We required external knowledge to determine that the data set would fit in about 10 tracks and should have 20 directory blocks.
Instead of using DD DUMMY for SYSIN we could this:
```
//SYSIN DD *
 COPY OUTDD=SYSUT2,INDD=SYSUT1
 SELECT MEMBER=(PGM1,PGM2)
/*
```

The OUTDD and INDD parameters specify the DD names to be used. In this case, we simply used the default names, but this is not required. The SELECT statement specifies the member names to be processed.

Restoring a partitioned data set from an unloaded copy automatically compresses (recovers lost space) the data set.

IEBDG

The IEBDG utility is used to create records in which fields can be generated with various types of data. IEBDG is typically used to create test data. A variety of fields and data can be generated and the fields can be changed for each record with ripple, wave, shift, roll, and other field permutations. IEBDG can accept input data records and overlay specified fields in the input with generated data.

Here is a simple example of IEGDB use:
```
//OGDEN7 JOB 1,BILL,MSGCLASS=X
// EXEC PGM=IEBDG
//SYSPRINT DD SYSOUT=*
//OUT DD DISP=(NEW,CATLG),DSN=OGDEN.TEST.DATA,UNIT=3390,
//            VOL=SER=WORK01,SPACE=(CYL,(10,1)),
//            DCB=(RECFM=FB,LRECL=80,BLKSIZE=8000)
//SYSIN DD *
  DSD OUTPUT=(OUT)
  FD NAME=FIELD1,LENGTH=30,FORMAT=AL,ACTION=RP
  FD NAME=FIELD2,LENGTH=10,PICTURE=10,'TEST DATA '
  FD NAME=FIELD3,LENGTH=10,FORMAT=RA
  CREATE QUANTITY=90000,NAME=(FIELD1,FIELD2,FIELD3)
  END
/*
```

This job creates a new data set, OGDEN.TEST.DATA, with 90,000 records. Each record is 80 bytes, as specified in the DCB parameters in the DD statement. The control statements specify three fields that occupy the first 50 bytes of each record. By default, IEBDG fills the remaining bytes with binary zeros. The three fields are:

► An alphabetic field ('ABCDEF...'), 30 bytes long. It is rippled (rotated left one byte) after each record is generated.

► The second field contains 10 bytes with the fixed constant 'TEST DATA '.

► The third field contains 10 bytes with random binary data.

The utility can generate more complex patterns, but this example is typical of simple usage. It also illustrates an estimate of the amount of disk space needed for data:

► We know that a 3390 track holds about 57 KB, less whatever space is lost to inter-record gaps.

► We know the DCB parameters (as specified in the JCL) are LRECL=80, BLKSIZE=8000, and RECFM=FB. We do not know why these DCB parameters were selected, but we assume they relate to the program that will use the test data.

► We can estimate that six blocks of 8000 each will probably fit on one track. This is not an efficient block size, because some track space is probably lost, but it is useful enough.

► Each block contains 100 records of 80 bytes each. Each track contains 600 records. (There is no space lost within a block of FB records.)

► A cylinder contains 15 tracks, therefore a cylinder will hold 9000 of these records.

Based on this setup, we need 10 cylinders to hold 90,000 records. We specified 10 cylinders as the primary allocation space in the JCL, with one cylinder as the secondary allocation increment. We should not require any secondary allocation, but it provides a safety factor. We could have asked for 150 tracks instead of 10 cylinders; the result would be the same.

IDCAMS

The IDCAMS program is not part of the basic set of z/OS utilities documented in *z/OS DFSMSdfp Utilities*, SC26-7414. The IDCAMS program is primarily used to create and manipulate VSAM data sets. It has other functions (such as catalog updates), but it is most closely associated with VSAM. It provides many complex functions and whole manuals are needed to describe all of them. The basic IBM manual, at the time of the writing of this book, is *DFSMS Access Method Services for Catalogs*, SC26-7394.

A typical example of a simple use of IDCAMS is as follows:

```
//OGDEN12 JOB 1,BILL,MSGCLASS=X
//DEL   EXEC PGM=IDCAMS
//SYSPRINT DD SYSOUT=*
//SYSIN DD *
  DELETE OGDEN.DATA.VSAM CLUSTER
/*
//LOAD  EXEC PGM=IDCAMS
//SYSPRINT DD *
//DATAIN DD DISP=OLD,DSN=OGDEN.SORTOUT
//SYSIN DD *
  DEFINE CLUSTER (NAME (OGDEN.DATA.VSAM) -
         VOLUMES(WORK02) CYLINDERS(1 1) -
         RECORDSIZE (72 100) KEYS(9 8) INDEXED)
  REPRO INFILE(DATAIN) OUTDATASET(OGDEN.DATA.VSAM) ELIMIT(200)
/*
```

This example illustrates a number of points:

▶ There are two job steps. The first step deletes the data set that will be created by the second step. This is a clean-up function. The data set might not exist at this point and the first step will have a completion code indicating the action failed. It is ignored.

▶ Note that there are no DD statements for the VSAM data set. IDCAMS performs dynamic allocation to create the necessary JCL.

▶ The second step performs two functions. It first creates a VSAM data set (using the DEFINE CLUSTER command), and then loads it from a sequential data set (using the REPRO command). The sequential data set does require a DD statement.

▶ The DEFINE CLUSTER command is continued over three records. The continuation indicators are the same as used for TSO commands.

- The VSAM data set is on volume WORK02, and uses one cylinder for primary space and one cylinder for secondary allocation. The average record size is 72 bytes and the maximum record size is 100 bytes. (VSAM data sets always use variable length records.) The primary key (for accessing records in the data set) is 8 bytes long and begins at an offset of 9 bytes into each record.

- Records for loading a VSAM data set this way should already be sorted into key order.

- The ELIMIT parameter specifies the number of error records that REPRO will ignore before terminating operation. An error record is usually due to a duplicate key value.

Many of IDCAMS functions can be entered as TSO commands. For example, DEFINE CLUSTER can be used as a TSO command. However, this is generally not recommended because these commands can be complex and the errors encountered can be complex. Entering the IDCAMS commands through a batch job allows the commands and resulting messages to be reviewed as often as necessary by using SDSF to view the output.

IEBUPDTE

The IEBUPDTE utility is used to create multiple members in a partitioned data set, or to update records within a member. Although it can be used for other types of records, its main use is to create or maintain JCL procedure libraries or assembler macro libraries. Today, this utility is used mostly for z/OS licensed program distributions and maintenance. It is seldom used by TSO users.

A basic example involves adding two JCL procedures to MY.PROCLIB. This task can easily be accomplished through ISPF, but if we assume the following job was sent on tape, then the usefulness is more apparent:

```
//OGDEN10 JOB 1,BILL,MSGCLASS=X
// EXEC PGM=IEBUPDTE
//SYSPRINT DD SYSOUT=*
//SYSUT1 DD DISP=OLD,DSN=MY.PROCLIB
//SYSUT2 DD DISP=OLD,DSN=MY.PROCLIB
//SYSIN DD DATA
./ ADD   LIST=ALL,NAME=MYJOB1
//STEP1 EXEC=BILLX1
//PRINT DD SYSOUT=A
//          (more JCL for MYJOB1)
//SYSUDUMP DD SYSOUT=*    (last JCL for MYJOB1)
./   REPL  LIST=ALL,NAME=LASTJOB
//LIST EXEC PGM=BILLLIST
//          (more JCL for this procedure)
//* LAST JCL STATEMENT FOR LASTJOB
```

```
./      ENDUP
/*
```

This example requires a few comments:

▶ When a library is to be updated, then SYSUT1 and SYSUT2 both point to that library. (If they point to different libraries, the SYSUT1 library is copied to the SYSUT2 library and then updated.)

▶ The SYSIN DD DATA format indicates that the data in the input stream contains // in columns one and two. It should not be interpreted as JCL. The end of the input stream is indicated by /*.

▶ The IEBUPDTE utility uses control statements with ./ in the first two columns.

▶ A member named MYJOB1 is added to MY.PROCLIB; this member should not already exist in the library.

▶ A member named LASTJOB is replaced with new contents.

The IEBUPDTE utility can also add or replace statements in a member based on the *sequence numbers* in the statements. This is one of the few remaining uses for sequence numbers in JCL or source statements.

Again, we stress that IEBUPDTE is typically used for program distribution and maintenance. For example, if a software vendor's product adds 25 JCL procedures to a customer's procedure library, the vendor might package the procedures as an IEBUPDTE job. One advantage is that all the material is in source format and the customer can easily review the contents before running the job.

System-oriented utilities

The programs discussed in this section provide several basic utility functions for system administrators and are only briefly described.

IEHLIST

The IEHLIST utility is used to list a partitioned data set directory or a disk volume table of contents (VTOC). It is normally used for VTOC listings and provides bit-level information. IEHLIST is not used often in most installations, but is needed in the rare cases where a VTOC is corrupted. It is sometimes used with the SUPERZAP program to patch or fix a broken VTOC.

IEHINITT

The IEHINITT utility is used to write standard labels on tapes. It can be used, as needed, to label a single tape or it can be used to label large batches of tapes. Many larger z/OS installations do not allow unlabeled tapes to be brought into the installation.

IEHPROGM

The IEHPROGM utility is almost obsolete. It is used primarily to manage catalogs, rename data sets, and delete data sets using a program instead of using JCL actions. It was primarily used during system installation or the installation of a major program product. These functions may involve dozens (or hundreds) of such catalog and data set actions. Having commands prepared beforehand (in a batch job with IEHPROGM) is much less error-prone than more dynamic approaches. Most of the IEHPROGM functions are available in IDCAMS and that is now the preferred utility for catalog and data set functions.

ICKDSF

The ICKDSF utility is used primarily to initialize disk volumes. At a minimum, this involves creating the disk label record and the VTOC. ICKDSF can also scan a volume to ensure that it is usable, reformat all the tracks, write home addresses and R0 records, and so on.

SUPERZAP

The SUPERZAP program (the actual name has changed a number of times) can be used to patch disk records. It understands the format of executable modules in PDS libraries, which is needed for its most common use, that is, applying patches to such executable modules. SUPERZAP is not often used for system maintenance now; its use was more common in earlier versions of the operating system.

SUPERZAP is used to patch VTOCs, executable programs, or almost any other disk record. In practice, it is mostly used to patch executable programs. It was extensively used in earlier days to install minor fixes in programs.

Consider, for example, a new release of a product. The new release may have been sent on tape to hundreds or thousands of customers. After shipping all these tapes, the developers may have discovered a minor bug that could be fixed by changing a few instructions. Instead of creating new distribution tapes and shipping them to all the customers (a massive and expensive undertaking for a major software product), the developers could create a SUPERZAP solution and mail, fax, or use FTP to download it to their customers.

SUPERZAP is a bit-level tool. Its use is practical where relatively few bits or bytes need to be changed. An example of SUPERZAP is:

```
//OGDEN15 JOB 1,BILL,MSGCLASS=X
//   EXEC PGM=AMASPZAP
//SYSPRINT DD SYSOUT=*
//SYSLIB DD DISP=OLD,DSN=OGDEN.LIB.LOAD
//SYSIN DD *
  NAME QSAM1
  VERIFY 004E 4780
  REP    004E 4700
/*
```

A SYSLIB DD statement must point to the data set containing the load module to be modified. The NAME control statement identifies the executable module (which is the PDS member name) to be altered. The VERIFY statement says to look at offset x'004E' in the module and verify that it contains x'4780'. If the verification is correct, then change the module to contain x'4700' at this same offset. This action changes a Branch Equal instruction to a No Operation and, we assume, changes the logic of the program.

We can make a SUPERZAP patch like this because we had an assembly listing of the program and could see the exact offset within the module containing the instruction we wanted to change. This would be much more difficult without a listing, although it has been done by reading hexadecimal storage dumps and reconstructing machine language operation from the dumps. Note that the format of executable programs on disk is complex and is not a simple image of the program when it is loaded into memory. (Relocation data, external symbols, and an optimized disk loading format form part of the complexity.) SUPERZAP understands this disk format and allows users to zap an executable program as though it were a memory image.

We have discussed SUPERZAP, but the program in the example is AMASPZAP. This is the current name of the program, although it is still widely known as SUPERZAP.

Application-level utilities

There are many application programs that could be considered utilities. We briefly describe a few of the common ones here. These are more complex to use than the basic programs above and we do not include usage examples.

ADRDSSU

This program is the primary *disk dump* and *disk restore* program provided with z/OS. It is capable of filtering and selecting which data sets to dump or restore, but it is used primarily as a full disk dump program. The purpose of dumping a disk is usually to provide a backup of the contents that can be restored, if needed. A common use is to dump complete volumes, but restore only a specific data set that was accidentally destroyed.

A backup is usually written to tape, but can be written to a disk data set. A disk can be dumped track-by-track (known as a *physical dump*) or data set-by-data set (known as a *logical dump*). When a logical dump is performed, multiple data set extents may be combined into a single extent, partitioned data sets are compressed, and free space is all in a single extent.

RMF

Resource Measurement Facility (RMF) is an optional IBM licensed program used to measure various aspects of system performance. Different RMF modules provide long-term statistical gathering, instantaneous data, long-term reporting, batch-type reports, TSO-oriented reports, and so on. The hardware I/O system maintains statistical counters about queuing time for each I/O device, amount of activity per device, and other low-level information. RMF accesses these hardware counters and includes them in its reports.

EBCDIC - ASCII table

In this appendix, we provide the correlations between EBCDIC and ASCII settings.

Hx	Dec	E	A	Hx	Dec	E	A	Hx	Dec	E	A	Hz	Dec	E	A
00	00	NUL		20	32		SP	40	64	SP	@	60	96	-	'
01	01			21	33		!	41	65		A	61	97	/	a
02	02			22	34		"	42	66		B	62	98		b
03	03			23	35		#	43	67		C	63	99		c
04	04			24	36		$	44	68		D	64	100		d
05	05			25	37		%	45	69		E	65	101		e
06	06			26	38		&	46	70		F	66	102		f
07	07			27	39		'	47	71		G	67	103		g
08	08			28	40		(	48	72		H	68	104		h
09	09			29	41		)	49	73		I	69	105		i
0A	10			2A	42		*	4A	74	^	J	6A	106			j
0B	11			2B	43		+	4B	75	.	K	6B	107	,	k
0C	12			2C	44		,	4C	76	<	L	6C	108	%	l
0D	13			2D	45		-	4D	77	(	M	6D	109	_	m
0E	14			2E	46		.	4E	78	+	N	6E	110	>	n
0F	15			2F	47		/	4F	79			O	6F	111	?	o
10	16			30	48		0	50	80	&	P	70	112		p
11	17			31	49		1	51	81		Q	71	113		q
12	18			32	50		2	52	82		R	72	114		r
13	19			33	51		3	53	83		S	73	115		s
14	20			34	52		4	54	84		T	74	116		t
15	21			35	53		5	55	85		U	75	117		u
16	22			36	54		6	56	86		V	76	118		v

Hx	Dec	E	A	Hx	Dec	E	A	Hx	Dec	E	A	Hz	Dec	E	A
17	23			37	55		7	57	87		W	77	119		w
18	24			38	56		8	58	88		X	78	120		x
19	25			39	57		9	59	89		Y	79	121		y
1A	26			3A	58		:	5A	90	!	Z	7A	122	:	z
1B	27			3B	59		;	5B	91	$	[	7B	123	#	{
1C	28			3C	60		<	5C	92	*	\	7C	124	@	|
1D	29			3D	61		=	5D	93	)	]	7D	125	'	}
1E	30			3E	62		>	5E	94	;	^	7E	126	=	~
1F	31			3F	63		?	5F	95	not	_	7F	127	"	

Hx	Dec	E	A	Hx	Dec	E	A	Hx	Dec	E	A	Hz	Dec	E	A
80	128			A0	160			C0	192	{		E0	224	\	
81	129	a		A1	161			C1	193	A		E1	225		
82	130	b		A2	162	s		C2	194	B		E2	226	S	
83	131	c		A3	163	t		C3	195	C		E3	227	T	
84	132	d		A4	164	u		C4	196	D		E4	228	U	
85	133	e		A5	165	v		C5	197	E		E5	229	V	
86	134	f		A6	166	w		C6	198	F		E6	230	W	
87	135	g		A7	167	x		C7	199	G		E7	231	X	
88	136	h		A8	168	y		C8	200	H		E8	232	Y	
89	137	i		A9	169	z		C9	201	I		E9	233	Z	
8A	138			AA	170			CA	202			EA	234		
8B	139			AB	171			CB	203			EB	235		
8C	140			AC	172			CC	204			EC	236		
8D	141			AD	173	[		CD	205			ED	237		
8E	142			AE	174			CE	206			EE	238		
8F	143			AF	175			CF	207			EF	239		
90	144			B0	176			D0	208	}		F0	240	0	
91	145	j		B1	177			D1	209	J		F1	241	1	
92	146	k		B2	178			D2	210	K		F2	242	2	
93	147	l		B3	179			D3	211	L		F3	243	3	
94	148	m		B4	180			D4	212	M		F4	244	4	
95	149	n		B5	181			D5	213	N		F5	245	5	
96	150	o		B6	182			D6	214	O		F6	246	6	
97	151	p		B7	183			D7	215	P		F7	247	7	
98	152	q		B8	184			D8	216	Q		F8	248	8	
99	153	r		B9	185			D9	217	R		F9	249	9	
9A	154			BA	186			DA	218			FA	250		
9B	155			BB	187			DB	219			FB	251		
9C	156			BC	188			DC	220			FC	252		
9D	157			BD	189	]		DD	221			FD	253		
9E	158			BE	190			DE	222			FE	254		
9F	159			BF	191			DF	223			FF	255		

Class programs

All the exercises here work with an employee file (or database); this file identifies all employees by an employee number and lists basic personnel information.

The exercise has the department number as input, selects all records from that department, and then does the sum of the salary fields of those records. Finally, the average salary is displayed.

The exercises that follow are written in different languages, executed in different environments and with different data sources, but all cover the functionality just described. The code, preparation jobs, and instructions are provided.

We assume students have installed an appropriate 3270 emulator and have the appropriate TSO, CICS, IBM DB2, and IBM WebSphere for z/OS authorizations. Pay attention to the system definitions (such as HLQs, DB2 database name, and so on) that each exercise might require.

COBOL-CICS-DB2 program

This section covers the program for COBOL, CICS, and DB2.

Source code

In this section, we list to the source code for this program.

Map definition

This definition is in the TMAP01 member in the LUISM.TEST.SAMPLIB library:

```
        PRINT NOGEN
TMAPSET DFHMSD TYPE=&SYSPARM,                                        X
               LANG=COBOL,                                           X
               MODE=INOUT,                                           X
               TERM=3270-2,                                          X
               CTRL=FREEKB,                                          X
               STORAGE=AUTO,                                         X
               TIOAPFX=YES
TMAP01  DFHMDI SIZE=(24,80),                                         X
               LINE=1,                                               X
               COLUMN=1,                                             X
               MAPATTS=COLOR
        DFHMDF POS=(1,1),                                            X
               LENGTH=9,                                             X
               ATTRB=(NORM,PROT),                                    X
               COLOR=BLUE,                                           X
               INITIAL='ABCD txid'
        DFHMDF POS=(1,26),                                          X
               LENGTH=28,                                            X
               ATTRB=(NORM,PROT),                                    X
               COLOR=GREEN,                                          X
               INITIAL='Average salary by department'
        DFHMDF POS=(9,1),                                            X
               LENGTH=41,                                            X
                ATTRB=(NORM,PROT),                                   X
               INITIAL='Type a department number and press enter.'
        DFHMDF POS=(11,1),                                          X
               LENGTH=18,                                            X
               ATTRB=(NORM,PROT),                                    X
               COLOR=GREEN,                                          X
               INITIAL='Department number:'
DPTONO  DFHMDF POS=(11,20),                                         X
               LENGTH=3,                                             X
               ATTRB=(NORM,UNPROT,IC),                               X
               COLOR=TURQUOISE,                                      X
               INITIAL='___'
        DFHMDF POS=(11,24),                                         X
```

```
                        LENGTH=1,                                    X
                        ATTRB=ASKIP
                DFHMDF POS=(13,1),                                   X
                        LENGTH=18,                                   X
                        ATTRB=(NORM,PROT),                           X
                        COLOR=GREEN,                                 X
                        INITIAL='Average salary($):'
AVGSAL    DFHMDF POS=(13,20),                                        X
                        LENGTH=11,                                   X
                        ATTRB=(NORM,PROT),                           X
                        COLOR=TURQUOISE
MSGLINE   DFHMDF POS=(23,1),                                         X
                         LENGTH=78,                                  X
                        ATTRB=(BRT,PROT),                            X
                        COLOR=BLUE
                DFHMDF POS=(23,79),                                  X
                        LENGTH=1,                                    X
                        ATTRB=(DRK,PROT,FSET),                       X
                        INITIAL=' '
                DFHMDF POS=(24,1),                                   X
                        LENGTH=7,                                    X
                        ATTRB=(NORM,PROT),                           X
                        COLOR=RED,                                   X
                        INITIAL='F3=Exit'
                DFHMSD TYPE=FINAL
                END
```

Program code

This program resides in the XYZ2 member in the LUISM.TEST.SAMPLIB library:

```
IDENTIFICATION DIVISION.
      *----------------------------------------------------------------
      *     COBOL-CICS-DB2 PROGRAM ZSCHOLAR RESIDENCY
      *     OBTAINS THE AVERAGE SALARY OF EMPLOYEES OF A GIVEN DEPART.
      *----------------------------------------------------------------
      *----------------------
       PROGRAM-ID.    XYZ2.
      /
       ENVIRONMENT DIVISION.
      *--------------------
       CONFIGURATION SECTION.
       INPUT-OUTPUT SECTION.
       FILE-CONTROL.
       DATA DIVISION.
      *-------------
       FILE SECTION.
      /
      *-------------
       WORKING-STORAGE SECTION.
```

```
******************************************************
* WORKAREAS                                          *
******************************************************
 01 SWITCH.
   05 DATA-IS          PIC X VALUE 'Y'.
      88 DATA-IS-0            VALUE 'Y'.
   05 SEND-IND         PIC X.
      88 SEND-IND-ERASE    VALUE '1'.
      88 SEND-IND-DATAO    VALUE '2'.
      88 SEND-IND-ALARM    VALUE '3'.
 01 COMMUNICATION-AREA PIC X.
 01 MSGLINET.
    02 MSGSQLC       PIC X(8).
    02 FILLER        PIC X.
    02 MSGREST       PIC X(69).
******************************************************
* DB2 HOST VARIABLES DECLARATION                     *
******************************************************
 01  WORKDEPT-HV  PIC X(3).
 01  SALARY-HV    PIC X(11).
 01  SALARY-IN    PIC S9(4) COMP-5.
******************************************************
* SQLCA DECLARATION                                  *
******************************************************
     EXEC SQL INCLUDE SQLCA END-EXEC.
******************************************************
* DFHAID                                             *
******************************************************
     COPY DFHAID.
******************************************************
* MAP COPY                                           *
******************************************************
     COPY MAPONL.
******************************************************
* DECLARE OF DB2 TABLE                               *
******************************************************
     EXEC SQL
     DECLARE DSN8810.EMP TABLE
     (EMPNO     CHAR(6)     NOT NULL,
      FIRSTNAME VARCHAR(12) NOT NULL,
      MIDINIT   CHAR(1)     NOT NULL,
      LASTNAME  VARCHAR(15) NOT NULL,
      WORKDEPT  CHAR(3)              ,
      PHONENO   CHAR(4)              ,
      HIREDATE  DATE                 ,
      JOB       CHAR(8)              ,
      EDLEVEL   SMALLINT             ,
      SEX       CHAR(1)              ,
      BIRTHDATE DATE                 ,
```

```
                SALARY    DECIMAL(9,2)         ,
                BONUS     DECIMAL(9,2)         ,
                COMM      DECIMAL(9,2)         )
            END-EXEC.
*****************************************************************
 LINKAGE SECTION.
*****************************************************************
 01 DFHCOMMAREA    PIC X.
/
 PROCEDURE DIVISION USING DFHCOMMAREA.
*****************************************************************
* MAIN ROGRAM ROUTINE
*****************************************************************
 MAINLINE.
*****************************************************************
* 2000-PROCESS
*****************************************************************
 2000-PROCESS.
     EVALUATE TRUE
       WHEN EIBCALEN = ZERO
          MOVE LOW-VALUE TO TMAP01O
          SET SEND-IND-ERASE TO TRUE
          PERFORM 2000-10-SEND
       WHEN EIBAID = DFHCLEAR
          MOVE LOW-VALUE TO TMAP01O
          SET SEND-IND-ERASE TO TRUE
          PERFORM 2000-10-SEND
       WHEN EIBAID = DFHPA1 OR DFHPA2 OR DFHPA3
          CONTINUE
       WHEN EIBAID = DFHPF3
           EXEC CICS RETURN
          END-EXEC
          GOBACK
       WHEN EIBAID = DFHENTER
          PERFORM 2000-00-PROCESS
       WHEN OTHER
          MOVE LOW-VALUE TO TMAP01o
          MOVE 'WRONG KEY' TO MSGLINEO
          SET SEND-IND-ALARM TO TRUE
          PERFORM 2000-10-SEND
     END-EVALUATE.
*
     EXEC CICS RETURN TRANSID('ABCD')
        COMMAREA(COMMUNICATION-AREA)
     END-EXEC.
     GOBACK.
 2000-00-PROCESS.
     EXEC CICS RECEIVE MAP('TMAP01')
                       MAPSET('TMAPSET')
```

```
                        INTO(TMAP01I)
        END-EXEC.
        IF DPTONOL = ZERO OR DPTONOI = SPACE
            MOVE 'N' TO DATA-IS
            MOVE 'ENTER A VALID DEPARTMENT NUMBER' TO MSGLINEO
        END-IF.
        IF DATA-IS-0
            MOVE DPTONOI TO WORKDEPT-HV
            PERFORM 2000-01-DB2
        END-IF.
        IF DATA-IS-0
            SET SEND-IND-DATAO TO TRUE
            PERFORM 2000-10-SEND
        ELSE
            SET SEND-IND-ALARM TO TRUE
            PERFORM 2000-10-SEND
        END-IF.
    *
      2000-01-DB2.
        EXEC SQL SELECT CHAR(DECIMAL(SUM(SALARY),9,2))
            INTO :SALARY-HV :SALARY-IN
            FROM DSN8810.EMP
            WHERE WORKDEPT=:WORKDEPT-HV END-EXEC.
        IF SQLCODE = 0
        THEN
            IF SALARY-IN = -1
            THEN
              MOVE 'N' TO DATA-IS
              MOVE 'NO EMPLOYEES EXIST IN THIS DEPARTMENT' TO MSGLINEO
              MOVE SPACES TO AVGSALO
            ELSE
              MOVE SALARY-HV TO AVGSALO
              MOVE SPACES TO MSGLINEO
            END-IF
        ELSE
            MOVE '0' TO DATA-IS
            MOVE SPACES TO AVGSALO
            MOVE 'SQLSTATE' TO MSGSQLC
            MOVE SQLSTATE TO MSGREST
            MOVE MSGLINET TO MSGLINEO
        END-IF.
    *
      2000-10-SEND.
        EVALUATE TRUE
        WHEN SEND-IND-ERASE
          EXEC CICS SEND MAP('TMAP01')
              MAPSET('TMAPSET')
              FROM (TMAP01O)
              ERASE
```

```
                END-EXEC
          WHEN SEND-IND-DATAO
            EXEC CICS SEND MAP('TMAP01')
                 MAPSET('TMAPSET')
                 FROM (TMAP01O)
                 DATAONLY
            END-EXEC
          WHEN SEND-IND-ALARM
            EXEC CICS SEND MAP('TMAP01')
                 MAPSET('TMAPSET')
                 FROM (TMAP01O)
                 DATAONLY
                 ALARM
            END-EXEC
       END-EVALUATE.
```

Preparation jobs

This section covers the preparation jobs for this program.

Assembling and link-editing the map

This job is in the MAPASSEM member in the LUISM.TEST.SAMPLIB library.
Both invoked procedures are in SYS1.PROCLIB.

```
//LUISM01 JOB (999,POK),'BMS Compilation',
//            CLASS=A,MSGCLASS=T,MSGLEVEL=(1,1)
//*****************************************************************
//*        ASSEMBLE MAP SET                                      *
//*****************************************************************
//STEP01   EXEC PROC=DFHASMV1,PARM.ASSEM='SYSPARM(MAP)'
//SYSLIN   DD DSN=LUISM.OBJETO,DCB=(LRECL=80),
//            SPACE=(2960,(10,10)),UNIT=SYSDA,DISP=(NEW,PASS)
//SYSIN    DD DSN=LUISM.TEST.SAMPLIB(TMAP01),DISP=SHR
/*
//*****************************************************************
//*        LINK EDIT                                             *
//*****************************************************************
//STEP02   EXEC PROC=DFHLNKV1,PARM='LIST,LET,XREF'
//SYSLIN   DD DSN=LUISM.OBJETO,DISP=(OLD,DELETE)
//         DD *
         MODE RMODE(ANY)
         NAME TMAPSET(R)
/*
```

Generating the map copy file

This job is in the MAPCOPYGM member in the LUISM.TEST.SAMPLIB library:

```
//LUISM02 JOB (999,POK),'BMS COPY',
//             CLASS=A,MSGCLASS=T,MSGLEVEL=(1,1)
//*********************************************************************
//*          MAP COPY GENERATION                                      *
//*********************************************************************
//STEP01   EXEC PROC=DFHASMV1,PARM.ASSEM='SYSPARM(DSECT)'
//SYSLIN   DD DSN=LUISM.TEST.SAMPLIB(MAPCOPY),DISP=OLD
//SYSIN    DD DSN=LUISM.TEST.SAMPLIB(TMAP01),DISP=SHR
/*
```

Preparing the program

This job is in the CICSDB2P member in the LUISM.TEST.SAMPLIB library:

```
//LUISM03 JOB (999,POK),'Cobol-CICS-DB2',
//             CLASS=A,MSGCLASS=T,MSGLEVEL=(1,1)
//*********************************************************************
//*  DB2 precompile, CICS translation, COBOL compile, pre-link,       *
//*  and link edit. Also DB2 Bind.                                    *
//*********************************************************************
//*********************************************************************
//*          DB2 Precompile                                           *
//*********************************************************************
//PC       EXEC PGM=DSNHPC,PARM='HOST(IBMCOB)'
//SYSIN    DD  DSN=LUISM.TEST.SAMPLIB(XYZ2),DISP=SHR
//DBRMLIB  DD  DISP=SHR,
//             DSN=DB8HU.DBRMLIB.DATA(XYZ2)
//STEPLIB  DD  DISP=SHR,DSN=DB8H8.SDSNEXIT
//         DD  DISP=SHR,DSN=DB8H8.SDSNLOAD
//SYSCIN   DD  DSN=&&DSNHOUT,DISP=(MOD,PASS),UNIT=SYSDA,
//             SPACE=(800,(500,500))
//SYSLIB   DD  DISP=SHR,DSN=DB8HU.SRCLIB.DATA
//SYSPRINT DD  SYSOUT=*
//SYSTERM  DD  SYSOUT=*
//SYSUDUMP DD  SYSOUT=*
//SYSUT1   DD  SPACE=(800,(500,500),,,ROUND),UNIT=VIO
//SYSUT2   DD  SPACE=(800,(500,500),,,ROUND),UNIT=VIO
/*
//*********************************************************************
//*          CICS Translator                                          *
//*********************************************************************
//TRN      EXEC PGM=DFHECP1$,
//             COND=(4,LT,PC)
//STEPLIB  DD DSN=CICSTS23.CICS.SDFHLOAD,DISP=SHR
//SYSPRINT DD SYSOUT=*
//SYSPUNCH DD DSN=&&SYSCIN,
//             DISP=(MOD,PASS),UNIT=SYSDA,
```

```
//              DCB=BLKSIZE=400,
//              SPACE=(400,(400,100))
//SYSUDUMP DD  SYSOUT=*
//SYSIN    DD  DSN=&&DSNHOUT,DISP=(OLD,DELETE)
//*
//*********************************************************************
//*        Compile                                                    *
//*********************************************************************
//COB      EXEC PGM=IGYCRCTL,
//              PARM=(NOSEQUENCE,QUOTE,RENT,'PGMNAME(LONGUPPER)'),
//              COND=(4,LT,TRN)
//SYSPRINT DD  SYSOUT=*
//SYSLIB   DD  DSN=CICSTS23.CICS.SDFHCOB,DISP=SHR
//         DD  DSN=CICSTS23.CICS.SDFHMAC,DISP=SHR
//         DD  DSN=CICSTS23.CICS.SDFHSAMP,DISP=SHR
//         DD  DSN=LUISM.TEST.SAMPLIB,DISP=SHR
//SYSTERM  DD  SYSOUT=*
//SYSLIN   DD  DSN=&&LOADSET,DISP=(MOD,PASS),UNIT=VIO,
//              SPACE=(800,(500,500))
//SYSIN    DD  DSN=&&SYSCIN,DISP=(OLD,DELETE)
//SYSUT1   DD  SPACE=(800,(500,500),,,ROUND),UNIT=VIO
//SYSUT2   DD  SPACE=(800,(500,500),,,ROUND),UNIT=VIO
//SYSUT3   DD  SPACE=(800,(500,500),,,ROUND),UNIT=VIO
//SYSUT4   DD  SPACE=(800,(500,500),,,ROUND),UNIT=VIO
//SYSUT5   DD  SPACE=(800,(500,500),,,ROUND),UNIT=VIO
//SYSUT6   DD  SPACE=(800,(500,500),,,ROUND),UNIT=VIO
//SYSUT7   DD  SPACE=(800,(500,500),,,ROUND),UNIT=VIO
//*********************************************************************
//*        Prelink                                                    *
//*********************************************************************
//PLKED    EXEC PGM=EDCPRLK,COND=(4,LT,COB)
//STEPLIB  DD  DISP=SHR,DSN=CEE.SCEERUN
//SYSMSGS  DD  DISP=SHR,
//              DSN=CEE.SCEEMSGP(EDCPMSGE)
//SYSIN    DD  DSN=&&LOADSET,DISP=(OLD,DELETE)
//SYSMOD   DD  DSN=&&PLKSET,UNIT=SYSDA,DISP=(MOD,PASS),
//              SPACE=(32000,(30,30)),
//              DCB=(RECFM=FB,LRECL=80,BLKSIZE=3200)
//SYSDEFSD DD  DUMMY
//SYSOUT   DD  SYSOUT=*
//SYSPRINT DD  SYSOUT=*
//SYSTERM  DD  SYSOUT=*
//*********************************************************************
//*        Linkedit                                                   *
//*********************************************************************
//LKED     EXEC PGM=IEWL,PARM='LIST,XREF',
//              COND=(4,LT,PLKED)
//SYSLIB   DD  DISP=SHR,DSN=CEE.SCEELKED
//         DD  DISP=SHR,DSN=DB8H8.SDSNLOAD
```

```
//         DD   DISP=SHR,DSN=CICSTS23.CICS.SDFHLOAD
//         DD   DISP=SHR,DSN=ISP.SISPLOAD
//         DD   DISP=SHR,DSN=GDDM.SADMMOD
//SYSLMOD  DD   DSN=CICSTS23.CICS.SDFHLOAD(XYZ2),
//              DISP=SHR
//SYSPRINT DD   SYSOUT=*
//SYSUT1   DD   SPACE=(1024,(50,50)),UNIT=VIO
//SYSLIN   DD   DSN=&&PLKSET,DISP=(OLD,DELETE)
//         DD   DDNAME=SYSIN
//CICSLOAD DD   DSN=CICSTS23.CICS.SDFHLOAD,
//              DISP=SHR
//SYSIN    DD   *
        INCLUDE CICSLOAD(DSNCLI)
        MODE RMODE(ANY)
        NAME XYZ2(R)
/*
//**********************************************************************
//*          Bind                                                     *
//**********************************************************************
//BIND     EXEC PGM=IKJEFT01,DYNAMNBR=20,COND=(4,LT,LKED)
//STEPLIB  DD DSN=DB8H8.SDSNLOAD,DISP=SHR
//DBRMLIB  DD DSN=DB8HU.DBRMLIB.DATA,DISP=SHR
//SYSUDUMP DD SYSOUT=*
//SYSTSPRT DD SYSOUT=*
//SYSPRINT DD SYSOUT=*
//SYSIN    DD *
   GRANT BIND, EXECUTE ON PLAN XYZP TO PUBLIC;
//SYSTSIN  DD *
DSN SYSTEM(DB8H)
BIND PACKAGE (DSN8CC81) MEMBER(XYZ2) -
     ACT(REP) ISO(CS) ENCODING(EBCDIC)
BIND PLAN(XYZP)  PKLIST(DSN8CC81.*) -
     ACT(REP) ISO(CS) ENCODING(EBCDIC)
RUN  PROGRAM(DSNTIAD) PLAN(DSNTIA81) -
     LIB('DB8HU.RUNLIB.LOAD')
END
/*
```

CICS definitions

All the CICS resources are defined online through a CEDA transaction. The group is PAZSGROU. The definitions are shown in Table E-1.

Table E-1 CICS definitions

Resource	Tipo
ABCD	Transaction
XYZ2	Program
TMAPSET	Program (map)
TMAPSET	Mapset
XYZE	DB2 entry (correlates ABCD transaction and XYZP planname)

Program execution

Enter ABCD into a CICS panel and press Enter. Then, type a department number and press Enter. When finished, press PF3. You should receive the following output:

```
ABCD txid                Average salary by department

Type a department number and press Enter.

Department number: ___

Average salary($):

F3=Exit
```

COBOL-Batch-VSAM program

This section covers the program for COBOL, batch, and VSAM.

Program code

This program is in the XYZ3 member in the LUISM.TEST.SAMPLIB library.

```
IDENTIFICATION DIVISION.
*---------------------------------------------------------------
*    COBOL VSAM PROGRAM ZSCHOLAR RESIDENCY
*---------------------------------------------------------------
```

```
*----------------------
 PROGRAM-ID.    XYZ3.
/
 ENVIRONMENT DIVISION.
*-------------------
 CONFIGURATION SECTION.
 SPECIAL-NAMES.
 INPUT-OUTPUT SECTION.
 FILE-CONTROL.
     SELECT I-FILE
       ASSIGN TO KSDATA
       ORGANIZATION IS INDEXED
       ACCESS IS DYNAMIC
       RECORD KEY IS I-FILE-RECORD-KEY
       ALTERNATE RECORD KEY IS I-FILE-ALTREC-KEY
       FILE STATUS IS FSTAT-CODE VSAM-CODE.
     SELECT DPTONO
       ASSIGN TO SYSIN
       ORGANIZATION IS SEQUENTIAL
       ACCESS IS SEQUENTIAL
        FILE STATUS IS DPTONO-CODE.
 DATA DIVISION.
*-------------
 FILE SECTION.
 FD I-FILE
     RECORD CONTAINS 101 CHARACTERS.
   01 I-FILE-RECORD.
     05 I-FILE-RECORD-KEY        PIC X(6).
     05 FILLER                   PIC X(32).
     05 I-FILE-ALTREC-KEY        PIC X(3).
     05 FILLER                   PIC X(42).
     05 SALARY                   PIC S9(7)V9(2) COMP-3.
     05 FILLER                   PIC X(13).
 FD DPTONO
     RECORDING MODE F
     BLOCK O RECORDS
     RECORD 80 CHARACTERS
     LABEL RECORD STANDARD.
   01 DPTONO-RECORD     PIC X(80).
/
 WORKING-STORAGE SECTION.
 01 STATUS-AREA.
   05 FSTAT-CODE                 PIC X(2).
     88 I-O-OKAY                 VALUE ZEROES.
   05 VSAM-CODE.
     10 VSAM-R15-RETURN-CODE     PIC 9(2) COMP.
     10 VSAM-FUNCTION-CODE       PIC 9(1) COMP.
     10 VSAM-FEEDBACK-CODE       PIC 9(3) COMP.
 77 DPTONO-CODE                  PIC XX.
```

```
     01 WS-DPTONO-RECORD.
        05 DPTONO-KEYED      PIC X(3).
        05 FILLER            PIC X(77).
     01 WS-SALARY            PIC S9(7)V9(2) COMP-3 VALUE 0.
     01 WS-SALARY-EDITED     PIC $ZZ,ZZZ,ZZ9.99.
/
 PROCEDURE DIVISION.
        OPEN INPUT DPTONO.
        READ DPTONO INTO WS-DPTONO-RECORD.
        DISPLAY DPTONO-KEYED.
        OPEN INPUT I-FILE.
        IF FSTAT-CODE NOT = "00"
           DISPLAY "OPEN INPUT VSAMFILE FS-CODE: " FSTAT-CODE
           PERFORM VSAM-CODE-DISPLAY
           STOP RUN
        END-IF.
        MOVE DPTONO-KEYED TO I-FILE-ALTREC-KEY.
        PERFORM READ-FIRST.
        IF FSTAT-CODE = "02"
           PERFORM READ-NEXT UNTIL FSTAT-CODE = "00"
        END-IF.
        IF FSTAT-CODE = "23"
           DISPLAY "NO RECORDS EXISTS FOR THIS DEPARTMENT"
        END-IF.
        MOVE WS-SALARY TO WS-SALARY-EDITED.
        DISPLAY WS-SALARY-EDITED.
        CLOSE DPTONO.
        CLOSE I-FILE.
        STOP RUN.

 READ-NEXT.
        READ I-FILE NEXT.
        IF FSTAT-CODE NOT = "00" AND FSTAT-CODE NOT = "02"
           DISPLAY "READ NEXT I-FILE FS-CODE: " FSTAT-CODE
           PERFORM VSAM-CODE-DISPLAY
        ELSE
           ADD SALARY TO WS-SALARY
        END-IF.

 READ-FIRST.
        READ I-FILE RECORD KEY IS I-FILE-ALTREC-KEY.
        IF FSTAT-CODE NOT = "00" AND FSTAT-CODE NOT = "02"
           DISPLAY "READ I-FILE FS-CODE: " FSTAT-CODE
           PERFORM VSAM-CODE-DISPLAY
        ELSE
           ADD SALARY TO WS-SALARY
        END-IF.

 VSAM-CODE-DISPLAY.
```

```
                DISPLAY "VSAM CODE -->"
                        " RETURN: " VSAM-R15-RETURN-CODE,
                        " COMPONENT: " VSAM-FUNCTION-CODE,
                        " REASON: " VSAM-FEEDBACK-CODE.
```

Preparation jobs

This section covers the preparation jobs for this program.

Creating the VSAM environment

This job is in the VSAMDEF member in the LUISM.TEST.SAMPLIB library.

The job performs the following steps:

► Unloads the employee DB2 table into a sequential file.

► Deletes and defines the VSAM KSDS file.

► Defines the alternate index (by department number).

► Defines the path.

► Performs the REPRO of the VSAM file from the sequential file (step1).

► Performs the BLDINDEX.

```
//LUISM06 JOB (999,POK),'UNLTAB/DEFVSAM/REPRO',
//           CLASS=A,MSGCLASS=T,MSGLEVEL=(1,1)
//*********************************************************************
//*        UNLOAD DB2 TABLE                                          *
//*********************************************************************
//STEP00   EXEC PGM=IKJEFT01,DYNAMNBR=20
//STEPLIB  DD DSN=DB8H8.SDSNLOAD,DISP=SHR
//SYSTSPRT DD SYSOUT=*
//SYSPRINT DD SYSOUT=*
//SYSUDUMP DD SYSOUT=*
//SYSREC00 DD DSN=LUISM.EMP.TABLE.UNLOAD,
//           SPACE=(TRK,(1,1)),DISP=(,CATLG)
//SYSPUNCH DD DSN=LUISM.EMP.TABLE.SYSPUNCH,
//           SPACE=(TRK,(1,1)),DISP=(,CATLG),
//           RECFM=FB,LRECL=120
//SYSIN    DD *
DSN8810.EMP
/*
//SYSTSIN  DD *
DSN SYSTEM(DB8H)
RUN  PROGRAM(DSNTIAUL) PLAN(DSNTIB81) -
     LIB('DB8HU.RUNLIB.LOAD')
END
/*
//*********************************************************************
```

```
//*          DELETE THE KSDS FILE                                     *
//**********************************************************************
//STEP01    EXEC PGM=IDCAMS,COND=(4,LT,STEP00)
//SYSPRINT DD  SYSOUT=*
//SYSIN     DD *
 DELETE LUISM.KSDATA
/*
//**********************************************************************
//*          DEFINE A KSDS FILE                                       *
//**********************************************************************
//STEP02    EXEC PGM=IEFBR14,COND=(4,LT,STEP01)
//DEFINE    DD  DSN=LUISM.KSDATA,DISP=(NEW,KEEP),
//              SPACE=(TRK,(1,1)),AVGREC=U,RECORG=KS,
//              KEYLEN=6,KEYOFF=0,LRECL=101
/*
//**********************************************************************
//*          DEFINE ALTERNATE INDEX                                   *
//**********************************************************************
//STEP03    EXEC PGM=IDCAMS,COND=(4,LT,STEP02)
//SYSPRINT DD  SYSOUT=*
//SYSIN     DD *
 DEFINE ALTERNATEINDEX                         -
       (NAME(LUISM.ALTINDEX)                   -
        RELATE(LUISM.KSDATA)                   -
        NONUNIQUEKEY                           -
        KEYS(3 38)                             -
        RECORDSIZE(23 150)                     -
        VOLUMES(TOTSSI)                        -
        KILOBYTES(100 100)                     -
        UPGRADE)
/*
//**********************************************************************
//*          DEFINE PATH                                              *
//**********************************************************************
//STEP04    EXEC PGM=IDCAMS,COND=(4,LT,STEP03)
//SYSPRINT DD  SYSOUT=*
//SYSIN     DD *
 DEFINE PATH                                   -
       (NAME(LUISM.PATH)                       -
        PATHENTRY(LUISM.ALTINDEX))
/*
//**********************************************************************
//*          REPRO INTO THE KSDS FROM DB2 UNLOAD SEQ FILE             *
//**********************************************************************
//STEP05    EXEC PGM=IDCAMS,COND=(4,LT,STEP04)
//SEQFILE  DD  DSN=LUISM.EMP.TABLE.UNLOAD,DISP=SHR
//SYSPRINT DD  SYSOUT=*
//SYSIN     DD *
 REPRO INFILE(SEQFILE)                         -
```

```
           OUTDATASET(LUISM.KSDATA)              -
           REPLACE
   /*
   //**********************************************************************
   //*          BLDINDEX                                                  *
   //**********************************************************************
   //STEP06    EXEC PGM=IDCAMS,COND=(4,LT,STEP05)
   //BASEDD    DD   DSN=LUISM.KSDATA,DISP=SHR
   //AIXDD     DD   DSN=LUISM.ALTINDEX,DISP=SHR
   //SYSPRINT  DD   SYSOUT=*
   //SYSIN     DD *
    BLDINDEX INFILE(BASEDD)                        -
            OUTFILE(AIXDD)                         -
            SORTCALL
   /*
```

Preparing the program

This job is in the BATVSAMP member in the LUISM.TEST.SAMPLIB library:

```
//LUISM07 JOB (999,POK),'Cobol-VSAM',
//             CLASS=A,MSGCLASS=T,MSGLEVEL=(1,1)
//**********************************************************************
//*          Compile the IBM COBOL program                            *
//**********************************************************************
//COB      EXEC PGM=IGYCRCTL,
//             PARM=(NOSEQUENCE,QUOTE,RENT,'PGMNAME(LONGUPPER)')
//SYSPRINT DD   SYSOUT=*
//SYSTERM  DD   SYSOUT=*
//SYSLIN   DD   DSN=&&LOADSET,DISP=(MOD,PASS),UNIT=VIO,
//             SPACE=(800,(500,500))
//SYSIN    DD   DSN=LUISM.TEST.SAMPLIB(XYZ3),DISP=SHR
//SYSUT1   DD   SPACE=(800,(500,500),,,ROUND),UNIT=VIO
//SYSUT2   DD   SPACE=(800,(500,500),,,ROUND),UNIT=VIO
//SYSUT3   DD   SPACE=(800,(500,500),,,ROUND),UNIT=VIO
//SYSUT4   DD   SPACE=(800,(500,500),,,ROUND),UNIT=VIO
//SYSUT5   DD   SPACE=(800,(500,500),,,ROUND),UNIT=VIO
//SYSUT6   DD   SPACE=(800,(500,500),,,ROUND),UNIT=VIO
//SYSUT7   DD   SPACE=(800,(500,500),,,ROUND),UNIT=VIO
//**********************************************************************
//*  PRELINK STEP.                                                     *
//**********************************************************************
//PLKED    EXEC PGM=EDCPRLK,COND=(4,LT,COB)
//STEPLIB  DD   DISP=SHR,DSN=CEE.SCEERUN
//SYSMSGS  DD   DISP=SHR,
//             DSN=CEE.SCEEMSGP(EDCPMSGE)
//SYSIN    DD   DSN=&&LOADSET,DISP=(OLD,DELETE)
//SYSMOD   DD   DSN=&&PLKSET,UNIT=SYSDA,DISP=(MOD,PASS),
//             SPACE=(32000,(30,30)),
//             DCB=(RECFM=FB,LRECL=80,BLKSIZE=3200)
```

```
//SYSDEFSD DD   DUMMY
//SYSOUT   DD   SYSOUT=*
//SYSPRINT DD   SYSOUT=*
//SYSTERM  DD   SYSOUT=*
//*********************************************************************
//*         Linkedit                                                  *
//*********************************************************************
//LKED     EXEC PGM=IEWL,PARM='LIST,XREF',
//         COND=(4,LT,PLKED)
//SYSLIB   DD   DISP=SHR,DSN=CEE.SCEELKED
//         DD   DISP=SHR,DSN=ISP.SISPLOAD
//         DD   DISP=SHR,DSN=GDDM.SADMMOD
//SYSLMOD  DD   DSN=LUISM.TEST.LOADLIB(XYZ3),
//              DISP=SHR
//SYSPRINT DD   SYSOUT=*
//SYSUT1   DD   SPACE=(1024,(50,50)),UNIT=VIO
//SYSLIN   DD   DSN=&&PLKSET,DISP=(OLD,DELETE)
//         DD   DDNAME=SYSIN
//SYSIN    DD   *
         MODE RMODE(ANY)
         NAME XYZ3(R)
/*
```

Program execution

The job execution is in the RUNXYZ3 member in the LUISM.TEST.SAMPLIB library:

```
//LUISM08 JOB (999,POK),'EJEC. COB-VSAM',
//            CLASS=A,MSGCLASS=T,MSGLEVEL=(1,1)
//*********************************************************************
//STEP01   EXEC PGM=XYZ3
//STEPLIB  DD   DSN=LUISM.TEST.LOADLIB,DISP=SHR
//KSDATA   DD   DSN=LUISM.KSDATA,DISP=SHR
//KSDATA1  DD   DSN=LUISM.PATH,DISP=SHR
//OUTPUTFI DD   SYSOUT=*
//SYSIN    DD   *
E01
/*
```

Following is the output for department E01:

```
****************************** TOP OF DATA ********************************
E01
$    40,175.00
*************************** BOTTOM OF DATA ********************************
```

The output for a department that have no employees is like the following:

```
****************************** TOP OF DATA ********************************
A01
READ I-FILE FS-CODE: 23
VSAM CODE --> RETURN: 08 COMPONENT: 2 REASON: 016
NO RECORDS EXISTS FOR THIS DEPARTMENT
$          0.00
****************************** BOTTOM OF DATA *****************************
```

DSNTEP2 utility

This PL/I program dynamically executes SQL statements read in from SYSIN.
This application can also execute non-SELECT statements.

Execution job

This execution job can be found in the DSNTEP2 member in the
LUISM.TEST.SAMPLIB library:

```
//LUISM04 JOB (999,POK),'Dsntep2',
//              CLASS=A,MSGCLASS=T,MSGLEVEL=(1,1)
//**********************************************************************
//*          DSNTEP2                                                   *
//**********************************************************************
//DSNTEP2  EXEC PGM=IKJEFT01,DYNAMNBR=20
//STEPLIB  DD DSN=DB8H8.SDSNLOAD,DISP=SHR
//SYSTSPRT DD SYSOUT=*
//SYSTSIN  DD *
DSN SYSTEM(DB8H)
RUN  PROGRAM(DSNTEP2) PLAN(DSNTEP81) -
     LIB('DB8HU.RUNLIB.LOAD')
END
/*
//SYSPRINT DD SYSOUT=*
//SYSUDUMP DD SYSOUT=*
//SYSIN    DD *
    SELECT CHAR(DECIMAL(SUM(SALARY),9,2))
    FROM DSN8810.EMP
    WHERE WORKDEPT='A00'
/*
```

Here is the output:

```
PAGE    1
***INPUT STATEMENT:
    SELECT CHAR(DECIMAL(SUM(SALARY),9,2))
```

```
         FROM DSN8810.EMP
         WHERE WORKDEPT='A00'
```

```
                                                       1_|  0204250.00 |
                                                          +------------+
```

```
SUCCESSFUL RETRIEVAL OF        1 ROW(S)
```

QMF batch execution

This exercise shows a QMF procedure, query, or form executed in batch. The
EMPQRY query contains the SQL statement of our class program. The
EMPPRO procedure invokes the query execution and the report printing. The job
invokes the QMF procedure and passes the department number to it; also, the
execution mode (batch, M=B) and the DB2 subsystem are specified.

The job is in the QMFBATCH member in the LUISM.TEST.SAMPLIB library.

QMF is invoked with ISPF option Q7 in the SC47TS system with ISPQMF71 in
the COMMAND field.

Execution job

```
//LUISM10 JOB (999,POK),'QMF in batch',
//            CLASS=A,MSGCLASS=T,MSGLEVEL=(1,1)
/*JOBPARM SYSAFF=SC47
//*******************************************************************
//QMFBAT   EXEC PGM=DSQQMFE,
//            PARM='M=B,I=LUISM.EMPPRO(&&DEP=''A00''),S=DB7D'
//STEPLIB  DD  DISP=SHR,DSN=DB7DU.SDSQLOAD
//         DD  DISP=SHR,DSN=DB7D7.SDSNLOAD
//         DD  DISP=SHR,DSN=DB7D7.SDSNEXIT
//ADMGGMAP DD  DSN=DB7DU.DSQMAPE,DISP=SHR
//DSQPRINT DD  SYSOUT=A,DCB=(RECFM=FBA,LRECL=133,BLKSIZE=1330)
//DSQDEBUG DD  SYSOUT=A,DCB=(RECFM=FBA,LRECL=121,BLKSIZE=1210)
//DSQUDUMP DD  SYSOUT=A,DCB=(RECFM=VBA,LRECL=125,BLKSIZE=1632)
//DSQSPILL DD  DSN=&&SPILL,DISP=(NEW,DELETE),
//    UNIT=VIO,SPACE=(TRK,(100),RLSE),
//    DCB=(RECFM=F,LRECL=4096,BLKSIZE=4096)
//*
```

QMF procedure

```
RUN QUERY EMPQRY (&&D=&DEP FORM=EMPFORM
PRINT REPORT
```

QMF query

```
SELECT CHAR(DECIMAL(SUM(SALARY),9,2))
FROM DSN8710.EMP
WHERE WORKDEPT=&D
```

Batch C program to access DB2

This section covers the batch program used to access DB2.

Source code

This program (Example E-1) is in the CDB2 member in the GMULLER.TEST.C library.

Example: E-1   C source code for accessing DB2

```
#include <stdio.h>
#include <stdlib.h>
#include <string.h>

EXEC SQL INCLUDE SQLCA;
EXEC SQL INCLUDE SQLDA;

EXEC SQL
    DECLARE DSN8810.EMP TABLE
    (EMPNO     CHAR(6)     NOT NULL,
    FIRSTNAME VARCHAR(12) NOT NULL,
    MIDINIT   CHAR(1)     NOT NULL,
    LASTNAME  VARCHAR(15) NOT NULL,
    WORKDEPT  CHAR(3)             ,
    PHONENO   CHAR(4)             ,
    HIREDATE  DATE                ,
    JOB       CHAR(8)             ,
    EDLEVEL   SMALLINT            ,
    SEX       CHAR(1)             ,
    BIRTHDATE DATE                ,
    SALARY    DECIMAL(9,2)        ,
    BONUS     DECIMAL(9,2)        ,
    COMM      DECIMAL(9,2)        );
```

```
EXEC SQL BEGIN DECLARE SECTION;
  long sum;
  long count;
  char deptno[4];
EXEC SQL END DECLARE SECTION;

int avg_sal(char*);
int record_read(FILE*,char*);

void main()
{
  FILE* cardin; /* for DD card CARDIN */
  int avgsal;
  char dept[4];

  cardin = fopen("DD:CARDIN","rb,recfm=FB,lrecl=80,type=record");
  if(cardin == NULL)
  {
    printf("Error opening DD CARDIN\n");
    exit(-2);
  }

  while(record_read(cardin, dept) != 0)
  {
    avgsal = avg_sal(dept);
    if(avgsal > 0)
      printf("Average salary of %s is %d\n",dept, avgsal);

  }
  fclose(cardin);
}

int avg_sal(char* dept)
{
  int avgsal;
  count = 0;
  strncpy(deptno, dept, 3);
  deptno[3] = 0;

  EXEC SQL SELECT SUM(SALARY), COUNT(*) INTO :sum, :count
           FROM DSN8810.EMP
           WHERE WORKDEPT = :deptno;

  if(count != 0)
  {
    avgsal = sum/count;
    return avgsal;
  } else
  {
```

```
        printf("DEPT %s does not exist\n", deptno);
        return -1;
    }
}

int record_read(FILE* file, char* dept)
{
    int readbytes;
    char linebuf[81], linebuf2[80];
    readbytes = fread(linebuf, 1, 81, file);
    strncpy(dept, linebuf, 3); /* first 3 bytes are dept. number */
    dept[3]=0; /* terminate string */
    return readbytes;
}
```

Preparing the program

This JCL (Example E-2) is in the CDB2 member in the GMULLER.TEST.CNTL library.

Example: E-2   GMULLER.TEST.CNTL(CDB2)

```
//GMULLERC JOB 1,GEORG,MSGLEVEL=(1,1),NOTIFY=&SYSUID
//* PRECOMPILE AND COMPILE THE SAMPLE C FILE
//PROCLIB JCLLIB ORDER=DB8HU.PROCLIB
/*JOBPARM SYSAFF=SCO4
//STEP1 EXEC PROC=DSNHC,MEM=CDB2,
//       PARM.PC=('HOST(C),CCSID(1047)')
//PC.DBRMLIB DD DSN=DB8HU.DBRMLIB.DATA(CDB2),DISP=SHR
//PC.SYSLIB  DD DSN=GMULLER.TEST.C,DISP=SHR
//PC.SYSIN   DD DSN=GMULLER.TEST.C(&MEM),DISP=SHR
//LKED.SYSLMOD DD DSN=GMULLER.TEST.LOAD(&MEM),DISP=SHR
//LKED.SYSIN DD *
 INCLUDE SYSLIB(DSNELI)
/*
//****************************************************
//* BIND AND RUN THE PROGRAM                        *
//****************************************************
//BIND      EXEC PGM=IKJEFT01,DYNAMNBR=20,COND=(4,LT)
//STEPLIB   DD DSN=DB8H8.SDSNLOAD,DISP=SHR
//DBRMLIB   DD DSN=DB8HU.DBRMLIB.DATA,DISP=SHR
//SYSUDUMP  DD SYSOUT=*
//SYSTSPRT  DD SYSOUT=*
//SYSPRINT  DD SYSOUT=*
//CARDIN    DD *
D11
XYZ
A00
```

```
/*
//SYSIN    DD *
   GRANT BIND,EXECUTE ON PLAN CDB2 TO PUBLIC;
//SYSTSIN DD *
 DSN SYSTEM(DB8H)
 BIND PACKAGE (CDB2PAK) MEMBER(CDB2) -
      ACT(REP) ISO(CS) ENCODING(EBCDIC)
 BIND PLAN(CDB2)  PKLIST(CDB2PAK.*) -
      ACT(REP) ISO(CS) ENCODING(EBCDIC)
 RUN  PROGRAM(CDB2) PLAN(CDB2) LIB('GMULLER.TEST.LOAD')
 END
/*
```

Where:

▶ This job requires the PDS GMULLER.TEST.LOAD with RECFM=U.

▶ The /*JOBPARM SYSAFF=SC04 statement points to the system where DB2 is running and has to be modified (or deleted, if not in a sysplex).

▶ DB8H has to be replaced with the name of the local DB2.

▶ HLQs for DB2 libs may differ.

Output

Example E-3 shows the output of CDB2.

Example: E-3   Output of CDB2

```
Average salary of D11 is 25147
DEPT XYZ does not exist
Average salary of A00 is 40850
```

Running the program

This JCL (Example E-4) is in the RUNJCL member in the GMULLER.TEST.CNTL library.

Example: E-4   GMULLER.TEST.CNTL(RUNJCL)

```
//GMULLERR JOB 1,GEORG,MSGLEVEL=(1,1),NOTIFY=&SYSUID
//* PRECOMPILE AND COMPILE THE SAMPLE C FILE
/*JOBPARM SYSAFF=SC04
//****************************************************
//* RUN THE PROGRAM                                  *
//****************************************************
//BIND    EXEC PGM=IKJEFT01,DYNAMNBR=20,COND=(4,LT)
//STEPLIB DD DSN=DB8H8.SDSNLOAD,DISP=SHR
//DBRMLIB DD DSN=DB8HU.DBRMLIB.DATA,DISP=SHR
```

```
//SYSUDUMP DD SYSOUT=*
//SYSTSPRT DD SYSOUT=*
//SYSPRINT DD SYSOUT=*
//CARDIN   DD DISP=SHR,DSN=GMULLER.TEST.CNTL(CARDIN)
//SYSTSIN  DD *
 DSN SYSTEM(DB8H)
 RUN  PROGRAM(CDB2) PLAN(CDB2) LIB('GMULLER.TEST.LOAD')
 END
/*
```

Where:

► This program requires the CARDIN member in the GMULLER.TEST.CNTL library.

► HLQ for DB2 libs may differ.

Input

Example E-5 shows the input for GMULLER.TEST.CNTL(CARDIN).

Example: E-5   GMULLER.TEST.CNTL(CARDIN)

```
D11
A00
XYZ
C01
ABC
E21
```

Output

Example E-6 shows the output of RUNJCL.

Example: E-6   Output of RUNJCL

```
Average salary of D11 is 25147
Average salary of A00 is 40850
DEPT XYZ does not exist
Average salary of C01 is 29722
DEPT ABC does not exist
Average salary of E21 is 24086
```

Java servlet access to DB2

This section covers the Java servlet used to access DB2.

Servlet source code

Example E-7 shows the Java servlet source code.

Example: E-7   SalaryServlet.java

```java
import java.io.IOException;
import java.io.PrintWriter;
import java.sql.Connection;
import java.sql.ResultSet;
import java.sql.SQLException;
import java.sql.Statement;

import javax.naming.Context;
import javax.naming.InitialContext;
import javax.naming.NamingException;
import javax.servlet.ServletException;
import javax.servlet.http.HttpServlet;
import javax.servlet.http.HttpServletRequest;
import javax.servlet.http.HttpServletResponse;
import javax.sql.DataSource;

public class SalaryServlet extends HttpServlet {

    private DataSource ds;
    private boolean dbProblem = false;

    public void init() throws ServletException {
        super.init();
        try { // get DataSource from Container
            Context context = new InitialContext();
            ds = (DataSource) context.lookup("jdbc/DB8H");
        } catch (NamingException e) {
            e.printStackTrace();
            this.dbProblem = true;
        }
    }

    protected void doGet(HttpServletRequest req, HttpServletResponse resp)
            throws ServletException, IOException {

        resp.setContentType("text/html");
        String deptno = req.getParameter("deptno"); // get from request string

        PrintWriter out = resp.getWriter();
        out.println("<html>\n<head>\n <title>Average
Salary</title>\n</head>\n<body>");
        out.println("<h1>Average Salary</h1>");
        out.println("<form action=\"salary\" method=\"get\">");
```

```
        out.println("Dept. No.: <input type=\"text\" name=\"deptno\" />");
        out.println(" <input type=\"submit\" />\n</form>");

        if (deptno != null) {
            try {
                int avgSal = getAvgSal(deptno);
                out.println("The average salary of <b>" + deptno + "</b> is
<b>$ " + avgSal
                    + "</b><br>");
            } catch (Exception e) {
                out.println("<b>Error: " + e.getMessage() + "</b><br>");
            }
        }
        out.println("</html>");
    }

    private int getAvgSal(String deptno) throws Exception {
        String sqlStatement = "SELECT SUM(salary), COUNT(*) "
            + "FROM DSN8810.EMP WHERE WORKDEPT = '" + deptno + "'";
        // Connect to database
        Connection con = null;
        try {
            con = ds.getConnection();
            Statement stmt = con.createStatement();
            ResultSet rs = stmt.executeQuery(sqlStatement); // Execute SQL
            // statement

            rs.next(); // get Values from result set
            int sum = rs.getInt(1);
            int count = rs.getInt(2);
            if (count == 0)
                throw new Exception("Department " + deptno
                    + " does not exist");
            return sum / count;

        } catch (SQLException e) {
            throw new Exception(e.getMessage());
        } finally {
            try {
                con.close();
            } catch (SQLException e) {}
        }
    }
}
```

This servlet requires a data source (here we use the JNDI name jdbc/DB8H)
defined in the web container, which points to the DB2 database.

Deployment descriptor

Example E-8 shows the deployment descriptor for this servlet.

Example: E-8   web.xml

```
<?xml version="1.0" encoding="UTF-8"?>
<!DOCTYPE web-app PUBLIC "-//Sun Microsystems, Inc.//DTD Web Application
2.3//EN" "http://java.sun.com/dtd/web-app_2_3.dtd">
<web-app id="WebApp_ID">
    <display-name>Salary</display-name>
    <servlet>
        <servlet-name>Salary</servlet-name>
        <servlet-class>SalaryServlet</servlet-class>
    </servlet>
    <servlet-mapping>
        <servlet-name>Salary</servlet-name>
        <url-pattern>/salary</url-pattern>
    </servlet-mapping>
</web-app>
```

C program to access MQ

This section covers the C program used to access MQ. The following steps accomplish this task:

1. MQPUT writes a message onto a queue (entered in TSO).

2. The program is started with TSO CALL 'ZSCHOLAR.PROGRAM.LOAD(MQPUT)', and then you have to enter a message.

3. MQGET receives the message back and displays it on the panel.

4. The program is started with TSO CALL 'ZSCHOLAR.PROGRAM.LOAD(MQGET)', and then you have to enter a message.

It is also possible to receive the message using the Java application shown in "Java program to access MQ" on page 699.

MQPUT

Example E-9 shows the MQPUT for ZSCHOLAR.PROGRAM.SRC.

Example: E-9   ZSCHOLAR.PROGRAM.SRC(MQPUT)

```c
#pragma csect(code,"CSQ4BCK1")
/*                                                                      */
/* Define static CSECT name                                            */
/*                                                                      */
#pragma csect(static,"BCK1WS")

#include <stdlib.h>
#include <string.h>
#include <stdio.h>
#include <cmqc.h>


/*                                                                      */
/* Function prototypes                                                 */
/*                                                                      */
void usageError( char* programName );
void errorMessage( char* msgStr, MQLONG CC, MQLONG RC );

int main( int argc, char** argv )
{
   /*                                                                   */
   /* API variables                                                    */
   /*                                                                   */
   MQHCONN HConn = MQHC_DEF_HCONN;
   MQHOBJ  HObj;
   MQLONG  OpenOptions;
   MQMD    MsgDesc = { MQMD_DEFAULT };
   MQOD    ObjDesc = { MQOD_DEFAULT };
   MQPMO   PutMsgOpts = { MQPMO_DEFAULT };
   MQLONG  CompCode;
   MQLONG  Reason;

   /*                                                                   */
   /* Parameter variables                                              */
   /*                                                                   */
   MQCHAR48 qMgr;
   MQCHAR48 qName;
   char     msgBuffer[255];
   int      msgLength;
   char     persistent = 'N';
   long     rc = 0;

   printf("Please enter message text:\n");
   fgets(msgBuffer, 255, stdin);
```

```
msgLength = strlen(msgBuffer);

strcpy( qMgr,  "MQ8H\0" );
strcpy( qName, "GMULLER\0" );
/*
memset( qMgr,  '\0', MQ_Q_MGR_NAME_LENGTH );
memset( qName, '\0', MQ_Q_NAME_LENGTH );
*/


/*                                                              */
/* Connect to Queue Manager (MQCONN)                            */
/*                                                              */
MQCONN( qMgr,
        &HConn,
        &CompCode,
        &Reason    );
/*                                                              */
/* If connect failed then display error message and exit        */
/*                                                              */
if( MQCC_OK != CompCode )
   {
   errorMessage( "MQCONN", CompCode, Reason );
   return Reason;
   }

printf( "MQCONN SUCCESSFUL\n" );

/*                                                              */
/* Open Queue for output (MQOPEN). Fail the call if the queue   */
/* manager is quiescing.                                        */
/*                                                              */
OpenOptions = MQOO_OUTPUT +
              MQOO_FAIL_IF_QUIESCING;

strncpy( ObjDesc.ObjectName, qName, MQ_Q_NAME_LENGTH );
MQOPEN( HConn,
        &ObjDesc,
        OpenOptions,
        &HObj,
        &CompCode,
        &Reason    );
/*                                                              */
/* If open failed then display error message,                   */
/* disconnect from the queue manager and exit                   */
/*                                                              */
if( MQCC_OK != CompCode )
   {
   errorMessage( "MQOPEN", CompCode, Reason );
   rc = Reason;
```

```
            MQDISC( &HConn,
                    &CompCode,
                    &Reason    );
            return rc;
            }


printf( "MQOPEN SUCCESSFUL\n" );

/*                                                                  */
/* Set persistence depending on parameter passed                    */
/*                                                                  */
if( 'P' == persistent )
   MsgDesc.Persistence = MQPER_PERSISTENT;
else
   MsgDesc.Persistence = MQPER_NOT_PERSISTENT;

/*                                                                  */
/* Put String format messages                                       */
/*                                                                  */
strncpy( MsgDesc.Format, MQFMT_STRING, MQ_FORMAT_LENGTH );

/*                                                                  */
/* Set the put message options to fail the call if the queue        */
/* manager is quiescing.                                            */
/*                                                                  */
PutMsgOpts.Options = MQPMO_FAIL_IF_QUIESCING;


strncpy( MsgDesc.MsgId,    MQMI_NONE, MQ_MSG_ID_LENGTH );
strncpy( MsgDesc.CorrelId, MQCI_NONE, MQ_CORREL_ID_LENGTH );

MQPUT( HConn,
       HObj,
       &MsgDesc,
       &PutMsgOpts,
       msgLength,
       msgBuffer,
       &CompCode,
       &Reason    );
/*                                                                  */
/* If put failed then display error message                         */
/* and break out of loop                                            */
/*                                                                  */
if( MQCC_OK != CompCode )
   {
   errorMessage( "MQPUT", CompCode, Reason );
   rc = Reason;
   }
```

```
        printf("MESSAGE PUT TO QUEUE\n");

        free( msgBuffer );

        /*                                                              */
        /* Close the queue and then disconnect from the queue manager   */
        /*                                                              */
        MQCLOSE( HConn,
                 &HObj,
                 MQCO_NONE,
                 &CompCode,
                 &Reason   );
        if( MQCC_OK != CompCode   )
           {
           errorMessage( "MQCLOSE", CompCode, Reason );
           rc = Reason;
           }
        else printf( "MQCLOSE SUCCESSFUL\n" );


        MQDISC( &HConn,
                &CompCode,
                &Reason   );
        if( MQCC_OK != CompCode )
           {
           errorMessage( "MQDISC", CompCode, Reason );
           return Reason;
           }
        else
           {
           printf( "MQDISC SUCCESSFUL\n" );
           return rc;
           }

     return(rc);
} /*end main*/

/*********************************************************************/
/* Functions to display error messages                              */
/*********************************************************************/
void errorMessage( char* msgStr, MQLONG CC, MQLONG RC )
{
   printf( "**********************************************\n" );
   printf( "* %s\n", msgStr );
   printf( "* COMPLETION CODE : %09ld\n", CC );
   printf( "* REASON CODE     : %09ld\n", RC );
   printf( "**********************************************\n" );
}
```

JCL to compile:

Example: E-10   ZSCHOLAR.PROGRAM.CNTL(MQPUT)

```
//GMULLERT JOB 1,GEORG,MSGCLASS=H,MSGLEVEL=(1,1),NOTIFY=&SYSUID
//* COMPILE MQ PROGRAM
//STEP1    EXEC PROC=EDCCB,
//              INFILE='ZSCHOLAR.PROGRAM.SRC(MQPUT)',
//              OUTFILE='ZSCHOLAR.PROGRAM.LOAD(MQPUT)',DISP=SHR'
//SYSLIB   DD DSN=MQ531.SCSQC370,DISP=SHR
//BIND.CSQBSTUB  DD DSN=MQ531.SCSQLOAD(CSQBSTUB),DISP=SHR
//BIND.SYSIN DD *
  INCLUDE CSQBSTUB
/*
```

MQGET

Example E-11 shows the MQGET source code.

Example: E-11   ZSCHOLAR.PROGRAM.SRC(MQGET)

```
#pragma csect(code,"CSQ4BCK1")
/*                                                              */
/* Define static CSECT name                                     */
/*                                                              */
#pragma csect(static,"BCK1WS")

#include <stdlib.h>
#include <string.h>
#include <stdio.h>
#include <cmqc.h>

#define maxMessageLength  65536

/*                                                              */
/* Function prototypes                                          */
/*                                                              */
void usageError( char* programName );
void errorMessage( char* msgStr, MQLONG CC, MQLONG RC );

int main( int argc, char** argv )
{
   /*                                                           */
   /* API variables                                             */
   /*                                                           */
   MQHCONN HConn = MQHC_DEF_HCONN;
   MQHOBJ  HObj;
   MQLONG  OpenOptions;
   MQMD    MsgDesc = { MQMD_DEFAULT };
```

```
MQOD    ObjDesc = { MQOD_DEFAULT };
MQGMO   GetMsgOpts = { MQGMO_DEFAULT };
MQLONG  CompCode;
MQLONG  Reason;

/*                                                          */
/* Parameter variables                                     */
/*                                                          */
MQCHAR48 qMgr;
MQCHAR48 qName;
char     msgBuffer[maxMessageLength];
int      msgLength = maxMessageLength;
char     persistent = 'N';
long     rc = 0;
long     dataLength;
char     browseGet = 'D'; /* destructive get */
char     syncpoint = 'N'; /* no Syncpoint */

memset( msgBuffer, '\0', msgLength );

strcpy( qMgr,  "MQ8H\0" );
strcpy( qName, "GMULLER\0" );

/*                                                          */
/* Connect to Queue Manager (MQCONN)                        */
/*                                                          */
MQCONN( qMgr,
        &HConn,
        &CompCode,
        &Reason   );
/*                                                          */
/* If connect failed then display error message and exit    */
/*                                                          */
if( MQCC_OK != CompCode )
   {
   errorMessage( "MQCONN", CompCode, Reason );
   return Reason;
   }

printf( "MQCONN SUCCESSFUL\n" );

/*                                                          */
/* Open Queue for input shared and browse. Fail the call if the */
/* queue manager is quiescing.                              */
/*                                                          */
OpenOptions = MQOO_INPUT_SHARED +
              MQOO_BROWSE +
              MQOO_FAIL_IF_QUIESCING;
```

```
          strncpy( ObjDesc.ObjectName, qName, MQ_Q_NAME_LENGTH );
          MQOPEN( HConn,
                  &ObjDesc,
                  OpenOptions,
                  &HObj,
                  &CompCode,
                  &Reason    );
          /*                                                          */
          /* If open failed then display error message,              */
          /* disconnect from the queue manager and exit              */
          /*                                                          */
          if( MQCC_OK != CompCode )
            {
            errorMessage( "MQOPEN", CompCode, Reason );
            rc = Reason;
            MQDISC( &HConn,
                    &CompCode,
                    &Reason    );
            return rc;
            }

          printf( "MQOPEN SUCCESSFUL\n" );

          /*                                                          */
          /* Set persistence depending on parameter passed           */
          /*                                                          */
          if( 'P' == persistent )
            MsgDesc.Persistence = MQPER_PERSISTENT;
          else
            MsgDesc.Persistence = MQPER_NOT_PERSISTENT;

          /*                                                          */
          /* Set GetMsgOpts .. don't wait if there are no messages on the */
          /* queue, truncate the message if it does not fit into our  */
          /* buffer, perform data conversion on the message if required */
          /* and if possible, and fail the call if the queue manager is */
          /* quiescing.                                               */
          /*                                                          */
          GetMsgOpts.Options = MQGMO_NO_WAIT +
                               MQGMO_ACCEPT_TRUNCATED_MSG +
                               MQGMO_CONVERT +
                               MQGMO_FAIL_IF_QUIESCING;

          strncpy( MsgDesc.MsgId,    MQMI_NONE, MQ_MSG_ID_LENGTH );
          strncpy( MsgDesc.CorrelId, MQCI_NONE, MQ_CORREL_ID_LENGTH );

          /*                                                          */
          /* Set additional GetMsgOpts depending on parameters passed */
          /* into program.                                            */
```

```c
/*                                                                */
if( ('S' == syncpoint) && ('B' != browseGet) )
   GetMsgOpts.Options += MQGMO_SYNCPOINT;
else
   GetMsgOpts.Options += MQGMO_NO_SYNCPOINT;

if( ('B' == browseGet) )
   GetMsgOpts.Options += MQGMO_BROWSE_FIRST;

MsgDesc.Encoding = MQENC_NATIVE;
MsgDesc.CodedCharSetId = MQCCSI_Q_MGR;

/* GET */
MQGET( HConn,
       HObj,
       &MsgDesc,
       &GetMsgOpts,
       msgLength,
       msgBuffer,
       &dataLength,
       &CompCode,
       &Reason     );

if( (MQCC_FAILED == CompCode) )
   {
   errorMessage( "MQGET", CompCode, Reason );
   rc = Reason;
   }
else
   {
   /*                                                              */
   /* Only character data messages are correctly displayed        */
   /* by this code                                                 */
   /*                                                              */
   if (MQRC_TRUNCATED_MSG_ACCEPTED == Reason)
      {
      msgBuffer??( msgLength - 1 ??) = 0;
      printf( "Message received (truncated):\n%s\n",
              msgBuffer );
      }
   else
      {
      msgBuffer??( dataLength ??) = 0;
      printf( "Message received:\n%s\n",
              msgBuffer );
      }
   }

free( msgBuffer );
```

```
        /*                                                              */
        /* Close the queue and then disconnect from the queue manager    */
        /*                                                              */
        MQCLOSE( HConn,
                 &HObj,
                 MQCO_NONE,
                 &CompCode,
                 &Reason    );

        if( MQCC_OK != CompCode  )
           {
           errorMessage( "MQCLOSE", CompCode, Reason );
           rc = Reason;
           }
        else printf( "MQCLOSE SUCCESSFUL\n" );


        MQDISC( &HConn,
                &CompCode,
                &Reason     );
        if( MQCC_OK != CompCode )
           {
           errorMessage( "MQDISC", CompCode, Reason );
           return Reason;
           }
        else
           {
           printf( "MQDISC SUCCESSFUL\n" );
           return rc;
           }

     return(rc);
} /*end main*/

/*********************************************************************/
/* Functions to display error messages                             */
/*********************************************************************/
void errorMessage( char* msgStr, MQLONG CC, MQLONG RC )
{
   printf( "***********************************************\n" );
   printf( "* %s\n", msgStr );
   printf( "* COMPLETION CODE : %09ld\n", CC );
   printf( "* REASON CODE     : %09ld\n", RC );
   printf( "***********************************************\n" );
}
```

Example E-12 shows the JCL that you must compile.

Example: E-12   ZSCHOLAR.PROGRAM.CNTL(MQGET)

```
//GMULLERT JOB 1,GEORG,MSGCLASS=H,MSGLEVEL=(1,1),NOTIFY=&SYSUID
//* COMPILE MQ PROGRAM
//STEP1    EXEC PROC=EDCCB,
//             INFILE='ZSCHOLAR.PROGRAM.SRC(MQGET)',
//             OUTFILE='ZSCHOLAR.PROGRAM.LOAD(MQGET),DISP=SHR'
//SYSLIB   DD DSN=MQ531.SCSQC370,DISP=SHR
//BIND.CSQBSTUB  DD DSN=MQ531.SCSQLOAD(CSQBSTUB),DISP=SHR
//BIND.SYSIN DD *
  INCLUDE CSQBSTUB
/*
```

Java program to access MQ

This section covers the Java program used to access MQ. The following steps accomplish this task:

1. The Java program receives a message from a queue (Example E-13). The MessageHandler class also contains a class to send messages (Example E-14 on page 700).

2. You have to add `com.ibm.mq.jar` and `connector.jar` to your CLASSPATH. All the files are in `program sample\mq`.

3. Run the program using **java -jar mqconnect.jar**.

Example: E-13   MQReceiver.java

```
import com.ibm.mq.MQException;

public class MQReceiver {

    public static void main(String[] args) {

        // Connection settings
        String hostname = "wtsc04.itso.ibm.com";
        String queueName = "GMULLER";
        int port = 1598; // mq port
        String channel = "GMULLER.SERV";

        MessageHandler handler = new MessageHandler(hostname, port, queueName,
                channel);

        String message;
        try {
```

```
            System.out.println("Sending message...");
            handler.sendMessage("Hello");
            //System.out.println("Receiving message...");
            //message = handler.receiveMessage();
            //System.out.println("Message: " + message);
            System.out.println("Finished");
        } catch (MQException e) {
            if (e.reasonCode == MQException.MQRC_NO_MSG_AVAILABLE)
                System.out.println("No message in queue");
            else {
                System.out.println("Error getting message");
                e.printStackTrace();
            }
        }
    }
}
```

Example: E-14   MessageHandler.java

```
import java.io.IOException;

import com.ibm.mq.*;

public class MessageHandler {

    private String hostname;
    private String queueName;

    public MessageHandler(String hostname, int port, String queueName, String
channel) {
        MQEnvironment.hostname = hostname;
        MQEnvironment.port = port;
        MQEnvironment.channel = channel;
        this.queueName = queueName;
    }

    public String receiveMessage() throws MQException {
        try {
            MQQueueManager mqm = new MQQueueManager(hostname);

            int openOptions = MQC.MQOO_INPUT_AS_Q_DEF + MQC.MQOO_OUTPUT;

            MQQueue queue = mqm.accessQueue(queueName, openOptions);
            // create new Message for receiving
            MQMessage message = new MQMessage();

            // get message from queue
            queue.get(message);
            // get the whole message string
```

```
            String messageString =
message.readString(message.getMessageLength());
            // close queue;
            queue.close();
            // disconnect from queue manager
            mqm.disconnect();

            return messageString;

        } catch (IOException e) {
            e.printStackTrace();
            return null;
        }
    }

    public void sendMessage(String messageString) throws MQException {
        try {
            MQQueueManager mqm = new MQQueueManager(hostname);

            int openOptions = MQC.MQOO_INPUT_AS_Q_DEF + MQC.MQOO_OUTPUT;


            MQQueue queue = mqm.accessQueue(queueName, openOptions);
            // create new Message for receiving
            MQMessage message = new MQMessage();


            // write message
            message.writeString(messageString);

            message.encoding = MQC.MQENC_NATIVE;
            message.characterSet = MQC.MQCCSI_INHERIT;

            // put message onto the queue
            queue.put(message);

            // close queue;
            queue.close();
            // disconnect from queue manager
            mqm.disconnect();

        } catch (IOException e) {
            e.printStackTrace();
        }
    }
}
```

Glossary

Numerics

3270 pass-through mode. A mode that lets a program running from the z/OS shell send and receive a 3270 data stream or issue TSO/E commands.

A

abend. See *abnormal end.*

abnormal end (abend). The end of a task, a job, or a subsystem because an error condition occurred that cannot be resolved by recovery facilities while the task is performed. See also *abnormal termination.*

abnormal termination. (1) The end of processing prior to scheduled termination. (2) A system failure or operator action that causes a job to end unsuccessfully. Synonymous with *abend* and *abnormal end.*

ACB. See *access control block.*

accept. In SMP/E, to install SYSMODs in the distribution libraries. This is done by using the ACCEPT command.

ACCEPT. The SMP/E command used to install SYSMODs in the distribution libraries.

accepted SYSMOD. A SYSMOD that has been successfully installed by the SMP/E ACCEPT command. Accepted SYSMODs do not have the ERROR flag set and are found as SYSMOD entries in the distribution zone.

access authority. An authority that sends a request for a type of access to protected resources. In RACF, the access authorities are NONE, READ, UPDATE, ALTER, and EXECUTE.

access control block (ACB). An ACB represents an application program to VTAM. It is part of the user application program and is initialized in response to an application program's OPEN ACB request. The ACB defines the interface between the problem state application program code (generated by macro instructions in the program) and the supervisor state VTAM routines that support the application program.

access list. A list within a profile of all authorized users and their access authorities.

access method. A technique for moving data between main storage and I/O devices.

ACID properties. The properties of a transaction: atomicity, consistency, isolation, and durability. In CICS, the ACID properties apply to a unit of work (UoW).

address space identifier (ASID). A unique number assigned to an address space during its creation to track and account for z/OS activity and functions.

address space. The complete range of addresses available to a program. In z/OS, an address space can range up to 16 EB of contiguous virtual storage addresses that the system creates for the user. An address space contains user data and programs, as well as system data and programs, some of which are common to all address spaces. See also *virtual address space.*

address. The unique code assigned to each device, workstation or system connected to a network.

addressing mode (AMODE). A program attribute that refers to the address length that is expected to be in effect when the program is entered. In z/OS, addresses can be 24, 31, or 64 bits in length.

administrator. A person responsible for administrative tasks such as access authorization and content management. Administrators can also grant levels of authority to users.

Advanced Peer-to-Peer Network (APPN). An extension to the Systems Network Architecture (SNA).

Advanced Program-to-Program Communications (APPC). A protocol that computer programs can use to communicate over a network.

ALLOCATE command. In z/OS, the TSO/E command that serves as the connection between a file's logical name (the ddname) and the file's physical name (the data set name).

allocate. To assign a resource for use in performing a specific task.

alphanumeric character. A letter or a number.

American Standard Code for Information Interchange (ASCII). A character-encoding scheme based on the ordering of the English alphabet. ASCII codes represent text in computers, communications equipment, and other devices that use text. Most modern character-encoding schemes are based on ASCII, though they support many more characters than ASCII does.

AMODE. See *addressing mode.*

ANSI. American National Standards Institute.

AOR. See *application-owning region.*

APAR fix. A temporary correction of a defect in an IBM system control program or licensed program that affects a specific user. An APAR fix is usually replaced later by a permanent correction called a PTF. APAR fixes are identified to SMP/E by the ++APAR statement.

APAR. See *authorized program analysis report.*

APF. See *authorized program facility.*

API. See *application programming interface.*

APPC. See *Advanced Program-to-Program Communications.*

application program. A collection of software components used to perform specific types of work on a computer, such as a program that does inventory control or payroll.

application programming interface (API). A particular set of rules and specifications that a software program can follow to access and make use of the services and resources provided by another particular software program that implements that API. It serves as an interface between different software programs and facilitates their interaction, similar to the way the user interface facilitates interaction between humans and computers.

application-owning region (AOR). In a CICSPlex® configuration, a CICS region devoted to running applications.

application. A program or set of programs that performs a task; some examples are payroll, inventory management, and word processing applications.

apply. In SMP/E, to install SYSMODs in the target libraries. This is done by using the APPLY command.

APPLY. The SMP/E command used to install SYSMODs in the target libraries.

APPN. See *Advanced Peer-to-Peer Network.*

ARM. See *automatic restart manager.*

ASCII. See *American Standard Code for Information Interchange.*

ASID. See *address space identifier.*

ASSEM entry. An SMP/E entry containing assembler statements that can be assembled to create an object module.

assembler language. A symbolic programming language that is composed of instructions for basic computer operations that are structured according to the data formats, storage structures, and registers of the computer.

assembler. A computer program that converts assembler language instructions into binary machine language (object code).

asynchronous processing. A series of operations that are done separately from the job in which they were requested; for example, submitting a batch job from an interactive job at a work station. See also *synchronous processing*.

ATM. automated teller machine.

audit. To review and examine the activities of a data processing system mainly to test the adequacy and effectiveness of procedures for data security and data accuracy.

authority. The right to access objects, resources, or functions.

authorization checking. The action of determining whether a user is permitted access to a RACF-protected resource.

authorized program analysis report (APAR). A request for correction of a problem caused by a defect in a current unaltered release of a program. The correction is called an *APAR fix*.

authorized program facility (APF). A facility that permits identification of programs authorized to use restricted functions. To maintain system security and integrity, a program must be authorized by the APF before it can access restricted functions, such as supervisor calls (SVC) or SVC paths. APF helps to avoid integrity exposures; the installation identifies which libraries contain special functions or programs.

automated operations. Automated procedures to replace or simplify actions of operators in both systems and network operations.

automatic call library. Contains load modules or object decks that are used as secondary input to the linkage editor to resolve external symbols left undefined after all the primary input has been processed.
The automatic call library may be:
► Libraries containing object decks, with or without linkage editor control statements
► Libraries containing load modules
► The library containing Language Environment runtime routines.

automatic call. The process used by the linkage editor to resolve external symbols left undefined after all the primary input has been processed. See also *automatic call library*.

automatic library call. Automatic call. See also *automatic call library*.

automatic restart manager (ARM). A z/OS recovery function that improves the availability of batch jobs and started tasks. When a job fails, or the system on which it is running unexpectedly fails, z/OS can restart the job without operator intervention. It is a sysplex-wide integrated restart mechanism that automatically restarts z/OS elements in place or remotely if they abend.

automatic restart. A restart that takes place during the current run, that is, without resubmitting the job. An automatic restart can occur within a job step or at the beginning of a job step. Contrast with *deferred restart*. See also *checkpoint restart*.

auxiliary storage. All addressable storage other than processor storage.

B

background job. (1) A low-priority job, usually a batched or non-interactive job. (2) Under TSO, a job entered through the SUBMIT command or through SYSIN. Contrast with *foreground job*.

background. (1) In multiprogramming, the environment in which low-priority programs are executed. (2) Under TSO/E, the environment in which jobs submitted through the SUBMIT command or SYSIN are executed. One job step at a time is assigned to a region of central storage, and it remains in central storage to completion. Contrast with *foreground*.

backout. A request to remove all changes to resources since the last commit or backout or, for the first unit of recovery, since the beginning of the application. Backout is also called *rollback* or *abort*.

backup. The process of creating a copy of a data set to ensure against accidental loss.

BAL. Basic Assembler Language.

base control program (BCP). Provides the essential services to process workloads reliably, securely, with complete data integrity and without interruption..

base function. In SMP/E, a SYSMOD defining elements of the base z/OS system or other products that were not previously present in the target libraries. Base functions are identified to SMP/E by the ++FUNCTION statement. SMP/E itself is an example of a base function of z/OS.

base level system. In SMP/E, the level of the target system modules, macros, source, and DLIBs created by system generation, to which function and service modifications are applicable.

batch job. A predefined group of processing actions submitted to the system to be performed with little or no interaction between the user and the system. Contrast with *interactive job*.

batch message processing (BMP) program. An IMS batch processing program that has access to online databases and message queues. BMPs run online, but like programs in a batch environment, they are started with job control language (JCL).

batch processing. A method of running a program or a series of programs in which one or more records (a batch) are processed with little or no action from the user or operator. Contrast with *interactive processing*.

batch. A group of records or data processing jobs brought together for processing or transmission. Pertaining to activity involving little or no user action. Contrast with *interactive*.

BCP. See *base control program*.

big endian. A format for the storage of binary data in which the most significant byte is placed first. Big endian is used by most hardware architectures including the z/Architecture. Contrast with *little endian*.

binary data. (1) Any data not intended for direct human reading. Binary data may contain unprintable characters that are outside the range of text characters. (2) A type of data consisting of numeric values stored in bit patterns of 0s and 1s. Binary data can cause a large number to be placed in a smaller space of storage.

bind. (1) To combine one or more control sections or program modules into a single program module, resolving references between them. (2) In SNA, a request to activate a session between two logical units (LUs).

binder. The z/OS program that processes the output of the language translators and compilers into an executable program (load module or program object). It replaces the linkage editor and batch loader used in earlier forms of the z/OS operating system, such as MVS and OS/390.

blade. A hardware unit that provides application-specific services and components. The consistent size and shape (or form factor) of each blade allows it to fit in a BladeCenter chassis.

BladeCenter chassis. A modular chassis that can contain multiple blades, allowing the individual blades to share resources, such as the management, switch, power, and blower modules.

BLK. A subparameter of the SPACE parameter in a DD statement. It specifies that space is allocated by blocks.

BLKSIZE. A command that provides for grouping of records into blocks for faster processing.

BLOB. binary large object.

block size. (1) The number of data elements in a block. (2) A measure of the size of a block, usually specified in units such as records, words, computer words, or characters. (3) Synonymous with *block length*. (4) Synonymous with *physical record size*.

BMP. See *batch message processing program*.

BPAM. basic partitioned access method.

BSAM. basic sequential access method.

buffer. A portion of storage used to hold input or output data temporarily.

bypass. In SMP/E, to circumvent errors that would otherwise cause SYSMOD processing to fail. This task is accomplished by using the BYPASS operand on an SMP/E command.

byte stream. A simple sequence of bytes stored in a stream file. See also *record data*.

byte. The basic unit of storage addressability. It has a length of 8 bits.

C

C language. A high-level language used to develop software applications in compact, efficient code that can be run on different types of computers with minimal change.

cabinet. Housing for panels organized into port groups of patchports, which are pairs of fibre adapters or couplers. Cabinets are used to organize long, complex cables between processors and controllers, which may be as far away as another physical site. Also known as *fiber management cabinets*.

cable "in inventory." Unused cables.

cache structure. A Coupling Facility structure that enables high-performance sharing of cached data by multisystem applications in a sysplex. Applications can use a cache structure to implement several different types of caching systems, including a store-through or a store-in cache.

cache. A random access electronic storage in selected storage controls used to retain frequently used data for faster access by the channel.

called routine. A routine or program that is invoked by another one.

carriage control character. An optional character in an input data record that specifies a write, space, or skip operation.

carriage return (CR). (1) A key stroke generally indicating the end of a command line. (2) In text data, the action that indicates to continue printing at the left margin of the next line. (3) A character that will cause printing to start at the beginning of the same physical line in which the carriage return occurred.

CART. See *command and response token*.

case-sensitive. Pertaining to the ability to distinguish between uppercase and lowercase letters.

catalog. (1) A directory of files and libraries, with reference to their locations. (2) To enter information about a file or a library into a catalog. (3) The collection of all data set indexes that are used by the control program to locate a volume containing a specific data set.

cataloged data set. A data set that is represented in an index or hierarchy of indexes that provide the means for locating it.

cataloged procedure. A set of job control language (JCL) statements placed in a library and retrievable by name.

CCA. See *channel connection address*.

CCW. See *channel command word*.

CEMT. The CICS-supplied transaction that allows the checking of the status of terminals, connections, and other CICS entities from a console or from CICS terminal sessions.

central processing unit (CPU). Synonymous with *processor*.

central processor (CP). The part of the computer that contains the sequencing and processing facilities for instruction execution, initial program load, and other machine operations.

central processor complex (CPC). A physical collection of hardware that consists of main storage, one or more central processors, timers, and channels. In the zEnterprise environment, the CPC consists of a System z zEnterprise mainframe and any attached IBM zEnterprise BladeCenter Extension (zBX).

central storage. (1) In z/OS, the storage of a computing system from which the central processing unit can directly obtain instructions and data, and to which it can directly return results. (Formerly referred to as "real storage".) (2) Synonymous with *processor storage*.

CF. See *Coupling Facility*.

CFRM. Coupling Facility resource management.

CGI. Common Gateway Interface.

channel adapter. A device that groups two or more controller channel interfaces electronically.

channel command word (CCW). Contains the channel commands used by VTAM to send data to and receive data from channel-attached non-SNA 3270 terminals.

channel connection address (CCA). The input/output (I/O) address that uniquely identifies an I/O device to the channel during an I/O operation.

channel interface. The circuitry in a storage control that attaches storage paths to a host channel.

channel path identifier (CHIPID). The logical equivalent of channels in the physical processor.

channel subsystem (CSS). A collection of subchannels that directs the flow of information between I/O devices and main storage. Logical partitions use subchannels to communicate with I/O devices. The maximum number of CSSs supported by a processor also depends on the processor type. If more than one CSS is supported by a processor, each CSS has a processor unique single hexadecimal digit CSS identifier (CSS ID).

channel-to-channel (CTC) connection. A connection between two CHPIDs on the same or different processors, either directly or through a switch. When connecting through a switch, both CHPIDs must be connected through the same or a chained switch.

channel-to-channel (CTC). The communication (transfer of data) between programs on opposite sides of a channel-to-channel adapter (CTCA).

channel-to-channel adapter (CTCA). An input/output device that is used a program in one system to communicate with a program in another system.

character. A letter, digit, or other symbol that is used as part of the organization, control, or representation of data. A character is often in the form of a spatial arrangement of adjacent or connected strokes.

checkpoint data set. A data set in which information about the status of a job and the system can be recorded so that the job step can be restarted later.

checkpoint write. Any write to the checkpoint data set. A general term for the primary, intermediate, and final writes that update any checkpoint data set.

checkpoint. (1) A place in a routine where a check, or a recording of data for restart purposes, is performed. (2) A point at which information about the status of a job and the system can be recorded so that the job step can be restarted later.

CHPID. See *channel path identifier*.

CI. See *control interval*.

CICS. See *Customer Information Control System*.

CICSplex. A configuration of interconnected CICS systems in which each system is dedicated to one of the main elements of the overall workload. See also *application owning region* and *terminal owning region*.

CKD. See *count-key data*.

client-server. In TCP/IP, the model of interaction in distributed data processing in which a program at one site sends a request to a program at another site and awaits a response. The requesting program is called a client; the answering program is called a server.

client. A functional unit that receives shared services from a server. See also *client-server*.

CLIST. command list.

CLOB. character large object.

CLPA. See *create link pack area*.

CMOS. See *complementary metal oxide semiconductor*.

CMS. See *conversational monitor system*.

COBOL. See *Common Business-Oriented Language*.

code page. (1) An assignment of graphic characters and control function meanings to all code points; for example, assignment of characters and meanings to 256 code points for an 8-bit code, or assignment of characters and meanings to 128 code points for a 7-bit code. (2) A particular assignment of hexadecimal identifiers to graphic characters.

code point. A 1 byte code representing one of 256 potential characters.

coexistence. Two or more systems at different levels (for example, software, service or operational levels) that share resources. Coexistence includes the ability of a system to respond in the following ways to a new function that was introduced on another system with which it shares resources: ignore a new function, terminate gracefully, or support a new function.

command and response token (CART). A parameter on WTO, WTOR, MGCRE, and certain TSO/E commands and REXX EXECs that allows you to link commands and their associated message responses. is a keyword and subcommand for the TSO/E CONSOLE command and an argument on the GETMSG function. You can use the CART to associate MVS system and subsystem commands you issue with their corresponding responses.

command prefix. A one to eight character command identifier. The command prefix distinguishes the command as belonging to an application or subsystem rather than to z/OS.

command. A request to perform an operation or run a program. When parameters, arguments, flags, or other operands are associated with a command, the resulting character string is a single command.

COMMAREA. A communication area made available to applications running under CICS.

commit. A request to make all changes to resources since the last commit or backout or, for the first unit of recovery, since the beginning of the application.

Common Business-Oriented Language (COBOL). A high-level language, based on English, that is primarily used for business applications.

common service area (CSA). In z/OS, a part of the common area that contains data areas that are addressable by all address spaces.

compatibility. The ability to work in the system or the ability to work with other devices or programs.

compilation unit. A portion of a computer program sufficiently complete to be compiled correctly.

compiler options. Keywords that can be specified to control certain aspects of compilation. Compiler options can control the nature of the load module generated by the compiler, the types of printed output to be produced, the efficient use of the compiler, and the destination of error messages. Also called *compiler-time options*.

compiler. A program that translates a source program into an executable program (an object deck).

Complementary Metal Oxide Semiconductor (CMOS). A technology that combines the electrical properties of positive and negative voltage requirements to use considerably less power than other types of semiconductors.

component. A functional part of an operating system, for example, the scheduler or supervisor.

condition code. A code that reflects the result of a previous input/output, arithmetic, or logical operation.

configuration. The arrangement of a computer system or network as defined by the nature, number, and chief characteristics of its functional units.

connection. In TCP/IP, the path between two protocol applications that provides a reliable data stream delivery service. In Internet communications, a connection extends from a TCP application on one system to a TCP application on another system.

consistent copy. A copy of a data entity (for example, a logical volume) that contains the contents of the entire data entity from a single instant in time.

console group. In z/OS, a group of consoles defined in CNGRPxx, each of whose members can serve as an alternate console in console or hardcopy recovery or as a console to display synchronous messages.

console. Any device from which operators can enter commands or receive messages.

control block. A storage area used by a computer program to hold control information.

control interval (CI). A fixed-length area or disk in which VSAM stores records and creates distributed free space. Also, in a key-sequenced data set or file, the set of records to which an entry in the sequence-set index record points. The control interval is the unit of information that VSAM transmits to or from disk. A control interval always includes an integral number of physical records.

control region. The main storage region that contains the subsystem work manager or subsystem resource manager control program.

control section (CSECT). The part of a program specified by the programmer to be a relocatable unit, all elements of which are to be loaded into adjoining main storage locations.

control statement. In programming languages, a statement that is used to alter the continuous sequential execution of statements; a control statement can be a conditional statement, such as IF, or an imperative statement, such as STOP. In JCL, a statement in a job that is used in identifying the job or describing its requirements to the operating system.

control unit (CU). Each physical controller contains one or more control units, which translate high level requests to low level requests between processors and devices. Synonymous with *device control unit.*

control unit address. The high order bits of the storage control address, which are used to identify the storage control to the host system.

controller. A device that translates high level requests from processors to low level requests for I/O devices, and vice versa. Each physical controller contains one or more logical control units, channel and device interfaces, and a power source. Controllers can be divided into segments, or grouped into subsystems.

conversation. A logical connection between two programs over an LU type 6.2 session that allows them to communicate with each other while processing a transaction.

conversational monitor system (CMS). A virtual machine operating system that provides general interactive time sharing, problem solving, and program development capabilities, and operates only under the control of the VM/370 control program.

conversational. Pertaining to a program or a system that carries on a dialog with a terminal user, alternately accepting input and then responding to the input quickly enough for the user to maintain a train of thought.

CORBA. Common Object Request Broker Architecture.

corequisite SYSMODs. SYSMODs that can be installed properly only if the other is present. Corequisites are defined by the REQ operand on the ++VER statement.

corrective service. Any SYSMOD used to selectively fix a system problem. Generally, corrective service refers to APAR fixes.

count-key data (CKD). A disk storage device for storing data in the format: count field, normally followed by a key field, and then followed by the actual data of a record. The count field contains, in addition to other information, the address of the record in the format CCHHR (where CC is the two-digit cylinder number, HH is the two-digit head number, and R is the record number) and the length of the data. The key field contains the record's key.

couple data set. A data set that is created through the XCF couple data set format utility and, depending on its designated type, is shared by some or all of the z/OS systems in a sysplex. See also *sysplex couple data set.*

Coupling Facility (CF). A special logical partition that provides high-speed caching, list processing, and locking functions in a sysplex.

Coupling Facility channel. A high bandwidth fiber optic channel that provides the high-speed connectivity required for data sharing between a Coupling Facility and the central processor complexes directly attached to it.

coupling services. In a sysplex, the functions of XCF that transfer data and status between members of a group residing on one or more z/OS systems in the sysplex.

CP. See *central processor.*

CPC. See *central processor complex.*

CPU. See *central processing unit.*

CR. See *carriage return.*

create link pack area (CLPA). An option that is used during IPL to initialize the link pack pageable area.

cross-memory linkage. A method for invoking a program in a different address space. The invocation is synchronous with respect to the caller.

cross-system Coupling Facility (XCF). A component of z/OS that provides functions to support cooperation between authorized programs running within a sysplex.

cross-system extended services (XES). A set of z/OS services that allow multiple instances of an application or subsystem, running on different systems in a sysplex environment, to implement high-performance and high-availability data sharing by using a Coupling Facility.

cross-system restart. If a system fails, automatic restart management restarts elements on another eligible system in the sysplex.

crossbar switch. A static switch that can connect controllers to processors with parallel (bus and tag) interfaces. The crossbar contains a number of channel interfaces on its top, which can connect to objects above it, such as processors or other crossbars. The crossbar switch also contains a number of control unit interfaces on its side, which can connect to objects below it, such as controllers or other crossbars.

cryptographic key. A parameter that determines cryptographic transformations between plaintext and ciphertext.

cryptography. The transformation of data to conceal its meaning.

CSA. See *common service area*.

CSECT. See *control section*.

CSI. consolidated software inventory data set. See *SMPCSI*.

CSS. See *channel subsystem*.

CTC connection. channel-to-channel connection.

CTC. See *channel-to-channel*.

CTCA. See *channel-to-channel adapter*.

CU. See *control unit*.

cumulative service tape. A tape sent with a new function order, containing all current PTFs for that function.

Customer Information Control System (CICS). An online transaction processing (OLTP) system that provides specialized interfaces to databases, files, and terminals in support of business and commercial applications. CICS enables transactions entered at remote terminals to be processed concurrently by user-written application programs.

D

daemon. In UNIX systems, a long-lived process that runs unattended to perform continuous or periodic system-wide functions, such as network control. Some daemons are triggered automatically to perform their task; others operate periodically. An example is the cron daemon, which periodically performs the tasks listed in the crontab file. The z/OS equivalent is a started task.

DASD volume. A DASD space identified by a common label and accessed by a set of related addresses. See also *volume*.

DASD. See *direct access storage device*.

DAT. See *dynamic address translation*.

data class. A collection of allocation and space attributes, defined by the storage administrator, that are used that are used when allocating a new SMS-managed data set.

data control block (DCB). A control block used by access method routines in storing and retrieving data. It also provides the physical attributes of a data set.

data definition (DD) statement. A job control statement that describes a data set associated with a particular job step. It is used in JCL to describe the data set, its disposition, and attributes.

data definition name (ddname). (1) The name of a data definition (DD) statement that corresponds to a data control block that contains the same name. (2) The symbolic representation for a name placed in the name field of a data definition (DD) statement. The data definition name is used in JCL to reference a data set relationship between the program and DD statement.

data definition statement. A JCL control statement that serves as the connection between a file's logical name (the ddname) and the file's physical name (the data set name).

data division. In COBOL, the part of a program that describes the files to be used in the program and the records contained within the files. It also describes any WORKING-STORAGE data items, LINKAGE SECTION data items, and LOCAL-STORAGE data items that are needed.

Data Facility Sort (DFSORT). An IBM licensed program that is a high-speed data-processing utility. DFSORT provides a method for sorting, merging, and copying operations, as well as providing versatile data manipulation at the record, field, and bit level.

data in transit. The update data on application system DASD volumes that is being sent to the recovery system for writing to DASD volumes on the recovery system.

data integrity. The condition that exists when accidental or intentional destruction, alteration, or loss of data does not occur.

data set backup. This is the backup that protects against the loss of individual data sets.

data set label. (1) A collection of information that describes the attributes of a data set and is normally stored on the same volume as the data set. (2) A general term for data set control blocks and tape data set labels.

data set. In z/OS, a named collection of related data records that is stored and retrieved by an assigned name. Equivalent to a file.

data sharing. The ability of concurrent subsystems (such as DB2 or IMS DB) or application programs to directly access and change the same data, while maintaining data integrity.

data stream. (1) All information (data and control commands) sent over a data link, usually in a single read or write operation. (2) A continuous stream of data elements being transmitted, or intended for transmission, in character or binary-digit form, using a defined format.

data type. The properties and internal representation that characterize data.

data warehouse. A system that provides critical business information to an organization. The data warehouse system cleanses the data for accuracy and currency, and then presents the data to decision makers so that they can interpret and use it effectively and efficiently.

database administrator (DBA). An individual who is responsible for designing, developing, operating, safeguarding, maintaining, and using a database.

database management system (DBMS). A software system that controls the creation, organization, and modification of a database and the access to the data that is stored within it.

database. A collection of tables, or a collection of table spaces and index spaces.

DB2 data sharing group. A collection of one or more concurrent DB2 subsystems that directly access and change the same data while maintaining data integrity.

DB2. Generally, one of a family of IBM relational database management systems and, specifically, the system that runs under z/OS.

DBA. See *database administrator.*

DBCS. See *double-byte character set.*

DBMS. See *database management system.*

DCB. See *data control block.*

DCE. See *Distributed Computing Environment.*

DCLGEN. See *declaration generator.*

DD statement. See *data definition (DD) statement.*

ddname. See *data definition name (ddname).*

deadlock. (1) An error condition in which processing cannot continue because each of two elements of the process is waiting for an action by or a response from the other. (2) Unresolvable contention for the use of a resource. (3) An impasse that occurs when multiple processes are waiting for the availability of a resource that does not become available because it is being held by another process that is in a similar wait state.

deallocate. To release a resource that is assigned to a specific task.

declarations generator (DCLGEN). A subcomponent of DB2 that generates SQL table declarations and COBOL, C, or PL/I data structure declarations that conform to the table. The declarations are generated from DB2 system catalog information.

dedicated. Pertaining to the assignment of a system resource (a device, a program, or a whole system) to an application or purpose.

default. A value that is used or an action that is taken when no alternative is specified by the user.

deferred restart. A restart performed by the system when a user resubmits a job. The operator submits the restart deck to the system through a system input reader. See also *checkpoint restart.* Contrast with *automatic restart.*

deleted function. In SMP/E, a function that was removed from the system when another function was installed. This is indicated by the DELBY subentry in the SYSMOD entry for the deleted function.

destination node. The node that provides application services to an authorized external user.

destination. A combination of a node name and one of the following: a user ID, a remote printer or punch, a special local printer, or LOCAL (the default if only a node name is specified).

device address. The field of an ESCON device-level frame that selects a specific device on a control unit image. The one or two left-most digits are the address of the channel to which the device is attached. The two right digits represent the unit address.

device control unit. A hardware device that controls the reading, writing, or displaying of data at one or more I/O devices or terminals.

device number. A four-hexadecimal-character identifier, for example 13A0, that you associate with a device to facilitate communication between the program and the host operator. The device number that you associate with a subchannel.

Device Support Facilities program (ICKDSF). A program used to initialize DASD volumes at installation and perform media maintenance.

device type. The general name for a kind of device; for example, 3390.

device. A computer peripheral or an object that appears to the application as such.

DFS. See *Distributed File Service.*

DFSMS. Data Facility Storage Management Subsystem.

DFSMShsm. An IBM product used for backing up and recovering data, and managing space on volumes in the storage hierarchy.

DFSORT. See *Data Facility Sort.*

dialog. An interactive window containing options that allow you to browse or modify information, take specific action relating to selected objects, or access other dialogs. For example, HCM provides a series of dialogs to help you create, edit, delete, and connect objects, as well as manipulate the configuration diagram.

direct access storage device (DASD). A device in which the access time is effectively independent of the location of the data.

directory. (1) A type of file containing the names and controlling information for other files or other directories. Directories can also contain subdirectories, which can contain subdirectories of their own. (2) A file that contains directory entries. No two directory entries in the same directory can have the same name. (POSIX.1). (3) A file that points to files and to other directories. (4) An index used by a control program to locate blocks of data that are stored in separate areas of a data set in direct access storage.

disaster recovery. Recovery after a disaster, such as a fire, that destroys or otherwise disables a system. Disaster recovery techniques typically involve restoring data to a second (recovery) system, then using the recovery system in place of the destroyed or disabled application system. See also *recovery, backup,* and *recovery system.*

DISP. Disposition (JCL DD parameter).

display console. In z/OS, an MCS console whose input/output function you can control.

Distributed Computing Environment (DCE). A comprehensive, integrated set of services that supports the development, use, and maintenance of distributed applications. DCE is independent of the operating system and network; it provides interoperability and portability across heterogeneous platforms.

distributed computing. Computing that involves the cooperation of two or more machines communicating over a network. Data and resources are shared among the individual computers.

distributed data. Data that resides on a DBMS other than the local system.

Distributed File Service (DFS). A DCE component. DFS joins the local file systems of several file server machines, making the files equally available to all DFS client machines. DFS allows users to access and share files stored on a file server anywhere in the network, without having to consider the physical location of the file. Files are part of a single, global namespace, so that a user can be found anywhere in the network by means of the same name. Distributed File Service provides file services for Unix System Services.

distribution library (DLIB). A library that contains the master copy of all the elements in a system. A distribution library can be used to create or back up a target library.

distribution zone. In SMP/E, a group of records in a CSI data set that describes the SYSMODs and elements in a distribution library.

DL/I. Data Language/Interface.

DLIB. See *distribution library.*

DLL. See *dynamic link library.*

double-byte character set (DBCS). A set of characters in which each character is represented by a two-bytes code. Languages such as Japanese; Chinese, and Korean, which contain more symbols than can be represented by 256 code points, require double-byte character sets. Because each character requires two bytes, the typing, display, and printing of DBCS characters requires hardware and programs that support DBCS. Contrast with *single-byte character set.*

doubleword. A sequence of bits or characters that comprises eight bytes (two 4 byte words) and is referenced as a unit.

downwardly compatible. The ability of applications to run on previous releases of z/OS.

drain. Allowing a printer to complete its current work before stopping the device.

driving system. The system used to install the program. Contrast with *target system.*

dsname. data set name.

DSORG. data set organization (a parameter of DCB and DD and in a data class definition).

dump. A report showing the contents of storage. Dumps are typically produced following program failures, for use as diagnostic aids.

dynamic address translation (DAT). The process of translating a virtual address during a storage reference into the corresponding real address.

dynamic allocation. Assignment of system resources to a program at the time the program is executed rather than at the time it is loaded into central storage.

dynamic link library (DLL). A file containing executable code and data bound to a program at load time or run time. The code and data in a dynamic link library can be shared by several applications simultaneously.

dynamic reconfiguration. The ability to make changes to the channel subsystem and to the operating system while the system is running.

E

e-business. (1) The transaction of business over an electronic medium such as the Internet. (2) The transformation of key business processes through the use of Internet technologies.

EB. See *exabyte.*

EBCDIC. See *Extended Binary Coded Decimal Interchange Code.*

EC. engineering change.

ECSA. extended common service area.

EDT. See *eligible device table.*

EIS. Enterprise Information System.

element. In SMP/E, part of a product, such as a macro, module, dialog panel, or sample code.

eligible device table (EDT). An installation defined representation of the devices that are eligible for allocation. The EDT defines the esoteric and generic relationship of these devices. During IPL, the installation identifies the EDT that z/OS uses. After IPL, jobs can request device allocation from any of the esoteric device groups assigned to the selected EDT. An EDT is identified by a unique ID (two digits), and contains one or more esoterics and generics.

enclave. A transaction that can span multiple dispatchable units (SRBs and tasks) in one or more address spaces and is reported on and managed as a unit.

encrypt. To systematically encode data so that it cannot be read without knowing the coding key.

endian. An attribute of data representation that reflects how certain multi-octet data is stored in memory. See big endian and little endian.

ensemble member. A zEnterprise node that has been added to an ensemble.

ensemble. A collection of one or more zEnterprise nodes (including any attached zBX) that are managed as a single logical virtualized system by the Unified Resource Manager, through the use of a Hardware Management Console.

Enterprise Systems Connection (ESCON). A set of products and services that provides a dynamically connected environment using optical cables as a transmission medium.

enterprise. The composite of all operational entities, functions, and resources that form the total business concern.

entry area. In z/OS, the part of a console panel where operators can enter commands or command responses.

entry name. In assembler language, a programmer-specified name within a control section that identifies an entry point and can be referred to by any control section. See also *entry point.*

entry point name. The symbol (or name) that represents an entry point. See also *entry point.*

entry point. The address or label of the first instruction that is executed when a routine is entered for execution. Within a load module, the location to which control is passed when the load module is invoked.

EOF. end of file.

ESCON. See *Enterprise Systems Connection.*

esoteric. Esoteric (or esoteric device group) is an installation-defined and named grouping of I/O devices of usually the same device group. Eligible device tables (EDTs) define the esoteric and generic relationship of these devices. The name you assign to an esoteric is used in the JCL DD statement. The job then allocates a device from that group instead of a specific device number or generic device group.

ETR. External Time Reference. See also *Sysplex Timer.*

exabyte. For processor, real and virtual storage capacities and channel volume: 1,152,921,504,606,846,976 bytes or $2^{(60)}$.

exception SYSMOD. A SYSMOD that is in error or that requires special processing before it can be installed. ++HOLD and ++RELEASE statements identify exception SYSMODs.

EXCP. execute channel programs.

executable program. (1) A program in a form suitable for execution by a computer. The program can be an application or a shell script. (2) A program that has been link-edited and can therefore be run in a processor. (3) A program that can be executed as a self-contained procedure. It consists of a main program and, optionally, one or more subprograms. (4) See also *executable file* and *load module.*

executable. A load module or program object that has yet to be loaded into memory for execution.

Extended Binary-Coded Decimal Interchange Code (EBCDIC). An encoding scheme that is used to represent character data in the z/OS environment. Contrast with *ASCII* and *Unicode.*

extended MCS console. In z/OS, a console other than an MCS console from which operators or programs can issue system commands and receive messages. An extended MCS console is defined through an OPERPARM segment.

extended remote copy (XRC). A hardware- and software-based remote copy service option that provides an asynchronous volume copy across storage subsystems for disaster recovery, device migration, and workload migration.

external reference. In an object deck, a reference to a symbol, such as an entry point name, defined in another program or module.

F

feature code. A four-digit code used by IBM to process hardware and software orders.

feature. A part of an IBM product that may be ordered separately by a customer.

fetch. The dynamic loading of a procedure.

Fiber Connection Environment (FICON). An optical fiber communication method offering channels with high data rate, high bandwidth, increased distance, and a large number of devices per control unit for mainframe systems. It can work with, or replace, ESCON links.

fiber link. The physical fiber optic connections and transmission media between optical fiber transmitters and receivers. A fiber link can be composed of one or more fiber cables and patchports in fiber management cabinets. Each connection in the fiber link is either permanent or mutable.

FICON. See *Fiber Connection Environment*.

FIFO. See *first in, first out*.

file. A named collection of related data records that is stored and retrieved by an assigned name. Equivalent to a z/OS data set.

FILEDEF. file definition statement.

firewall. An intermediate server that functions to isolate a secure network from an insecure network.

firmware. Licensed internal code (LIC) that is shipped with hardware. Firmware is considered an integral part of the system and is loaded and run at power on. Firmware is not open for customer configuration and is expected to run without any customer setup.

first in, first out. A queuing technique in which the next item to be retrieved is the oldest item in the queue.

fix. A correction of an error in a program, usually a temporary correction or bypass of defective code.

fixed-length record. A record having the same length as all other records with which it is logically or physically associated. Contrast with *variable-length record*.

FlashCopy. A point-in-time copy services function that can quickly copy data from a source location to a target location.

FMID. See *function modification identifier*.

foreground job. (1) A high-priority job, usually a real-time job. (2) Under TSO, any job executing in a swapped region of central storage, such as a command processor or a terminal user's program. Contrast with *background job*.

foreground. (1) in multiprogramming, the environment in which high-priority programs are executed. (2) Under TSO, the environment in which programs are swapped in and out of central storage to allow CPU time to be shared among terminal users. All command processor programs execute in the foreground. Contrast with *background*.

foreign key. A column or set of columns in a dependent table of a constraint relationship. The key must have the same number of columns, with the same descriptions, as the primary key of the parent table. Each foreign key value must either match a parent key value in the related parent table or be null.

fork. To create and start a child process. Forking is similar to creating an address space and attaching. It creates a copy of the parent process, including open file descriptors.

Fortran. A high-level language used primarily for applications involving numeric computations. In previous usage, the name of the language was written in all capital letters, that is, FORTRAN.

frame. For a mainframe microprocessor cluster, a frame contains one or two central processor complexes (CPCs), support elements, and AC power distribution.

FRCA. Fast Response Cache Accelerator.

FTP. File Transfer Protocol.

fullword boundary. A storage location whose address is evenly divisible by 4.

fullword. A sequence of bits or characters that is composed of four bytes (one word) and is referenced as a unit.

function modification identifier (FMID). A code that identifies the release levels of a z/OS licensed program.

function. In SMP/E, a product (such as a system component or licensed program) that can be installed in a user's system if desired. Functions are identified to SMP/E by the ++FUNCTION statement. Each function must have a unique FMID.

G

gateway node. A node that is an interface between networks.

GB. See *gigabyte*.

GDG. See *generation data group*.

GDPS. See *Geographically Dispersed Parallel Sysplex*.

generalized trace facility (GTF). Like system trace, gathers information that used to determine and diagnose problems that occur during system operation. Unlike system trace, however, GTF can be tailored to record specific system and user program events.

generation data group (GDG). A collection of historically related non-VSAM data sets that are arranged in chronological order; each data set is called a generation data set.

generic. A z/OS-defined grouping of devices with similar characteristics. For example: the device types 3270-X, 3277-2, 3278-2, -2A, -3, -4, and 3279-2a, -2b, -2c, -3a, -3b belong to the same generic. Every generic has a generic name that is used for device allocation in the JCL DD statement. z/OS interprets this name as "take any device in that group." In a given z/OS configuration, each eligible device table (EDT) has the same list of generics.

Geographically Dispersed Parallel Sysplex (GDPS). An application that integrates Parallel Sysplex technology and remote copy technology to enhance application availability and improve disaster recovery. GDPS topology is a Parallel Sysplex cluster spread across two sites, with all critical data mirrored between the sites. GDPS manages the remote copy configuration and storage subsystems, automates Parallel Sysplex operational tasks, and automates failure recovery from a single point of control.

gigabyte. 1,073,741,824 bytes, or 2^{30} bytes. This is approximately a billion bytes in American English.

global access checking. The ability to allow an installation to establish an in-storage table of default values for authorization levels for selected resources.

global resource serialization complex. One or more z/OS systems that use global resource serialization to serialize access to shared resources (such as data sets on shared DASD volumes).

global resource serialization. A function that provides a z/OS serialization mechanism for resources (typically data sets) across multiple z/OS images.

global zone. A group of records in a CSI data set used to record information about SYSMODs received for a particular system. The global zone also contains information that (1) enables SMP/E to access target and distribution zones in that system, and (2) enables you to tailor aspects of SMP/E processing.

GPMP. See *guest platform management provider.*

Gregorian calendar. The calendar in use since Friday, 15 October 1582 throughout most of the world.

group. A collection of RACF users who can share access authorities for protected resources.

GTF. See *generalized trace facility.*

guest platform management provider (GPMP). An optional suite of applications that is installed in specific z/OS, Linux, and AIX operating system images to support platform management functions. For example, the guest platform management provider collects and aggregates performance data for virtual servers and workloads

H

hardcopy log. In systems with multiple console support or a graphic console, a permanent record of system activity.

hardware configuration dialog (HCD). In z/OS, a panel program that is part of the hardware configuration definition. The program allows an installation to define devices for z/OS system configurations.

Hardware Management Console (HMC). A user interface through which data center personnel configure, control, monitor, and manage IBM System z hardware and software resources. The HMC communicates with each central processor complex (CPC) through the Support Element. On an IBM zEnterprise mainframe, using the Unified Resource Manager on the HMCs or Support Elements, personnel can also create and manage an ensemble.

hardware unit. A central processor, storage element, channel path, device, and so on.

hardware. Physical equipment, as opposed to the computer program or method of use; for example, mechanical, magnetic, electrical, or electronic devices. Contrast with *software.*

HASP. See *Houston Automatic Spooling Priority.*

HCD. See *hardware configuration dialog.*

head of string. The first unit of devices in a string. It contains the string interfaces that connect to controller device interfaces.

hexadecimal. A base 16 numbering system. Hexadecimal digits range from 0 through 9 (decimal 0 to 9) and uppercase or lowercase A through F (decimal 10 to 15) and A through F, giving values of 0 through 15.

HFS. See *hierarchical file system.*

hierarchical file system (HFS) data set. A data set that contains a POSIX-compliant hierarchical file system, which is a collection of files and directories organized in a hierarchical structure, that can be accessed using z/OS UNIX System Services facilities.

hierarchical file system (HFS). A data set that contains a POSIX-compliant file system, which is a collection of files and directories organized in a hierarchical structure, that can be accessed using z/OS UNIX System Services.

high-level language (HLL). A programming language above the level of assembler language and below that of program generators and query languages. Examples are C, C++, COBOL, Fortran, and PL/I.

highly parallel. Refers to multiple systems operating in parallel, each of which can have multiple processors. See also *n-way.*

HLL. See *high-level language.*

HMC. See *Hardware Management Console.*

HOLDDATA. In SMP/E, one or more MCSs used to indicate that certain SYSMODs contain errors or require special processing before they can be installed. ++HOLD and ++RELEASE statements are used to define HOLDDATA. SYSMODs affected by HOLDDATA are called exception SYSMODs.

Houston Automatic Spooling Priority (HASP). A computer program that provides supplementary job management, data management, and task management functions, such as control of job flow, ordering of tasks, and spooling. See also *JES2*.

hypervisor. A program that allows multiple instances of operating systems or virtual servers to run simultaneously on the same hardware device. A hypervisor can run directly on the hardware, can run within an operating system, or can be embedded in platform firmware. Examples of hypervisors include PR/SM, z/VM, and PowerVM™ Enterprise Edition.

I

I/O cluster. A sysplex that owns a managed channel path for a logically partitioned processor configuration.

I/O device. A printer, tape drive, hard disk drive, and so on. Devices are logically grouped inside units, which are in turn grouped into strings. The first unit, known as the head of string, contains string interfaces that connect to controller device interfaces and eventually to processor CHPIDs. Devices are represented as lines of text within the appropriate unit object in the configuration diagram.

I/O. input/output.

IBM Support Center. The IBM organization responsible for software service.

IBM System z Application Assist Processor (zAAP). A specialized processor that provides a Java execution environment, which enables Java-based web applications to be integrated with core z/OS business applications and back-end database systems.

IBM System z Integrated Information Processor (zIIP). A specialized processor that provides computing capacity for selected data and transaction processing workloads, and for selected network encryption workloads.

IBM Systems Engineer (SE). An IBM service representative who performs maintenance services for IBM software in the field.

IBM zEnterprise System (zEnterprise). A heterogeneous hardware infrastructure that can consist of a IBM zEnterprise mainframe and an attached IBM Enterprise BladeCenter Extension (zBX) managed as a single logical virtualized system by the Unified Resource Manager.

IBM zEnterprise BladeCenter Extension (zBX). A heterogeneous hardware infrastructure that consists of a BladeCenter chassis attached to a IBM zEnterprise mainframe. A BladeCenter chassis can contain POWER blades or optimizers.

IBM zEnterprise Unified Resource Manager (zManager). Licensed internal code (LIC), also known as firmware, that is part of the Hardware Management Console. The Unified Resource Manager provides energy monitoring and management, goal-oriented policy management, increased security, virtual networking, and data management for the physical and logical resources of a given ensemble.

ICSF. Integrated Cryptographic Service Facility.

IDCAMS. An IBM program used to process access method services commands. It can be invoked as a job or job step, from a TSO terminal, or from within a user's application program.

image. A single instance of the z/OS operating system.

IMS DB data sharing group. A collection of one or more concurrent IMS DB subsystems that directly access and change the same data while maintaining data integrity.

IMS DB. Information Management System Database Manager.

IMS TM. Information Management System Transaction Manager

IMS. See *Information Management System*.

Information Management System (IMS). IBM product that supports hierarchical databases, data communication, translation processing, and database backout and recovery.

initial program load (IPL). The initialization procedure that causes the z/OS operating system to begin operation. During IPL, system programs are loaded into storage and z/OS is made ready to perform work. Synonymous with *boot* and *load*.

initial storage allocation. The amount of central to be assigned to a logical partition.

initiator. That part of an operating system that reads and processes operation control language statements from the system input device.

initiator/terminator. The job scheduler function that selects jobs and job steps to be executed, allocates input/output devices for them, places them under task control, and at completion of the job, supplies control information for writing job output on a system output unit.

input/output configuration data set (IOCDS). A file that contains different configuration definitions for the selected processor. Only one IOCDS is used at a time. The IOCDS contains I/O configuration data for the files associated with the processor controller on the host processor, as it is used by the channel subsystem. The channel subsystem (CSS) uses the configuration data to control I/O requests. The IOCDS is built from the production IODF.

input/output definition file (IODF). A VSAM linear data set that contains I/O definition information, including processor I/O definitions and operating system I/O definitions, including all logical objects and their connectivity in the hardware configuration.

install. In SMP/E, to apply a SYSMOD to the target libraries or to accept a SYSMOD into the distribution libraries.

installation exit. The means by which an IBM software product may be modified by a customer's system programmers to change or extend the functions of the product.

instruction line. In z/OS, the part of the console panel that contains messages about console control and input errors.

Interactive Problem Control System (IPCS). A component of z/OS that permits online problem management, interactive problem diagnosis, online debugging for dumps, problem tracking, and problem reporting.

Interactive System Productivity Facility (ISPF). A dialog manager for interactive applications. It provides control and services to permit execution of dialogs.

interactive. Pertaining to a program or system that alternately accepts input and responds. In an interactive system, a constant dialog exists between user and system. Contrast with *batch*.

internal reader. A facility that transfers jobs to JES.

interrupt. A suspension of a process, such as the execution of a computer program, caused by an event external to that process, and performed in such a way that the process can be resumed.

IOCDS. See *input/output configuration data set*.

IODF. See *input/output definition file*.

IPCS. See *Interactive Problem Control System*.

IPL. See *initial program load*.

IPv6. Internet Protocol Version 6.

IRLM. Internal Resource Lock Manager.

ISMF. interactive storage management facility.

ISPF. See *Interactive System Productivity Facility*.

ISPF/PDF. Interactive System Productivity Facility/Program Development Facility.

IVP. installation verification procedure.

J

JCL. See *job control language*.

JES. See *job entry subsystem*.

JES2. A z/OS subsystem that receives jobs into the system, converts them to internal format, selects them for execution, processes their output, and purges them from the system. In an installation with more than one processor, each JES2 processor independently controls its job input, scheduling, and output processing. Contrast with *JES3*.

JES3. A z/OS subsystem that receives jobs into the system, converts them to internal format, selects them for execution, processes their output, and purges them from the system. In complexes that have several loosely-coupled processing units, the JES3 program manages processors so that the global processor exercises centralized control over the local processors and distributes jobs to them via a common job queue. Contrast with *JES2*.

job class. Any one of a number of job categories that can be defined. With the classification of jobs and direction of initiator/terminators to initiate specific classes of jobs, it is possible to control the mixture of jobs that are performed concurrently.

job control language (JCL) statements. Statements placed into an input stream to define work to be done, methods to be used, and the resources needed.

job control language (JCL). A sequence of commands used to identify a job to an operating system and to describe a job's requirements.

job entry subsystem (JES). A system facility for spooling, job queuing, and managing I/O.

job entry subsystem 2. See *JES2*.

job entry subsystem 3. See *JES3*.

job priority. A value assigned to a job that is used as a measure of the job's relative importance while the job contends with other jobs for system resources.

job separator pages. Those pages of printed output that delimit jobs.

job step. The job control (JCL) statements that request and control execution of a program and that specify the resources needed to run the program. The JCL statements for a job step include one EXEC statement, which specifies the program or procedure to be invoked, followed by one or more DD statements, which specify the data sets or I/O devices that might be needed by the program.

job. A unit of work for an operating system. Jobs are defined by JCL statements.

Julian date. A date format that contains the year in positions 1 and 2, and the day in positions 3 through 5. The day is represented as 1 through 366, right-adjusted, with zeros in the unused high-order position.

jumper cable. Fiber used to make mutable connections between patchports.

K

kernel. The part of an operating system that performs basic functions, such as allocating hardware resources.

key-sequenced data set (KSDS). A VSAM file or data set whose records are loaded in ascending key sequence and controlled by an index. Records are retrieved and stored by keyed access or by addressed access, and new records are inserted in key sequence by means of distributed free space. Relative byte addresses can change because of control interval or control area splits.

keyword. A part of a command operand that consists of a specific character string (such as DSNAME=).

KSDS. See *key-sequenced data set*.

L

LAN. See *local area network*.

Language Environment. Short form of z/OS Language Environment. A set of architectural constructs and interfaces that provides a common runtime environment and runtime services for C, C++, COBOL, Fortran, PL/I, VisualAge PL/I, and Java applications compiled by Language Environment-conforming compilers.

last in, first out (LIFO). A queuing technique in which the next item to be retrieved is the item most recently placed in the queue.

LCSS. logical channel subsystem.

LCU. See *logical control unit*.

LDAP. See *Lightweight Directory Access Protocol*.

library. A partitioned data set (PDS) that contains a related collection of named members. See *partitioned data set*.

LIC. See *licensed internal code*.

licensed internal code (LIC). Microcode that IBM does not sell as part of a machine, but licenses to the customer. LIC is implemented in a part of storage that is not addressable by user programs. Some IBM products use it to implement functions as an alternative to hardwired circuitry.

licensed program. A software package that can be ordered from the program libraries, such as IBM Software Distribution (ISMD). IMS and CICS are examples of licensed programs.

LIFO. See *last in, first out*.

Lightweight Directory Access Protocol (LDAP). An Internet protocol standard, based on the TCP/IP protocol, which allows the access and manipulation of data organized in a Directory Information Tree (DIT).

link library. A data set containing link-edited object modules.

link pack area (LPA). An area of virtual storage that contains reenterable routines that are loaded at IPL (initial program load) time and can be used concurrently by all tasks in the system.

link-edit. To create a loadable computer program by means of a linkage editor or binder.

linkage editor. An operating system component that resolves cross-references between separately compiled or assembled modules and then assigns final addresses to create a single relocatable load module. The linkage editor then stores the load module in a load library on disk.

linked list. A list in which the data elements may be dispersed but in which each data element contains information for locating the next. Synonymous with *chained list*.

list structure. A Coupling Facility structure that enables multisystem applications in a sysplex to share information organized as a set of lists or queues. A list structure consists of a set of lists and an optional lock table, which can be used for serializing resources in the list structure. Each list consists of a queue of list entries.

little endian. A format for storage of binary data in which the least significant byte is placed first. Little endian is used by the Intel hardware architectures. Contrast with *big endian*.

LMOD. See *load module*.

load module. An executable program stored in a partitioned data set program library. See also *program object*.

local area network (LAN). A network in which communication is limited to a moderate-sized geographical area (1 to 10 km), such as a single office building, warehouse, or campus, and which does not generally extend across public rights-of-way. A local area network depends on a communication medium capable of moderate to high data rate (greater than 1 Mbps), and normally operates with a consistently low error rate.

local system queue area (LSQA). In z/OS, one or more segments associated with each virtual storage region that contain job-related system control blocks.

lock structure. A Coupling Facility structure that enables applications in a sysplex to implement customized locking protocols for serialization of application-defined resources. The lock structure supports shared, exclusive, and application-defined lock states, as well as generalized contention management and recovery protocols.

logical control unit (LCU). A single control unit (CU) with or without attached devices, or a group of one or more CUs that share devices. In a channel subsystem (CSS), an LCU represents a set of CUs that physically or logically attach I/O devices in common.

logical partition (LPAR). A subset of the processor hardware that is defined to support an operating system. See also *logically partitioned mode*.

logical partitioning. A function of an operating system that enables the creation of logical partitions.

logical record length (LRECL) Used by JCL to describe the size of logical records used by an application program.

logical subsystem. The logical functions of a storage controller that allow one or more host I/O interfaces to access a set of devices. The controller aggregates the devices according to the addressing mechanisms of the associated I/O interfaces. One or more logical subsystems exist on a storage controller. In general, the controller associates a given set of devices with only one logical subsystem.

logical unit (LU). In SNA, a port through which an user accesses the SNA network to communicate with another user, and through which the user accesses the functions provided by system services control points (SSCPs).

logical unit type 6.2. The SNA logical unit type that supports general communication between programs in a cooperative processing environment.

logically partitioned mode. A central processor complex (CPC) power-on reset mode that enables use of the PR/SM feature and allows an operator to allocate CPC hardware resources (including central processors, central storage, and channel paths) among logical partitions.

logoff. (1) The procedure by which a user ends a terminal session. (2) In VTAM, a request that a terminal be disconnected from a VTAM application program.

logon. (1) The procedure by which a user begins a terminal session. (2) In VTAM, a request that a terminal be connected to a VTAM application program.

loop. A situation in which an instruction or a group of instructions execute repeatedly.

loosely coupled. A multisystem structure that requires a low degree of interaction and cooperation between multiple z/OS images to process a workload. See also *tightly coupled*.

LP. A logical partition or server instance that is configured for CPU, storage, and channels.

LPA. See *link pack area*.

LPAR. See *logical partition*.

LRECL. See *logical record length*.

LSQA. See *local system queue area*.

LU-to-LU. logical unit to logical unit.

LU. See *logical unit*.

M

machine check interruption. An interruption that occurs as a result of an equipment malfunction or error.

machine readable. Pertaining to data a machine can acquire or interpret (read) from a storage device, a data medium, or other source.

macro. An instruction in a source language that is replaced by a defined sequence of instructions in the same source language.

main task. In the context of z/OS multitasking, the main program in a multitasking environment.

MAS. See *multi-access spool configuration*.

master catalog. A catalog that contains extensive data set and volume information that VSAM requires to locate data sets, to allocate and deallocate storage space, to verify the authorization of a program or operator to gain access to a data set, and to accumulate usage statistics for data sets.

master IODF. A centrally kept IODF containing I/O definitions for several systems or even for a complete enterprise structure. Master IODFs help maintain consistent I/O data and can provide comprehensive reports.

master trace. A centralized data tracing facility of the master scheduler, used in servicing the message processing portions of z/OS.

MB. See *megabyte*.

MCS console. A non-SNA device defined to z/OS that is locally attached to a z/OS system and is used to enter commands and receive messages.

MCS. (1) See *multiple console support*. (2) See *modification control statement* (in SMP/E).

mean time between failure (MTBF). The estimated or actual average time period between failures in a computer component or system.

megabyte (MB). 1,048,576 bytes, or 2^{20} bytes.

member. A partition of a partitioned data set (PDS) or partitioned data set extended (PDSE).

message processing facility (MPF). A facility used to control message retention, suppression, and presentation.

message queue. A queue of messages that are waiting to be processed or waiting to be sent to a terminal.

message text. The part of a message consisting of the actual information that is routed to a user at a terminal or to a program.

microcode. Stored microinstructions, not available to users, that perform certain functions.

microprocessor. A processor implemented on one or a small number of chips.

migration. Refers to activities, often performed by the system programmer, that relate to the installation of a new version or release of a program to replace an earlier level. Completion of these activities ensures that the applications and resources on a system will function correctly at the new level.

mixed complex. A global resource serialization complex in which one or more of the systems in the global resource serialization complex are not part of a multisystem sysplex.

modification control statement (MCS). An SMP/E control statement used to package a SYSMOD. MCSs describe the elements of a program and the relationships that program has with other programs that may be installed on the same system.

modification level. A distribution of all temporary fixes that have been issued since the previous modification level. A change in modification level does not add new functions or change the programming support category of the release to which it applies. Contrast with *release* and *version*. Whenever a new release of a program is shipped, the modification level is set to 0. When the release is reshipped with the accumulated services changes incorporated, the modification level is incremented by 1.

module. The object that results from compiling source code. A module cannot be run. To be run, a module must be bound into a program.

monoplex. A sysplex consisting of one system that uses a sysplex couple data set.

MP. See *multiprocessor*.

MPF. See *message processing facility*.

MTBF. See *mean time between failure*.

multi-access spool configuration (MAS). Multiple systems sharing the JES2 input, job, and output queues (through a checkpoint data set or Coupling Facility).

multiple console support (MCS). The operator interface in a z/OS system.

Multiple Virtual Storage (MVS). An earlier form of the z/OS operating system.

multiprocessing. The simultaneous execution of two or more computer programs or sequences of instructions. See also *parallel processing*.

multiprocessor (MP). A CPC that can be physically partitioned to form two operating processor complexes.

multisystem application. An application program that has various functions distributed across z/OS images in a multisystem environment.

multisystem console support. Multiple console support for more than one system in a sysplex. Multisystem console support allows consoles on different systems in the sysplex to communicate with each other (send messages and receive commands)

multisystem environment. An environment in which two or more z/OS images reside in one or more processors, and programs on one image can communicate with programs on the other images.

multisystem sysplex. A sysplex in which two or more z/OS images are allowed to be initialized as part of the sysplex.

multitasking. Mode of operation that provides for the concurrent, or interleaved, execution of two or more tasks, or threads. Synonymous with *multithreading*.

mutable connection. Connections made with fiber jumper cables between patchports in a cabinet or between cabinets and active objects, such as CHPIDs, switches, converters, and controllers with ESCON or FICON interfaces. Mutable connections are broken when the patchports they connect are not in use.

MVS. See *Multiple Virtual Storage*.

MVS/ESA. Multiple Virtual Storage/Enterprise Systems Architecture.

N

n-way. The number (n) of CPs in a CPC. For example, a 6-way CPC contains six CPs.

NCP. network control program.

Network File System. A component of z/OS that allows remote access to z/OS host processor data from workstations, personal computers, or any other system on a TCP/IP network that is using client software for the Network File System protocol.

network job entry (NJE). A JES2 facility that provides for the passing of selected jobs, system output data, operator commands, and messages between communicating job entry subsystems connected by binary-synchronous communication lines, channel-to-channel adapters, and shared queues.

network operator. (1) The person responsible for controlling the operation of a telecommunication network. (2) A VTAM application program authorized to issue network operator commands.

network. A collection of data processing products connected by communications lines for exchanging information between stations.

next sequential instruction. The next instruction to be executed in the absence of any branch or transfer of control.

NIP. See *nucleus initialization program*.

NJE. See *network job entry*.

nonpageable region. In MVS, a subdivision of the nonpageable dynamic area that is allocated to a job step or system task that is not to be paged during execution. In a nonpageable region, each virtual address is identical to its real address. Synonymous with *V=R region*.

nonreentrant. A type of program that cannot be shared by multiple users.

nonstandard labels. Labels that do not conform to American National Standard or IBM System/370 standard label conventions.

nucleus initialization program (NIP). The stage of z/OS that initializes the control program; it allows the operator to request last minute changes to certain options specified during initialization.

nucleus. That portion of a control program that always remains in central storage.

null. Empty. A byte containing no value (binary zeroes).

O

object deck. A collection of one or more control sections produced by an assembler or compiler and used as input to the linkage editor or binder. Also called object code or simply OBJ.

object module. A module that is the output from a language translator (such as a compiler or an assembler). An object module is in relocatable format with machine code that is not executable. Before an object module can be executed, it must be processed by the link-edit utility.

offline. Not connected to a central computer.

offset. The number of measuring units from an arbitrary starting point in a record, area, or control block, to some other point.

OLTP. See *online transaction processing*.

online transaction processing (OLTP). Refers to a class of systems that facilitate and manage transaction-oriented applications, typically for data entry and retrieval transaction processing.

online. Connected to a central computer.

operating system. Software that controls the running of programs; in addition, an operating system may provide services such as resource allocation, scheduling, I/O control, and data management. Although operating systems are predominantly software, partial hardware implementations are possible.

operations log. In z/OS, the operations log is a central record of communications and system problems for each system in a sysplex.

operator commands. Statements that system operators may use to get information, alter operations, initiate new operations, or end operations.

operator message. A message from an operating system directing the operator to perform a specific function, such as mounting a tape reel, or informing the operator of specific conditions within the system, such as an error condition.

optimizer. A special-purpose hardware component or appliance that can perform a limited set of specific functions, with optimized performance when compared to a general-purpose processor. Because of its limited set of functions, an optimizer is an integrated part of a processing environment, rather than a stand-alone unit. One example of an optimizer is the IBM Smart Analytics Optimizer for DB2 for z/OS.

OS/390. An earlier form of the z/OS operating system.

output group. A set of a job's output data sets that share output characteristics, such as class, destination, and external writer.

output writer. A part of the job scheduler that transcribes specified output data sets onto a system output device independently of the program that produced the data sets.

overlay. To overwrite existing data in storage.

P

page fault. In z/OS or S/390 virtual storage systems, a program interruption that occurs when a page that is marked "not in central storage" is referred to by an active page.

page. (1) In virtual storage systems, a fixed-length block of instructions, data, or both, that can be transferred between central storage and external page storage. (2) To transfer instructions, data, or both, between central storage and external page storage.

pageable region. In MVS, a subdivision of the pageable dynamic area that is allocated to a job step or a system task that can be paged during execution. Synonymous with *V=V region*.

paging device. In z/OS, a direct access storage device on which pages (and possibly other data) are stored.

paging. In z/OS, the process of transferring pages between central storage and external page storage.

parallel processing. The simultaneous processing of units of work by many servers. The units of work can be either transactions or subdivisions of large units of work (batch). See also *highly parallel*.

Parallel Sysplex. A sysplex that uses one or more Coupling Facilities.

parameter. A data item that is received by a routine.

PARMLIB member. One of the members in the SYS1.PARMLIB PDS that contain parameters setting the limits and controlling the behavior of z/OS.

PARMLIB. All the members in the SYS1.PARMLIB PDS that contain parameters setting the limits and controlling the behavior of z/OS.

partially qualified data set name. A data set name in which the qualifiers are not spelled out. Asterisks and percent signs are used in place of the undefined qualifiers.

partitionable CPC. A CPC that can be divided into two independent CPCs. See also *physical partition*, *single-image mode*, and *side*.

partitioned data set (PDS). A data set in direct access storage that is divided into partitions, called members, each of which can contain a program, part of a program, or data. Synonymous with *program library*. Contrast with *sequential data set*.

partitioned data set extended (PDSE). A
system-managed data set that contains an indexed
directory and members that are similar to the
directory and members of partitioned data sets. A
PDSE can be used instead of a partitioned data set.

partitioning. The process of forming multiple
configurations from one configuration.

password. A unique string of characters known to a
computer system and to a user, who must specify
the character string to gain access to a system and
to the information stored within it.

patchport. A pair of fibre adapters or couplers. Any
number of patchports can participate in a fiber link.
To determine the total number of patchports in a
cabinet, you must add the number of patchports of
each defined panel of the cabinet.

PC. personal computer.

PCHID. See *physical channel identifier.*

PDS. See *partitioned data set.*

PDSE. See *partitioned data set extended.*

PE-PTF. See *program error PTF.*

peer-to-peer remote copy (PPRC). A direct
connection between DASD controller subsystems
that is used primarily to provide a hot standby
capability. These connections can be point-to-point
from one DASD controller to another, or they can
pass through switches, just as connections from
CHPIDs to control units can.

percolate. The action taken by the condition
manager when the returned value from a condition
handler indicates that the handler could not handle
the condition, and that the condition will be
transferred to the next handler.

performance administration. The process of
defining and adjusting workload management goals
and resource groups based on installation business
objectives.

permanent.connection. Permanent connections
are usually made between cabinets with fiber trunk
cables. Patchports that are permanently connected
remain so even when they are not in use.

permanent data set. A user-named data set that is
normally retained for longer than the duration of a
job or interactive session. Contrast with *temporary
data set.*

PFK capability. On a display console, indicates that
program function keys are supported and were
specified at system generation.

PFK. See *program function key.*

physical channel identifier (PCHID). The physical
address of a channel path in the hardware. Logical
CHPIDs have corresponding physical channels.
Real I/O hardware is attached to a processor
through physical channels. Channels have a
physical channel identifier (PCHID) that determines
the physical location of a channel in the processor.
The PCHID is a three hexadecimal digit number and
is assigned by the processor.

physical partition. Part of a CPC that operates as
a CPC in its own right, with its own copy of the
operating system.

physical unit (PU). (1) The control unit or cluster
controller of an SNA terminal. (2) The part of the
control unit or cluster controller that fulfills the role of
a physical unit as defined by systems network
architecture (SNA).

physically partitioned (PP) mode. The state of a
processor complex when its hardware units are
divided into two separate operating configurations or
sides. The A-side of the processor controller
controls side 0; the B-side of the processor controller
controls side 1. Contrast with *single-image (SI)
configuration.*

PL/I. A general purpose scientific/business high-level language. PL/I is a powerful procedure-oriented language that is especially well suited for solving complex scientific problems or running lengthy and complicated business transactions and record-keeping applications.

platform. The operating system environment in which a program runs.

PLPA. pageable link pack area.

pointer. An address or other indication of location.

portability. The ability to transfer an application from one platform to another with relatively few changes to the source code.

Portable Operating System Interface (POSIX). Portable Operating System Interface for computing environments is an interface standard governed by the IEEE and based on UNIX. POSIX is not a product. Rather, it is an evolving family of standards describing a wide spectrum of operating system components ranging from C language and shell interfaces to system administration.

POSIX. See *Portable Operating System Interface.*

PPRC. See *peer-to-peer remote copy.*

PPT. In z/OS, the program properties table.

PR/SM. See *Processor Resource/Systems Manager.*

preprocessor. A routine that examines application source code for preprocessor statements that are then executed, resulting in the alteration of the source.

preventive service planning (PSP). Installation recommendations and HOLDDATA for a product or a service level. PSP information can be obtained from the IBM Support Center.

preventive service. (1) The mass installation of PTFs to avoid rediscoveries of the APARs fixed by those PTFs. (2) The SYSMODs delivered on the program update tape.

primary key. One or more characters within a data record used to identify the data record or control its use. A primary key must be unique.

printer. A device that writes output data from a system on paper or other media.

procedure. A set of self-contained high-level language (HLL) statements that performs a particular task and returns to the caller. Individual languages have different names for this concept of a procedure. In C, a procedure is called a function. In COBOL, a procedure is a paragraph or section that can only be performed from within the program. In PL/I, a procedure is a named block of code that can be invoked externally, usually through a a call.

processor controller. Hardware that provides support and diagnostic functions for the central processors.

Processor Resource/Systems Manager (PR/SM). The feature that allows the processor to use several z/OS images simultaneously and provides logical partitioning capability. See also *LPAR.*

processor storage. See *central storage.*

processor. The physical processor, or machine, has a serial number, a set of channels, and a logical processor associated with it. The logical processor has a number of channel path IDs (CHPIDs), which are the logical equivalent of channels. The logical processor may be divided into a number of logical partitions.

profile. Data that describes the significant characteristics of a user, a group of users, or one or more computer resources.

program error PTF (PE-PTF). A PTF that has been found to contain an error. A PE-PTF is identified on a ++HOLD ERROR statement, along with the APAR that first reported the error.

program fetch. A program that prepares programs for execution by loading them at specific storage locations and readjusting each relocatable address constant.

program function key (PFK). A key on the keyboard of a display device that passes a signal to a program to call for a particular program operation.

program interruption. The interruption of the execution of a program due to some event such as an operation exception, an exponent-overflow exception, or an addressing exception.

program level. The modification level, release, version, and fix level.

program library. A partitioned data set that always contains named members.

program management. The task of preparing programs for execution, storing the programs, load modules, or program objects in program libraries, and executing them on the operating system.

program mask. In bits 20 through 23 of the program status word (PSW), a 4-bit structure that controls whether each of the fixed-point overflow, decimal overflow, exponent-overflow, and significance exceptions should cause a program interruption. The bits of the program mask can be manipulated to enable or disable the occurrence of a program interruption.

program module. The output of the binder. A collective term for program object and load module.

program number. The seven-digit code (in the format xxxx-xxx) used by IBM to identify each licensed program.

program object. All or part of a computer program in a form suitable for loading into virtual storage for execution. Program objects are stored in PDSE program libraries and have fewer restrictions than load modules. Program objects are produced by the binder.

program status word (PSW). A 64-bit structure in central storage used to control the order in which instructions are executed, and to hold and indicate the status of the computing system in relation to a particular program. See also *program mask*.

program temporary fix (PTF). A temporary solution or bypass of a problem diagnosed by IBM as resulting from a defect in a current unaltered release of the program.

PSP. See *preventive service planning*.

PSW. See *program status word*.

PTF. See *program temporary fix*.

PU. See *physical unit*.

Q

QM. queue manager.

QSAM. See *queued sequential access method*.

qualified name. A data set name consisting of a string of names separated by periods. For example, "TREE.FRUIT.APPLE" is a qualified name.

qualifier. A modifier in a qualified name other than the rightmost name. For example, "TREE" and "FRUIT" are qualifiers in "TREE.FRUIT.APPLE."

queue. A line or list formed by items in a system waiting for processing.

queued sequential access method (QSAM). An extended version of the basic sequential access method. Input data blocks awaiting processing or output data blocks awaiting transfer to auxiliary storage are queued on the system to minimize delays in I/O operations.

R

RACF. See *Resource Access Control Facility*.

RAID. See *redundant array of independent disks*.

RAS. See *Reliability, Availability, Serviceability.*

RDW. record descriptor word.

read access. Permission to read information.

reader. A program that reads jobs from an input device or data base file and places them on the job queue.

real address. In virtual storage systems, the address of a location in central storage.

real storage. See *central storage.*

reason code. A return code that describes the reason for the failure or partial success of an attempted operation.

RECEIVE processing. An SMP/E process that is necessary to install new product libraries. During this process, the code, organized as unloaded partition data sets, is loaded into temporary SMPTLIB data sets. SMP/E RECEIVE processing automatically allocates the temporary partitioned data sets that correspond to the files on the tape, and loads them from the tape.

receive. In SMP/E, receive means to read SYSMODs and other data from SMPPTFIN and SMPHOLD and store them on the global zone for subsequent SMP/E processing. This is done by using the RECEIVE command.

RECEIVE. The SMP/E command used to read in SYSMODs and other data from SMPPTFIN and SMPHOLD.

RECFM. See *record format.*

record data. Data sets with a record-oriented structure that are accessed record by record. This data set structure is typical of data sets on z/OS and other mainframe operating systems. See also *byte stream.*

record. (1) A group of related data, words, or fields treated as a unit, such as one name, address, and telephone number. (2) A self-contained collection of information about a single object. A record is made up of a number of distinct items called fields. A number of shell programs (for example, awk, join, and sort) are designed to process data consisting of records separated by newlines, where each record contains a number of fields separated by spaces or some other character. awk can also handle records separated by characters other than newlines. See *fixed-length record* and *variable-length record.*

recording format (RECFM). For a tape volume, the format of the data on the tape, for example, 18, 36, 128, or 256 tracks.

recovery system. A system that is used in place of a primary application system that is no longer available for use. Data from the application system must be available for use on the recovery system. This task is usually accomplished by using backup and recovery techniques, or by using various DASD copying techniques, such as remote copy.

recovery. The process of rebuilding data after it has been damaged or destroyed, often by restoring a backup version of the data or by reapplying transactions recorded in a log.

recursive routine. A routine that can call itself or be called by another routine that it has called.

redundant array of independent disks (RAID). A disk subsystem architecture that combines two or more physical disk storage devices into a single logical device to achieve data redundancy.

reenterable. The reusability attribute that allows a program to be used concurrently by more than one task. A reenterable module can modify its own data or other shared resources, if appropriate serialization is in place to prevent interference between using tasks. See *reusability* and *reentrant.*

reentrant. The attribute of a routine or application that allows more than one user to share a single copy of a load module.

refreshable. The reusability attribute that allows a program to be replaced (refreshed) with a new copy without affecting its operation. A refreshable module cannot be modified by itself or any other module during execution. See *reusability*.

register save area (RSA). Area of main storage in which contents of registers are saved.

register. An internal computer component capable of storing a specified amount of data and accepting or transferring this data rapidly.

related installation material (RIM). In IBM custom-built offerings, task-oriented documentation, jobs, sample exit routines, procedures, parameters, and examples developed by IBM.

release. A distribution of a new product or new function and APAR fixes for an existing product. Contrast with *modification level* and *version*.

Reliability, Availability, Serviceability (RAS). Design features that enable mainframe computers to run for months and years with little or no downtime.

remote copy. A storage-based disaster recovery and workload migration function that can copy data in real time to a remote location. Two options of remote copy are available. See *peer-to-peer remote copy* and *extended remote copy*.

remote job entry (RJE). Submission of job control statements and data from a remote terminal, causing the jobs described to be scheduled and executed as though encountered in the input stream.

remote operations. Operation of remote sites from a host system.

reserved storage allocation. The amount of central that you can dynamically configure online or offline to a logical partition.

residency mode (RMODE). The attribute of a program module that specifies whether the module, when loaded, must reside below the 16 MB virtual storage line or may reside anywhere in virtual storage.

Resource Access Control Facility (RACF). An IBM security manager product that provides for access control by identifying and verifying the users to the system, authorizing access to protected resources, logging the detected unauthorized attempts to enter the system, and logging the detected accesses to protected resources.

resource recovery services (RRS). The z/OS system component that provides the services that a resource manager calls to protect resources. RRS is the z/OS system level sync point manager.

restore. In SMP/E, to remove applied SYSMODs from the target libraries by using the RESTORE command.

RESTORE. The SMP/E command used to remove applied SYSMODs from the target libraries.

restructured extended executor (REXX). A general-purpose, procedural language designed to be easily used by both casual users and computer professionals. It is also useful for application macros. REXX includes the capability of issuing commands to the underlying operating system from these macros and procedures.

resynchronization. A track image copy from the primary volume to the secondary volume of only the tracks that have changed since the volume was last in duplex mode.

return code. A code produced by a routine to indicate its success or failure. It may be used to influence the execution of succeeding instructions or programs.

reusability. The attribute of a module or section that indicates the extent to which it can be reused or shared by multiple tasks within the address space. See *refreshable*, *reenterable*, and *serially reusable*.

REXX. See *restructured extended executor.*

RIM. See *related installation material.*

RJE. See *remote job entry.*

RMF. Resource Measurement Facility.

RMODE. See *residency mode.*

rollback. The process of restoring data changed by an application to the state of its last commit point.

routine. (1) A program or sequence of instructions called by a program. Typically, a routine has a general purpose and is frequently used. CICS and programming languages use routines. (2) A database object that encapsulates procedural logic and SQL statements, is stored on the database server, and can be invoked from an SQL statement or by using the CALL statement. The three main classes of routines are procedures, functions, and methods. (3) In REXX, a series of instructions called with the CALL instruction or as a function. A routine can be either internal or external to a user's program. (4) A set of statements in a program that causes the system to perform an operation or a series of related operations.

routing code. A code assigned to an operator message and used to route the message to the proper console.

routing. The assignment of the communications path by which a message will reach its destination.

RRS. See *resource recovery services.*

RSA. See *register save area.*

run time. Any instant at which a program is being executed. Synonymous with *execution time.*

run. To cause a program, utility, or other machine function to be performed.

runtime environment. A set of resources that are used to support the execution of a program. Synonymous with *execution environment.*

S

SAF. system authorization facility.

save area. An area of main storage in which contents of registers are saved.

SCE. See *system control element.*

SCSI. See *small computer system interface.*

SDLC. Synchronous Data Link Control.

SDSF. System Display and Search Facility.

SE. See *IBM Systems Engineer.*

security administrator. A programmer who manages, protects, and controls access to sensitive information.

sequential data set. (1) A data set whose records are organized on the basis of their successive physical positions, such as on magnetic tape. Contrast with *direct data set.* (2) A data set in which the contents are arranged in successive physical order and are stored as an entity. The data set can contain data, text, a program, or part of a program. Contrast with *partitioned data set (PDS).*

serially reusable. The reusability attribute that allows a program to be executed by more than one task in sequence. A serially reusable module cannot be entered by a new task until the previous task has exited. See *reusability.*

server address space. Any address space that does work on behalf of a transaction manager or a resource manager. For example, a server address space could be a CICS AOR, or an IMS control region.

server. (1) On a network, the computer that contains programs, data, or provides the facilities that other computers in the network can access. (2) The party that receives remote procedure calls. Contrast with *client.*

service level agreement (SLA). A written agreement about the information systems (IS) service to be provided to the users of a computing installation.

service level. The FMID, RMID, and UMID values for an element. The service level identifies the owner of the element, the last SYSMOD to replace the element, and all the SYSMODs that have updated the element since it was last replaced.

service processor. The part of a processor complex that provides for the maintenance of the complex.

service unit. The amount of service consumed by a work request as calculated by service definition coefficients and CPU, SRB, I/O, and storage service units.

service. PTFs and APAR fixes.

session. (1) The period of time during which a user of a terminal can communicate with an interactive system; usually, the elapsed time from when a terminal is logged on to the system until it is logged off the system. (2) The period of time during which programs or devices can communicate with each other. (3) In VTAM, the period of time during which a node is connected to an application program.

severity code. A part of operator messages that indicates the severity of the error condition (I, E, or S).

shared DASD option. An option that enables independently operating computing systems to jointly use common data residing on shared direct access storage devices.

shared storage. An area of storage that is the same for each virtual address space. Because it is the same space for all users, information stored there can be shared and does not have to be loaded in the user region.

side. One of the configurations formed by physical partitioning.

SIGP. signal processor.

simultaneous peripheral operations online (spool). The reading and writing of input and output streams on auxiliary storage devices, concurrently while a job is running, in a format convenient for later processing or output operations.

single point of control (SPOC). The characteristic a sysplex displays when you can accomplish a given set of tasks from a single workstation, even if you need multiple IBM and vendor products to accomplish that particular set of tasks.

single point of failure (SPOF). A part of a system which, if it fails, will stop the entire system from working. SPOFs are undesirable in any system whose goal is high availability, be it a network, software application or other industrial system. Systems are made robust by adding redundancy to all potential SPOFs. Redundancy is generally achieved in computing through high-availability clusters. Redundancy can be achieved at the internal component level, at the system level (multiple machines), or site level (replication).

single system image. The characteristic a product displays when multiple images of the product can be viewed and managed as one image.

single-image (SI) mode. A mode of operation for a multiprocessor (MP) system that allows it to function as one CPC. By definition, a uniprocessor (UP) operates in single-image mode. Contrast with *physically partitioned (PP) configuration*.

single-processor complex. A processing environment in which only one processor (computer) accesses the spool and comprises the entire node.

single-system sysplex. A sysplex in which only one z/OS system is allowed to be initialized as part of the sysplex. In a single-system sysplex, the cross-system Coupling Facility (XCF) provides XCF services on the system but does not provide signalling services between z/OS systems. See also *multisystem sysplex*.

SLA. See *service level agreement.*

small computer system interface (SCSI). A standard hardware interface that enables a variety of peripheral devices to communicate with one another.

SMF. See *system management facilities.*

SMP/E. See *System Modification Program/Extended.*

SMPCSI. The SMP/E data set that contains information about the structure of a user's system and information needed to install the operating system on a user's system. The SMPCSI DD statement refers specifically to the CSI that contains the global zone. This is also called the master CSI.

SMS. See *Storage Management Subsystem.*

SNA. See *Systems Network Architecture.*

software. (1) All or part of the programs, procedures, rules, and associated documentation of a data processing system. (2) A set of programs, procedures, and, possibly, associated documentation concerned with the operation of a data processing system, for example, compilers, library routines, manuals, and circuit diagrams. Contrast with *hardware.*

sort/merge program. A processing program that can be used to sort or merge records in a prescribed sequence.

source code. The input to a compiler or assembler, which is written in a source language.

source program. A set of instructions written in a programming language that must be translated to machine language before the program can be run.

spin data set. A data set that is deallocated (available for printing) when it is closed. Spin off data set support is provided for output data sets just prior to the termination of the job that created the data set.

SPOC. See *single point of control.*

SPOF. See *single point of failure.*

spool. See *simultaneous peripheral operations online.*

spooled data set. A data set written on an auxiliary storage device and managed by JES.

spooling. The reading and writing of input and output streams on auxiliary storage devices, concurrently with job execution, in a format convenient for later processing or output operations.

SPUFI. SQL Processing Using File Input.

SQA. See *system queue area.*

SQL. Structured Query Language.

SR. servant region

SREL. system release identifier.

SRM. system resources manager.

SSI. See *subsystem interface.*

SSID. subsystem identifier.

SSL. Secure Socket Layer.

started task. In z/OS, an address space that runs unattended as the result of a START command. Started tasks are generally used for critical applications. The UNIX equivalent is a daemon.

status-display console. An MCS console that can receive displays about the system status but from which an operator cannot enter commands.

step restart. A restart that begins at the beginning of a job step. The restart may be automatic or deferred, where deferral involves resubmitting the job. Contrast with *checkpoint restart.*

storage administrator. A person in the data processing center who is responsible for defining, implementing, and maintaining storage management policies.

storage class. A collection of storage attributes that identify performance goals and availability requirements, defined by the storage administrator, that are used to select a device that can meet those goals and requirements.

storage group. A collection of storage volumes and attributes defined by the storage administrator. The collections can be a group of DASD volume or tape volumes, or a group of DASD, optical, or tape volumes treated as single object storage hierarchy.

Storage Management Subsystem (SMS). A facility used to automate and centralize the management of storage. Using SMS, a storage administrator describes data allocation characteristics, performance and availability goals, backup and retention requirements, and storage requirements to the system through data class, storage class, management class, storage group, and ACS routine definitions.

storage management. The activities of data set allocation, placement, monitoring, migration, backup, recall, recovery, and deletion. These tasks can be done either manually or by using automated processes. The Storage Management Subsystem automates these processes for you, while optimizing storage resources. See also *Storage Management Subsystem*.

string. A collection of one or more I/O devices. The term usually refers to a physical string of units, but may mean a collection of I/O devices that are integrated into a control unit.

structure. A construct used by z/OS to map and manage storage on a Coupling Facility. See *cache structure*, *list structure*, and *lock structure*.

subchannel set. Installation-specified structure that defines the placement of devices either relative to a channel subsystem or to an operating system.

subpool storage. All of the storage blocks allocated under a subpool number for a particular task.

subsystem interface (SSI). A component that provides communication between z/OS and its job entry subsystem.

subsystem. A secondary or subordinate system, or programming support, usually capable of operating independently of or asynchronously with a controlling system. Examples are CICS and IMS.

subtask. In the context of z/OS multitasking, a task that is initiated and terminated by a higher order task (the main task). Subtasks run the parallel functions, that is, those portions of the program that can run independently of the main task program and each other.

superuser authority. The unrestricted ability to access and modify any part of the operating system, usually associated with the user who manages the system.

superuser. (1) A system user who operates without restrictions. A superuser has the special rights and privileges needed to perform administrative tasks. The z/OS equivalent is a user in privileged, or supervisor, mode. (2) A system user who can pass all z/OS UNIX security checks. A superuser has the special rights and privileges needed to manage processes and files.

supervisor call instruction (SVC). An instruction that interrupts a program being executed and passes control to the supervisor so that it can perform a specific service indicated by the instruction.

supervisor. The part of z/OS that coordinates the use of resources and maintains the flow of processing unit operations.

support element. A hardware unit that provides communications, monitoring, and diagnostic functions to a central processor complex (CPC).

suspended state. A state where only one of the devices in a dual copy or remote copy volume pair is being updated because of either a permanent error condition or an authorized user command. All writes to the remaining functional device are logged. This allows for automatic resynchronization of both volumes when the volume pair is reset to the active duplex state.

SVC interruption. An interruption caused by the execution of a supervisor call instruction, causing control to be passed to the supervisor.

SVC routine. A control program routine that performs or begins a control program service specified by a supervisor call instruction.

SVC. See *supervisor call instruction*.

SWA. scheduler work area.

swap data set. A data set dedicated to the swapping operation.

swapping. A z/OS paging operation that writes the active pages of a job to auxiliary storage and reads pages of another job from auxiliary storage into central storage.

switch. A device that provides connectivity capability and control for attaching any two ESCON or FICON links together.

synchronous messages. WTO or WTOR messages issued by a z/OS system during certain recovery situations.

sync point manager. A function that coordinates the two-phase commit process for protected resources, so that all changes to data are either committed or backed out. In z/OS, RRS can act as the system level sync point manager. A sync point manager is also known as a transaction manager, sync point coordinator, or a commit coordinator.

syntax. The rules governing the structure of a programming language and the construction of a statement in a programming language.

SYSIN. A system input stream; also, the name used as the data definition name of a data set in the input stream.

SYSLIB. (1) A subentry used to identify the target library in which an element is installed. (2) A concatenation of macro libraries to be used by the assembler. (3) A set of routines used by the link-edit utility to resolve unresolved external references.

SYSLOG. system log.

SYSMOD. See *system modification*.

SYSOUT class. A category of output with specific characteristics and written on a specific output device. Each system has its own set of SYSOUT classes, designated by a character from A to Z, a number from 0 to 9, or a *.

SYSOUT. A system output stream; also, an indicator used in data definition statements to signify that a data set is to be written on a system output unit.

sysplex couple data set. A couple data set that contains sysplex-wide data about systems, groups, and members that use cross-system Coupling Facility services. All z/OS systems in a sysplex must have connectivity to the sysplex couple data set. See also *couple data set*.

Sysplex Timer. An IBM unit that synchronizes the time-of-day (TOD) clocks in multiple processors or processor sides.

sysplex. A set of z/OS systems communicating and cooperating with each other through certain multisystem hardware components and software services to process customer workloads. See also Parallel Sysplex.

SYSRES. system residence disk.

system abend. An abend caused by the operating system's inability to process a routine; it may be caused by errors in the logic of the source routine.

system console. In z/OS, a console attached to the processor controller used to initialize a z/OS system.

system control element (SCE). Hardware that handles the transfer of data and control information associated with storage requests between the elements of the processor.

system data. The data sets required by z/OS or its subsystems for initialization.

system library. A collection of data sets or files in which the parts of an operating system are stored.

system management facilities (SMF). A z/OS component that provides the means for gathering and recording information for evaluating system usage.

system modification (SYSMOD). The input data to SMP/E that defines the introduction, replacement, or updating of elements in the operating system and associated distribution libraries to be installed. A system modification is defined by a set of MCS.

System Modification Program Extended (SMP/E). An IBM program product, or an element of OS/390 or z/OS, used to install software and software changes on z/OS systems. SMP/E consolidates installation data, allows more flexibility in selecting changes to be installed, provides a dialog interface, and supports dynamic allocation of data sets. SMP/E is the primary means of controlling changes to the z/OS operating system.

system queue area (SQA). In z/OS, an area of virtual storage reserved for system-related control blocks.

system-managed data set. A data set that has been assigned a storage class.

system-managed storage. Storage managed by the Storage Management Subsystem (SMS) of z/OS.

system. The combination of a configuration (hardware) and the operating system (software).

Systems Network Architecture (SNA). A description of the logical structure, formats, protocols, and operational sequences for transmitting information units through, and controlling the configuration and operation of networks.

T

tape volume. Storage space on tape, identified by a volume label, which contains data sets or objects and available free space. A tape volume is the recording space on a single tape cartridge or reel. See also *volume*.

target library (TGTLIB or TLIP). In SMP/E, a collection of data sets in which the various parts of an operating system are stored. These data sets are sometimes called system libraries.

target zone. In SMP/E, a collection of VSAM records describing the target system macros, modules, assemblies, load modules, source modules, and libraries copied from DLIBs during system generation, and the SYSMODs applied to the target system.

task control block (TCB). A data structure that contains information and pointers associated with the task in process.

task. In a multiprogramming or multiprocessing environment, one or more sequences of instructions treated by a control program as an element of work to be accomplished by a computer.

TCB. See *task control block.*

TCO. See *total cost of ownership.*

TCP/IP. See *Transmission Control Protocol/Internet Protocol.*

temporary data set. A data set that is created and deleted in the same job.

terminal owning region (TOR). A CICS region devoted to managing the terminal network.

terminal. A device, usually equipped with a keyboard and some kind of display, capable of sending and receiving information over a link.

TGTLIB. See *target library*.

tightly coupled multiprocessing. Two computing systems operating simultaneously under one control program while sharing resources.

tightly coupled multiprocessor. Any CPU with multiple CPs.

tightly coupled. Multiple CPs that share storage and are controlled by a single copy of z/OS. See also *loosely coupled* and *tightly coupled multiprocessor*.

Time Sharing Option/Extensions (TSO/E). The facility in z/OS that allows users to interactively share computer time and resources.

timeout. The time in seconds that the storage control remains in a "long busy" condition before physical sessions are ended.

TLIB. See *target library*.

TLS. See *Transport Layer Security*.

TOR. See *terminal owning region*.

total cost of ownership (TCO). A financial estimate whose purpose is to help customers and enterprise managers determine direct and indirect costs of a product or system.

transaction. A unit of work performed by one or more transaction programs, involving a specific set of input data and initiating a specific process or job.

Transmission Control Protocol/Internet Protocol (TCP/IP). A hardware independent communication protocol used between physically separated computers. It was designed to facilitate communication between computers located on different physical networks.

Transport Layer Security (TLS). A protocol that provides communications privacy over the Internet.

TRK. A subparameter of the SPACE parameter in a DD statement. It specifies that space is to be allocated by tracks.

trunk cable. Cables used to make permanent connections between cabinets and which remain in place even when not in use.

TSO. See *Time Sharing Option/Extensions (TSO/E)*.

TSO/E. See *Time Sharing Option/Extensions*.

U

UCB. unit control block.

UCLIN. In SMP/E, the command used to initiate changes to SMP/E data sets. Actual changes are made by subsequent UCL statements.

UIM. unit information module.

Unicode Standard. A universal character encoding standard that supports the interchange, processing, and display of text that is written in any of the languages of the modern world. It can also support many classical and historical texts and is continually being expanded.

Unified Resource Manager. See *IBM zEnterprise*.

uniprocessor (UP). A processor complex that has one central processor.

unit of recovery (UR). A set of changes on one node that is committed or backed out as part of an ACID transaction. A UR is implicitly started the first time a resource manager touches a protected resource on a node. A UR ends when the two-phase commit process for the ACID transaction changing it completes.

UNIX file system. A section of the UNIX file tree that is physically contained on a single device or disk partition and that can be separately mounted, dismounted, and administered. See also *hierarchical file system*.

UNIX. See *z/OS UNIX System Services*.

unload. In SMP/E, to copy data out of SMP/E data-set entries in the form of UCL statements, by using the UNLOAD command.

UNLOAD. The SMP/E command used to copy data out of SMP/E data set entries in the form of UCL statements.

unused cable. Physical cables that have been recently disconnected, but not yet placed in inventory.

UP. See *uniprocessor*.

upwardly compatible. The ability for applications to continue to run on later releases of z/OS, without the need to recompile or relink.

UR. See *unit of recovery*.

user abend. A request made by the user code to the operating system to abnormally terminate a routine. Contrast with *system abend*.

user catalog. An optional catalog used in the same way as the master catalog and pointed to by the master catalog. It also lessens the contention for the master catalog and facilitates volume portability.

user exit. A routine that takes control at a specific point in an application. User exits are often used to provide additional initialization and termination functions.

user ID. See *user identification*.

user identification (user ID). A one to eight character symbol identifying a system user.

user modification (USERMOD). A change constructed by a user to modify an existing function, add to an existing function, or add a user-defined function. USERMODs are identified to SMP/E by using the ++USERMOD statement.

USERMOD. See *user modification*.

V

V=R region. Synonymous with *nonpageable region*.

V=V region. Synonymous with *pageable region*.

variable-length record. A record having a length independent of the length of other records with which it is logically or physically associated. Contrast with *fixed-length record*.

VB. variable blocked.

vendor. A person or company that provides a service or product to another person or company.

version. A separate licensed program that is based on an existing licensed program and that usually has significant new code or new functions. Contrast with *release* and *modification level*.

VIO. See *virtual input/output*.

virtual address space. In virtual storage systems, the virtual storage assigned to a job, terminal user, or system task. See also *address space*.

virtual input/output (VIO). The allocation of data sets that exist in paging storage only.

virtual server. A logical construct that is composed of processor, memory, and I/O resources conforming to a particular architecture. A virtual server can support an operating system, associated middleware, and applications. A hypervisor creates and manages virtual servers.

Virtual Storage Access Method (VSAM). An access method for direct or sequential processing of fixed-length and varying-length records on direct access devices. The records in a VSAM data set or file can be organized in logical sequence by a key field (key sequence), in the physical sequence in which they are written on the data set or file (entry-sequence), or by relative-record number.

virtual storage. (1) The storage space that can be regarded as addressable main storage by the user of a computer system in which virtual addresses are mapped into real addresses. The size of virtual storage is limited by the addressing scheme of the computer system and by the amount of auxiliary storage available, not by the actual number of main storage locations. (2) An addressing scheme that allows external disk storage to appear as main storage.

virtual telecommunications access method (VTAM). A set of programs that maintain control of the communication between terminals and application programs running under z/OS.

VM. virtual machine.

VOLSER. See *volume serial number*.

volume backup. Backup of an entire volume to protect against the loss of the volume.

volume serial number. A number in a volume label that is assigned when a volume is prepared for use in the system.

volume table of contents (VTOC). A table on a direct access storage device (DASD) volume that describes the location, size, and other characteristics of each data set on the volume.

volume. (1) The storage space on DASD, tape, or optical devices, which is identified by a volume label. (2) That portion of a single unit of storage which is accessible to a single read/write mechanism, for example, a drum, a disk pack, or part of a disk storage module. (3) A recording medium that is mounted and demounted as a unit, for example, a reel of magnetic tape or a disk pack.

VPN. virtual private network.

VSAM. See *virtual storage access method*.

VTAM. See *virtual telecommunications access method*.

VTOC. See *volume table of contents*.

W

wait state. Synonymous with *waiting time*.

waiting time. (1) The condition of a task that depends on one or more events to enter the ready condition. (2) The condition of a processing unit when all operations are suspended.

WAP. wireless access point.

wild carding. The use of an asterisk (*) as a multiple character replacement in classification rules.

WLM. A function in z/OS that is used to classify workloads.

work request. A piece of work, such as a request for service, a batch job, an APPC, CICS, or IMS transaction, a TSO LOGON, or a TSO command.

workload. A group of work to be tracked, managed, and reported as a unit.

wrap mode. The console display mode that allows a separator line between old and new messages to move down a full panel as new messages are added. When the panel is filled and a new message is added, the separator line overlays the oldest message and the newest message appears immediately before the line.

write-to-operator (WTO) message. A message sent to an operator console informing the operator of errors and system conditions that may need correcting

write-to-operator-with-reply (WTOR) message. A message sent to an operator console informing the operator of errors and system conditions that may need correcting. The operator must enter a response.

WTO. See *write-to-operator*.

WTOR. See *write-to-operator-with-reply*.

X

XA. Extended Architecture is a reference to the 31-bit addressing capability that was first introduced in MVS in 1981. On a virtual storage map, the highest point of 31 bit addresses is referred to as the "bar".

XCF. See *cross-system Coupling Facility.*

XES. See *cross-system extended services.*

Z

z/Architecture. An IBM architecture for mainframe computers and peripherals. The System z family of servers uses the z/Architecture.

z/OS Language Environment. An IBM software product that provides a common runtime environment and common runtime services for high-level language compilers.

z/OS UNIX System Services (z/OS UNIX). z/OS services that support a UNIX-like environment. Users can switch between the traditional TSO/E interface and the shell interface. UNIX-skilled users can interact with the system using a familiar set of standard commands and utilities. z/OS-skilled users can interact with the system using familiar TSO/E commands and interactive menus to create and manage hierarchical file system files and to copy data back and forth between z/OS data sets and files. Application programmers and users have both sets of interfaces to choose from and, by making appropriate trade-offs, can choose to mix these interfaces.

z/OS. A widely used operating system for IBM mainframe computers that uses 64-bit central storage.

zAAP. See *IBM System z Application Assist Processor.*

zBX. See *IBM zEnterprise BladeCenter Extension.*

zEnterprise. *See IBM zEnterprise System (zEnterprise).*

zFS. The IBM System z file system. It is a UNIX System Services file system.

zIIP. See *IBM System z Integrated Information Processor.*

zManager. See *IBM zEnterprise Unified Resource Manager.*

zSeries File System (zFS). A z/OS UNIX file system that stores files in VSAM linear data sets.

Related publications

The publications listed in this section are considered particularly suitable for a more detailed discussion of the topics covered in this book.

IBM Redbooks

The following IBM Redbooks publications provide additional information about the topic in this document. Note that some publications referenced in this list might be available in softcopy only.

- ► *ABCs of z/OS System Programming Volume 1*, SG24-6981
- ► *ABCs of z/OS System Programming Volume 2*, SG24-6982
- ► *ABCs of z/OS System Programming Volume 3*, SG24-6983
- ► *ABCs of z/OS System Programming Volume 4*, SG24-6984
- ► *ABCs of z/OS System Programming Volume 5*, SG24-6985
- ► *ABCs of z/OS System Programming Volume 6*, SG24-6986
- ► *ABCs of z/OS System Programming Volume 7*, SG24-6987
- ► *ABCs of z/OS System Programming Volume 8*, SG24-6988
- ► *ABCs of z/OS System Programming Volume 9*, SG24-6989
- ► *ABCs of z/OS System Programming Volume 10*, SG24-6990
- ► *ABCs of z/OS System Programming Volume 11*, SG24-6327
- ► *ABCs of z/OS System Programming Volume 12*, SG24-7621
- ► *ABCs of z/OS System Programming Volume 13*, SG24-7717
- ► *Creating Java Applications using NetRexx*, SG24-2216
- ► *IBM WebSphere Application Server V5.1 System Management and Configuration WebSphere Handbook Series*, SG24-6195
- ► *WebSphere Application Server for z/OS V5 and J2EE 1.3 Security Handbook*, SG24-6086

You can search for, view, or download Redbooks, Redpapers, Technotes, draft publications and Additional materials, as well as order hardcopy Redbooks publications, at this website:

ibm.com/redbooks

745

Other publications

The publications listed in this section are considered particularly suitable for a more detailed discussion of the topics covered in this book.

IBM provides access to z/OS manuals on the Internet. To view, search, and print z/OS manuals, visit the z/OS Internet Library at:

`http://www-03.ibm.com/systems/z/os/zos/bkserv/`

Mainframe architecture references

- *z/Architecture Principles of Operation*, SA22-7832

z/OS data management references

- *DFSMS Access Method Services for Catalogs*, SC26-7394
- *z/OS DFS Administration*, SC24-5989
- *z/OS DFSMS: Using Data Sets*, SC26-7410
- *z/OS Diagnosis Reference*, GA22-7588

z/OS JCL and utilities references

- *z/OS DFSMSdfp Utilities*, SC26-7414
- *z/OS MVS JCL Reference*, SA22-7597
- *z/OS MVS JCL User's Guide*, SA22-7598

z/OS system programming

- *JES2 Initialization and Tuning Guide*, SA22-7532
- *SMP/E User's Guide*, SA22-7773
- *z/OS MVS Authorized Assembler Services Guide*, SA22-7605
- *z/OS MVS Initialization and Tuning Guide*, SA22-7591
- *z/OS MVS Initialization and Tuning Reference*, SA22-7592
- *z/OS MVS Programming: Assembler Services Guide*, SA22-7605
- *z/OS MVS Programming: Extended Addressability Guide*, SA22-7614
- *z/OS MVS System Data Set Definition*, SA22-7629
- *z/OS V1R12.0 MVS System Messages, Vol 1 (ABA-AOM)*, SA22-7631

z/OS UNIX references

- ▸ *z/OS UNIX System Services Command Reference*, SA22-7802
- ▸ *z/OS UNIX System Services Planning*, GA22-7800
- ▸ *z/OS UNIX System Services User's Guide*, SA22-7801

z/OS Communications Server references

- ▸ *z/OS Communications Server IP Configuration Guide*, SC31-8775
- ▸ *z/OS Communications Server IP Configuration Reference*, SC31-8776
- ▸ *z/OS Communications Server IP System Administrators Commands*, SC31-8781
- ▸ *z/OS Communications Server SNA Operations*, SC31-8779

Language references

- ▸ *C/C++ Language Reference*, SC09-4764
- ▸ *C/C++ Programming Guide*, SC09-4765
- ▸ *Enterprise COBOL for z/OS and OS/390 V3R2 Language Reference*, SC27-1408
- ▸ *Enterprise COBOL for z/OS and OS/390 V3R2 Programming Guide*, SC27-1412
- ▸ *Enterprise PL/I Language Reference*, SC27-1460
- ▸ *Enterprise PL/I for z/OS V3R3 Programming Guide*, SC27-1457
- ▸ *HLASM General Information*, GC26-4943
- ▸ *HLASM Installation and Customization Guide*, SC26-3494
- ▸ *HLASM Language Reference*, SC26-4940
- ▸ *IBM SDK for z/OS V1.4 Program Directory*, GI11-2822
- ▸ *The REXX Language*, ZB35-5100
- ▸ *REXX on zSeries V1R4.0 User's Guide and Reference*, SH19-8160
- ▸ *z/OS TSO/E REXX Reference*, SA22-7790
- ▸ *z/OS V1R5.0 Language Environment Concepts Guide*, SA22-7567
- ▸ *z/OS V1R5.0 Language Environment Programming Guide*, SA22-7561

For more information about the REXX manuals listed in this section, go to:

`http://www.ibm.com/software/awdtools/REXX/language/REXXlinks.html`

CICS references

- *CICS Application Programming Primer*, SC33-0674
- *CICS Application Programming Reference*, SC34-6434
- *CICS C++ OO Class Libraries*, SC34-6437
- *CICS External Interfaces Guide*, SC34-6006
- *CICS Internet Guide*, SC34-6007
- *CICS Resource Definition Guide*, SC34-6430
- *CICS Transaction Server for z/OS - CICS Application Programming Guide*, SC34-6231
- *CICS Transaction Server for z/OS - CICS System Programming Reference*, SC34-6233
- *CICS Web Services Guide*, SC34-6458

IMS references

- *Connecting IMS to the World Wide Web: A Practical Guide to IMS Connectivity*, SG24-2220
- *IMS Application Programming: Database Manager*, SC18-7809
- *IMS Application Programming: Design Guide*, SC18-7810
- *IMS Application Programming: Transaction Manager*, SC18-7812
- *IMS Java Guide and Reference*, SC18-7821
- Meltz, et al., *An Introduction to IMS*, IBM Press, 2005, ISBN 0131856715

For more information about IMS, go to:

http://www.ibm.com/ims

DB2 references

- *DB2 UDB for z/OS: Administration Guide*, SC18-7413
- *DB2 UDB for z/OS: Application Programming and SQL Guide*, SC18-7415
- *DB2 UDB for z/OS: SQL Reference*, SC18-7426
- *DB2 for z/OS Utility Guide and Reference*, SC18-9855.

WebSphere MQ references

- ► *WebSphere MQ Application Programming Guide*, SC34-6064
- ► *WebSphere MQ Bibliography and Glossary*, SC34-6113
- ► *WebSphere MQ System Administration Guide*, SC34-6068

For more information about IBM WebSphere MQ, go to:

`http://www.ibm.com/software/integration/mqfamily/library/manualsa/`

Online resources

These websites are also relevant as further information sources:

- ► IBM Terminology

  `http://www.ibm.com/ibm/terminology/`

- ► z/OS website:

  `http://www-03.ibm.com/systems/z/`

- ► z/OS Basic Skills Information Center:

  `http://publib.boulder.ibm.com/infocenter/zoslnctr/v1r7/index.jsp`

- ► z/OS Communications Server website:

  `http://www.software.ibm.com/network/commserver/support/`

- ► z/OS Internet Library:

  `http://www-03.ibm.com/systems/z/os/zos/bkserv/`

Help from IBM

IBM Support and downloads

ibm.com/support

IBM Global Services

ibm.com/services

Index

Numerics

A

B

C

compiler 155, 279
language program 34, 209, 281
cold start IPL 536, 561
collating sequence
EBCDIC versus ASCII 311
command
RESERVE and RELEASE 66
XCTL 422
command list 345
COMMAREA 423
commit 408
common area 560
compatibility 11, 19
compilation unit 339
compiled language 347, 350
compiling a REXX source program 348
compiling and linking language programs 392
Complementary Metal Oxide Semiconductor
(CMOS) 637
compress partition data sets 652
computer language 324–325
consolidated software inventory (CSI) 567, 580
constraints of the project 301, 307
Control Area (CA) 221
control block 97
Control Interval (CI) 221
control unit
definition 47
conversational model of CICS programming 414
copybook 364
Count Key Data (CKD) format 207
Coupling Facilities (CFs) 71
coupling technology 74, 88
CP See central processor
CPU See central processing unit
cross-memory
communication 605
services 104
CSS See Channel Subsystem
CTC See channel-to-channel
CUoD See Capacity Upgrade on Demand
customer engineer (CE) 36
Customer Information Control System (CICS) 410
command 416, 420
preprocessor 340–341
programming roadmap 424
region 411
terminal owning region (TOR) 81
transaction flow 417

D
DASD See direct access storage device
data control block (DCB) 212
data security 601
data types 446
database
request module 459
table 444
view 444
Database Manager 427
DB2 optimizer 460
DBCLOB 446
DBCS See double byte character set
DBRM 459
DCB See data control block
DCE Security Server 598
DDNAME
definition 251
Debug Tool 329
declaratives for COBOL 331
default logon procedure 608
design documents 305
design phase 303
designing applications for z/OS 299
device number 50, 52
definition 50
device type
DD 248
devices
I/O 48
DFS See Distributed File Service
DFSMS component 131
DFSORT 170
product 170
direct access storage device (DASD) 207, 337
directory 447, 460
disk
controller 561
drive 207
dump 660
pack 207
restore 660
volume 207
disposition parameters
DD 247
Distributed File Service (DFS) 231
Distributed File Service Server Message Block
(SMB) 232
DLL 336

double byte character set (DBCS) 311, 341
DSNAME
    definition 251
dump
    logical 660
    physical 660
Dump and Trace Control 421
dynamic workload management 74

E

EBCDIC character set 310, 479, 484
ECKD See *Extended Count Key Data*
EIM See *Enterprise Identity Mapping*
emerging requirements 308
enclave 354
enqueue 132
Enterprise Identity Mapping (EIM) 598
Entry Sequence Data Set (ESDS) 220
ESCON
    channels 51
    director 52
ESDS See *Entry Sequence Data Set*
esoteric name 248
EXEC CICS 416
EXEC SQL interface 420
EXECUTE CICS 416
Extended Count Key Data (ECKD) 207
extended MCS console 602
extents
    disk data sets 211

F

FastCGI 480
Fault Analyzer 316
FICON channels 51
field technical sales support (FTSS) 37
file-owning region (FOR) 411
firewall 605
fixed link pack area (FLPA) 535
FLPA See *fixed link pack area*
FOR See *file-owning region*
FREEMAIN macro 116
FTSS See *field technical sales support*
functional requirements for an application 308

G

gathering requirements 303, 308

generation data set (GDS) 226
Generic Resource Management 81
Geographically Dispersed Parallel Sysplex (GDPS) 86
GETMAIN macro 116
global resource serialization (GRS) 68, 141
go production 303
GRS ring 68

H

hacker 597
Hardware Configuration Definition (HCD) 550
Hardware Configuration Manager (HCM) 550
Hardware Management Console (HMC) 56, 555
HDA See *Head Disk Assembly*
Head Disk Assembly (HDA) 207

I

I/O connectivity
    overview 50
I/O Control Data Set (IOCDS) 52
IBM Enterprise COBOL for z/OS and OS/390 328
IBM SDK for z/OS 343
IBM Security Server 597
ICF See *Integrated Coupling Facility*
ICKDSF utility 207, 223, 658
IDCAMS utility 210, 655
IDE See *Interactive Development Environment*
IEAFIXxx PARMLIB member 537
IEASYMxx PARMLIB member 544
IEBCOPY utility 652
IEBDG utility 653
IEBGENER utility 651
IEBUPDTE utility 656
IEFBR14 utility 650
IEHINITT utility 658
IEHLIST utility 657
IEHPROGM utility 658
IEXEC 349
IFL See *Integrated Facility for Linux*
image 68
IMS 427
    APPC feature 429
    Java dependent region 329
    messages 429
    transaction 429
in-backout 408
Include preprocessor 341

in-commit 408
independent software vendor (ISV) 36
index space 445
in-flight 408
initialization process 557
initializing real storage management 556
initializing the system control program 560
initiator 276
in-prepare 408
input-output coding 332
in-reset 408
Integrated Coupling Facility (ICF) 47, 61
Integrated Facility for Linux (IFL) 47, 59
integration testing 303, 318
Intelligent Resource Director (IRD) 639
Interactive Development Environment (IDE) 317
Interactive System Productivity Facility (ISPF) 166
interfacing with Java 342
interpreted language 325, 347, 350
interrupt 131
interval control 421
IOCDS See I/O Control Data Set
IPLable disk 556
IRD See Intelligent Resource Director
ISPF See Interactive System Productivity Facility
ISV See independent software vendor

J

Java 343
Java Certification Kit 344
Java class definition 336
Java Development Kits 344, 375
Java Native Interface (JNI) 335, 344
   services 335
Java Software Development Kit 343–344
Java Virtual Machine (JVM) 344
JCK 344
JES2 275, 286, 289, 291, 539
JES2 cataloged procedure 540
JES3 275, 289, 291, 539
JNI See Java Native Interface
job entry subsystem (JES) 275
journaled VIO data set 561
JVM See Java Virtual Machine

K

Kerberos security services 598
Key Sequence Data Set (KSDS) 220

KSDS See Key Sequence Data Set

L

Language Environment 351
large objects 446
latch 132
LCSS (Logical Channel SubSystem) 639
libraries, system 262, 535
licensed program 156, 343, 606, 656, 660
Lightweight Directory Access Protocol Server (LDAP) 487
LINK command 422
link pack area (LPA) 535
linkage editor 327
linker 327
linklist concatenation 537
load modules 327
LOB 446
locking 132
Logical Channel SubSystem (LCSS) 639
logical dump 660
LPA (link pack area) 535
LPA pages, storage protection 604
LPALST concatenation 536
LPALSTxx member 536
LPAR (logical partition) 56, 62
LPAR characteristics 57
LRECL, logical record length 212

M

machine instructions 326
machine language 324
machine-dependent 325
macro 327
macro preprocessor 341
mainframe consolidation 58
mainframe security 596
mainframe, defined 9
maintenance phase 319
master JCL 539
master scheduler 539
   address space 125, 539
   subsystem 125
MCM (Multiple Chip Module) 639
message queue 517
Message Queue Interface (MQI) 515
metadata 447
microcode 5